Managerial Economics

Managerial Economics

Third Edition

Ivan Png and Dale Lehman

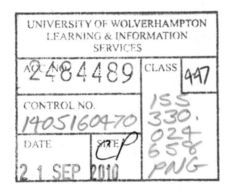

Blackwell
Publishing

BLACKWELL PUBLISHING
350 Main Street, Malden, MA 02148–5020, USA
9600 Garsington Road, Oxford OX4 2DQ, UK
550 Swanston Street, Carlton, Victoria 3053, Australia

First edition published 1998
Second edition published 2002
Third edition published 2007 by Blackwell Publishing Ltd

4   2009

Library of Congress Cataloging-in-Publication Data

Png, Ivan, 1957–
   Managerial economics / Ivan Png and Dale Lehman.—3rd ed.
      p. cm.
   Includes bibliographical references and index.
   ISBN 978-1-4051-6047-6 (pbk. : alk. paper)   1. Managerial economics.
I. Lehman, Dale E.   II. Title.

   HD30.22.P62 2007
   338.5024′658—dc22

                                        2006103321

A catalogue record for this title is available from the British Library.

Set in 10/12pt Times
by Graphicraft Limited, Hong Kong
Printed and bound in the United Kingdom
by CPI Antony Rowe, Chippenham, Wiltshire

For further information on
Blackwell Publishing, visit our website:
www.blackwellpublishing.com

For my parents, and three Cs – CW, CY, CH
(I. P.)

And for my parents, Pearl and Sid
(D. L.)

Brief Contents

Contents

Preface

Managerial economics is the science of directing scarce resources in management of a business or other organization. This book presents tools and concepts from managerial economics that practicing managers can and do use. The book is aimed at business students as well as practitioners. Accordingly, it is deliberately written in a simple and accessible style. There is a minimum of technical jargon, complicated figures, and high-brow mathematics. The emphasis is on simple, practical ideas.

The distinguishing features of this book include conceptual rigor without mathematical complexity, integration of global business issues and practices, emphasis on the role of information in business decisions, minimal economic ideology, and focus on application to business decision-making.

The book starts with the very basics. It presumes no prior knowledge of economics and only very elementary mathematics. While the mathematics is minimal, the economics is rigorous. The application of economic concepts to business practice will challenge readers with some background in economics.

Managerial economics is unique in integrating the various functions of management. In addition to presenting the essentials of managerial economics, this book includes many links to other management functions. Some examples are accounting (statistical cost analysis and transfer pricing), finance (opportunity cost of capital and takeover strategies), human resource management (incentives and organization), and marketing (brand extensions, promotion, and pricing). Readers can think of these as hyperlinks to other management functions.

The book's coverage of economic efficiency and related concepts (externalities, public goods) is somewhat non-traditional. Efficiency is shown to be as relevant within an organization as it is to an economy. The book eschews the usual examples of externalities, such as pollution and education, instead showing how externalities are relevant to business decision-making such as organization, location, and joint venturing.

In addition to the managerial focus, two features are worth emphasizing. First, the same principles of managerial economics apply globally. Reflecting this unity, the book includes examples and cases from throughout the world. Second, the book uses examples from both consumer and industrial markets. The reasons are simple: a customer is as likely to be another business as a human being and likewise for suppliers.

For most readers, this may be their only formal book on economics. Accordingly, the book omits sophisticated theories and models, such as indifference curves and production functions, which are more useful in advanced economics courses. Further, the book recognizes that many topics traditionally covered by managerial economics textbooks are now the domain of other basic management courses. Accordingly, the book omits linear programming, and capital budgeting.

Regarding language, this book refers to *businesses* rather than *firms*. Realistically, many firms are involved in a wide range of businesses. In economics, the usual unit of analysis is a business, industry, or market rather than a firm. Also, the book refers to *buyers* and *sellers* rather than *consumers* and *firms*, since in most real markets, demand and supply do not neatly divide among households and businesses. To cite just two examples, in the market for telecommunications, the demand side consists of businesses and households, while in the market for human resources, the supply side comprises households and businesses. Outsourcing has reinforced this diversity of suppliers.

Finally, some comments on how to use this book are in order. Managerial economics is a practical science. Just as no one has learned swimming or tennis simply by watching a professional, no one can learn managerial economics merely by reading this book. Every chapter of this book includes progress checks, and review and discussion questions. The progress checks and review questions are to help the reader check and reinforce the chapter material. It is essential that new-found skills be practiced on these checks and questions. The discussion questions are intended to challenge, provoke, and stretch. They will be useful for class and group discussions.

Some chapters include suggestions for further reading. These are practical references for the typical reader, rather than academic journal articles intended for PhD economists.

Some chapters include mathematical supplements. These provide reinforcement to the text using algebra and calculus. The supplements will benefit students with a mathematics background.

Managerial economics is a science that is driven by data. Accordingly, the text and discussion questions frequently refer to actual data and the companion website lists many useful sources of data.

Key Features

- Integrates managerial economics into finance, accounting, human resources, and other management functions.
- Every chapter begins with a real mini-case.
- Every chapter is reinforced with progress checks, review questions, and discussion questions.
- Cases and examples from around the world.
- Minimum technical jargon, figures, and mathematics.
- Complete instructor's supplements – transparency masters, answers to discussion questions, casebank, and testbank.

New to This Edition

- Introductory case on Managerial Economics: Airbus vs Boeing (chapter 1).
- Section on Timing, including discounting and net present value (chapter 1).
- Section on Behavioral Economics (chapter 1).
- Section on Global Integration (chapter 1).
- Introductory case on Demand: General Motors and gasoline prices (chapter 2).

- Introductory case on Elasticity: New York MTA (chapter 3).
- Introductory case on Supply: Bestar, a Canadian furniture manufacturer (chapter 4).
- Introductory case on Economic Efficiency: China's food consumption (chapter 6).
- Chapter on Oligopoly (chapter 11).
- Introductory case on Externalities: General Growth real estate investment trust (chapter 12).
- Introductory case on Asymmetric Information: life insurance with Hartford (chapter 13).
- New box cases and discussion questions throughout.

Organization

This book is organized in three parts. Following the Introduction, part I presents the framework of perfectly competitive markets. Chapters 2–6 are the basic starting point of managerial economics. These are presented at a very gradual pace, accessible to readers with no prior background in economics.

The book moves faster in parts II and III. These are relatively self-contained, so the reader may skip part II and go directly to part III. Part II broadens the perspective to situations of market power, while part III focuses on the issues of management in imperfect markets. Chapter 15 on regulation is the only chapter in part III that depends on understanding part II.

A complete course in managerial economics would cover the entire book. If time is limited, there are three possible shorter alternatives. One is a course focusing on the managerial economics of strategy, which would consist of chapters 1–11. Another alternative focuses on the managerial economics of organization and would consist of chapters 1–7 and 12–14. The third alternative focuses on modern managerial economics – strategy and organization – and would consist of chapters 1–4 and 7–14.

Websites

Please visit the website at http://www.comp.nus.edu.sg/~ipng/mecon.htm for online support to this book. The site contains updates and corrections to the book, a study guide, and a guide to data sources. The site also contains a link to resources for instructors, including transparencies, answers to discussion questions, a testbank, and a casebank.

The book's Wiki site can be found at http://polar.alaskapacific.edu/dlehman. It is organized according to the book's table of contents and contains additional examples, as well as contributions from readers. Instructors can use this site for additional cases, or to have students contribute their own examples or updates.

Acknowledgments

Third edition: I would like to acknowledge my appreciation to Ivan Png for providing me with the opportunity to work on this project. It has been fulfiling to contribute to such a high quality product designed to enhance business education and practice. I would also like to thank my students who assisted with finding many fine examples of economics at work: Eric Anderson, Jana Fedakova, Leatha Merculieff, Christopher Newman, Elizabeth Vazquez, Edgars Vimba, and Romero Wilkin. I am also grateful to Dennis Weisman for a lifetime of discussions regarding the application of economics to a range of business issues. Finally, my deepest thanks go to my wife Nancy, and son Jesse, for patience, support, and inspiration.
D. L.

I welcome Dale Lehman to this book. I also wish to record appreciation to various individuals who have helped us with this edition: Arindam Dasgupta (Goa Institute of Management), Samuel Huang (Macau University of Science and Technology), Eunice Tai, Zhigang Tao (University of Hong Kong), Jenny Wong, and Wen Zhou (Hong Kong University of Science and Technology).   I. P.

We both wish to thank the reviewers of this edition for their careful and constructive comments.

About the Authors

Ivan Png is Kwan Im Thong Hood Cho Temple Professor and Professor of Business Policy at the National University of Singapore. He graduated with a BA with First Class Honours in Economics from Cambridge University (1978) and a PhD from the Graduate School of Business, Stanford (1985).

Dr Png was previously a faculty member at the Anderson School, University of California, Los Angeles (1984–96) and the Hong Kong University of Science & Technology (1993–6). Dr Png received the Outstanding Teaching Award from UCLA's MBA Program for Fully Employed Students, Class of '91, and Teaching Excellence Award, National University of Singapore (1998).

His research has been published in leading scholarly journals including the *American Economic Review*, *Economic Journal*, *Journal of Political Economy*, *Management Science*, *Marketing Science*, and the *RAND Journal of Economics*.

Dr Png was a Nominated MP (10th Parliament of Singapore, Second Session), 2005–6. He is a member of the Trustworthy Computing Academic Advisory Board of Microsoft Corporation, and independent director of Hartford Education Corporation.

Dale Lehman is an Associate Professor of Economics, Director of the MBA in Information and Communication Technology, and Chair of the Business Administration Department at Alaska Pacific University. He received a BA in Economics from the State University of New York at Stony Brook (1972) and a MA (1975) and PhD (1981) in Economics from the University of Rochester.

Professor Lehman previously taught at Fort Lewis College, Villanova University, the University of Colorado, Willamette University, California State University at San Luis Obispo, University of Santa Clara, and Saint Mary's University. He was also Member of Technical Staff at Bellcore and Senior Economist at Southwestern Bell Telephone Company. His research in the areas of telecommunications and information demand, policy, and strategy has been published in journals such as the *Review of Network Economics*, the *Review of Industrial Organization*, *Journal of Regulatory Economics*, and *Information Economics and Policy*. He co-authored, with Dennis Weisman, *The Telecommunications Act of 1996: The "Costs" of Managed Competition*, Kluwer Academic Publishers, 2000.

Chapter 1

Introduction to Managerial Economics

1 What is Managerial Economics?

Boeing and Airbus are the world's two leading manufacturers of large commercial jets. Until 2001, Airbus was a marketing consortium established under French law as a "Groupe d'Intérêt Economique." The four shareholders – Aerospatiale–Matra (37.9%), British Aerospace (20%), Construcciones Aeronauticas (4.2%) and Daimler Aerospace (37.9%) – performed dual roles as owners and industrial contractors.

Most major decisions required unanimous approval of the shareholders. Airbus was obliged to distribute production work among its shareholders according to political as well as economic considerations.

Then, Airbus was re-organized into a single fully integrated limited company. The objective was to streamline operations across national boundaries, reduce costs, and speed production. The re-organization coincided with a consolidation of Airbus market position. As figure 1.1 shows, Airbus had steadily increased its share of the market from 31% in 1996 to 57% in 1999, but then dipped sharply to 47% in 2000. Following the re-organization, Airbus recovered and maintained its share in the mid- to high 50s until 2005.

In April 2004, Boeing launched the new 7E7 Dreamliner jet with a firm order for 50 aircraft from All Nippon Airways of Japan. The deal was worth about $6 billion at list prices, with deliveries scheduled to begin in 2008. The Dreamliner was targeted to serve the market segment of twin-engine medium to long range jets with capacity of 200–300 passengers.

Eight months later, in December 2004, following considerable speculation, Airbus announced that it would develop the A350 to compete with the Boeing 7E7. Airbus Chief Commercial Officer John Leahy predicted that the A350 would attract a substantial number of Boeing customers and "put a hole in Boeing's Christmas stocking."[1]

The December 2004 announcement from Airbus raised several questions for Boeing. Should Boeing proceed with its plan to develop the Dreamliner or should it alter its development plans? Should Boeing respond by changing its pricing for its new jet? How much would development and manufacturing cost, and how do these costs depend on sales volume? Finally, did Airbus respond correctly to Boeing's Dreamliner?

---

[1] "A350: Airbus's Counter-Attack," *Flight International*, January 25, 2005.

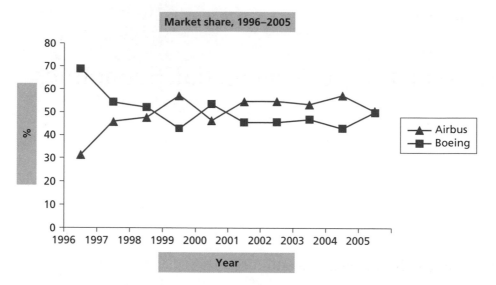

Figure 1.1   Airbus and Boeing market shares

Managerial economics
is the science of
directing scarce
resources to manage cost
more effectively.

All of these are questions of managerial economics. **Managerial economics** is the science of directing scarce resources to manage effectively. Wherever resources are scarce, a manager can make more effective decisions by applying the discipline of managerial economics. These may be decisions with regard to customers, suppliers, competitors, or the internal workings of the organization. It does not matter whether the setting is a business, non-profit organization, or home. In all of these settings, managers must make the best of scarce resources.

Boeing has limited financial, human, and physical resources. Boeing managers seek to maximize the financial return from these limited resources. They should apply managerial economics to develop pricing and R&D strategies, design their organizations, and manage purchasing. The same is true of Airbus.

While Boeing is a publicly traded company, Airbus was organized more like a cooperative with a tax-free status. Despite the differences in organization, the principles of managerial economics apply to Airbus and Boeing. Each needs to understand how they can influence the demand through price and advertising, how to compete effectively against the other, and what is the best organizational architecture.

Managerial economics also applies to the "new economy." Many of the challenges that confront management in the "new economy" are the same as those in the "old" economy. Consequently, the economic analysis and appropriate managerial solutions are similar. For instance, in pricing, airlines use differences in fare conditions to segment their market between business and leisure travelers. Some analysts claim that the Internet is the ultimate segmentation tool: using online auctions, a seller can charge a different price to every buyer.

In competitive strategy, when Boeing announces development of a new plane, Airbus must consider whether to follow. Similarly, in the "new economy," Google competes fiercely with Yahoo. To better meet the challenge from Yahoo, over 2005–6, Google launched various personal services including Gmail, chat, and calendar. In terms of organizational architecture, Airbus cut several hundred million euros in costs by transforming itself from a marketing joint venture into a fully-integrated corporation. In the new economy, Amazon.com faced a similar issue: it decided to vertically integrate from being a "virtual retailer" and spent hundreds of millions of dollars on warehouses.

Given the many similarities, how then does the "new" economy differ from the old? The most obvious is the essential role of *network effects* in demand – where the benefit provided to any user depends on the total number of other users. Network effects explain the growth of the Internet from an academic curiosity to a ubiquitous business platform in just five years. When only one person had email, she had no one to communicate with. With 1 billion users online, the demand for email, ICQ, and other communications services mushroomed. Another reason for the feverish growth of the Internet was its open technology, which freely admitted developers of content and applications.

The other distinctive feature of the new economy is the importance of scale and scope economies. A recurring theme in the new economy is "scalability" – the degree to which the scale and scope of a business can be increased without a corresponding increase in costs. The information in Google is eminently scalable: the same information can serve 100 as well as 100 million users. It is, in economic language, a *public good*, for which one person's consumption does not reduce the quantity available to others. To serve a larger number of users, Google needs only to increase the capacity of its computers and communications links. By contrast, a traditional library is less scalable: a library must incur additional costs to serve a larger number of readers.

Managerial economics consists of three branches: competitive markets, market power, and imperfect markets. Accordingly, this book is organized in three parts, one part for each branch. Before discussing these three branches, let us first develop some background.

Progress Check 1A How is the managerial economics of the "new economy" different from that of the "old economy"?

---

2   Preliminaries

To appreciate when and how to apply managerial economics, we should understand the scope and methodology of the discipline. We also need to understand several basic analytical concepts that are used throughout the three branches of managerial economics. This preliminary background is a necessary first step toward mastering the discipline.

Scope

First, we should distinguish managerial economics from *microeconomics* and *macroeconomics*. **Microeconomics** is the study of individual economic behavior where resources are costly. It addresses issues such as how consumers respond to changes in prices and income and how businesses decide on employment and sales. Microeconomics also extends to such issues as how voters choose between political parties and how governments should set taxes. Managerial economics has a more limited scope – it is the application of microeconomics to managerial issues.

> **Microeconomics** is the study of individual economic behavior where resources are costly.

Macroeconomics is the study of aggregate economic variables.

By contrast with microeconomics, the field of **macroeconomics** focuses on aggregate economic variables. Macroeconomics addresses such issues as how a cut in interest rates will affect the inflation rate and how a depreciation of the U.S. dollar (or more pointedly, an appreciation in the Chinese Renminbi, RMB) will affect unemployment, exports, and imports. While it is certainly true that the whole economy is made up of individual consumers and businesses, the study of macroeconomics often considers economic aggregates directly rather than as the aggregation of individual consumers and businesses. This is the key distinction between the fields of macroeconomics and microeconomics.

Some issues span both macroeconomics and microeconomics. For instance, energy is such an important part of the economy that changes in the price of energy have both macroeconomic and microeconomic effects. If the price of oil were to rise by 10%, it would trigger increases in other prices and hence generate price inflation, which is a macroeconomic effect. The increase in the price of oil would also have microeconomic effects; for instance, power stations might switch to other fuels, drivers might cut back on using their cars, and oil producers might open up new fields.

Methodology

Having defined the scope of managerial economics, let us now consider its methodology. The fundamental premise of managerial economics is that individuals share common motivations that lead them to behave systematically in making economic choices. This means that a person who faces the same choices at two different times will behave in the same way at both times.

An **economic model** is a concise description of behavior and outcomes.

If economic behavior is systematic, then it can be studied. Managerial economics proceeds by constructing models of economic behavior. An **economic model** is a concise description of behavior and outcomes. By design, the model omits considerable information so as to focus on a few key variables. Economic models are abstractions, like maps: a map with too much detail is confusing rather than helpful. Imagine driving around Chicago with a map that included every pothole on the street. The map would not fit into the car! To be useful, a map must be less than completely realistic.

Economic models are like maps in another way. Different maps of Chicago serve different purposes: street maps for drivers, guides to main attractions for tourists, and charts of underground utility lines for builders. Likewise, there may be different economic models of the same situation, each of them focusing on a different issue.

Models are constructed by inductive reasoning. For instance, inductive reasoning suggests that the demand for new software increases with the amount that the publisher spends on advertising. We can build a model in which the demand for a product depends on advertising expenditure. The model should then be tested with actual empirical data. If the tests support the model, it can be accepted; otherwise, it should be revised.

The **marginal value** of a variable is the change in the variable associated with a unit increase in a driver.

Marginal vis-à-vis Average

In managerial economics, many analyses resolve to a balance between the marginal values of two variables. Accordingly, it is important to understand the concept of a *marginal value*. Generally, the **marginal value** of a variable is the change in the variable associated with a unit increase in a driver. By contrast, the **average value** of a variable is the total value of the variable divided by the total quantity of a driver.

> The **average value** of a variable is the total value of the variable divided by the total quantity of a driver.

What is a *driver*? To explain, consider the following example. Alan and Hilda are clerks at a department store. The store pays each clerk $10 per hour for a basic eight-hour day, $15 per hour for overtime of up to four hours, and $20 for overtime exceeding four hours a day. Suppose that Alan works 10 hours a day. Then he earns $10 per hour for eight hours and $15 per hour for two hours of overtime, which adds up to a total of ($10 × 8) + ($15 × 2) = $110.

With respect to Alan's pay, the driver is the number of hours worked. Hence, Alan's marginal pay is the amount that he could earn by working one additional hour. His marginal pay is $15 per hour. By contrast, Alan's average pay is his total pay divided by the total number of hours worked, which is $110/10 = $11 per hour. The marginal pay exceeds the average pay because the store pays higher rates for additional hours beyond the basic eight. Since the marginal pay is the pay for an additional hour of overtime, it is higher than the average pay.

Note that the marginal and average pay depend on the number of hours worked. Suppose that Hilda works 14 hours a day. She earns $10 per hour for eight hours, $15 per hour for the first four hours of overtime, and $20 per hour for the fifth and sixth hours of overtime, which sums to ($10 × 8) + ($15 × 4) + ($20 × 2) = $180. Her marginal pay is $20 per hour, while her average pay is $180/14 = $12.86 per hour. Hilda's marginal pay exceeds Alan's because she works four hours longer, which puts her into the $20 per hour overtime bracket.

Generally, the marginal value of a variable may be less than, equal to, or greater than the average value. The relation between the marginal and average values depends on whether the average value is decreasing, constant, or increasing with respect to the driver.

Stocks and Flows

Another important distinction in managerial economics is that between *stocks* and *flows*. A **stock** is the quantity at a specific point in time. By contrast, a **flow** is the change in a stock over some period of time. While stocks are measured in units of the item, flows are measured in units per time period.

> A **stock** is the quantity of a given item at a specific point in time.

Every manager must understand the distinction between stocks and flows. A balance sheet represents the financial status of a business at a specific point in time, hence the items on a balance sheet – assets and liabilities – are stocks. By contrast, the income statement reports changes in the financial status of a business. The items in an income statement – receipts and expenses – are flows. An annual income statement reports flows over a year, while a quarterly income statement reports flows over three months.

> A **flow** is the change in a given item over a period of time.

Consider two other examples. The world's oil reserves at the beginning of the current year is a stock. This stock may be measured in billions of barrels. By contrast, the world's current production of oil is a flow. This flow may be measured in millions of barrels per day. Northwest Airlines' inventory of jet fuel on December 31, 2007, is a stock while its purchases and consumption of jet fuel during the period January 1–March 31, 2008, are flows.

> Holding **other things equal** is the assumption that all other relevant factors do not change, made so that changes due to the factor being studied may be examined independently of those other factors.

Other Things Equal

The final basic concept in managerial economics is the device of holding **other things equal**. At any one time, the environment of business may change in several different ways. It would be difficult to analyze the implications of all the various changes together. The difficulty is compounded if the separate changes have conflicting effects.

An alternative approach is to simplify the problem by analyzing each change separately, holding other things equal. Having analyzed the separate effects, we can then put them together for the complete picture.

For instance, a silver mine may be confronted with an increase in the price of electricity, a drop in the price of silver, and a change in labor laws, all in the same week. How should the mine adjust its production? The most practical way to address this question is to consider each change separately, holding "other things equal." Having understood each of the separate effects, the next step is to assemble them to get the complete picture.

Either explicitly or implicitly, almost every piece of managerial economics analysis holds other things equal. This usage is so close to being universal that we will not explicitly state the proviso. Nevertheless, it is always important to bear the proviso in mind when applying the results of some analysis to a practical managerial issue.

3   Timing

Managerial economics analysis includes two types of models. Static models describe behavior at a single point of time, or equivalently, disregard differences in the sequence of actions and payments. Examples include the model of competitive markets (chapters 2–5) and the analysis of organizational architecture (chapter 14).

By contrast, dynamic models explicitly focus on the timing and sequence of actions and payments. Examples include games in extensive form (chapter 10), one seller's commitment to increase production and so persuade competitors to produce less (chapter 11), and the effect of critical mass in a market with network effects (chapter 12).

In dynamic settings, receipts and expenditures often occur at different times. In principle, one dollar now is different from one dollar in the future. To put the two amounts on the same basis, the dollar in the future must be discounted to its present value. While the analysis of present value is the subject of financial theory and outside the scope of this book, we do provide a brief introduction.

Discounting

> **Discounting** is a procedure used to transform future dollars into an equivalent number of present dollars.

Investments necessarily involve using resources at some times in order to receive benefits at other times. In order to account correctly for the importance of time for managerial decisions, it is necessary to **discount** future values so that they can be compared with the present.

If we put $1 in the bank today and it earns 10% interest, it will become $1.10 next year. This year's dollars and next year's dollars are treated as if they are measured in different units (just as if they were different currencies). Since $1 now is equivalent to $1.10 next year, we can divide by 1.10 to show that $1/1.10 this year, which is approximately $0.91, is equivalent to $1 next year.

The reason that $1 next year is only worth 91 cents now, is that the 91 cents, after growing for one year at 10% interest will become $1 next year. For similar reasons, $1 two years from now is only worth around $0.83 today (since $0.83 today, growing at 10% interest, will become $1 in two years time).

Present value can be calculated over any period of time – years, months, and even weeks. Whatever the period, the key is to apply an appropriate discount rate for that period.

Net Present Value

Evaluating a series of flows over time requires repeated application of the principle of discounting. Every dollar amount should be discounted according to how far in the future it occurs to evaluate its present value. The **net present value** (NPV) is the sum of the discounted values of a series of inflows and outflows over time. Intuitively, the NPV represents the current valuation of a flow of dollars over time.

> The **net present value** is the sum of the discounted values of a series of inflows and outflows over time.

For instance, in chapter 10, we shall consider whether members of an agreement to restrain competition have an incentive to produce more than their agreed quota. By doing so, the individual seller would gain sales and profit in the first period, but, in subsequent periods, suffer punishment as other sellers retaliate.

Suppose that the gain is $3 million in the first month, and the punishment is $2 million for the next two months. Should a seller produce more than quota? The net present value provides the answer. Suppose that the discount rate is 1% per month? Then, the net present value would be

$$\$3 - \frac{\$2}{1.01} - \frac{\$2}{(1.01)^2} = -\$0.94 \text{ million.}$$

The NPV permits evaluation of a series of inflows and outflows that occur at different points of time from the vantage point of a single point of time – the present. If the NPV is positive, then the inflows exceed the outflows after accounting for the timing of the inflows and outflows of the opportunity. Conversely, if the NPV is negative, then the outflows exceed the inflows. In the case of the seller above, the NPV = $-\$940,000$, which means that the seller should not produce more than quota.

We present a general formula for NPV in the math supplement. The most critical piece of information in an NPV calculation is the discount rate. In many applications the choice will be clear: when borrowing money to purchase a car, the discount rate should generally be the interest rate on the loan. When using money from your bank account to invest in real estate, the discount rate should be the interest rate you were earning in the bank (since that represents the opportunity cost – you forgo the opportunity to earn the bank's interest rate).

In some applications, however, the choice of the discount rate may not be so obvious. In these circumstances, an alternative approach avoids calculating the net present value, which would require a discount rate. This alternative is to use the *internal rate of return* of the series of inflows and outflows. We explain the concept of internal rate return in the math supplement to this chapter.

Progress Check 1B Referring to the seller's incentive to produce more than the agreed quota, show that the NPV would be $-\$880,000$ if the discount rate were 2% per month.

---

4 Organization

Throughout this book, we will take the viewpoint of an organization, which may be a business, nonprofit, or a household. Managers of all such organizations face the same issue of how to effectively manage costly resources. Since our analysis focuses on the organization, we first must identify its boundaries. We briefly discuss this issue here, while leaving the detailed analysis to chapters 7 and 14. Further, since organizations comprise individual persons, we discuss various limitations in individual decision-making.

Organizational Boundaries

> **Vertical** boundaries delineate activities closer to or further from the end user.

The activities of an organization are subject to two sets of boundaries. One is **vertical**, which delineates activities closer to or further from the end user. Members of the same industry may choose different vertical boundaries.

For instance, the vertical chain in the automobile industry runs from production of steel and other materials, electrical and electronic components, tires and other parts to assembly of the vehicle to distribution. Both General Motors (GM) and Toyota are principally manufacturers of automobiles. Historically, Toyota did not produce electrical and electronic components, while GM did. Then, in 1999, GM spun off Delphi Automotive Systems, which manufactures automotive components, systems and modules. By contrast, Toyota has been acquiring shares in Denso, its principal supplier of electrical and electronic parts.

In the US telecommunications industry, judicial action prompted the divestiture of AT&T into one long-distance company (AT&T) and seven regional companies (RBOCs, the Regional Bell Operating Companies) in 1984. This vertical disintegration of communications services has subsequently been reversed with the acquisition of AT&T by SBC (one of the RBOCs) in 2005.

The vertical chain in the Internet runs from provision of content such as information, entertainment, and e-commerce, to Internet access, and to the telephone or cable service over which users access the Internet. America Online merged with Time Warner to become a provider of the entire vertical chain, including content, Internet access, and cable service. By contrast, Google provides Internet content, but neither telephone nor cable service.

> **Horizontal** boundaries are defined by the scale and scope of an organization's operations.

An organization's other set of boundaries is *horizontal*. The organization's **horizontal** boundaries are defined by its scale and scope of operations. Scale refers to the rate of production or delivery of a good or service, while scope refers to the range of different items produced or delivered. Just as members of the same industry may choose different vertical boundaries, they may also choose different horizontal boundaries.

For instance, in the sale of personal computers, HP and Lenovo operate on a much larger scale than the numerous small businesses that advertise generic machines in *PC Week*. Hence, in terms of scale, HP and Lenovo have wider horizontal boundaries than the generic suppliers. At the time of writing, however, HP and Lenovo differ in scope. HP manufactures a wide range of computers, including personal computers, and it also manufactures printers and provides consulting services. By contrast, Lenovo focuses on servers and personal computers. Accordingly, in terms of scope, HP has wider horizontal boundaries than Lenovo.

The horizontal boundaries in the telecommunications industry have also been changing rapidly. Shortly after passage of the Telecommunications Act of 1996, SBC merged with Pacific Telesis and NYNEX merged with Bell Atlantic (to become Verizon). Further changes in horizontal boundaries occurred as SBC merged with Ameritech, Verizon merged with GTE, and SBC (as of April, 2006) was attempting to merge with BellSouth. Thus, the original seven RBOCs created in 1984 (along with the independent GTE) had become three entities essentially covering the same geographical footprint.

> **Progress Check 1C** Explain the difference between the vertical and horizontal boundaries of an organization.

⊢ LCD manufacturing: cost and organization ⊢

The cost of setting up a plant to manufacture thin-film transistor liquid crystal displays (TFT-LCDs) exceeds $1 billion. With such high fixed costs, plants operate efficiently only on a large scale.

The high fixed costs have had another consequence – consolidation of the industry. In 1999, Korean conglomerate LG and Dutch diversified electronics and electrical manufacturer, Koninklijke Philips Electronics N.V., merged their LCD manufacturing businesses to form LG Philips LCD. In 2004, LG Philips LCD was listed through an initial public offering on both the Korean and New York stock exchanges.

Continuing the same trend, in 2004, Japanese diversified electronics and electrical manufacturers Seiko Epson and Sanyo Electric merged their LCD manufacturing businesses to form Sanyo Epson Imaging Devices.

By spinning off LCD manufacturing, the various parent companies – LG, Philips, Seiko Epson, and Sanyo – were shrinking both vertical and horizontal boundaries. The parent companies continued to manufacture semiconductors and consumer and industrial-oriented electronic goods.

Individual Behavior

As mentioned, our analysis takes the viewpoint of any organization. This book mostly focuses on decision-making by businesses and we assume that these aim to maximize profit. Of course, this is just a working assumption. As we discuss in chapter 14, businesses are managed by individuals, and their interests may diverge from those of the organization. Further, as we discuss next, managers, being human, are subject to *bounded rationality.*

The standard assumption in managerial economics is that people make decisions rationally. Rationality means that, when presented with various alternatives, individuals choose the alternative that gives them the greatest difference between value and cost. This means that their behavior will follow some predictable patterns based on what they judge to be in their best interest. For instance, when price rises, their consumption should fall (how much depends on their unique tastes, but it should fall to some extent for all buyers).

However, many experimental studies show that people do not always behave rationally, and indeed, they make systematic errors in decisions. The studies have grown out of collaboration between economists and psychologists which combine analyses of the psychology of human behavior with economic incentives.

For instance, two groups of experimental subjects were posed the following scenario: "[Y]ou have decided to see a play where admission is $10 per ticket. As you enter the theater you discover that you have lost . . . Would you pay $10 for another ticket?".[2] One

---

[2]   Amos Tversky and Daniel Kahneman, "The Framing of Decisions and the Psychology of Choice," *Science*, New Series, 211, no. 4481 (January 30, 1981), pp. 453–8.

group was told that they had lost a $10 bill: 88% of them responded that they would buy a replacement ticket. The other group was told that they had lost the ticket: only 46% of these would buy a replacement.

This experiment revealed an error in decision-making. People seemed to distinguish between losing a ticket and losing money, although tickets and money are fungible. Apparently, individuals account for tickets and money separately in their psychological accounts. Within the mental account for tickets, individuals suffered from a fallacy of sunk cost (we explain sunk costs in chapter 7). If it was correct to buy the first ticket, it should still have been correct to buy a replacement ticket – the cost of the first ticket is sunk and should not affect forward-looking decisions.

> Human beings behave with **bounded rationality** because they have limited cognitive abilities and cannot fully exercise self-control.

Why do people make systematic errors? Human beings behave with **bounded rationality** because they have limited cognitive abilities and cannot fully exercise self-control. Processing and analyzing information, especially under conditions of uncertainty, causes people to adopt simplified rules for decision-making. One such simplification is separate accounting for different categories of benefits and costs, for instance, entertainment and money. In addition, people may lack self-control: they may show addictive behavior and may have difficulty postponing immediate gratification for longer-term benefits.

Uncertainty causes special difficulties for individual decision-making. As we discuss in chapter 13, the standard assumption is that people are risk averse: they will reject a fair bet (one with an equal probability of a loss or an equivalent gain). However, many experimental studies show that people are much more sensitive to losses than to gains, and that their decisions may depend on how choices are "framed," i.e., presented as potential losses or absence of potential gain.

⊣ Libertarian paternalism: overcoming bounded rationality ⊢

401(k) plans are the primary vehicle for retirement savings for Americans. Many companies will match employee contributions to these plans, so there is a great benefit to enrolling in one. While most employees in companies with matching plans will eventually enroll, it often takes them a long while to do so. Often their savings rates are lower than they could be (with an attendant loss of matching funds from their employer).

Companies that have used automatic enrollment in 401(k) plans, rather than asking employees to "opt-in" to such plans, have seen increased initial participation jump from 49% to 86%. This has led to a concept called Save More Tomorrow (SMarT), in which employees precommit to have a portion of their salary raises put into their retirement accounts. Companies involved in the SMarT initiative reported an increase in average retirement savings from 3.5% to 13.6% over a 40-month period.

Efforts to alter people's behavior by channeling their choices, have been dubbed "libertarian paternalism."

Sources: Richard H. Thaler and Cass R. Sunstein, "Libertarian Paternalism," *American Economic Review*, 93 no. 2 (2003), pp. 175–9; S. Benartzi and R. H. Thaler, "Save More Tomorrow: Using Behavioral Economics to Increase Employee Saving," *Journal of Political Economy*, 112, no. 1 (2004), pp. S164–S186.

That individuals are subject to bounded rationality has two implications for managerial economics:

- The first implication is that individuals will be relatively sluggish in responding to changes in business and economic conditions. For instance, the theater-goers who lost their tickets are "mentally locked-in" and would be less responsive to a last-minute cut in the price of movie tickets.
- The second implication is that the role for managerial economics is even larger. Besides showing how to make better decisions in the context of market interaction, the discipline has also an important role in correcting systematic biases in individual decision-making.

5 Markets

One basic concept of managerial economics – the *market* – is so fundamental that it appears in the names of each branch of the discipline. A **market** consists of the buyers and sellers that communicate with one another for voluntary exchange. In this sense, a market is not limited to any physical structure or particular location. The market extends as far as there are buyers or sellers who can communicate and trade at relatively low cost.

> A **market** consists of the buyers and sellers that communicate with one another for voluntary exchange.

Consider, for instance, the market for cotton. This extends beyond the New York Board of Trade to growers in the Carolinas and textile manufacturers in East Asia. If the price on the Board of Trade increases, then that price increase will affect Carolina growers and Asian textile manufacturers. Likewise, if the demand for cotton in Asia increases, this will be reflected in the price on the Board of Trade.

In markets for consumer products, the buyers are households and sellers are businesses. In markets for industrial products, both buyers and sellers are businesses. Finally, in markets for human resources, buyers are businesses and sellers are households.

By contrast with a market, an **industry** is made up of the businesses engaged in the production or delivery of the same or similar items. For instance, the clothing industry consists of all clothing manufacturers, and the textile industry consists of all textile manufacturers. Members of an industry can be buyers in one market and sellers in another. The clothing industry is a buyer in the textile market and a seller in the clothing market.

> An **industry** consists of the businesses engaged in the production or delivery of the same or similar items.

Competitive Markets

The global cotton market includes many competing producers and buyers. How should a producer respond to an increase in the price of water, a drop in the price of cotton, or a change in labor laws? How will these changes affect buyers? The basic starting point of managerial economics is the model of competitive markets. This applies to markets with many buyers and many sellers. The market for cotton is an example of a competitive market. In a competitive market, buyers provide the demand and sellers provide the supply. Accordingly, the model is also called the *demand–supply model*.

The model describes the systematic effect of changes in prices and other economic variables on buyers and sellers. Further, the model describes the interaction of these choices. In the cotton example, the model can describe how the cotton producer should adjust prices when the price of water increases, the price of cotton drops, and labor laws change. These changes affect all cotton producers. The model also describes the interaction among the adjustments of the various cotton producers and how these affect buyers.

Part I of this book presents the model of competitive markets. It begins with the demand side, considering how buyers respond to changes in prices and income (chapter 2). Next, we develop a set of quantitative methods that support precise estimates of changes in economic behavior (chapter 3). Then, we look at the supply side of the market, considering how sellers respond to changes in the prices of products and inputs (chapter 4). We bring demand and supply together and analyze their interaction in chapter 5, then show that the outcome of market competition is efficient (chapter 6).

⊣ The extent of e-commerce markets ⊢

A bricks-and-mortar bookstore serves a geographical area defined by a reasonable traveling time. By contrast, an Internet bookstore serves a much larger market – defined by the reach of telecommunications and the cost of shipping.

In June 2006, the market value of Internet bookstore Amazon.com was six times greater than that of America's leading bricks-and-mortar bookstore, Barnes and Noble. The vast disparity reflected the stock market's assessment of the difference in the long-term profitability of the two companies. An e-commerce business can reach a much larger market than a traditional bricks-and-mortar retailer. Further, by avoiding the costs of inventory and store rental, the e-commerce business may achieve lower costs.

At the end of 2004, e-commerce accounted for 55.3% of total book and magazine sales (15.1% growth 2003–04), 35% of computer hardware and software sales (23% growth), and 50.2% of music and video sales (13.5% growth). Total e-commerce retail sales were only 2% of total retail sales in the U.S., but grew by 25.2% from 2003 to 2004.

Source: U.S. Census Bureau, E-Stats, *2004 E-Commerce Multi-Sector Data Tables*.

Market Power

In a competitive market, an individual manager may have little freedom of action. Key variables such as prices, scale of operations, and input mix are determined by market forces. The role of a manager is simply to follow the market and survive. Not all markets, however, have so many buyers and sellers to qualify as competitive.

> **Market power** is the ability of a buyer or seller to influence market conditions.

Market power is the ability of a buyer or seller to influence market conditions. A seller with market power will have relatively more freedom to choose suppliers, set prices, and use advertising to influence demand. A buyer with market power will be able to influence the supply of products that it purchases.

A business with market power must determine its horizontal boundaries. These depend on how its costs vary with the scale and scope of operations. Accordingly, businesses with market power – whether buyers or sellers – need to understand and manage their costs.

In addition to managing costs, sellers with market power need to manage their demand. Three key tools in managing demand are price, advertising, and policy toward competitors. What price maximizes profit? A lower price boosts sales, while a higher price brings in higher margins. A similar issue arises in determining advertising expenditure. With regard to other businesses, what are the benefits of cooperating rather than competing?

Part II of this book addresses all of these issues. We begin by analyzing costs (chapter 7), then consider management in the extreme case of market power, where there is only one seller or only one buyer (chapter 8). Next, we discuss pricing policy (chapter 9), strategic thinking in general (chapter 10) and particularly in the context of competition among several sellers or buyers (chapter 11).

Imperfect Markets

Businesses with market power have relatively more freedom of action than those in competitive markets. Managers will also have relatively more freedom of action in markets that are subject to imperfections. A market may be **imperfect** in two ways: when one party directly conveys a benefit or cost to others, and where one party has better information than others. The challenge for managers operating in imperfect markets is to resolve the imperfection and, so, enable the cost-effective provision of their products.

> In an **imperfect market**, one party directly conveys a benefit or cost to others, or one party has better information than others.

Consider the market for residential mortgages. Applicants for mortgages have better knowledge of their ability and willingness to repay than potential lenders. In this case, the market is imperfect owing to differences in information. The challenge for lenders is how to resolve the informational differences so that they can provide loans in a cost-effective way.

Managers of businesses in imperfect markets need to think strategically. For instance, a residential mortgage lender may require all loan applicants to pay for a credit evaluation, with the lender refunding the cost if the credit evaluation is favorable. The lender might reason that bad borrowers would not be willing to pay for a credit evaluation because they would fail the check. Good borrowers, however, would pay for the evaluation because they would get their money back from the lender. Hence, the credit evaluation requirement will screen out the bad borrowers. This is an example of strategic thinking in an imperfect market.

Differences in information and conflicts of interest can cause a market to be imperfect. The same imperfection can arise within an organization, where some members have better information than others and interests diverge. Accordingly, another issue is how to structure incentives and organization.

Part III of this book addresses all of these issues. We begin by considering the sources of market imperfections – where one party directly conveys a benefit or cost to others (chapter 12) and where one party has better information than others (chapter 13), then the appropriate structure of incentives and organization (chapter 14). Finally, we consider how government regulation can resolve market imperfections (chapter 15).

6 Global Integration

A market extends as far as there are buyers or sellers who can communicate and trade at relatively low cost. Owing to the relatively high costs of communication and trade, some markets are local. Examples include grocery retailing, housing, and live entertainment. The price in one local market will be independent of prices in other local markets. For instance, an increase in the price of apartments in New York City does not affect the housing market in Houston.

By contrast, some markets are global because the costs of communication and trade are relatively low. Examples include commodities, financial services, and shipping. In the case of an item with a global market, the price in one place will move together with the prices elsewhere. For instance, when the price of gold increases in London, the price will also rise in Tokyo.

Whether a market is local or global, the same managerial economics principles apply. For instance, when the price of fresh vegetables in Britain increases, consumers will switch to frozen vegetables. The same will be true in Japan, the United States, and elsewhere. An airline with market power in France will use that power to raise prices above the competitive level, and a mortgage lender in Australia will act strategically to resolve differences in information relative to borrowers. The same will be true all over the world.

Communications Costs and Trade Barriers

With developments in technology and deregulation, costs of international transport and communication have systematically fallen. The Internet operates over national and international telecommunications links. The explosive growth of the Internet is due in large part to cheap telecommunications.

Further, bilateral and multilateral agreements between governments have reduced barriers to trade. The World Trade Organization actively promotes the lowering of tariffs and other barriers to trade.

⊢ New business model: peer-to-peer ⊢

Some of the fastest growing businesses today challenge conventional thinking about business strategy and organization. Janus Friis and Niklas Zennstrom developed Kazaa, a peer-to-peer technology for distribution of digital content, including text, music, and videos. Launched in 2001 and distributed free of charge, Kazaa grew explosively.

Unlike conventional businesses, Kazaa is located nowhere and everywhere – it operates from the computers of its 60 million users world wide and over the Internet. As for organizational architecture, its vertical chain is short, as it comprises just one product, while its horizontal boundaries are large in terms of scale but narrow in terms of scope.

In 2002, Sharman Networks purchased Kazaa. While Sharman Networks owned and sold the technology, the Kazaa service continued to be provided by its world wide users. Kazaa has attracted legal attention, with restrictions on its use imposed by the Supreme Court of the United States (June 27, 2005) and the Federal Court of Australia (December 5, 2005).

In 2003, Friis and Zennstrom moved on to a new target – international telephony: "The telephony market is characterized both by what we think is rip-off pricing and a reliance on heavily centralized infrastructure. We just couldn't resist the opportunity to help shake this up a bit."

Again, applying peer-to-peer technology, Friis and Zennstrom developed Skype, software that provides telephone calls from one computer to another over the Internet. Launched in August 2003, the free Skype software was downloaded 60,000 times within just the first week. By May 2006, Skype had been downloaded over 200 million times and had 100 million registered users. Skype was acquired on October 14, 2005 by eBay, Inc. for $2.5 billion. Skype has also attracted legal attention, in particular from the governments of France and China.

Sources: Kazaa History (http://www.kazaa.com/revolution/history/htm); "Kazaa Founders Tout PTP VoIP," *CNET*, October 19, 2004.

These trends have caused many markets to become relatively more integrated across geographical boundaries. For instance, Canadian insurers sell life insurance and mutual funds in Asia, Israeli growers ship fresh flowers by air to Europe, and Internet telephony services offer cheap international telephone calls throughout the world.

With the trend toward greater integration, managers must pay increasing attention to markets in other places. Some markets may be similar, while others are different. In all cases, managers must not allow their planning to be limited by traditional geographical boundaries.

Outsourcing

One implication of greater international integration is *outsourcing* to other countries. **Outsourcing** is the purchase of services or supplies from external sources. The external sources could be within the same country or foreign.

> **Outsourcing** is the purchase of services or supplies from external sources.

Reductions in international communications costs and trade barriers have been especially dramatic. The result has been rapid growth in international outsourcing. For instance, U.S. financial services businesses outsource customer service to contractors in the Philippines and India, and European manufacturers outsource production to contractors in Eastern Europe. We discuss outsourcing in detail in chapter 14 on incentives and organizations.

7 Summary

Managerial economics is the science of directing scarce resources to manage cost effectively. It consists of three branches: competitive markets, market power, and imperfect markets. A market consists of buyers and sellers that communicate with each other for voluntary exchange. Whether a market is local or global, the same managerial economics principles apply.

A seller with market power will have freedom to choose suppliers, set prices, and use advertising to influence demand. A market is imperfect when one party directly conveys a benefit or cost to others, or when one party has better information than others.

An organization must decide its vertical and horizontal boundaries. For effective management, it is important to distinguish marginal from average values, stocks from flows, and to consider the timing of actions. Managerial economics applies models that are necessarily less than completely realistic. Typically, a model focuses on one issue, holding other things equal.

Key Concepts

managerial economics	flow	horizontal boundaries
microeconomics	other things equal	industry
macroeconomics	discounting	market power
economic model	net present value	imperfect market
marginal value	bounded rationality	outsourcing
average value	market	
stock	vertical boundaries	

Further Reading

Robert H. Frank's *Microeconomics and Behavior*, 6th ed. (Boston, MA: McGraw-Hill Irwin, 2006), chapters 1 and 8, discusses behavioral economics in greater detail and provides key references.

Review Questions

1. Amazon markets books and recorded music over the Internet, and delivers them by conventional means such as the United Parcel Service. Which of Amazon's activities are relatively more scalable?

2. "Managerial economics uses less than completely realistic models." Is this necessarily bad?

3. A Hong Kong mobile telephone operator set the following rates for calls from Japan back to Hong Kong during peak hours: HK$20 (Hong Kong dollars) for the first minute and HK$14.70 for each subsequent minute. Wong makes a five-minute call.
    (a) What is the average price per minute of Wong's call?
    (b) What is the price of Wong's marginal minute?

4. Explain the relation among the number of cars in service on January 1, 2007, the number in service on January 1, 2008, and the production, imports, exports, and scrappage of cars. Which of the variables are stocks and which are flows?

5. True or false? If the discount rate is higher, then the NPV of a series of inflows and outflows will be lower.

6. Explain why an employer expecting $1 million of future pension costs need not provide $1 million today in order to meet the pension fund's future obligations.

7. Describe the vertical and horizontal boundaries of your university. In what ways could the vertical boundaries be expanded or reduced? What about the horizontal boundaries?

8. Why do economies of scale affect the horizontal boundaries of an organization?

9. Why do people not behave completely rationally in making decisions?

10. Explain the difference between
    (a) the market for electricity;
    (b) the electricity industry.

11. True or false?
    (a) In every market, all the buyers are consumers.
    (b) In every market, all the sellers are businesses.

12. Which of the following manufacturers has relatively more market power in its market?
    (a) Intel, which accounts for more than 50% of world wide production of microprocessors for personal computers.
    (b) Datamini, which has less than a 1% share of the global market for personal computers.

13. Managers operating in an imperfect market must (choose a or b).
    (a) Set high prices to make up for the imperfection.
    (b) Act strategically to resolve the imperfection.

14. Which of the following are consequences of the falling costs of international communication and trade?
    (a) Buyers can obtain products from a wider range of suppliers.
    (b) Sellers can market their products to a wider set of customers.

15. Explain the distinctions among the three branches of managerial economics.

Discussion Questions

1. Nancy's savings consist of $10,000 in a savings account that yields 2% a year interest and another $10,000 in a money market fund that pays interest of 5% a year. Nancy has just received a gift of $10,000 from her mother. Her bank pays 4% interest on savings accounts with a minimum deposit of $20,000. The money market fund pays 5% interest on investments up to $100,000.

(a)   Calculate the average interest rate (= dollar amount of interest divided by amount of investment) from the savings account if Nancy deposits the additional $10,000 in the savings account and qualifies for the higher interest rate.

(b)   Calculate the average interest rate if Nancy deposits the additional $10,000 in the money market fund.

(c)   Calculate the marginal interest rate (= increase in dollar amount of interest divided by additional investment) from the savings account if Nancy deposits the additional $10,000 in the savings account.

(d)   Calculate the marginal interest rate if Nancy deposits the additional $10,000 in the money market fund.

(e)   From the viewpoint of maximizing his total interest income, where should Nancy deposit the additional money?

2.   Ford offers a 3-year or 36,000 mile warranty on its Ford Explorer. Consumers must pay for extended warranties beyond the manufacturer's warranty period. For example, the Auto Club (www.autoclub.com) offers a 5-year or 100,000 mile extended warranty for a Ford Explorer 4 × 4 in Dartmouth, New Hampshire, at a price of $1,259. This would cover years 4 and 5, after the manufacturer's warranty has expired.

(a)   Explain the role of discounting in your decision whether or not to purchase the extended warranty.

(b)   Suppose that the expected repair costs for years 4 through 5 are $800. If your discount rate is 6% per year, should you purchase the extended warranty?

(c)   Suppose you finance the car purchase at 1% per year, with a special financing deal from the manufacturer. The manufacturer is willing to include the extended warranty in the amount that is financed. Should you purchase the extended warranty?

3.   In each of the following instances, discuss whether horizontal or vertical boundaries have been changed, and whether they were extended or shrunk.

(a)   General Motors divested Delphi Automotive Systems, which manufactures automotive components, systems, and modules.

(b)   Online auction service eBay acquired Skype, a provider of Internet telephony services.

(c)   Following the September 11, 2001 attacks, the U.S. government established the Department of Homeland Security. The new Department took over the Customs and Secret Services from the Department of the Treasury and the Immigration Service from the Department of Justice.

4.   Referring to the definition of a *market*, answer the following questions:

(a)   Opponents of the Iraqi government periodically sabotage the pipelines through which Iraq exports oil to the rest of the world. Is Iraq part of the world market for oil?

(b)   Prisoners cannot freely work outside the jail. Do prisoners belong to the national labor market?

(c)   The Australian national electricity transmission grid links eastern states including New South Wales, South Australia, and Victoria, but does not link Western Australia. How would price changes in Western Australia affect the other states?

5.   The recorded music industry is undergoing a transition from the compact disc to digital formats for online delivery. CDs are pressed from masters created from the original soundtrack and distributed through retailers and other channels. By contrast, digital titles can be delivered directly to consumers over the Internet. In 1999, the leading music publisher EMI decided to close all CD manufacturing facilities in North America and outsourced production of CDs to specialist manufacturers.

(a)   By considering the relative costs of transporting CD masters and pressed CDs, explain why music publishers arrange for CDs to be pressed in various regional centers throughout the world rather than in one central factory.

(b)   How would the shift from CDs to online digital delivery affect the extent of the market that EMI can serve economically from its headquarters in Britain?

(c)   Relate the changes in EMI's vertical boundaries to your discussion in (b).

6.   This question refers to the internal rate of return developed in the math supplement. Consider an individual who has decided to enter medical school but is not sure whether to specialize. Physician education requires 4 years of medical school for general practice, and 3–8 years of additional training (say 5 years as an average) to be a specialist. In 2004, the average income for physicians with less than 2 years experience was $141,912 for general practice, $173,922 for psychiatrists, and $228,839 for general surgery. Malpractice premiums averaged $15,389, $9,000, and $37,696 for these three practice areas, respectively. In addition, average medical school tuition is $33,000 per year. (*Source*: Bureau of Labor Statistics, *Occupational Outlook Handbook*.)

(a)   Estimate the internal rate of return for the investment in each of the three practice areas? (*Hints*: Begin the IRR calculation from the time when the person has just completed the 4 years of basic medical education. Excel provides an IRR function.)

(b)   Discuss qualitatively any biases in the data that you used in the IRR calculations.

(c)   Some of the doctors who undergo specialist training will fail to qualify. Discuss qualitatively how this should affect a person's choice among the three practice areas.

Chapter 1

Math Supplement

Present Value

In general, if the *discount rate* is $d\%$ per year, the present value of $1 available n years from now, is given by the formula $1/(1 + d)^n$ (since $1 now will grow to become $(1 + d)^n$ in n years time). The greater the discount rate, or the further in the future the dollars are spent or received, the lower their present value.

If we denote inflows at period t by B_t, and outflows at time t by C_t, then the net present value of a series of inflows and outflows from now until period n with a discount rate of d per period, is given by the formula,

$$NPV = (B_0 - C_0) + \frac{(B_1 - C_1)}{(1 + d)^1} + \frac{(B_2 - C_2)}{(1 + d)^2} + \ldots + \frac{(B_n - C_n)}{(1 + d)^n} = \sum_{t=0}^{t=n} \frac{(B_t - C_t)}{(1 + d)^t}. \tag{1.1}$$

The last expression in equation (1.1) is simply shorthand for the summation of the series.

Internal Rate of Return

Consider the decision of whether or not to invest in a college education. Suppose you have already graduated from high school. According to 2005 data from the U.S. Census Bureau, your average yearly earnings with a high school degree, but without a college degree, are $27,915. If you graduate from college, your average annual earnings would be $51,206. Going to college involves an opportunity cost – you forgo the earnings from spending your time working rather than attending college. In addition, you would incur out-of-pocket expenses: average tuition, fees, and books were $9,700 per year in 2005.[3]

---

[3]   Average tuition and fees at 4-year private colleges was $19,710 and at 4-year public colleges was $4,694. About one-third of students attend private colleges, so the $9,700 figure is a weighted average of private and public college tuition and fees. Room and board expenses have been excluded, as they would be incurred whether an individual were to attend college or not.

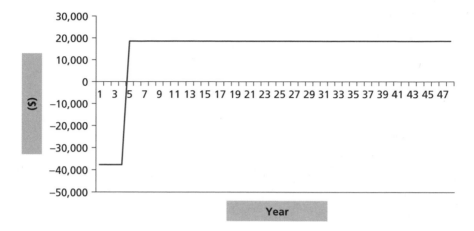

Figure 1.2   Yearly cash flow from college

Using these averages, we can show the yearly cash flow (benefits and costs) for a student at age 18 who would earn their college degree in four years, and retire at age 65. This is illustrated in figure 1.2.

The first four years show the college costs that would be incurred, as well as the foregone earnings. If we apply equation 1.1 to this series, using a discount rate of 10%, the NPV for this investment is $6,109.48. However, it is not clear what discount rate a prospective college student should use to evaluate this investment.

An alternative way to evaluate this investment is to calculate the **internal rate of return** (IRR): the discount rate that would make the NPV equal zero.[4] This can be easily calculated in a spreadsheet or on a calculator. Intuitively, we know that, with a discount rate of zero, the NPV is positive: we would just add up the annual benefits and costs, ignoring their timing, since we would not be discounting the future. We would have 4 years of $37,615 costs (including opportunity costs) and 43 years of $18,633 of annual benefits (the difference between the average salary with and without a college degree). On the other hand, as the discount rate becomes very large, we ignore the future costs and benefits and are left with only the first year opportunity costs, which is the NPV = −$37,615.

> The **internal rate of return** (IRR) is the discount rate that would make the net present value of a series of inflows and outflows equal to zero.

Figure 1.3 illustrates the relationship between the NPV and the discount rate for this example.

The IRR is the discount rate that makes the NPV = 0, in this case 10.5%. It measures the earnings opportunity inherent in this investment opportunity. For discount rates greater than the IRR, the NPV is negative, and there are better earnings opportunities elsewhere (in this case, by not going to college and earning more money now). For discount rates less than the IRR, the NPV is positive, and this investment is worth its opportunity cost.

In the current example, 10.5% is certainly higher than the returns on the safest investments, like Treasury Bills. It is lower than the returns typically associated with very risky investments, like venture capital. Of course, investing in college carries its own risks. This is a good illustration of the

---

[4]   Care must be taken when using the IRR. It is safe to apply the IRR when the investment decision has a time profile similar to figure 1.2 – when the net benefits cross zero only once (either they start negative and become positive, or the reverse). If the net benefits change from positive to negative (or the reverse) more than once, then the IRR will not be unique. In general, there will be as many values for the IRR as there are sign changes for the annual net benefits. In this case, the NPV will be positive over several disconnected ranges of values for the discount rate, and negative over others. Figure 1.2 is a typical pattern for investment decisions, however.

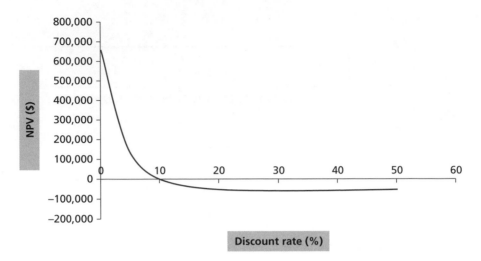

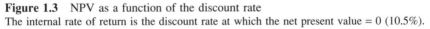

Figure 1.3 NPV as a function of the discount rate
The internal rate of return is the discount rate at which the net present value = 0 (10.5%).

principle of average and marginal concepts discussed in this chapter. This college investment was analyzed using average costs and benefits associated with investing in a college education. For any individual, these averages may not be representative of the incremental cost or benefits that they will actually experience.

Part I

Competitive Markets

Chapter 2

Demand

1 Introduction

Jung and Nelson Chai live in Lake Forest, Illinois, with their three children. Until 2004, they drove a Ford Expedition jumbo SUV and an Isuzu Trooper compact SUV respectively. Jung was appalled by the cost of refueling the Expedition and the jumbo SUV's emissions. She traded it in for a Ford Freestar minivan, which provided 19 miles per gallon (mpg), which was 25% better than the Expedition. Then, Nelson, an executive with an e-trading business, decided to sell his Isuzu Trooper compact SUV and buy a 55-mpg Toyota Prius gas-electric hybrid. *BusinessWeek* reported Jung's remark: "I look at gas prices now, and I just laugh . . . I'm very happy I made the switch."[1]

The yearly average retail price of gasoline in the U.S. fell from $1.56 per gallon in 2000 to a low of $1.44 per gallon in 2002. Since then, it has climbed each year to $2.34 per gallon in 2005. Gasoline is essential to car owners. Nevertheless, in early 2004, General Motors (GM) Vice-Chairman Robert A. Lutz still dismissed the impact of rising gasoline prices: "It sounds cavalier, but in any household budget, gasoline isn't a factor."

Light truck sales (including SUVs) comprise over half of all U.S. auto sales. SUVs alone account for over 23% of total sales. Rising gasoline prices have wrought major changes in the auto market. Between September 2004 and September 2005, the monthly average retail price of gasoline jumped from $1.85 per gallon to $3.08 per gallon. Sales of full-size SUVs dropped 16.8% over the same time period (with a particularly sharp 42.5% drop for full-size GM SUVs).

Meanwhile sales of hybrid gasoline-electric vehicles soared by 333%. A hybrid vehicle uses electric power from an on-board rechargeable energy storage system to economize gasoline or diesel fuel to propel the vehicle. Rising gasoline prices have accentuated the fuel-efficiency of hybrids.

How important are gasoline prices to the sales of SUVs and other types of automobiles, and how should the auto manufacturers respond to the increasing price of gasoline? Are

---

[1] This and following quotations are from "Steering Away From Guzzlers, *BusinessWeek* online, May 31, 2004, with additional data from www.greencarcongress.com and the US Energy Information Administration, www.eia.doe.gov.

manufacturer incentives an effective response? What are the combined effects of incentives (i.e., price reductions) and increasing gas prices?

In this chapter, we introduce the concept of a demand curve, which describes the quantity demanded of an item given its price, buyer's income, seller's advertising expenditure, and other relevant parameters such as the prices of complementary and substitutable goods. We apply demand to show how the rising price of gasoline has caused decreases in large SUV sales, and how manufacturer incentives can offset these reductions.

We begin with the demand curve of an individual buyer. This shows the quantity of the item that an individual will purchase as a function of its price. Next, we consider how demand depends on other factors, including income, the prices of other products, and advertising. Then, we extend from the demand of an individual to the demand curve of the entire market. With the model of demand, businesses can identify factors that affect the demand for their products, and how to influence that demand.

Using the individual buyer's demand curve, a seller can determine the maximum that the buyer is willing to pay for any specified quantity, and thereby extract the highest possible price. Finally, we highlight the important differences between consumer and business demand.

2   Individual Demand

> The **individual demand curve** is a graph showing the quantity that the buyer will purchase at every possible price.

To understand how a price cut will affect sales, we need to know how the cut in price will affect the purchases of the individual buyers and, generally, how an individual's purchases depend on the price of the item. The *individual demand curve* provides this information: it is a graph that shows the quantity that the buyer will purchase at every possible price. We shall present the concept of a demand curve with reference to an individual consumer.

Construction

The basic issue is how to determine an individual's demand curve. Let us address the issue by considering Joy's demand for movies. We must ask Joy a series of questions that elicit her responses to changes in price, while holding other things equal.

We first ask, "Other things equal, how many movies would you attend a month at a price of $20 per movie?" Suppose that Joy's answer is, "None." We must add the proviso of "other things equal" because Joy's decision may depend on other factors, such as her income and the price of popcorn in the movie theater. When constructing Joy's demand curve for movies, we focus on the effect of changes in the price of movies and hold all other factors constant.

We then pose similar questions to Joy for other possible prices for a movie: $19, $18, ... $1, and 0. For each of these prices, Joy will tell us how many movies she would attend a month. We can tabulate this information as shown in table 2.1. This table represents Joy's demand for movies.[2]

Next we graph the information from table 2.1 as shown in figure 2.1. We represent the price of movies on the vertical axis and the quantity in movies a month on the horizontal axis. At a price of $20, Joy says that she would not go to any movies, so we mark the point where

---

[2]   Table 2.1 is constructed assuming each consumer's demand relationship is *linear*. The constant slope allows us to complete the table without needing to complete all the rows of the table.

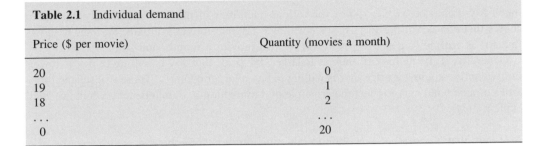

Table 2.1   Individual demand

Price ($ per movie)	Quantity (movies a month)
20	0
19	1
18	2
. . .	. . .
0	20

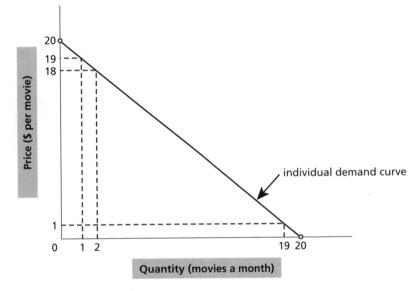

Figure 2.1   Individual demand curve
The individual demand curve shows, for every possible price, the quantity of movies that Joy will attend.
It also shows how much Joy would be willing to pay for various quantities.

the price is $20 and quantity of movies is 0. Continuing with the information from table 2.1,
we mark every pair of price and quantity that Joy reports. Joining these points, we then have
Joy's demand curve for movies.

The demand curve in figure 2.1 shows, for every possible price, the quantity of movies
that Joy will attend. Knowing Joy's demand curve, a movie theater can predict how Joy will
respond to changes in its price. For instance, if presently, the theater charges $12 per movie,
Joy goes to eight movies a month. If the theater reduces its price to $11 per movie, it knows
that Joy will increase her consumption to nine movies a month. By contrast, if the theater
raises its price to $13 per movie, Joy would cut back to seven movies a month.

Slope

The individual demand curve shows the quantity that the buyer will purchase at every possible price. Let us now consider the individual demand curve from another perspective.

Referring to Joy's demand curve in figure 2.1, we can use the curve to determine how much Joy would be *willing to pay* for various quantities of movies. Specifically, the curve shows that she is willing to pay $19 per movie for one movie a month. Further, it shows that Joy is willing to pay $18 per movie for two movies a month, and so on.

Generally, if the number of movies is larger, the price that Joy is willing to pay is lower. Equivalently, at a lower price, Joy is willing to buy a larger quantity. These two related properties of a demand curve reflect the principle of diminishing marginal benefit, which we shall explain next.

Any item that a consumer is willing to buy must provide some benefit, which may be psychic or monetary. We measure the benefit in monetary terms as we are interested in goods and services that are bought and sold. The **marginal benefit** is the benefit provided by an additional unit of the item. The marginal benefit of the first movie is the benefit from one movie a month. Similarly, the marginal benefit of the second movie is the additional benefit from seeing a second movie each month.

> The **marginal benefit** is the benefit provided by an additional unit of the item.

By the principle of **diminishing marginal benefit**, each additional unit of consumption or usage provides less benefit than the preceding unit. In Joy's case, this means that the marginal benefit of the second movie is less than the marginal benefit of the first movie, the marginal benefit of the third movie is less than the marginal benefit of the second movie, and so on.

> Principle of **diminishing marginal benefit**: each additional unit provides less benefit than the preceding unit.

Accordingly, the price that an individual is willing to pay will decrease with the quantity purchased. In terms of a graph, this means that the demand curve will slope downward. This is a general property of all demand curves: the lower the price, the larger will be the quantity demanded. Hence, demand curves slope downward. The fundamental reason for this downward slope is diminishing marginal benefit.

Progress Check 2A Suppose that the movie theater presently charges $11 per movie. By how much must the theater cut its price for Joy to increase her consumption by three movies a month?

Preferences

Our procedure for constructing a demand curve relies completely on the consumer's individual preferences. The individual decides how much he or she wants to buy at each possible price. The demand curve then displays information in a graphical way.

There are two implications of this approach. First, the demand curve will change with changes in the consumer's preferences. As a person grows older, her or his demand for rock videos and junk food will decline, while the demand for adult contemporary music CDs and healthcare will increase.

Second, different consumers may have different preferences and hence different demand curves. One consumer may like red meat while another is a vegetarian. We get the demand curve for each consumer from her or his individual responses to the questions regarding the quantity she or he would buy at each possible price.

┌─ **Gasoline prices and driving** ─┐

With average gasoline prices well above $2.50 per gallon, an ABC News poll reported that 94% of Americans were disappointed about gasoline prices and 44% were angry. The proportion of people with lower incomes (earning less than $100,000 a year) who were angry was 46%, while the proportion among higher-income people (earning $100,000 a year or more) was lower at 32%.

Despite higher gasoline bills, just 22% of survey respondents said that they were driving less. However, 63% said that they would cut back on driving if gasoline prices rose above $3 per gallon.

Source: ABC News, "Many Angry about Gas Prices, and Are Cutting Back Elsewhere," August 22, 2005.

3   Demand and Income

We have mentioned that Joy's demand for movies may depend on other factors besides the price of such movies. For instance, if she gets a raise, she might spend more on movies. Her demand for movies will also depend on the price of alternative forms of entertainment such as video rentals.

The individual demand curve shows explicitly how the quantity that a person buys depends on the price of the item. The demand curve, however, does not explicitly display the effect of changes in income and other factors that affect demand. How do changes in these other factors affect an individual's demand curve? In this section, we focus on the effect of changes in the buyer's income and consider the impact of other factors in the next section.

Income Changes

Let us consider the effect of changes in income on demand in the context of Joy's demand for movies. Suppose that Joy's income is presently $50,000 a year. Table 2.1 and figure 2.1 represent Joy's demand curve for movies when her income is $50,000 a year.

We then ask Joy a series of questions. These questions probe the effect of changes in income as well as price: "Suppose that your income were $40,000 a year. Other things equal, how many movies would you buy a month at a price of $20 per movie?" We then pose the same question with other possible prices and tabulate the information.

Suppose that table 2.2 represents Joy's answers. We also represent this information in figure 2.2, with the price of movies on the vertical axis and number of movies a month on the horizontal axis. Marking the pairs of prices and quantities, and joining the points, we have Joy's demand curve with an income of $40,000 a year. We can see that Joy's demand curve for movies with a $40,000 income lies to the left of her demand curve with a $50,000 income. At every price, Joy's quantity demanded with a $40,000 income is less than or equal to her quantity demanded with a $50,000 income.

The effect of a change in income on the demand curve is very different from that of a change in price. Recall that an individual demand curve shows the quantity that the person will buy for every possible price, other things equal. Referring to figure 2.1, if the price of movies drops from $12 to $11 per movie, while Joy's income remains unchanged at $50,000 a year, we can trace Joy's response by moving along her demand curve from the $12 level to the $11 level.

Table 2.2   Individual demand with lower income

Price ($ per movie)	Quantity (movies a month)
20	0
19	0
. . .	0
10	0
9	2
8	4
. . .	. . .
0	20

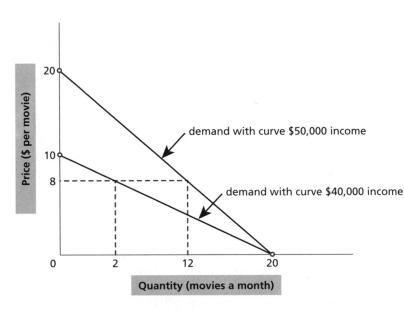

Figure 2.2   Individual demand curve with lower income
As Joy's income falls from $50,000 to $40,000, her entire demand curve shifts toward the left.

Suppose, however, that Joy's income drops from $50,000 to $40,000 a year. This change in income will affect her purchases of movies at all price levels – $20, $19, $18, . . . , 0. Accordingly, the drop in income will shift her entire demand curve. Figure 2.2 shows that, when Joy's income drops from $50,000 to $40,000 a year, her entire demand curve for movies shifts toward the left.

Let us understand the difference between a change in price and a change in income from another perspective. On figure 2.2, at the $8 level, we can mark two quantities: a quantity of 12 movies a month when Joy's income is $50,000, and another quantity of four movies a month when Joy's income is $40,000. Can we join these points to form a demand curve? The answer is definitely "no," because each point corresponds to a different income. A demand curve shows how a buyer's purchases depend on changes in the price of some item, holding income and all other factors unchanged. Accordingly, for each of the points that we have marked, there is a separate demand curve.

In general, a change in the price of an item will cause a movement along the demand curve for that item. By contrast, a change in income or any factor other than the price of the item will cause a shift in the entire demand curve.

Normal vis-à-vis Inferior Products

When Joy's income drops from $50,000 to $40,000 a year, her demand for movies shifts to the left. As Joy's income falls, her demand for movies also falls. By contrast, if her income were to rise, her demand would increase.

Let us compare Joy's demand for movies in general with her demand for afternoon matinees. Many movie theaters offer afternoon matinees at a cheaper price than their regular evening showings. If Joy's income falls, it is quite possible that she will substitute cheaper forms of entertainment for more expensive ones. In particular, the drop in her income may lead to an increase in her demand for afternoon matinees.

By contrast, when Joy's income increases, we can expect her to switch away from cheaper forms of entertainment and toward more expensive alternatives. So, as her income rises, Joy's demand for afternoon matinees will fall.

Goods and services can be categorized according to the effect of changes in income on demand. If the demand for an item increases as the buyer's income increases, while the demand falls as the buyer's income falls, then the item is considered a *normal product*. Equivalently, the demand for a **normal product** is positively related to changes in the buyer's income.

> For a **normal product**, demand is positively related to changes in buyer's income.

By contrast, the demand for an **inferior product** is negatively related to changes in the buyer's income. This means that the demand falls as the buyer's income increases, while the demand increases as the buyer's income falls.

> For an **inferior product**, demand is negatively related to changes in buyer's income.

We can apply this classification to Joy. For her, movies in general are a normal product, while afternoon matinees are an inferior product. Generally, broad categories of products tend to be normal, while particular products within the categories may be inferior.

Consider, for instance, transportation services. The entire category is probably a normal product: the higher a person's income, the more he or she tends to spend on transportation. Public transportation, however, may be an inferior product: with a higher income, the typical commuter switches from public transport to a private car. Similarly, higher education tends to be a normal good, but public higher education is estimated to be an inferior good while private higher education is strongly normal.

Consumer electronics provide another example. While consumer electronics as a category is a normal product, particular products such as all-in-one stereos may be inferior.

The distinction between normal and inferior products is important for business strategy. When the economy is growing and incomes are rising, the demand for normal products will rise, while the demand for inferior products will fall. By contrast, when the economy is in recession and incomes are falling, the demand for normal products will fall, while the demand for inferior products will rise.

The normal-inferior product distinction is also important for international business. The demand for normal products is relatively higher in richer countries, while the demand for inferior products is relatively higher in poorer countries. For instance, in developed countries, relatively more people commute to work by car than bicycle. The reverse is true in very poor countries.

Progress Check 2B Draw a curve to represent an individual consumer's demand for all-in-one stereos. (a) Explain why it slopes downward. (b) How will a drop in the consumer's income affect the demand curve?

⊣ T-Mobile USA: pre-paid vis-à-vis post-paid ⊢

With pre-paid mobile service, subscribers pay for specific quantities of air-time in advance. By contrast, with contract (also called "post-paid") service, subscribers enter into an agreement for a minimum period which may be 12 or 24 months and may use any quantity of air-time subject to payment of the end-of-month bill.

Pre-paid service caters to different market segments from contract service. Typical customers for pre-paid service include people that the service provider would consider a bad risk for contract service – those without a regular high income, migrant workers, and travelers. To the extent that it caters to customers with relatively lower income, pre-paid service is an inferior product. As incomes rise, users would upgrade from pre-paid to contract service.

T-Mobile USA, based in Bellevue, Washington, is a subsidiary of Deutsche Telekom and provides wireless voice, messaging, and data services across the United States. T-Mobile's pre-paid service covers a more limited area than its post-paid service. In 2005, T-Mobile earned an average revenue of $25 per month from 3.266 million pre-paid customers, and $55 per month from 18.424 million post-paid customers.

Source: T-Mobile USA, Press Release, March 2, 2006.

4   Other Factors in Demand

The individual demand for an item may depend on other factors besides the price of the item and the buyer's income. The other factors include the prices of related products, advertising, durability, season, weather, and location. In this section, we focus on the prices of related products, durability, and advertising. The principles for the other factors are similar, hence we do not analyze each one of them explicitly.

Complements and Substitutes

Assume that Joy always eats popcorn when she goes to the movies. How will an increase in the price of popcorn affect Joy's demand for movies? Recall that Joy's demand curve for movies shows the quantity that she will purchase for every possible price of a movie, other things equal. A change in the price is represented by a movement along the demand curve. By contrast, a change in any other factor such as the price of popcorn will affect Joy's purchases of movies at all prices of movies. Hence, it will cause a shift in the entire demand curve.

Suppose that, presently, the price of popcorn is $1. Figure 2.3 represents Joy's demand curve for movies when the price of popcorn is $1.

We next construct Joy's demand when the price of popcorn is $2. To do so, we ask Joy a series of questions to probe the effect of changes in the prices of both popcorn and movies:

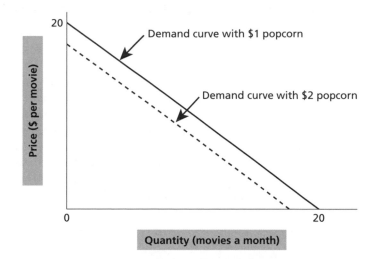

Figure 2.3 Individual demand curve with a more expensive complement
As the price of popcorn increases, Joy's entire demand curve shifts toward the left.

"Suppose that the price of popcorn is $2. Other things equal, how many movies would you attend a month at a price of $20 per movie?"

By repeating this question for all other prices of movies and marking the pairs of prices and quantities on a graph, we can obtain Joy's demand curve when the price of popcorn is $2. Figure 2.3 shows this demand curve: When the price of popcorn is higher, the demand curve for movies is further to the left.

In general, related products can be classified as either complements or substitutes according to the effect of a price increase in one product on the demand for the other. Two products are **complements** if an increase in the price of one causes the demand for the other to fall. By contrast, two products are **substitutes** if an increase in the price of one causes the demand for the other to increase.

> Two products are **complements** if an increase in the price of one causes a fall in the demand for the other.

> Two products are **substitutes** if an increase in the price of one causes an increase in the demand for the other.

In Joy's case, popcorn and movies are complements. The more movies that she sees, the more popcorn she will want. Hence, if the price of popcorn is higher, the price of the overall movie experience will be higher, and she will go to fewer movies.

How will an increase in the price of video rentals affect Joy's demand for movies? Instead of seeing a movie, Joy could watch a rented video. Accordingly, these two products are substitutes. If there is an increase in the price of video rentals, Joy's demand for movies will increase.

Generally, a demand curve will shift to the left if there is either an increase in the price of a complement or a fall in the price of a substitute. By contrast, a demand curve will shift to the right if there is either a fall in the price of a complement or an increase in the price of a substitute.

> **Progress Check 2C** Referring to figure 2.1, how will a fall in the price of video rentals affect the original demand curve?

⊣ Gasoline prices and the demand for SUVs vis-à-vis hybrids ⊢

Large SUVs like the Ford Expedition and Isuzu Trooper consume much more gasoline per mile than gas-electric hybrid cars like the Toyota Prius. Gasoline is a complement to motor vehicles, while hybrid cars are a substitute for SUVs.

Sustained increases in the price of gasoline have resulted in a substantial decline in the demand for large SUVs and a corresponding increase in the demand for hybrids.

General Motors and other American manufacturers of SUVs have responded to the drop in demand by offering incentives. Incentives are essentially are price cuts, and led to movements along the demand curve towards higher quantities demanded.

On balance, the net effect of higher gasoline prices and manufacturer incentives has been a reduction in large SUV sales. In the next chapter, we will see how these two somewhat offsetting effects (decreased demand and increasing quantity demanded) can be further quantified and compared.

⊣ Financing new vehicle purchases ⊢

A key way by which the auto industry has promoted sales of new vehicles is through leasing programs. These leasing programs provide buyers a lower cost of entry for new vehicles compared to bank loans.

The promotion of leases provided a substitution for bank loans and increased the percentage of vehicle under a loan or lease agreement from 26.3% in 1992 to 34.5% in 2001. Leases became attractive to buyers; who typically could not get bank loans, by providing an opportunity to upgrade to higher priced models and who regularly replace vehicles in 2–4 year increments.

Leases provided for increased demand but also caused substitution of bank loans. In 1992 8.5% of recent model vehicles were under lease, and this increased to 17.5% in 2001. Leasing peaked in 1999, decreased by almost 20% by 2003, and then began to increase again. One reason for the recent declines in leasing is falling interest rates which made loans relatively cheaper than leases for new car buyers. Forecasts for 2006 are for 16.8% of new cars to be leased in 2006, up from 15.4% in 2003.

Sources: Ana Aizcorbe, Martha Starr, and James T. Hickman, "Vehicle Purchases, Leasing, and Replacement Demand: Evidence from the Federal Reserve's Survey of Consumer Finances," *Business Economics*, April 2004; Automotive Lease Guide, March 2006 at www.blcassociates.com/e-newsletters/0306-ALG-Forecast.html.

Advertising

Advertising expenditure is another factor in demand. For instance, Joy's demand for movies may depend on advertising by the theater. Advertising may be informative as well as persuasive. Informative advertising communicates information to potential buyers and sellers. For instance, movie theaters list the movies that they are showing and their show times in the daily newspapers. These listings inform potential customers.

Persuasive advertising aims to influence consumer choice. Manufacturers of cigarettes and cosmetics, for instance, use commercials to retain the loyalty of existing consumers and attract others to switch brands. Marketers may also use persuasive advertising to promote new products.

Generally, an increase in advertising expenditure, whether informative or persuasive, will increase demand. Conversely, a reduction in advertising expenditure will cause demand to fall. The effect of advertising expenditure on demand may be subject to a diminishing marginal product, which means that each additional dollar spent on advertising has a relatively smaller effect on demand. (We will elaborate on the concept of a diminishing marginal product in chapter 4.)

The effect of advertising on a consumer's demand depends on the medium. TV commercials during football games will have more effect on male consumers, while those during cartoons will have relatively more effect on children. Print advertisements in women's magazines will have more effect on female consumers, while those in car magazines will have relatively more effect on auto enthusiasts.

Durable Goods

Durable goods, such as automobiles, home appliances, and machinery, provide a stream of services over an extended period of time. In addition to price, income, the prices of complements and substitutes, and advertising, three factors are particularly significant in the demand for durable goods. They are expectations about future prices and incomes, interest rates, and the price of used models.

By the very nature of durable goods, buyers have some discretion over the timing of purchase. Hence, the demand for durables depends significantly on buyer expectations about future prices and incomes. For instance, a consumer who is pessimistic about his future income may postpone replacing his car. A consumer who expects automobile manufacturers to cut prices at the end of the model year may delay a purchase until the price is cut.

In addition, many buyers need to finance their purchases of durable goods. Accordingly, the demand for durables depends significantly on interest rates. If interest rates are low, then the cost of buying a car or home will be lower; hence, the demand for these durables will be higher. By contrast, if interest rates are high, then the cost of buying a durable will be higher and the demand will be lower.

Finally, an important factor in the demand for new "big-ticket" durable goods such as homes, automobiles and machinery is the price of used models. Used cars are a substitute for new automobiles and, likewise, used machinery is a substitute for new equipment. A higher price for used cars affects the demand for new cars in two ways. First, the higher price makes the used car less attractive; hence, it increases the demand for a new car. Second, the higher price signals a higher resale value and so will encourage consumers to purchase new cars.

⊢ A textbook case of durable goods demand ⊢

College textbooks are an example of a durable good – buyers have the option of purchasing a new or used textbook. Textbook demand is simpler than many other durable goods (e.g., refrigerators, autos, etc.) in that purchases are rarely delayed. A student will generally purchase the required text when it is time to enroll in the course.

A typical college student spends around $900 per year on textbooks. In 2003, the used book market represented 28.5% of the total textbook market. Students often sell back their texts at the end of a semester. Most college bookstores buy back books at 50% of the price, if they will be used by future instructors, and if a new edition has not been issued. When a new edition is issued, the resale value of a text typically collapses. Critics claim that publishers issue new editions principally in order to limit the resale market for books.

Buyers of textbooks can choose between new and used books, and their effective cost will depend on the likelihood that a new edition will be issued. Research in behavioral economics suggests that consumers are often excessively myopic, and may have difficulty evaluating decisions that have a time dimension (such as later resale). If this is the case, then textbook publishers may be able to exploit this behavior by releasing new editions to undermine their resale value.

On the other hand, if textbook buyers behave rationally, they should take into account the future resale opportunity for the books. In this case, the resale market will not threaten publishers, provided that they can commit to not lowering the prices of the books over time. Buyers would then incorporate the future resale value into their current values for the books.

A recent study tested whether textbook buyer behavior conforms to the rational consumer model or the alternative behavioral economics model. It rejected the behavioral model and found that students are not myopic, having discount rates with reasonable values (20% or less).

The study found that prices of new and used textbooks remain fairly constant over the life of an edition, although the revision probability of the edition varies significantly. Used book sales exceed new sales by about 3 or 4 semesters into the life of an edition. As the probability of revision increases, the price sensitivity of consumers increases.

Hence, publishers must establish a balance when considering acceleration of the revision cycle of textbooks (typically, a new edition is issued every three years). Shorter cycles would increase the proportion of new textbook sales, but would decrease the willingness to pay of students, since the revision probability would be larger. The study concludes that the net effect on publisher profits would be negative.

Source: J. A. Chevalier and A. Goolsbee, 2005 draft, "Are Durable Goods Consumers Forward Looking? Evidence from College Textbooks," available at http://gsbwww.uchicago.edu/fac/austan.goolsbee/research/texts.pdf.

5   Market Demand

The **market demand curve** is a graph showing the quantity that all buyers will purchase at every possible price.

Businesses that deal with many different customers may determine their strategy on the basis of the entire market rather than individual customers. Such businesses need to understand the demand of the entire market. The *market demand curve* is a graph that shows the quantity that all buyers will purchase at every possible price. The analysis of a **market demand curve** is essentially similar to that for an individual demand curve.

Construction

To construct the market demand for an item, we must interview all the potential consumers and ask each person the quantity that he or she would buy at every possible price. For each price, we then add the reported individual quantities to get the quantity that the market as a whole will demand.

Let us apply this procedure to construct the market demand for movies. Suppose that there are only three potential consumers: Joy, Max, and Lucas. We ask each of them, "Other things equal, how many movies would you attend a month at a price of $20 per movie?" Table 2.3 reports their answers. The market quantity demanded is 0.

Table 2.3 Market demand

Price ($ per movie)	Quantity (movies a month)			
	Joy	Max	Lucas	Market
20	0	0	0	0
19	1	0	0	1
18	2	0	0	2
. . .	. . .	0	0	. . .
10	10	10	0	20
8	12	14	2	28
. . .	. . .	. . .	. . .	. . .
0	20	30	10	60

We then repeat these questions for other possible prices: $19, $18, . . . , $0 per movie. At each price, we add the reported individual quantities to get the market quantity demanded. For instance, at a price of $8, Joy would go to 12 movies, Max would go to 14 movies, and Lucas would go to two; hence, the market quantity demanded is 12 + 14 + 2 = 28 movies.

We represent the market demand on a graph, with the price of movies on the vertical axis and quantity on the horizontal axis, in figure 2.4. Joining the pairs of prices and quantities, we have the market demand for movies. This market demand curve is in bold.

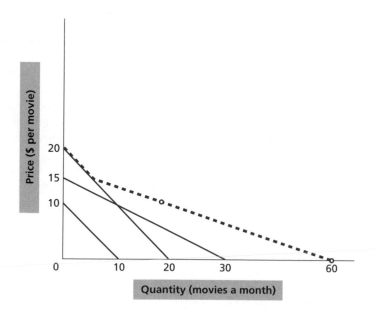

Figure 2.4 Market demand curve
The market demand curve is the horizontal summation of the individual demand curves. At every price, the market quantity demanded is the sum of the individual quantities demanded.

Another way to construct the market demand curve is by *horizontal summation* of the individual demand curves. On figure 2.4, we draw the individual demand curves of the three potential consumers: Joy, Max, and Lucas.

To do a **horizontal summation**, add the demand curves in the horizontal direction.

Horizontal summation means that we add the curves in the horizontal direction. The individual demand curves show the number of movies that each of the three consumers will buy at every possible price. So, at every price, we add the quantities that the three consumers buy to obtain the quantity that the market will buy.

Since the individual demand curves slope downward, the market demand curve also slopes downward. The fundamental reason is that all consumers get diminishing marginal benefit; hence, at a lower price, the market as a whole will buy a larger quantity.

Other Factors

Like individual demand, the market demand depends on other factors, including buyers' incomes, the prices of related products, and advertising. The market demand curve for an item shows explicitly only the effect of price on the quantity that the market wishes to buy. So, a change in the price of the item will cause a movement along the market demand curve from one point to another on the same curve.

By contrast, the market demand curve does not explicitly show other factors, such as incomes, the prices of related products, and advertising. Accordingly, changes in these factors will shift the entire market demand curve. In the math supplement to this chapter, we use algebra to explain how changes in the various factors affect a special type of smooth demand curve: a straight-line demand curve.

The directions of the effects of changes in the other factors on the market demand curve are similar to those for the individual demand curve. We will not repeat the discussion here. Instead, we focus on the key differences. An important application of demand analysis is to compare market demands in different countries. In each country, the market demand will depend on incomes as well as other factors. Let us discuss how to measure incomes in different countries.

Generally, there are two ways of measuring the income of an entire country: the gross national product (GNP) and the gross domestic product (GDP). Broadly, the GNP and GDP measure the total amount produced in a country for a given year. Since employers must pay workers, landlords, and lenders, the total value of production is also the total income of the country. The GNP is the GDP plus net income from foreign sources; hence, the two measures are closely related.

The average income of the residents of some country may be estimated by dividing either the GNP or the GDP by the population, which yields the GNP and GDP per capita, respectively. This can be converted into U.S. dollars by using the relevant exchange rate between the domestic currency and the U.S. dollar.

Income Distribution

Market researchers frequently take a shortcut when assessing market demand. Instead of considering the demand of all individual consumers and adding these individual demands, a common simplification is to estimate the demand for an individual with average income and multiply that by the number of buyers.

This simple approach ignores the distribution of income; that is, whether consumers have very similar or very disparate incomes. The distribution of income may have an important effect on the demand for particular items.

For instance, suppose that Northland and Southland have identical national incomes of $29.8 billion and populations of 1 million. In both countries, the average per capita income is $29,800. In Northland, 1% of the people earn $100,000 a year, while the other 99% earn $20,000 a year; however, in Southland, everyone has an equal income. Northland may have a substantial demand for cosmetic surgery, luxury cars, and designer clothing. By contrast, there will be no demand for these items in Southland.

Generally, the more uneven is the distribution of income, the more important it is to consider the actual distribution of income and not merely the average income when estimating market demand.

Progress Check 2D Referring to figure 2.4, show how an increase in the price of a complement would affect the market demand.

⊣ Who buys washing machines in India? ⊢

With an average income of less than $1000 a year, the people of India are among the poorest in the world. How could they afford to buy 1.3 million units of washing machines in 2002? The answer to this question is that many people earn much more than the average income.

In India, income is less evenly distributed than in major developed countries. The top 10% of the population receive 33% of national income, and the next 10% of the population receive over 22% of income. Sales of washing machines grew quickly in the 1990s, and then stagnated in the new decade. Market researchers Euromonitor explained, "the cost of washing machines is still prohibitive to the majority of households in India. The number of households able to afford washing machines has probably been exhausted."

Although the overall picture was bleak, sales in southern India were relatively strong. Water shortages in the south persuaded households to replace their machines with models that used less water.

Sources: Euromonitor, "Home Laundry Appliances," 2003; "What Is Middle Class?" in Pictures @ India, August 2003.

---

6   Buyer Surplus

An individual buyer's demand curve shows the quantity that the buyer will purchase at every possible price. We now consider the buyer's demand curve from another perspective, which is to show the maximum amount that a buyer is willing to pay for each unit of the item. This perspective is important for business strategy as it shows how a seller can calculate the maximum price that the buyer can be charged for a given purchase.

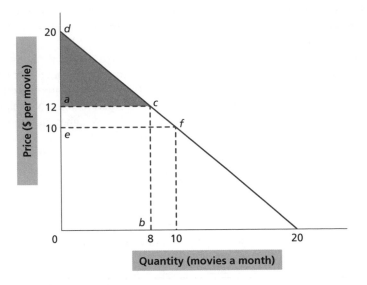

Figure 2.5 Individual buyer surplus
The individual buyer surplus is the buyer's total benefit from some quantity of purchases less the actual expenditure. At a price of $12, Joy's buyer surplus is the shaded area between the demand curve and the $12 line.

Benefit

Recall that the marginal benefit is the benefit provided by an additional unit of an item. It can be measured as the maximum amount of money that the buyer is willing to pay for that unit. To illustrate, consider Joy's demand curve for movies, reproduced in figure 2.5. This shows that Joy is willing to pay $19 for the first movie; hence, her marginal benefit from one movie is $19. Similarly, Joy is willing to pay $18 for the second movie; hence, her marginal benefit from the second movie is $18, and so on.

In effect, Joy's demand curve is also her marginal benefit curve. This perspective also implies that the demand curve slopes downward. By the principle of diminishing marginal benefit, each additional movie gives less benefit than the one before. Hence, Joy's marginal benefit curve will slope downward. Since the marginal benefit curve is identical with Joy's demand curve, this means that Joy's demand curve will slope downward.

> The **total benefit** is the benefit yielded by all the units that the buyer purchases.

We have just seen how the demand curve shows the marginal benefit from each unit that a buyer purchases. Using this information, we can then calculate the buyer's **total benefit**, which is the benefit yielded by all the units that the buyer purchases. The total benefit is the marginal benefit from the first unit plus the marginal benefit from the second unit, and so on, up to and including marginal benefit from the last unit that the buyer purchases.

A buyer's total benefit from some quantity of purchases is the maximum that the buyer is willing to pay for that quantity. Graphically, the total benefit is represented by the area under the buyer's demand curve up to and including the last unit purchased.[3] Let us apply this approach to calculate Joy's total benefit from eight movies a month. Her total benefit is

---

[3] Technically, this is only true if prices and quantities can take infinitely small values. For simplicity, we ignore this detail. The area will approximate the sum of the discrete values if prices and quantities cannot vary continuously.

the area under her demand curve up to and including eight movies a month. In figure 2.5, this is area $0bcd = \frac{1}{2}(\$8 \times 8) + \$12 \times 8 = \$128$. Hence, the maximum that Joy would be willing to pay for four movies a month is $128.

Benefit vis-à-vis Price

Suppose that the price of a movie is $12. Then Joy goes to eight movies a month. As already calculated, her total benefit would be $128. Joy, however, needs to pay only $12 × 8 = $96, which is substantially less than her total benefit. The difference between a buyer's total benefit from some quantity of purchases and the actual expenditure is called the **buyer surplus**. At a price of $12 per movie, Joy's buyer surplus is $128 − $96 = $32.

Referring to figure 2.5, Joy's total benefit from eight movies a month is represented by the area $0bcd$ under her demand (marginal benefit) curve up to and including eight movies a month. At a price of $12, her expenditure on eight movies a month is represented by the area $0bca$ under the $12 line up to and including eight movies a month. Joy's **buyer surplus** is the difference between these two areas, that is, the area acd between her demand curve and the $12 line.

> The **buyer surplus** is the difference between a buyer's total benefit from some quantity of purchases and the buyer's actual expenditure.

Generally, provided that purchases are voluntary, a buyer must get some surplus; otherwise, he or she will not buy. Hence, the maximum that a seller can charge is the buyer's total benefit. If a seller tries to charge more, then the buyer will walk away.

Progress Check 2E Suppose that the price of movies is $8. In figure 2.5, mark Joy's buyer surplus at that price.

Price Changes

Referring to Joy's demand for movies, at the price of $12, Joy goes to eight movies a month, and her buyer surplus is area acd. Now suppose that the price drops to $10. Then Joy will raise her attendance from eight to ten movies a month. Her buyer surplus will increase by area $efca$. The increase in buyer surplus can be attributed to two effects – she gets the eight original movies at a lower price, and she goes to more movies.

⊢ Price promotions: the more you buy, the more you save? ⊣

Students at the University of California, Los Angeles, enjoy several privileges. One is a good education at a low price. Another is California's unbeatable weather, and a third is discounted movie tickets. Suppose that Alan buys 12 tickets a year at $7 rather than the full price of $10. By how much does he gain from the discount scheme?

One answer is that Alan "saves" $10 − $7 = $3 on each ticket, which adds to a total of $3 × 12 = $36. This answer, however, implicitly assumes that Alan would buy 12 tickets a year whether the price is $7 or $10.

For the correct answer, we apply the concept of buyer surplus. Figure 2.6 represents Alan's demand curve for movies. At the $10 full price, Alan would buy six tickets a year and get the buyer surplus of the shaded area bac. By contrast, at the discount price of $7, Alan buys 12 tickets a year and gets the buyer surplus of the shaded area bac plus the area $deab$.

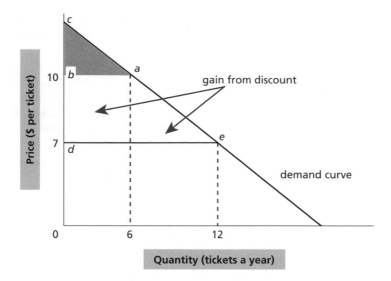

Figure 2.6 Value of discount movie tickets
The reduction in the price of movie tickets from $10 to $7 increases Alan's buyer surplus by the area *deab*.

Thus, the discount scheme increases Alan's buyer surplus by the area *deab*. This represents $(10 − 7) × 0.5(6 + 12) = $27, which is Alan's gain from the discount scheme.

We can analyze this $27 gain in two parts. First, Alan can buy six tickets (the number that he would have bought at the full $10 price) at a lower price. He gains $10 − $7 = $3 on each of these six tickets, or a total of $3 × 6 = $18. Second, the discount scheme induces Alan to increase his purchases to 12 tickets a year. Alan will get some buyer surplus on each of the additional tickets. In figure 2.6, the buyer surplus on the seventh through twelfth tickets is 0.5 × $(10 − 7) × 6 = $9.

Generally, a buyer gains from a price reduction in two ways. First, the buyer gets a lower price on the quantity that he or she would have purchased at the original higher price. Second, he or she can buy more, gaining buyer surplus on each of the additional purchases. The extent of the second effect depends on the buyer's response to the price reduction. The greater the increase in purchases, the larger will be the buyer's gain from the price reduction.

Similarly, a buyer loses from a price increase in two ways – the buyer must pay a higher price, and he or she will buy less.

Package Deals and Two-Part Pricing

A seller who has complete flexibility over pricing maximizes its profit by charging each buyer just a little less than his or her total benefit. Suppose, for instance, that figure 2.7 describes Jania's demand for mobile telephone calls. If the mobile telephone service charges a price of 50 cents per minute, Jania will make 30 minutes of calls a month. The service would earn a revenue of 30 × 50 cents = $15. Jania would get buyer surplus of 0.5 × 30 × 150 cents = $22.50.

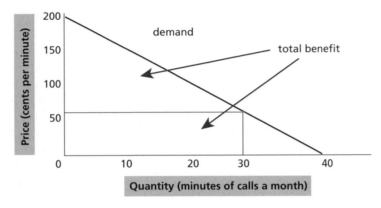

Figure 2.7 Package deal
Jania will buy a package deal of 30 minutes of calls for any price not exceeding her total benefit of $37.50.

Jania's total benefit from 30 minutes of calls a month is the area under her demand curve from 0 to 30 minutes, or $30 \times 0.5(200 + 50) = \$37.50$. Suppose that the mobile telephone service offers Jania a *package deal* of 30 minutes of calls at $37 with no other alternative. The package deal will give Jania a buyer surplus of $37.50 – $37 = 50 cents. Since there is no other alternative, Jania will buy this package. The service will earn $37 in revenue, which is more than double the revenue from the 50-cent pricing policy. The package deal enables the service to soak up almost all of Jania's buyer surplus.

> A **two-part price** is a pricing scheme consisting of a fixed payment and a charge based on usage.

The mobile telephone service could also extract Jania's buyer surplus through a *two-part price*. A **two-part price** is a pricing scheme comprising a fixed payment and a charge based on usage.

Suppose that the mobile telephone provider offers a two-part price comprising a $22 monthly charge and an airtime charge of 50 cents a minute. Referring to figure 2.7, Jania would choose 30 minutes of calls a month. Her total benefit would be the area under her demand curve from 0 to 30 minutes, which we earlier calculated to be $37.50. She would pay $22 in monthly charge and 30×50 cents = $15 in airtime charges. Hence, her buyer surplus would be $37.50 – $22 – $15 = 50 cents. Just like the package deal, the two-part price enables the service provider to soak up most of the consumer's buyer surplus.

Providers of many services, including banking, car rentals, telecommunications and Internet access make widespread use of package deals and two-part pricing. They also combine the two pricing techniques so that the monthly charge covers a specified quantity of "free" usage while the user must pay a usage charge beyond the free quantity. Table 2.4 reports several examples.

Market Buyer Surplus

We have introduced the concept of buyer surplus for individual buyers. To see how the concept applies at the market level, let us consider the market demand for movies reproduced in figure 2.8. At a price of $8, the market quantity demanded is 28 movies. The market's total benefit is the area under the market demand curve up to and including 28 movies. By contrast, the market's expenditure for 28 movies is the area under the $8 line up to and including 28 movies a month.

Table 2.4 Two-part prices

Business	Provider	Fixed payment	Usage charge
Check-writing bank account, California	Bank of America, VERSATEL checking	Nil	$2 per teller transaction
Broadband Access, Hong Kong	PCCW Netvigator 3M Single User Plan	HK$298 per month	Includes 100 free hours; HK$2 per additional hour
Weekday car rental, Melbourne Airport	Airport Rent-a-Car, Toyota Camry Sedan	A$70 for one day	Includes 100 free km; A$0.25 per additional km
Mobile telephone service, United Arab Emirates	Etisalat Corporation, GSM Standard Service	125 dirham connection fee; 60 dirham subscription per quarter	0.24 dirham per minute at peak time; 0.18 dirham per minute at off peak

Sources: Company websites.

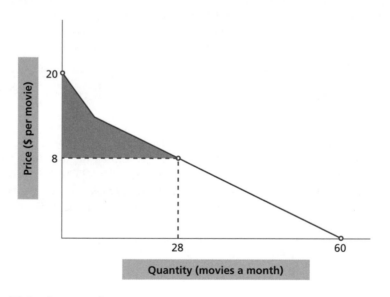

Figure 2.8 Market buyer surplus
At a price of $8, the market buyer surplus is the shaded area between the market demand curve and the $8 line.

The total benefit exceeds the expenditure; that is, the market as a whole is not paying the maximum that it would be willing to pay for that quantity of purchases. The difference is the market buyer surplus. Graphically, it is the area between the market demand curve and the $8 line. (Recall that, likewise, the buyer surplus of an individual consumer is the area between his or her demand curve and the price line.)

The principles underlying the market buyer surplus are the same as those for the individual buyer surplus. When the market price rises, the market buyer surplus drops as buyers suffer from the higher price and cut their purchases. By contrast, when the market price falls, the market buyer surplus increases as buyers enjoy the lower price and expand their purchases.

The concept of market buyer surplus will be useful in analyzing the impact of price changes on the market as a whole and in developing pricing policies to maximize a seller's profit.

7 Business Demand

We have introduced the concepts of individual and market demand through the example of movies. Movies are a consumer good. By contrast, some items are purchased only by businesses. Examples include TV commercials, heavy trucks, machine tools, and human resources. Some items, such as gasoline and telephone calls, are purchased by both consumers and businesses.

Accordingly, it is important to understand the principles of business demand. In many ways, these principles are similar to those underlying consumer demand. Therefore, we will focus on the important differences between business and consumer demand.

Inputs

Consumers buy goods and services for final consumption or usage. By contrast, businesses do not purchase goods and services for their own sake but to use them as inputs in the production of other goods and services. We will make a detailed analysis of business operations in chapter 4. Here, we will review only the essentials necessary to understand the business demand for inputs.

For convenience, the inputs purchased by a business can be classified into materials, energy, labor, and capital. Businesses use these inputs to produce outputs for sale to consumers or other businesses. For example, an express delivery service uses human resources, equipment, vehicles, planes, and energy to deliver documents and packages for consumers and businesses.

The inputs may be substitutes or complements. Consider, the express delivery service. Its trucks and drivers are complements: a truck without a driver is quite useless, as is a driver without a truck. Other inputs may be substitutes. For example, the service may use machines or workers to sort packages. Similarly, operations such as loading and packing could be performed by machine or manually.

Demand

A business produces items for sale to consumers or other businesses. The business earns revenues from sales. By raising the quantity of inputs, the business can produce a larger output and hence a change in revenue. Accordingly, the business can measure its marginal benefit from an input as the increase in revenue arising from an additional unit of the input.

Using the marginal benefit of an input, we can construct the individual demand curve of a business. This shows the quantity of the input that the business will purchase at every possible price. A business should buy an input up to the quantity that its marginal benefit from the input exactly balances the price.

We suppose that, when the quantity of an input is larger, each additional unit of the input will generate a smaller increase in revenue. This means that the input provides a diminishing marginal benefit to the business.

Hence, when the price is lower, the business will buy a larger quantity, and conversely, when the price is higher, the business will buy a smaller quantity. Thus, the demand curve for the input slopes downward.

⊣ **General Motors' demand for aluminum** ⊢

Aluminum is a strong, lightweight metal made from bauxite ore. By substituting aluminum for steel and other materials, automobile manufacturers can reduce vehicle weight, and so, improve fuel economy and thereby reduce emissions.

Alcoa is one of the world's leading aluminum manufacturers. According to President of Alcoa Advanced Transportation Systems, Misha Riveros-Jacobson, reducing vehicle weight by 10% improves fuel consumption by 9%. Further, she contended that: "Pound for pound, aluminum can be stiffer than steel."

With sustained increases in oil prices, car buyers have sought lighter vehicles. Consequently, auto-makers have systematically replaced steel and iron with aluminum. In 1973, the average aluminum content per vehicle manufactured in North America was 81 lb. By 2005, the average content had risen to 319 lb.

In 1998, to address the volatility of aluminum prices, GM signed several long-term billion-dollar purchase agreements. These included a 10-year contract with Alcan and a 13-year deal with IMCO Recycling.

Sources: "GM Commits to Buy Aluminum in an Unusual Pact with Alcan," *Wall Street Journal*, November 8, 1998; and "General Motors Inks Long-Term Pact to Buy IMCO's Recycled Aluminum," *Wall Street Journal*, March 11, 1999; "Aluminum Claims No. 2 Ranking," WardsAuto.com, March 10, 2006.

Factors in Demand

A change in the price of an input is represented by a movement along the demand curve. By contrast, changes in other factors will lead to a shift of the entire demand curve. A major factor in consumer demand is income. Business demand does not depend on income but rather on the quantity of the output. If the output is larger, then the business will increase its demand for inputs. This is a shift of the entire demand curve because the increase occurs at all prices. If, however, the output is lower, then the demand for inputs will be lower.

The demand of a business for an input also depends on the prices of complements and substitutes in the production of the output. For instance, delivery trucks and drivers are complements, hence an increase in the drivers' wages will reduce the demand for trucks.

As we have outlined, business demand is derived from calculations of marginal benefit. On the whole, purchasing decisions of businesses are relatively less subject to impulse buying than those of consumers. Hence, advertising plays a smaller role in business demand, and emphasizes information rather than persuasion. Other promotional methods such as exhibiting at conferences and trade shows and personal selling figure more prominently in business demand.

8 Summary

A demand curve shows the quantity demanded as a function of price, other things equal. Generally, the demand curve slopes downward. Changes in price are represented by movements along the demand curve; changes in other factors, such as income, the prices of related products, and advertising, are represented by shifts of the entire demand curve. The market demand curve is the horizontal summation of the individual demand curves of the various buyers.

Buyer surplus is the difference between a buyer's total benefit from some quantity of purchases and his or her actual expenditure. Changes in price affect buyer surplus through the price changes themselves as well as through changes in the quantity demanded.

Key Concepts

individual demand curve	complement	total benefit
marginal benefit	substitute	buyer surplus
normal product	market demand curve	two-part price
inferior product	horizontal summation	

Further Reading

For the behavior of consumer and business buyers, see Philip Kotler's classic, *Marketing* *Management*, 12th ed. (Englewood Cliffs, NJ: Prentice-Hall, 2006), chapters 6 and 7.

Review Questions

1. Define each of the following terms and give an example to illustrate your definition:
   (a) substitute;
   (b) complement;
   (c) normal product;
   (d) inferior product.
2. Name a good or service that you bought recently. Would you have bought less of the item if the price had been lower? Explain why or why not.
3. A new birth control device protects women against pregnancy but not sexually transmitted diseases. How will the introduction of this product affect each of the following:
   (a) the demand for male condoms;
   (b) the demand for birth-control pills.
4. For many years, the government of Taiwan imposed tight controls on the newspaper and free-to-the-air broadcast television industries. Explain how these controls helped the growth of illegal cable television services.
5. The penetration of mobile telephony (number of subscribers per thousand people) is relatively high in wealthy countries like Finland and also in some very poor countries like Cambodia. Are mobile and fixed-line telephone service complements or substitutes?

6. How does Pepsi advertising affect the demand for the soft drink?
7. Suppose that there is a general increase in incomes. Compare the effect of this increase on the demand faced by the following two chains:
   (a) Marriott, a luxury hotel chain with properties throughout the world.
   (b) Motel 6, a chain of low-price motels.
8. Real per capita income in South Africa is much lower than in Britain. For which product is it more important to know South Africa's distribution of income when estimating demand (choose a or b)?
   (a) Bic disposable ballpoint pens.
   (b) Mont Blanc fountain pens.
9. Which of the following are important factors in the demand for new homes?
   (a) interest rates;
   (b) household incomes;
   (c) expectations of future home prices;
   (d) the current price of building materials.
10. Explain how a long-distance telecommunications carrier can use the concept of buyer surplus to price a 1-hour package of long-distance calls.
11. The price of mobile telephone calls is 10 cents a minute. Antonella buys 200 minutes a month. Illustrate her demand curve and identify her buyer surplus.

12. "Summer sale: the more you buy, the more you save." Please comment.

13. How do the factors in demand for inputs such as advertising differ from the factors in the demand for end-user items such as Internet access?

14. Why are automated teller machines (ATMs) relatively more common in countries with higher labor costs?

15. Why do shipbuilders pay close attention to the prices of secondhand vessels and interest rates?

Discussion Questions

1. Using data from 93 countries, *The Economist* ("Population: Battle of the Bulge," September 3, 1994, pp. 19–21) estimated a relationship between the literacy rate of women and the number of births per woman (fertility rate). When the literacy rate is 0%, the fertility rate is 8 per woman; and when the literacy rate is 100%, the birth rate is 2.5 per woman.
   (a) Construct a diagram with literacy rate on the vertical axis and fertility rate on the horizontal axis. Mark the two points that *The Economist* estimated. Join the two points with a straight line.
   (b) Perhaps the largest cost of having a baby is the time that the mother must invest to bear and rear the child. For a more educated woman, is the value of this time higher or lower?
   (c) Returning to your diagram, mark "cost of child" on the vertical axis. Does your diagram have any relation to a demand curve? Please explain.

2. Between 2001 and 2003, China Mobile's customer base grew from 90.6 million to 141.6 million, as the company added subscribers and acquired service providers in the poorer inland regions of China. However, over the same period, its average revenue per user (ARPU) fell from 141 to 102 yuan per month and its proportion of subscribers using pre-paid service rose from 48% to 64%.
   (a) How would the entry of China Unicom into mobile services affect the demand for China Mobile service?
   (b) How would China Mobile's provision of pre-paid service affect the demand for its post-paid (contract) service?
   (c) Compare the demand for pre-paid service in the inland regions with that in the wealthier coastal regions.
   (d) Relate your discussion in (b) and (c) to China Mobile's decline in ARPU.

3. In 1998, the value of world wide sales of recorded music in the form of singles, music cassettes, and CDs was $38.7 billion. Americans bought 3.1 CDs and 0.6 music cassettes per capita, while Mexicans bought 0.5 CDs and 0.3 music cassettes per capita.
   (a) Explain why per capita CD sales were relatively higher while per capita sales of music cassettes were relatively lower in the United States than in Mexico.
   (b) On a suitable diagram, draw the U.S. demand for music CDs. Explain how the following changes would affect the demand curve: (i) increase in the price of CDs; (ii) rise in the ownership of CD players; and (iii) fall in the price of music cassettes.
   (c) On another diagram, draw the demand for music CDs in Mexico. Explain how the following changes would affect the demand curve: (i) fall in advertising by music publishers such as Sony and Time Warner; (ii) reduction in the penalty for copyright infringement; and (iii) increase in the price of hamburgers.

4. In fall 2005, an ABC News poll reported that 46% of lower-income Americans (earning less than $100,000 a year) were angry about gasoline prices, while just 32% of higher-income people (earning $100,000 a year or more) were angry. Despite higher gasoline bills, just 22% of survey respondents said that they had reduced driving. However, 63% said that they would cut back on driving if gasoline prices rose above $3 per gallon.
   (a) Use a demand curve to explain why the proportion of people who would reduce driving is higher if the price of gasoline is higher.

(b)   Explain how people can adjust to higher gasoline prices by replacing their cars rather than driving less.

(c)   Why were relatively fewer higher-income people "angry" about high gasoline prices?

5.   The price of Chanel perfume is around $200 per fluid ounce, while the price of Arrowhead bottled water is $1 per gallon. Nancy buys 2 fluid ounces of Chanel and 10 gallons of bottled water a month.

(a)   Using relevant demand curves, illustrate Nancy's choices. Illustrate how the following changes will affect Nancy's demand for Chanel perfume: (i) a price increase to $220 per fluid ounce, and (ii) a cut in the price of another of Nancy's favorite perfumes.

(b)   Nancy spends more money each month on perfume than bottled water. Does this necessarily mean that perfume gives her more total benefit than water? Use appropriate demand curves to address this question.

6.   In June 1999, AOL had 17.6 million subscribers, and Compuserve had 2 million. By September 2000, AOL had grown to 24 million, and Compuserve to 2.8 million. Subscribers continued to be attracted by America Online's content and services, including chat rooms, instant messaging services (AOL Instant Messenger and ICQ), and specialized services like Digital City, Moviefone, and MapQuest.

(a)   With more people joining AOL Instant Messenger, each subscriber has more persons to communicate with. Using a suitable diagram, illustrate how growth of the AOL Instant Messenger subscriber base raises the individual demand curve of a typical AOL member.

(b)   In 1999, AOL raised the price for its unlimited access plan from $19.95 to $21.95 a month. Using the diagram in (a), illustrate how AOL might have determined the new price.

(c)   Compuserve kept its price at $9.95 a month. How might changes in AOL's content and services have affected the individual demand curve of a typical Compuserve member?

7.   PCCW provides broadband Internet access in Hong Kong under the brand name, Netvigator. Table 2.5 lists several of the plans offered in April 2004.

(a)   Wong subscribes to the 6M plan and uses 150 hours per month. Suppose that Wong's demand curve is a straight line such that if the price of access is HK$20 per hour, her quantity demanded drops to zero. Draw her demand curve and calculate her buyer surplus.

(b)   Suppose that Wong switches to the 3M plan. Referring to her demand curve, how many hours would she use each month? Calculate her buyer surplus.

8.   The Coca-Cola Company markets the Coke brand and manufactures concentrate for sale to regional bottlers. Coke bottlers mix concentrate with sweetener and water to produce the soft drink for supermarkets, restaurants, and other retail outlets. Possible sweeteners include corn syrup and sugar. Owing to federal restrictions against imports, sugar is relatively more expensive in the United States than the rest of the world.

(a)   Why do U.S. soft drink bottlers use relatively more corn syrup than bottlers elsewhere in the world?

Table 2.5   Netvigator broadband Internet access plans

Plan	Monthly subscription	Included hours	Charge per additional hour	Bandwidth
Basic	HK$198	20	HK$2	Up to 1.5 Mbps
3M Single User Plan	HK$298	100	HK$2	Up to 3.0 Mbps
6M Single User Plan	HK$398	200	HK$2	Up to 6.0 Mbps

(b)   Explain how the following changes would affect a Coke bottler's demand curve for corn syrup: (i) removal of the federal restrictions against sugar imports; (ii) fall in the price of corn syrup; and (iii) increase in the sales of Pepsi.

(c)   How would an increase in Pepsi advertising affect the demand for Coke?

9.   By substituting aluminum for steel and other materials, automobile manufacturers can reduce vehicle weight, and so, improve fuel economy. In 1998, General Motors used 1.7 billion pounds of aluminum, with an average of 210 pounds per vehicle. By the following year, its average usage had increased to 271 pounds. Automobile manufacturers as a group accounted for 18% of 25 million tons world wide aluminum consumption.

(a)   Using a suitable figure, draw GM's demand curve for aluminum. (Strictly, this requires an assumption that GM is a small buyer and cannot affect the price of aluminum.) The price of aluminum fell from $1,476 per metric ton in 1997 to $1,303 in 1998 and $1,314 in 1999. Illustrate the effect of the price changes on your figure.

(b)   Show how GM's demand curve for aluminum depends on the prices of gasoline and steel.

(c)   Manufacturers of beverage cans also use large quantities of aluminum. Does GM's demand for aluminum depend on the sales of soft drinks and beer?

10.   This question applies the techniques introduced in the math supplement. Suppose that a typical household's demand for long-distance calls is represented by the equation

$$D = 200 - 4p + 0.4Y, \tag{2.1}$$

where D is the quantity demanded in minutes a month, p is the price of calls in cents per minute, and Y is the household's income in thousands of dollars a year. Assume that $Y = 100$.

(a)   Draw the household's demand curve.

(b)   How many minutes will the household buy at a price of 25 cents a minute?

(c)   What is the maximum lump sum that a long-distance carrier can charge the household for a package of 140 minutes of calls?

11.   This question applies the techniques introduced in the math supplement. Suppose that the market demand for car rentals is represented by the equation

$$D = 50 - p + 0.2Y, \tag{2.2}$$

where D is the quantity demanded in rentals a month, p is the price in dollars per rental, and Y is the average consumer's income in thousands of dollars a year. Assume that $Y = 50$.

(a)   Draw the market demand curve. Show the effect of a cut in price, from $p = 30$ to $p = 20$.

(b)   Show the effect on demand of an increase in income from $Y = 50$ to $Y = 60$.

Chapter 2

Math Supplement

Individual Demand Curve

Using a little mathematics, we can reinforce our understanding of the individual demand curve, especially the effect of changes in price vis-à-vis other factors. Let the individual's demand for some item be represented by the equation

$$D = 30 - 2p + 0.04Y + 4s, \tag{2.3}$$

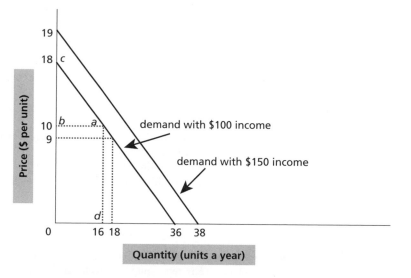

Figure 2.9   Straight-line individual demand curve

where D is the quantity demanded in units a year, p is the price of the item in dollars per unit, Y is the buyer's income in thousands of dollars a year, and s is the value of another factor.

This demand curve is a straight line. To explain, suppose that $Y = 100$ and $s = 0.5$. Then, substituting in (2.3),

$$D = 30 - 2p + 4 + 2 = 36 - 2p. \tag{2.4}$$

Differentiating (2.4) with respect to price

$$\frac{dD}{dp} = -2 \tag{2.5}$$

which means that the demand equation has a constant slope, or equivalently, that the demand curve is a straight line.

To sketch the demand curve, we consider two points on the curve. First, when the price $p = 0$, the quantity demanded $D = 36$. Next, if $D = 0$, $p = 36/2 = 18$. Marking and joining these two points on figure 2.9, we have the buyer's demand curve. As shown in the figure, the demand curve is drawn with price on the vertical axis and quantity on the horizontal axis.

The demand curve can be used to illustrate the effect of a change in price. By (2.4), when the price $p = 9$, the quantity demanded $D = 36 - (2 \times 9) = 18$. When the price is higher, $p = 10$, the quantity demanded $D = 36 - (2 \times 10) = 16$. We represent this change by a movement along the demand curve from the point where $p = 9$ and $D = 18$ to the point where $p = 10$ and $D = 16$.

This demand curve can be used to illustrate the effect of a change in income. Recall that, originally, the buyer's income was $Y = 100$. Suppose that the buyer's income rises to $Y = 150$. The other factor remains $s = 0.5$. Then, by (2.3), the demand curve becomes

$$D = 30 - 2p + 6 + 2 = 38 - 2p. \tag{2.6}$$

In this case, when the price $p = 0$, the quantity demanded $D = 38$, while if the quantity demanded $D = 0$, the price $p = 38/2 = 19$.

Marking and joining these two points on figure 2.9, we have the demand curve with the income of $Y = 150$. This is a straight line that lies to the right of the demand curve with the income of $Y = 100$. By contrast to a change in price, the change in income is represented by a shift of the entire demand curve.

Recall that s is the value of another factor in demand. Originally, $s = 0.5$. Suppose that the other factor increases to $s = 0.6$, while income remains $Y = 100$. Then, by (2.3), the demand curve becomes

$$D = 30 - 2p + 4 + 2.4 = 36.4 - 2p. \tag{2.7}$$

Accordingly, the change in the other factor is also represented by a shift of the entire demand curve. This other factor could be the price of a related product, advertising expenditure, season, weather, or location. A change in any of these factors would shift the entire demand curve.

With the equation of the demand curve, we can calculate the total benefit and buyer's surplus. Recall the demand curve, with $Y = 100$ and $s = 0.5$ was

$$D = 36 - 2p. \tag{2.8}$$

At the price $p = 10$, the buyer purchases quantity $D = 16$. The buyer's total benefit is represented by trapezium $0dac$, while the buyer's expenditure is represented by rectangle $0dab$. Hence, at the price $p = 10$, the buyer's surplus is represented by the triangle bac. The area of this triangle is $1/2 \times \$(18 - 10) \times 16 = \$64$.

Market Demand Curve

Using a mathematical approach, it is very simple to see the relation between individual and market demand curves. Suppose that the market for some item has two buyers, Alan and Jania. Alan's demand for the item is

$$D_a = 18 - 2p + 0.02Y_a, \tag{2.9}$$

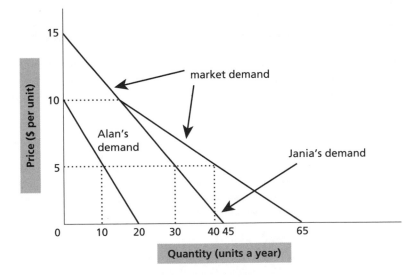

Figure 2.10   Horizontal summation of straight-line individual demand curves

while Jania's demand is

$$D_j = 42 - 3p + 0.01Y_j. \tag{2.10}$$

To draw the curves, suppose that $Y_a = 100$ and $Y_j = 300$. Then

$$D_a = 20 - 2p, \text{ and} \tag{2.11}$$

$$D_j = 45 - 3p. \tag{2.12}$$

We draw these curves in figure 2.10.

Notice that Jania's quantity demanded is 0 for prices above 15, while Alan's quantity demanded is 0 for prices above 10. By horizontal summation, the market demand curve has two segments. The upper segment covers prices between 10 and 15, where the market quantity demanded $D = D_j = 45 - 3p$. The lower segment covers prices of 10 or less, where the market quantity demanded $D = D_a + D_j = 65 - 5p$. We draw the market demand curve in figure 2.10.

We can check this market demand curve for the price $p = 5$. With $p = 5$, the individual quantities demanded are $D_a = 20 - 10 = 10$, and $D_j = 45 - 15 = 30$; hence, $D_a + D_j = 40$. This is exactly the quantity from the market demand curve in figure 2.10.

Just as for an individual demand curve, a price change is represented by a movement along the market demand curve, while a change in income or any factor is represented by a shift of the entire demand curve.

Chapter 3

Elasticity

1 Introduction

The New York Metropolitan Transportation Authority (MTA) provides public transportation and vehicular access to and around New York City through six operating agencies – New York City Transit Authority (subway and bus), Staten Island Rapid Transit Operating Authority, Long Island Rail Road Company, Metropolitan Suburban Bus Authority, Metro-North Commuter Railroad Company, and Triborough Bridge and Tunnel Authority.

In 2002, the MTA's total operating budget was $7.635 billion, of which fares and operating revenues (other than tolls) contributed 40.9% and tolls a further 12.2%, while state, regional, and local taxes and subsidies accounted for the remainder. MTA's rail and bus systems transported 2.37 billion passengers, with average weekday ridership of 7.7 million, while MTA's bridges and tunnels conveyed over 299.8 million vehicles.

In May 2003, faced with a projected budget shortfall of $1 billion over the next two years, the MTA raised subway prices for the first time since 1995.[1] Single-ride fares increased 33%, from $1.50 to $2, while a number of discount fares also increased. One-day unlimited passes rose from $4 to $7; while 30-day unlimited passes rose from $63 to $70. The $10 Metrocard would cover six trips after the fare increase (at an average of $1.67 per ride as compared with the $2 single-ride fare).

The MTA expected to raise an additional $286 million in revenue between May and December of 2003. Management projected that average fares would increase from $1.04 to $1.30, and that total subway ridership would decrease by 2.9%.

In order to gauge the effects of the price increases, the MTA needed to predict how the new fares would impact total subway use, as well as how it would affect subway riders' use of discount fares. Would the MTA forecasts be realized?

---

[1] The following discussion is based, in part, on "Because of Heavy Use of Discount Fares, M.T.A. Raised Less Than Expected in 2003," *New York Times*, January 11, 2005; R. L. Hickey, "Impact of Transit Fare Increase on Ridership and Revenue: Metropolitan Transportation Authority, New York City," *Transit: Planning, Management and Maintenance, Technology, Marketing and Fare Policy, and Capacity and Quality of Choice*, Transportation Research Board, 2005; and Metropolitan Transportation Authority *Annual Reports, 2002 and 2003*. The projected deficit turned out to be the product of creative accounting and was challenged in court. While the MTA projections were found to be incorrect, the fare increase was upheld.

To address these questions, we develop the concept of *elasticity*. The **elasticity of demand** measures the responsiveness of demand to changes in an underlying factor, such as the price of the product, income, the prices of related products, or advertising expenditure. There is an elasticity corresponding to every factor that affects demand.

> **Elasticity of demand** is the responsiveness of demand to changes in an underlying factor.

The *own-price elasticity of demand* measures the responsiveness of the quantity demanded to changes in the price of the item. With the own-price elasticity, a manager can tell the extent to which buyers will respond to a price increase or reduction. The MTA could apply this concept to gauge the impacts of its 2003 fare increases.

We will show how elasticities can be used to forecast the effect of single as well as multiple changes in the factors underlying demand. Accordingly, a transport industry analyst can use elasticities to consider how changes in price, income, and other factors will affect the demand for public and private transport. We will also discuss how elasticities depend on the time available for adjustment. Finally, we consider the data and statistical methods to use in estimating elasticities.

In this chapter, we present elasticities in the context of demand. The same analysis applies to the supply side of a market as well. In chapter 4, we discuss the factors underlying supply and their corresponding elasticities.

2   Own-Price Elasticity

To address the issue of whether to raise price, we need a measure of buyers' sensitivity to price changes. The *own-price elasticity* of demand provides this information. The **own-price elasticity** of demand is the percentage by which the quantity demanded will change if the price of the item rises by 1%, other things equal. Equivalently, the own-price elasticity is the ratio,

> The **own-price elasticity** of demand is the percentage by which the quantity demanded will change if the price of the item rises by 1%.

$$\frac{\text{percentage change in quantity demanded}}{\text{percentage change in price}}$$

or

$$\frac{\text{proportionate change in quantity demanded}}{\text{proportionate change in price}}.$$

Understanding the own-price elasticity of demand is fundamental to the management of a business. Indeed, this concept is so basic that it is often called simply the *price elasticity* or *demand elasticity*. In chapter 2, we distinguished the demand curve of an individual buyer and the market demand curve. Every demand curve has a corresponding own-price elasticity. Before discussing how to apply this concept, let us first consider how it can be calculated.

Construction

Generally, there are two ways of deriving the own-price elasticity of demand. One is the *arc approach*, in which we collect records of a price change and the corresponding change in quantity demanded. Then we calculate the own-price elasticity as the ratio of the proportionate (percentage) change in quantity demanded to the proportionate (percentage) change in price.

> The **arc approach** calculates the own-price elasticity of demand from the average values of observed price and quantity demanded.

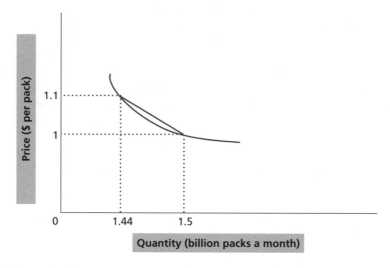

Figure 3.1   Arc approach
By the arc approach, the own-price elasticity of the demand for cigarettes is the proportionate change in
quantity demanded divided by the proportionate change in price = (−0.041)/0.095 = −0.432.

To illustrate, figure 3.1 represents the demand for cigarettes. Presently, the price of cigarettes
is $1 a pack and quantity demanded is 1.5 billion packs a month. According to figure 3.1,
if the price rises to $1.10 per pack, the quantity demanded would drop to 1.44 billion packs.
The proportionate change in quantity demanded is the change in quantity demanded divided
by the average quantity demanded. Since the change in quantity demanded is 1.44 − 1.5 =
−0.06 billion packs and the average quantity demanded is 0.5 × (1.44 + 1.5) = 1.47 billion
packs, the proportionate change in quantity demanded is −0.06/1.47 = −0.041. Similarly, the
proportionate change in price is the change in price divided by the average price. The change
in price is $1.10 − $1 = $0.10 per pack, while the average price is 0.5 × (1.10 + 1) = $1.05
per pack. Hence, the proportionate change in price is 0.1/1.05 = 0.095.

By the arc approach, the own-price elasticity of the demand for cigarettes is the proportionate change in quantity demanded divided by the proportionate change in price, or
(−0.041)/0.095 = −0.432. Equivalently, in this example, the percentage change in quantity
demanded was −4.1%, while the percentage change in price was 9.5%; hence, the own-price
elasticity is −4.1/9.5 = −0.432.

An alternative way of calculating the own-price elasticity of demand is the **point
approach**, which sets up a mathematical equation with quantity demanded as a function of the
price and other variables. The own-price elasticity can then be derived from the coefficient
of price in this equation. We illustrate this procedure later in the chapter.

The **point approach**
calculates own-price
elasticity from a
mathematical equation,
in which the quantity
demanded is a function
of the price and other
variables.

The point approach calculates the elasticity at a specific point on
the demand curve. By contrast, the arc approach calculates the elasticity
between two points on the demand curve. In principle, as we consider shorter
and shorter arcs, the estimate from the arc approach will tend to the point
estimate. Thus, for an infinitesimally short arc, the arc and point approaches
will provide identical numbers for the elasticity.

The arc and point approaches are the two ways of calculating the elasticity of demand with respect to all the factors that affect demand.

Properties

The cigarette example illustrates several properties of the own-price elasticity of demand. First, as discussed in chapter 2, demand curves generally slope downward: if the price of an item rises, the quantity demanded will fall. Hence, the own-price elasticity will be a negative number. For ease of interpretation, some analysts report own-price elasticities as an absolute value, that is, without the negative sign. Accordingly, when applying the concept, it is very important to bear in mind that the own-price elasticity is a negative number.

Second, the own-price elasticity is a pure number, independent of units of measure. In our example, we measured the quantity demanded of cigarettes in packs per month. The percentage change in quantity demanded, however, is the change in quantity demanded divided by the average quantity demanded. It is a pure number that does not depend on any units of measure: the percentage change will be the same whether we measure quantity demanded in packs or individual cigarettes.

Likewise, the percentage change in price is a pure number. Since the own-price elasticity is the percentage change in quantity demanded divided by the percentage change in price, it is also a pure number. Thus, the own-price elasticity of demand provides a handy way of characterizing price sensitivity that does not depend on units of measure.

Third, recall that the own-price elasticity is the ratio

$$\frac{\text{percentage change in quantity demanded}}{\text{percentage change in price}}.$$

If a very large percentage change in price causes no change in quantity demanded, then the elasticity will be 0. By contrast, if an infinitesimal percentage change in price causes a large change in quantity demanded, then the elasticity will be negative infinity. Accordingly, the own-price elasticity ranges from 0 to negative infinity.

Table 3.1 reports the own-price elasticities of the market demand for several product categories, while table 3.2 reports the own-price elasticities of the demand for some individual brands. We say that the demand for an item is **price elastic** or *elastic with respect to price* if a 1% increase in price leads to more than a 1% drop in quantity demanded. Equivalently, demand is price elastic if a price increase causes a proportionately larger drop in quantity demanded.

We say that demand is **price inelastic** or *inelastic with respect to price* if a 1% price increase causes less than a 1% drop in quantity demanded. An alternative definition is that demand is price inelastic if a price increase causes a proportionately smaller drop in quantity demanded.

> The demand is price **elastic** if a 1% increase in price leads to more than a 1% drop in the quantity demanded.

From table 3.1, the own-price elasticity of the market demand for domestic compact cars is −3.4. This means that a 1% price increase will reduce the quantity demanded by 3.4%. So, the demand for domestic compact cars is elastic. The own-price elasticity of the market demand for foreign-made compact cars is −4.0. This indicates that the demand for foreign compact cars is more elastic than the demand for domestic makes.

> The demand is price **inelastic** if a 1% increase in price leads to less than a 1% drop in the quantity demanded.

By contrast, the own-price elasticity of the market demand for liquor is −0.2. This means that a 1% increase in the price of liquor will reduce the quantity demanded by 0.2%. The demand for liquor is inelastic.

Progress Check 3A Referring to table 3.1, is the United States' residential demand for water relatively more or less elastic than the industrial demand?

Table 3.1   Own-price elasticities of market demand

Product	Market	Own-price elasticity	Source (see References)
Automobiles			
Domestic compacts	U.S.	−3.4	Koujianou-Goldberg (1995)
Foreign compacts	U.S.	−4.0	Koujianou-Goldberg (1995)
Domestic intermediates	U.S.	−4.2	Koujianou-Goldberg (1995)
Foreign intermediates	U.S.	−5.2	Koujianou-Goldberg (1995)
Consumer products			
Coffee	U.S.	−3.06	Bell et al. (1999)
Cigarettes	U.S.	−0.2, −0.4	Becker et al. (1994); Tegene (1991)
Liquor	U.S.	−0.2	Baltagi and Griffin (1995)
Margarine	U.S.	−2.34	Bell, et al. (1999)
Soft Drinks	U.S.	−3.09	Bell, et al. (1999)
Services			
Electricity (residential)	Quebec	−0.7	Bernard et al. (1996)
Telephone service	Spain	−0.1	Garin Munoz (1996)
Water (residential)	U.S.	−0.2, −0.3	Williams and Suh (1986)
Water (industrial)	U.S.	−0.7, −1.0	Williams and Suh (1986)

Table 3.2   Product-level own-price elasticities

Brand/product	Own-price elasticity
Honda Civic	−3.4
Ford Escort	−3.4
Buick Century	−4.8
Cadillac Fleetwood	−0.9
Ferrari	−1

Source: Koujianou-Goldberg (1995).

Intuitive Factors

Managers can consider several intuitive factors to gauge whether demand will be relatively more elastic or inelastic:

- *Availability of direct or indirect substitutes*. The fewer substitutes that are available, the less elastic will be the demand. People who are dependent on alcoholic drinks or cigarettes feel that they cannot do without them; hence, the demand for these products is relatively inelastic. For the image-conscious teenager, sporting a pair of the "in" athletic shoes is the only way to gain peer acceptance, so teenage demand for the shoes is very inelastic.

   In many countries, the Post Office has a legally established monopoly over carriage of letters. Hence, there are no direct substitutes for the Post Office letter service. Indirect substitutes, however, are popping up all over the world. With the spread of email and fax machines, the demand for Post Office letter service is becoming relatively more elastic.

By considering the availability of substitutes, we can conclude that the demand for a product category will be relatively less elastic than the demand for specific products within the category. The reason is that there are fewer substitutes for the category than for specific products. Consider, for instance, the demand for cigarettes compared with the demand for a particular brand. The particular brand has many more substitutes than the category as a whole. Accordingly, the demand for the brand will tend to be more elastic than the demand for the category. This means that, if cigarette manufacturers can raise prices collectively by 10%, their sales will fall by a smaller percentage than if only one manufacturer increases its price by 10%.

• *Buyer's prior commitments.* A person who has bought an automobile becomes a captive customer for spare parts. Automobile manufacturers understand this very well. Accordingly, they set relatively higher prices on spare parts than on new cars. The same applies as well in the software business. Once users have invested time and effort to learn one program, they become captive customers for future upgrades. Whenever there is such a commitment, demand is less elastic.

• *Benefits/costs of economizing.* Buyers have limited time to spend on searching for better prices, so they focus attention on items that account for relatively larger expenditures. Families with toddlers, for instance, spend more time economizing on diapers than Q-tips. Similarly, office managers focus attention on copying paper rather than paper clips. Marketing practitioners have given the name *low involvement* to products that get relatively little attention from buyers.

The balance between the benefit and cost of economizing also depends on a possible split between the person who incurs the cost of economizing and the person who benefits. Almost everyone who has driven a damaged car to a repair shop has been asked the question, "Are you covered by insurance?" Experienced repair managers know that car owners who are covered by insurance care less about price. In this example, the car owner gets the benefit of the repair work, while the insurer pays most or all the costs. A car owner who bargains over the repairs must spend his or her own time, while the insurer will get most of the saving.

Elasticity and Slope

When comparing the demands for different products or even quantities demanded of the same product at different prices, it is important to remember that these comparisons are relative. The reason is that the own-price elasticity describes the shape of only one portion of the demand curve. A change in price, by moving from one part of a demand curve to another part, may lead to a change in own-price elasticity.

Let us show this by considering the demand curve for cars in figure 3.2. This demand curve is a straight line. Suppose that, initially, the price is $70,000 per car and the quantity demanded is 22,000 cars a month. When the price increases to $80,000, the quantity demanded falls to 20,000 cars. The proportionate change in quantity demanded is $-2,000/21,000 = -0.1$, while the proportionate change in price is $10,000/75,000 = 0.13$. Hence, by the arc approach, the own-price elasticity is $-0.1/0.13 = -0.8$.

Now, suppose that the price increases from $80,000 to $90,000; then the quantity demanded falls from 20,000 to 18,000 cars. The proportionate change in quantity demanded is now $-2,000/19,000 = -0.11$, while the proportionate change in price is $10,000/85,000 = 0.12$. Hence, by the arc approach, the own-price elasticity is $-0.11/0.12 = -0.9$. Thus, the demand curve in figure 3.2 is inelastic at both prices of $80,000 and $70,000. It is relatively more elastic at the price of $80,000 per car than at a price of $70,000.

Auto buyer loyalty: American versus Japanese manufacturers

Between 1970 and 2005, American automobile manufacturers' market shares (for cars and light trucks) fell from 87% to 57%, while Japanese manufacturers' shares increased from 4% to 32%, and European manufacturer shares held constant at 7%. The American manufacturer loss to the Japanese manufacturers has been consistent throughout that time frame. What are its causes?

A recent study estimated the demand elasticities for individual manufacturers. Based on a random sample of 458 households out of 250,000 in the Current Population Survey, it found an average price elasticity of −2.32 for all vehicles. Individual makes and models elasticities were mostly in the range of −2 to −3. The study found significant effects of vehicle attributes on demand.

The study found that brand loyalty was strongest towards the Japanese automakers, and that General Motors had the weakest loyalty. Vehicle attributes (e.g., horsepower, weight, length, fuel consumption, etc.) could account for 6.34 of the 6.8 percentage point loss of American automakers over the 1990 to 2000 period. It was estimated that it would take a 50% price decrease to maintain the 1990 market share of American autos in 2000.

Source: K. E. Train and C. Winston. "Vehicle Choice Behavior and the Declining Market Share of U.S. Automakers," *International Economic Review* (forthcoming).

Shared costs: frequent flyer programs

Whenever there is a split between the person who pays and the person who chooses the product, the demand will be less elastic. In 1981, American Airlines established its AAdvantage program for frequent flyers. This program records each member's travel on American Airlines and awards free flights according to the number of miles that the member accumulates. The AAdvantage program does not give mileage credit for travel on competing airlines such as United or Delta, hence it provides members with a strong incentive to concentrate travel on American Airlines.

The AAdvantage program is especially attractive to travelers, such as business executives, who fly at the expense of others. Such travelers are relatively less price sensitive than those who pay for their own tickets. AAdvantage gives them an incentive to choose American Airlines even if the fare is higher. Among customers who fly at the expense of others, the program makes demand relatively less elastic. AAdvantage was a brilliant marketing strategy, and all of American's competitors soon established their own frequent flyer programs.

The concept has spread to retailers, supermarkets, restaurants, and many other retail industries. In 2003, it was estimated that at least 75% of American consumers had at least one "loyalty" card, and over 33% had at least two.

Source: "CRM Strategies: Loyalty Programs That Are Working," eWeek.com, December 30, 2003.

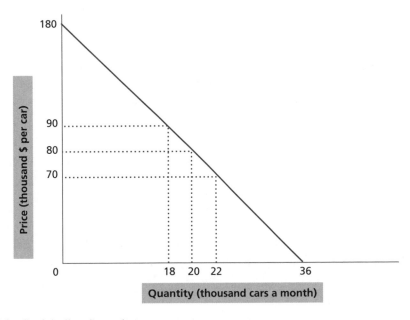

Figure 3.2 Straight-line demand
By the arc approach, the own-price elasticity at a price of $70,000 is −0.1/0.13 = −0.8, and the own-price elasticity at a price of $80,000 is −0.11/0.12 = −0.9.

Generally, whether the demand curve is a straight line or curved, the own-price elasticity can vary with changes in the price of the item. In the case of a straight line demand curve, the demand becomes more elastic at higher prices. For demand curves with other shapes, the demand may become less elastic at higher prices.

Another point worth noting is that the own-price elasticity can also vary with changes in any of the other factors that affect demand. Recall that the own-price elasticity is the percentage by which the quantity demanded will change if the price of the item rises by 1%. If there are changes in any of the other factors that affect demand, then the demand curve will shift; hence, the own-price elasticity may also change.

A frequently asked question is the relation between own-price elasticity and the slope of the demand curve. The math supplement shows that, other things equal, where the demand curve is steeper, the demand is less elastic, and where the demand curve is less steep, the demand is more elastic. It is very important to stress that the price and quantity demanded are the "other things equal." To illustrate, let us consider again the straight line demand curve in figure 3.2. The slope of this curve is the rate of change of price for changes in the quantity demanded. The slope is −180/36 = −5. The demand curve is a straight line; hence, it has the same slope throughout.

By contrast, as we have already shown, the own-price elasticity is −0.8 at a price of $70,000, and −0.9 at a price of $80,000. Generally, the own-price elasticity varies throughout the length of a straight-line demand curve.

If the own-price elasticity varies throughout the demand curve, while the slope is the same everywhere, what explains the difference? The answer is the price and quantity demanded. Even though the slope remains constant, the changes in price and quantity demanded along the demand curve mean that the own-price elasticity will vary. Thus, the own-price elasticity and slope are related but are not equivalent.

Progress Check 3B Referring to figure 3.2, suppose that the price increases from $110,000 to $120,000. Calculate the own-price elasticity of demand using the arc approach.

---

3   Forecasting Quantity Demanded and Expenditure

The own-price elasticity of demand can be applied to forecast the effect of price changes on quantity demanded and buyer expenditure. Expenditure is related to the quantity demanded, since expenditure equals the quantity demanded multiplied by the price.[2] The own-price elasticity can be applied at the level of an entire market as well as for individual sellers. From the standpoint of an individual seller, the quantity demanded is sales, while buyer expenditure is revenue. Hence, using the own-price elasticity of demand, the seller can forecast the effect of price changes on sales and revenue.

Quantity Demanded

Let us first consider how to use the own-price elasticity of demand to forecast the effect of price changes on the quantity demanded. Refer, for instance, to the demand for automobiles at a price of $70,000 in figure 3.2. How will a 10% increase in price affect the quantity of cars that buyers demand?

We have already calculated the own-price elasticity of demand at the $70,000 price to be -0.8. By definition, the own-price elasticity is the percentage by which the quantity demanded will change if the price rises by 1%. Hence, if the price of cars increases by 10%, then the quantity demanded will change by $-0.8 \times 10 = -8\%$; that is, the quantity demanded will fall by 8%.

To forecast the change in quantity demanded in terms of the number of cars, we should multiply the percentage change of -8% by the quantity demanded before the price change. By this method, the change in quantity demanded is $-0.08 \times 22,000$, that is, a drop of 1,760 cars. (Note that $8\% = 0.08$.) The new quantity demanded would be $22,000 - 1,760 = 20,240$ cars a month.

We can also use the elasticity method to estimate the effect of a reduction in the price on quantity demanded. Referring to figure 3.2, suppose, for instance, that the price of cars is initially $70,000 and then drops by 5%. The quantity demanded will change by $-0.8 \times (-5) = 4\%$; that is, it will increase by 4%. This example shows that it is important to keep track of the signs of the own-price elasticity and the price change.

Expenditure

Let us next see how to use the own-price elasticity of demand to estimate the effect of changes in price on buyer expenditure. Buyer expenditure equals the quantity demanded multiplied by the price. Hence, a change in price will affect expenditure through the price itself as well as through the related effect on quantity demanded.

---

[2]   In chapter 9 on pricing, we consider the possibility of price discrimination. With price discrimination, different buyers pay different prices so expenditure is not simply quantity demanded multiplied by price.

Consider the effect of a small increase in price. By itself, the price increase will tend to raise the expenditure. The price increase, however, will reduce the quantity that buyers demand and so tend to reduce the expenditure. Hence, the net effect on expenditure depends on which effect is relatively larger.

This is where the concept of own-price elasticity is useful. Recall that demand is elastic with respect to price if an increase in price causes a proportionately larger fall in quantity demanded, while demand is inelastic if a price increase causes a proportionately smaller fall in quantity demanded. The own-price elasticity enables us to compare the relative magnitude of changes in price and quantity demanded.

If demand is price elastic, then the drop in the quantity demanded will be proportionately larger than the increase in price; hence, the small price increase will reduce expenditure. If, however, demand is price inelastic, the drop in quantity demanded will be proportionately smaller than the increase in price; hence, the small price increase will increase expenditure.

Generally, if demand is price elastic, a small price increase will reduce expenditure while a small price reduction will increase expenditure. By contrast, if demand is price inelastic, a small price increase will increase expenditure while a price reduction will reduce expenditure.

Whenever managers are asked to raise prices, their most frequent response is, "But my sales would drop!" Since demand curves slope downward, it certainly is true that a higher price will reduce sales. The real issue is the *extent* to which the price increase will reduce sales. A manager ought to be thinking about the own-price elasticity of demand.

To explain, suppose that a cement manufacturer's demand is price inelastic at the current price. What if the manufacturer raises price? Since demand is price inelastic, the price increase will lead to a proportionately smaller reduction in the quantity demanded. The buyers' expenditure will increase, which means that the manufacturer's revenue will increase.

Meanwhile, owing to the reduction in quantity demanded, the manufacturer can reduce production, cutting its costs. Since revenues will be higher and costs will be lower, the manufacturer's profits definitely will be higher. Accordingly, if demand is price inelastic, a seller can increase profit by raising price.

This discussion shows that, under the right conditions, a price increase can raise profits even though it may cause sales to drop. Therefore, when setting the price for an item, managers ought to focus on the own-price elasticity of demand. Generally, the price should be raised until the demand becomes price elastic. We will develop this idea further in chapter 9 on pricing.

Accuracy

We have used the own-price elasticity of demand to forecast that, in figure 3.2, if the price of cars rises by 10% from $70,000, then the quantity demanded would drop to 20,240 cars a month. We can calculate the effect of the price increase in another way – directly from the demand curve. After a 10% increase, the new price would be $77,000. From the demand curve, the quantity demanded at that price would be 20,600 cars a month.

What explains the discrepancy between the quantities of 20,240 and 20,600? The reason for the discrepancy is that, as we have emphasized previously, the own-price elasticity may vary along a demand curve. Accordingly, the forecast using the own-price elasticity will not be as precise as a forecast directly from the demand curve. The same applies to forecasting changes in expenditure with the own-price elasticity.

Generally, the error in a forecast based on the own-price elasticity will be larger for larger changes in the price and the other factors that affect demand. Elasticities do not provide as much information as the entire demand curve. In many cases, however, managers do not know the entire demand curve. Their information is limited to the quantity demanded around the current values of the factors that affect the demand.

For many business decisions, however, managers do not need to know the full demand curve. The manufacturer of a luxury car, for instance, would never consider cutting the price to the level of a subcompact. So, it need not know the quantity demanded at such a low price. Likewise, the manufacturer of a subcompact would never consider raising the price to the level of a luxury car. Hence, the elasticities often provide sufficient information for business decisions.

4   Other Elasticities

In addition to price, the demand for an item also depends on buyers' incomes, the prices of related products, and advertising among other factors. Changes in any of these factors will lead to a shift in the demand curve. There is an elasticity to measure the responsiveness of demand to changes in each factor. Managers can use these elasticities to forecast the effect of changes in these factors. In particular, the elasticities can be used to forecast the effect of changes in multiple factors that occur at the same time.

The analyses of elasticities of demand with respect to income, the prices of related products, and advertising are very similar. Accordingly, we will focus on the elasticity of demand with respect to income and discuss only the key differences for the other elasticities.

Income Elasticity

The **income elasticity** of demand is the percentage by which the demand will change if the buyer's income rises by 1%.

The *income elasticity* of demand measures the sensitivity of demand to changes in buyers' incomes. By definition, the **income elasticity** of demand is the percentage by which the demand will change if the buyer's income rises by 1%, other things equal. In this case, the price of the item is one of the other things that must remain unchanged. Equivalently, the income elasticity is the ratio

$$\frac{\text{percentage change in demand}}{\text{percentage change in income}}.$$

The income elasticity may be calculated using either the arc or point approach. (Since the demand curve diagram does not explicitly show income, we cannot draw a picture of the arc approach for calculating income elasticity.) For an infinitesimally small change in income, the arc estimate equals the point elasticity. Like the own-price elasticity, the income elasticity of demand varies with changes in the price and any other factor that affects demand.

By definition, the income elasticity is a ratio of two proportionate changes; hence, it is a pure number and independent of units of measure. In the case of a normal product, if income rises, the demand will rise, so the income elasticity will be positive. By contrast, for an inferior product, if income rises, demand will fall, so the income elasticity will be negative. So, depending on whether the product is normal or inferior, the income elasticity can be either positive or negative. Hence, it is important to note the sign of the income elasticity. Income elasticity can range from negative infinity to positive infinity.

Table 3.3 Income elasticities of market demand

Product	Market	Income elasticity	Source (see References)
Consumer products			
Cigarettes	U.S.	0.1	Tegene (1991)
Liquor	U.S.	0.2	Baltagi and Griffin (1995)
Automobiles			
Domestic-made	U.S.	1.62	McCarthy (1996)
European-made	U.S.	1.93	McCarthy (1996)
Asian-made	U.S.	1.65	McCarthy (1996)
Services			
Electricity (residential)	Quebec	0.1	Bernard et al. (1996)
Telephone service	Spain	0.5	Garin Munoz (1996)

We say that demand is *income elastic* or *elastic with respect to income* if a 1% income increase causes more than a 1% change in demand. Demand is said to be *income inelastic* or *inelastic with respect to income* if a 1% income increase causes less than a 1% change in demand.

The demand for necessities tends to be relatively less income elastic than the demand for discretionary items. Consider, for instance, the demand for food as compared with restaurant meals. Eating in a restaurant is more of a discretionary item. Accordingly, we expect the demand for food to be relatively less income elastic than the demand for restaurant meals.

Table 3.3 reports the income elasticities of the market demand for various items. In the United States, the demand for cigarettes and liquor hardly changes with income, while, in Quebec, the residential demand for electricity is also extremely inelastic with respect to income.

We can apply the income elasticity of demand to forecast the effect of changes in income on demand and expenditure. Suppose that, presently, the price of cigarettes is $1 per pack, the quantity demanded is 1.5 billion packs a month, and the income elasticity of demand is 0.1. How will a 3% increase in income affect the demand?

By definition, the income elasticity of demand is the percentage by which the demand will change if the buyer's income rises by 1%, other things equal. In the present case, the income rises by 3%; hence, the percentage change in demand will be $0.1 \times 3 = 0.3\%$; that is, demand will increase by 0.3%. Since the initial quantity was 1.5 billion packs, the increase in quantity is 0.003×1.5 billion = 4.5 million packs a month. Provided that the price remains at $1 per pack, this increase in demand will mean an increase in expenditure of $4.5 million.

Progress Check 3C Referring to table 3.3, is the demand for liquor relatively more or less income elastic than the demand for cigarettes?

Table 3.4 Cross-price elasticities of market-demand

Products	Market	Cross price elasticity	Source (see References)
Consumer products			
Newspapers/competing newspapers	U.S. midwest	0.44	Fu (2003)
Gasoline at competing stations	Boston, MA	1.2	Png and Reitman (1994)
Automobiles			
Domestic/other makes	U.S.	0.28	McCarthy (1996)
European/other makes	U.S.	0.76	McCarthy (1996)
Asian/other makes	U.S.	0.61	McCarthy (1996)
Services			
Electricity/gas (residential)	Quebec	0.1	Bernard et al. (1996)
Electricity/oil (residential)	Quebec	0.0	Bernard et al. (1996)
Bus/subway	London	0.0, 0.5	Gilbert and Jalilian (1991)

Cross-Price Elasticity

> The **cross-price elasticity** of demand is the percentage by which the demand will change if the price of another item rises by 1%.

Just as the income elasticity of demand measures the sensitivity of demand to changes in income, the *cross-price elasticity* measures the sensitivity of demand to changes in the prices of related products. By definition, the **cross-price elasticity** of demand with respect to another item is the percentage by which the demand will change if the price of the other item rises by 1%, other things equal. In this case, the (own) price of the item is one of the other things that must remain unchanged.

If two products are substitutes, an increase in the price of one will increase the demand for the other, so the cross-price elasticity will be positive. By contrast, if two products are complements, an increase in the price of one will reduce demand for the other; hence, the cross-price elasticity will be negative. The cross-price elasticity can range from negative infinity to positive infinity.

Generally, the more two items are substitutable, the higher their cross-price elasticity will be. Table 3.4 reports the cross-price elasticities of the demand for various items.

Cross-price elasticity and the demand for postal services

Competition from new communications technologies is perceived to be a major threat to provision of mail services by established postal providers. World wide demand for domestic letter items rose from 300 billion in 1980 to 425 billion in 2003, a compound annual growth rate of 2.7%. In the past 5 years, however, this growth rate has slowed to 0.5% per year.

Might this slowdown be caused by increased use of electronic technologies such as fax and email? The interactions between old and new technologies can be both subtle and complex: consider the following four patterns of demand relationships:

- *Pure substitution*: the new technology fully displaces the old method.
- *Complementarity*: the new and old methods both grow, although they may coexist for long periods of time.
- *Creation of additional demand*: the new medium generates important new growth adding to the growth of traditional methods, which also continue to be used.
- *Stalling*: after a promising start, the new method reaches a limit, stagnates, and poses little subsequent threat to the traditional one.

In keeping with these complex interactions, the evidence is mixed. One study of household demand finds that a 10% increase in the probability of computer ownership decreases mail demand by 1.6% while others show complementary relationships between mail and fax or PC ownership but substitution with internet connectivity.

Source: Pitney Bowes, *Electronic Substitution for Mail*, 2005, www.postinsight.pb.com.

⊢ Gas prices: cars versus SUVs ⊢

Most households in the U.S. have more than one vehicle. As gas prices increase, they may change their desired bundle of vehicles to hold. One study explicitly examined the patterns of vehicle bundle ownership among a sample of 9,027 households. Of these, 38% had one car, while 13% had two cars, 15% one car and one SUV, and 3% two SUVs.

The cross elasticities for holding various bundles with respect to gasoline prices was estimated. Of note is the estimated cross-price elasticity for holding the bundle (car + SUV) of −0.793 and for holding the bundle (two cars) of +0.695. This indicates a considerable shift in preferred patterns as gas prices rise. In particular, a relatively large number of households may substitute a second car for their SUV.

Since automobiles are durable goods, this shift will not be instantaneous. Rather, the replacement decision should take into account the net present value of the costs associated with keeping the SUV versus the net present value of the costs associated with its sale and replacement with a car.

Source: Y. Feng, D. Fullerton, and L. Gan, "Vehicle Choices, Miles Driven, and Pollution Policies," National Bureau of Economic Research, Working Paper 11553 (2005).

Advertising Elasticity

The *advertising elasticity* measures the sensitivity of demand to changes in the sellers' advertising expenditure. By definition, the **advertising elasticity** of demand is the percentage by which the demand will change if the sellers' advertising expenditure rises by 1%, other things equal. In this case, the (own) price of the item is one of the other things that must remain unchanged.

> The **advertising elasticity** of demand is the percentage by which the demand will change if the seller's advertising expenditure rises by 1%.

Table 3.5 reports the advertising elasticities of the demand for several consumer product categories. The advertising elasticity for beer is 0, which means that a 1%

⊣ MTA: More riders, less revenue ⊢

The MTA predictions for the impacts of the subway fare increase, turned out to be off the mark. Ridership fell by less than 1% (it was predicted to drop by 2.9%). Average fares rose from $1.04 to $1.26, rather than the predicted $1.30. The expected revenue gain of $286 million by the end of 2003 fell short by up to $20 million.

Substitution of discount fares for regular fares accounted for the unexpected consequences. Metrocard discount riders rose from 24.7% to 32% of the total subway rides. The 30-day unlimited passes, whose price increased by only 11%, rose from 14.3% to 20% of the rides. The one-day unlimited pass, which rose in price by 75%, showed a decrease in rides from 6% to 1.7% of the total.

As a result, the overall price elasticity was less than expected. The primary shift was that riders were induced to move from regular fares to discounted fares. Most of the discounted fares experienced smaller price increases than did the regular fare. At the higher regular fares, the discounted fares became a more attractive substitute.

Table 3.5 Advertising elasticities of market demand

Product	Market	Advertising elasticity	Source (see References)
Beer	U.S.	0.0	Franke and Wilcox (1987)
Wine	U.S.	0.08	Franke and Wilcox (1987)
Cigarettes	U.S.	0.04	Tegene (1991)
Antihypertensive drugs	U.S.	0.26–0.27	Rizzo (1999)
Clothing	U.S.	0.01	Baye et al. (1992)
Recreation	U.S.	0.08	Baye et al. (1992)

increase in advertising expenditure will not change the demand for beer. The advertising elasticity for cigarettes is 0.04, which means that a 1% increase in advertising expenditure will increase the demand for cigarettes by 0.04%.

Given these small elasticities, it may seem surprising that beer and cigarette manufacturers spend so much on advertising. Note that the advertising elasticities reported in table 3.5 pertain to market demand. Most advertising, however, is undertaken by individual sellers to promote their own business. By drawing buyers away from competitors, advertising has a much stronger effect on the sales of an individual seller than on the market demand. Accordingly, the advertising elasticity of the demand faced by an individual seller tends to be larger than the advertising elasticity of the market demand.

Forecasting the Effects of Multiple Factors

The business environment will often change in conflicting ways. For instance, the prices of substitutes may rise, but the prices of complements may rise as well. The only way to discern the net effect of factors pushing in different directions is to use the elasticities with respect to each of the variables.

⊣ Dairy advertising elasticity ⊢

The Dairy Production and Stabilization Act of 1983 and the Fluid Milk Promotion Act of 1990 provide promotion programs to increase awareness and the sale of fluid milk and related dairy products. The Fluid Milk program had the largest impact on consumption, estimated to be 4.3% lower without the advertising. In comparison if the Dairy Program was enacted but the Fluid Milk program was not, consumption is estimated to drop 0.9%.

Other variables significantly impact advertising effectiveness. The elasticity of advertising effectiveness with respect to the population under 6 years of age was estimated to be 6.661 between 1998 and 2002. This implies that parents with children under 6 are significantly impacted by generic advertising provided by the Fluid Milk Promotion Act.

Is this expense worth the returns in demand and price? Advertising expenditures were $61 million per year on average with an average increase in revenues of $535 million.

Source: U.S. Department of Agriculture, Report to Congress, chapter 3, "Impact of Generic Fluid Milk and Dairy Advertising on Dairy Markets: An Independent Analysis," www.ams.usda.gov/dairy/prb/rtc_2003.

To illustrate, suppose that the price of cigarettes is $1 per pack and sales are 1.5 billion packs a month. Then the price increases by 5% while income rises by 3%. What would be the impact on demand?

We have shown how to apply the own-price elasticity to forecast the effect of a change in price on quantity demanded and similarly to apply the income elasticity to forecast the effect of a change in income on demand. To calculate the net effect of the increases in both price and income, we simply add the changes due to each of the factors.

Suppose that the own-price elasticity of the demand for cigarettes is −0.4. Then, a 5% increase in price would change quantity demanded by $-0.4 \times 5 = -2\%$. We have already calculated that a 3% increase in income would increase demand by 0.3%. Therefore, the net effect of the increases in price and income is to change demand by $-2 + 0.3 = -1.7\%$. Originally, the quantity demanded of cigarette services was 1.5 billion packs per month. After the increases in price and income, the quantity demanded will be 1.475 billion packs per month.

We can use similar techniques to forecast the effects of changes in other factors, such as the prices of related products and advertising expenditures. Generally, the percentage change in demand due to changes in multiple factors is the sum of the percentage changes due to each separate factor.

⊣ Advertising and the demand for pharmaceuticals ⊢

The demand for prescription drugs differs from that for many other products in that it derives from the decision of possibly three persons – one who recommends the item (physician), another who consumes it (patient), and possibly another who pays for it (medical insurer or health maintenance organization).

Pharmaceutical manufacturers spend up to 30% of sales on advertising. Most of this takes the form of "detailing," which is visits by sales representatives to physicians in their offices and hospitals. What is the effect of this advertising on the demand for prescription drugs?

Research into the demand for antihypertensive drugs has shown that the advertising elasticity of demand ranged between 0.26 and 0.27. The advertising elasticity for antihypertensive drugs covered by patents ranged between 0.23 and 0.25. This suggests that advertising has a smaller effect for drugs covered by patents.

Further, advertising caused the demand for antihypertensive drugs to become less price elastic. For all antihypertensive drugs, the own-price elasticity ranged between −2.0 and −2.1 without advertising, while ranging between −1.5 and −1.7 in the long run with advertising.

Recall that, if demand is inelastic, a seller can increase profit by raising price. Hence, advertising helps a prescription drug manufacturer to raise profit in two ways – by directly increasing the demand, and by rendering the demand less price elastic.

Source: John A. Rizzo, "Advertising and Competition in the Ethical Pharmaceutical Industry: The Case of Anti-hypertensive Drugs," *Journal of Law and Economics* 62 (1999), pp. 89–116.

SUV demand, manufacturer rebates, and the price of gas

We can now revisit the SUV case in the introduction to chapter 2. The price of gasoline rose by 66%. At the same time, manufacturer rebates (incentives) increased by $500, which amounted to a 1.4% decrease in price, based on the average large SUV price of $36,000. What does this imply for SUV sales?

For the price elasticity of the demand for SUVs, we use −2.5, which is the midpoint of the estimates by Train and Winston. For the cross-elasticity of the demand for SUVs with respect to the gasoline price, we use the long-run demand elasticity for vehicle ownership with respect to fuel prices, which is −0.25.

Using the formula,

% change in demand = % change in price × price elasticity of demand + % change in gasoline price × cross-elasticity = (−1.4%)(−2.5) + (66%) × (−0.25) = 13.0%

Accordingly, we estimate that the demand change would be −13%. This is close to the actual reduction of 16.8% in new SUV demand reported in chapter 2.

Sources: Goodwin, Dargay, and Hanly, "Elasticities of Road Traffic and Fuel Consumption with Respect to Price and Income: A Review," *Transport Reviews* 24, no. 3 (2004), pp. 275–92; K. E. Train and C. Winston, "Vehicle Choice Behavior and the Declining Market Share of U.S. Automakers," *International Economic Review* (forthcoming).

5   Adjustment Time

The **short run** is a time horizon within which a buyer cannot adjust at least one item of consumption or usage.

The **long run** is a time horizon long enough for buyers to adjust all items of consumption or usage.

We have analyzed the elasticities of demand with respect to changes in price, income, the prices of related products, and advertising expenditures. We have discussed the intuitive factors that underly these elasticities. In addition, another factor affects all elasticities: the time available for buyers to adjust.

With regard to adjustment time, it is important to distinguish the *short run* from the *long run*. The **short run** is a time horizon within which a buyer cannot adjust at least one item of consumption or usage. By contrast, the **long run** is a time horizon long enough for buyers to adjust all items of consumption or usage.

To illustrate the distinction, consider how Max commutes into Chicago. He does not have a car, so he takes the train. To switch from the train to a car, he needs time to buy or lease a car. Accordingly, with regard to Max's choice of transportation mode, a short run is any period of time shorter than that which he needs to get a car. A long run is any period of time longer than that which he needs to get a car.

We shall now discuss the effect of adjustment time on the elasticities of demand, and how the effect depends on whether the item is durable or nondurable.

Nondurables

Consider an everyday item like commuter train services. Suppose that one Monday morning, the local railway operator announces a permanent 10% increase in fares. Many commuters may have already made plans for that day, so the response to the higher fare may be quite weak on that day. Over time, however, the response will be stronger: as more commuters acquire cars, the demand for the railway service will drop.

Generally, for nondurable items, the longer the time that buyers have to adjust, the bigger will be the response to a price change. Accordingly, the demand for such items will be more elastic in the long run than in the short run. This applies to all nondurable items, including both goods and services.

Figure 3.3 illustrates the short- and long-run demand for a nondurable item. Suppose that the current price is $5 and quantity demanded is 1.5 million units. If the price drops to $4.50, the quantity demanded will rise to 1.6 million units in the short run and 1.75 million units in the long run.

Table 3.6 reports the short- and long-run own-price elasticities of market demand for several non-durables. Consistent with our analysis, the demand for these items is relatively more elastic in the long run than in the short run.

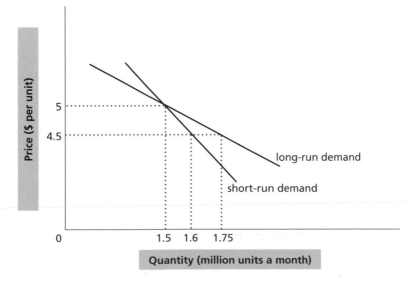

Figure 3.3 Short- and long-run demand for a nondurable item
If the price drops from $5 to $4.50, the quantity demanded will rise to 1.6 million units in the short run and 1.75 million units in the long run.

Table 3.6   Short- vis-a-vis long-run elasticities

Product	Demand factor	Market	Short-run elasticity	Long-run elasticity	Source (see References)
Nondurable goods					
Cigarettes	Price	U.S.	−0.2, −0.4	−3.3	Becker et al. (1994); Tegene (1991)
Liquor	Price	U.S.	−0.2	. . .	Baltagi and Griffin (1995)
		Canada	−1.8	. . .	Johnson and Oksanen (1977)
Antihypertensive drugs	Price	U.S.	−0.5	−1.6	Rizzo (1999)
Gasoline	Price	International	−0.23	−0.43	Espey (1998)
	Income	International	0.39	0.81	Espey (1998)
Services					
Electricity (residential)	Price	New Zealand	−0.18	−0.44	Fatai et al. (2003)
Bus	Price	London	−0.8	−1.3	Gilbert and Jalilian (1991)
Subway	Price	London	−0.4	−0.7	Gilbert and Jalilian (1991)
Railway	Price	Philadelphia	−0.5	−1.8	Voith (1987)
Durables					
Automobiles	Price	U.S.	−0.2	−0.5	Pindyck and Rubinfeld (1995)
	Income	U.S.	3	1.4	Pindyck and Rubinfeld (1995)

Two nondurable goods worth highlighting are alcohol and tobacco. To the extent that consumption of these items is addictive, the demand will be relatively inelastic. The effect of price changes on the quantity demanded will work through discouraging new people from taking up smoking and drinking. Accordingly, the demand for alcohol and tobacco will be relatively more elastic in the long run.

Durables

The effect of adjustment time on the demand for durable items such as automobiles is somewhat different. For both durables and nondurables, buyers need time to adjust, which leads demand to be relatively more elastic in the long run. However, for durables only, a countervailing effect leads demand to be relatively more elastic in the short run. This countervailing effect is especially strong for changes in income.

Consider, for instance, the demand for cars. Most drivers buy cars at intervals of several years. Suppose that there is a drop in incomes. Then, drivers will plan to keep their cars longer. Some drivers, who were just about to replace their cars, will keep their cars longer. So, the drop in incomes will cause purchases to dry up until sufficient time passes that these drivers want to replace their cars at the new lower income.

By contrast, in the long run, the effect on sales will be more muted: eventually, all drivers will replace their cars but less frequently. Thus, the drop in income will cause demand to fall more sharply in the short run than in the long run.

Similarly, if income rises, drivers will replace their cars more frequently. Some drivers will find that they want to replace their cars immediately, causing a boom in purchases. This boom, however, will last only as long as it takes all such drivers to adjust to their new replacement frequency. Thus, the increase in income will tend to cause demand to increase more sharply in the short run than in the long run.

Accordingly, for durable items, the difference between short- and long-run elasticities of demand depends on a balance between the need for time to adjust and the replacement frequency effect. Adjustment time has a similar effect on the own-price and other elasticities of the demand for durable items.

Referring to table 3.6, we see that, for automobiles, the demand is more price elastic in the long run than the short run, indicating that the need for time to adjust outweighs the replacement frequency effect. By contrast, the demand for automobiles is more income elastic in the short run than the long run, suggesting that the replacement frequency effect is relatively stronger for changes in income.

Forecasting Demand

In the preceding section, we showed how short-run elasticities can be used to forecast the effect of multiple (short-run) changes in the factors that affect demand. We can apply the same method to forecast the effect of long-run changes, using long-run elasticities in place of short-run elasticities.

Progress Check 3D Draw a figure, analogous to figure 3.3, showing the short- and long-run demand for a durable.

---

6   Estimating Elasticities[3]

We have seen how elasticities can be applied to forecast changes in demand and expenditure for entire markets as well as individual products. Tables 3.1 to 3.6 present various elasticities of demand. As we have emphasized, an elasticity can change with a change in any one of the factors that affect demand. Further, to the extent that businesses sell different products or cater to different buyers, they will face different demand curves; hence, they will also face different elasticities. Accordingly, managers may not be able to rely on "off-the-shelf" estimates of elasticities.

Suppose, for instance, that the management of an auto lubrication service chain would like to know the sensitivity of the demand for its service to changes in price and advertising. In this section, we outline the data and statistical techniques that can be used to estimate the elasticities of demand. We focus on an intuitive explanation of the basic concepts. For a detailed presentation, the reader should consult the Further Reading section at the end of the chapter.

---

[3]   This section is more advanced. It may be omitted without loss of continuity.

Data

Generally, there are two sources of data. One is records of past experience, including published statistics as well as private records. The other source of data is surveys and experiments specifically designed to discover buyers' preferences. An experiment conducted with genuine buyers making actual purchases is said to be done on a *test market*.

The data from past experience or surveys and experiments can be collected in two ways. One way is to focus on a particular group of buyers and observe how their demand changes as the factors affecting demand vary over time. For instance, using this method, the lube service chain could compile year-by-year records of sales, prices, and advertising expenditures. This type of data is called a **time series**, as it records changes over time.

> A **time series** is a record of changes over time in one market.

The other way of collecting data is to compare the quantities purchased in markets with different values of the factors affecting demand. Using this method, the chain would collect records of sales, prices, and advertising expenditures in each of its markets. This type of data is called a **cross section**, because it records all the data at one time.

> A **cross section** is a record of data at one time over several markets.

Just as time series or cross-section data can be compiled from records of past experience, the same applies to surveys and experiments.

Specification

Suppose that the lube service chain has selected 15 outlets as test markets. In each market, it set different levels of price and advertising expenditure for one week and recorded the corresponding sales.

As chapter 2 suggests, however, the demand for lube service may depend on other factors. To obtain accurate estimates of elasticities, it is important to specify all the factors that have a significant effect on demand and the mathematical relationship between demand and the various factors.

> The **dependent variable** is the variable whose changes are to be explained.

The mathematical relationship can be specified in a number of ways. In a relationship, the **dependent variable** is that whose changes are to be explained, while an **independent variable** is a factor affecting the dependent variable. A common specification is a linear equation in which the dependent variable is equal to a constant plus the weighted sum of the independent variables.

> An **independent variable** is a factor affecting the dependent variable.

In the case of a lube service outlet, the other factors affecting demand may include the number of cars in the area, and the price of competing lube services. Many factors, however, can safely be ignored. These include the weather, the prices of groceries, and the number of schoolchildren in the area. Table 3.7 records the test market data.

As for the mathematical form, the following is a linear equation relating the demand for lube service with four independent variables:

$$D = b_0 + b_1 \times p + b_2 \times N + b_3 \times A + b_4 \times c + u \tag{3.1}$$

where D represents the quantity demanded; p, the price of lube service; N, the number of cars; A, the advertising expenditure; and c, the average price at competing lube services. In equation (3.1), b_0 is a constant, while $b_1, \ldots, b_4$ are the coefficients of quantity demanded,

Table 3.7 Test market data

Market	Quantity	Price ($)	No. of cars (thousands)	Advertising Spendng	Avereage competing price ($)
1	86	30	22.00	500	20
2	87	35	23.00	550	29
3	93	28	23.40	430	31
4	92	25	23.00	400	35
5	86	30	23.60	500	29
6	93	20	24.00	400	30
7	88	29	24.10	300	35
8	89	31	24.50	450	28
9	88	35	25.00	430	25
10	93	29	25.60	500	30
11	87	35	26.00	400	29
12	89	40	26.00	570	31
13	88	47	26.70	520	35
14	82	34	27.30	300	29
15	93	35	28.00	450	35
Average	*88.93*	*32.20*	*24.81*	*446.67*	*30.07*

the price of lube service, the number of cars, and the average competing price, respectively. The variable u represents the collective effect of other factors.

Multiple Regression

Referring to table 3.7, we see variations in all the independent variables among the 15 test markets. To estimate the own-price elasticity of the demand for lube service, we need some way to isolate the effect of price on quantity demanded from the effects of the other variables; we need a similar procedure for estimating the advertising elasticity of demand.

> **Multiple regression** is a statistical technique to estimate the separate effect of each independent variable on the dependent variable.

The statistical technique of **multiple regression** can estimate the separate effect of each independent variable on the dependent variable. Essentially, multiple regression operationalizes the "other things equal" condition needed to estimate an elasticity.

Multiple regression aims to determine values for the constant and the coefficients. To explain the technique, we denote the estimates for the constant and the coefficients by $\hat{b}_0, \hat{b}_1, \hat{b}_2, \hat{b}_3$, and $\hat{b}_4$. Using these values and the corresponding records of p, N, A, and c, we can calculate the *predicted value* of the dependent variable,

$$\hat{b}_0 + (\hat{b}_1 \times p) + (\hat{b}_2 \times N) + (\hat{b}_3 \times A) + (\hat{b}_4 \times c), \tag{3.2}$$

for each test market.

The predicted value may diverge from the actual quantity demanded, D, for the corresponding market. Let us call this difference the *residual*; that is, the residual is the actual value of the dependent variable, D, minus the predicted value:

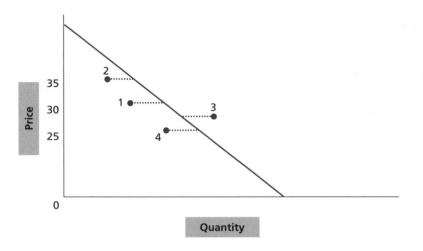

Figure 3.4   Multiple regression
In market 3, the actual quantity exceeds the predicted value, hence the residuals are positive; in markets 1, 2, and 4, the actual quantity is less than the predicted value, so the residuals are negative.

$$D - [\hat{b}_0 + (\hat{b}_1 \times p) + (\hat{b}_2 \times N) + (\hat{b}_3 \times A) + (\hat{b}_4 \times c)].\tag{3.3}$$

Figure 3.4 presents a simplified version of the demand for lube service with only one independent variable, the price. The straight line represents the predicted values of the demand, using the estimated constant and coefficient. We also mark the actual values for several markets. In market 3, the actual quantity exceeds the predicted value, hence the residual is positive. By contrast, in markets 1, 2, and 8, the actual quantity is less than the predicted value, so the residuals are negative.

Ideally, the estimates of the constant and the coefficients will be such that every predicted value equals the corresponding actual value. Then, all the residuals will be 0. Referring to figure 3.4, this would mean that every point would lie along the straight line.

Realistically, however, it is not likely that all the residuals will be 0. This leads to the question of what is the best way to determine the constant and estimates, and the line in figure 3.4. The most common approach is called the *method of least squares*. This is based on the view that positive residuals are as bad as negative residuals while large residuals are disproportionately bad.

The method of least squares seeks a set of estimates for the constant and the coefficients to minimize the sum of the squares of the residuals. Since equally large positive and negative residuals have identical squares, the method treats them identically. By squaring the residuals, the method gives relatively greater weight to large residuals. Least-squares multiple regression analysis is available in common spreadsheet programs as well as specialized statistical packages.

Interpretation

By applying least-squares multiple regression to estimate the equation for the lube service demand, we obtain the results in table 3.8. The estimates of the constant and coefficients are $\hat{b}_0 = 63.48$, $\hat{b}_1 = -0.48$, $\hat{b}_2 = 0.65$, $\hat{b}_3 = 0.03$, and $\hat{b}_4 = 0.42$.

Table 3.8   Multiple regression results

Regression statistics				
R²	0.65			
Standard error	2.29			
Number of observations	15			
F-statistic	4.68			
Significance	0.02			
Independent variable	Coefficient	Standard error	t-statistic	Significance
Constant	63.48	11.60	5.47	0.001
Price	−0.48	0.14	−3.31	0.008
Number of cars	0.65	0.51	1.28	0.242
Advertising spending	0.03	0.01	2.85	0.022
Competing price	0.42	0.17	2.53	0.036

Using these estimates, we can calculate the elasticities of demand. In equation (3.1), the coefficient of price, b_1, is the rate of change of the quantity demanded with respect to changes in price. From table 3.8, the estimate of this rate of change, $\hat{b}_1 = -0.48$. The math supplement shows that the own-price elasticity is this rate of change multiplied by price and divided by quantity. From table 3.7, the average price is \$32.20 and the average quantity is 88.93. Hence, the own-price elasticity at the average price and quantity is

$$-0.48 \times 32.20/88.93 = -0.17. \qquad (3.4)$$

We can use the same approach to calculate the elasticity of demand with respect to advertising and other independent variables.

Statistical Significance

Next, we use this example to discuss how to evaluate the significance of least-squares multiple regression results. The estimates of the constant and coefficients depend on the particular sample of observations in table 3.7. With another sample, we would obtain somewhat different estimates. By repeating the regression many times with different samples, we will obtain many sets of estimates. Using the probability distributions of these estimates, we can calculate measures to assess the significance of the regression estimates.

F *Statistic*

The *F*-statistic measures the overall significance of the independent variables. The statistic is computed on the assumption that there is no relationship between the dependent variable and the set of independent variables, meaning that the coefficients are all 0. The *F*-statistic ranges from 0 to infinity.

Using the probability distributions of these estimates, we can calculate the probability of obtaining any particular value for the *F*-statistic if the constant and coefficients are all 0. If this probability falls below a specific benchmark, then we say that the regression estimates are statistically significant. The conventional benchmarks are 1% and 5%.

From table 3.8, the F-statistic is 4.68 and the significance is $0.02 = 2\%$, which meets the 5% benchmark. We can be fairly confident that the regression estimates are statistically significant.

R^2

Related to the F-statistic is the R^2. This statistic uses the squared residuals to measure the extent to which the independent variables account for the variation of the dependent variable. R^2 ranges from 0 to 1. An R^2 value of 1 means that all the residuals are exactly 0, or equivalently, that every predicted value is exactly equal to the corresponding actual value. By contrast, an R^2 value of 0 means that the independent variables account for none of the variation in the dependent variable.

From table 3.8, R^2 is 0.65. This means that the regression equation accounts for 65% of the variation of the dependent variable. This is a reasonably large part of the variation.

t *statistic and p-value*

The t-statistic is used to evaluate the significance of a particular independent variable. Specifically, the t-statistic is the estimated value of the coefficient divided by the standard error. The standard error measures the dispersion of the estimate of the coefficient.

The t-statistic will be negative or positive according to the sign of the estimated coefficient. It ranges from negative to positive infinity. Using the probability distribution of the estimate, we can calculate the probability of obtaining any particular value for the t-statistic if the coefficient is 0. If this probability falls below a specific benchmark, then the estimated coefficient is statistically significant. The conventional benchmarks are 1% and 5%.

Most statistical software packages compute this probability directly, and report it as the p-value. The p-value directly measures the likelihood that the estimated coefficient could be the result of chance, under the assumption that the true coefficient is zero. That is, if there really were no effect of the particular independent variable on the dependent variable, then the p-value gives the probability that random sampling errors could produce a coefficient as large as found by the least-squares multiple regression model.

If the p-value is acceptably low, then the chance that the coefficient is a spurious finding is also low; when the p-value is high, then there is a large chance that the coefficient's sign (positive or negative) is the result of a random sampling error rather than demonstration of a real effect.

In table 3.8, the t-statistic for the price of lube service is -3.31 and the p-value is 0.008 $= 0.8\%$, which meets both the 1% and 5% benchmarks. The t-statistic for advertising spending is 2.85 and the p-value is $0.022 = 2.2\%$, which meets the 5% benchmark. By contrast, the t-statistic for the number of cars is 1.28 and the p-value is $0.242 = 24.2\%$, which does not meet even the 5% benchmark.

Accordingly, we infer that the price of lube service and advertising spending have significant effects on the demand for lube service, but the effect on the number of cars is questionable.

Progress Check 3E Referring to tables 3.7 and 3.8, calculate the advertising elasticity of demand at the average quantity and advertising spending.

⊢ Waiting time and "price elasticity" ⊢

A multiple regression study of the demand for gasoline at individual Boston-area service stations found that the elasticity of demand with respect to the price of gasoline was −3.3.

Customers of service stations, however, pay two prices: one in money to the seller and another in the form of waiting time. Estimates of demand must take into account the customers' sensitivity to waiting. If a station raises its price by 1%, its customers must pay 1% more in money. But this tends to reduce customer purchases. Given the station's fueling capacity, the reduction in purchases will reduce waiting times, which tends to increase the quantity demanded.

Accordingly, the estimated "price elasticity" of −3.3 combines the responsiveness to an increase in price alone together with the responsiveness to a reduction in waiting time. After adjusting for the effect on waiting time, Png and Reitman estimated that the pure own-price elasticity ranged between −6.3 and −8.4.

Other businesses that serve randomly arriving customers from a fixed capacity include Internet service providers, banks, hospitals, and supermarkets. In estimating the own-price elasticity of demand at any such business, an analyst must take care to adjust for the effect of price changes on waiting times.

Source: I. P. L. Png and David Reitman, "Service Time Competition," *RAND Journal of Economics* 25, no. 4 (Winter, 1994), pp. 619–34.

7 Summary

The elasticity of demand measures the responsiveness of demand to changes in a factor that affects demand. Elasticities can be estimated for price, income, prices of related products, and advertising expenditures. The own-price elasticity is the ratio of the percentage change in quantity demanded to the percentage change in price, and is a negative number. Demand is price elastic if a 1% increase in price leads to more than a 1% drop in quantity demanded, and inelastic if it leads to less than a 1% drop in quantity demanded.

The own-price elasticity can be used to forecast the effects of price changes on quantity demanded and buyer expenditure. Elasticities can be used to forecast the effects on demand of simultaneous changes in multiple factors. All elasticities vary with adjustment time. The long-run demand is generally more elastic than the short-run demand in the case of non-durables, but not necessarily for durables.

Elasticities can be estimated from records of past experience or test markets by the statistical technique of multiple regression.

Key Concepts

elasticity of demand	income elasticity	cross section
own-price elasticity	cross-price elasticity	dependent variable
arc approach	advertising elasticity	independent variable
point approach	short run	multiple regression
elastic	long run	
inelastic	time series	

Further Reading

Ramu Ramanathan covers the details of econometrics, which is the application of statistical techniques to economic issues, in *Introductory* *Econometrics with Applications* (Fort Worth, TX: Harcourt College Publishers, 2002).

Review Questions

1. Why is the demand for business travel less elastic than that for leisure travel?
2. The demand for medical services is price inelastic. Explain in terms of the split between the person who decides on the service (doctor/patient) and the person who pays (patient/medical insurer/health maintenance organization).
3. Explain why the own-price elasticity is a pure number with no units and is negative.
4. Consider a service that you buy frequently.
    (a) Suppose that the price was 5% lower and all other factors do not change. How much more would you buy each year?
    (b) Using this information, calculate the own-price elasticity of your demand.
5. Suppose that the own-price elasticity of the demand for food is -0.7 and that, as a result of a nationwide drought, the price of food rises by 10%. Will this cause expenditure on food to rise or fall?
6. Consider a good that you buy frequently.
    (a) Suppose that your income was 10% higher and all other factors do not change. How much more would you buy each year?
    (b) Using this information, calculate the income elasticity of your demand.
    (c) Is the good an inferior product or normal product for you?
7. True or false?
    (a) The income elasticity of demand can be estimated by either the arc approach or the point approach.
    (b) Changes in the price of an item will affect the income elasticity of demand.
8. Manufacturers such as Dunlop and Goodyear use both natural and synthetic rubber to produce tires. If the elasticity of the demand for natural rubber with respect to changes in the price of synthetic rubber is negative, then the two types of rubber are (choose a or b):
    (a) Substitutes.
    (b) Complements.
9. Suppose that the elasticity of the demand for Nike sports shoes with respect to changes in the price of Adidas sports shoes is 1.3. Do you expect the elasticity with respect to changes in the price of Ferragamo shoes to be a smaller or larger number?
10. Suppose that the advertising elasticity of the demand for one brand of cigarettes is 1.3. If the manufacturer raises advertising expenditure by 5%, by how much will the demand change?
11. Explain why the advertising elasticity of the market demand for beer may be smaller than the advertising elasticity of the demand for one particular brand.
12. Consider the effect of changes in fares on the quantity demanded of taxi services. Do you expect demand to be more elastic with respect to fare changes in the short run or the long run?
13. Why is the long-run demand for a nondurable item more elastic than the short-run demand? Why might the same rule not apply to the demand for a durable item?
14. This question relies on the section on estimating elasticities. Explain why the method of least-squares multiple regression aims to minimize the sum of the squares of the residuals and not the sum of just the residuals.
15. This question relies on the section on estimating elasticities. Explain the difference between cross-section and time series data.

Discussion Questions

1. Among commercial users such as apartment buildings, hotels, and offices, the demand for water is estimated to have an own-price elasticity of −0.36, elasticity with respect to the number of commercial establishments of 0.99, and elasticity with respect to the average summer temperature of 0.02 (Williams and Suh, 1986).
   (a) Intuitively, would an increase in the number of commercial establishments increase or reduce the demand for water? Is the estimated elasticity consistent with your explanation?
   (b) Intuitively, would a rise in the average summer temperature increase or reduce the demand for water? Is the estimated elasticity consistent with your explanation?
   (c) By considering the own-price elasticity of demand, explain how the water company could increase its profit.

2. At Boston-area service stations, the elasticity of the demand for gasoline with respect to price (combining the pure price effect with the effect on waiting times) was −3.3, the elasticity with respect to station fueling capacity was 0.7, and the elasticity with respect to the average price at nearby stations was 1.2 (Png and Reitman, 1994).
   (a) Explain why the elasticity with respect to the average price at nearby stations is a positive number.
   (b) Amy's station is the only competitor to Al's. Al's station has 3% more fueling capacity. Originally, both stations charged the same price. Then Amy reduced her price by 2%. What will be the percentage difference in quantity demanded between the two stations?
   (c) If Amy raises capacity from 6 to 7 fueling places, by how much could she increase price without affecting sales?

3. Suppose that, at the current price of $1.50 per gallon and average household income of $100,000 a year, the quantity demanded of bottled water is 200 million gallons a week. If the price were increased to $1.68, the quantity demanded would fall to 158.7 million gallons a week. If the household income were increased to $110,500 a year, the quantity demanded would rise to 208 million gallons a week.
   (a) Calculate the own-price elasticity of demand.
   (b) Calculate the income elasticity of demand.
   (c) According to these estimates, is bottled water a normal or inferior product?

4. Drugs that are not covered by patent can be freely manufactured by anyone. By contrast, the production and sale of patented drugs is tightly controlled. The advertising elasticity of the demand for antihypertensive drugs was around 0.26 for all drugs, and 0.24 for those covered by patents. For all antihypertensive drugs, the own price elasticity was about −2.0 without advertising, and about −1.6 in the long run with advertising.
   (a) Consider a 5% increase in advertising expenditure. By how much would the demand for a patented drug rise? What about the demand for a drug not covered by patent?
   (b) Why is the demand for patented drugs less responsive to advertising than the demand for drugs not covered by patent?
   (c) Suppose that a drug manufacturer were to increase advertising. Explain why it should also raise the price of its drugs.

5. Electric power producers have a choice of several fuels, including oil, natural gas, coal, and uranium. Once an electric power plant has been built, however, the scope to switch fuels may be very limited. Since power plants last for 30 years or more, producers must consider the relative prices of the alternative fuels well into the future when choosing a generating plant.
   (a) Do you expect the cross-price elasticity between the demand for oil-fired power plants and the price of oil to be positive or negative?
   (b) Will the cross-price elasticity between the demand for oil-fired power plants and the price of coal be positive or negative?

(c)   Would the demand for oil-fired power plants be more or less elastic in the long run as compared with the short run?

6.   Automobile travel demand (measured in total number of miles driven) is estimated to have short- and long-run elasticities with respect to the price of gasoline of -0.10 and -0.29, respectively. The demand for automobile travel also depends on total travel time: the short- and long-run elasticities are estimated to be -0.27 and -0.57, respectively (*Source*: Victoria Transport Policy Institute, www.vtpi.org/elasticities.pdf).

(a)   Explain why the long-run elasticities of the demand for automobile travel are more negative than the short-run elasticities. How does consumer choice of automobile affect the difference?

(b)   Suppose that the gasoline price rises by 20% and construction of new roads reduces travel time by 10%. Calculate the impact on the total number of miles driven in the (i) short run and (ii) long run.

7.   According to a study of U.S. cigarette sales between 1955 and 1985, when the price of cigarettes was 1% higher, consumption would be 0.4% lower in the short run and 0.75% lower in the long run (Becker et al., 1994).

(a)   Calculate the short- and long-run own-price elasticities of the demand for cigarettes.

(b)   Is demand more or less elastic in the long run than in the short run? Explain your answer.

(c)   If the government were to impose a tax that raised the price of cigarettes by 5%, would total consumer expenditure on cigarettes rise or fall in the short run? What about in the long run?

8.   In May 2003, the New York MTA increased subway fares by 33%. Total ridership fell by 1%, while discount ridership increased from 24.7% to 32%. Assume the average discount fare increased by 10%, and that the cross-elasticity of demand for regular rides with respect to discount prices is equal to the cross-price elasticity of discount rides with respect to regular fares.

(a)   Historically, the MTA used an estimated own-price elasticity for regular rides of -0.1. Based on the given information and assumptions, estimate the own-price elasticity for discount tickets and the cross-price elasticity.

(b)   Compare the magnitudes of the own-price elasticities for regular and discount fares. Do their relative magnitudes make sense? Explain.

9.   This question relies on the section on estimating elasticities. Suppose that the government has just announced a revision to the data in table 3.7. The new data increases the number of cars in markets 11–15 by 10%. All other data remain valid.

(a)   Use multiple regression to estimate the demand with (i) the original data and (ii) the revised data.

(b)   Calculate the new estimates for the elasticities with respect to price, number of cars, and advertising expenditure at the average values of quantity, price, number of cars, and advertising expenditure.

10.   An Australian telecommunications carrier wants to estimate the own-price elasticity of the demand for international calls to the United States. It has collected annual records of international calls and prices. In each of the following groups, choose the one factor that you would also consider in the estimation. Explain your reasoning.

(a)   *Consumer demographics*: (i) average per capita income, (ii) average age.

(b)   *Complements*: (i) number of telephone lines, (ii) number of mobile telephone subscribers.

(c)   *Prices of related items*: (i) price of electricity, (ii) postage rate from Australia to the United States.

(d)   *What other variables* would be relevant?

11.   This question applies techniques introduced in the math supplement to chapter 2. Suppose that a car rental business faces a demand represented by the equation

$$D = 30 - p + 0.4Y, \tag{3.5}$$

where D is the quantity demanded in rentals a month, p is the price in dollars per rental, and Y is the average consumer's income in thousands of dollars a year. Use the arc approach in the following calculations.

(a) Suppose that income $Y = 100$ and the car rental business raises the price from $p = 30$ to $p = 35$. Calculate the own-price elasticity of demand.

(b) Suppose that income $Y = 110$ and the car rental business raises the price from $p = 30$ to $p = 35$. Calculate the own-price elasticity of demand.

(c) Suppose that the price $p = 30$ and that income rises from $Y = 100$ to $Y = 110$. Calculate the income elasticity of demand.

(d) Suppose that the price $p = 35$ and that income rises from $Y = 100$ to $Y = 110$. Calculate the income elasticity of demand.

References

Badi H. Baltagi and James M. Griffin. 1995. "A Dynamic Demand Model for Liquor: The Case for Pooling." *Review of Economics and Statistics* 77, no. 3 (August), pp. 545–54.

Michael R. Baye, Dennis W. Jansen, and Jae-Woo Lee. 1992. "Advertising Effects in Complete Demand Systems." *Applied Economics* 24, no. 10, pp. 1087–96.

Gary Becker, Michael Grossman, and Kevin Murphy. 1994. "An Empirical Analysis of Cigarette Addiction." *American Economic Review* 84 (June), p. 396.

David R. Bell, Jeongwen Chiang, and V. Padmanabhan. 1999. "The Decomposition of Promotional Response: An Empirical Generalization." *Marketing Science* 18, no. 4, pp. 504–26.

Jean-Thomas Bernard, Denis Bolduc, and Donald Belanger. 1996. "Quebec Residential Electricity Demand: A Microeconometric Approach." *Canadian Journal of Economics* 29, no. 1 (February), pp. 92–113.

Molly Espey. 1998. "Gasoline Demand Revisited: An International Meta-analysis of Elasticities." *Energy Economics* 20, no. 3 (June 1998), pp. 273–95.

Koli Fatai, Les Oxley, and Frank G. Scrimgeour. 2003. "Modeling and Forecasting the Demand for Electricity in New Zealand: A Comparison of Alternative Approaches." *Energy Journal*, 24, no. 1, pp. 75–102.

George R. Franke and Gary B. Wilcox. 1987. "Alcoholic Beverage Advertising and Consumption in the United States." *Journal of Advertising* 16, no. 3, pp. 22–30.

W. Wayne Fu. 2003. "Multimarket Contact of US Newspaper Chains: Circulation Competition and Market Coordination." *Information Economics and Policy* 15, no. 4 (December), pp. 501–19.

Teresa Garin Munoz. 1996. "Demand for National Telephone Traffic in Spain from 1985–1989: An Econometric Study Using Provincial Panel Data." *Information Economics and Policy* 8, no. 1 (March), pp. 51–73.

Christopher Gilbert and Hossein Jalilian. 1991. "The Demand for Travel and for Travelcards on London Regional Transport." *Journal of Transport Economics and Policy* 25, no. 1 (January), pp. 3–29.

James A. Johnson and Ernest H. Oksanen. 1977. "Estimation of Demand for Alcoholic Beverages in Canada from Pooled Time Series and Cross Sections." *Review of Economics and Statistics* 59 (February), pp. 113–18.

Pinelopi Koujianou-Goldberg. 1995. "Product Differentiation and Oligopoly in International Markets: The Case of the U.S. Automobile Industry." *Econometrica* 63, no. 4 (July), pp. 891–951.

Patrick S. McCarthy. 1996. "Market Price and Income Elasticities of New Vehicle Demands." *Review of Economics and Statistics*, 78, no. 3 (August), pp. 543–7.

National Income and Product Accounts of the United States (1986).

Robert S. Pindyck and Daniel L. Rubinfeld. 1995. *Microeconomics*, 3d ed., p. 37. Englewood Cliffs, NJ: Prentice-Hall.

I. P. L. Png and David Reitman. 1994. "Service Time Competition." *RAND Journal of Economics* 25, no. 4 (Winter), pp. 619–34.

John A. Rizzo. 1999. "Advertising and Competition in the Ethical Pharmaceutical Industry: The Case of Anti-hypertensive Drugs." *Journal of Law and Economics* 62, pp. 89–116.

Abebayehu Tegene. 1991. "Kalman Filter and the Demand for Cigarettes." *Applied Economics* 23, pp. 1175–82.

Richard Voith. 1987. "Commuter Rail Ridership: The Long and Short Haul," *Business Review*, Federal Reserve Bank of Philadelphia (November–December), pp. 13–23.

Martin Williams and Byung Suh. 1986. "The Demand for Urban Water by Customer Class." *Applied Economics* 18, pp. 1275–89.

Chapter 3

Math Supplement

Own-Price Elasticity

By definition, the own-price elasticity of demand is the proportionate change in quantity demanded divided by the proportionate change in price. Let Q represent the quantity demanded; dQ, the change in quantity demanded; p, the price; and dp, the change in price. Then dQ/Q is the proportionate change in quantity demanded, while dp/p is the proportionate change in price. Thus, in algebraic terms, the own-price elasticity is

$$e_p = \frac{dQ/Q}{dp/p} = \frac{p}{Q}\frac{dQ}{dp}. \tag{3.6}$$

Using this definition, we can study the relationship between the own-price elasticity and the slope of the demand curve. Rearrange the definition of the own-price elasticity as follows:

$$e_p = \frac{p}{Q}\bigg/\frac{dp}{dQ}. \tag{3.7}$$

The variable dp/dQ is the change in price divided by the change in quantity demanded, that is, the slope of the demand curve. So, by (3.7), the own-price elasticity is (p/Q) divided by the slope of the demand curve. Clearly, the own-price elasticity and slope are related but are not the same.

Changes in Price

Let us now show how to use the definition in (3.6) to forecast changes in quantity demanded and buyer expenditure as a function of the own-price elasticity, percentage change in price, and the quantity demanded. Rearranging the definition in (3.6),

$$\frac{dQ}{Q} = e_p \times \frac{dp}{p}. \tag{3.8}$$

This says that the proportionate change in quantity demanded is the own-price elasticity multiplied by the proportionate change in price.

Let $\%Q$ represent the percentage change in quantity demanded and $\%p$ represent the percentage change in price. Then $\%Q = 100 \cdot dQ/Q$, and $\%p = 100 \cdot dp/p$. Multiplying both sides of (3.8) by 100 and substituting, we have

$$\%Q = e_p \times \%p, \tag{3.9}$$

which says that the percentage change in the quantity demanded is the own-price elasticity multiplied by the percentage change in the price.

Chapter 4

Supply

1 Introduction

Founded in 1948, Bestar is listed on the Toronto Stock Exchange.[1] It designs, manufactures, and distributes ready-to-assemble and fully assembled furniture. The company's plant and offices are located in Lac-Megantic (Quebec). Bestar exports 70% of its annual production, principally to the United States. It distributes through mass retailers, office superstores, warehouse clubs, and catalog retailers.

With annual revenue of C$38.7 million and 199 employees in 2005, Bestar is larger than the industry average. The average business in Canada's furniture industry generated revenue of C$2.87 million and employed 25 persons. Furniture manufacturing is relatively intensive in wood and labor: on average, materials and supplies accounted for 68% of manufacturing costs, and wages accounted for 31%.

Between 2003 and 2004, Bestar's revenue fell slightly from C$44.3 million to C$43.7 million. However, net earnings of C$254,000 fell to a loss of C$442,000, in part due to C$1.4 million in restructuring costs. The company secured additional financing through a private placement of C$975,000, an unsecured debenture of C$975,000 from the Fonds de solidarité des travailleurs du Québec, and a C$1.5 million loan from Investissement-Québec.

Between 2004 and 2005, the company's revenue fell by more than 11% to $38.7 million, while it reversed the loss to net earnings of C$174,000. Chief Executive Officer, Jacques Hetu, attributed the fall in revenue to: "Delayed introduction of our new products, growing Asian competition and an average exchange rate of C$0.08 higher than in 2004."

Indeed, Bestar forecast that first-quarter 2006 revenues would be lower than the corresponding 2005 quarter as a key retailer had re-allocated display space from Bestar to an Asian supplier. Asian manufacturers pose a direct challenge to the Canadian furniture industry. Further, with lower labor costs, Asian manufacturers posed an indirect challenge – their fully assembled furniture competes with Canadian-produced ready-to-assemble furniture.

Canada is a major international producer of lumber and wood. This partly explains Canada's leading position in furniture manufacturing. How would changes in the prices of lumber and

---

[1] The following analysis is based, in part, on Bestar, Inc., Press Release, February 21, 2006; Bestar, Inc., Annual Report, 2005; Industry Canada, statistics for NAISC (North American Industry Classification System) 3371.

wood affect the furniture industry? How do Asian competitors affect the supply of furniture to the United States and the prospects for Canadian manufacturers like Bestar? How should Bestar shareholders decide between shutting down the company and continuing operations?

To address these questions, we need to understand how a seller determines the quantity that it will supply and the price at which it breaks even. In this chapter, we first consider the relation between costs and the production rate and how a business will adjust its production rate to changes in the prices of its output and inputs. We also analyze whether a business should continue in business. This provides the foundation for the the individual supply curve, which is the seller-side counterpart to the demand curve, and the individual demand for inputs.

Then, we compare supply in the short run, when businesses are restricted in the extent to which they can adjust inputs, with supply in the long run, when businesses can freely adjust all inputs. Using this analysis, we can explain why Bestar shareholders did not shut down the company in the face of the appreciating Canadian dollar and Asian competition.

Next, extending from the individual seller to the market, we examine the market supply curve. This enables us to explain the impact of Asian manufacturers on the U.S. supply of furniture and the prospects for Canadian manufacturers like Bestar, and also the impact of lumber and wood prices on the furniture industry.

Following this, we introduce the concept of seller surplus, which is the seller-side counterpart to buyer surplus, and then elasticities of supply, which measure the responsiveness of quantity supplied to changes in various factors.

2   Short-Run Costs

Two key decisions of a business, whether to continue in operation and the rate at which to operate, both depend on the length of the time horizon. In chapter 3, we introduced the concepts of short run and long run in relation to buyers. The same concepts apply to sellers as well. A **short run** is a time horizon in which a seller cannot adjust at least one input. In the short run, the business must work within the constraints of past commitments such as employment contracts and investment in facilities and equipment. Over time, however, these commitments expire. A **long run** is a time horizon long enough for the seller to adjust all inputs.

The **short run** is a time horizon within which a seller cannot adjust at least one input.

The difference between the short run and long run depends on the circumstances. For instance, if a building contractor has just engaged 100 workers on a 12-month contract, then the employment of these workers cannot be adjusted until the expiration of the contract. Hence, the contractor's short run is at least 12 months long. By contrast, a contractor that has hired workers on a daily basis could adjust its workforce every day. Similarly, a contractor who has purchased construction equipment has committed to a relatively longer horizon than one who has rented the equipment on a weekly contract.

The **long run** is a time horizon long enough for the seller to adjust all inputs.

In this and the next section, we focus on short-run business decisions; we consider long-run behavior in the fourth section.

Fixed vis-à-vis Variable Costs

To determine its production rate, a business needs to know the cost of delivering an additional unit of product. To decide whether to continue in operation, a business needs to know how shutting down will affect its costs. An important factor in both decisions is the

Table 4.1 Short-run weekly expenses

Weekly production rate	Rent	Wages	Cost of supplies	Total
0	$2,000	$200	$0	$2,200
1,000	$2,000	$529	$100	$2,629
2,000	$2,000	$836	$200	$3,036
3,000	$2,000	$1,216	$300	$3,516
4,000	$2,000	$1,697	$400	$4,097
5,000	$2,000	$2,293	$500	$4,793
6,000	$2,000	$3,015	$600	$5,615
7,000	$2,000	$3,870	$700	$6,570
8,000	$2,000	$4,862	$800	$7,662
9,000	$2,000	$5,996	$900	$8,896

distinction between fixed and variable costs. The **fixed cost** is the cost of inputs that do not change with the production rate. By contrast, the **variable cost** is the cost of inputs that change with the production rate.

> The **fixed cost** is the cost of inputs that do not change with the production rate.

Let us consider the distinction between fixed and variable costs in the context of Luna Farm, which produces eggs. Like those of most businesses, Luna's financial and accounting records do not classify expenses into fixed and variable. Rather, the records organize expenses according to the type of input: rent, wages, and payments for supplies. By interviewing Luna's management, we can learn the costs required for alternative short-run production rates. Table 4.1 presents this information.

> The **variable cost** is the cost of inputs that change with the production rate.

To distinguish between fixed and variable costs, a business must analyze how each category of expense varies with changes in the scale of operations. Referring to table 4.1, we can perform this analysis for Luna. Luna cannot adjust the size of its facility, so the rent does not vary with the production rate. The rent is $2,000 whether Luna produces nothing or 9,000 dozen eggs a week; hence, it is a fixed cost. Wages vary with the production rate, but even when Luna produces no eggs, it incurs wages of $200. Hence, the wages include a fixed component of $200, while the remainder is variable. Finally, the cost of supplies is completely variable.

In table 4.2, we assign Luna's expenses – rent, wages, and cost of supplies – into the two categories of fixed costs and variable costs. As the production rate increases from nothing to 9,000 dozen eggs a week, the fixed cost is always $2,200. By contrast, the variable cost increases from nothing for no production to $6,696 for 9,000 dozen eggs a week.

Total cost is the sum of fixed cost and variable cost. Algebraically, if we represent total cost by C, fixed cost by F, and variable cost by V, then

> **Total cost** is the sum of the fixed and variable costs.

$$C = F + V. \tag{4.1}$$

Provided that there are some variable costs, then total cost will increase with operations. In Luna's case, referring to table 4.2, the total cost is $2,200 for no production, and rises to $8,896 for production of 9,000 dozen eggs a week.

Table 4.2   Analysis of short-run costs

Weekly production rate	Fixed cost	Variable cost	Total cost	Marginal cost	Average fixed cost	Average variable cost	Average cost
0	$2,200	$0	$2,200				
1,000	$2,200	$429	$2,629	$0.43	$2.20	$0.43	$2.63
2,000	$2,200	$836	$3,036	$0.41	$1.10	$0.42	$1.52
3,000	$2,200	$1,316	$3,516	$0.48	$0.73	$0.44	$1.17
4,000	$2,200	$1,897	$4,097	$0.58	$0.55	$0.47	$1.02
5,000	$2,200	$2,593	$4,793	$0.70	$0.44	$0.52	$0.96
6,000	$2,200	$3,415	$5,615	$0.82	$0.37	$0.57	$0.94
7,000	$2,200	$4,370	$6,570	$0.95	$0.31	$0.62	$0.94
8,000	$2,200	$5,462	$7,662	$1.09	$0.28	$0.68	$0.96
9,000	$2,200	$6,696	$8,896	$1.23	$0.24	$0.74	$0.99

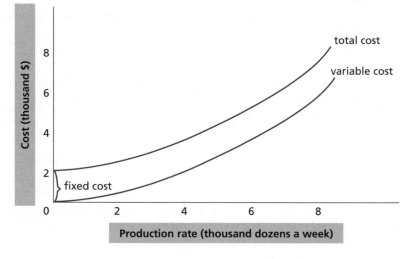

Figure 4.1   Short-run total cost
The total cost curve is the variable cost curve shifted up by the amount of the fixed cost.

It is helpful to illustrate the concepts of total, fixed, and variable costs. In figure 4.1, the vertical axis represents cost, while the horizontal axis represents the scale of operations. We draw a curve representing variable cost. The total cost curve is the variable cost curve, shifted up everywhere by the amount of the fixed cost. In particular, the fixed cost is represented by the height of the total cost curve at the zero production rate.

By analyzing its costs as fixed and variable, the management of a business can understand which cost elements will be affected by changes in the scale of operations. The distinction between fixed and variable costs is important whether the business is growing or shrinking. For instance, suppose that management is planning to reduce costs by downsizing. Downsizing will have no effect on fixed costs and will only reduce the variable costs. Hence, in a business whose costs are mostly fixed, downsizing may have relatively little effect on costs.

> **Progress Check 4A** In figure 4.1, if the fixed cost were higher, how would that affect the total and variable cost curves?

Marginal Cost

To determine the scale at which it should operate, a business needs to know the cost of making an additional unit of product. Then, the business can see whether selling the additional unit will add to or subtract from its total profit. The change in total cost due to the production of an additional unit is the **marginal cost**. The marginal cost can be derived from the analysis of fixed and variable costs.

> The **marginal cost** is the change in total cost due to the production of an additional unit.

Let us derive the marginal cost in the case of Luna Farm. Referring to table 4.2, as the production rate increases from none to 1,000 dozen eggs a week, the total cost increases from $2,200 to $2,629. The increment $2,629 − $2,200 = $429 is the additional cost of producing the 1,000 dozen eggs. Hence, the marginal cost is $429/1,000 = 43 cents per dozen.

Notice that, as the production rate increases from none to 1,000 dozen a week, the fixed cost remains unchanged; only the variable cost increases. Hence, we can also calculate the marginal cost from the increase in variable cost. Using this approach, as the production rate increases from none to 1,000 dozen eggs a week, the variable cost increases from $0 to $429. Therefore, the marginal cost is $429/1,000 = 43 cents per dozen.

Similarly, as the production rate increases from 1,000 to 2,000 dozen eggs a week, the variable cost increases from $429 to $836. The marginal cost is now $407 for 1,000 dozen eggs, or 41 cents per dozen. With each increase in the production rate, the marginal cost increases, reaching $1.23 at the rate of 9,000 dozen eggs a week. In Luna's case, each additional dozen requires more variable cost than the one before. We display this information in table 4.2.

Average Cost

The marginal cost is the cost of producing an additional unit. A related concept is **average cost**, which is the total cost divided by the production rate. The average cost is also called the *unit cost*. Given the scale of operations, the average cost reflects the cost of producing a typical unit.

> The **average cost** (unit cost) is the total cost divided by the production rate.

Let us derive the average cost in the case of Luna Farm. Referring to table 4.2, we can obtain the average cost as total cost divided by the production rate. At 1,000 dozen eggs a week, the average cost is $2,629/1,000 = $2.63, while at 2,000 dozen a week, the average cost is $3,036/2,000 = $1.52. The average cost continues to fall with increases in the production rate until it reaches a minimum of 94 cents at 6,000–7,000 dozen a week. Thereafter, it increases with the production rate. At 9,000 dozen a week, the average cost is 99 cents.

To understand why the average cost first drops with increases in the production rate and then rises, recall that the total cost is the sum of the fixed cost and the variable cost:

$$C = F + V. \tag{4.2}$$

If q represents the production rate, then dividing throughout by q, we have

$$\frac{C}{q} = \frac{F}{q} + \frac{V}{q}. \tag{4.3}$$

In words, the average cost is the average fixed cost plus the average variable cost. The average fixed cost is fixed cost divided by the production rate. So, if the production rate is higher, the fixed cost will be spread over more units; hence, the average fixed cost will be lower. This factor causes the average cost to fall with increases in the production rate.

The other element in average cost is the average variable cost, which is the variable cost divided by the production rate. In the short run, at least one input is fixed; hence, to raise the production rate, the business must combine increasing quantities of the variable inputs with an unchanged quantity of the fixed input.

> The **marginal product** is the increase in output arising from an additional unit of the input.

The increase in output arising from an additional unit of an input is called the **marginal product** from that input. At low production rates, there is a mismatch between the variable inputs and the fixed input. Owing to the mismatch, the marginal product is low and the average variable cost is high. With a higher production rate, the variable inputs match the fixed input relatively better, and the average variable cost is lower.

As more of the variable inputs are added in combination with the fixed input, there will be a mismatch again. Eventually, there will be a *diminishing marginal product* from the variable inputs. This means that the marginal product becomes smaller with each increase in the quantity of the variable input. With a diminishing marginal product from the variable inputs, the average variable cost will increase with the production rate.

In Luna's case, table 4.2 shows that the average variable cost first drops from 43 cents to 42 cents as the production increases from 1,000 to 2,000 dozen eggs a week. Then, the average variable cost rises from 42 cents to 74 cents as the production increases from 2,000 to 9,000 dozen a week.

Recall that the average cost is the average fixed cost plus the average variable cost. While the average fixed cost falls with the production rate, the average variable cost falls and then increases. Accordingly, where the average variable cost is increasing, the relationship between the average cost and the production rate depends on the balance between the declining average fixed cost and the increasing average variable cost.

If the fixed cost is not too large and the average variable cost increases sufficiently, the average cost will first decline with the production rate and then increase. As table 4.2 shows, this is the case for Luna.

In figure 4.2, we graph the marginal, average, and average variable costs against the production rate. The marginal cost curve falls from 43 cents at 1,000 dozen a week, to reach a minimum of 41 cents at 2,000 dozen a week, and rises thereafter. The average variable cost curve falls from 43 cents at 1,000 dozen a week, to a minimum of 42 cents at 2,000 dozen a week, and then rises. Similarly, the average cost curve falls from $2.63 at 1,000 dozen a week, to a minimum of 94 cents at 6,000–7,000 dozen a week, and then rises. The graphs of the marginal, average variable, and average cost curves are each shaped like the letter *U*.

***

Progress Check 4B In figure 4.2, if the fixed cost were lower, how would that affect the marginal, average variable, and average cost curves?

***

Technology

In the preceding analysis, we derived the information about costs by asking the seller for the cost of producing at various rates. Accordingly, at every production level, the total, average, and marginal cost depend on the seller's individual operating technology.

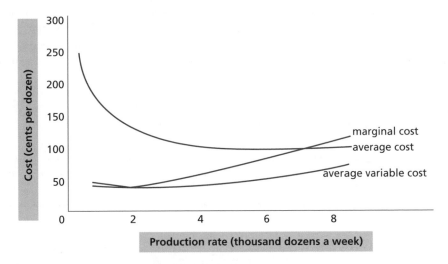

Figure 4.2   Short-run marginal, average variable, and average costs
The marginal, average variable, and average cost curves are U-shaped. The curves decrease at low production rates, reach a minimum, and then increase for high production rates.

There are two implications of this approach. First, the curves will change with adjustments in the seller's technology. For instance, a seller that discovers a technology involving a lower fixed cost will lower its average cost curve. A seller that uses a technology with a lower variable cost will lower its average, average variable, and marginal cost curves.

Second, different sellers may have different technologies and, hence, different cost curves. They may differ in the structure of fixed vis-à-vis variable costs. Some may have better technologies and hence lower costs than others.

⊣ Hospitals: transition from fixed to variable costs ⊢

Managed care has become the predominant form of health insurance in the United States, increasing from 27% of the health insurance market in 1988 to 71% in 2001. About one-third of the population covered by "managed care" plans belong to Health Maintenance Organizations (HMOs) and the other two-thirds are covered by Preferred Provider Organizations (PPOs).

While these two types of managed care plans differ in detail, they share the common trait that they detach the payment to healthcare providers from the actual provision of healthcare services (for example, using a "capitation" system, where providers receive a fixed payment per covered person, regardless of actual treatments provided). The incentives under such systems are to carefully control the cost of care since the providers fully bear the cost of any care provided (or, alternatively, they get to keep any difference between their capitated payments and their actual costs).

Indeed, average length of stay in hospitals has dramatically declined, from 7.3 days in 1980 to 4.9 days in 2001, as managed care has expanded. To an extent, there has been a consumer backlash against managed care, based on perceptions that cost reductions may have come at the expense of compromised quality of care.

The reduction in demand has challenged hospitals financially. Hospitals have high fixed costs, particularly as they remain staffed to meet an uncertain demand for treatment. Fixed costs are costs that do not vary with the number of occupied beds. To reduce fixed costs and accommodate lower in-patient utilization expected under managed care, many hospitals downsized nursing staff, retaining a smaller permanent core staff and supplementing with part-time or temporary nurses to cover fluctuations in patient census.

These moves have transformed some of the hospital fixed costs into variable costs. However, they have given rise to other problems, as the shortage of nurses has been exacerbated by reductions in the permanent nursing staffs.

Sources: Linda R. Brewster, Liza Rudell, and Cara S. Lesser, "Emergency Room Diversions: A Symptom of Hospitals Under Stress," issue brief no. 38, May 2001, Center for Studying Health System Change; Kaiser Family Foundation, *Employer Health Benefits 2004 Annual Survey*; *National Hospital Discharge Survey*, National Center for Health Statistics.

3 Short-Run Individual Supply

Costs are one dimension of the short-run decisions whether to continue in operation and how much to produce. The other side to these decisions is revenue. We now consider the revenues of a business.

In analyzing revenues, we shall assume that the business aims to maximize profit. Realistically, of course, managers may pursue a number of objectives in addition to maximizing profit. We maintain the assumption of profit maximization because it is enough to account for a wide variety of common business practices.

Further, we assume that the business is so small relative to the market that it can sell as much as it would like at the going market price. We need this assumption to construct individual and market supply, which are the counterparts to individual and market demand.

Production Rate

> The **total revenue** of a business is the price of its product multiplied by the number of units sold.

Supposing that the price of eggs is 70 cents a dozen, how much should Luna produce? Generally, the profit of a business is its total revenue less its total cost, and in turn, **total revenue** is the price multiplied by sales.[2]

In table 4.3, we show Luna's cost and revenue at different production rates, with the assumption that the price is 70 cents. For instance, if sales are 1,000 dozen a week, then Luna's total revenue will be $0.70 \times 1,000 = $700. If sales are 2,000 dozen a week, then Luna's total revenue will be $0.70 \times 2,000 = $1,400. Similarly, we can calculate the total revenue at other production rates. From table 4.3, the highest profit is a *loss* of $1,293, which comes from producing at a rate of 5,000 dozen a week. (Later, we will explain why it makes sense for Luna to produce "at a loss.")

We can derive a general rule for the profit-maximizing production rate by illustrating cost and revenue with a diagram. In figure 4.3, we draw the cost curves from figure 4.1, adding a line to represent Luna's total revenue at a price of 70 cents. The line rises at a rate of $700 for every increase of 1,000 dozen in the production rate. Equivalently, the slope of the line is 0.70. For instance, one point on the total revenue line is at a production rate of 4,000 dozen and revenue of $0.70 \times 4,000 = $2,800.

---

[2] In chapter 9 on pricing, we consider the possibility of price discrimination. With price discrimination, different units are sold at different prices, so total revenue is not simply price multiplied by sales.

Table 4.3   Short-run profit

Weekly production rate	Variable cost	Total cost	Total revenue	Profit	Marginal cost	Marginal revenue
0	$0	$2,200	0	−$2,200		
1,000	$429	$2,629	$700	−$1,929	$0.43	$0.70
2,000	$836	$3,036	$1,400	−$1,636	$0.41	$0.70
3,000	$1,316	$3,516	$2,100	−$1,416	$0.48	$0.70
4,000	$1,897	$4,097	$2,800	−$1,297	$0.58	$0.70
5,000	$2,593	$4,793	$3,500	−$1,293	$0.70	$0.70
6,000	$3,415	$5,615	$4,200	−$1,415	$0.82	$0.70
7,000	$4,370	$6,570	$4,900	−$1,670	$0.95	$0.70
8,000	$5,462	$7,662	$5,600	−$2,062	$1.09	$0.70
9,000	$6,696	$8,896	$6,300	−$2,596	$1.23	$0.70

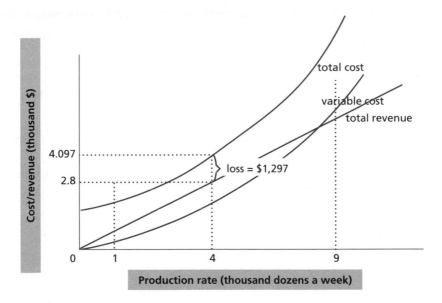

Figure 4.3   Short-run profit
At a production rate of 4,000 dozen, the total revenue is $2,800 and the total cost is $4,097; hence, the vertical difference between revenue and cost is a loss of $1,297. Marginal revenue is represented by the slope of the total revenue line, while marginal cost is represented by the slope of the total cost curve.

Using figure 4.3, we can measure the difference between the total revenue and the total cost at any production rate. In the figure, the vertical difference between the total revenue line and the total cost curve represents the profit. For instance, at a production rate of 4,000 dozen a week, the height of the total revenue line is $2,800, while the height of the total cost curve is $4,097. Hence, the vertical difference is a loss of $1,297.

Generally, to maximize profit, a business should produce at that rate where its marginal revenue equals its marginal cost. The **marginal revenue** is the change in total revenue arising from selling an additional unit.

> The **marginal revenue** is the change in total revenue arising from selling an additional unit.

To explain the rule for maximizing profit, consider figure 4.3. Graphically, the marginal revenue is represented by the slope of the total revenue line. Similarly, since marginal cost is the change in total cost due to the production of an additional unit, the marginal cost is represented by the slope of the total cost curve.

At a production rate such as 1,000 dozen a week, the total revenue line climbs faster than the total cost curve, or equivalently, the marginal revenue exceeds the marginal cost. Then, an increase in production will raise the profit. Wherever the marginal revenue exceeds the marginal cost, Luna can raise profit by increasing production.

By contrast, at a production rate of 9,000 dozen a week, the total revenue climbs more slowly than the total cost curve, or equivalently, the marginal revenue is less than the marginal cost. Then, a reduction in production will increase profit. Wherever the marginal revenue is less than the marginal cost, Luna can raise profit by reducing production.

> The **profit-maximizing** scale of production is where marginal revenue equals marginal cost.

Thus, Luna will **maximize profit** at the production rate where its marginal revenue equals marginal cost. At that point, the total revenue line and the total cost curve climb at exactly the same rate. Hence, a small change in production (either increase or reduction) will affect both total revenue and total cost to the same extent. Accordingly, it is not possible to increase profit any further.

We can use another approach to explain why a business maximizes profit by balancing marginal revenue and marginal cost. By definition, the marginal revenue is the change in total revenue arising from selling an additional unit. For a business that can sell as much as it would like at the market price, the change in total revenue arising from selling an additional unit is exactly equal to the price. Hence, the marginal revenue equals the price of the output.

In figure 4.4, we draw the marginal and average cost curves from figure 4.2 and also include the marginal revenue line. The marginal revenue line also represents the price. Where the price exceeds the marginal cost, Luna can increase profit by raising production. By contrast, where the price is less than the marginal cost, Luna can increase profit by cutting production. Therefore, Luna will maximize profit by producing at 5,000 dozen a week, a rate at which its marginal cost just balances the price.

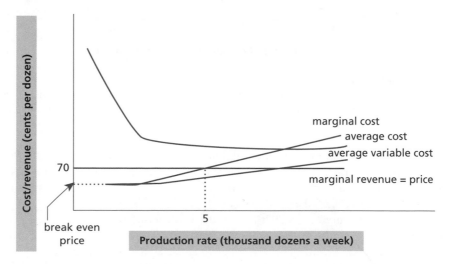

Figure 4.4   Short-run production rate
Given the price of 70 cents, the seller maximizes profits by producing at the rate of 5,000 dozen a week, where marginal cost equals the price.

Break even

Our discussion of the profit-maximizing production rate assumed that the business is continuing in operation. To decide whether to continue production, the business needs to compare the profit from continuing in production with the profit from shutting down. We shall see that the key factor in this comparison is the composition of fixed vis-à-vis variable costs.

Suppose that a business continues production. Let the revenue from the profit-maximizing production rate be R, while the fixed cost is F and the variable cost is V. Then, the maximum profit is $R - F - V$.

Now suppose that the business shuts down. Clearly, this will reduce its total revenue to 0. How will the shutdown affect its costs? We assume that the entire fixed cost, F, of the business is also *sunk* in the short run. A cost is **sunk** if it has been committed and cannot be avoided. The opposite of "sunk" is "avoidable."

> A **sunk cost** is a cost that has been committed and cannot be avoided.

By assumption, the entire fixed cost, F, is also sunk. This means that, even if the business shuts down, it must still pay the fixed cost, F. In contrast to the fixed cost, the variable cost is avoidable. Hence, if the business shuts down, it need not pay anything in variable cost. Thus, if it shuts down, the profit will be the zero revenue minus the fixed cost, that is, $-F$.

The business should continue in production if the maximum profit from continuing in production is at least as large as the profit from shutting down. Algebraically, this break even condition is

$$R - V - F \geq -F, \tag{4.4}$$

which simplifies to

$$R \geq V. \tag{4.5}$$

Because the fixed cost is sunk, it drops out of the condition for continuing in production. The business should continue in production so long as its revenue covers the variable cost.

Recall that revenue is the price multiplied by sales, $R = p \times q$. We can divide the break even condition (4.5) throughout by sales (or the production rate) to obtain

$$p \geq V/q \tag{4.6}$$

Hence an equivalent way of stating the **short-run break even condition** is that the price must cover the average variable cost.

> The **short-run break even condition** is that price covers average variable cost.

To summarize, in the short run, a business maximizes profit by producing at the rate where the marginal cost equals the price, provided that the price covers the average variable cost. Otherwise, it should shut down.

Let us apply the short-run break even analysis to Luna Farm. Suppose that Luna continues production. Then, from table 4.3, by producing at a rate of 5,000 dozen eggs a week, Luna will operate at a loss of $1,293. By assumption, Luna's entire $2,200 fixed cost is also sunk, while if Luna shuts down, it need not pay anything in variable cost. Thus, if Luna shuts down, its profit will be the zero revenue minus the $2,200 fixed cost, that is, a loss of $2,200. Clearly, Luna is better off continuing in production.

Another way to make this decision simply ignores the fixed cost. Table 4.3 shows the variable cost and total revenue. If Luna produces 5,000 dozen a week, it will earn a total revenue of $3,500, while its variable cost would be $2,593. Since the revenue exceeds the variable cost, Luna should continue in production. Thus, we have explained why it makes sense for Luna to produce "at a loss" – the reason is that the "loss" includes a sunk cost that should be ignored.

Alaska Ferry System: sailings and losses

The Alaska Marine Highway System (the State Ferry System), like many public transport systems, operates at a loss, covered by subsidies from the State government. This prompted the need for a "$22 million bailout" in 2005. The bailout was attributed to increased costs from fuel cost increases, new labor contracts, and increased scheduled sailings.

The last reason is controversial. Governor Frank Murkowski attributed part of the cost increase to an increase in scheduled sailings, particularly in winter. The director of the state ferry system, Robin Taylor, disagreed, saying "All things considered, it is cheaper to operate a boat than it is to tie it up. Even when a vessel is tied up, expenses are still incurred as a captain and crew must be on board and line handlers must be available. When those expenses are coupled with the loss of revenue, the more economical choice would be to operate the vessel rather than to tie it up."

The costs of the ships are largely fixed costs, and the profitability (or lack thereof) of winter sailings depends solely on the comparison of variable costs with the revenues. Interestingly, part of the ferry's finanical losses appear to be related to its pricing policy. Between 1993 and 2005, it raised prices and ridership decreased from 400,000 to 296,000. In 2005, prices were increased by 17% but revenue declined. In 2006, new price promotions (decreases) began, and the ferry registered an 18% increase in winter revenue.

Thus, a combination of raising prices with relatively elastic demand, and idling ships when revenues could exceed variable costs (but not total costs), resulted in larger losses.

Source: Alaska State Senate Finance Committee hearing, March 2, 2006, Alaska Public Radio, October 17, 2005, www.publicbroadcasting.net/apti/news.newsmain?action=article&ARTICLE_ID=832141

Delphi: fixed labor costs

In 1999, General Motors Corporation (GM) spun off its auto-parts business, Delphi Corporation. At the time, Delphi's prospects seemed good: it was the world's largest auto-parts maker, its top customers were generating large profits selling trucks and SUVs, and orders from fast-growing foreign automakers were rapidly increasing. But, in 2005 it filed for Chapter 11 bankruptcy protection.

Delphi was dragged under by a combination of GM's falling market share and its inherited legacy labor contracts (the same costs that threaten GM, its former parent). CEO Robert S. "Steve" Miller explained: "We got a tremendous blessing and a tremendous curse at the time of the spin-off." The tremendous blessing was the technology and capability that came with the company. The curse was that Delphi inherited the automaker's labor contract package, which was uncompetitive with any other automotive supplier.

An increasing portion of Delphi's U.S. workforce is in a paid but nonproductive status; i.e., a sunk cost. Under the terms of Delphi's collective bargaining agreements with the United Auto Workers (UAW) union, Delphi is generally not permitted to permanently lay off idled workers. The number of idled hourly workers that receive nearly full pay and benefits has been as high as 4,000.

Historically, under the terms of the spin-off from GM, Delphi's UAW employees could "flow back" to GM. However, with GM production falling, flowback has been severely limited. Consequently, although Delphi cut its U.S. hourly workforce by 15% over the 15-month period ending December 31, 2004, it still retained 12% of its hourly workforce in a non-productive status. In 2004, the non-productive workers "cost" Delphi $170 million.

Sources: "Delphi's Troubles Have Deep Roots," *Detroit News*, October 10, 2005; *Delphi Bankruptcy News*, issue no. 1, October 10, 2005, Bankruptcy Creditors' Service, Inc.

Individual Supply Curve

Using the rule for profit-maximizing production, we can determine how much a business should produce at other prices for its output. This is the information needed to construct a seller's *individual supply curve*. The **individual supply curve** is a graph showing the quantity that one seller will supply at every possible price.

> The **individual supply curve** is a graph showing the quantity that one seller will supply at every possible price.

For every possible price of its output, a business should produce at the rate that balances its marginal cost with the price, provided that the price covers the average variable cost. Referring to figure 4.4, if the price is 80 cents rather than 70 cents a dozen, Luna should expand production to the rate where the new price equals the marginal cost.

Indeed, by varying the price, we can trace out the quantity that Luna should supply at every possible price and, hence, construct Luna's individual supply curve. The individual supply curve is identical with the portion of the seller's marginal cost curve that lies above the average variable cost curve.

Following the marginal cost curve, the individual supply curve slopes upward. If the seller is to expand production, then it will incur a higher marginal cost. Hence, the seller should expand production only if it receives a higher price. Accordingly, the individual supply curve slopes upward.

The individual supply curve shows how a seller should adjust its production in response to changes in the price of its output. Hence, the effect of any change in the output price will be represented by a movement along the supply curve.

> **Progress Check 4C** Using figure 4.4, show the quantity that Luna should produce at a price of 75 cents per dozen eggs.

Input Demand

We can now explain the individual seller's demand for inputs. We have derived the seller's marginal cost from its total cost, which in turn was derived from the estimates of the expenses on rent, wages, and other supplies needed at various production rates. These estimates depend on the prices of the various inputs.

Suppose, for instance, that table 4.1 assumes a wage of $10 per hour. The calculations in tables 4.2 and 4.3 and figures 4.3 and 4.4 are based on a wage of $10 per hour. What if the wage is $9 per hour? Then, we must go back to adjust tables 4.1–4.3 and figures 4.3–4.4 using the new wage rate.

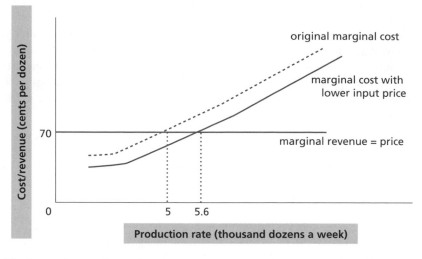

Figure 4.5   Lower input price
With a lower input price, the marginal cost curve will shift downward; hence the seller will increase the production rate from 5,000 to 5,600 dozen.

Intuitively, as we show in figure 4.5, the marginal cost curve will shift downward. The profit-maximizing production rate increases from 5,000 to 5,600 dozen. From the new production rate of 5,600 dozen, we can go back to determine the corresponding quantity of the labor input. With a higher production, the quantity of labor demanded will also be higher.

By varying the wage rate, we can determine the quantity demanded of labor at every possible wage rate. This will allow us to construct the individual seller's demand for labor. As we have just shown, the quantity demanded will be higher at a lower wage; hence, the demand curve for labor will slope downward. The same method can be used to derive the individual seller's demand for every other input.

Organizing production at multiple facilities

Echo Bay Mines has gold mines at Lupin in Canada as well as Cove in Nevada. How should it organize production at the two mines? Assuming that it can sell as much as it would like at the market price, Echo Bay Mines could simply direct each mine to produce at a rate balancing the price of gold with its marginal cost.

Another, more general approach applies even to sellers that are large enough to affect the market price. These should organize production so as to *equalize* the marginal cost at every facility. By doing so, the seller will minimize its companywide production cost.

To explain this rule, suppose that Echo's marginal cost at Lupin is $370 per ounce, while its marginal cost at Cove is $350 per ounce. If Echo reduced production at Lupin by one ounce and increased production at Cove by one ounce, it could reduce total cost by $370 − $350 = $20. These adjustments would not affect the total production of the entire company. Generally, if the two mines have different marginal costs of production, the company can always reduce costs by switching production between the mines.

Therefore, to minimize the companywide cost of production, a seller should organize production so as to equalize the marginal cost at every facility.

4   Long-Run Individual Supply

In the short run, a business must work within the constraints of past commitments such as employment contracts and investment in facilities and equipment. Over time, however, contracts expire and investments wear out. With sufficient time, all inputs become avoidable. A long-run planning horizon is a time frame far enough into the future that all inputs can be freely adjusted. Then the business will have complete flexibility in deciding on inputs and production.

How should a business make two key decisions – whether to continue in operation and how much to produce – in the long run? To address these issues, we first analyze the long-run costs and then look at the revenue.

Long-Run Costs

Let us analyze long-run costs in the context of Luna Farm. We ask the management to estimate the costs of producing at various rates when all inputs are avoidable. Suppose that table 4.4 presents the expenses classified into rent, wages, and cost of supplies.

In the long run, Luna can vary the size of its facility. The rent is $250 at zero production and increases to $2,500 for production of 9,000 dozen eggs a week. Similarly, the wages are $200 at zero production and rise to $5,289 at a production rate of 9,000. The cost of supplies rises from nothing for zero production to $900 at a production rate of 9,000.

As this example shows, in the long run, the business may incur some cost even at production levels close to zero. For instance, it may not be possible to build an egg-producing facility smaller than some minimum size. The $250 is the rent associated with a facility of the minimum size. Similarly, Luna's owner must work at least 20 hours a week. At a wage of $10 per hour, the minimum labor cost is $10 × 20 = $200 a week. Extracting the relevant information from table 4.4, we can compile the long-run marginal and average costs in table 4.5. We draw the long-run marginal and average costs in figure 4.6.

Comparing the short-run and long-run average cost curves, the long-run average cost curve is lower and has a gentler slope. The reason is that, in the long run, the seller has more flexibility in adjusting inputs to changes in the production rate. Accordingly, it can produce at a relatively lower cost than in the short run, when one or more inputs cannot be changed.

Table 4.4   Long-run weekly expenses

Weekly production rate	Rent	Wages	Cost of supplies	Total
0	$250	$200	$0	$450
1,000	$500	$279	$100	$879
2,000	$750	$461	$200	$1,411
3,000	$1,000	$757	$300	$2,057
4,000	$1,250	$1,176	$400	$2,826
5,000	$1,500	$1,722	$500	$3,722
6,000	$1,750	$2,403	$600	$4,753
7,000	$2,000	$3,221	$700	$5,921
8,000	$2,250	$4,182	$800	$7,232
9,000	$2,500	$5,289	$900	$8,689

Table 4.5   Analysis of long-run costs

Weekly production rate	Total cost	Marginal cost	Average cost
0	$450		
1,000	$879	$0.43	$0.88
2,000	$1,411	$0.53	$0.71
3,000	$2,057	$0.65	$0.69
4,000	$2,826	$0.77	$0.71
5,000	$3,722	$0.90	$0.74
6,000	$4,753	$1.03	$0.79
7,000	$5,921	$1.17	$0.85
8,000	$7,232	$1.31	$0.90
9,000	$8,689	$1.46	$0.97

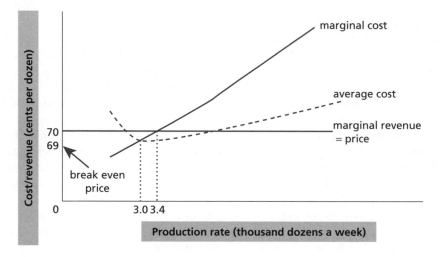

Figure 4.6   Long-run production rate
Given a price of 70 cents, the seller maximizes profits by producing 3,400 dozen, where the long-run marginal cost equals the price.

Production Rate

Let us now consider how much the business should produce in the long run. We can apply the general rule derived for short-run production: to maximize profit, a business should produce at that rate where its marginal cost equals the price of its output. In the long run, however, we use the long-run marginal cost.

The reasoning for this rule is the same as before. Where the price exceeds the long-run marginal cost, the seller can increase profit by raising production. By contrast, where the price is less than the long-run marginal cost, the seller can increase profit by cutting production. Thus, the seller will maximize profit by producing at the rate such that its long-run marginal cost just equals the price.

For Luna Farm, table 4.6 shows the long-run cost, revenue, and profit. The profit column shows that profit reaches a maximum at a production rate of 3,400. The marginal cost at a

Table 4.6   Long-run profit

Weekly production rate	Total cost	Total revenue	Profit	Marginal cost	Marginal revenue
0	$450	0	−$450		
1,000	$879	$700	−$179	$0.43	$0.70
2,000	$1,411	$1,400	−$11	$0.53	$0.70
3,000	$2,057	$2,100	$43	$0.65	$0.70
4,000	$2,826	$2,800	−$26	$0.77	$0.70
5,000	$3,722	$3,500	−$222	$0.90	$0.70
6,000	$4,753	$4,200	−$553	$1.03	$0.70
7,000	$5,921	$4,900	−$1,021	$1.17	$0.70
8,000	$7,232	$5,600	−$1,632	$1.31	$0.70
9,000	$8,689	$6,300	−$2,389	$1.46	$0.70

production rate of 3,400 is 70 cents. Since the price is 70 cents, this confirms that the production rate of 3,400 maximizes profit.

Break Even

We next analyze the break even condition under which a business should continue in long-run production. Combining this with the profit-maximizing production rate, we can derive the long-run individual supply curve.

In the long run, a business should continue in production if the maximum profit from continuing in production is at least as large as the profit from shutting down. In the long run, all costs are avoidable; hence, if the business shuts down, it will incur no costs and so its profit from shutting down is nothing.

Let $(R - C)$ represent the maximum profit from continuing in production. Then the business should continue in production if

$$R - C \geq 0, \tag{4.7}$$

which simplifies to

$$R \geq C. \tag{4.8}$$

This break even condition says that the business should continue in production so long as total revenue covers total cost.

Since total revenue is price multiplied by sales, $R = p \times q$, we can divide the break even condition throughout by sales (or the production rate) to obtain

$$p \geq C/q \tag{4.9}$$

An equivalent way of stating the **long-run break even condition** is that the price must cover the average cost.

Referring to table 4.5, Luna's lowest average cost is 69 cents. It attains this cost at a production rate of 3,000. Hence, if the price of eggs falls below 69 cents, then Luna should go out of business.

> The **long-run break even condition** is that price covers average cost.

Individual Supply Curve

A seller maximizes profits by producing at the rate where its long-run marginal cost equals the price of the output. By varying the price, we can determine the quantity that the seller will supply at every possible price. We have also shown that the seller should remain in business only if the price covers its average cost. Thus, the seller's long-run individual supply curve is that part of its long-run marginal cost curve, which lies above its long-run average cost curve.

Progress Check 4D Referring to table 4.5, if the market price of eggs is $1.31, how much should Luna produce and what will be its profit?

⊣ Bestar: re-structuring ⊢

Located in Lac-Megantic (Quebec), Bestar designs, manufactures, and distributes ready-to-assemble and fully assembled furniture. Between 2003 and 2004, under pressure from Asian competitors and the appreciation of the Canadian dollar, Bestar's revenue fell slightly from C$44.3 million to C$43.7 million, and net earnings of C$254,000 fell to a loss of C$442,000.

Following the downturn, Bestar decided to restructure at a cost of C$1.4 million. It secured financing from a private placement, the Fonds de solidarité des travailleurs du Québec, and Investissement-Québec. Why didn't Bestar simply shut down? Why did investors and the two Quebec agencies finance the restructuring?

The short-run break-even condition for a business is that the (short-run) price covers the average variable cost. By contrast, the long-run break-even condition is that the (long-run) price covers the average cost.

If Bestar had continued in business without new financing, that would have indicated that the short-run price covered the average variable cost, but that the long-run price fell below the average cost. However, Bestar succeeded in procuring new financing. This suggests that investors, the Quebec agencies, and Bestar shareholders projected that the long-run demand for Bestar's products was so strong that prices would cover average costs.

Source: Bestar, Inc., Annual Report, 2005.

⊣ Oil: to produce or not to produce? ⊢

In the oil industry, production is the activity of extracting crude oil from the ground. The cost of producing oil from small wildcat sites in Texas is relatively high. High-cost producers must carefully consider the relation between the long-run price and their average cost.

Figure 4.7 shows year-by-year percentage changes in the price of the benchmark West Texas Intermediate crude oil, and the numbers of active drilling rigs in Canada and Texas over the period between 1995 and 2003. The changes in the number of Texas drilling rigs tracked the changes in the oil price very closely. More dramatic was how the change in the number of Canadian drilling rigs tracked and amplified changes in the oil price.

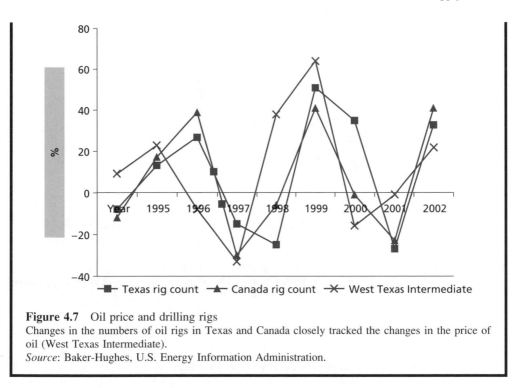

Figure 4.7 Oil price and drilling rigs
Changes in the numbers of oil rigs in Texas and Canada closely tracked the changes in the price of oil (West Texas Intermediate).
Source: Baker-Hughes, U.S. Energy Information Administration.

5 Market Supply

If the price of eggs is 70 cents a dozen, how much will be produced by the market as a whole? To address this question, we need to know the market supply curve of eggs. The **market supply curve** of an item is a graph showing the quantity that the market will supply at every possible price. At any particular price, the quantity that the market will supply is the sum of the quantities supplied by each individual seller.

> The **market supply curve** is a graph showing the quantity that the market will supply at every possible price.

The market supply is the seller-side counterpart to the market demand, which we introduced in chapter 2. Together, supply and demand constitute a market. We first analyze the short-run market supply, and then consider the long-run supply.

Short Run

To construct the market supply, we can draw an analogy from our analysis of market demand. Recall that the market demand curve is the horizontal sum of the individual demand curves. Similarly, the market supply curve is the horizontal sum of the individual supply curves. At any particular price, each seller's individual supply curve shows the quantity that seller will supply. The sum of these quantities is the quantity supplied by the market as a whole. By varying the price, we can get the information needed to construct the market supply curve.

A seller's short-run individual supply curve is the portion of its marginal cost curve that lies above its average variable cost curve. Hence, the market supply curve begins with the seller that has the lowest average variable cost. The market supply curve then gradually blends in sellers with higher average variable cost.

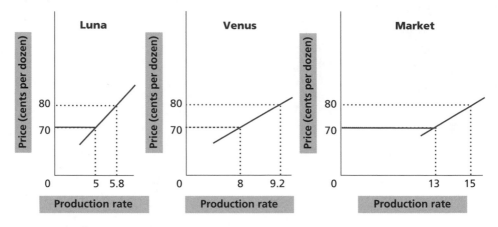

Figure 4.8   Market supply
The market supply curve is the horizontal summation of the individual supply curves. At a price of 70 cents per dozen, the market quantity supplied is 5,000 + 8,000 = 13,000 dozen. At a price of 80 cents per dozen, the market quantity supplied is 5,800 + 9,200 = 15,000 dozen.

In figure 4.8, we assume that there are just two producers of eggs: Luna Farm and Venus Farm. We draw the individual supply curves of the two producers and sum these horizontally to obtain the market supply curve. This shows that, at a price of 70 cents, the market as a whole will supply 5,000 + 8,000 = 13,000 dozen a week.

Our analysis of individual supply showed that the higher the price of the output, the more the seller will wish to produce. Since each seller will produce more, the market as a whole will also produce a larger quantity. Accordingly, the market supply curve slopes upward.

The market supply curve shows how market production responds to changes in the price of the output. Hence, the effect of a change in the output price is represented by a movement along the supply curve. Suppose, for instance, that the price of eggs rises from 70 to 80 cents per dozen. Then, referring to the market supply curve in figure 4.8, the market quantity supplied increases from 13,000 to 15,000.

The supply of an individual seller depends on the prices of all inputs, including labor, equipment, and supplies. A change in an input price will affect the seller's marginal cost at all production levels. The change will shift the entire marginal cost curve and hence the entire individual supply curve.

Since the market supply curve is the horizontal summation of the various individual supply curves, the change in the input price will also shift the entire market supply curve. Specifically, an increase in the price of an input will shift the market supply up, while a reduction in an input price will shift the market supply down.

We can apply this analysis to predict how an increase in the price of animal feed would affect the market supply of eggs. The higher price of feed will raise each seller's marginal cost of production and shift up its individual supply curve. Hence, the market supply curve will shift up.

In general, a change in the price of the output is represented by a movement along the market supply curve, while a change in the price of any input will cause a shift of the entire market supply curve.

Progress Check 4E In figure 4.8, show how a fall in the price of animal feed would affect the market supply of eggs.

Long Run

The principles of long-run market supply are somewhat different from those underlying short-run supply. In the long run, every business will have complete flexibility in deciding on inputs and production. This flexibility implies that existing sellers can leave the industry, and new sellers can enter. The freedom of entry and exit is the key difference between the short run and long run.

We have shown that, for a seller to break even in the long run, its total revenue must cover its total cost. If a seller's total revenue does not cover the total cost, then the seller should leave the industry. Hence, the seller's individual supply will reduce to zero. This departure will reduce the market supply, hence raise the market price and the profits of the other sellers. Sellers that cannot cover their total costs will leave the industry until all the remaining sellers break even.

By contrast, an industry where businesses can make profits, in the sense that total revenue exceeds total cost, will attract new entrants. Each of the new entrants will contribute its individual supply and so add to the market supply. The increase in the market supply will push down the market price and hence reduce the profits of all the existing sellers. If the existing sellers continue making profits, new entrants will enter the industry until all the sellers just break even.

Accordingly, in the long run, when there is a change in the market price, the quantity supplied will adjust in two ways: first, all existing sellers will adjust their quantities supplied along their individual supply curves, and second, some sellers may enter or leave the market.

Let us apply this analysis to understand how producers of eggs will respond to an increase in the market price from 70 to 80 cents. Referring to figure 4.9, when the price rises from 70 to 80 cents, the short-run quantity supplied will increase from 13,000 to 15,000. Further, the price increase will raise the profits of the existing producers.

Over time, however, the higher profits will attract new producers to enter the industry. The new entrants will add to the market supply; hence, in the long run, the quantity supplied will increase from 13,000 to 20,000. As this example shows, for a given increase in price, the long-run market supply slopes more gently than the short-run market supply.

How will producers respond to a fall in the market price from 70 to 65 cents? Referring to figure 4.9, when the price drops from 70 to 65 cents, the short-run quantity supplied will drop from 13,000 to 12,000. In the short run, a business will continue to produce so long as the price covers its average variable cost.

Over time, however, producers for whom the price is below average cost will leave the industry. The departures will reduce the market supply. So, in the long run, the quantity supplied will drop relatively more, from 13,000 to, say, 7,400. This example shows that, for a price reduction, the long-run market supply slopes more gently than the short-run market supply.

Accordingly, for any change in price, the long-run market supply slopes more gently than the short-run market supply. Using terminology that we will introduce later in the chapter, we say that the long-run market supply is *more elastic* than the short-run supply.

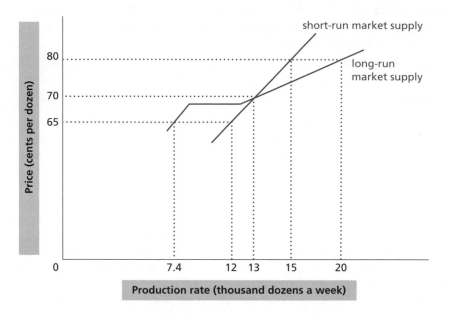

Figure 4.9 Short- vis-à-vis long-run market supply
If the price rises from 70 to 80 cents per dozen, the quantity supplied will increase from 13,000 to 15,000 in the short run and to 20,000 in the long run. If the price falls from 70 to 65 cents per dozen, the quantity supplied will fall from 13,000 to 12,000 in the short run and to 10,000 in the long run.

Properties

While the short-run market supply generally slopes upward, the long-run market supply may be flat. In the long run, new businesses can enter and existing businesses can leave. Specifically, in the long run, the quantity supplied can expand through replication of existing businesses, and, hence, the long-run supply should be completely flat.

⊣ U.S. furniture supply ⊢

The U.S. supply of furniture combines supply by domestic manufacturers and Canadian and Asian manufacturers. Furniture manufacturing is relatively intensive in resources and labor. Canada is a major international producer of lumber and wood. This partly explains Canada's leading position in the furniture industry.

With the advantage of substantially lower labor costs, Asian manufacturers pose direct and indirect challenges to the Canadian furniture industry. Asian manufacturers can directly challenge the Canadian industry in both fully assembled and ready-to-assemble furniture. In this regard, the Asian manufacturers have increased U.S. supply at the lower-cost end of the supply curves for fully assembled and ready-to-assemble furniture.

Moreover, Asian manufacturers pose an *indirect* challenge to Canadian and U.S. domestic manufacturers of ready-to-assemble furniture. Fully assembled furniture from Asia is cheap enough to compete with ready-to-assemble furniture made in Canada and the United States.

There is, however, a reason why the long-run market supply may slope upward. The resources – human, natural, and knowledge – available to the various suppliers may vary in quality. New entrants may not be able to replicate the resources of existing suppliers; hence, the new entrants must incur higher costs.

The long-run market supply curve shows the quantity that the market will supply at every possible price. Hence, the effect of a change in the output price is represented by a movement along the market supply curve. By contrast, a change in wage or any factor other than the price of the output will cause a shift of the entire market supply curve.

6   Seller Surplus

We derived the individual supply curve by asking a seller how much it would supply at every possible price. Another way to interpret the supply curve is to view it as showing the minimum price that the seller will accept for each unit of production. Using this approach, we can explain how a seller benefits or suffers from changes in the price of its output, and how a seller's profit varies with the price of its output.

Price vis-à-vis Marginal Cost

In the case of Luna, referring to figure 4.10, the marginal cost of producing 1,000 dozen eggs a month is 43 cents. This is the minimum price that Luna will accept for the first 1,000 dozen. At a market price of 70 cents, however, Luna receives 70 cents for each unit

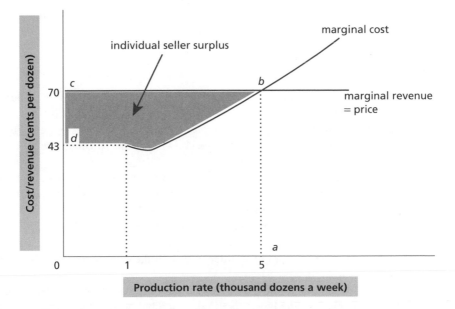

Figure 4.10   Individual seller surplus
The marginal cost of producing 1,000 eggs is 43 cents per dozen. At a price of 70 cents per dozen, the seller receives a surplus of $(0.70 − 0.43) × 1,000 = 270 for that production. At the 70 cent price, the seller will produce 5,000 dozen a week. The individual seller surplus is the shaded area *dbc* between the price line and the marginal cost curve.

The **seller surplus** is the difference between a seller's revenue from some production rate and the minimum amount necessary to induce the seller to produce that quantity.

of production. The difference of $(0.70 − 0.43) × 1,000 = 270 is a surplus for the seller. Generally, the **seller surplus** is the difference between a seller's revenue from some quantity of production and the minimum amount necessary to induce the seller to produce that quantity. Luna receives seller surplus on all production up to the marginal unit.

We will show that the short-run seller surplus can also be defined as the difference between the seller's revenue from some production rate and the variable cost. The minimum amount sufficient to induce a seller to deliver some production rate is the minimum that it requires for each unit up to the specified quantity. The minimum that a seller requires for each unit is the marginal cost. Hence, the minimum amount sufficient to induce a seller to deliver some production rate is the sum of the marginal costs for each unit up to the specified quantity.

The sum of the marginal costs for each unit up to some specified quantity is the variable cost. Accordingly, in the short run, the minimum amount necessary to induce a seller to deliver some production is the variable cost. Graphically, this is the area under the marginal cost curve up to the specified production rate. Thus, the seller surplus is the difference between the seller's revenue from some production rate and the variable cost, or $R − V$.

To illustrate, let us consider Luna's seller surplus at the price of 70 cents. Referring to figure 4.10, the revenue is represented by the area of the rectangle 0*abc* under the price line up to the quantity of 5,000. The variable cost can be represented by the area 0*abd* under Luna's marginal cost curve up to 5,000 dozen a month. The shaded area *dbc* between the price line and the marginal cost curve represents the seller surplus.

In the short run, a seller breaks even where total revenue covers the variable cost; hence, the *short-run* seller surplus is equal to total revenue less variable cost. In the long run, however, total revenue must cover total cost for the seller to break even. Hence, the *long-run* seller surplus is equal to total revenue less total cost.

Purchasing

An important application of the concept of seller surplus is in the management of purchasing. Suppose, for instance, that Speedy Foods is a large dairy manufacturer. It buys eggs as an input into manufacturing confectionery and ice cream. Presently, Speedy pays 70 cents per dozen to suppliers such as Luna Farm. We have shown that the 70-cent price gives Luna the area *dbc* in seller surplus.

Speedy can use the analysis of seller surplus to reduce the cost of its purchases and hence raise its own profit. Referring to figure 4.10, the minimum amount of money necessary to induce Luna to sell 5,000 dozen eggs a month is the area 0*abd* under Luna's marginal cost curve. Speedy should offer Luna a lump sum equal to area 0*abd* plus $1 to supply a bulk order of 5,000 dozen eggs. This amount of money leaves Luna with $1 of seller surplus and is just enough to induce Luna to supply the order. Through the bulk order, Speedy saves an amount represented by area *dbc* less $1.

The foregoing example illustrates how a buyer can apply the concept of seller surplus to reduce the cost of its purchases. The buyer should design a bulk order that extracts the seller surplus and pay the seller the minimum amount of money necessary to induce production of the desired quantity of output. Essentially, the buyer is purchasing up the seller's marginal cost curve.

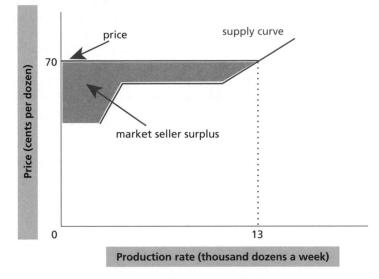

Figure 4.11   Market seller surplus
At a price of 70 cents, the market seller surplus is the shaded area between the price line and the market supply curve.

Market Seller Surplus

The seller surplus for an individual is the difference between its revenue from some production rate and the minimum amount necessary for it to produce that quantity. The seller surplus for the whole market is the sum of the individual seller surpluses. It is the difference between the market revenue from some production rate and the minimum amount necessary for the market to produce that quantity. Graphically, the market seller surplus is represented by the area between the price line and the market supply curve. This concept applies in both the short run and the long run.

Figure 4.11 shows a short-run market supply curve. For example, at a price of 70 cents, the short-run market seller surplus is represented by the shaded area between the price line and the short-run market supply curve.

We have mentioned previously that, in the long run, the market supply curve may be flat. In this case, there will be no market seller surplus. If, however, the long-run market supply curve slopes upward, then there will be some market seller surplus. The seller surplus accrues to those who own the superior resources.

7   Elasticity of Supply

Consider a typical issue for an industry analyst: If the price of gasoline and wages increases by 5 and 10%, respectively, what would be the effect on the short-run supply of gasoline by oil refineries? The analyst could answer this question with the market supply curve. In practice, however, analysts seldom have sufficient information to construct the entire market supply curve.

> The **elasticity of supply** is the responsiveness of supply to changes in an underlying factor.

Another way of responding to the question applies the **elasticities of supply**, which measure the responsiveness of supply to changes in underlying factors such as the prices of the item and inputs. The elasticities of supply are the supply-side counterparts to the elasticities of demand, which we introduced in chapter 3.

There is an elasticity corresponding to every factor that affects supply. Further, the elasticity can be estimated for individual supply curves as well as the market supply.

Price Elasticity

> The **price elasticity of supply** is the percentage by which the quantity supplied will change if the price of the item rises by 1%.

The *price elasticity of supply* measures the responsiveness of the quantity supplied to changes in the price of the item. By definition, the **price elasticity of supply** is the percentage by which the quantity supplied will change if the price of the item rises by 1%, other things being equal. Equivalently, the price elasticity is the ratio

$$\frac{\text{percentage change in quantity supplied}}{\text{percentage change in price}}.$$

We can estimate the price elasticity of supply by either the arc or point approach. Let us apply the arc approach to calculate the price elasticity of Luna's short-run supply of eggs. Referring to figure 4.12, at a price of 70 cents, Luna produces 5,000 dozen. If the price increases to 80 cents, Luna would increase production to 5,800 dozen.

The proportionate change in quantity supplied is the change in quantity supplied divided by the average quantity supplied. The change in quantity supplied is $5,800 - 5,000 = 800$

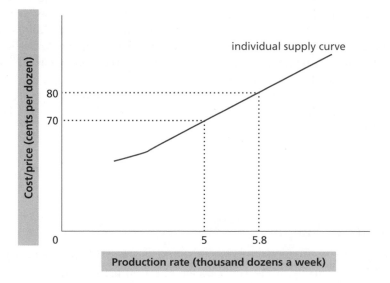

Figure 4.12   Price elasticity of supply
The proportionate change in quantity supplied is 15%, while the proportionate change in price is 13%. Hence the price elasticity of supply is 0.15/0.13 = 1.15.

dozen a year, and the average quantity supplied is (5,800 + 5,000)/2 = 5,400 dozen a year; hence the proportionate change in quantity supplied is 800/5,400 = 0.15 = 15%.

Similarly, the proportionate change in price is the change in price divided by the average price. The change in price is 80 − 70 = 10 cents, while the average price is (70 + 80)/2 = 75 cents. Hence, the proportionate change in price is 10/75 = 0.13 = 13%. Accordingly, the price elasticity of Luna's short-run supply is 0.15/0.13 = 1.15.

Properties

The price elasticity of supply is a pure number that does not depend on any units of measure. Generally, the individual supply curves of businesses selling goods and services slope upward. Hence, the price elasticity of supply is a positive number that ranges from 0 to infinity.

If the price elasticity is less than 1, then a 1% increase in price will lead to less than a 1% increase in quantity supplied. In this case, the supply is inelastic. By contrast, if the price elasticity is more than 1, then a 1% increase in price will lead to more than a 1% increase in quantity supplied. Then, the supply is elastic.

From a managerial standpoint, the price elasticity is a handy way of characterizing the sensitivity of sellers to changes in price without worrying about choosing appropriate units of measure. For instance, a human resource manager may want to know whether unionized workers are more or less sensitive to changes in wages than nonunion workers. The manager can address this question by comparing the wage elasticities of the two groups.

When comparing the supplies of different items or even quantities supplied of the same item at different prices, it is important to remember that these comparisons are relative, because the price elasticity may vary along the same supply curve. A change in price, by moving from one point on a supply curve to another, may lead to a change in the price elasticity. Similarly, a change in any of the factors that affect supply may affect the price elasticity.

Intuitive Factors

The price elasticity of supply depends on the extent of capacity relative to current production. For instance, a seller that has considerable excess capacity will step up production in response to even a small increase in price. In this case, the individual supply will be relatively elastic. On the other hand, if capacity is tight, the seller may not increase production very much even if the price rises substantially. Hence, when capacity is tight, the individual supply will be relatively inelastic. Capacity utilization affects the elasticity of both individual and market supply.

The price elasticity of supply also depends on time. In the short run, some inputs may be costly or impossible to change. Consequently, the marginal cost of production is very steep. For instance, a factory wishing to step up production immediately may have to engage the workforce on overtime. Since overtime rates are 50–100% higher than regular wage rates, the marginal cost of overtime work is relatively high. With sufficient time, however, the factory could hire more workers at the regular wage. Accordingly, in the long run, the marginal cost of production will slope more gently.

Generally, the long-run supply is relatively more elastic than the short-run supply. This applies to both individual and market supply. Table 4.7 presents the price elasticities of the market supply for several items.

Table 4.7 Price elasticities of supply

Product	Country	Time horizon	Price elasticity	Source
Distillate (heating oil)	U.S.	Short run	1.57	Considine (1992)
Gasoline	U.S.	Short run	1.61	Considine (1992)
Tobacco	U.S.	Long run	7.0	Fulginiti and Perrin (1993)
Housing	U.S.	Long run	1.6–3.7	Blackley (1999)

Sources: Dixie M. Blackley, "The Long-Run Elasticity of New Housing Supply in the United States: Empirical Evidence for 1950 to 1994," *Journal of Real Estate Finance and Economics* 18, no. 1 (January 1999), pp. 25–42; Timothy J. Considine, "A Short-Run Model of Petroleum Product Supply," *Energy Journal* 13, no. 2 (1992), pp. 61–91; Lilyan Fulginiti and Richard Perrin, "The Theory and Measurement of Producer Response Under Quotas," *Review of Economics and Statistics* 75, no. 1 (February 1993), pp. 97–105.

⊣ Retail space: supply elasticity ⊢

A study of retail space supply used data from 56 Metropolitan Statistical Areas (MSAs) with populations greater than 250,000 in 1991, and retail sales data from 1972 to 1991 normalized to 1987 dollars. This study found retail space elasticity with respect to retail sales to be inelastic in the short run for all MSAs. However, in some MSAs, the supply was highly inelastic due to factors such as a shortage of available developable land and local and state regulatory restrictions. In the long run, retail space supply is much more elastic: in 21 of the 34 MSAs, the elasticity of retail space was greater than 1.

It is important to understand the supply elasticity. In areas with elastic supply, there tends to be more development and the potential for over-supply for the market. Developers starting late in developing retail space in an elastic market could be faced with large vacancies or reduced rents by the time their projects are completed.

Source: John D. Benjamin, G. Donald Jud, and Daniel T. Winkler, "The Supply Adjustments Process in Retail Space Markets," *Journal of Real Estate Research* 15, no. 3 (1998), pp. 297–307.

Forecasting Quantity Supplied

We can use the price elasticity of supply to calculate the effect of changes in price on quantity supplied for an individual seller as well as the entire market. To illustrate, let us calculate how a 5% increase in the price of eggs will affect Luna's production. Earlier, we estimated that the price elasticity of Luna's short-run supply was 1.15. The price elasticity of supply is the percentage by which the quantity supplied will change if the price rises by 1%. Hence, if the price of eggs increases by 5%, the quantity supplied will change by $1.15 \times 5 = 5.8\%$; that is, the quantity supplied will increase by 5.8%.

Progress Check 4F Referring to figure 4.12, suppose that, if the price were 90 cents per dozen, Luna would supply 6,500 dozen. Calculate the price elasticity of supply for an increase in price from 80 to 90 cents.

8   Summary

A small seller, which cannot affect the market price, maximizes profit by producing at a rate where its marginal cost equals the price. In the short run, at least one input cannot be adjusted. The business breaks even when total revenue covers variable cost. In the long run, the business can adjust all inputs and leave or enter the industry. It breaks even when total revenue covers total cost.

The supply curve shows the quantity supplied as a function of price, other things equal. The effect of a change in price is represented by a movement along the supply curve to a new quantity. Changes in other factors such as wages and the prices of other inputs are represented by shifts of the entire supply curve.

Seller surplus is the difference between revenue from some production rate and the minimum amount necessary to induce the seller to produce that quantity. Elasticities of supply measure the responsiveness of supply to changes in underlying factors that affect supply.

Key Concepts

short run	average (unit) cost	individual supply curve
long run	marginal product	market supply curve
fixed cost	marginal revenue	seller surplus
variable cost	profit maximizing	elasticity of supply
total cost	total revenue	price elasticity of supply
marginal cost	sunk cost	

Review Questions

1. Explain the distinction between the short run and long run. How is this related to the distinction between fixed and variable costs?

2. Comment on the following statement: "It costs our factory an average of $2 to produce a piece of clothing. If you ask me how much it would cost to step up the production rate, I would say $2 per piece."

3. Farmer John's fixed cost of growing corn is higher than that of Farmer Jill. What does this imply for the difference in their marginal costs of growing corn?

4. Consider a business that can sell as much as it wants at the market price. Explain why its marginal revenue equals the market price.

5. Presently, an oil producer is producing 2,000 barrels of crude oil a day. The price is $15 per barrel. Its marginal cost is $20 per barrel. How can the company increase its profit?

6. Does the following analysis under- or overestimate the change in profit? Presently, the price of eggs is 60 cents per dozen. A farm is producing 10,000 dozen eggs a month with a profit of $2,000. If the price of eggs rises to 70 cents a dozen, the farm's profit will rise by $1,000.

7. A silver mine uses diesel-powered excavators and dump trucks. How will the following changes affect the mine's average and marginal cost curves?
   (a) An increase in the price of diesel fuel.
   (b) A drop in the price of silver.
   (c) A cut in the wages of workers.

8. Advertising is an important input into marketing most consumer products. Explain why the profit generated by an additional dollar of advertising will diminish with the total amount of advertising.

9. Some companies continue in business even though they are losing money. Are they making a mistake?

10. Following an increase in the price of diesel fuel, which was expected to be temporary, one bus operator suspended operations, while another continued in business. Explain this disparity in terms of the short-run break even condition.

11. Consider the market supply curve of new apartments. For each of the following changes, identify whether the change will cause a movement along the curve or a shift of the entire curve.
    (a) An increase in the price of new apartments.
    (b) An increase in the price of building materials.
    (c) A cut in the wages of construction workers.

12. How can a buyer use the concept of seller surplus to reduce the cost of its purchases?

13. True or false?
    (a) When capacity is tight, a seller's supply will be relatively more elastic.
    (b) If the supply curve slopes upward, the price elasticity of supply will be positive.

14. For a given increase in price of the product, will the increase in seller surplus be smaller or larger if the supply is more elastic? (Hint: draw two supply curves, one more elastic than the other.)

15. Consider the price elasticity of the market supply of a taxi service. Do you expect supply to be relatively more elastic with respect to fare changes in the short run or long run?

Discussion Questions

1. Ole Kirk Kristiansen, invented "Lego" in 1949. Since then, Lego has produced over 200 billion bricks. "Lego" bricks are made from acrylonitrile butadinese styrene. The raw material is melted at around 235 degrees Celsius, molded under high pressure, and then cooled. In 2005, Lego out-sourced production of "Duplo" bricks to Flextronics, a contract manufacturer with a plant in Hungary. Then, in 2006, Lego sold its factory at Kladno, Czech Republic, used to manufacture "Lego" bricks, to Flextronics. Lego would produce only the more complicated products including Technic and Bionicles in Billund, Denmark.
   (a) Compare the equipment and labor costs of producing "Duplo" and "Lego" bricks in the Czech Republic and Hungary vis-à-vis Denmark, where wages are relatively higher.
   (b) By selling its Kladno factory to Flextronics, how would Lego affect its fixed relative to variable costs of production?

2. A typical bank's sources of funds include savings deposits, certificates of deposit (CDs), and checking (demand) deposits.
   (a) Obtain the current interest rates on savings and checking accounts and CDs from a local bank. Suppose that the bank incurs an additional 1% cost to administer checking accounts. There are no additional administrative costs for savings accounts and CDs. List the three sources of funds in ascending order of annual cost per dollar of funds.
   (b) Suppose that the bank has equal amounts of savings and checking deposits and CDs. Compare its average cost of funds with its marginal cost of funds.

3. Table 4.1 shows the weekly expenses of the Luna Farm. Suppose that wages are 5% higher, increasing the cost of labor by 5%.
   (a) By recalculating tables 4.1 and 4.2, explain how the increase in wages will affect the (i) average variable cost and (ii) average cost.
   (b) Luna's management claims that it needs a 5% higher price to make up for the wage increase. Assess whether this claim is valid in the (i) short run and (ii) long run.

4. Barrick Gold owns the Bulyanhulu mine in Tanzania and the Karlgoolie mine in Australia. Table 4.8 reports information on selling prices and costs for the two mines. Barrick's selling price of gold differs from the spot price as some production is sold through long-term contract and also

Table 4.8   Barrick Gold

	Bulyanhulu			Karlgoolie
	2002	2003	2004	2004
Production (thousand ounces)	356	314	350	444
Selling price ($ per ounce)	339	366	391	391
Average cash cost ($ per ounce)	198	246	284	234
Average cost ($ per ounce)	300	369	384	278

Source: Barrick Gold Corporation, Annual Reports.

owing to the company's use of hedging. The "average cash cost" includes operating cost, royalties, and taxes, while the "average cost" includes the cash cost as well as amortization.

(a) Suppose that the Bulyanhulu mine always produces at the scale where its marginal cost equals the selling price of gold. Its marginal cost curve, however, shifts with changes in electricity prices, wages, and other factors. Using the data from table 4.8, illustrate the shifts in Bulyanhulu's marginal cost curve, the selling price, and profit-maximizing scale of production between 2002 and 2004.

(b) In 2003, Barrick continued to produce from the Bulyanhulu mine even though the selling price of gold, $366 per ounce, was less than its average production cost of $369 per ounce. Was this a mistake?

(c) Use Barrick's 2004 data to compare the (i) short-run break even conditions for Bulyanhulu and Karlgoolie; and (ii) the long-run break even conditions for the two mines.

5. Dynamic random access memory (DRAM) chips are an essential component of personal computers, mobile telephones, and other electronic devices. Over the course of the 1990s, DRAM technology evolved through several generations – from 4 Megabits to the present state-of-the-art 4 Gigabit chips. Until 1998, there were two major American manufacturers of DRAMs – Texas Instruments (TI) and Micron Technology. Then, TI sold its factories in Avezzano (Italy), Richardson (Texas), and Singapore, and interests in two Asian joint ventures to Micron Technology. TI shut the remainder of its DRAM production facilities including one in Midland, Texas.

(a) Which probably had the higher average cost – the Richardson or Midland plant?

(b) Compare the effects on the world wide long-run DRAM supply of TI's sale of the Richardson plant with its closure of the Midland factory.

(c) Explain Micron's decision to buy TI's plants in terms of differences between the two companies in their expectations of long-run DRAM prices.

6. In January 2005, the world's total supply of oil tankers amounted to 304.1 million deadweight tons (dwt). During 2005, 28.0 million dwt of new tankers were delivered into service, while 5.1 million dwt were scrapped or otherwise removed from service. Hence, at the end of the year, the world's total supply was 326.9 million dwt. Among tankers and chemical carriers in operation of 200,000 dwt or larger, 60% by tonnage was less than 10 years old, 37% was 10–20 years old, and the remainder was more than 20 years old. (*Source*: *Platou Report*, 2006.) Typically, older tankers are more costly to operate.

(a) Identify the following as either a short- or long-run decision: (i) lay-up (idling the vessel); (ii) scrapping.

(b) Explain how the owner of a tanker should decide whether to continue to operate, lay-up, or scrap a vessel.

(c) The marginal cost of keeping a tanker in service ("lay-up equivalent") is the tanker's operating cost minus the cost of lay-up. When tanker rates fall, identify which tanker owners
would first lay up.

7. Referring to the U.S. Energy Information Administration (www.eia.doe.gov), Historical Data
Overview: Prices, compile monthly prices of West Texas Intermediate crude oil for the last five
years. Referring to Baker Hughes (www.bakerhughes.com), Rig Counts, compile monthly counts
of active rotary drilling rigs in Canada and Texas for the last five years.
   (a) For each of Canada and Texas, calculate the standard deviation of the number of rigs divided
        by the average number of rigs.
   (b) A higher standard deviation relative to average number of rigs means that the number of
        rigs is relatively more volatile. Does this imply that the fixed costs of drilling are relatively
        smaller or larger?
   (c) Compute the monthly changes in the price of West Texas Intermediate crude oil and the
        number of active rotary drilling rigs in Canada and Texas. Use your data to draw graphs
        corresponding to figure 4.7.
   (d) Comment on the relation, if any, between the changes in price and the changes in the
        number of active rigs.

8. With annual revenue of C$38.7 million and 199 employees in 2005, Bestar is larger than the typ-
ical Canadian furniture manufacturer. Furniture manufacturing is relatively intensive in wood and
labor. Canada is a leading international producer of lumber and wood. It is also a major exporter
of furniture to the United States.
   (a) Relate Canada's success in exporting furniture to its abundant forest resources.
   (b) How would the cost of labor affect the decision by Bestar and other Canadian manufac-
        turers to produce fully assembled as compared with ready-to-assemble furniture?
   (c) Asian furniture manufacturers face substantially lower labor costs than the Canadian indus-
        try. In which market segment – fully assembled or ready-to-assemble – do lower labor costs
        give the Asian manufacturers the relatively greater advantage?

9. The short-run supply of gasoline has been estimated to have an elasticity with respect to price
of 1.61, and with respect to wages of −0.05.
   (a) Explain why the elasticity of supply with respect to price is positive while the elasticity
        with respect to wages is negative.
   (b) How would a 5% increase in the price of gasoline and a 10% increase in wages affect the
        short-run supply of gasoline.
   (c) Do you expect the impact to be smaller or larger in the long run? Explain your answer.

10. This question applies the techniques presented in the math supplement. Let the market supply
for aluminum be represented by the equation

$$S = p - 0.5z - 2,$$

where S is the quantity supplied in tons a year, p is the price of the aluminum in dollars per ton,
and z is the price of electricity.
   (a) Suppose that that $z = 5$. Sketch the supply curve.
   (b) Illustrate the effect of a change in the price of aluminum from $p = 20$ to $p = 16$.
   (c) Illustrate the effect of a change in the price of electricity from $z = 5$ to $z = 2$.

Chapter 4

Math Supplement

Market Supply Curve

Using algebra, we can reinforce our understanding of the market supply curve and especially the effect of changes in price vis-à-vis other factors. Let the market supply for some item be represented by the equation

$$S = p - 0.5z - 3, \tag{4.10}$$

where S is the quantity supplied in units a year, p is the price of the item in dollars per unit, and z is the price of an input.

This supply curve is a straight line. To explain, suppose that $z = 2$. Then, substituting in equation (4.16),

$$S = p - 1 - 3 = p - 4. \tag{4.11}$$

Differentiating (4.17) with respect to price,

$$\frac{ds}{dp} = 1 \tag{4.12}$$

which means that the supply equation has a constant slope, or equivalently, that the supply curve is a straight line.

To sketch the supply curve, we consider two points on the curve. First, when the price $p = 10$, the quantity supplied is $S = 10 - 4 = 6$. Next, if the quantity supplied is $S = 0$, the price, $p = 4$. Marking and joining the two points $p = 10$, $S = 6$, and $p = 4$, $S = 0$ on figure 4.13, we have the market supply curve.

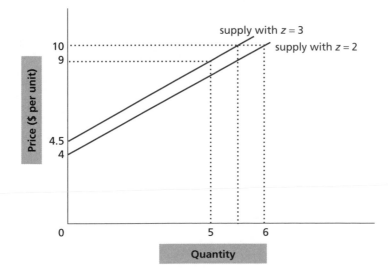

Figure 4.13   Straight-line market supply curve

We can use the supply curve to illustrate the effect of a change in price. For instance, when the price $p = 9$, the quantity supplied is $S = 9 - 4 = 5$. When the price is higher, $p = 10$, the quantity supplied is $S = 10 - 4 = 6$. We represent this change by a movement along the supply curve from the point at which $p = 9$ and $S = 5$ to the point at which $p = 10$ and $S = 6$.

The market supply curve in (4.16) can also illustrate the effect of a change in the price of an input. Recall that, originally, the price of the input was $z = 2$. Suppose that the price rises to $z = 3$. Then, referring to (4.16), the supply curve would become

$$S = p - 1.5 - 3 = p - 4.5. \tag{4.13}$$

In this case, when the price $p = 10$, the quantity supplied $S = 5.5$; if the quantity supplied $S = 0$, the price $p = 4.5$. Marking and joining these two points on figure 4.13, we have the supply curve with the input price of $z = 3$. This is a straight line that lies to the left of the supply curve with the input price of $z = 2$. By contrast to a change in price, the change in the input price is represented by a shift of the entire supply curve.

Generally, a change in any factor other than the price of the item is represented by a shift of the entire market supply curve.

Forecasting Quantity Supplied

We can also use algebra to derive a general formula with which to calculate changes in quantity supplied as a function of the price elasticity and percentage changes in price. Let S represent the average quantity supplied; $\%S$, the percentage change in the quantity supplied; p, the average price; and $\%p$, the percentage change in price. Then, by definition, the price elasticity of supply is

$$s_p = \frac{\%\Delta S}{\%\Delta p} \tag{4.14}$$

We can rearrange the price elasticity as follows:

$$\% \Delta S = s_p \, \% \, \Delta p, \tag{4.15}$$

which says that the percentage change in quantity supplied is the price elasticity multiplied by the percentage change in price.

If there are multiple changes in the factors affecting the quantity supplied, then the net percentage effect on quantity supplied is the sum of the separate effects. Each separate effect is the corresponding elasticity multiplied by the percentage change in the factor.

Chapter 5

Competitive Markets

1 Introduction

The fleets of integrated oil producers such as BP, Exxon, and Saudi Aramco comprise one-third of the global oil tanker industry.[1] Independent owner-operators such as Frontline Ltd, headquartered in Bermuda, account for the other two-thirds.

The global tanker industry is quite fragmented. In 2006, total tonnage amounted to almost 327 million tons. With total capacity of 17.9 million deadweight tons in 2006, Frontline claimed "the largest and most modern [fleet] in the world." Its fleet included 42 very large crude carriers (VLCCs) with capacities of around 300,000 tons and 35 Suezmax tankers with capacities of around 160,000 tons.

Following disastrous oil spills by the tankers *Exxon Valdez*, *Erika*, and *Prestige*, international and national authorities imposed progressively more stringent standards on tanker safety. Industry researchers R. S. Platou report that tankers with capacity of 86.4 million tons were scrapped between 2000 and 2005.

The demand for oil tanker services depends on the quantity and distance of oil exports. Global oil consumption is projected to increase by 2% in 2006, driven by 2.3% growth in U.S. consumption and 7% growth in China's consumption. Meanwhile, the United States is reducing imports from the Middle East and increasing imports from nearer sources in West Africa, Latin America, and Russia. By contrast, China is diversifying its imports towards more distant sources in West Africa and Russia.

The supply of tanker services depends on the cost of fuel, which accounts for one-third of tanker operating costs. In ten years, the fuel consumption of VLCCs fell from 200 tons per day by over two-thirds. However, a countervailing factor has been the rising price of oil.

Changes in the oil market and tanker regulations pose important questions for the managements of integrated as well as independent tanker fleets. How would increasing oil prices, increasing Chinese and U.S. oil consumption, and tighter regulations affect the market for tanker services? To answer each of these questions, we must understand demand, supply, and the interaction between the two sides of the market.

---

[1] The following discussion is based in part on data from Frontline Ltd, www.frontline.bm, "The Giant Tankers That Transport Oil by Sea," Royal Dutch/Shell Group of Companies, www.shell.com, and Platou Report 2006, www.platou.com.

At first glance, the need to understand both demand and supply may seem surprising. The increased cost of fuel and tighter regulation affect the supply of tanker service but not the demand. The increase in Chinese and U.S. consumption affects the demand for tanker service but not the supply. Yet, as we shall see, in all these cases, we cannot get a complete answer unless we consider both sides of the market. The same applies to many other managerial issues: although the initial change affects only one side of a market, it is necessary to consider the interaction with the other side to obtain a sensible and complete picture.

In this chapter, we combine our earlier analyses of demand and supply to understand how they interact in competitive markets. The central concept is that of market equilibrium. Applying this concept, we can understand the short- and long-run effects of changes in demand and supply. Within this framework, we can explain the effects of the increasing cost of fuel, increasing Chinese and U.S. consumption, and tighter regulations on the price and quantity of tanker service.

The demand–supply framework is the core of managerial economics. It can be applied to address business issues in a wide range of markets, including both goods and services, consumer as well as industrial products, and domestic and international markets.

2   Perfect Competition

In the preceding chapters, we developed the concepts of demand and supply. Recall that a market demand curve shows, for every possible price, the quantity that all buyers will purchase. When deriving a demand curve, we assume that every buyer can purchase as much as he or she would like at the going price and that all buyers pay the same price. Similarly, when deriving a market supply curve, we assume that every seller can deliver as much as he or she would like at the going price and that all sellers receive the same price.

> A market is said to be in **perfect competition** if
>
> - its products are homogeneous;
> - it includes many buyers, each purchasing a small quantity;
> - it includes many sellers, each supplying a small quantity;
> - buyers and sellers can enter and exit freely;
> - all buyers and all sellers have symmetric information.

Let us now make explicit the assumptions underlying the concepts of demand and supply. Generally, demand–supply analysis applies to markets in which competition is very keen in the sense of the following five conditions: the product is homogeneous; there are many buyers, each of whom purchases a quantity that is small relative to the market; there are many sellers, each of whom supplies a quantity that is small relative to the market; new buyers and sellers can enter freely, and existing buyers and sellers can exit freely; and all buyers and all sellers have symmetric information about market conditions.

Collectively, these five conditions define **perfect competition**. We shall treat the terms *perfect competition* and *demand–supply framework* as synonymous. Let us now review the five conditions for perfect competition.

Homogeneous Product

Competition in a market where products are differentiated is not as keen as that in a market where products are homogeneous. Gold is a homogeneous commodity. Gold mined in North America is a perfect substitute for gold from Australia, Brazil, South Africa, or any other part of the world. If a North American gold producer tries to sell its gold at even 1% above the prevailing world market price, absolutely no one would buy. By the same token, if it offered its gold at 1% less than the market price, it would be swamped with orders. The price of gold from any source is exactly the same.

In contrast, mineral water is not homogeneous. Water from different sources has different chemical composition and hence different taste and therapeutic effect. A mineral water producer can raise its price by 1% without worrying that all its consumers would switch to other brands. Likewise, if it reduced its price by 1%, its sales would increase, but by only a limited degree. Consequently, there is no uniform price for mineral water: different manufacturers may charge different prices. In general, competition among manufacturers of mineral water is relatively weaker than competition among gold mines.

Many Small Buyers

The second condition for perfect competition is that there are many buyers, each of whom purchases a quantity that is small relative to the market. In such a market, no buyer can get a lower price than others; hence, all buyers face the same price. This means that all buyers compete on the same level playing field.

Consider a market where some buyers have market power and get lower prices. Then, different buyers pay different prices. A buyer with market power cannot answer the question, "How much would you buy, assuming that you could buy as much as you would like at the going price?" Such a buyer cannot answer this question because it can affect the going price. Thus, when some buyers have market power, it is not possible to construct a market demand curve, which is fundamental to the demand–supply framework.

In the market for cotton, there are countless buyers of cotton, ranging from Indian villagers to Paris designers. The purchases of each buyer are very small relative to the world supply. No one buys enough to get an especially low price. Rather, every buyer pays the same world price.

By contrast, the demand for Pacific yew bark is dominated by a few pharmaceutical manufacturers who use it to produce the anti-cancer drug, Taxol. These buyers are so big that they have market power. As a result, they are able to procure better prices for their purchases.

Many Small Sellers

The third condition for perfect competition is that there are many sellers, each of whom supplies a quantity that is small relative to the market. The logic for this condition is similar to that for requiring many small buyers. In a market where there are many sellers, all of whom are small, no seller has market power. This means that no seller can get a higher price than others; hence, they all face the same price. All sellers compete on the same level playing field. The condition that there are many sellers supplying small quantities is necessary to construct a market supply curve.

Compare the markets for haircuts and cable television. In any city, there are many barbers, none of whom has market power. By contrast, there would be one or two providers of cable television, each of which has substantial market power. Accordingly, the market for haircuts is much more competitive than that for cable television.

Free Entry and Exit

The fourth condition for perfect competition is that new buyers and sellers can enter freely, and existing buyers and sellers can exit freely. In particular, this means that no technological, legal, or regulatory barriers constrain entry or exit. To explain this condition, let us focus on free entry by new sellers and free exit by existing sellers. The logic for free entry and exit among buyers is quite similar.

Consider a market with free entry and exit. As we saw in chapter 4 on market supply, if the market price rises above a seller's average cost, then new sellers will be attracted to enter. This will add to the market supply and bring down the price. Hence, with free entry and exit, the market price cannot stay above a seller's average cost for very long. The market will be very competitive.

To illustrate, let us compare the markets for telephone service and telemarketing. Telephone service providers require a license to operate. By contrast, there is relatively little regulation of telemarketing. As a result, there is much more competition among telemarketers.

The degree of competition also depends on barriers to exit. Suppose that a telephone service provider must pay the government a compensation fee to cease service. It must consider this exit cost when deciding whether to enter the market. Therefore, the higher the exit costs, the less likely new providers are to enter the market; hence, the less competitive the market will be.

Symmetric Information

The fifth condition for perfect competition is that all buyers and all sellers have symmetric information about market conditions such as prices, available substitutes, and technology. With symmetric information, every seller or buyer will be subject to intense competition. If, for instance, a new supplier offers a key input at a lower price, then, immediately, every producer will get the same lower price. No seller can enjoy the privilege of secret information.

Photocopying service is a mature industry. Information about market conditions is widely and evenly available among buyers as well as sellers. As a result, the market is extremely competitive.

By contrast, information is not symmetric in the market for medical services. Patients rely on their doctors for advice. In this market, sellers (doctors) have better information than buyers (patients). There may be differences in information on the supply side as well as between the two sides of the market. Doctors who attend continuing education and follow the latest journals may have better information and provide better advice and treatment than others.

Markets where there are differences in information among buyers, or among sellers, or between buyers and sellers are not as competitive as those where all buyers and all sellers have symmetric information.

Progress Check 5A Explain why it is possible to construct a market supply curve only if there are many sellers, each of whom supplies a quantity that is small relative to the market.

Regulatory barriers to competition: the Australian electricity industry

Until the late 1980s, the Australian electricity industry consisted of publicly owned vertically integrated monopoly suppliers which operated in an extensively regulated market. The government had set regulations to prevent the market from moving towards perfect competition: in fact, the laws were in place to uphold the government's monopoly. The government concluded that electricity costs were inflated and that monopoly might not be the most efficient industry structure. This conclusion was reached due to pressure from the manufacturing industry which had opposed the state owned monopoly for a long time.

In July 1991, the government established a National Grid Management Council (NGMC) which was in charge of restructuring the electricity market. The major changes implemented by NGMC were: separation of generation, transmission and distribution of electricity; privatization of the government run suppliers; and liberalizing laws which prevented entry of new suppliers (such as lengthy application procedures for licenses, unreasonably high qualification requirements for workers, high minimum investment requirements over the first 3 years of operation, and high requirements for equity capital).

As a result of these reforms:

- In New South Wales, three competing generation entities were created, an independent transmission business was privatized, and the distributors were consolidated into six new distribution utilities.
- In Western Australia, the government has sold all the power stations to private operators and separated water supply from electricity supply.

Business users are now able to choose from many suppliers and average prices have fallen by 25–30%. Inefficiencies have been reduced: employment in the industry fell from over 80,000 in 1985 to 37,000 in 1997. As industry conditions moved closer to perfect competition, workers with low marginal productivity were laid off. The resulting cost reductions have improved the efficiency of the industry under deregulation.

Source: Year Book Australia, 2002, Energy: Special Article – Reforms in the Australian Electricity and Gas Industries, www.abs.gov.au/Ausstats/abs@.nsf/0/c50cabc70c99e249ca2569e3001ff8a5?OpenDocument.

3 Market Equilibrium

We have reviewed the five conditions for perfect competition. If a market meets these conditions, we can validly apply the concepts of demand and supply. We now introduce the concept of *market equilibrium*, which unifies demand and supply. **Market equilibrium** is the price at which the quantity demanded equals the quantity supplied. The concept of equilibrium is the basis for all analyses of how changes in demand or supply affect market prices and quantities.

> **Market equilibrium** is the price at which the quantity demanded equals the quantity supplied.

Demand and Supply

To illustrate the concept of equilibrium, consider the market for tanker service. Shippers generate the demand, and tanker lines provide the supply. Using a graph, we mark the price of tanker service in dollars per ton-mile on the vertical axis and the quantity of tanker service in billions of ton-miles a year on the horizontal axis. (One ton-mile represents the carriage of one ton over a distance of one mile.) Then, we draw the demand for and the supply of tanker service.

As emphasized in chapter 2, the demand curve slopes downward. From chapter 4, we know that, depending on the circumstances, the supply curve is flat or slopes upward. In this case,

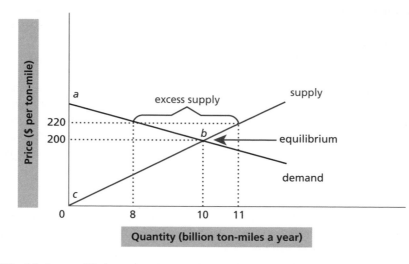

Figure 5.1   Market equilibrium
At the price of $200 per ton-mile, the quantity demanded is 10 billion ton-miles a year and the quantity supplied is the same. When the price is $220 per ton-mile, the quantity supplied exceeds the quantity demanded by 3 billion ton-miles a year.

we suppose that the supply curve slopes upward. In figure 5.1, consider the point at which the demand and the supply curves cross. That point represents the market equilibrium: the price at which the quantity demanded just balances the quantity supplied.

Suppose that the equilibrium in the market for tanker service is at a price of $200 per ton-mile and quantity of 10 billion ton-miles a year. Referring to figure 5.1, the demand curve shows that, at the price of $200, buyers want to purchase a total of 10 billion ton-miles a year. The supply curve in figure 5.1 shows that, at the price of $200, sellers want to supply a total of 10 billion ton-miles a year. The quantity that buyers want to purchase exactly balances the quantity that sellers want to supply.

At the market equilibrium, there is no tendency for price, purchases, or sales to change. The price will not tend to change because the quantity demanded of 10 billion ton-miles just balances the quantity supplied of 10 billion ton-miles. Purchases will not tend to change because, at the price of $200, buyers (shippers) maximize benefits less expenditure by purchasing 10 billion ton-miles. Further, sales will not tend to change because, at the price of $200, sellers (tanker lines) maximize profits by supplying 10 billion ton-miles.

Excess Supply

What happens when the market is not in equilibrium? Then, generally, the market price will tend to change in such a way as to restore equilibrium. For instance, suppose that the market price is $20 above equilibrium, at $220 per ton-mile. Then, referring to the demand curve in figure 5.1, buyers would cut back purchases to 8 billion ton-miles a year. The supply curve in figure 5.1 shows that, at a price of $220, sellers would supply more, specifically 11 billion ton-miles a year.

Hence, at a price of $220 per ton-mile, the quantity supplied would exceed the quantity demanded by $11 - 8 = 3$ billion ton-miles a year. In more colorful terms, there would be too many ships chasing too few customers. The amount by which the quantity supplied exceeds the quantity demanded is called **excess supply**. So, at a price of $220, there would be an excess supply of 3 billion ton-miles a year. In a situation of excess supply, the market price will tend to fall. Tanker lines would compete to clear their extra capacity and the market price would drop back toward the equilibrium level of $200.

> The **excess supply** is the amount by which the quantity supplied exceeds the quantity demanded.

From figure 5.1, it is clear that, if the price were even higher, at $250 per ton-mile, the excess supply would be even larger than the excess supply at a price of $220. Generally, the higher is the price above the equilibrium level, the larger will be the excess supply.

Excess Demand

Another way in which the market can be out of equilibrium is when the price is below the equilibrium level. In this case, the market price will tend to rise. To illustrate, suppose that in the market for tanker service, the price is $180 per ton-mile. Further, suppose that, at the price of $180, buyers would purchase 12 billion ton-miles a year, and sellers would supply 9 billion ton-miles a year. Then, the quantity demanded would exceed the quantity supplied by 12 − 9 = 3 billion ton-miles a year.

The amount by which the quantity demanded exceeds the quantity supplied is called the **excess demand**. At a price of $180 per ton-mile, there would be excess demand of 3 billion ton-miles a year. Faced with this excess demand, buyers would compete for the limited capacity and the market price would rise toward the equilibrium level of $200. Generally, the lower the price is below the equilibrium level, the larger will be the excess demand.

> The **excess demand** is the amount by which the quantity demanded exceeds the quantity supplied.

Progress Check 5B In figure 5.1, illustrate the excess demand if the price is $160 per ton-mile. Mark the quantities demanded and supplied.

Significance of Equilibrium

We focus on equilibrium for two reasons. First, as we have seen, if a market is not in equilibrium, either buyers or sellers will push the market toward equilibrium. Second, by comparing equilibria, we can address a wide range of questions like, "If the price of a related product, the cost of inputs, or government policy was different, how would that affect the market for my product?" To address such questions, we compare the market equilibrium under the original circumstances to the equilibrium under the new set of parameters. When prices are quite flexible, the market will adjust to the new equilibrium fairly quickly, so comparing equilibria is a fairly accurate method of analysis.

For a market to be in equilibrium, both the quantity demanded and the quantity supplied must be the result of voluntary choices by buyers and sellers, respectively. Neither buyers nor sellers may face rationing.

In practice, very few markets exactly satisfy the five conditions for perfect competition. This means that demand–supply analysis does not precisely apply. Nevertheless, we can still apply this method of analysis: many of the managerial implications are the same even if a market is not perfectly competitive. However, we must be careful to check the implications against the conditions that the market does not satisfy.

4   Supply Shift

In general, changes in economic variables such as the prices of inputs or changes in government policies will cause shifts in demand, supply, or both. Even if the change superficially appears to affect only one side of the market, it is essential to analyze the effects on the other side as well. As we shall soon see, an analysis that ignores the other side of the market could be seriously misleading.

In this section, we consider the effect of a change that shifts the supply curve. Specifically, the introduction to this chapter asked how a drop in the cost of fuel would affect the price of tanker service. Let us apply the demand–supply framework to address this question.

We need to start from the equilibrium before the change in fuel cost. Suppose that, before the change in fuel cost, the price of tanker service was $200 per ton-mile and the quantity purchased was 10 billion ton-miles a year.

Equilibrium Change

The supply curve of tanker service does not explicitly show the cost of fuel. Accordingly, any change in the cost of fuel will shift the entire supply curve. Suppose that the average fuel cost of tanker service was $40 per ton-mile, and that the cost of fuel drops by 15% or $6 per ton-mile. This would cause the entire supply curve of tanker service to shift downward by $6 per ton-mile. We represent this shift in figure 5.2.

The entire supply curve shifts down because the reduction in fuel cost affects sellers' marginal costs whatever the quantity that they supply. Another way of looking at the impact of the change in fuel cost is that it shifts the supply curve to the right: at every possible price, sellers want to supply more.

The change in fuel cost, however, does not affect the demand for tanker service. Referring to figure 5.2, the new supply curve crosses the unchanged demand curve at a new

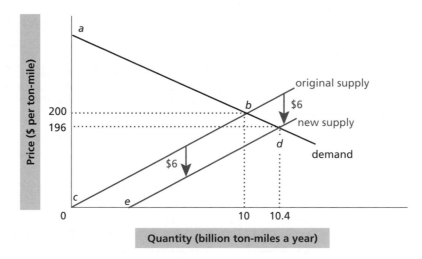

Figure 5.2   Supply shift
When the cost of fuel drops $6 per ton-mile, the entire supply curve shifts downward by $6. At the new equilibrium, the price is $196 per ton-mile and the quantity is 10.4 billion ton-miles a year.

equilibrium point *d*, where the price is $196 per ton-mile. The fall in price from $200 to $196 increases the quantity demanded from 10 to 10.4 billion ton-miles a year. On the new supply curve, at the price of $196, the quantity supplied is 10.4 billion ton-miles a year. The price of $196 is the new market equilibrium.

Price Elasticities

In the example of the tanker market, when the supply curve shifted down by $6, the equilibrium price fell by only $4. Generally, a downward or upward shift in the supply curve will change the equilibrium price by no more than the amount of the supply shift. What determines the extent of the change in price? We shall show that the change in the equilibrium price depends on the price elasticities of demand and supply.

Consider figure 5.3(a), which depicts an extremely inelastic demand. This means that buyers are completely insensitive to the price: they purchase the same quantity regardless of the price. Accordingly, when the supply curve shifts, the buyers do not change their behavior – they continue to purchase exactly the same quantity. In figure 5.3(a), when the supply curve shifts down by $6, the equilibrium price drops by exactly $6 to $194 per ton-mile.

Regarding the market demand curve, the other extreme is an extremely elastic demand, as depicted in figure 5.3(b). This means that buyers are extremely sensitive to price. When the supply curve shifts, the buyers soak up all the additional quantity supplied. Consequently, the equilibrium price does not change at all. In figure 5.3(b), when the supply shifts down by $6, the equilibrium price remains unchanged at $200 per ton-mile. The new equilibrium quantity is 10.6 billion.

Realistically, however, the market demand is probably somewhat but not extremely sensitive to price. If there is an increase in supply, some buyers will switch from other forms of transport to tanker service, while existing buyers may purchase more. Hence, when the supply curve shifts down, the price will fall but by less than the downward shift. Likewise, if the supply curve should shift up, the market price will rise but by less than the upward shift.

By comparing figures 5.3(a) and (b), we can see the relationship between the price elasticity of demand and the price response to a shift in supply. Generally, if the demand is more elastic, then the change in the equilibrium price resulting from a shift in supply will be smaller.

Let us next see how the change in the equilibrium price depends on the price elasticity of supply. Figure 5.3(c) depicts an extremely inelastic supply. This means that sellers are completely insensitive to the price: they provide the same quantity regardless of the price. In particular, if their costs change, they will not change the quantity supplied. Referring to figure 5.3(c), tanker lines supply 10 billion ton-miles a year whatever the market price. Consequently, the change in fuel cost does not change the equilibrium price.

Regarding the market supply curve, the other extreme is an extremely elastic supply, as depicted in figure 5.3(d). This means that, essentially, the marginal cost of production is constant. Accordingly, if the cost of an input changes, the marginal cost changes by the same amount at all production levels. Then, the equilibrium price changes by exactly the same amount. Referring to figure 5.3(d) for the tanker services market, when the supply curve shifts down by $6, the equilibrium price drops by exactly $6 per ton-mile. The quantity rises to 11 billion ton-miles a year.

Realistically, however, the supply of tanker services is sensitive to price: to supply more service requires more capacity and, so, higher costs. An elastic supply means that sellers can

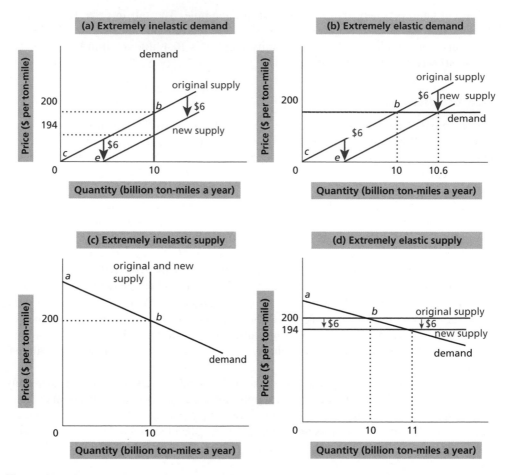

Figure 5.3   Price elasticities of demand and supply
(a)   When demand is extremely inelastic, the supply curve shift reduces the price by exactly $6 but does not affect the quantity.
(b)   When demand is extremely elastic, the supply curve shift does not affect the price but raises the quantity to 10.6 billion.
(c)   When supply is extremely inelastic, the supply curve does not shift.
(d)   When supply is extremely elastic, the supply curve shift reduces the price by exactly $6 and raises the quantity to 11 billion.

increase service with some increase in costs. So, when the supply curve shifts down, the price will fall. Likewise, if the supply curve should shift up, the market price will rise.

By comparing figures 5.3(c) and (d), we can see that, generally, if the supply is more elastic, then the change in the equilibrium price resulting from a shift in supply will be larger.

Progress Check 5C Which of (1) and (2) is true? For a given downward shift of the market supply curve, the drop in the equilibrium price will be larger if (1) the demand is more price elastic or (2) the supply is more price elastic.

Common Misconception

A common misconception is that, if sellers' costs fall by some amount, then the market price will fall by the same amount. For instance, a change in the cost of fuel affects only the supply side of the tanker service market. Does this mean that, if the cost of tanker service drops by $6, then the price would fall by the same amount?

Such simple thinking overlooks the impact of the shift in supply on buyers. If they are extremely insensitive to price, then they will not buy more; hence, the price will drop by the entire $6. If, however, they are very sensitive to price, then the shift in supply would result in no change to the equilibrium price.

The simple thinking also overlooks the price sensitivity of sellers. If sellers are insensitive to price, then the drop in cost will not induce them to sell more; hence, the price of tanker service will not change at all. If, however, sellers are very sensitive to price, then the shift in supply would cause the price to fall by the entire $6.

Generally, the effect of a change in costs on the market price depends on the price elasticities of both demand and supply.

Progress Check 5D In figure 5.2, show how an $8 drop in the cost of fuel would affect the supply curve and the equilibrium price.

The demand for French products: foie gras vis-à-vis butter

France's agricultural exports include foie gras and butter. The supplies of French products to world markets depend on the exchange rate between the euro and other world currencies, such as the U.S. dollar. If the euro becomes more expensive, the supply curves of French products to world markets will be higher. If, however, the euro becomes cheaper, then the supply curves will be lower.

Suppose that the euro becomes 10% more expensive, causing the supply curves of French foie gras and butter to shift up by 10%. How will these shifts affect the prices of foie gras and butter on world markets?

There are few substitutes for French foie gras; hence, the demand is relatively inelastic. The upward shift of the supply curve will result in a relatively large increase in the world price. By contrast with foie gras, butter is a relatively homogeneous product. There are many close substitutes for French butter, so that the demand is relatively elastic. Accordingly, the upward supply shift curve will result in a relatively small increase in the world price.

Retail competition and wholesale price cuts

A frequent complaint among consumer goods manufacturers is that, when they reduce wholesale prices, their retailers do not reduce retail prices by the same amount. The retailers take bigger margins instead of passing on the full reduction to consumers. Some marketing consultants believe that the cause of the problem is a lack of competition among retailers and claim that, if retailing were competitive, retailers would pass on the full amount of reductions in the wholesale price.

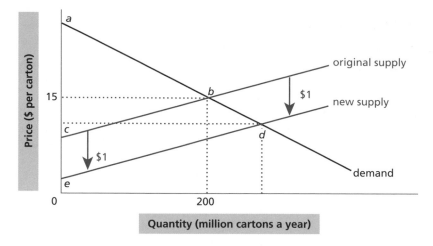

Figure 5.4 Wholesale price cut
A $1 cut in the wholesale price shifts down the retail supply curve by $1 and results in a lower retail price and larger quantity.

Let us apply the demand–supply framework to study this argument. Consider, for instance, the retail market for tissues. In this market, consumers generate the demand, while retailers provide the supply. We make the extreme assumption that the market is perfectly competitive. Figure 5.4 represents the demand and supply. The equilibrium is a price of $15 per carton and quantity of 200 million cartons a year.

Now suppose that tissue manufacturers reduce the wholesale price by $1 a carton. In the retail market, this will reduce the cost of supplying tissues by $1 at all quantities. Hence, the supply curve will shift down by $1.

Does the market price fall by $1? Only if either the market demand is extremely inelastic or the market supply is extremely elastic. In all other cases, the market price will fall by less than $1.

Recall that we assumed that the retail market was perfectly competitive. And yet we found that, in most cases, the retail price would fall by less than $1 when manufacturers reduce the wholesale price by $1. Accordingly, the reason why retailers absorb part of a cut in wholesale prices is not a lack of competition. The explanation lies in the price elasticities of retail demand and supply.

5   Demand Shift

In the case of the market for tanker service, we saw that, to understand the impact of a shift in supply, we had to consider the interaction between supply and demand. Our next application begins with a change that shifts demand. To get a complete understanding of the final outcome, however, it is necessary to consider the supply side as well.

How would an increase in oil shipments affect the price and quantity of tanker service? Figure 5.5 shows the original equilibrium at point *b*, with a price of $200 and quantity of 10 billion ton-miles a year. Suppose that the demand rises by 1 billion ton-miles at all price levels. Accordingly, in figure 5.5, the entire demand curve shifts to the right by 1 billion

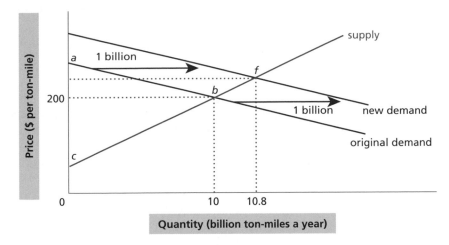

Figure 5.5 Demand shift
A 1-billion ton-mile increase in demand shifts the demand curve to the right and results in a higher price and larger quantity.

ton-miles. The increase in oil shipments, however, does not directly affect the supply of tanker service. So, the supply curve does not change.

From figure 5.5, we see that the new demand curve crosses the unchanged supply curve at a new market equilibrium (point *f*). The new equilibrium has a higher price and a larger quantity of tanker service. By how much will the price rise and by how much will the quantity of tanker service increase? The answer depends on the price elasticities of both demand and supply.

⊣ Demand and supply on Valentine's Day ⊢

People buy greeting cards and roses throughout the year. As Valentine's Day approaches, however, cards and roses become necessities. The demand for both products jumps. Applying demand–supply analysis, we expect the prices of both products to rise. The price of roses, however, always increases much more sharply than the price of greeting cards. Why?

We can explain this disparity by considering the price elasticities of supply in the two markets. The supply of greeting cards on Valentine's Day is much more elastic than the supply of roses. Greeting cards can be stored, so manufacturers can easily step up production and prepare larger stocks ahead of Valentine's Day. This means that the supply of cards is relatively elastic; hence, an increase in demand has little effect on price.

By contrast, roses are perishable. Only roses maturing around Valentine's Day will be suitable for that day. It is relatively costly to increase the quantity supplied on Valentine's Day. This means that the supply is relatively inelastic, and consequently, the increase in demand causes the price to increase sharply.

Source: B. Peter Pashigian, "Demand and Supply on Valentine's Day," in *Price Theory and Applications* (New York: McGraw-Hill, 1995), p. 19.

⊣ China and the tanker services market ⊢

China's rapid economic expansion powered a 33% increase in oil imports in 2003, and a further 34% increase in 2004. While increasing overall imports, Chinese importers also sought to diversify away from traditional Middle East sources to new sources in West Africa and Russia.

As a result, the demand for tanker services to China has increased for two reasons – increases in oil imports and longer distances of transportation. Owing to economies of scale, the average cost of transportation is lower with larger vessels. VLCCs, however, cannot transit the Danish Straits and the Suez canal, and cannot enter most Chinese terminals, and so must transfer their cargoes to and from smaller ships when shipping oil from northwest Europe to China.

Given this trade-off, VLCCs tend to dominate long-haul routes, while smaller Suezmax and Aframax tankers cater to shorter routes. Owing to the shift in the pattern of demand towards longer distances between 2003 and 2004, average rates for VLCCs rose by 75%, while rates for Suezmax and Aframax tankers increased by the relatively smaller proportions of 63% and 48%, respectively.

These were short-term changes in daily rental rates – the long-term tanker market behaves somewhat differently. Increased demand for tanker services drove up second-hand prices of VLCCs, Suezmax, and Aframax tankers by 20%, 30%, and 26% respectively.

Source: *Platou Report 2005*, www.platou.com.

6 Adjustment Time

Earlier, we studied the effects of shifts in demand and supply on the market equilibrium. An important factor in the size of these effects is the time horizon. Specifically, the elasticities of demand and supply vary with the time horizon. Accordingly, shifts in demand and supply may have different short-run and long-run effects.

To consider these differences, we start from a market that is in short- and long-run equilibrium. Generally, in equilibrium, each individual buyer purchases the quantity where her or his marginal benefit equals the price, and each individual seller provides the quantity where its marginal cost equals the price. Figure 5.6 represents the interactions among individual buyers and sellers in a market equilibrium.

The market demand curve is the horizontal summation of the individual demand curves, and the market supply curve is the horizontal summation of the individual supply curves. At the equilibrium price, the market demand curve crosses the market supply curve. The price then signals to each buyer how much to purchase and to each seller how much to provide. Figure 5.6 applies to both short- and long-run equilibria.

Suppose that, originally, the market for tanker service was in short- and long-run equilibrium, with a price of $200 per ton-mile and quantity of 10 billion ton-miles. Let us now analyze the short-run vis-à-vis long-run effects of an increase in demand by 1 billion ton-miles.

Short-Run Equilibrium

Short-run market equilibrium is the price at which the short-run quantity demanded equals the short-run quantity supplied.

Figure 5.7 depicts the *short-run market equilibrium* at a price of $200 per ton-mile. Figure 5.7(a) shows the cost and demand curves of an individual seller. The short-run supply curve of any individual seller is that portion of its short-run marginal cost curve that lies above its short-run average variable cost curve.

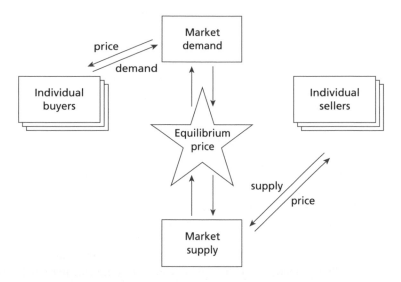

Figure 5.6 Market and individual equilibrium
The individual demands add up to market demand, and individual supplies add up to market supply. The equilibrium price signals to each buyer how much to purchase and to each seller how much to provide.
Source: Adapted from Michael Katz and Harvey Rosen, *Microeconomics*, 1994 edition, p. 53. Reprinted by permission of Richard D. Irwin, Homewood, Illinois.

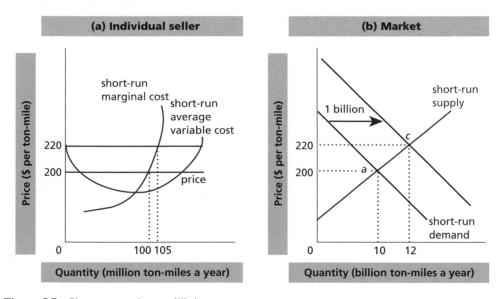

Figure 5.7 Short-run market equilibrium
(a)   An individual seller operates at 100 million ton-miles a year, where the short-run marginal cost equals the market price.
(b)   The market is in equilibrium at a price of $200, where the short-run demand crosses the short-run supply.

By the assumption of perfect competition, each seller supplies a quantity that is small relative to the market. Equivalently, it has a small market share. Hence, the demand facing the seller is extremely elastic at the $200 market price. In the short run, the seller maximizes profit by operating at the point where its short-run marginal cost equals the market price. In figure 5.7(a), the profit-maximizing scale of short-run operations is 100 million ton-miles a year.

Figure 5.7(b) shows the short-run market equilibrium at point *a*. At the $200 equilibrium price, the short-run market demand curve crosses the short-run market supply curve. The short-run market demand curve is the horizontal summation of the short-run individual demand curves. Similarly, the short-run market supply curve is the horizontal summation of the short-run individual supply curves.

Long-Run Equilibrium

Long-run market equilibrium is the price at which the long-run quantity demanded equals the long-run quantity supplied.

Figure 5.8 depicts the *long-run market equilibrium* at a price of $200 per ton-mile. Figure 5.8(a) shows the cost and demand curves of an individual seller. The long-run supply curve of any individual seller is that portion of its long-run marginal cost curve that lies above its long-run average cost curve. As each seller has a small market share, it faces a demand that is extremely elastic at the $200 market price. In the long run, it maximizes profit by operating at the point where its long-run marginal cost equals the market price. By figure 5.8(a), the profit-maximizing scale of long-run operations is 100 million ton-miles a year.

Figure 5.8(b) shows the long-run market equilibrium at point *a*. At the $200 equilibrium price, the long-run market demand curve crosses the long-run market supply curve. The long-run market demand curve is the horizontal summation of the long-run individual demand curves. Similarly, the long-run market supply curve is the horizontal summation of the long-run individual supply curves.

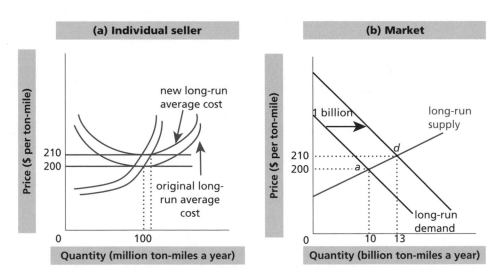

Figure 5.8   Long-run market equilibrium
(a)   An individual seller operates at 100 million ton-miles a year, where the long-run marginal cost equals the market price.
(b)   The market is in equilibrium at a price of $200, where the long-run demand crosses the long-run supply.

Demand Increase

Starting from the short- and long-run equilibria, we suppose that the demand curve shifts to the right by 1 billion ton-miles. For simplicity, we assume that the short- and long-run demand curves are the same.

Let us first consider the new short-run equilibrium. Referring to figure 5.7(b), the shift in demand will move the short-run market equilibrium to point c, with a higher price of $220. At the same time, referring to figure 5.7(a), every seller expands its operations to the scale of 105 million ton-miles, where its short-run marginal cost equals the new market price of $220. This means operating service capacity more intensively; for instance, by delaying routine maintenance on ships and postponing annual vacations for crews.

Generally, the extent to which a seller expands its operations depends on the slope of its short-run marginal cost curve. If the short-run marginal cost curve is steep, then the price increase will not lead the seller to expand operations by very much. By contrast, if the short-run marginal cost curve is gentle, then the price increase will induce a large expansion of operations. The steepness of the short-run marginal cost curve depends on such factors as the availability of excess production capacity and the cost of overtime relative to standard wage rates.

Let us next consider the new long-run equilibrium. In a long-run horizon, there is enough time for all costs to become avoidable, for new sellers to enter the market, and for existing sellers to leave. Accordingly, as we have shown in chapter 4, the market supply tends to be more elastic in the long run than in the short run.

With regard to the tanker service market, the increase in demand raises the market price and hence each seller's profits. Over the long run, this will induce existing sellers to expand capacity and enlist additional crew members and also will attract new sellers to enter the market. The industry will expand along the long-run market supply curve. To the extent that the expansion will attract sellers with relatively less favorable resources, the long-run market supply will slope upward.

Referring to figure 5.8(b), the shift in demand will move the long-run market equilibrium to point d with a price of $210. Figure 5.8(a) shows the new long-run equilibrium for an individual seller. Although the price is higher than in the original equilibrium, higher input prices result in higher marginal and average cost curves. Accordingly, in the new long-run equilibrium, each individual seller just breaks even. No other sellers will wish to enter the industry, and no seller will wish to leave.

Figure 5.9 depicts both the short- and long-run market equilibria. The original equilibrium is point a, the new short-run equilibrium is point c, and the new long-run equilibrium is point d. The price in the new long-run equilibrium is lower than in the new short-run equilibrium but higher than in the original equilibrium. The quantity in the new long-run equilibrium is higher than in the new short-run equilibrium, which in turn is higher than in the original equilibrium. The basic reason for these differences is that the supply is more elastic in the long run than the short run.

In the new long-run equilibrium, there will be more sellers than in the new short-run equilibrium or the original equilibrium. The higher price attracts new sellers to enter and supports a larger number of sellers; hence, a larger industry.

Progress Check 5E Suppose that the demand for tanker service increases by 2 billion ton-miles. Use figure 5.9 to illustrate the short- and long-run effects on the market equilibrium.

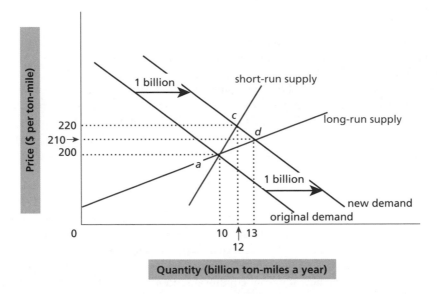

Figure 5.9   Demand increase: short and long run
Following an increase in demand, the new short-run equilibrium is at point c and the new long-run equilibrium is at point d. The price rises more in the short run than in the long run. The quantity increases less in the short run than in the long run.

Demand Reduction

We have considered the short- and long-run impacts of an increase in demand. We can apply the same approach to study the effects of a fall in demand. Figure 5.10 illustrates a 1 billion ton-mile reduction in the demand for tanker service. The original equilibrium is at point b.

The reduction in demand will move the short-run market equilibrium to point e, with a lower price of \$170. Those sellers whose average variable cost exceeds the price will shut down. In the tanker market, this means laying up their ships. Those sellers for whom the price covers their average variable cost will continue in business. Each will cut back operations to the scale where its short-run marginal cost equals the new market price of \$170.

The extent of the cutback depends on two factors. One factor is the extent of sunk costs. If a seller has many prior commitments, most costs are sunk. It will continue to produce so long as the price covers its average variable cost. In this case, the price reduction will lead to a relatively minor cutback in operations. Generally, in an industry involving substantial sunk costs, the reduction in demand will translate into a relatively large drop in price and a small reduction in quantity.

The second factor is the slope of the seller's short-run marginal cost curve. If the short-run marginal cost curve is steep, then the price reduction will not induce the seller to cut back operations by very much. By contrast, if the short-run marginal cost curve is gentle, then the price reduction will have a relatively larger impact on quantity.

In the long run, there is enough time for all costs to become avoidable, for new sellers to enter the market, and for existing sellers to leave. Referring to figure 5.10, the shift in demand will move the long-run market equilibrium to point f with a price of \$190. For some sellers, the long-run price is below their average total cost. These will exit the industry, which

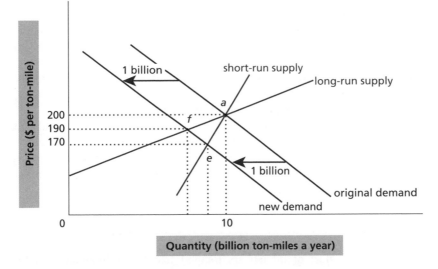

Figure 5.10   Demand reduction: short and long run
Following a reduction in demand, the new short-run equilibrium is at point *e* and the new long-run equilibrium is at point *f*. The price falls further in the short run than in the long run. The quantity drops less in the short run than the long run.

means scrapping their ships and dismissing all workers. The entire industry will contract along the long-run market supply curve. In the new long-run equilibrium, there will be a smaller number of sellers and each will exactly break even with average total cost equal to the market price.

Referring to figure 5.10, the price in the new long-run equilibrium is higher than in the new short-run equilibrium but lower than in the original equilibrium. Further, the quantity in the new long-run equilibrium is less than in the new short-run equilibrium, which in turn is less than in the original equilibrium. The basic reason for these differences is that the market supply is more elastic in the long run than the short run.

Price and Quantity over Time

Our analysis of the short- and long-run effects of shifts in the demand illustrates two general points. First, in response to shifts in demand, the market price will be more volatile in the short run than the long run. Specifically, if there is an increase in demand, the market price will increase more in the short run than in the long run. By contrast, if there is a reduction in demand, then the market price will fall more in the short run than in the long run.

Second, in response to shifts in demand, there is a greater change in the market quantity over the long run than in the short run. If there is an increase in demand, the quantity will increase more in the long run than in the short run. Likewise, if there is a reduction in demand, the quantity will drop more in the long run than the short run.

The distinction between the short run and long run is that, in the short run, some costs are sunk. Accordingly, the disparity between the short run and long run is relatively sharper in industries where operations involve substantial sunk costs. In such industries, the price will be relatively volatile, as the market adjusts to shifts in demand. When demand increases, the short-run price will exceed the long-run price. When, however, there is a fall in demand, the short-run price will be less than the long-run price.

Further, in industries with substantial sunk costs, the adjustment of production will be concentrated in the long run. Owing to the substantial sunk costs, relatively little adjustment can be made in the short run.

By contrast, in industries where sunk costs are minor, the adjustment to shifts in demand will be relatively smoother. The market price will be relatively less volatile. The adjustment of production will be spread through the short run and long run.

Like the elasticity of the market supply, the elasticity of the market demand depends on the time horizon. Recall from chapter 3 that, depending on the nature of the item, the long-run demand may be more or less elastic than the short-run demand. Just as we analyzed the short- and long-run effects of shifts in demand, we can apply the same approach to consider the short- and long-run effects of shifts in supply.

⊣ Frontline ⊢

In 1996, Frontline's fleet of oil tankers totalled just 5.5 million tons deadweight capacity. It adopted a new strategy to build one of the most modern fleet of tankers. Frontline aimed to be a "consolidator within a highly fragmented industry . . . through acquisitions, mergers and market cooperation, the latter preferably in the form of pool arrangements."

In March 1999, OPEC successfully cut back production. In the short run, given the available tanker tonnage, the reduction in the demand for tanker services caused charter rates to fall. Between 1998 and 1999, the average daily charter rate for modern VLCCs fell by 41% to $19,600. Frontline's bottom line dropped from after-tax income of $31.9 million to an after-tax loss of $86.9 million.

However, the recession in the tanker services market bore a silver lining for Frontline. Charter rates for older VLCCs fell relatively more than those for modern VLCCs. The drop in rates prompted a significant long-run adjustment. Under the pressure of low charter rates, high operating costs, and the looming costs of retrofitting to meet new regulations, the owners of many older tankers decided to scrap their vessels. Tonnage scrapped rose from 7.0 million in 1998 to 16.4 million in 1999.

Frontline's management concluded, "The weak market over the last two years has reduced new ordering, increased scrapping and will most likely lead to a stronger and longer upturn in the market."

Sources: *Platou Report 1999*, www.platou.com, Frontline Ltd., *Annual Report 1999*.

⊣ Texas Instruments, Micron, and the DRAM market ⊢

In 1998, following three years of continuously falling prices for dynamic random access memories (DRAMs), Texas Instruments (TI) decided to quit the industry. It sold plants in Avezzano (Italy), Richardson (Texas), and Singapore, as well as interests in two Asian joint ventures to Micron Technology. TI sold its share of a Taiwanese factory to joint-venture partner Acer. It shut all other DRAM production facilities including one in Midland, Texas. TI's exit left Micron as the United States' only significant DRAM manufacturer.

Why did Micron buy TI's production capacity at a time of tremendous excess supply in the market? One possible reason was that, with its increased size, Micron would command significantly more power over the DRAM market. We discuss market power in chapter 8.

Another possible explanation is that TI and Micron differed in their long-run expectations of DRAM prices. Micron may have been more optimistic, and hence viewed the purchase of TI's plants at a depressed time as a good deal.

Indeed, the demand for DRAMs recovered with Asia's emergence from its economic crisis and a general shift from 32 to 64 megabytes as the standard memory for personal computers (one megabyte is made up of 8 megabits). In addition, Korean manufacturers reduced their investment as their government cut back low-interest financing. The price of 64-megabit DRAMs bottomed out at $7.50 in the autumn of 1998 and then recovered to $10 by January 1999. Subsequently, the price fluctuated between $5 and $15, and then ended 1999 at $8.50.

Source: *Standard & Poor's Industry Surveys: Semiconductors 167*, no. 41, section 2 (October 14, 1999).

7 Summary

How will an increase in demand and a reduction in marginal costs affect the market for an item? Questions such as these are commonplace. The answers, however, are not so simple. To understand the complete effect of a shift in demand or supply, it is necessary to consider both sides of the market. Generally, the effect of any change in demand or supply depends on the elasticities of both demand and supply.

The time horizon is a key factor affecting elasticities of demand and supply. Prices are more volatile and quantity adjustment takes relatively longer in industries where production involves substantial sunk costs.

Key Concepts

perfect competition	excess supply	short-run market equilibrium
market equilibrium	excess demand	long-run market equilibrium

Further Reading

A useful reference on the economics of competitive markets is Steven E. Landsburg, *Price Theory and Applications*, 6th ed. (Mason, OH: South-Western College Publishing, 2005), chapter 7.

Review Questions

1. Explain which market better fits the model of perfect competition at the retail level (choose a or b)?
   (a) cable television;
   (b) video rentals.
2. What are the conditions for a market to be in perfect competition?
3. True or false? If some sellers have market power, then it is not possible to construct a supply curve. Explain your answer.
4. The California Public Utilities Commission regulates airport shuttle services. License applicants must have liability insurance and satisfy standards of financial responsibility. How does such regulation affect the degree of competition in the market for airport shuttle services?
5. True or false? The assumptions of perfect competition are unrealistic, so the model is useless.
6. How would the following changes affect the market for sugar?
   (a) development of a new zero-calorie sweetener;
   (b) a cut in the wages of farm workers.
7. If the market price exceeds the equilibrium price, what will be the consequences?
8. If the market price is less than the equilibrium price, what will be the consequences?
9. How would the following changes affect the market for new apartments?
   (a) an increase in the price of building materials;
   (b) an increase in household incomes.
10. Under what circumstances would an increase in household incomes have the least effect on the market price of air travel? Please state conditions in terms of the price elasticities of demand and supply.
11. Suppose that wages in the hotel industry are rising at the rate of 3% a year. Explain why the effect of an increase in wages on hotel room rates depends on both the price elasticity of demand and the price elasticity of supply.
12. Consider the effect of an increase in demand on the market for restaurant meals. Compare the short-run changes in price and quantity with the long-run changes.
13. Consider the effect of a cut in mortgage rates on the market for new housing. Compare the short-run changes in price and quantity with the long-run changes.
14. True or false? Prices will be relatively less volatile in industries with substantial sunk costs. Explain your answer.
15. Compare two natural gas markets: in one, gas is supplied by pipeline, while in the other, gas is supplied by tanker. In which market would prices be relatively more volatile?

Discussion Questions

1. At times, a major problem for Japanese consumer electronics manufacturers has been the appreciation of the yen against the U.S. dollar. This means that the yen is more expensive in terms of the U.S. dollar.
   (a) Explain how the appreciation of the yen from ¥150 to ¥100 per U.S. dollar affects the wholesale cost of supplying Japanese consumer electronics to the United States.
   (b) Suppose that the Japanese yen rises by one-third against the U.S. dollar. Which of the following are plausible explanations of why the U.S. retail price of Japanese-made DVD players will rise by less than one-third: (i) the wholesale cost accounts for only part of retailers' costs, (ii) American retail demand for Japanese-made DVD players is inelastic, (iii) American retail supply of Japanese-made DVD players is inelastic?
   (c) How would the appreciation of the yen affect the price and sales of Korean DVD players in the United States?

2. Seasonal changes can affect demand and supply. In the market for fresh fruit and vegetables, the supply varies with the season. By contrast, in the market for heating oil, the demand varies with the season.

(a)   Using suitable demand and supply curves, explain how prices of fruit and vegetables would vary over the four seasons of the year.

(b)   Using suitable demand and supply curves, explain how the price of heating oil would vary through the seasons.

(c)   Referring to the U.S. Department of Agriculture, Economic Research Service (www.ers.usda.gov) Data Sets: Data Products by Title: Vegetable and Melons Yearbook Data tables, obtain monthly producer prices for vegetables in the most recent year. Referring to the U.S. Department of Energy, Energy Information Administration (www.eia.doe.gov) Historical Data Overview: Prices, obtain monthly refiner prices of no. 2 fuel oil for resale in the most recent year. Graph the two series and compare their seasonal variation. No. 2 fuel oil is the grade used for heating.

3. Using figure 5.3 as a basis, construct a series of four figures to show the effect of an increase in the demand for tanker service on the market price when (a) demand is extremely inelastic, (b) demand is extremely elastic, (c) supply is extremely inelastic, and (d) supply is extremely elastic.

4. Manufacturers of cardboard cartons and other packaging use a combination of wood pulp and wastepaper in production. The supply of wastepaper comes from households and businesses. An issue in environmental policy is the effectiveness of price incentives in encouraging recycling of wastepaper. The price elasticity of the demand for wastepaper has been estimated to be −0.07, while the price elasticity of the supply has been estimated to be 0 (*Source*: John A. Edgren and Kemper W. Moreland, "An Econometric Analysis of Paper and Wastepaper Markets," *Resources and Energy* 11 (1989), pp. 299–319).

(a)   Consider a government policy that reduces the price of wastepaper to manufacturers by 5%. How will this affect the quantity demanded?

(b)   Consider a government policy that increases the price of wastepaper to sellers by 5%. How will this affect the quantity supplied?

(c)   Are price incentives an effective way of increasing the recycling of wastepaper?

5. Industry researchers R.S. Platou predicted that, between 2003–04, oil prices would fall by 5%, production of oil by OPEC and the former Soviet Union would increase, and deliveries of new tankers would exceed scrappage of older vessels. (*Source*: *Platou Report 2004*, www.platou.com).

(a)   Using suitable diagrams, explain how each of the following would affect the market for tanker services: (i) a fall in oil prices; (ii) an increase in production by OPEC and the former Soviet Union; (iii) new tanker deliveries; and (iv) scrappage of older vessels.

(b)   Suppose that the net effect is to increase tanker rates. Illustrate the net effect on a single diagram. Explain the impact on the quantity of tanker services used.

(c)   In actuality, oil prices increased by 25% between 2003 and 2004 and OPEC and the former Soviet Union production increased by about 10%. Modify your analyses in (a) for these changes.

6. Housing is a sensitive issue in China. Many blame speculators for rapid increases in housing prices. To cool speculation, in May 2006, the China Banking Regulatory Commission publicly discouraged financial institutions from lending to investors buying more than one residential unit. The Commission was expected to raise the minimum down-payment for mortgage loans from 30% to 50%.

(a)   How do the following factors affect the demand for housing: (i) rising incomes, (ii) population growth, and (iii) trend away from multi-generational to single-generation households?

(b)   Is the supply of housing more elastic in the short run or in the long run?

(c)   How would the government's mortgage restrictions affect the rate of new construction, housing prices, and the housing stock in (i) the short run and (ii) the long run?

7. In 2002, Iraq's Kirkuk region exported 0.5–0.8 million barrels of crude oil per day (mpd) by pipeline to the Turkish port of Ceyhan. Following the U.S.-led coalition attack against Iraq, the pipeline was sabotaged and Kirkuk oil exports were disrupted. Refineries in western Europe switched to buying oil from the Urals in Russia, which produce oil that is chemically similar to Kirkuk.

Urals oil is shipped to western Europe by tanker from the Black Sea through the Bosporus and Dardanelles. However, by early 2004, the surge in European demand and congestion in the Bosporus and Dardanelles had lifted spot tanker rates to €39,000 per day (*Source*: "Bosporus Tanker Congestion Threatens Shortage of Oil," *Financial Times*, January 12, 2004).

(a)   Using suitable demand and supply curves, illustrate the short-run effects of pipeline disruption on the tanker services market.

(b)   Using your diagram for (a), illustrate the long-run effects of the pipeline disruption.

(c)   When political conditions in Iraq are restored to normal, exports by pipeline will resume, and the demand for tanker services will fall. With lower charter rates, the owner of a tanker must decide whether to continue operating, temporarily lay up, or scrap the vessel. Explain how the owner should choose among these alternatives.

8.   With January 1, 2000 heralding a new millennium, many predicted world wide shortages of champagne, lobster, and other New Year delicacies. New England and Canadian wholesalers began stockpiling lobsters in the first half of 1999. Boston dealer James Hook ordered 675,000 kilograms, 50% more than the previous year. The anticipated shortages, however, did not materialize. In early December, with just weeks to the New Year, the wholesale price of lobster fell 12% to $11.70 per kilogram (*Source*: "Lobster Dealers Net Meager Sales on New Year Celebration Stockpile," *Asian Wall Street Journal*, December 29, 1999, pp. 1 and 7).

(a)   On a suitable diagram, draw the long-run supply of lobster for New Year's Eve. In gauging the price elasticity of supply, note that lobster can be stockpiled for over 6 months.

(b)   Illustrate the effect of an increase in demand from 1998 to 1999. How would the increase in demand affect the price? How would the price effect depend on the price elasticity of supply?

(c)   Processors have developed a method to freeze whole lobsters in a plastic sleeve of brine that provides a quality almost equal to the fresh animal. How would this new technology affect the elasticity of long-run supply?

9.   Lexington Corporation is one of North Carolina's largest furniture manufacturers. North Carolina produces half of all home furniture used in the United States. Furniture manufacturing is intensive in wood, lumber, and labor. The furniture industry has faced fierce competition from Asian, and especially Chinese, manufacturers which have the advantage of lower labor costs. In 2003, Lexington closed Factory no. 1, the oldest company plant, located in Piedmont for over 100 years. The next year, it laid off 75 workers at Plant no. 5 in Lexington. Lexington itself has outsourced production to factories in Asia.

(a)   How is the demand for furniture related to sales of new and existing residential housing?

(b)   Compare the impact of a short-term vis-à-vis long-term appreciation of the Chinese Renminbi against the U.S. dollar on the North Carolina furniture industry.

(c)   How should Lexington decide between shutting down a plant and reducing capacity by laying off workers?

10.   This question applies the techniques for solving equilibrium explained in the math supplement. Let p and w represent the price of new construction (in dollars per square foot) and a laborer's wage (in dollars per hour), respectively. Further, let the demand for new construction be represented by the equation

$$D = 40 - p, \tag{5.2}$$

and the supply be represented by the equation

$$S = 5 + 1.5\,p - w. \tag{5.3}$$

All quantities are in millions of square feet a year.

(a)   Suppose that, initially, $w = 5$. Calculate the market equilibrium price and quantity.

(b)   Next, suppose that a laborer's wage increases to 7. Calculate the new market equilibrium price and quantity. Does the price of new construction increase by the same proportion as the increase in the wage?

Chapter 5

Math Supplement

Market Equilibrium

Earlier, we used graphs to analyze the equilibrium in the market for tanker service. To reinforce our understanding, we now derive the market equilibrium using algebraic methods. Let p and f represent the price of tanker service and the cost of fuel, respectively. Further, let the demand for tanker service be represented by the equation

$$D = 30 - 0.1\,p, \tag{5.4}$$

and the supply be represented by the equation

$$S = 4 + 0.05p - f. \tag{5.5}$$

Suppose that, initially, $f = 4$. Then, the supply equation simplifies to

$$S = 0.05p. \tag{5.6}$$

Before calculating the equilibrium, it is useful to graph the equilibrium. From the demand equation, when $D = 0$, $p = 30/0.1 = 300$, and when $p = 0$, $D = 30$. This gives us two points on the demand curve. Moreover, differentiating the demand equation with respect to price,

$$dD/dp = 0.1 \tag{5.7}$$

which means that the demand equation has a constant slope, or equivalently, that the demand curve is a straight line. This is enough information to draw the demand curve.

Similarly, we can draw the supply curve. From the supply equation, when $S = 0$, $p = 0$, and when $p = 200$, $S = 10$. Further, by differentiating the supply equation with respect to price, we can show that the supply curve is also a straight line. This completes figure 5.1.

In market equilibrium, the quantity demanded equals the quantity supplied, that is,

$$D = S. \tag{5.8}$$

Substituting from (5.4) and (5.6), this means

$$30 - 0.1\,p = 0.05p, \tag{5.9}$$

which implies that

$$p = 200 \tag{5.10}$$

and, hence, that

$$D = S = 10. \tag{5.11}$$

Therefore, as depicted in figure 5.1, the market equilibrium occurs at a price of $200 per ton-mile and quantity of 10 billion ton-miles.

Demand and Supply Shifts

We can also use an algebraic method to analyze the impact of shifts in demand or supply. Consider, for instance, the effect of a 15% drop in the cost of fuel. As the original cost is 4, the 15% drop will reduce the cost to $4 \times 0.85 = 3.40$. Substituting $f = 3.40$ in the supply equation (5.5)

$$S = 4 + 0.05p - 3.40$$
$$= 0.60 + 0.05p. \qquad (5.12)$$

In market equilibrium, the quantity demanded equals the quantity supplied: that is,

$$D = S. \qquad (5.13)$$

Substituting from (5.4) and (5.12), this means

$$30 - 0.1\,p = 0.60 + 0.05p, \qquad (5.14)$$

which implies that

$$p = 196 \qquad (5.15)$$

and, hence, that

$$D = S = 10.4. \qquad (5.16)$$

Therefore, as depicted in figure 5.2, the new market equilibrium occurs at a price of $196 per ton-mile and quantity of 10.4 billion ton-miles.

Chapter 6

Economic Efficiency

1 Introduction

In 1995, then Worldwatch Institute President Lester R. Brown famously warned "For the first time in History, the environmental collision between expanding human demand for food and some of the earth's natural limits will have an economic effect that will be felt around the world. . . . China's emergence as a massive grain importer . . . may well force a redefinition of security, a recognition that food scarcity and the associated economic instability are far greater threats to security than military aggression. . . . Rising food prices and the associated economic and political disruptions within China could bring that nation's economic miracle to a premature end."[1]

Having painted this ominous scenario, Mr. Brown called for urgent world wide action, including a tax on the consumption of meat, milk, eggs, and other livestock products. "If the 630 million tons of grain used for feed were reduced by 10 percent, by whatever means, it would free up 63 million tons of grain for consumption as food, enough to cover world population growth for 28 months."[2] He also called for land to be diverted from production of cotton to grain: "If consumers could be persuaded to replace half of the cotton clothing they buy with clothes made from synthetic fibers, some 9 million hectares of land would be freed up, providing enough grain for 11 months of world population growth."[3]

The government of China was sufficiently alarmed to curb exports and raise the procurement prices for wheat, soybeans, and corn above international levels. It even launched the "Governor's Grain Bag," a policy aimed to ensure that each province became self-sufficient in food.

What, in fact, happened? Referring to figure 6.1, in the case of wheat, a key grain, China's consumption and imports increased until 1996. At the same time, the price and production of wheat also increased in the U.S. However, from 1997 onward, China's consumption, imports,

---

[1] Lester R. Brown, *Who Will Feed China?* (New York: Norton, 1995), pp. 24, 32, 134. The following discussion is also based on Fred Gale, Francis Tuan, Bryan Lohmar, Hsin-Hui Hsu, and Brad Gilmour, *China's Feed and Agriculture: Issues for the 21st Century*, U.S. Department of Agriculture Economic Research Service Bulletin no. AIB775, April 2002; and Mark W. Rosegrant, Michael S. Painer, Siet Meijer, and Julie Witcover, *Global Food Projections to 2020*, International Food Policy Research Institute, Washington, DC, 2001.
[2] Brown, *Who Will Feed China?*, p. 140.
[3] Brown, *Who Will Feed China?*, p. 139.

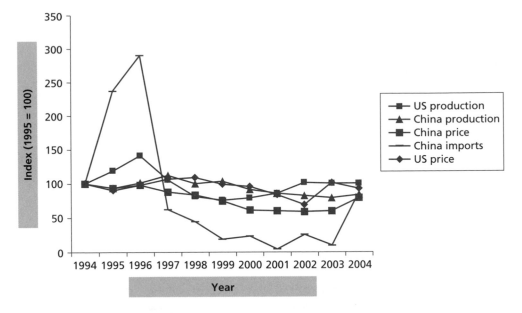

Figure 6.1   U.S. and China: wheat

and wheat prices fell, and soon thereafter, wheat production also declined. Only in 2003 and 2004 were there any increases, and these did not restore the 1995 levels.

Mr. Brown's ominous scenario did *not* materialize. An important reason is that the world production of wheat responded to the price increase. The price elasticity of the supply of wheat has been estimated to be 0.28 in China and 0.35 in developed countries. Accordingly, a 10% price increase would raise wheat production by 2.8% in China and 3.5% in developed countries.

In the presence of impending shortages, why do economists hail price increases as good news, although technology experts believe that they signal imminent disaster? How does free trade, such as between China and the U.S., improve the well-being of *all* participating nations? How would government price supports affect grain markets? And, how would government-dictated changes in food and clothing consumption affect consumer welfare?

A firm understanding of economic efficiency is important to every manager because it provides the intellectual foundation for the market system. We show that market prices allocate scarce resources in an economically efficient way. This efficiency is the reason why economists welcome the increases in the prices of items in short supply. The price increases motivate users to conserve and producers to expand supply.

The same concept of economic efficiency is also fundamental in management for two reasons. First, it provides a guide to managing resources within an organization. Second, it provides a guide to opportunities for profit. Whenever the allocation of resources is not economically efficient, there is a way to make money by resolving the inefficiency. This is a simple yet very powerful rule. In this chapter, we focus on the concept of economic efficiency. Later, in chapters 9, 12, and 13 on pricing, externalities, and asymmetric information, we apply the rule extensively to identify opportunities for profit in different contexts.

Finally, in this chapter, we apply the demand–supply framework and the concept of economic efficiency to two sets of issues in competitive markets. One is the impact of intermediation. We will address such questions as the impact of shifting transportation costs from buyers to sellers. A similar analysis will apply to the shifting of taxes between buyers and sellers. The other set of issues is the effect of price ceilings and floors. We will consider how these affect demand, supply, and market prices. We can use the analysis to predict the impact of government price supports on the markets for wheat and other essential grains.

2   Conditions for Economic Efficiency

Before discussing economic efficiency, we must define this concept. An allocation of resources is **economically efficient** if no reallocation of resources can make one person better off without making another person worse off. In this definition, persons may be human beings or businesses.

> An allocation of resources is **economically efficient** if no reallocation of resources can make one person better off without making another person worse off.

To appreciate the concept of economic efficiency, let us consider an allocation of resources that is not economically efficient. Then, by some reallocation of resources, it is possible to make one person better off without making another person worse off. Clearly, the original allocation of resources is undesirable. Accordingly, it seems very reasonable to aim for economic efficiency in the allocation of resources.

Sufficient Conditions

The concept of economic efficiency seems very reasonable. The definition, however, is difficult to apply in practice. It is easier to consider economic efficiency in terms of three sufficient conditions that are based on users' benefits and suppliers' costs.

An allocation of resources is economically efficient if, for every item,

1. all users achieve the same marginal benefit,
2. all suppliers operate at the same marginal cost,
3. every user's marginal benefit is equal to every supplier's marginal cost.

For economic efficiency, every product and resource – consumer as well as industrial, goods as well as services, and domestic as well as imported – must satisfy these conditions.

Let us review these three conditions in the context of Russian passenger airlines operating under central planning.

- *Equal marginal benefit.* The first condition for economic efficiency is that all users receive the same marginal benefit. Consider two people in the city of Novosibirsk, Siberia. Mikhail, a senior Communist party official, can take any number of flights anywhere in Russia free of charge. Raisa works in a factory and, every year, pays one month's wages for a flight to visit her family in Moscow. In this example, Mikhail will fly so much that the marginal flight provides almost no benefit. By contrast, Raisa's annual flight is worth at least one month's wages. If the Russian government reallocated a flight from Mikhail to Raisa, Mikhail's loss would be less than Raisa's gain, so society as a whole would be better off. This shows that an allocation of resources is economically efficient only if all users of a product achieve the same marginal benefit.
- *Equal marginal cost.* The second condition for efficiency is that all suppliers of an item must be operating at the same marginal cost. Suppose that the Central Planning Bureau has designated two airlines, Narodny Airways and Siberia Airlines, to serve the

Novosibirsk–Moscow route. Owing to higher fuel efficiency and better allocation of personnel, however, Siberia Airlines' marginal cost on the route is 10% lower than that of Narodny Airways. In this case, society as a whole could reduce the cost of airline travel while maintaining the number of flights if Siberia Airlines were to expand its services and Narodny Airways were to shrink. This shows that an allocation of resources is economically efficient only if all suppliers operate at the same marginal cost.

• *Marginal benefit equals marginal cost.* The final condition for efficiency ties together users and suppliers: for a resource allocation to be economically efficient, the users' marginal benefit must balance the suppliers' marginal cost. Suppose that, in accordance with a Russian government policy of encouraging migration to Siberia, the Central Planning Bureau allocated more aircraft, fuel, and human resources to the two airlines and ordered them to increase service. To fill the extra seats, the Central Planning Bureau had to distribute free airline tickets to all factories in the Novosibirsk area. Not all the free tickets were used, which indicates that, for some passengers, the marginal benefit of flying was 0.

Under these circumstances, the marginal benefit of flying to passengers will be lower than the airlines' marginal cost. Since marginal benefit is less than marginal cost, society overall could benefit by reducing the number of flights provided to Siberia. The cut in service will reduce the benefit by less than it reduces the cost. The difference between the marginal cost and the marginal benefit is a gain to society. Likewise, if the marginal benefit from some product exceeds the marginal cost of providing it, society should increase provision. Accordingly, an allocation of resouces is economically efficient only if users' marginal benefit balances suppliers' marginal cost.

Philosophical Basis

> **Technical efficiency** is the provision of an item at the minimum possible cost.

We have presented the concept of economic efficiency. Let us review two aspects of this concept. The first is the distinction between economic efficiency and technical efficiency. **Technical efficiency** means providing an item at the minimum possible cost. Technical efficiency alone, however, does not imply that scarce resources are being well used. For instance, an airline may be providing service at the minimum possible cost. These, however, may be flights that no one wants. The concept of economic efficiency extends beyond technical efficiency. For economic efficiency, the quantity of the item must be such that the marginal benefit equals the marginal cost.

The other important aspect of the concept of economic efficiency is that it assesses resource allocations in terms of each individual user's evaluation of the benefit. So, for instance, if air travelers strongly prefer non-stop flights and do not like stop-overs, the concept takes these preferences as a given in assessing the efficiency of resource allocation. By contrast, in a centrally planned economy, the central planners may disregard individual preferences and instead impose their own view of what people should or should not consume. For instance, the Central Planning Bureau may dictate that only senior Communist party officials should be allowed to fly non-stop.

Progress Check 6A Referring to the market for wheat, explain the difference between economic efficiency and technical efficiency.

Internal Organization

Let us now see how to apply the same concept of economic efficiency within an organization. Suppose that Saturn Bank has two divisions – commercial banking and individual banking. Each division takes deposits and makes loans. Saturn must decide how to allocate resources across the two divisions.

The concept of economic efficiency provides a guide to how Saturn should use its scarce resources. Production will be efficient if all users achieve the same marginal benefit, all suppliers operate at the same marginal cost, and every user's marginal benefit balances every supplier's marginal cost.

Let us explain these three conditions in the context of Saturn's two divisions. In this case, the users are the lending units and the suppliers are the deposit-taking units of the two divisions. The first condition for efficiency is that all users receive the same marginal benefit. This means that each of the company's lending units must get the same profit from an additional dollar of funds. If one lending unit could get more profit than another, the company should switch some funds to the lending unit that gets the higher profit. Then, the company's overall profit will be higher.

The second condition for efficiency is that all suppliers of an item must be operating at the same marginal cost. If one deposit-taking unit can produce funds at a lower marginal cost than another, then the company should direct the lower-cost deposit-taking unit to produce more and the higher-cost deposit-taking unit to produce less. This would increase the company's overall profit.

The final condition for efficiency is that the marginal benefit must balance the marginal cost. If the marginal benefit of funds to the lending unit is less than the marginal cost of producing the funds, then the company should cut back deposit-taking. The reduction in cost would be greater than the reduction in benefit, so overall profit would rise. By contrast, if the marginal benefit of funds is greater than the marginal cost, then the company should increase deposit-taking. The company will maximize profit when the marginal benefit equals the marginal cost.

The concept of economic efficiency is very useful. It provides a guide to making the best use of scarce resources within individual organizations as well as across entire economies.

3   Adam Smith's Invisible Hand

He intends only his own gain, and he is . . . led by an invisible hand to promote an end which was no part of his intention.[4]

Although published over 200 years ago, Adam Smith's insight is no less valid today. In a competitive market, buyers and sellers, all acting independently and selfishly, will channel scarce resources into economically efficient uses. The **invisible hand** that guides the multitude of buyers and sellers is the market price. This invisible hand is a simple and practical way of achieving economic efficiency.

> The **invisible hand** that guides multiple buyers and sellers, acting independently and selfishly, to channel scarce resources into economically efficient uses, is the market price.

---

[4]   Adam Smith, *The Wealth of Nations*, vol. II, book IV, p. 35, first published in 1776.

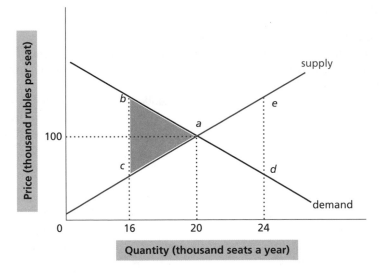

Figure 6.2 Air travel market
In equilibrium, the demand crosses the supply at a price of 100,000 rubles. Each consumer purchases up to the quantity where the marginal benefit is 100,000 rubles. Each provider supplies the quantity where marginal cost is 100,000 rubles.

Competitive Market

Suppose that Russia privatizes airline travel and, as a result, the Novosibirsk–Moscow route becomes a perfectly competitive market. Let us see how the invisible hand will work in this market. Demand comes from individual persons and supply from airlines. Figure 6.2 shows the market equilibrium with a price of 100,000 rubles and quantity of 20,000 seats a year.

On the demand side, as we explained in chapter 2, each person will buy enough to balance his or her marginal benefit with the price of travel, and this is true for every buyer. In a perfectly competitive market, all buyers face the same price; hence, their respective marginal benefits will be equal. This is the first condition for economic efficiency. Note that, in deciding on his or her purchases, every individual is acting selfishly – no one is thinking about economic efficiency.

What about the airlines? On the supply side, as we explained in chapter 4, each airline will expand up to the point where the marginal cost at a larger scale of operations just balances the price. This scale of operations maximizes profit. Again, in a perfectly competitive market, all airlines face the same price. Thus, with each airline selfishly maximizing profits, every airline will be operating at the same marginal cost. This is the second condition for economic efficiency.

We have seen that all buyers balance marginal benefit with price and all airlines balance marginal cost with price. But, in a market equilibrium, all buyers and all airlines face the same price. Therefore, marginal benefit and marginal cost must balance. This is the third condition for economic efficiency. So, a perfectly competitive market satisfies all three requirements for economic efficiency.

This example illustrates the power of Adam Smith's "invisible hand." The market price guides multiple buyers and sellers, all acting independently and selfishly, to achieve economic efficiency.

Market System

Adam Smith's invisible hand is the market price. A price performs two roles. First, it communicates all the necessary information: the price tells buyers how much to purchase and tells sellers how much to supply. Second, it provides a concrete incentive for each buyer to purchase the quantity that balances marginal benefit with the market price: by purchasing this quantity, the buyer achieves the maximum net benefit. Similarly, the price provides a concrete incentive for every seller to supply the quantity that balances marginal cost with the market price: by supplying this quantity, the seller maximizes its profit.

> The **market** or **price system** is the economic system in which resources are allocated through the independent decisions of buyers and sellers, guided by freely moving prices.

The name **market system** or **price system** describes an economic system in which resources are allocated through the independent decisions of buyers and sellers, guided by freely moving prices. The alternative names, market system or price system, recognize the key role of prices in markets. The role of the invisible hand in achieving economic efficiency is the intellectual foundation of the market system.

The invisible hand explains, in part, why China and eastern Europe abandoned central planning. Prior to World War II, East and West Germany were a single country with the same income throughout the nation. When Germany was defeated in 1945, it was divided into a western part that adopted a market system, and an eastern part that came under Communist central planning. After 50 years of central planning, East Germany had fallen far behind West Germany. It reunited with the west to regain an equal standard of living. The example of East and West Germany clearly proved the superiority of a market system in allocating resources. By switching to a market system, China and eastern Europe hoped to replicate the economic success of West Germany and other market economies.

Progress Check 6B Lester Brown forecast that China's continuing economic and population growth would lead to severe world wide shortages of grain. Explain how the invisible hand helped avoid this.

⊣ The limits to growth: 30 years afterward ⊢

One of the most influential books of the 1970s, *The Limits to Growth*, predicted that the world supply of oil would be exhausted by 2003. The book's scary prediction has not even come close to being realized. Far from presaging disaster, sharp increases in oil prices were a critical step by which resource markets adjusted to increasing consumption and diminishing stocks.

On the demand side, higher prices encouraged users to conserve, switch to other sources of energy, and use alternative materials. For instance, between 1975 and 2005, the average fuel efficiency of American light-duty vehicles rose by 60% from 13.1 to 21 miles per gallon.

On the supply side, higher prices stimulated producers to seek out new sources of supply, and encouraged businesses to develop new energy sources and alternative materials. Between 1973 and 2005, the world's proven reserves of oil increased by

106% from 577 to 1,189 billion barrels. Note that reserves increased even as the world continued to consume over 29 billion barrels of oil a year.

Dramatic increases in oil prices in 2005 and 2006 have prompted new warnings of impending exhaustion of the world's oil supplies. Calls for government regulation of oil prices and/or forced conservation of oil have increased. Is there any reason to believe the current "crisis" is different from the "crisis" of the 1970s?

Sources: Donella H. Meadows et al., *The Limits to Growth: A Report of the Club of Rome's Project on the Predicament of Mankind* (New York: Universe Books, 1972); U.S. Department of Transportation, Bureau of Transportation Statistics *National Transportation Statistics 2005*, www.bts.gov/ntda/nts/; *BP Statistical Review of World Energy, 2005*, www.bp.com/worldenergy/index.htm.

The invisible hand in government allocations: licenses for personal communications services and import quotas

The Federal Communications Commission (FCC) regulates telecommunications and broadcasting in the United States. As the electromagnetic spectrum is limited, one of the FCC's major responsibilities is to allocate licenses to use frequencies for wireless telecommunications and broadcasting. Until 1994, the FCC assigned licenses by administrative fiat. Administrative law judges held hearings to decide which of the many applicants deserved the limited number of licenses. When this method proved too time consuming, the FCC turned to allocating licenses by lottery. Some lotteries attracted over 500,000 applications!

In August 1993, with a view to developing a new source of revenue, Congress mandated the FCC to award licenses by competitive auction. The FCC adopted an auction procedure suggested by Stanford University professors Paul Milgrom and Robert Wilson and University of Texas (Austin) professor Preston McAfee. In July 1994, the auction for narrowband Personal Communications Services (PCS) licenses raised $617 million, while in March 1995, the auction for broadband PCS licenses raised $7.7 billion.

The 2000 auctions for "3G" licenses in OECD countries collected over $94 billion. This was a dramatic increase from $1 billion in 1999, and markedly higher than the $4 billion received in 2001. This "bubble" proved to be unsustainable – telecommunications operators reduced their intangible assets by $243 billion in 2001. Since the auction expenditures are sunk costs, they had severe financial consequences, but little real consequence for the use of the licenses.

There are two major differences between allocation by administrative fiat and by auction. One, as emphasized by governments, is revenue. The other is that the auction will be much more likely to assign licenses to the applicants with the highest marginal benefit. Those applicants will be willing to pay the highest bids. Even bankruptcy of bidders may still permit the spectrum licenses to be used by those with the highest marginal benefit. Thus far, secondary markets for auctioning unused spectrum (due to bankruptcy or other reasons) are relatively less developed.

When there is a limited number of items, it is economically efficient to allocate the items to the users with the highest marginal benefit. The auction will be more likely than administrative fiat to allocate licenses in an economically efficient way.

Auctions can be used in other government allocations as well. The European Union has adopted auctions for distributing quota rights. For example, licenses to import bananas used to be allocated through administrative methods and are now auctioned to the highest bidders. The World Bank estimated that the total value of the banana quotas is about $2 billion a year. This value is now being collected by the government, and more importantly, ensures that the import rights for bananas (and many other goods) go to the highest valued users.

Sources: Peter C. Cramton, "Money Out of Thin Air: The Nationwide Narrowband PCS Auction," *Journal of Economics and Management Strategy* 4 (1995), pp. 267–343; European Commission 1998, *OECD Communications Outlook, 2003 and 2005*; *Reforming the EU Banana Import Regime: Auctioning Import Licenses as the Best Option for a Sustainable Banana Industry.*

4 Decentralized Management

We have shown that the concept of economic efficiency can guide the best use of scarce resources within individual organizations as well as across whole economies. An entire economy can apply the invisible hand to achieve economic efficiency. Let us now see how an individual organization can also apply the invisible hand.

Internal Market

Recall that Saturn Bank needs to organize production and its use of funds. Suppose that there is a competitive market for funds. One approach is central planning: the bank headquarters can collect information about deposit-taking and lending unit costs and revenues from all lending units, and then decide how much funds each unit should accept and how much each lending unit should lend.

An alternative for Saturn is to decentralize management of deposit-taking in the following way. Saturn should direct the managers of every deposit-taking unit to maximize profit and sell funds at the market price, whether to the company's own lending units or outside buyers. Similarly, Saturn should direct every lending unit to maximize profit and allow them the freedom to procure funds from any source, whether it be one of the bank's own deposit-taking units or external to the bank.

As these sales are a transfer within the same organization, the corresponding price is called a **transfer price**. Saturn should set the transfer price for funds equal to the market price. With the decentralized policy, each lending unit will buy funds up to the point that its marginal benefit balances the market price. Since all lending units face the same market price, their marginal benefits will be equal. Similarly, each deposit-taking unit will produce up to the point that its marginal cost balances the market price. As all deposit-taking units face the same market price, their marginal costs will be equal.

> A **transfer price** is the price charged for the sale of an item within an organization.

Since the deposit-taking and lending units face the same market price, marginal benefit will be equal to marginal cost. Thus, the decentralized policy achieves the three conditions for economic efficiency within the same organization. Essentially, by decentralizing the management of funds, Saturn is establishing an internal market that is integrated with the external market.

Implementation

The Saturn Bank example illustrates two general rules that an organization should follow when decentralizing control over an internal resource. First, if there is a competitive market for the item, the transfer price should be set equal to the market price. If there is no competitive market for the item, then the appropriate transfer price is more complicated. We discuss transfer pricing more generally in chapter 7.

> **Outsourcing** is the purchase of services or supplies from external sources.

The second general rule of decentralized management is that producing units should be allowed to sell the product to outside buyers and consuming units should be allowed to buy the product from external sources. Purchase of services or supplies from external sources is described as **outsourcing**.

To explain why the right of outsourcing is crucial, suppose that Saturn required all lending units to source funds internally. Then, Saturn's deposit-taking units would have market power, and as we show in chapter 8, they would charge a price above the competitive market level. As a result, the lending units would no longer secure the economically efficient quantity of funds. A similar argument shows why it is necessary to allow producing units to sell the product to outside buyers.

Any organization that uses resources or products for which there are competitive markets can apply decentralization to achieve internal economic efficiency. For example, energy producers can apply the technique to manage production and use of crude oil and natural gas, and auto manufacturers can apply it to manage production and use of components.

Progress Check 6C Jupiter Electronics manufactures semiconductors, consumer electronics, and mobile phones. Explain how the company can use decentralization to ensure that its consumer electronics and mobile phone divisions can make efficient use of the output of the semiconductor division.

⊣ Sinopec: transfer pricing ⊢

China Petroleum & Chemical Corporation ("Sinopec") is an integrated energy and chemical company including Exploration and Production and Refining segments. It is listed on stock exchanges in Hong Kong, London, New York, and Shanghai.

Historically, the Chinese government regulated the domestic price of crude oil. In June 1998, the government relaxed its policy to allow buyers and sellers to negotiate prices. In January 2000, Sinopec revised its crude oil transfer pricing policy to align the prices for internal sales with those for external sales of similar grades.

Table 6.1 reports prices and sales volumes for Sinopec's Exploration and Production segment. Following the policy change, in 2000, the price for inter-segment sales

Table 6.1 Sinopec Exploration and Production segment

		1999	2000	2001	2002
Inter-segment sales	Price (yuan/ton)	901	1,640	1,385	1,360
	Volume (million tons)	27.41	27.19	31.27	28.98
External sales	Price (yuan/ton)	1,444	1,664	1,256	1,189
	Volume (million tons)	4.50	4.90	4.74	6.55
Operating profit (yuan billion)		3.9	24.7	23.2	14.8

Source: Sinopec, *Annual Reports*, various years.

leapt from 901 to 1,640 yuan per ton. Thereafter, the price for inter-segment sales followed the price for external sales closely.

When Sinopec changed its transfer pricing policy, the price for inter-segment sales increased sharply. However, the higher price appears to have had no effect on the *volume* of inter-segment sales. This suggests that the Exploration and Production segment had been limited in its sales to external buyers. It may have been required to meet the requirements of the Refining segment before selling externally.

5 Incidence

An important application of the demand–supply framework is to understand the impact of the costs of transportation, brokerage, and other forms of intermediation on the market for the final good or service.

For instance, a typical issue for manufacturers of industrial products is whether to include the cost of shipment in the price to the customer. One approach is to set an "ex-works" or "free on board" price and leave the customer to pay the freight, while the alternative is to charge a price including freight. Using the demand–supply framework, we will show that both pricing methods have exactly the same impact on the manufacturer and customer.

Freight Inclusive Pricing

We begin by considering the cement market with freight inclusive pricing. A price that includes freight is called **cost and freight**, abbreviated CF. In the market for cement, the buyers are building contractors and the sellers are cement manufacturers. Suppose that all manufacturers set CF prices that include a freight cost of 25 cents. The market price is $4.50 per bag,

> The **cost and freight (CF) price** includes the cost of delivery to the buyer.

at which price, the buyers purchase 1 billion bags a year. Figure 6.3 illustrates the market equilibrium at point *a*. In this equilibrium, the marginal benefit of cement is $4.50 per bag and the marginal cost (inclusive of freight) is also $4.50 per bag.

Ex-Works Pricing

Next, suppose that all cement manufacturers switch to *ex-works pricing*. An **ex-works price** does not include the freight cost: it literally means "the price at the gate to the works." Since the manufacturers no longer incur the 25-cent freight cost, the switch will shift the entire supply curve of cement

> The **ex-works price** does not include the cost of delivery to the buyer.

down by 25 cents. In figure 6.3, the entire supply curve shifts down because each manufacturer's marginal cost of supplying cement is reduced whatever the quantity that it actually supplies.

The switch to ex-works pricing also affects the market demand. With ex-works pricing, each buyer must pay 25 cents a bag to obtain the cement. In figure 6.3, this can be represented by shifting the entire retail demand curve down by 25 cents. To explain this shift, recall that the market demand curve is the horizontal sum of the individual demand curves. In turn, each buyer's demand curve shows the amount that the consumer is willing to pay for each bag of cement. Since each buyer must pay 25 cents in freight for every bag, the buyer's willingness to pay will be 25 cents lower at all quantities. This means that the entire demand curve will shift down by 25 cents.

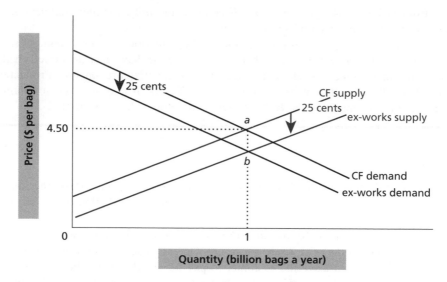

Figure 6.3 Pricing and freight cost
If all manufacturers switch to ex-works pricing, the supply curve shifts down by 25 cents and the demand also shifts down by 25 cents. The equilibrium quantity remains unchanged at 1 billion bags.

There is another way to confirm that the switch to ex-works pricing will shift down the demand curve. Consider the buyer of the 1 billionth bag. By the original demand curve, that buyer would be willing to pay exactly $4.50 for that bag. If, however, the buyer must incur a 25-cent freight cost, it will now be willing to pay $4.50 − $0.25 = $4.25 for the 1 billionth pound. The same 25 cent reduction in willingness to pay applies to all the inframarginal units as well. Hence, the entire demand curve shifts down by 25 cents.

In figure 6.3, the new demand and supply curves cross at point *b*. Relative to the original equilibrium at point *a*, the price is lower. The new demand curve is the original demand curve shifted down by 25 cents. Likewise, the new supply curve is the original supply curve shifted down by 25 cents. Hence, the new equilibrium point *b* must be vertically below the original equilibrium point *a*, and the vertical distance *ab* must be 25 cents.

Thus, in the new equilibrium, each buyer pays $4.25 to the seller and $0.25 in freight, making a "total price" of $4.25 + $0.25 = $4.50, which is exactly the price under freight-inclusive pricing. Further, the quantity of sales is exactly the same in the old and new equilibria. Generally, the price and sales are the same whether the sellers do or do not include the freight cost in their prices.

Further, in the new equilibrium, the marginal benefit of cement is $4.50 per bag, while the marginal cost (inclusive of freight) is also $4.50 per bag. Accordingly, from the viewpoint of economic efficiency, the new and old equilibria are identical.

Incidence

Incidence is the change in the price for a buyer or seller resulting from a shift in demand or supply.

When demand or supply shift, the consequent change in the price for a buyer or seller is called the **incidence** on that party. In the cement example, when manufacturers switch from freight-inclusive to ex-works pricing, the market price drops by 25 cents to $4.25; hence, the net effect on buyers is zero. This shows that, although the switch in pricing method requires buyers to "pay" the freight cost, there is no net effect after we consider adjustments in both demand and supply.

Equivalently, whether manufacturers set prices that do or do not include the freight cost, the incidence is the same. The incidence does not depend on which side – buyer or seller – initially pays the freight cost.

In fact, the incidence of the freight cost depends only on the price elasticities of demand and supply. This analysis reflects common sense. If sellers pay the freight cost, the buyers would be willing to pay a higher price. By contrast, buyers that must pay the freight cost would insist on paying less to sellers.

The distinction between receiving or paying an amount of money and the incidence of the receipt or payment is a very fundamental economic concept. We have applied this distinction in the context of industrial pricing. The distinction is also important for understanding the effect of brokerage fees and government taxes.

Using demand–supply analysis, it can be shown that, regardless of whether buyers or sellers pay brokerage fees, the market price and quantity will be the same, and there will be no impact on economic efficiency. Similarly, as we show next, regardless of whether a tax is initially imposed on buyers or sellers, the market price and quantity will be the same. The incidence of brokerage fees and taxes depends only on the price elasticities of demand and supply.

Progress Check 6D Using figure 6.3 as a basis, construct a series of four figures to compare the market equilibria with freight-inclusive pricing and ex-works pricing when (a) demand is extremely inelastic, (b) demand is extremely elastic, (c) supply is extremely inelastic, and (d) supply is extremely elastic.

Taxes

Governments depend on tax revenues to support public services such as national defense, administration of justice, and public health. Some taxes are levied on consumers, others on businesses, and some are levied on both. For instance, the United States government imposes an airport tax on airlines for every passenger that they carry. The September 11 security fee is $2.50 one-way ($5 for multi-leg trips). By contrast, many Asian governments collect the airport tax from the passenger. What difference would it make if the U.S. government switched to the Asian system?

To address this question, we must first understand the impact of taxes on a market. Let us apply the demand–supply framework to investigate the effect of taxes on market price and quantity. Specifically, suppose that the U.S. government levies a $10 tax on airline tickets. How would this affect the market for air travel between Chicago and Paris?

Buyer's vis-à-vis Seller's Price

We assume that the market is perfectly competitive. The demand comes from business and leisure travelers, while American and foreign airlines provide the supply. Since this market is subject to a tax, it is necessary to make one change to the usual demand–supply analysis. We must distinguish the price that buyers pay (buyer's price) from the price that sellers receive (seller's price). The seller's price is the buyer's price minus the amount of the tax.

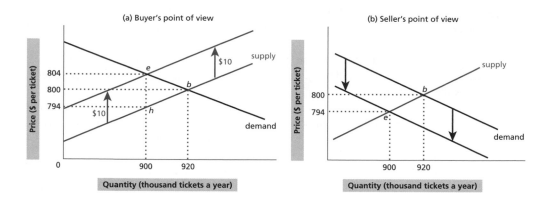

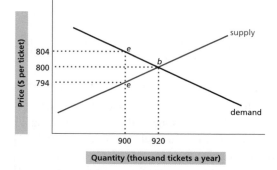

Figure 6.4   Airline travel tax
The tax of $10 per ticket (a) raises the marginal cost of supplying air travel, (b) reduces the willingness to pay by $10, or (c) drives a $10 wedge between buyers' willingness to pay and the marginal cost of air travel. In all these cases the buyers end up paying $804, the sellers keep $794, and the quantity is reduced to 900,000 tickets a year.

We draw the demand and supply curves in figure 6.4. Suppose that, initially, there is no tax on airline tickets and the equilibrium is at point *b*, with a price of $800. Since there is no tax, $800 is the buyer's price as well as the seller's price. At the price of $800, airlines sell 920,000 tickets a year.

Now the federal government requires airlines to pay a tax of $10 on each ticket. Refering to figure 6.4, we can represent this graphically in one of three equivalent ways: (a) we can shift the supply curve vertically up by $10, showing the market from airline buyers' point of view; (b) we can shift the demand curve vertically down by $10, showing the market from airlines' point of view; or (c) we shift neither demand nor supply, but show the $10 tax as a wedge between the demand and supply curves.

As a result of the tax, there will be a new equilibrium at point *e* in each diagram, with a price of $804 and quantity of 900,000 tickets a year. The price is higher and the quantity of travel is smaller. Now that there is a tax, the buyer's price differs from the seller's price. The buyer's price is $804, while the seller's price is the buyer's price less the $10 tax, or $794. In the new equilibrium, the seller's price of $794 is lower than the original seller's price with no tax, which was $800.

Tax Incidence

What determines the extent to which the buyer's price increases, the seller's price falls, and the quantity falls? In general, the effect on prices and quantity depends on the price elasticities of demand and supply. With moderate demand and supply elasticities, the buyer's price will rise by less than the amount of the tax, the seller's price will drop by less than the amount of the tax, and the quantity will fall by some amount.

We are now ready to address the introductory question of the effects of a switch to collecting an airport tax from passengers rather than airlines. This is just one specific case of the general issue of whether a tax should be imposed on the buyers or the sellers.

Obviously, there may be differences in administrative costs and perhaps psychological differences between collecting the tax from passengers rather than airlines. For instance, since there are relatively fewer airlines than passengers, it may be less costly to collect the tax from airlines.

Aside from administrative and psychological differences, however, we claim that the effect of a tax will be the same, whether it is collected from the buyers or the sellers. Further, the tax is generally shared between buyers and sellers according to their relatively price elasticities. The side of the market that is relatively less sensitive to price changes will bear the relatively larger portion of the tax. Generally, the effect of a tax will be the same, whether it is collected from the buyers or the sellers.

> **Progress Check 6E** In figure 6.4, draw in a more inelastic demand curve. How does this affect the incidence of tax on travelers relative to airlines?

Promoting retail sales: cents-off coupons

Some consumer marketing consultants suggest that cents-off coupons are more effective in lowering retail prices than cuts in wholesale prices. According to this suggestion, manufacturers should distribute coupons widely. Then, when consumers make purchases, they can redeem the coupons and get the full price reduction. This argument, however, overlooks the possibility that retailers will raise their prices when consumers use coupons. So, are coupons more effective than direct cuts in wholesale prices?

To address this question, we consider the retail market for a brand of shampoo, where consumers provide the demand and competitive grocery stores provide the supply. Figure 6.5 illustrates the market equilibrium at point s, with a price of $4 per bottle and quantity of 500 million bottles a year.

First, we suppose that the manufacturer cuts the wholesale price of its shampoo by 25 cents. In the retail market, this wholesale price cut will shift the supply curve down by 25 cents. The entire supply curve shifts down because the wholesale price cut affects retailers' marginal costs of supplying the shampoo at all quantities. The cut in the wholesale price does not affect the retail demand. At the new equilibrium (point t), the price is lower and the quantity of sales is higher. Suppose that the price is $3.80 and the quantity is 550 million bottles a year.

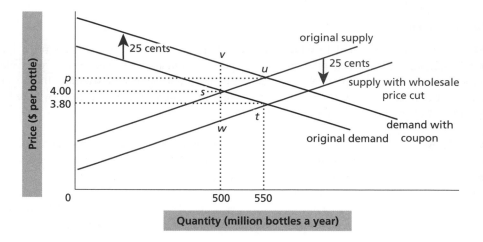

Figure 6.5 Wholesale price cut vis-à-vis coupons
If the wholesale price is cut by 25 cents, the retail supply curve shifts down by 25 cents and the quantity increases to 550 million bottles. If every consumer uses a 25-cent coupon, the retail demand curve shifts up by 25 cents and the quantity increases to 550 million bottles. In both cases, the effective retail price and sales are the same.

Next, suppose that, instead of cutting the wholesale price, the manufacturer maintains the wholesale price, while distributing 25-cent coupons to all consumers. Supposing that every consumer will cash in a 25-cent coupon for every bottle purchased, the consumer's willingness to pay will be 25 cents higher at all purchase levels. This means that each consumer's and hence the market demand curve will shift up by 25 cents.

The coupons, however, do not affect the supply curve. Referring to figure 6.5, the new demand curve crosses the original supply curve at point u. Relative to the original equilibrium, the price is higher, and the quantity of sales is higher.

In figure 6.5, compare the triangle vsu with the triangle swt. Line sv represents a 25-cent upward shift of the demand curve, and line sw represents a 25-cent downward shift of the supply curve. Accordingly, lines sv and sw are of equal length.

Curve st is a segment of the original demand curve, and curve vu is the same segment shifted up by 25 cents. Further, curve su is a segment of the original supply curve, and curve wt is the same segment shifted down by 25 cents. Accordingly, the triangles vsu and swt must be identical. This means that the point u must be vertically above the point t and the vertical distance tu must be 25 cents. Since the quantity at point t is 550 million bottles, the quantity at point u also is 550 million bottles.

Since the price at point t is \$3.80, the price at point u must be \$3.80 + 0.25 = \$4.05. This is the retail price with coupons. Hence, the effective price to consumers is \$4.05 − 0.25 = \$3.80. The effective price with a coupon is identical to the price when the manufacturer directly cuts the wholesale price by 25 cents. This means that, in the new equilibrium, the price and sales are the same whether the manufacturer cuts the wholesale price or all consumers use coupons.

Assuming that all consumers use coupons, there is no difference between coupons and a direct cut in the wholesale price. Hence, there must be a different reason for using coupons. In chapter 9 on Pricing Policy, we explain how coupons can be used to discriminate between consumers with different willingness to pay for a product.

⊣ Taxation of mobile telephony in emerging markets ⊢

The prices of cell phones have been steadily falling: from $50 at the beginning of 2004 to an estimated $20 in 2007. Although the price is dropping, taxes have become a barrier to increased sales. Cell phones are taxed in several ways. Most countries charge a value-added tax (VAT) and many impose customs duties on imported phones (e.g., 45.6% in Syria). Other taxes may also be imposed. Taxes will generally impact usage. For example, monthly subscriber growth in Bangladesh fell from 11% to 7% after the introduction of a $14 connection tax in June 2005.

A recent study examined taxes on mobile phones and their usage in 50 emerging markets, comprising 4.83 billion people (80% of the world's total population and 50% of all mobile subscribers). Taxes as a share of total mobile service costs ranged from 3% in China to 55% in Turkey, with an average of around 20%. Using elasticity estimates of −0.5 for mobile penetration with respect to subscription and usage fees, −0.5 to −0.76 for mobile minutes with respect to the price per minute, and −1.04 for legitimate handsets with respect to the price of legitimate handsets, the study estimated the effects of cutting various taxes on mobile telephony.

The study found that cutting the telecommunications-specific taxes (24% of the total tax on mobile phones) would increase subscribers by 8%. A 1% reduction in the VAT was estimated to lead to a 2.4% increase in subscription. Exempting handsets and services from the VAT would increase mobile penetration by 9.8% to 19.6%.

Sources: "Making the Connection," September 29, 2005, *The Economist*; "Tax and the Digital Divide," GSM Association Mobile Tax Report.

6 Summary

The central idea in this chapter was Adam Smith's invisible hand. Free-market competition will ensure that the allocation of resources is economically efficient. Although the buyers and sellers act selfishly, the net outcome is at least as good as the best efforts of the most enlightened and well-informed central planner.

The same principle applies within an organization. Through decentralization, management can achieve efficient use of scarce internal resources. This means charging a transfer price for items produced and consumed within the organization.

It is important to distinguish a payment or receipt from incidence. A payment or receipt can be shifted from one to the other side of the market. Incidence is fundamental and depends only on the elasticities of demand and supply. As an example, the incidence of taxes generally does not depend on whether the tax is collected from the buyers or the sellers in a market. It will be shared, according to the relatively elasticities of demand and supply, in either case.

Key Concepts

economic efficiency	outsourcing	transfer price
technical efficiency	cost and freight price	tax incidence
invisible hand	ex-works price	
market or price system	incidence	

Further Reading

For a vigorous rebuttal of the doomsday scenarios painted by some environmentalists, read Bjorn Lomborg's *The Skeptical Environmentalist* (Cambridge, UK: Cambridge University Press, 2001).

Review Questions

1. In 1987, Soviet leader Mikhail Gorbachev complained that children were kicking bread in games of football. Consider this observation in terms of the conditions for economic efficiency. Note that bread was subsidized.

2. The external auditor of the local school system has found that some schools are paying 20% more for cleaning services than other schools in the same area. Which condition of economic efficiency is being violated?

3. Consider a competitive labor market. Explain how the invisible hand ensures that the allocation of labor is economically efficient.

4. In a Communist system, all resources are allocated by a central planning agency. If no resources are scarce, would central planning be less effective than a market system?

5. Using relevant examples, explain the concept of a transfer price.

6. Venus Fruit produces apples that the company uses to make juice as well as for sale to external customers. The apple market is perfectly competitive. How much should Venus charge the juice division for apples?

7. Regulated firms often sell wholesale services to competitors as well as using such services internally to produce a downstream retail service. Regulators usually require that such firms pay themselves the same price for these wholesale services as they charge competitors. Does this requirement impose a burden on the regulated firm?

8. Venus Paper is cutting the wholesale price of its tissues. Which of the following situations is better for consumers?

   (a) There are many other attractive brands, and hence the retail demand for Venus tissue is very elastic.

   (b) Venus tissue is quite special and has an inelastic demand.

9. On-line air reservations avoid the use of intermediary services, such as travel agents. Who benefits from the avoidance of these costs?

10. If e-commerce retailers offer free shipping, what would be the effect on the retail demand and supply?

11. Explain the difference between the payment and incidence of a gasoline tax.

12. The market for telephones is competitive. Demand is very inelastic, while supply from factories in Asia is very elastic. Suppose that the government were to impose a tax on telephones. How much will this affect a manufacturer of telephones?

13. The state of Pennsylvania has a 5% state sales tax and the city of Philadelphia has an additional 1% city sales tax. Delaware, less than 30 miles from Philadelphia has no state sales tax. When a buyer purchases a $1,000 stereo in a Philadelphia electronics store, who pays the sales tax?

14. In times of budget crises, governments often apply special taxes to luxury items, such as expensive new boats, cars, and aircraft. The logic is that only rich individuals and corporations purchase such items and they can afford to bear the additional tax burden. Assess the validity of this belief.

15. In the late 1970s, there were tax credits (up to 70%) for households that installed solar energy systems. As a result the solar industry expanded rapidly, only to contract sharply when the credits expired. Supposea household installed a $10,000 solar system and received a $7,000 tax credit for its installation. Discuss who effectively received the $7,000 tax credit by thinking about supply and demand conditions in the solar market.

Discussion Questions

1. The Japanese consume relatively more fish and less meat than people in other developed countries. In 1995, then Worldwatch Institute President Lester R. Brown pronounced "[I]f the Chinese were to consume seafood at the same rate as the Japanese do, China would need the annual world fish catch." (*Source*: Brown, *Who Will Feed China?*, p. 30.)
   (a) Compare the Japanese marginal benefit from eating fish with that of other people. Which aspect of the philosophical basis of economic efficiency did Mr. Brown overlook?
   (b) How would increases in the Chinese demand for fish affect the world price of fish and Japanese fish consumption?
   (c) Is it likely that China would consume the entire world fish catch?

2. Tickets to popular sporting events, like the FIFA World Cup and the Super Bowl, often sell out. Devoted fans must either spend long hours waiting in line for a limited supply of tickets or pay a premium price to scalpers or touts. Scalpers and touts buy tickets to resell.
   (a) When tickets sell out, which condition(s) for economic efficiency might not be satisfied?
   (b) Do scalpers and touts improve economic efficiency?

3. Consider a company that manages a network of hospitals across several counties in one state. Household incomes and the cost of living are higher in urban than rural areas. The company, however, has set the same prices for pharmaceuticals and services in all of its hospitals. It has also paid the same salaries for doctors, nurses, and other professional staff throughout the state.
   (a) Management has noticed that there are long waiting lists for treatment at its urban hospitals. Can you explain this problem?
   (b) The company has had great difficulty in recruiting professional staff for its urban hospitals. Can you explain this problem?
   (c) What advice would you give to management?

4. LaGuardia Airport is one of three major airports that serve New York City. The heavy demand for flights to and from the airport has caused systematic delays. The entry of new carriers and expansion of service by existing carriers would increase congestion. In 2000, the airport authority decided to allocate a limited number of new takeoff and landing slots among the various airlines by lottery. Incumbent carriers that had been allocated slots were allowed to retain them.
   (a) With a limited number of takeoff and landing slots allocated among the various airlines by lottery, which condition for economic efficiency might be violated?
   (b) Explain how the following measures would increase efficiency: (i) giving the incumbent carriers ownership over their slots and allowing them to lease or sell their slots, (ii) Auctioning the right to new slots.

5. Consider a company that operates silver mines in Colorado and Peru. Until recently, corporate headquarters set production targets for each mine based on average production costs. Then, management consultants recommended a new policy: each mine must aim to maximize profits given the prevailing price of silver.
   (a) Under the company's old production policy, which condition(s) for economic efficiency might not be satisfied?
   (b) Does the new production policy improve economic efficiency?
   (c) Explain the role of price under the new policy.

6. China Petroleum & Chemical Corporation ("Sinopec") is an integrated energy and chemical company including Exploration and Production and Refining segments. In January 2000, Sinopec revised its crude oil transfer pricing policy to align the prices for internal sales with those for external

sales of similar grades. Table 6.1 reports prices and sales volumes for Sinopec's Exploration and Production segment.

(a)   Compare the prices and sales volumes for inter-segment and external sales before and after the policy change.

(b)   Suppose that Sinopec's Exploration and Production segment had been maximizing its segment profit. Comment on your findings in (a).

(c)   Suppose instead that the Exploration and Production segment had been directed to meet the requirements of the Refining segment before selling externally. What are the shortcomings of such a policy?

(d)   Explain how Sinopec should decentralize inter-segment sales.

7.   Typical real-estate broker: "In California, the seller always pays the broker's commission, so, buyers get brokerage services free."

   MBA: "If the custom were for the buyer to pay the commission, then would sellers get brokerage services free?"

   Real-estate broker, clearly losing patience: "That is a purely hypothetical scenario, but if that situation were to arise, yes, I guess you're right."

(a)   Assume that each seller pays a brokers' commission of $18,000. Then, the supply of houses includes the cost of brokerage. Illustrate the market equilibrium with a price of $310,000 per house and sale of 200,000 houses a year.

(b)   Now suppose that buyers rather than sellers pay the $18,000 commission. Using your figure, illustrate the following: (i) shift the supply curve down by $18,000 since sellers do not pay the commission, and (ii) shift the demand curve down by $18,000 since buyers now pay the commission.

(c)   Compare the market equilibria of (a) and (b) in terms of (i) the net price received by sellers and (ii) the net price paid by buyers. (Net prices are net of brokerage commission, if any.)

8.   Many e-commerce sites include free shipping while others assess shipping charges separately. For example, a recent search for a Sony high definition TV found that bajangles.com offered free shipping, while MBsuperstore charged $299.50 for shipping (to Alaska).

(a)   If consumers view these sellers as equivalent (in terms of quality of service), how should their prices for the same TV compare?

(b)   Prices for the same 60-inch rear projection TV were $2,968.99 at bajangles.com and $2,692.95 at MBsuperstore (priced on July 10, 2006). Does this comport with your answer in (a)?

(c)   A search of 30 stores for this TV revealed that prices ranged from $2,639 to $4,000, while shipping charges ranged from $0 to $315. How can you explain this?

9.   United States federal income tax is progressive: the higher your income, the higher your tax rate. Skilled workers are generally paid higher wages than unskilled worders, and so pay more income tax on average.

(a)   Consider the markets for skilled and unskilled workers. How do the elasticities of demand and supply compare in these two markets?

(b)   Suppose there was a flat $10,000 tax on annual income. Compare the effective tax incidence on skilled and unskilled labor.

(c)   Suppose there was a flat 20% tax on annual income. Compare the effective tax incidence on skilled and unskilled labor.

   Use a diagram (such as figure 6.4) in your answers.

10.   In Switzerland, the federal government levies a social security tax, partly on employers and partly on employees. Employers and employees pay equal percentages of the employee's salary in tax.

(a)   Using relevant demand–supply analysis, explain the effect of the social security tax on wages, employment, and the buyer and seller surpluses.

(b) Suppose that the government changed its policy and decided to collect the entire tax from employees. How would this new policy benefit employers?

11. E-commerce is predicted to reduce the cost of intermediary services such as those of travel agencies, real-estate brokers, and investment advisors. Consider the market for air travel. Suppose that, with conventional travel agencies, the market equilibrium price is $300 per ticket, including a $15 intermediation cost. The quantity bought is two million tickets a year. With e-commerce, however, the intermediation cost falls to $2 per ticket.

(a) Using suitable demand and supply curves, illustrate the original equilibrium with conventional travel agencies. Represent the intermediation cost by shifting the supply curve.

(b) Illustrate the new equilibrium with e-commerce.

(c) What factors determine the extent to which consumers will benefit from e-commerce? Explain your answer with demand and supply curves.

Part II

Market Power

Part III

Market Power

Chapter 7

Costs

1 Introduction

Airbus and Boeing compete in manufacturing large commercial airliners. Airbus's product line includes the A330, A340, and the mammoth A380 which first flew in April 2005. In 2005, Airbus received orders for 1,111 aircraft and earned revenue of €22.3 billion. Boeing's product line includes the 737, 777, and 747. In 2005, Boeing received orders for 1,031 aircraft and earned revenue of $22.7 billion from sales of commercial aircraft.

In April 2004, Boeing launched the new 787 Dreamliner with 50 firm orders from All Nippon Airways of Japan. The deal was worth about $6 billion at list prices, with deliveries scheduled to begin in 2008. With domestic and international capacity of 70.0 billion and 25.4 billion available seat kilometres respectively, All Nippon Airways is a major Japanese and international carrier.

Boeing had earlier denoted the 787 Dreamliner as the 7E7, and targeted the new plane at the market segment of twin-engine medium- to long-range jets with capacity of 200–300 passengers. The 787 is a completely new design with a development cost estimated at $8–10 billion.

In December 2004, following considerable speculation, Airbus announced that it would develop the A350 to compete with Boeing's 787. The A350 was planned to be a derivative of the existing A330, enhanced with a new wing, more fuel-efficient engines, and other new technologies. The development cost was estimated to be just €4 billion.

At that time, Boeing had secured just 52 firm orders, far below its target of 200 orders by the end of 2004. Richard Aboulafia of industry consultants Teal Group remarked that Airbus had succeeded in its goal of "disrupt[ing] the business case for the 7E7."[1] Airbus Chief Commercial Officer John Leahy predicted that the A350 would attract a substantial number of Boeing customers and "put a hole in Boeing's Christmas stocking."[2]

However, in 2005, orders for the Boeing 787 gathered momentum. One of the new customers was Northwest Airlines, which placed a firm order for 18 Boeing 787s and secured options for 50 additional planes. The deal was worth about $2.2 billion at list prices. The planes were to be delivered between 2008 and 2010.

---

[1] "Airbus Pushes Ahead with Rival to 7E7," *Seattle Post-Intelligencer*, December 11, 2004.
[2] "A350: Airbus's Counter-Attack," *Flight International*, January 25, 2005.

Northwest Airlines and Northwest Airlink operate a total of 1,200 flights daily from hubs in Detroit, Minneapolis/St. Paul, Memphis, Tokyo and Amsterdam. With capacity of 91.4 million available seat-miles and operating revenue of $12.3 billion in 2005, Northwest Airlines is one of the world's largest carriers. Yet, in recent years, Northwest has consistently incurred losses. In 2005, Northwest's operating loss was $919 million, while its net loss was $1.376 billion. Northwest's losses have been aggravated by a sharp and sustained increase in oil prices.

How could Airbus develop the A350 so much more cheaply than Boeing's cost of developing the 787? In what sense had Airbus succeeded in disrupting the business case for the Boeing 787? Why was Northwest buying new planes amidst continuing losses?

For many important business decisions – including pricing, deciding whether to outsource, assessing performance, and planning investments – managers must have accurate information about costs. In chapter 4, we introduced concepts of fixed, variable, marginal, and average costs. Now, we build on that foundation and develop concepts particularly relevant to businesses with market power.

We first analyze three drivers that could affect operational costs – they are the scale and scope of the business and accumulated experience. Economies of scope across the development of multiple products explain why Airbus expected to develop the A350 at substantially lower cost than Boeing's cost of developing the 787. The experience curve can explain why it was essential for Boeing to meet its target of 200 orders for the 787.

Then, we apply the principle of relevance – that, in operational decisions, managers should consider only relevant costs and ignore all others. To identify what costs are relevant, a manager needs to consider the alternative courses of action. This approach will reveal costs not shown in accounting statements, called *opportunity costs*. This approach also reveals that some expenses shown in accounting statements, called *sunk costs*, are not relevant. The concept of sunk costs explains Northwest Airlines' decision to order new planes despite sustained losses in the past.

2   Economies of Scale

A fundamental issue for any business is whether to operate on a small scale or large scale. Large-scale production means mass marketing and relatively low pricing; by contrast, small-scale production is associated with niche marketing and relatively high pricing. Here, we shall analyze how costs depend on the scale or rate of production. (We shall treat the *scale* and *rate* of production as synonymous.) It is important, however, to note that the decision on scale also depends on market demand and competition. We will analyze these factors in chapters 8 and 10.

To understand how costs depend on the scale of production, let us recall the distinction between the fixed and variable costs introduced in chapter 4. The *fixed cost* is the cost of inputs that do not change with the production rate. The *variable cost* is the cost of inputs that change with the production rate.

In chapter 4, we introduced fixed and variable costs in a short-run planning horizon. The same distinction applies in the long run as well and explains how costs depend on the scale of production.

Fixed and Variable Costs in the Long Run

To illustrate the distinction between long-run fixed and variable costs, let us consider the production of a layout of a newspaper, the *Daily Globe*. The production process begins when

Table 7.1 Daily expenses

Daily production (thousands)	Labor	Printing press	Ink and paper	Electric power	Total
0	$5,000	$1,000	$0	$200	$6,200
10	$5,000	$1,500	$1,200	$300	$8,000
20	$5,000	$2,000	$2,400	$400	$9,800
30	$5,000	$2,500	$3,600	$500	$11,600
40	$5,000	$3,000	$4,800	$600	$13,400
50	$5,000	$3,500	$6,000	$700	$15,200
60	$5,000	$4,000	$7,200	$800	$17,000
70	$5,000	$4,500	$8,400	$900	$18,800
80	$5,000	$5,000	$9,600	$1,000	$20,600
90	$5,000	$5,500	$10,800	$1,100	$22,400

the printing department receives a photographic negative containing the text of the forthcoming edition. The negative is "burned" on to an aluminum plate, which is then mounted on electric-powered printing presses. The presses can be switched on and fed a continuous flow of newsprint and ink to produce the newspaper.

Table 7.1 reports the daily expenses for production rates up to 90,000 copies a day, in the four categories of labor, printing press, ink and paper, and electric power. For simplicity, we ignore other costs.

Consider each category of expense. The cost of labor is $5,000, and does not vary with the size of the print run. The labor required to produce the paper is the same whether the newspaper plans to print 10,000 or 90,000 copies a day. Accordingly, the labor is a fixed cost of newspaper production.

Next, the cost of the printing press ranges from $1,000 with no production up to $5,500 at a production rate of 90,000. The cost of the press includes a fixed cost of $1,000. The remainder is a variable cost.

The cost of ink and paper is nothing with no production; hence, this item is completely variable. For a print run of 10,000 copies, the cost of ink and paper is $1,200, while for a run of 20,000 copies, the cost is $2,400. The cost of ink and paper is proportional to the production rate.

The cost of electricity is also partly fixed and partly variable. There is a $200 cost of power for lighting which does not vary with the production rate. It is a fixed cost. By contrast, the cost of powering the presses is variable. It increases by $100 for every 10,000 copy increase in the production rate.

In table 7.2, we assign the costs of newspaper production – labor, printing press, ink and paper, and electric power – into the two categories of fixed and variable costs. There is a fixed cost of $6,200. A substantial fixed cost is a fact in producing a newspaper. The industry has given the name *first copy cost* to the fixed cost. It is the cost of producing just one copy a day.

By contrast, as the print run increases from 0 to 90,000 copies a day, the variable cost rises from nothing to $16,200. By distinguishing between fixed and variable costs, the management of a business can understand which cost elements will be affected by changes in the scale of production.

Table 7.2   Analysis of fixed or variable costs

Daily production (thousands)	Fixed cost	Variable cost	Total cost	Marginal cost	Average fixed cost	Average variable cost	Average cost
0	$6,200	$0	$6,200				
10	$6,200	$1,800	$8,000	$0.18	$0.62	$0.18	$0.80
20	$6,200	$3,600	$9,800	$0.18	$0.31	$0.18	$0.49
30	$6,200	$5,400	$11,600	$0.18	$0.21	$0.18	$0.39
40	$6,200	$7,200	$13,400	$0.18	$0.16	$0.18	$0.34
50	$6,200	$9,000	$15,200	$0.18	$0.12	$0.18	$0.30
60	$6,200	$10,800	$17,000	$0.18	$0.10	$0.18	$0.28
70	$6,200	$12,600	$18,800	$0.18	$0.09	$0.18	$0.27
80	$6,200	$14,400	$20,600	$0.18	$0.08	$0.18	$0.26
90	$6,200	$16,200	$22,400	$0.18	$0.07	$0.18	$0.25

Marginal and Average Costs

Applying the analysis of fixed and variable costs, we can see how costs depend on the scale of production. In chapter 4, we also introduced the concepts of marginal and average costs. Recall that the marginal cost is the change in total cost due to the production of an additional unit. The average (or unit) cost is the total cost divided by the production rate or scale.

Let us study the marginal and average costs of production of the *Daily Globe*. Referring to table 7.2, as the print run increases from 0 to 90,000 copies a day, the total cost of production increases from $6,200 to $22,400.

The marginal cost of the first 10,000 copies is $8,000 − $6,200 = $1,800, or $1,800/10,000 = 18 cents per copy. The marginal cost is constant at 18 cents at all scales of production. From chapter 4, we know that the marginal cost equals the rate of change of the variable cost. For the *Daily Globe*, the average variable cost remains constant at 18 cents per copy. Hence, the marginal cost is also constant at 18 cents per copy.

Dividing total cost by the scale of production, we can obtain the average cost. The average cost drops from 80 cents at a scale of 10,000 copies a day to 25 cents at 90,000 copies a day. To understand why the average cost decreases with the scale of production, recall that the average cost is the average fixed cost plus the average variable cost. The average fixed cost is the fixed cost divided by the production scale. With a larger scale of production, the fixed cost will be spread over more units of production and the average fixed cost will be lower.

The average variable cost is constant at 18 cents per copy. Therefore, the average cost declines as the scale of production increases. In figure 7.1, we graph the marginal, average variable, and average costs against the scale of production. The marginal and average variable cost curves are identical and flat. The average cost curve slopes downward.

> **Economies of scale** (increasing returns to scale) means that the average cost decreases with the scale of production.

A business for which the average cost decreases with the scale of production is said to exhibit **economies of scale** or **increasing returns to scale**. With economies of scale, the marginal cost will be lower than the average cost. Since the marginal unit of production costs less than the average, any increase in production will reduce the average. Therefore, the average cost curve slopes downward.

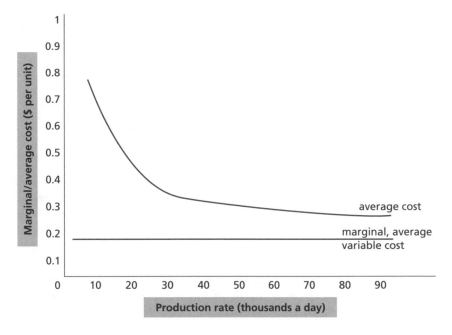

Figure 7.1 Economies of scale
The marginal and average variable costs are identical and do not change with the scale of production. The average cost decreases with the scale of production.

Intuitive Factors

Scale economies arise from two possible sources. One is substantial fixed inputs, that is, those that can support any scale of production. At a larger scale, the cost of the fixed inputs will be spread over more units of production, so that the average fixed cost will be lower. If the average variable cost is constant or does not increase very much with the scale of production, then the average cost will fall with the scale. Newspaper production illustrates economies of scale arising from substantial fixed inputs.

Any business with a strong element of composition, design, or invention has substantial fixed inputs. For instance, the cost of developing a new pharmaceutical is fixed. Regardless of the production rate, the development cost will remain the same. Similarly, the cost of preparing the computer code for a software package is fixed. It is the same whether the publisher distributes 1 million copies or only one. Accordingly, there are strong economies of scale in these businesses. Indeed, for pharmaceuticals, software and other knowledge-intensive industries, the marginal production cost is tiny compared with the average cost.

The other reason for scale economies is if the average variable cost falls with the scale of production. Generally, an increase in scale may increase or reduce the average variable cost. Whether the average variable cost increases or falls depends on the particular techno-logy of the business.

For example, a distributor of gas needs a pipeline to transport its product. The transmis-sion capacity of a pipeline depends on its cross-sectional area, which increases with the of the radius of the cross section. By contrast, the amount of material required to pipeline depends on the circumference of the pipeline, which increases with t the cross section. Accordingly, a 10% increase in the transmission capacity of the pipeline requires less than 10% additional materials. In this case, the average variable cost falls with the scale of operations. This factor tends to generate economies of scale in pipeline operations.

> **Progress Check 7A** Using the data in table 7.2, draw the average fixed cost in figure 7.1.

Economies of scale in tanker construction

In 1833, Marcus Samuel opened a shop in London to sell seashells. While procuring shells in the Caspian Sea, Marcus Samuel's son spotted a new business opportunity – to export kerosene from Russia to the Far East. This business grew into Shell Transport and Trading. Historically, oil had been transported in wooden barrels on cargo ships. In 1892, Marcus Samuel Junior conceived the idea of building a ship in the shape of a tank. This became the world's first oil tanker.

An oil tanker is like a pipeline in the sense that its capacity increases with the cross-sectional area, and hence the square of the radius of the cross section, but the material and construction costs increase with the circumference, and hence the radius of the cross section.

Figure 7.2 shows the price of new tankers per deadweight ton for four standard tanker sizes. Clearly, larger tankers are cheaper, presumably because they are less costly to build.

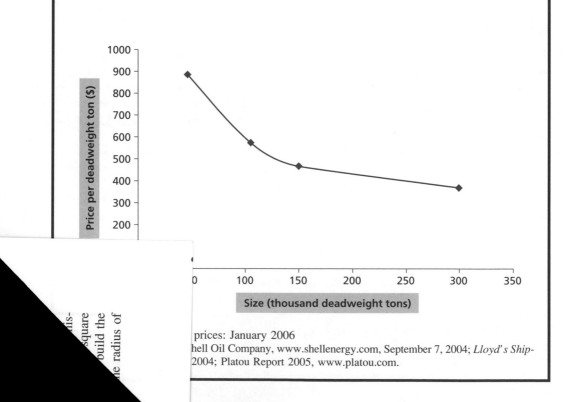

prices: January 2006
hell Oil Company, www.shellenergy.com, September 7, 2004; *Lloyd's Ship-* 2004; Platou Report 2005, www.platou.com.

Diseconomies of Scale

A business where the average cost increases with the scale of production is said to exhibit **diseconomies of scale** or **decreasing returns to scale**. A business will have diseconomies of scale if the fixed cost is not substantial and the variable cost rises more than proportionately with the scale of production.

> **Diseconomies of scale** (decreasing returns to scale) means that the average cost increases with the scale of production.

To illustrate diseconomies of scale, let us consider a hair-dressing salon. The salon does not involve a significant fixed cost. The main variable cost is labor. To the extent that additional workers are less productive, the cost of labor rises more than proportionately with the scale of production.

The average cost is the average fixed cost plus the average variable cost. For the salon, the average cost initially decreases with the scale because of the decreasing average fixed cost. Since the variable cost rises more than proportionately with the scale of production, the average variable cost is increasing. Hence, there is a scale where the decreasing average fixed cost is outweighed by the increasing average variable cost. Then, the average cost reaches a minimum and rises with further increases in the scale. The average cost curve is shaped like the letter U. As we explained in chapters 4 and 5, the average cost curve of a perfectly competitive business is U-shaped.

Strategic Implications

The relation between average cost and the scale of production influences the structure of the industry. If there are economies of scale, a business operating on a relatively large scale will achieve a lower average cost than smaller-scale competitors. Large-scale production means mass marketing and relatively low pricing. An industry where individual suppliers have economies of scale tends to be concentrated, with a few suppliers serving the entire market. In chapter 8, we analyze the extreme case of a monopoly, where there is only one supplier.

By contrast, in a business with diseconomies of scale, the management should aim at a relatively small scale. Small-scale production is associated with niche marketing and relatively high pricing. Industries where individual suppliers have diseconomies of scale tend to be fragmented. The extreme case is the model of perfect competition in chapter 5, where there are many sellers, none of whom can influence the market demand.

Technology and economies of scale: processing credit card transactions

Changes in technology can affect the extent of scale economies. Consider, for instance, the processing of credit card transactions. Credit cards are issued by businesses ranging from banks and credit unions to department stores and gasoline retailers. In the past, every transaction made with a credit card was processed manually.

Automation, however, has changed the processing of credit card transactions into a production-line operation. Automated processing requires significant fixed investments in computer systems. Consequently, the processing of credit card transactions is now a business with economies of scale. It is no longer cost-efficient for each issuer of credit cards to process its own transactions on a small scale.

The efficient scale of processing exceeds the volume of transactions at many individual credit card issuers. As a result, specialized firms have arisen to process the credit card transactions of issuers.

In line with scale economies, the credit card processing industry has become increasingly concentrated. For instance, in six years, Nova Corporation and PMT acquired over 130 other credit card processors, and finally, in June 1998, Nova acquired PMT. Nova Chairman Edward Grzedzinski explained: "This is a scale business, and by adding PMT's volume to our operating platform there is a tremendous advantage economically."

The following year, Nova had become the third largest processor with an 8% market share. The largest processor was giant First Data, with a commanding 44% market share, followed by National Processing with 13%.

Sources: "Credit-Card Processor Nova to Buy PMT in Stock Accord Valued at $1.23 Billion," *Wall Street Journal*, June 19, 1998, p. A4; Nilson Report.

3 Economies of Scope

> **Economies of scope** means that the total cost of production is lower with joint than with separate production.

> **Diseconomies of scope** means that the total cost of production is higher with joint than with separate production.

A fundamental strategic issue for any business is whether to offer many different products or focus on a single item. The answer to this question depends in part on the relation between cost and the scope of production. There are **economies of scope** across two products if the total cost of production is lower when two products are produced together than when they are produced separately. Conversely, there are **diseconomies of scope** across two products if the total cost of production is higher when two products are produced together.

Joint Cost

Let us consider how costs depend on the scope of production through the following example. Suppose that the management of the *Daily Globe* is considering whether to launch an afternoon paper, the *Afternoon Globe*. Table 7.3 shows three categories of expenses required to produce the *Daily Globe* and the *Afternoon Globe*, assuming a print run of 50,000 copies a day for each paper.

If the two newspapers are printed in separate facilities, then the total production cost is $15,200 a day for each paper, or $30,400 for the two papers. If, however, both newspapers are printed in the same facility, then the total cost of producing the two newspapers is $26,900. The cost of producing both newspapers in the same facility is 11.5% lower than if they were produced separately.

What explains the difference in cost? The key is that the same printing press can be used in the night to print the morning paper, and in the late morning to print the afternoon paper.

Table 7.3 Expenses for two products

Organization	Daily production (thousands)	Labor	Printing press	Ink, paper, electric power	Total cost
Separate production					
Daily Globe	50	$5,000	$3,500	$6,700	$15,200
Afternoon Globe	50	$5,000	$3,500	$6,700	$15,200
Combined production	100	$10,000	$3,500	$13,400	$26,900

To produce the *Daily Globe* by itself, the publisher must spend $3,500 a day on the printing press. Likewise, to produce the *Afternoon Globe* by itself, the publisher must spend $3,500 a day on the printing press. To produce both newspapers from the same facility, however, the publisher spends $3,500 only once.

The expense of the printing press is a *joint cost* of the morning and afternoon newspapers. The **joint cost** is the cost of inputs that do not change with the scope of production. Economies of scope arise wherever there are significant joint costs.

> The **joint cost** is the cost of inputs that do not change with the scope of production.

Strategic Implications

Where two products are linked by economies of scope, it will be relatively cheaper to produce the products together. Then, a supplier of both items can achieve a relatively lower cost than competitors that specialize in one or the other product. Subject to conditions of market demand and competition, the management should offer both products. Multiproduct suppliers dominate industries with economies of scope.

Telecommunication and broadcasting provide an important example of scope economies. Fixed-line telephone service requires a wire network connecting all potential subscribers. Similarly, cable television requires a wire network connecting all potential subscribers. In this case, the cost of building and maintaining the network is a significant joint cost. Consquently, there are very substantial economies of scope across the telephone and television businesses. Combined providers of telephone and television service can deliver the services at relatively lower cost than specialized services. Throughout the world, telephone and cable television companies are expanding into each other's businesses.

Economies of scope in advertising and promotion are essential for the strategy of *brand extension* in marketing. When Sony spends $1 to advertise Sony, it is promoting the sales of every product carrying the Sony brand, including computers, TV sets, and playstations. Accordingly, the expenditure on advertising a brand is a joint cost of marketing all the products marked with the brand. This joint cost gives rise to economies of scope in advertising and promotion. Through a brand extension, the owner of an established brand can introduce new products at relatively lower cost than a competitor with no established brand.

Economies of scope also underlie the strategic concept of *core competence*. A *core competence* is generalized expertise in the design, production, and marketing of products based on common or closely related technologies. For instance, a manufacturer with a core competence in small liquid crystal displays can apply this as a basis for digital watches and mobile phone displays. It can produce these items at a relatively lower cost than a specialized competitor. Essentially, a core competence is a joint cost that gives rise to economies of scope.[3]

Diseconomies of Scope

There are **diseconomies of scope** across two products if the total cost of production is higher when the two items are produced together than when they are produced separately. Diseconomies of scope arise where joint costs are not significant and making one product increases the cost of making the other in the same facility.

[3]   This discussion is based on Paul Milgrom and John Roberts, *Economics, Organization, and Management* (Englewood Cliffs, NJ: Prentice-Hall, 1992), pp. 107–9.

To illustrate diseconomies of scope, consider two retail businesses: basic clothing and fast food. Both cater to a similar mix of customers looking for good value. Why then does some entrepreneur not sell clothing together with fast food?

Such a combined business would probably encounter diseconomies of scope. There is no significant joint cost between the two products. Further, people consuming fast food might wander over to the clothing section and spill food and drinks on the merchandise. So, the fast food service increases the cost of selling clothing in the same facility. Given these difficulties, it would be less costly to sell the two products in separate facilities.

Where diseconomies of scope prevail, it will be relatively cheaper to produce the various items separately. Hence, specialized producers can achieve relatively lower costs than competitors that combine production. In such circumstances, the management should aim for a narrow scope and focus on one product.

Progress Check 7B Referring to table 7.3, suppose that, with combined production, the expenses on the printing press would be $7,000 a day. Are there economies or diseconomies of scope?

⊣ Samsung Electronics: economies of scale and scope ⊢

In the first half of 2004, the average cost of new 300-millimeter wafer fabrication plants announced by Fujitsu, Chartered Semiconductor, Promos, Matsushita Electronics, Semiconductor Manufacturing International, and Hynix was $1.4 billion. The average planned production rate was 30,900 wafers per month.

Meanwhile, Samsung announced an investment of 1 trillion Won ($852 million) just to set up its 14th and 15th semiconductor manufacturing lines without definite production plans. Evidently, there are substantial fixed costs in manufacturing semiconductors. The same is true in TFT-LCD production. Consequently, it is cost-effective to manufacture semiconductors and TFT-LCDs only on a large scale.

Samsung gains advantage by manufacturing both semiconductors and TFT-LCDs to the extent of economies of scope between the two products. The manufacturing processes for both products involve deposition, photo-lithography, and etching of integrated circuits. The key differences are that TFT-LCDs are built on a glass substrate and at a relatively lower temperature.

Further, both semiconductors and TFT-LCDs are used in manufacturing computers, mobile phones, and digital cameras. Accordingly, Samsung enjoys an economy of scope in marketing the semiconductors and LCDs. Practically, however, the economies of scope may not be very substantial. Samsung Electronics produces both semiconductors and TFT-LCDs, but in separate facilities. Other manufacturers specialize, like Infineon in semiconductors and LG Philips in TFT-LCDs.

Sources: L. G. Philips, 2004, "Technology: Manufacturing Process," http://global.lgphilips-lcd.com/en/technology/manufacture.html, September 8, 2004; "Chipmakers Expected to Make Heavy Investments This Year," *Korea Times*, January 4, 2004.

Financial services: economies of scale but not economies of scope?

During the 1990s, there was a flurry of mergers to create a small number of giant diversified banks (megabanks). The goal of these mergers was to provide customers with a wide range of services and products, including retail, commercial, and investment banking, insurance, mutual funds, and brokerage services. It was anticipated that the added sales of these services and products would increase profits through economies of scale and economies of scope.

In general, the megabanks have not generated more profits than the smaller banks. Size does matter but not for the reasons generally understood by the banking community. Megabanks have not realized the economies of scale and economies of scope expected. The larger customers do not appear to care whether their banks offer a full range of services. In addition, cross-selling to retail customers has proven difficult at best.

Successful giants such as the American International Group and Axa in insurance and Goldman Sachs in investment banking are specialists, and realize economies of scale by focusing on narrow slices of the industry. These economies of scale lie in areas such as brand management. Specifically, the cost of establishing the brand name can be accomplished at an average cost far lower than for smaller businesses.

So, size does matter in the banking industry and can provide economies of scale. However, it appears that the economies of scope expected by megabanks offering a wide range of services may not be so easily realized. In recent years, Citibank spun off its Travelers Insurance unit, and the Credit Suisse Group sold its Winterthur insurance group.

Source: "The Trials of Megabanks," *The Economist*, October 29, 1998.

Economies of scale and scope in telecommunications

As the telecommunications industry continues to change rapidly, there are opportunities to gain economies of scale and scope. According to industry consultant, Raul Katz, the economies of scale in the wireless industry are very high. This comes from the consolidation of national carriers as well as national with regional carriers whose networks complement each other. One example of this was the consolidation of Voicestream and Powertel which resulted in a 15% reduction in operating cost per subscriber within six quarters after the merger.

Telecommunications providers can further improve their operations by taking advantage of ecomomies of scope. Mergers among providers of wireline and wireless telecommunications, Internet access, and television broadcasting allow the consolidated company to provide a basket of goods while improving operations and reducing customer churn. Bundling (which we will discuss in chapter 9) is one way that churn can be reduced. This type of integration works particularly well for wireline providers whose customers substitute wireless for wireline usage, since it keeps the customers usage within the same network.

Source: Raul Katz, "Can Mergers Save Telecom? Why M&As Are Inevitable, Where the Biggest Economies of Scale Are, and What Pitfalls to Avoid," http://www.findarticles.com/p/articles/mi_m0 FGI/is_11_14/ai_111694661/print.

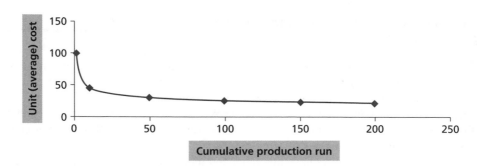

Figure 7.3 Experience curve

4 Experience Curve

Scale and scope are drivers that can affect costs of production within any time period. Another driver – accumulated experience – can affect costs of production over time. Accumulated experience matters in industries characterized by relatively short production runs and a relatively substantial input of human resources.

Such industries include aerospace manufacturing and shipbuilding. For instance, Boeing's 727 was one of the most successful large civilian jets of all time. Yet, by 1983, with the last delivery of 15 aircraft to Federal Express, Boeing had built a cumulative total of just 1,831 units of the 727.

In such industries, as engineers and workers gain experience in production, they become more proficient individually and as teams. They also devise new ways to reduce cost, including developing better tools and more cost-effective procedures.

> The **experience curve** shows how the unit (average) cost of production falls with cumulative production over time.

Accordingly, the unit cost of production falls with accumulated experience, which motivates the concept of the *experience curve*, which is also called the *learning curve*. Typically, experience is measured by cumulative production, hence the **experience curve** shows how the unit (average) cost of production falls with cumulative production over time.

Figure 7.3 illustrates an experience curve, where the unit (average) cost of production is indexed to 100 for the first unit produced. The unit cost falls most sharply with the initial units of cumulative production. Referring to figure 7.3, by the 50th unit of cumulative production, the unit cost will have dropped by more than half, and then flattens out. The rate at which the unit cost falls with cumulative production and then flattens out depends on the particular technology of the industry and product.

The experience curve is distinct from economies of scale. The experience curve relates cumulative production over *preceding periods* to production costs in one period. By contrast, economies of scale relate the scale of production within one period to production costs in the *same period*.

Strategic Implications

In any industry where production costs are subject to a substantial experience curve, it is crucial to forecast cumulative production accurately. For instance, referring to figure 7.3, if cumulative production is 10 units, the unit (average) cost would be slightly less than 50, while if cumulative production is 100, the unit cost would be around 25.

Accurate forecasting of cumulative production would be crucial for both planning investments and setting prices. The challenge is especially great to the extent that sales, and hence, cumulative production depend on pricing and competitor's strategies.

Progress Check 7C On figure 7.3, draw a gentler experience curve that begins at 100 for the first unit produced and flattens to 50 with cumulative production of 200 units.

⊣ Airbus and Boeing's Christmas stocking ⊢

In April 2004, Boeing launched the new 787 Dreamliner with 50 firm orders from All Nippon Airways of Japan. The Dreamliner was targeted at the market segment of twin-engine medium- to long-range jets with capacity of 200–300 passengers. The 787 is a completely new design with a development cost estimated at $8–10 billion.

In December 2004, Airbus introduced the A350 to compete with Boeing's 787. The A350 was planned to be a derivative of the existing A330, enhanced with a new wing, more fuel-efficient engines, and other new technologies. The development cost was estimated to be just €4 billion.

By designing the A350 as a derivative of the A330, Airbus could realize economies of scope across the two planes, and reduce its cost of developing the new A350. Boeing did not plan on similar economies of scope, hence the cost of developing the Dreamliner was much higher.

At the A350 introduction, Airbus Chief Commercial Officer John Leahy predicted that the A350 would draw Boeing customers and so "put a hole in Boeing's Christmas stocking." The experience curve explains Mr Leahy's remark.

The cost of aircraft manufacturing is substantially affected by accumulated experience. Hence, Airbus and Boeing must set prices for aircraft based on projections of forecast cumulative sales. If the sales fall short of target, unit costs will be higher than planned, and the manufacturer may incur a substantial loss on the plane.

Boeing had planned to secure 200 orders for the Dreamliner by December 2004, but fell short of the target by almost 75%. However, Mr Leahy may have spoken too soon. Airbus' announcement of the A350 design was indeed a Christmas present for Boeing. Once airlines could compare the Airbus and Boeing offers, they streamed to Boeing with orders for the Dreamliner.

Source: "A350: Airbus's Counter-Attack," *Flight International*, January 25, 2005.

5 Opportunity Cost

We have seen how business costs depend on economies of scale and scope, and cumulative production. To actually determine the extent of scale and scope economies and the experience curve, we must know how to measure costs. Analyses of costs usually begin with the accounting statements. These, however, do not always provide the information appropriate for effective business decisions. It is often necessary to look beyond the conventional accounting statements.

Principle of **relevance**:
managers should
consider only relevant
costs.

Here, we present a key principle to guide managers in measuring costs. That principle is **relevance**: managers should consider only relevant costs and ignore all others. There is no simple definition of which costs are relevant. Which costs are relevant depends on the alternative courses of action for the decision at hand.

Alternative Courses of Action

The following example shows how an analysis of the alternative courses of action will uncover relevant costs that conventional accounting statements leave out. Suppose that, in 1980, Eleanor bought a warehouse in an industrial area that has since been transformed into a tourist zone. Eleanor paid $300,000 for the warehouse, using $200,000 of her own money and a bank loan of $100,000. She has since repaid the loan in full.

Table 7.4 presents the most recent income statement for her warehouse. Eleanor's annual sales revenue is $700,000, her cash outlays are $220,000, hence her profit is $480,000. She is making a return on sales of 480/700 = 69%. Eleanor's warehouse business seems to be doing very well.

We contend, however, that this assessment of performance overlooks some significant costs of Eleanor's warehouse business. To evaluate Eleanor's business, we should investigate her alternative courses of action. Since the area has become a tourist zone, an obvious alternative is to redevelop the warehouse into a tourist facility such as a shopping center or entertainment complex.

Suppose that a developer were willing to buy the warehouse for $2 million. If Eleanor sells the warehouse, she could invest the proceeds in government bonds and get a secure income of, say, 8% a year, which works out to $2 million $\times$ 0.08 = $160,000. Moreover, Eleanor could then work elsewhere for a salary of, say, $400,000. Thus, if Eleanor were to sell the warehouse, she could earn $560,000 a year. This is more than she earns from continuing in the warehouse business. So, if Eleanor considers the alternative of selling the warehouse, she will soon see that this is better than continuing in business.

This example highlights a major deficiency of the conventional income statement: it does not present the revenues and costs of the alternative courses of action. In table 7.5, we

Table 7.4   Conventional income statement

Revenue	$700,000
Expenses	$220,000
Profit	$480,000

Table 7.5   Income statement showing alternatives, I

	Continue warehouse operations	Shutdown
Revenue	$700,000	$560,000
Expenses	$220,000	$0
Profit	$480,000	$560,000

Table 7.6   Income statement reporting opportunity costs

Revenue	$700,000
Cost	$780,000
Profit	−$80,000

present an expanded income statement that explicitly shows the revenues and costs of Eleanor's two alternatives. It is then very clear that Eleanor should sell the warehouse.

Opportunity Cost Defined

By continuing in the warehouse business, Eleanor forgoes the opportunity to earn $560,000 a year. The **opportunity cost** of the current course of action is the net revenue from the best alternative course of action. In Eleanor's case, the opportunity cost of continuing in the warehouse business is $560,000 a year.

> The **opportunity cost** is the net revenue from the best alternative course of action.

We can apply the concept of opportunity cost to present the revenues and costs of continuing in the warehouse business in another way. This includes opportunity costs among the costs of the business. Table 7.6 presents a single income statement, in which costs include both the cash outlays and the opportunity cost. The cost of $780,000 consists of $220,000 in outlays plus $560,000 in opportunity cost.

Using the opportunity cost approach, we find that Eleanor is incurring a loss of $80,000 a year; hence, she should get out of the warehouse business. This approach leads to the same decision as in table 7.5, where we explicitly show the two alternative courses of action.

Uncovering Relevant Costs

Thus, there are two ways to uncover relevant costs: explicitly consider the alternative courses of action or use the concept of opportunity cost. When applied correctly, both approaches lead to the same business decision.

In Eleanor's case, there was one alternative to the existing course of action. Where there is more than one alternative, the explicit approach still works well. The opportunity cost approach, however, becomes more complicated: we must first identify the best of the alternatives and then charge the net revenues from that alternative as an opportunity cost of the existing course of action.

Conventional methods of cost accounting focus on the cash outlays associated with the course of action that management has adopted. This means that they do not consider the revenues and costs of alternative courses of action; hence, they ignore costs that are relevant but do not involve cash outlays. One reason for these omissions is that alternative courses of action and opportunity costs change with the circumstances and hence are more difficult to measure and verify. Conventional methods of cost accounting focus on easily verifiable costs. Accordingly, they overlook opportunity costs.

> **Progress Check 7D** Suppose that government bonds pay an interest rate of 3% a year. Revise tables 7.5 and 7.6. Should Eleanor continue in the warehouse business?

⊣ Opportunity cost: downtown department store ⊢

The main store of the Wing On chain is one of the few department stores in Hong Kong's central district. The store occupies 25,000 square feet on the ground floor and 64,000 square feet on three other floors of the Wing On Center. The tenants of street-level floors of other nearby buildings include banks, fast-food chains, and jewelers. In 2003, the Wing On department stores reported revenues of HK$2,623 million, expenses of HK$1,239 million, and a before tax profit of HK$384 million.

At the time, the market rent for retail space around the Wing On Center was HK$50–100 per square foot per month for ground floors and HK$15–25 for other floors. Let us use this data to estimate the opportunity cost of the premises used by Wing On's main store. To be conservative, we use the lower figures of HK$50 and HK$15 a month. Then, on an annual basis, the opportunity cost of the ground-floor space was HK$(25,000 × 50 × 12) = HK$15 million, while the opportunity cost of the other floors was HK$(64,000 × 15 × 12) = HK$11.52 million. The total opportunity cost was HK$26.52 million a year.

To evaluate the performance of its department stores, the Wing On Group should take account of the HK$26.52 million a year income that it could earn by leasing space to other tenants such as banks and fast-food chains.

Source: Wing On Group, *2003 Annual Report*.

⊣ Free lunch: Picasso versus Rockefeller ⊢

The following story is apocryphal. Nelson Rockefeller (a member of the wealthy New York family that controlled the Chase Manhattan Bank) and the famous European artist Pablo Picasso had lunch at the Four Seasons restaurant in New York City. At the end of a fine meal, Picasso reached for the bill, "Let me pay. I'll write a personal check, draw a few squiggles, and sign it. The manager won't ever cash it. She will display it as a work of art. And we'll have a free lunch."

Rockefeller would not agree. "No, allow me to write a personal check. Remember, this is New York City. Here, our Rockefeller name is as good as gold. The manager won't cash my check. She can use it just like money and our lunch will be free."

Who was right? Picasso or Rockefeller? The correct answer to the puzzle is that neither Picasso nor Rockefeller was right. By drawing a few squiggles, Picasso was adding to the world's stock of his works. The increase in the supply would reduce the price that he could get for future works. Picasso would not get a free lunch – he was bartering a picture for a lunch.

Rockefeller was also wrong. Each check that he wrote added to his stock of debts and, ultimately, reduced his creditworthiness. He could not create an unlimited number of checks. So, by creating a check, Rockefeller was exchanging a lunch for a reduction in his creditworthiness. In believing that they could get a free lunch, both Pablo Picasso and Nelson Rockefeller overlooked opportunity cost.

Source: Frank Rabinovitch, personal communication, 1984.

Opportunity Cost of Capital

Conventional accounting methods require the expensing of interest payments but do not require expensing of expected dividends. Consequently, a business that is partly financed by debt will appear to be "less profitable" than an otherwise identical business that is completely financed by equity. Indeed, many loss-making businesses have returned to profit by persuading their creditors to convert their loans to shares.

However, from a managerial perspective, equity capital is not costless; it has an opportunity cost. The shareholders of a business would like management to earn a rate of return on equity that at least matches the return from other investments with the same risk profile. Managers who evaluate business performance in terms of accounting profit will tend to be biased in favor of capital-intensive activities.

Management consultants Stern Stewart developed and trademarked the concept of *economic value added* as a better measure of business performance than accounting earnings. The definition of **economic value added** is net operating profit after tax subject to adjustments for accounting conventions less a charge for the cost of capital. Managers who evaluate business performance in terms of economic value added will make better decisions. In particular, they are less likely to be biased in favor of capital-intensive activities.

> **Economic value added** is net operating profit after tax subject to adjustments for accounting conventions less a charge for the cost of capital.

The appropriate mix between debt and equity as sources of investment funds is a deep and complicated issue of corporate finance. It is beyond the scope of a managerial economics book. Here, we confine ourselves to the point that a complete measure of business performance should take account of the opportunity cost of equity capital.

⊢ Loewen Group: life after death ⊢

In June 1999, the Loewen Group operated more than 1,100 funeral homes and 400 cemeteries in Canada, the United Kingdom, and the United States. Historically, the group had emphasized the operation of funeral homes. It then expanded into cemeteries, partly financed by $2 billion of bonds and $300 million of bank loans.

For the six months ending June 30, 1999, Loewen's revenues were $566 million, operating expenses were $493 million, and operating earnings were $73 million. However, interest expenses of $77 million, and other non-operational expenses dragged the group down to a pre-tax loss of $88 million. Faced with the prospect of further losses, Loewen filed for bankruptcy protection in Canada and the United States.

Chairman John Lacey explained that Loewen would refocus on funeral home operations and away from cemeteries. Saying that bondholders supported the bankruptcy filing, he called on them to convert their bonds into equity.

Following the conversion of bonds into equity, Loewen's interest expense would be reduced. But the financial engineering alone would not change the revenues and operational expenses of the group. Conversion of debt to equity would "reduce" losses only in a financial sense and only because accounting standards do not require expensing of expected dividends. However, the debt–equity conversion would not change the group's business situation.

> In 2002, the group emerged from bankruptcy protection. By then, it was operating 798 funeral homes and 62 cemeteries. The shift away from diversification into cemeteries had a real impact on the group's business situation.
>
> *Sources*: "Loewen Group Seeks Bankruptcy Protection in U.S., Canada," *Dow Jones Business News*, June 1, 1999; "The Loewen Group Reports Second Quarter 2000 Results," The Loewen Group, Inc., Press Release, July 31, 2000.

6 Transfer Pricing

Chapter 6 introduced the concept of a transfer price, which is charged for the sale of an item within an organization. Suppose that the Mercury Group consists of two divisions – semiconductors and consumer electronics. The semiconductor division supplies chips to the consumer electronics division for use in manufacturing personal digital assistants. How should these chips be priced?

Figure 7.4 shows the semiconductor division's marginal cost of manufacturing the chip. It also shows the consumer electronics division's marginal benefit from the chip, which reflects the additional profit generated by one more chip. Mercury's overall profit would be maximized at a quantity of 160,000 chips per month, where the consumer electronics division's marginal benefit equals the semiconductor division's marginal cost.

Suppose that Mercury sets the transfer price at $2 per chip, and allows the consumer electronics division to buy as many chips as it wants at that price. Comparing its marginal benefit with the transfer price, the consumer electronics division will buy 160,000 chips per month, which is exactly the quantity that maximizes Mercury's overall profit.

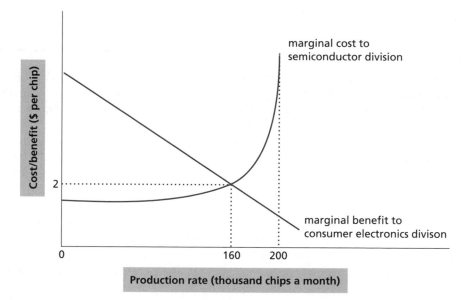

Figure 7.4 Transfer price
Mercury's semiconductor division has a maximum capacity of 200,000 chips a month. Mercury maximizes its overall profit at a production rate of 160,000 chips a month, where the semiconductor division's marginal cost equals the consumer electronics division's marginal benefits.

Generally, to maximize the profit of the entire organization, the **transfer price** of an internally produced input should be set equal to its marginal cost, which is the change in total cost due to the production of an additional unit. There are two important special cases, which we discuss below.

> The **transfer price** of an internally produced input should be set equal to its marginal cost.

Perfectly Competitive Market

One special case is where there is a perfectly competitive market for the input. We discussed this case in chapter 6 when considering decentralized management. Rather than measure the marginal cost, it is simpler to set the transfer price equal to the market price. A profit-maximizing business would produce the input at a rate where its marginal cost equals the market price. Hence, the transfer price (set at the market price) will also be the marginal cost.

Full Capacity

The other special case is where the (upstream) division that supplies the input is operating at full capacity. Then, the marginal cost of the input is not well defined. For instance, referring to figure 7.4, if Mercury's semiconductor division is producing at a rate of 200,000 chips a month, the marginal cost curve is vertical and hence the marginal cost of a chip is not defined.

In this case, the transfer price should be set equal to the opportunity cost of the input, which is the marginal benefit that the input provides to the current user. To understand why, suppose that Mercury re-allocates one chip away from the consumer electronics division to some other use. Since the semiconductor division's total production remains the same, there will be no effect on its production costs. However, the re-allocation will result in an opportunity cost – the reduction in profit for the consumer electronics division.

To ensure that the alternative use of the chip raises overall profit, the transfer price should be set equal to the consumer electronics division's marginal benefit from that chip. The alternative user will only buy the chip if the benefit exceeds the transfer price, and hence only if its benefit exceeds the consumer electronics division's benefit. Accordingly, this rule will maximize the profit of the entire organization.

7 Sunk Costs

For effective business decisions, managers should take account of all relevant costs. We have just seen that, because conventional accounting methods do not present alternative courses of action, they may fail to reveal important relevant costs. We shall next consider situations where some of the costs reported in conventional accounting statements are not relevant, and should be ignored.

In chapter 4, we introduced the concept of a sunk cost, which is a cost that has been committed and so cannot be avoided. Since sunk costs cannot be avoided, they are not relevant to business decisions. As with opportunity costs, the easiest way to identify sunk costs is to consider the alternative courses of action.

Alternative Courses of Action

The following example shows how an analysis of the alternative courses of action will identify sunk costs in a conventional accounting statement. Suppose that Sol Athletic is about

Table 7.7 Income statement showing alternatives, II

	Continue product launch	Cancel launch
Contribution margin	$280,000	$0
Advertising agency fee	$50,000	$50,000
Magazine charge	$250,000	$50,000
Profit	($20,000)	($100,000)

to launch a line of new athletic shoes. Some months before, management prepared an advertising campaign and booked space in *Road Runner* magazine. The total budget for the new advertisements was $300,000.

Management forecasts that the advertisements would generate sales of 20,000 units. The unit contribution margin, which is price less average variable cost, would be $20. Hence the contribution margin, which is revenue less variable cost, would be $20 × 20,000 = $400,000. Thus, the new product would yield a profit of $400,000 − $300,000 = $100,000.

Recently, however, one of Sol's major competitors launched a new athletic shoe. Sol now estimates that its own launch will generate sales of only 14,000 units. The unit contribution margin would still be $20; hence, the contribution margin would only be $20 × 14,000 = $280,000. This seems to be less than the cost of the advertisements. Should Sol cancel the launch?

To address this question, we should carefully lay out the revenues and costs associated with the alternative courses of action. Table 7.7 shows the required information.

Supposing that management continues with the launch, the contribution margin would be $280,000. Sol must pay $50,000 to an advertising agency and $250,000 to *Road Runner* magazine, hence the total advertising cost would be $300,000. Thus, Sol's profit would be −$20,000.

By contrast, if Sol cancels the launch, the contribution margin would be $0. Even if it cancels the launch, Sol must still pay the advertising agency, as well as some payment to the magazine as shown in table 7.7. Hence, if management decides to cancel the launch, the total advertising cost would be $100,000; thus, its profit would be −$100,000.

By this analysis, Sol should continue with the product launch. Continuation yields a loss of $20,000, which is less than the loss of $100,000 from cancellation.

Avoidable Costs

By canceling the launch, Sol does not save the entire advertising budget of $300,000. Some expenses have already been committed and are now sunk and so are not relevant. Another way by which Sol can correctly decide whether or not to continue the launch is to use a single income statement that omits sunk costs and includes only avoidable costs.

Table 7.8 presents this information, showing only avoidable costs rather than cash outlays. The contribution margin is $280,000. The total avoidable cost of the advertising plan is $200,000. If Sol continues with the launch, it will earn a profit of $80,000. Accordingly, the correct decision is to continue with the launch.

Table 7.8 Income statement omitting sunk costs

Contribution margin	$280,000
Advertising agency cost	$0
Magazine cost	$200,000
Profit	$80,000

Strategic Implications

Generally, managers should ignore sunk costs and consider only avoidable costs. Sunk costs, once incurred, are not relevant for pricing, investment, or any other business decision. Managers who consider sunk costs may stumble into serious mistakes.

From a prospective viewpoint, managers should be very careful before committing to costs that will become sunk, since such commitments cannot be reversed. In chapter 10, we discuss how businesses can exploit investments in sunk costs as a way to strategically influence the behavior of competitors.

We have shown two ways of dealing with sunk costs: explicitly consider the alternative courses of action or remove all sunk costs from the income statement. When applied correctly, both approaches lead to the same business decision.

In Sol's case, there was one alternative to the existing course of action. Where there is more than one alternative, the explicit approach still works well. The sunk cost approach, however, becomes more complicated. Which costs are sunk depends on the alternative at hand. Accordingly, it is easier to consider the alternative courses of action explicitly.

Conventional methods of cost accounting focus on the cash outlays associated with the course of action that management has adopted. These methods report all costs that involve cash outlays, even sunk costs. To make effective business decisions, managers must look beyond conventional accounting statements to consider only relevant costs. This means ignoring sunk costs.

Commitments and the Planning Horizon

To identify sunk costs, managers should consider two factors: past commitments and the planning horizon. Suppose that Sol Athletic has engaged an advertising agency on a retainer basis with a minimum monthly fee. The contract requires six months' notice of termination. Then, from the current standpoint, the advertising agency's minimum fee is sunk for a six-month planning horizon but not for the seventh and following months.

If Sol's commitment had been different, the sunk cost picture would also be different. Suppose that the contract provided for only three months' notice of termination. Then, from the current standpoint, the advertising agency's minimum fee is sunk for only the next three months. For planning beyond the fourth month, the fee is avoidable.

This example also illustrates how the extent to which a cost is sunk depends on the planning horizon. Generally, the longer the planning horizon, the more time there will be for past commitments to unwind and hence the greater will be management's freedom of action.

In chapter 4, we distinguished between short-run and long-run planning horizons. The short run is a time horizon in which at least one input cannot be adjusted. By contrast, the long run is a time horizon long enough that all inputs can be freely adjusted. Consequently, in a short-run planning horizon, there will be some sunk costs, while in a long-run horizon, there will be no sunk costs.

Progress Check 7E Suppose that Sol has made no commitments to the agency, magazine, or newspaper. Revise tables 7.7 and 7.8. Should Sol cancel the launch?

Northwest Airlines: awash in red ink yet buying new Dreamliners

In 2004, Northwest Airlines incurred an operating loss of $505 million and net loss of $862 million. Yet in May 2005, it placed a firm order for 18 Boeing 787 Dreamliners, worth approximately $2.2 billion at list prices, plus options for 50 additional planes. The first planes would be delivered in August 2008, with 6 planes delivered in each of 2008, 2009, and 2010.

Why did Northwest buy new Dreamliners amidst continuing losses? Investment decisions must be forward-looking, and ignore current losses, which are sunk costs. Having experienced a sharp and sustained increase in oil prices, Northwest's management believed that higher oil prices would persist. With persistently high oil prices, it was imperative to upgrade the fleet towards more fuel-efficient aircraft.

Northwest noted that the Dreamliner would consume 20% less fuel than comparable aircraft in service. Further, it would provide up to 45% more cargo capacity, and provide passengers with more comfort, including higher humidity, wider seats and aisles, and larger windows.

Source: "Northwest Airlines Orders Boeing 787," Press Release, Northwest Airlines, May 5, 2005.

Dampier–Bunbury pipeline: your loss, my profit

The 1,530 kilometer Dampier–Bunbury pipeline transports natural gas from the vast North Western Shelf gas fields into the state of Western Australia. The pipeline is the state's largest. In 1998, the state government sold the pipeline to Epic Energy, a joint venture of U.S. companies El Paso and Dominion Resources, for A$2.4 billion. Epic financed the purchase with A$1.85 billion of loans from a consortium of 28 banks.

The Dampier pipeline business, however, did not perform well. In October 2003, Epic announced that it would sell the pipeline after Western Australia's independent gas regulator imposed tariffs that the company considered to be unacceptably low. Both federal and state officials, however, blamed Epic. Australian Competition and Consumer Commissioner Edward Willett remarked that Epic had overpaid for the pipeline by A$1 billion. Western Australia Energy Minister Eric Ripper refused to intervene in the regulatory process.

In April 2004, with Epic's pipeline company failing to meet its debt obligations, the consortium of banks forced the company into receivership. In August, the receivers named a consortium led by Diversified Utility and Energy Trusts (DUET) as their preferred buyer at a price of A$1.86 billion. The consortium also included Western Australia's largest gas retailer Alinta, and the pipeline's largest customer, aluminum manufacturer Alcoa of Australia, each with a 20% share.

DUET Chief Executive Peter Barry remarked that "with the appropriate acquisition structure" the pipeline would yield very attractive returns.

How could the pipeline be unprofitable for Epic Energy while being "attractive" to DUET? One reason is that Epic Energy was unwilling to write down the value of the pipeline to its market value. If the market value was A$1.86 billion, while the pipeline had A$1.85 billion of debt outstanding, then the net equity of the pipeline would have been just A$10 million.

Another reason might be that the DUET consortium did not fully take into account the cost of its equity.

Sources: "Receivers Looming for Epic Energy," Sydney Morning Herald, April 12, 2004; "Joint Venture to Buy Australian Pipeline," International Herald Tribune, September 1, 2004.

Sunk vis-à-vis Fixed Costs

In popular as well as professional discussion, the term *fixed cost* is often used in two different senses: a cost that cannot be avoided once incurred (what we call *sunk cost*) and the cost of inputs that do not change with the production rate (what we call *fixed cost*).

For the sake of clarity, we distinguish these two meanings with two different terms. It is important to understand this distinction very clearly because the two types of costs have very different implications for business decisions. Managers should ignore sunk costs that have been incurred, as these cannot be avoided. By contrast, the presence of fixed costs in the long run tends to give rise to economies of scale, and so management should aim to operate on a large scale.

Some fixed costs become sunk once incurred. Consider, for instance, a manufacturer of rubber shoes. For each size of shoe, the manufacturer must have at least one pair of molds (left and right). So, the cost of designing the molds is a fixed cost. Moreover, once the molds have been designed, the cost has been committed and cannot be avoided. Hence, the design cost is a sunk cost, once incurred.

Not all sunk costs, however, are fixed in the sense of supporting any scale of operations. Having designed the molds, the manufacturer needs one set of molds to begin production of shoes. The cost of making the molds is sunk, once incurred. If the demand for the shoes is sufficiently high, the manufacturer might have to invest in a second production line. Then it will need a second set of molds, which requires an additional investment. So, the cost of making molds is not a fixed cost. Rather, it depends on the scale of operations.

Likewise, not all fixed costs become sunk when incurred. For instance, the manufacturer must have at least one production operator on each production line. Accordingly, the wage of a production operator is a fixed cost of making a particular model of shoes. If, however, the demand for that model of shoes should fall, the line can be closed and the operator shifted to another model. Thus, the production operator's wage need not be sunk.

Figure 7.5 illustrates a basic approach to analyzing costs. First, we divide costs into sunk and avoidable. This division depends on past commitments and the current planning horizon. Managers should ignore all costs that are sunk for the planning horizon at hand. Next, we can analyze avoidable costs into variable and fixed elements. This division depends on the technology of the business. The presence of substantial long-run fixed costs gives rise to economies of scale. Then, management should aim to operate on a relatively large scale.

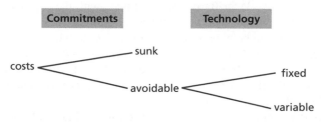

Figure 7.5   Classification of costs
The division of costs into sunk and avoidable depends on past commitments and the current planning horizon. The division of avoidable costs into variable and fixed elements depends on the technology of the business.

8   Statistical Methods[4]

We have presented two principles to guide managers in analyzing business costs. While these principles are very clear, in practice, managers are often confronted with a mass of disparate information. Under these circumstances, it helps to use statistical methods, specifically, multiple regression, to understand the data. These methods are also useful in making forecasts about costs.

Multiple regression can help in many analyses of costs, including researching the relationship between costs and the scale and scope of production.

Multiple Regression

In the following example, we show how to use multiple regression analysis to investigate the extent of fixed costs and economies of scale. Suppose that, from past experience, the management of an elevator manufacturer has identified four major factors in the manufacturing cost of producing an elevator system: the rated capacity and speed, the distance through which the elevator travels, and the number of landings.

To support its pricing, management would like to understand how its production cost depends on the four factors. It would also like to know whether there are significant fixed elements in the cost. Fixed costs would give rise to economies of scale in production.

We can use multiple regression to address these questions. First, we collect data on the manufacturing cost and the corresponding characteristics for some recent projects (see table 7.9).

In the multiple regression analysis, we specify cost as the dependent variable and four independent variables: capacity (in thousand kilograms), speed (in meters per second), travel (in meters), and number of landings. Table 7.10 reports the results of the analysis.

Referring to table 7.10, the F-statistic is 27.79, and the probability that all the coefficients are 0 is 0.00. Accordingly, we can be very confident that the regression equation is statistically valid. The R-squared is 0.95; hence, the equation explains a very high percentage of the variation of the cost.

The intercept is −5.51, which is negative. The probability that the intercept is 0 is 0.41. If there is a fixed cost in manufacturing, then the cost would be positive even with all the independent variables being equal to 0. Hence, the fixed cost would be reflected in the

---

[4]   This section is more advanced. It may be omitted without loss of continuity.

Table 7.9 Elevator manufacturing costs

Cost (thousand $)	Capacity (thousand kg)	Speed (m/s)	Travel (m)	Landings
65	1.60	1.6	21.0	2
63	0.71	1.6	47.5	8
64	0.85	1.6	47.5	8
39	1.00	0.6	15.0	6
59	0.90	1.0	45.2	9
50	0.90	1.0	28.6	6
56	0.90	1.6	60.9	6
35	0.80	1.0	6.9	2
58	0.54	1.0	40.6	15
45	0.54	1.0	40.7	8
68	0.82	1.0	43.8	16

Table 7.10 Multiple regression analysis estimates

Regression statistics				
R-square	0.95			
Standard error	3.23			
Number of observations	11			
F-statistic	27.79			
Significance	0.00			

Independent variable	Coefficient	Standard error	t-statistic	Significance
Intercept	−5.51	6.16	−0.89	0.41
Capacity	21.20	4.77	4.44	0.00
Speed	19.63	4.80	4.09	0.01
Travel	0.04	0.12	0.35	0.74
Landings	2.19	0.36	6.12	0.00

intercept. We find, however, that the intercept is negative and not statistically significant. This suggests that there are no significant fixed elements in manufacturing.

The coefficients for capacity, speed, and landings are positive. The probability that each of these coefficients is 0 is less than 0.05. Hence, we can be very confident that these variables are significant factors in the cost of manufacturing an elevator.

The coefficient for travel is positive, but the probability that this coefficient is 0 is 0.74. This suggests that, contrary to management's belief, the distance of travel is not a significant factor in the manufacturing cost.

Forecasting

A multiple regression equation can be used to forecast the dependent variable when the independent variables take different values. For this, we need a statistically significant multiple regression equation that explains a high percentage of the variation of the dependent variable.

Referring to table 7.10, the equation meets these conditions. Management can use the equation to forecast the cost of any future project. For instance, suppose that a client has requested a quotation for a system with the following characteristics: capacity of 1,000 kilograms, speed of 1.0 meter per second, travel of 20 meters, and four landings. Then, the estimated cost (in thousands of dollars) would be

$$-5.51 + (21.20 \times 1) + (19.63 \times 1) + (0.04 \times 20) + (2.19 \times 4) = 44.88, \tag{7.1}$$

or \$44,880.

Other Applications

We have just seen how multiple regression can be used to research the presence of fixed costs. Managers can also apply multiple regression to investigate the presence of joint costs across two products. To research this question, we need data about total costs when different quantities of the two products are produced together and when they are produced separately.

In the regression equation, the dependent variable should be the total cost and there should be three independent variables: the quantities of the two products and an indicator that takes the value of 1 where the two products are produced together and the value of 0 where the two products are produced separately. If there are joint costs, then the coefficient of the indicator should be negative and statistically significant.

> **Progress Check 7F** Referring to table 7.9, forecast the cost of an elevator with capacity of 750 kilograms, speed of 1.5 meters per second, travel of 40 meters, and 10 landings.

9 Summary

Conventional accounting statements do not always provide all the information on costs necessary for effective business decisions. Managers should use the principles presented in this chapter to develop accurate information about costs.

Economies of scale arise from either significant fixed costs or variable costs that diminish with the scale of production. An industry where businesses exhibit scale economies will tend to be concentrated. Economies of scope arise from significant joint costs across the production of two or more items. Scope economies drive businesses to supply multiple products. The experience curve shows how average costs decline with cumulative production.

Opportunity cost is the net revenue from the best alternative course of action. Sunk costs are costs that have been committed and cannot be avoided. For effective business decisions, managers should consider opportunity costs and ignore sunk costs. The transfer price of an item within an organization should be set equal to the marginal cost.

Key Concepts

economies of scale	joint cost	economic value added
diseconomies of scale	experience curve	transfer price
economies of scope	relevance	
diseconomies of scope	opportunity cost	

Further Reading

For a general introduction to cost accounting, refer to Charles Horngren, George Foster, and Srikant Datar's *Cost Accounting: A Managerial Emphasis*, 11th ed. (Englewood Cliffs, NJ: Prentice-Hall, 2003). Chapters 2, 3, 10, 11, and 14 are closely related to the concepts presented here. C. K. Prahalad and Gary Hamel launched the concept of core competence in "The Core Competence of the Corporation," *Harvard Business Review* 68, no. 3 (May–June 1990), pp. 79–91. Alfred Rappaport explains the concept of shareholder value added in *Creating Shareholder Value: A Guide for Managers and Investors* (New York: Free Press, 1998).

Review Questions

1. Explain the difference between economies of scale and economies of scope.

2. Generation of electric power involves significant short-run fixed costs. Owing to the entry of several independent power producers, the demand for Southern Power's electricity has dropped. Management has reduced production. How will this cutback affect Southern Power's average fixed costs?

3. Identify the situation for which economies of scale are more significant (choose a or b).
   (a) Tre Stagioni, which has a permanent staff of two chefs and five waiters.
   (b) Campus Deli, which relies mainly on part-time workers, hired on a monthly basis.

4. The most significant cost in family medicine practice is human resources. To treat twice as many patients, a clinic will probably need twice as many doctors, nurses, and other professional staff. Does this business have economies of scale?

5. Banks and insurers both need distribution networks to sell products and serve their customers. An office that takes deposits and makes loans can just as easily sell insurance policies. In France, many banks sell life insurance. Is the combination of banking and insurance, called *bancassurance*, a result of economies of scale or scope?

6. Hindus must not eat beef, while Muslim people must not consume pork. A restaurant catering to both Hindu and Muslim customers must have separate facilities for preparing Hindu and Muslim meals. Are there economies or diseconomies of scope across the Hindu and Muslim restaurant businesses?

7. Explain the difference between economies of scale and the experience curve.

8. A salesman buys lunch for a potential client. Why is this lunch *not* free for the client?

9. Discuss whether business performance should be measured in terms of economic value added rather than accounting profit.

10. The Director of Executive Education at your school has reported that revenue increased from $5 to $5.5 million, while profit rose from $2 to $2.1 million. How would you consider the free use of school facilities in evaluating these results?

11. There is a perfectly competitive market for lumber. How much should Saturn's residential development group pay the building materials division for lumber?

12. "Our costs are very high because of the huge pensions of our retirees." Are the pensions

of retired employees relevant for prospective business decisions?

13. For which of the following businesses are sunk labor costs more significant (choose a or b)?
    (a) A Japanese conglomerate that guarantees lifetime employment.
    (b) A U.S. manufacturer that employs workers at will, which means that workers can be dismissed without cause.

14. Consider the costs of offering a freight transport service. In which of the following situations are sunk costs relatively largest?
    (a) The railway company owns the tracks.
    (b) The railway company pays another company to use the track on a long-term contract.
    (c) The truck operator pays tolls to use the highway as and when necessary.

15. Referring to table 7.10, if you were to repeat the regression with only three independent variables, which ones would you choose?

Discussion Questions

1. Qantas operates a fleet of over 100 Boeing jet aircraft. Many jets carry cargo in their "bellies," under the passenger seating areas. Consider each of the following costs. Identify which are joint costs of the passenger and belly cargo services, which are fixed costs of passenger services, and which are both.
    (a) *Cockpit personnel*. All jets, large and small, require a pilot and co-pilot. Belly cargo service requires no additional officers in the cockpit.
    (b) *Airport landing fees*. Some airports charge landing fees by weight of the aircraft, while others levy a fixed fee regardless of weight.
    (c) *Fuel*. Larger aircraft and those carrying heavier loads consume relatively more fuel.

2. Elevators generally break down at random times and for different reasons. Elevator maintenance contractors must have trained service personnel to provide routine and emergency service. Shan On Elevator has 200 service personnel to maintain 1,000 elevators.
    (a) Suppose that Shan On has received a contract to maintain an additional 1,000 elevators. Do you expect that Shan On will need to double service personnel? Why or why not?
    (b) Does the example in (a) illustrate economies of scale or scope?
    (c) Escalators and elevators use quite different technology and parts. But many clients operate both escalators and elevators. Are there any economies of scope for a contractor to maintain both escalators and elevators?

3. Applying Internet Protocol technology, Qwest provides nationwide long-distance voice and data communications over a single network. Other carriers provide voice and data communications over separate networks. In 1999, while building networks for local telecommunications access in 25 metropolitan areas, Qwest acquired US West. US West dominated the market for local telephone and high bandwidth Internet access in the West and Midwest. Qwest forecast that the acquisition would bolster "scope and scale" through reducing operating expenses by $4.4 billion and capital expenditure by $2.2 billion over the period 2000–2005.
    (a) Discuss whether the acquisition would expand Qwest's horizontal or vertical boundaries or both.
    (b) To what extent do you expect the acquisition to yield gains from economies of scale?
    (c) To what extent do you expect the acquisition to yield gains from economies of scope?

4. Traditionally, electric power utilities generated electricity in large-scale plants with capacities of hundreds of megawatts. However, the economies of scale in generation had to be balanced against power losses in distribution of electricity, which increase with the distance of transmission. New gas-fired turbine technology allows cost-effective generation of electric power at small scales of 50–100 kilowatts.

(a) Explain the trade-off between economies of scale in power generation and power losses in the distribution of electricity.

(b) How did the development of the new gas-turbine technology affect economies of scale in the generation of electric power?

(c) How will the new gas-turbine technology affect the demand for electricity transmission equipment?

5. Semiconductor manufacturing requires billion-dollar investments. In August 2004, Infineon announced a deal with Taiwan's Winbond Electronics to build a new dynamic random-access memory (DRAM) factory. Infineon would provide the technology while Winbond would pay for the construction and equipping. Infineon executive Ralph Heinrich hoped that the deal would help Infineon to secure 25% of the global DRAM market. It was remarked that "the fight to survive in the DRAM industry depends largely on size – since the more chips a company churns out, the lower the cost per chip" (*Source*: "Infineon's Deal with Winbond Reaffirms Outsourcing Strategy," *Asian Wall Street Journal*, August 10, 2004).

(a) A 300 mm wafer is 2.25 times larger than a 200 mm wafer. Since wafers are just silicon, the variable cost of increasing wafer size is quite small. Suppose that the cost of processing a 300 mm wafer is less than 2.25 times that of a 200 mm wafer. Explain the economy of scale in manufacturing semiconductors from larger wafers.

(b) The cost of establishing a 300 mm wafer fabrication facility is higher than that of a 200 mm wafer fabrication facility. Explain how this affects the average cost of producing from 200 mm vis-à-vis 300 mm wafers.

(c) Infineon produces memory chips from multiple factories, some of which are joint ventures with Taiwanese manufacturers. Does the cost per chip depend on the total produced by the entire company or each factory?

6. In April 2004, Boeing launched the new 787 Dreamliner with 50 firm orders from All Nippon Airways of Japan. Boeing aimed to secure 200 firm orders by December. However, perhaps due to speculation about a competing Airbus offering, Boeing fell short – it had only 52 orders in December 2004. Industry consultant Richard Aboulafia remarked that Airbus had succeeded in its goal of "disrupt[ing] the business case for the 7E7[787]" (*Source*: "Airbus Pushes Ahead with Rival to 7E7," *Seattle Post-Intelligencer*, December 11, 2004).

(a) Would the costs of developing the 787 Dreamliner vary with the total quantity manufactured?

(b) Referring to figure 7.3, compare Boeing's average cost with cumulative production of 50 vis-à-vis 200 units. (Note that, in figure 7.3, the average cost is not absolute but rather indexed to 100 with production of the first unit.)

(c) Suppose that the price of a Boeing 787 is $120 million and that Boeing would just break even on the costs of development ($10 billion) and manufacturing with cumulative production of 200 units. How much would Boeing lose with cumulative production of 50 units?

7. Consider a retailer of consumer electronics that imports European and Korean DVD players to the United States. In January 2004, it bought a shipment of Korean DVD players for $200,000 and another 1,000 DVD players from Europe for $180,000.

(a) By August 2004, the Korean won had appreciated by 2%. For purposes of pricing, what is the relevant cost of the DVD players?

(b) By August 2004, the euro had depreciated by 3%. For purposes of pricing, what is the relevant cost of the European machines?

(c) Use the examples in (a) and (b) to explain the concepts of opportunity cost and sunk cost.

8. Over the 1990s, the Loewen Group expanded from funeral homes to cemeteries, partly financed by $2 billion of bonds and $300 million of bank loans. For the six months ending June 30, 1999, Loewen's operating earnings were $73 million. However, interest expenses of $77 million, and other non-operational expenses dragged the group down to a $88 million pre-tax loss. Faced with the prospect of further losses, Loewen filed for bankruptcy protection in Canada and the United

Table 7.11   Micropolis: Assets, December 1997 (S$ million)

	Estimated book value	Realizable value
Inventories and work-in-progress	130	13
Production equipment	34	4
Factory	70	45
Other items	40	14
Total	274	76

Source: "STPL's Micropolis Venture May Cost it $575m Loss," *Straits Times*, December 24, 1997, p. 1.

States. Chairman John Lacey called on bondholders to convert hundreds of millions of dollars of bonds into equity.

(a)   Discuss whether the Loewen Group expansion from funeral homes to cemeteries affected its horizontal or vertical boundaries or both.

(b)   If you had to justify the expansion, would you rely on economies of scale or scope or neither?

(c)   Suppose that bondholders converted $500 million worth of bonds to equity. How would this affect Loewen's earnings before income taxes as compared with its economic value added?

9.   In April 1996, the Singapore Technologies Group acquired disk-drive manufacturer Micropolis for S$80 million. Micropolis was hit by a severe downturn in the disk drive industry, and despite S$550 million in loans, the company had to be liquidated in late 1997. Liquidators estimated the market value of Micropolis's assets to be S$76 million as compared with their S$274 million book value. Table 7.11 lists the estimates for various categories of assets.

(a)   Which of the following best describes the difference between book value and estimated realizable value: (i) sunk cost, (ii) opportunity cost, (iii) fixed cost? Explain your answer.

(b)   Define "specificity" as the ratio of book value less estimated realizable value to book value, in percentage terms. Calculate the specificity of (i) inventories and work-in-progress, (ii) production equipment, and (iii) factory.

(c)   Explain the relation between sunk costs and specificity.

(d)   Explain why Micropolis's inventories and work-in-progress and production equipment have a higher specificity than the factory.

10.   This question relies on the statistical methods section. Suppose that Mercury Elevator has just discovered a mistake in the data of table 7.9. In the first column, every entry for cost should be $14,000 higher. All other data remain valid.

(a)   Estimate the cost equation with the original data (before the revision of the first column).

(b)   Estimate the cost equation with the revised data. Does production involve substantial fixed elements?

(c)   Using the revised estimates in (b), calculate the cost of a system with the following characteristics: capacity of 1,000 kilograms, speed of 1.0 meter per second, travel of 20 meters, and four landings.

Chapter 8

Monopoly

1 Introduction

Depression is associated with an imbalance of neurotransmitters, the chemicals that enable nerve cells in the brain to communicate with one another. The selective serotonin re-uptake inhibitor (SSRI) class of drugs helps to control the symptoms of depression by increasing the brain's supply of the neurotransmitter serotonin. Leading SSRIs include Eli Lilly's Prozac, Pfizer's Zoloft, and GlaxoSmithKline's Paxil.[1]

In December 1987, Prozac became the first SSRI to receive U.S. government approval for treatment of depression. The drug quickly became a blockbuster. By 1999, Lilly's world wide revenues from Prozac were $2.6 billion a year including $2.1 billion in the United States. Sales were supported by $60.2 million of detailing (visits to) physicians in offices and hospitals, $8.2 million of advertising in medical journals, and just $151,000 of direct-to-consumer advertising. However, Prozac was losing market share to Zoloft and Paxil.

In 1996, generic drug manufacturer Barr Laboratories began legal action to challenge Lilly's patent over Prozac. In the U.S. District Court, Judge Sarah Barker held that Lilly's patent was valid until December 2003. However, the U.S. Court of Appeals for the Federal Circuit overruled the lower court and cleared the way for generic competition from February 2001. Analysts expected Lilly to receive an additional six months' protection by testing Prozac on children and, so, competition would effectively begin only in August 2001.

Lilly priced Prozac at $2.63 for a day's supply. Typically, incremental margins on patented prescription drugs are about 90%, and generics are sold at half the price of branded drugs. Following the U.S. Appeals Court decision, Lilly's stock price fell by $31.86 from $108.55 to $76.69, reducing the company's market capitalization by $36 billion. Barr's stock price rose from $45.75 to $77, raising the company's market capitalization by $1.1 billion.

With the expiry of its patent and the advent of competition from generics, Eli Lilly had to consider whether, and if so, how to revise the price and advertising policy for Prozac. Why did the Appeals Court decision raise Barr's market value by less than the amount by

[1] This discussion is based, in part, on "Court Ruling Means Cheaper, Generic Prozac to Hit Market in 2001," *AP Business News*, August 11, 2000; "Prozac® Patent Ruled Invalid by U.S. Court of Appeals," Barr Laboratories Press Release, August 9, 2000; and "Hard to Swallow: America's Soaring Drug Costs," *Wall Street Journal*, November 16, 1998, p. A1.

which it reduced Lilly's value? How would the expiry of the Prozac patent affect the market for the ingredients used in the manufacturing of Prozac?

To address these questions, we must understand the behavior of buyers or sellers that have the power to influence market conditions. A buyer or seller that can influence market conditions is said to have *market power*. A buyer with market power can influence market supply, in particular, the price and quantity supplied. A seller with market power can influence market demand, in particular, the price and quantity demanded.

For simplicity, we will focus on markets in which there is either just one seller or one buyer. If there is only one seller in a market, that seller is called a **monopoly**. If there is only one buyer in a market, that buyer is called a **monopsony**. Monopoly and monopsony are extreme cases: at the opposite extreme lies perfect competition, where there are numerous buyers and sellers, all of whom are small relative to the market. The knowledge of these extremes helps us to understand the intermediate case where there are several buyers or sellers who are large enough to influence market conditions.

> A **monopoly** is the only seller in a market.

> A **monopsony** is the only buyer in a market.

We begin by discussing the sources of market power. Then, we analyze how a profit-maximizing monopoly sets its price and scale of production. This allows us to show how the monopoly should adjust price and production in response to changes in demand and costs. Applying this analysis, we can address the issue of whether and, if so, how Lilly should adjust the price of Prozac when generics enter the market.

Next, we consider how much a monopoly should spend on advertising and R&D. Then, we compare prices, production rates, and profits under a monopoly with perfect competition. This explains how competing sellers can benefit by restricting competition among themselves through cartels or horizontal integration. We can apply this analysis to explain why the Appeals Court decision raised Barr's market value by less than it reduced Lilly's.

Finally, we focus on monopsony and analyze how a monopsony that maximizes net benefit will set its price and scale of purchases. This analysis explains how the expiry of the Prozac patent would affect the market for the ingredients in Prozac production.

2   Sources of Market Power

Before analyzing how monopolies and monopsonies use market power, we first review the sources of this power. To understand the reasons for a monopoly, we need to ask why other sellers do not enter the market to compete for the business. Generally, the sources of market power are the barriers that deter or prevent entry by other competing sellers. Similarly, the sources of market power for a monopsony are the barriers that deter entry of competing buyers.

Monopoly

Unique resource

One barrier to entry by competing sellers is access to unique physical, natural, or human resources. For instance, football teams are limited to one quarterback and soccer teams to one goalkeeper. A football manager cannot field two quarterbacks nor can a soccer team have two goalkeepers. Under such circumstances, teams with better players enjoy market power.

The minerals industry provides an example of natural resources giving rise to market power. MMC Norilsk Nickel of Russia accounts for over 90% of the world production of nickel. Norilsk Nickel is also the world's leading producer of palladium.

Intellectual property

A second source of market power is control over intellectual property; that is, property over inventions or expressions. To encourage research and development of new products and processes, most governments award patents for new inventions. A patent gives the owner an exclusive right to the invention for a specified period of time. This exclusive right may be a source of market power. Eli Lilly's patent to Xigris, a drug for the treatment of sepsis, provides it with a monopoly over the drug.

Another form of intellectual property is a copyright. A copyright establishes property in published expressions, including computer software and engineering drawings. Microsoft, for example, has the copyright over Office XP, which gives Microsoft a monopoly over the software. In chapter 11, we discuss the economics of patents and copyrights in greater detail.

Economies of scale and scope

A third source of market power is economies of scale or scope, as discussed in chapter 7. Electricity distribution illustrates economies of scale. This service requires an extensive network of cables leading from generating stations to the various users, including factories, residences, and offices. To have two competing distributors of electricity would mean duplication of the cable network. So, in electricity distribution, one provider can achieve lower costs than multiple providers. Hence, the industry will tend to be dominated by a single provider.

Cable television and local telephone service illustrate economies of scope. Both services depend on a network of cables from the service provider to the individual subscribers. Owing to economies of scope, a combined provider of television and telephone service can achieve lower average costs than specialized providers. Consequently, these industries will tend to be dominated by a single provider.

Product differentiation

A seller may be able to establish market power by differentiating itself from competitors. Sellers can differentiate their products through product design, distribution, and advertising and promotion. Coca-Cola provides an excellent example. There are many competing colas in the retail market. To differentiate its product, Coca-Cola has made intensive investments in its brand that support a price premium over generic colas.

Pharmaceuticals provide another example. Although its patents on aspirin have long expired, Bayer still commands a higher price for its aspirin than generic manufacturers.

Regulation

Finally, market power may derive from government regulation. In businesses where economies of scale or scope are strong, the government may decide to award an exclusive franchise to one provider. By deliberately prohibiting competition, the government hopes to avoid duplication and, so, reduce the cost of the service. Examples of businesses in which governments may award exclusive franchises include local telephone service, and distribution of electricity, natural gas, water, and postal services.

Monopsony

So far, we have discussed why a seller may be a monopoly or, more generally, have market power. These same factors explain why a buyer may have market power. There is one additional reason for the presence of a monopsony: the existence of a monopoly. A seller

The U.S. Federal Reserve System: monopoly money machine

In 1913, the U.S. Congress established the Federal Reserve System. The system consists of 12 Federal Reserve Banks, which have the exclusive right to issue currency notes. As of December 2004, $719 billion worth of U.S. currency was in public circulation.

Considering that currency notes are merely high-quality printed paper, it is not surprising that the Federal Reserve's monopoly is extremely profitable. In 2004, the Federal Reserve Banks earned $21.3 billion on revenue of $23.5 billion – a performance that would be the envy of any business.

Although the Federal Reserve System has a monopoly within the United States, it has no such privilege overseas. International business can be transacted in any currency. Despite competition from other currencies, the greenback has held up very well in international transactions. It has been estimated that about two-thirds of the U.S. currency circulates outside the United States.

The profitability of producing U.S. currency attracts competition. In 2003, U.S. and other authorities seized about $63 million worth of counterfeit currency, including $31 million in Colombia.

Sources: Board of Governors of the Federal Reserve System, *2004 Annual Report*; Bruce A. Townsend, "Statement Before U.S. House of Representatives," Committee on Financial Services, Subcommittee on Domestic and International Monetary Policy, Trade and Technology, April 28, 2004.

that has a monopoly over some good or service is also likely to have market power over the inputs into that item. For instance, a monopoly electricity distributor would have market power over suppliers of electricity meters and high-voltage switch-gear. It would probably also be a monopsony in the market for the services of power engineers.

Defense provides another example. Generally, national governments monopolize defense. By this monopoly, the government would have market power over suppliers of military equipment and supplies, as well as the services of military personnel.

Brand-level vis-à-vis market demand elasticities

Generally, the products of an entire market have fewer close substitutes than the product of an individual seller. Accordingly, the individual seller's demand will tend to be more elastic than the market demand. At one extreme, if the market is perfectly competitive, the individual seller's demand will be extremely elastic. At the other extreme, if the market is a monopoly, the individual seller's demand will be the same as the market demand; hence, it will have the same price elasticity as the market demand.

Table 8.1 reports the price elasticities of demand for representative brands of consumer products as compared with their respective markets. The brand-level elasticity of the demand for margarine is almost 20 times higher than the market-level elasticity. By contrast, the brand-level elasticity of the demand for coffee is just twice the market-level elasticity. These data suggest that U.S. manufacturers of margarine have much less market power than those of coffee.

Table 8.1 U.S. consumer products: market and brand-level elasticities

Product	Price elasticity of demand	
	Market	Brand-level
Coffee	−1.42	−3.06
Ice cream	−0.74	−2.58
Margarine	−0.12	−2.34
Paper towels	−0.74	−4.74
Liquid detergents	−1.70	−5.66

Source: Authors' calculations based on David R. Bell, Jeongwen Chiang, and V. Padmanabhan, "The Decomposition of Promotional Response: An Empirical Generalization," *Marketing Science* 18, no. 4 (1999), pp. 504–26.

3   Monopoly Pricing

Having reviewed the sources of market power, let us now consider how a seller can use market power. Suppose that Solar Pharmaceutical has just received a patent for a new drug, Gamma-1, that cures bone-marrow cancer. How should Solar set the price for this drug? The essence of market power is that the seller faces a demand curve that slopes downward. Solar Pharmaceutical, being a monopoly, faces the market demand curve. Unlike a perfectly competitive seller, a monopoly has to consider how its sales will affect the market price.

Given the market demand curve, a monopoly can either set the price and let the market determine how much it will buy, or decide how much to sell and let the market determine the price at which it is willing to buy that quantity. If the monopoly tries to set both the price and sales, the price and the sales may be inconsistent in the sense that, at that price, the market wants to buy more or less than the quantity the monopoly is selling. In terms of a graph, inconsistency means that the monopoly is choosing a combination of price and sales off the demand curve. Accordingly, a monopoly can set either the price or sales but not both.

How does Solar's price affect its revenue and cost?

Revenue

First, let us look at the relationship between price and revenue. Table 8.2 shows the demand for Gamma-1: specifically, the second column shows, for every price, the quantity of Gamma-1 that Solar expects to sell. We see that the quantity demanded increases by 200,000 units for every $10 reduction in price. Using this information, we can then calculate Solar's *total revenue* for every price, which is price multiplied by sales.[2] From the total revenue, we can then calculate *marginal revenue*, which is the change in total revenue arising from selling an additional unit.

To sell additional units, Solar Pharmaceutical must reduce its price. So, when increasing sales by one unit, Solar will gain revenue from selling the additional (or marginal) unit, but

---

[2]   In chapter 9 on pricing, we consider the possibility of price discrimination. With price discrimination, different units are sold at different prices, so total revenue is not simply price multiplied by sales.

Table 8.2 Monopoly revenue, cost, and profit

Price ($)	Sales	Total revenue ($)	Marginal revenue ($)	Total cost ($)	Marginal cost ($)	Profit ($)
200	0.0	0		50		−50
190	0.2	38	190	52	10	−14
180	0.4	72	170	56	20	16
170	0.6	102	150	62	30	40
160	0.8	128	130	70	40	58
150	1.0	150	110	80	50	70
140	1.2	168	90	92	60	76
130	1.4	182	70	106	70	76
120	1.6	192	50	122	80	70
110	1.8	198	30	140	90	58
100	2.0	200	10	160	100	40
90	2.2	198	−10	182	110	16

Sales in millions of units; total revenue, total cost, and profit in millions of dollars.

Inframarginal units are those other than the marginal unit.

it will lose revenue on the *inframarginal units*. The **inframarginal** units are those other than the marginal unit. Solar would have sold the inframarginal units without reducing the price.

For example, referring to table 8.2, to increase sales from 200,000 to 400,000 units, Solar must reduce the price from $190 to $180. Hence, Solar will gain revenue of $180 × 200,000 = $36 million on the additional units, but lose $(190 − 180) × 200,000 = $2 million on the inframarginal 200,000 units that it could have sold at $190. Thus, Solar's revenue for the additional 200,000 units is $36 − $2 = $34 million, which means that marginal revenue is $170 per unit.

In general, the marginal revenue from selling an additional unit will be less than the price of that unit. The reason, as we have explained, is that the marginal revenue is the price of the marginal unit minus the loss of revenue on the inframarginal units.

The difference between the price and the marginal revenue depends on the price elasticity of demand. If demand is very elastic, then the seller need not reduce the price very much to increase sales; hence, the marginal revenue will be close to the price. If, however, demand is very inelastic, then the seller must reduce the price substantially to increase sales; so, the marginal revenue will be much lower than the price.

We should also emphasize that the marginal revenue can be negative, if the loss of revenue on the inframarginal units exceeds the gain on the marginal unit. Table 8.2 shows that, if Solar cut the price from $100 to $90, sales would increase from 2.0 to 2.2 million units. The change in revenue, however, is −$2 million for the additional 200,000 units, which means that marginal revenue is −$10 per unit.

Progress Check 8A If demand is extremely elastic, what will be the difference between the price and the marginal revenue?

Costs

We have considered the relation between price and revenue. The other side to profit is cost. Table 8.2 also shows data for Solar Pharmaceutical's production costs. It reports only avoidable costs and omits sunk costs. From the total cost at a zero production scale, we can infer that production requires a fixed cost of $50 million.

Total cost increases with the scale of production. Table 8.2 shows Solar's marginal cost, which is the change in total cost due to the production of an additional unit. The change in total cost arises from change in the variable cost.

Profit-Maximizing Price

With information on both revenue and cost, we can calculate Solar's profit. Profit is total revenue less total (fixed and variable) cost. The last column of table 8.2 reports profit at every quantity of sales. Looking down the column, we see that Solar's maximum profit is $76 million. It achieves this profit with a price of $130 and sales of 1.4 million units.

In addition to calculating the profit from all possible prices or quantities of sales, the *profit-maximizing scale of operation* can be identified in another way: it is the scale at which the marginal revenue balances the marginal cost. At the price of $130, Solar's sales are 1.4 million units. The marginal revenue is $70 per unit. The marginal cost is also $70 per unit. So, at the **profit-maximizing scale**, the marginal revenue equals the marginal cost.

> The **profit-maximizing scale of operation** is where marginal revenue equals marginal cost.

This suggests a general rule: to maximize profit, a monopoly should operate at a scale where its marginal revenue balances its marginal cost. This rule applies to any seller and not only a monopoly. It can be expressed in another way. The **contribution margin** is the total revenue less the variable cost. If the seller sells an additional unit, then its contribution margin will change by the difference between the marginal revenue and the marginal cost. Hence, a seller maximizes profit by operating at a scale where the sale of an additional unit will result in no change to the contribution margin.

> The **contribution margin** is the total revenue less variable cost.

Let us illustrate the profit-maximizing price and operation scale with a diagram. Figure 8.1 shows Solar Pharmaceutical's demand, marginal revenue, and marginal cost curves. The demand curve shows, for every price, the quantity that the market will buy. Equivalently, it shows, for every quantity of purchases (on the horizontal axis), the maximum price (on the vertical axis) that the market will pay for that quantity.

The marginal revenue curve shows, for every quantity (on the horizontal axis), the marginal revenue (on the vertical axis). As we have explained, for every quantity, the marginal revenue is less than the price. Accordingly, at all quantities, the marginal revenue curve lies below the demand curve.

The marginal revenue and marginal cost curves cross at the quantity of 1.4 million units. From the demand curve, we see that the price at that quantity is $130. This is the profit-maximizing price.

Let us understand why a seller maximizes profit at a production scale where marginal revenue balances marginal cost. Suppose that Solar produces at a scale, such as 1.2 million units, where the marginal revenue exceeds the marginal cost. Then, if Solar increases production by 200,000 units, its revenue will increase by more than its cost; indeed, it will increase its profit by the area shaded *bca*.

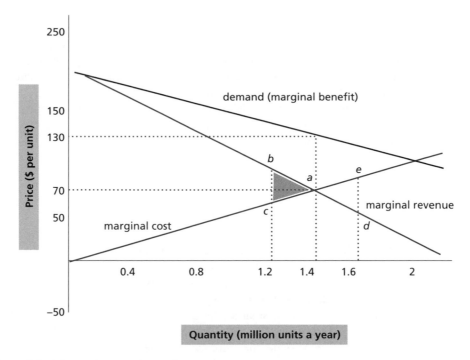

Figure 8.1   Monopoly operating scale
The marginal revenue and marginal cost curves cross at the quantity of 1.4 million units. Reading from the demand curve, the profit-maximizing price is $130. The demand curve also shows the marginal benefit. At 1.2 million units, the marginal benefit exceeds the marginal cost.

By contrast, suppose that Solar produces at a scale such as 1.6 million units, where the marginal revenue is less than the marginal cost. Then, if Solar cuts production by 200,000 units, its revenue will fall by less than its cost; hence it will increase its profit by the area *ade*. Generally, a seller will maximize profit if it produces at a scale where its marginal revenue balances its marginal cost.

Progress Check 8B   Suppose that, at the current scale of production, Solar's marginal revenue is less than its marginal cost. How should management adjust its price?

Economic Inefficiency

Figure 8.1 reveals an important aspect of a monopoly's profit-maximizing operating scale. At the quantity of 1.4 million units, the price is $130. Recall that the demand curve also shows the marginal benefit for every quantity of purchases. Hence, the marginal benefit at 1.4 million units is $130.

By contrast, the marginal cost at 1.4 million units is $70. Hence, the marginal benefit exceeds the marginal cost. This means that some buyers are willing to pay more than the marginal cost for the item but cannot get it. In chapter 6, we explained that such a divergence between the marginal benefit and the marginal cost is economically inefficient.

| Life-and-death monopoly: Glaxo Wellcome and the pricing of AZT |

GlaxoSmithKline owns the patent to the antiviral drug AZT (Zidovudine). AZT blocks the enzyme that stimulates the HIV virus to proliferate. While the drug does not cure AIDS, it may relieve symptoms and prolong remission.

At one time, Glaxo's drug meant the difference between life and death for many people. Even well-informed analysts have been confused into thinking that such a monopoly can make unlimited profit: "Once its products were approved, a big drug firm such as Glaxo could sell them at almost whatever price it wanted."

Although AZT was critical for a person with AIDS, Glaxo could not charge an unlimited price for the drug. Glaxo could actually set the price as high as it liked, but it could not force people with AIDS to buy the drug. Glaxo knew that, if it set a higher price, the quantity demanded would be lower.

In 2004, AZT was available in combination with Lamivudine as Combivir, at a retail price of $10 per tablet. Meanwhile, Glaxo provided Combivir at a special price of 65 cents to more than 60 of the world's poorest countries.

Sources: "Waging Sykological Warfare," *The Economist*, January 28, 1995, pp. 61–2; "GlaxoSmithKline Takes Further Action to Help the World's Poorest Fight HIV/AIDS," Press Release, Glaxo SmithKline, October 16, 2003.

The managerial implication of this economic inefficiency is that a profit can be made through bridging the gap to provide the item to those buyers. Since they are willing to pay more than the marginal cost, the difference is the potential profit to be made by supplying them. In chapter 9, we discuss various pricing policies through which a seller can increase profit by bridging the inefficiency.

4   Demand and Cost Changes

How should a monopoly respond to changes in demand? For instance, suppose that demand for Solar's Gamma-1 shifts outward. How should Solar adjust its price? To address this question, figure 8.2 shows the new demand curve. From the new demand curve, we can calculate the new marginal revenue curve.

The new marginal revenue curve lies further to the right. Since the upward-sloping marginal cost curve does not change, the new marginal revenue curve crosses the marginal cost curve at a larger scale. Specifically, the two curves cross at a scale of about 1.5 million units, and the new profit-maximizing price is around $135.

Although the change was only in demand, we must consider both the new marginal revenue and the original marginal cost to obtain the new profit-maximizing sales and price.

Marginal Cost Change

We can use a similar approach to understand how a monopoly should respond to a change in the marginal cost. Suppose, for instance, that, relative to the data reported in table 8.2, the marginal cost drops by half at all scales of production. Should Solar reduce the price of the drug by half as well?

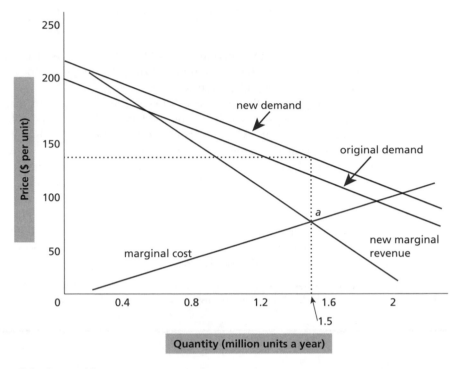

Figure 8.2   Demand increase
The new marginal revenue curve crosses the marginal cost curve at the quantity of 1.5 million units. The new profit-maximizing price is around $135.

To address this question, consider figure 8.3, which shows Solar's marginal revenue and the new marginal cost. The marginal revenue and the new marginal cost cross at a quantity of about 1.7 million units. The new profit-maximizing price is around $120. Notice that Solar maximizes profits by cutting its price by about $10, which is proportionately less than the fall in the marginal cost. Further, although the change was only in the marginal cost, Solar must consider the marginal revenue as well as the new marginal cost to obtain the new profit-maximizing price and sales.

Generally, when there is a change in either demand or cost, the extent to which a monopoly should adjust its price depends on the shapes of both its marginal revenue and marginal cost curves. It should adjust the price until its marginal revenue equals its marginal cost.

Fixed Cost Change

We should stress that a monopoly's profit-maximizing price and scale do not depend in any way on the fixed cost (so long as it is not too large). Suppose that Solar Pharmaceutical must incur an additional fixed cost of $40 million a year to maintain its production line. In table 8.3, we show Solar's revenues and costs with the higher fixed cost. The profit-maximizing price and scale are still $130 and 1.4 million units, respectively.

There is another way to see that the profit-maximizing price and sales do not depend on the fixed cost. Recall that a monopoly maximizes profit by operating at the scale where its

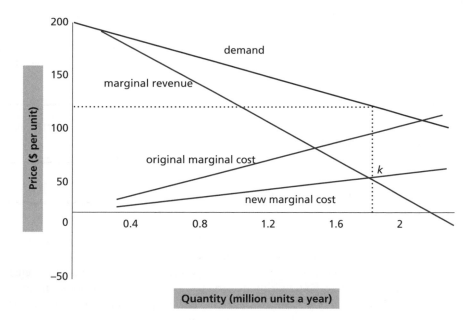

Figure 8.3 Reduction in marginal cost
The marginal revenue and the new marginal cost cross at a quantity of about 1.7 million units. The new profit-maximizing price is around $120.

Table 8.3 Increase in fixed cost

Price ($)	Sales	Total revenue ($)	Marginal revenue ($)	Total cost ($)	Marginal cost ($)	Profit ($)
200	0.0	0		90		−90
190	0.2	38	190	92	10	−54
180	0.4	72	170	96	20	−24
170	0.6	102	150	102	30	0
160	0.8	128	130	110	40	18
150	1.0	150	110	120	50	30
140	1.2	168	90	132	60	36
130	1.4	182	70	146	70	36
120	1.6	192	50	162	80	30
110	1.8	198	30	180	90	18
100	2.0	200	10	200	100	0
90	2.2	198	−10	222	110	−24

Sales, total revenue, total cost, and profit in millions of dollars.

marginal revenue equals its marginal cost. Changes in the fixed cost will not affect the marginal cost curve; hence, they will not affect the profit-maximizing price.

If, however, the fixed cost is so large that the total cost exceeds total revenue, then the monopoly will prefer to shut down. In Solar's case, if the fixed cost exceeds $126 million, the company will close. Unless the fixed costs are so large, they do not affect the profit-maximizing price and scale.

The general point that the profit-maximizing price and scale do not depend on the level of fixed cost is crucial in knowledge-intensive industries. These businesses are characterized by relatively high fixed costs and low marginal costs.

Progress Check 8C In figure 8.1, show how the monopoly should adjust price if marginal cost increases everywhere by $10.

License auctions and the cost of mobile telecommunications

Telecommunications regulators around the world are concerned about how to allocate new licenses for mobile services. The German, U.K., and U.S. Governments have used multiple-round sealed bid auctions. Other regulators worry about the impact of license auctions on the cost of telecommunications services. Hong Kong Director-General of Telecommunications, Anthony Wong, remarked, "There's good and bad in auctioning off spectrum . . . it may raise costs for telecoms providers."

In fact, regulators need not worry at all. Typically, the auction price is a lump sum that does not vary with the quantity or variety of services that the telecommunications provider will offer. Accordingly, the auction price is a fixed cost with respect to the scale and scope of operations, and would not affect the marginal cost at all. Hence, the auction price would not affect the price of telecommunications services to end-users.

Even if a telecommunications provider were to over-bid and eventually suffer losses and become bankrupt, the license would still exist and could be sold to another provider. At that stage, the price originally paid for the license at auction would be a sunk cost, and would not affect its resale price to the new licensee.

Source: "Telecoms Chief Sees Further Fall in Long-Distance Tariffs," *South China Morning Post*, December 31, 1999, Business 1.

---

5 Advertising

Promotion is the set of marketing activities that a business undertakes to communicate with its customers and sell its products.

A monopoly, and more generally, any seller with market power can influence the demand for its products. **Promotion** is the set of marketing activities that a business undertakes to communicate with its customers and sell its products. It encompasses advertising, sales promotion, and public relations. Let us now consider how much a business should spend on promotion. For convenience, we focus the analysis on advertising by a monopoly. The same principles apply to the other dimensions of promotion and any seller with market power.

Benefit of Advertising

How much should Solar Pharmaceutical spend on advertising its new drug, Gamma-1? Advertising can influence the market demand. Specifically, given Solar's price, expenditure on advertising can increase the quantity of sales by shifting out the demand curve as well as causing it to be less elastic. The additional sales in turn affect Solar's total revenue and variable cost and hence its contribution margin. The benefit of advertising is the change in the contribution margin.

Accordingly, the net benefit from advertising is the change in the contribution margin less the advertising expenditure. To maximize profits, Solar should advertise up to the point that the increase in the contribution margin from an additional dollar of advertising is exactly $1.

Let us understand why this rule maximizes profit. Consider a point at which the increase in the contribution margin from an additional dollar of advertising is more than $1. Then, if Solar spends an additional dollar on advertising, its contribution margin will increase by more than $1, hence Solar will increase its profit. By contrast, at a point where an additional dollar of advertising increases Solar's contribution margin by less than $1, Solar can increase profit by cutting back on advertising expenditure.

Essentially, the rule advises the seller to invest in advertising up to the point that the marginal benefit just balances the marginal cost. To keep a clear distinction between the benefits and the costs of advertising, we measure the benefits by the effect on the contribution margin.

By contrast, some marketing specialists measure the benefit of advertising by the effect on awareness and recall of the featured product or on product sales. We emphasize that it is more appropriate to consider the effect of advertising on the contribution margin generated by the product. The reason is that, ultimately, the aim of most advertisers is to increase the seller's profit rather than awareness or sales as such. Managers who focus on awareness and recall or even sales may overlook the effect on profit.

Advertising–Sales Ratio

We have just presented a rule for advertising expenditure: to maximize profits, a monopoly should advertise up to the point that the increase in the contribution margin from an additional dollar of advertising is $1. Using the concepts of the *incremental margin percentage* and the *advertising elasticity of demand*, we can derive a simpler version of the rule for the profit-maximizing level of advertising expenditure.

We define the **incremental margin** as the price less the marginal cost. The incremental margin is the increase in the contribution margin from selling an additional unit, holding the price constant. Further, the **incremental marginal percentage** is the ratio of the price less the marginal cost to the price.

> The **incremental margin** is the price less the marginal cost.

> The **incremental marginal percentage** is the ratio of the price less the marginal cost to the price.

Recall from chapter 3 that the advertising elasticity of demand is the percentage by which the demand will change if the seller's advertising expenditure rises by 1%, other things equal. When the marginal benefit equals the marginal cost of advertising, the **advertising–sales ratio** (the ratio of the advertising expenditure to sales revenue) equals the incremental margin percentage multiplied by the advertising elasticity of demand. This provides a simple rule for the profit-maximizing level of advertising expenditure.

> The **profit-maximizing advertising–sales ratio** is the incremental margin multiplied by the advertising elasticity of demand.

Strictly, the rule stipulates the ratio of advertising expenditure to sales *revenue*. So, the ratio should be called the advertising–revenue ratio. However, in practice, it is usually called the advertising–sales ratio.

We can apply the advertising–sales rule to determine the profit-maximizing level of advertising expenditure for Solar's new drug Gamma-1. Recall that, with the demand and costs in table 8.2, the profit-maximizing price is $130 per unit and the marginal cost is $70. This means that the incremental margin percentage is $(130 − 70)/$130 = 6/13. Suppose that, at the price of $130, the advertising elasticity of the demand is 0.26. Then the profit-maximizing advertising–sales ratio is 6/13 × 0.26 = 0.12 or 12%.

At the $130 price, Gamma-1 sales are 1.4 million units. Hence, the profit-maximizing advertising expenditure is 0.12 × $130 × 1.4 million = $21.84 million.

The rule for advertising expenditures implies that, if the incremental margin percentage is higher, then the seller should spend relatively more on advertising. The reason is that each dollar of advertising produces relatively more benefit as measured by the incremental margin percentage. Accordingly, when the incremental margin percentage is higher, the seller should increase advertising. This means that, whenever a seller raises its price or its marginal cost falls, it should also increase advertising expenditure. By contrast, if a seller reduces its price or its marginal cost rises, it should reduce advertising expenditure.

Further, the rule for advertising expenditures implies that, if either the advertising elasticity of demand or the sales revenue is higher, then the seller should spend relatively more on advertising. Essentially, a higher advertising elasticity of demand or sales revenue means that the influence of advertising on buyer demand is relatively greater. In these circumstances, it makes sense to advertise more.

⊣ Food and beer: advertising–sales ratios ⊢

Table 8.4 lists the advertising–sales ratios for various food and beer manufacturers. Unilever manufactures personal care products such as Dove, and cleaning products such as Surf, as well as foods. It is relatively more diversified than General Mills and Kellogg. Unilever's advertising–sales ratio is the highest at 12.6%.

Table 8.4 Advertising–sales ratios, 2005

Industry/company	Currency	Sales (revenue)	Advertising	Advertising–sales ratio
Food				
General Mills	$ million	11,244	477	4.2%
Kellogg	$ million	10,177	858	8.4%
Unilever	€ million	39,672	4,999	12.6%
Beer				
Anheuser Busch	$ million	15,036	850	5.7%
Fosters	A$ million	3,972	380	9.6%

Sources: Company Annual Reports, various years.

Progress Check 8D Suppose that the profit-maximizing scale of production for Gamma-1 is 1.4 million units. At that scale, the price is $140 per unit, the marginal cost is $70, and the advertising elasticity of demand is 0.14. How much should Solar spend on advertising?

⊣ Dollar General's new advertising policy ⊢

Discount retailer Dollar General operates over 4,000 stores in 24 states, mainly in the midwest and southeast of the USA. The chain targets low and fixed-income families. Two-thirds of customers have household incomes below $30,000. Shoppers spend an average of $8.06 a trip. Of the 3,200 items that Dollar General sells, it prices 1,500 at $1 or lower, and the most expensive at $35. The average size of a Dollar General store is 6,700 square feet, which is smaller than the typical Wal-Mart or Kmart.

In 1998, Dollar General made a significant change to its advertising policy. It discontinued all advertising other than announcements of new stores. Financial analysts worried that sales would drop. With advertising expenditure dropping from 3.8% to 0.2% of sales revenue, sales indeed did fall. However, sales fell by less than analysts feared, and the company's profit rose.

Dollar General Chief Executive, Cal Turner, Jr., explained the new advertising policy: "Our customer lives within three to five miles of the store, knows we're there, knows who we are and appreciates the everyday low price."

Source: "Dollar General Sticks to Plan for Prosperity," *Wall Street Journal*, August 16, 1999, p. B11E.

---

6 Research and Development

A monopoly, and more generally, any seller with market power can influence its demand through research and development (R&D). Generally, and especially in knowledge-intensive industries, R&D drives the pipeline of new products.

How much should a business invest in R&D? The principles are the same as for advertising and promotion. The benefit of R&D arises from shifting out the demand curve and causing it to be less elastic. This will increase sales and the contribution margin. Hence, the net benefit from R&D is the change in the contribution margin less the R&D expenditure.

Accordingly, a simple rule for the *profit-maximizing* level of R&D expenditure is that the **R&D–sales ratio** (the ratio of the R&D expenditure to sales revenue) equals the incremental margin percentage multiplied by the R&D elasticity of demand.

By this rule, when the incremental margin percentage is higher (higher price or lower marginal cost), the seller should increase R&D expenditure relative to sales revenue. Conversely, when the incremental margin percentage is lower (lower price or higher marginal cost), the seller should reduce R&D expenditure relative to sales revenue.

> The **profit-maximizing R&D–sales ratio** is the incremental margin percentage multiplied by the R&D elasticity of demand.

Further, if either the R&D elasticity of demand or the sales revenue is higher, then the seller should increase R&D, and if either the R&D elasticity of demand or the sales revenue is lower, then the seller should reduce R&D.

Progress Check 8E If both price and marginal cost are higher, how should R&D expenditure be adjusted?

Project Evaluation

We have discussed how a business should determine its overall R&D expenditure. A related question is how to evaluate individual R&D projects. Like any other investment, decisions

⊣ Food and IT: R&D–sales ratios ⊢

Table 8.5 lists the R&D–sales ratios for various food manufacturers and information technology (IT) vendors. Generally, IT vendors spend relatively more on R&D than food manufacturers. This suggests that incremental margin percentages or R&D elasticities or both are higher in the IT than in the food industry.

Table 8.5   R&D–sales ratios, 2005

Industry/company	Units	Sales (revenue)	R&D expenditure	R&D–sales ratio
Food				
General Mills	$ million	11,244	168	1.5%
Kellogg	$ million	10,177	181	1.8%
Unilever	€ million	39,672	953	2.4%
Information Technology				
IBM	$ million	91,134	5,842	6.4%
Microsoft	$ million	39,788	6,184	15.5%
SAP	€ million	8,512	1,089	12.8%

on individual R&D projects should account for the timing of costs and benefits. Often, there is a somewhat smaller commitment of resources initially, with significantly larger expenditures if technical feasibility and demand conditions are favorable.

Suppose that Neptune Tech is considering a $1 million R&D project this year, that may result in a profitable commercial product next year. We will assume that the R&D costs are all incurred this year, and that all future benefits and costs occur next year and are given in present discounted values. Due to uncertainty in market demand, the benefits next year will either be $3 million, with probability p, or $1 million, with probability $(1 - p)$. In addition, the costs next year will be $1.5 million with certainty. Then, the net present value (NPV) of the R&D project, in millions of dollars, is[3]

$$NPV = -1 + 3p + 1(1 - p) - 1.5 = 2p - 1.5.$$

This NPV will be positive if the probability of the higher valued outcome is at least 75%.

Most R&D projects are multi-stage, however. There may be an opportunity to abandon or modify a project as more information about costs, technical feasibility, and market demand becomes available. Suppose that Neptune has an opportunity to abandon the project next year before incurring further costs, if demand conditions produce the low valued outcome. In this case, if benefits turn out to be $1 million, no futher development will take place (since the benefits of $1 million are less than the further costs of $1.5 million). Thus, there is a probability $(1 - p)$ that next year's benefits and costs will be zero. Then, the NPV, in millions of dollars, would be

$$NPV = -1 + p(3 - 1.5) + (1 - p)0 = 1.5p - 1.$$

---

[3]   The reader may wish to refer to chapter 1 for a refresher on net present value.

This NPV will be positive if $p > 67\%$. Thus, the opportunity to revise the R&D project over time, as learning takes place, yields a more favorable investment rule than a static once and for all R&D project would call for.

This is the rationale behind the *real options* approach to investment decisions. R&D is viewed as analogous to a European call option, where the purchaser has the right, but not the obligation, to exercise the option at a future date. Investing in R&D today gives Neptune the opportunity to continue development next year.

⊣ Pharmaceutical R&D: accelerating costs and benefits ⊢

The pharmaceutical industry spent $38 billion on R&D in 2004, which amounted to 19% of sales, which is the highest of any industry. Recent estimates by DiMasi et al. report that R&D costs average $802 million per new chemical entity, two thirds of which occurs in the preclinical phase. On average, the time between discovery of a drug to FDA approval for public use is 14 years.

It is estimated that the internal rate of return on pharmaceutical R&D is around 11%, only slightly higher than the estimated cost of capital for pharmaceutical firms. Five out of every 10,000 compounds investigated are tested as potential medicines in a clinical trial, and only one of those five is ever approved for patient use. Of these, only 30% produce revenues that exceed average R&D costs. Drug firms are dependent on these "blockbusters." For example, in 2001, eight of Pfizer's products accounted for 76% of its total sales, while four were expected to lose their patent protection by 2007.

Part of the controversy over the cost estimates concerns the fact that many drugs are line extensions rather than totally new substances (and thus, less expensive to develop). There is little disagreement, however, that pharmaceuticals have played an important role in improving human health. Recent estimates show that a 10% increase in pharmaceutical consumption (about $25 per person) would extend the disability-adjusted life expectancy of an average 60 year old by 0.9% (about 2 months).

Sources: "What Goes into the Cost of Prescription Drugs?" PhRMA, 2005; J. A. Di Masi, R. W. Hansen, and H. G. Grabowski, "The Price of Innovation: New Estimates of Drug Development Costs," *Journal of Health Economics* 22 (2003), pp. 151–85; editorial by R. G. Frank, "New Estimates of Drug Development Costs," *Journal of Health Economics* 22 (2003), pp. 325–30; R. D. Miller Jr. and H. E. Frech III, *Health Care Matters: Pharmaceuticals, Obesity, and the Quality of Life* (Washington, DC: AEI Press, 2004).

---

7 Market Structure

Monopoly, the case of a single seller, is one extreme of a range of market structures. At the other extreme lies perfect competition, where there are numerous sellers, each of whom is too small to affect market conditions. How do price and production depend on the competitive structure of the market? Monopoly and perfect competition are extreme cases. Knowledge of these extremes helps us understand the intermediate case, where there are several sellers who are large enough to influence market conditions.

Effects of Competition

To address the question of how price and production depend on the market structure, consider the following example. We take a long-run perspective. Assume that the production of

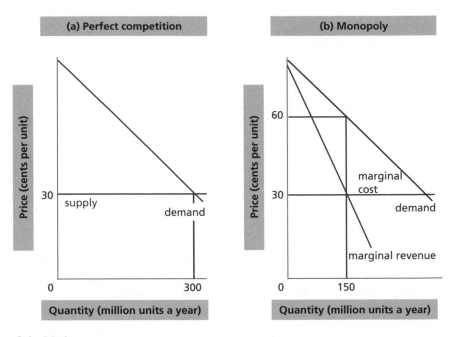

Figure 8.4 Market structure
(a) Under perfect competition, competition drives the market price down toward the long-run average cost of 30 cents. Production is 300 million units.
(b) Under a monopoly, the monopoly restricts production below the competitive level and sets a higher price of 60 cents to obtain larger profit.

oranges involves no fixed cost and the marginal cost is constant at 30 cents per unit. We will compare price and production when orange growing is perfectly competitive with the outcome when the same industry is a monopoly.

First, suppose that the orange industry is perfectly competitive. Since production requires only a constant marginal cost of 30 cents, all growers will be willing to supply unlimited quantities at 30 cents per orange. Hence, the market supply will be perfectly elastic at 30 cents per orange. Given the market demand, the supply will balance demand at a price of 30 cents. Figure 8.4(a) illustrates the market equilibrium. The sales and production will be the quantity demanded at a price of 30 cents, say, 300 million units a year. In equilibrium, each grower earns zero profit.

Next, suppose that the orange industry is a monopoly. The monopoly will produce at a scale that balances marginal revenue and the marginal cost of 30 cents. Since the marginal revenue curve lies below the demand curve, marginal revenue equals marginal cost at a quantity of less than 300 million a year. Accordingly, the monopoly will set the price above 30 cents. Suppose that the monopoly price is 60 cents and sales are 150 million units a year. Figure 8.4(b) depicts the monopoly price and sales. The monopoly will enjoy profits of $(0.60 - 0.30) \times 150 = \$45$ million a year.

The orange-growing example illustrates several general points. First, a monopoly restricts production below the competitive level, and by doing so, it can set a relatively higher price, extracting larger profit. By contrast, competition drives the market price down toward the long-run average cost and results in more production. Further, the profit of a monopoly exceeds what would be the combined profit of all the sellers if the same market were perfectly competitive.

Potential Competition

We have just seen that competition will push down the market price toward the long-run average cost. It is worth emphasizing that, under specific conditions, even *potential* competition will be sufficient to keep the market price close to the long-run average cost.

Consider a market in which sellers can enter and exit at no cost. Such a market is called **perfectly contestable**. A monopoly in a perfectly contestable market cannot raise its price substantially above its long-run average cost.

> A **perfectly contestable market** is a market in which sellers can enter and exit at no cost.

To understand why, suppose that Venus Trucking is the only truck service on the coastal route and that other truckers can easily switch their trucks from other routes to the coast. Now, if Venus raises its price above the long-run average cost, other truckers can profit by entering the coastal route. They will quickly enter to compete for a share of the market. The resulting increase in supply will drive the market price back toward the long-run average cost.

We have shown that a monopoly in a perfectly contestable market cannot raise price substantially above its long-run average cost. The degree to which a market is contestable depends on the extent of barriers to entry and exit. The introduction to this chapter reviewed barriers to entry. To the extent that there are barriers to entry, it will be more difficult for competing sellers to enter and, hence, it will be easier for a monopoly to raise its price above the long-run average cost.

The degree to which a market is contestable also depends on the extent of barriers to exit. Recall that, if Venus Trucking raises its price above long-run average cost, it might attract other truckers to enter the coastal market. These other truckers are lured by the attraction of temporary profits, made possible by Venus's relatively high price. Once Venus lowers its price back toward long-run average cost, these other truckers will leave. But their brief presence in the market will have been profitable.

Now, suppose that these other truckers must incur liquidation costs to exit the coastal market. When deciding whether to enter the market, these other truckers must consider these exit costs. The higher such exit costs are, the less likely these other truckers are to enter when Venus raises its price. This illustrates how barriers to exit affect the degree to which a market is contestable.

Lerner Index

Having understood the potential effect of monopoly on price and production, it is worth considering how to measure monopoly power. One measure is the **Lerner Index**, which is simply the incremental margin percentage. (This Index was proposed by the economist Abba Lerner.)

> The **Lerner Index** is the incremental margin percentage (ratio of the price less marginal cost to the price).

In a perfectly competitive market, every seller operates at a scale where its marginal cost equals the market price; hence, its incremental margin is 0. By contrast, a monopoly restricts sales to raise its price above its marginal cost. The more inelastic is market demand, the higher a monopoly can raise its price above its marginal cost. Accordingly, the Lerner Index focuses on the incremental margin, which is the difference between the price and the marginal cost.

The Lerner Index is defined as a ratio (incremental margin divided by price) so that it can be used to compare the degree of monopoly power in markets with different prices. For instance, the price of a recordable DVD is around $1 per unit, while the price of a database program may be well over $100. It would not make sense to directly compare the incremental margins in floppy disks and database programs. Even if the market for database programs were almost perfectly competitive, the price would be a few dollars above the marginal cost. This difference would exceed the incremental margin in a floppy disk monopoly. Accordingly, to enable comparison of monopoly power in markets with different price levels, the Lerner Index is defined as a ratio.

The Lerner Index also captures the impact of potential competition. If, owing to the presence of potential competitors, a monopoly sets a price close to its marginal cost, then its Lerner Index will also be relatively low. One problem with the index, however, is that it will not detect the power that a monopoly does not exercise. Specifically, if a monopoly faces an inelastic demand but nevertheless sets a price close to its marginal cost, then the Lerner Index will be relatively low, indicating that the market is close to perfectly competitive.

Progress Check 8F Referring to table 8.2, calculate the Lerner Index when Solar Pharmaceutical sets a price of $130.

⊢ Prozac: value of a monopoly ⊢

Eli Lilly's Prozac and other selective serotonin re-uptake inhibitors control the symptoms of depression by increasing the brain's supply of the neurotransmitter serotonin. In 1999, Lilly's world wide revenues from Prozac were $2.6 billion a year including U.S. revenues of $2.1 billion. In August 2000, the U.S. Court of Appeals overturned the District Court's finding that Lilly's patent over Prozac was valid until December 2003.

Under the extreme assumptions that Lilly would lose its entire sales of Prozac to generics, Lilly would lose its incremental margin on every unit sold. Supposing this to be 90%, Lilly's loss would be 0.9 × $2.6 billion = $2.34 billion a year.

The U.S. Appeals Court decision effectively shortened Lilly's patent by 26 months (the period between August 2001 and December 2003). Disregarding that a dollar in the future is worth less than a dollar in the present, the Appeals Court decision reduced Lilly's future earnings by $2.34 × 26/12 = $5.07 billion. However, the decision reduced Lilly's market capitalization by $36 billion. Apparently, Wall Street had over-reacted.

By contrast, the Appeals Court decision raised the market capitalization of generic drug manufacturer Barr Laboratories by only $1.1 billion. Why did Barr's market value rise by less than the drop in Lilly's value? One reason is that with the expiry of Lilly's patent, any generic drug manufacturer, and not only Barr, could produce Prozac. The other reason is that the new competitors would reduce drug prices, which would hurt drug manufacturers, while benefiting those who pay for medicine.

Eli Lilly then secured a new patent for Prozac weekly (a weekly version of Prozac), set to expire in 2017. Eli Lilly is currently suing Barr Laboratories for infringement of its patent on this new drug.

Sources: "Court Ruling Means Cheaper, Generic Prozac to Hit Market in 2001," *AP Business News*, August 11, 2000; "Prozac® Patent Ruled Invalid by U.S. Court of Appeals," Barr Laboratories, Press Release, August 9, 2000; "Hard to Swallow – America's Soaring Drug Costs," *Wall Street Journal*, November 16, 1998, p. A1.

8 Monopsony

A monopoly and, more generally, any seller with market power will restrain sales to raise the price and so increase profit. Let us now consider how the behavior of a buyer with market power will differ from that of a perfectly competitive buyer. We focus on a market where there is only one buyer, that is, a *monopsony*. Since there are close parallels between monopoly and monopsony, we will briefly highlight the similarities, while focusing on the important differences.

Benefit and Expenditure

Suppose that a key input into the production of Gamma-1 is a tropical leaf that grows in South America. Solar is the only buyer of this leaf; hence, it is a monopsony. By contrast, many growers produce the leaf. Each grower is too small to affect market conditions, so the supply of the leaf is perfectly competitive.

Since the leaf is a key input into Solar's manufacturing process, it provides a benefit that can be measured as the revenue generated less the costs of other associated inputs. The leaf, however, must be bought from the South American growers. Solar's expenditure is the market price of the leaf multiplied by the quantity purchased. Accordingly, Solar's net benefit from the leaf is its benefit less expenditure. We suppose that Solar's objective is to maximize its net benefit.

Let us determine the quantity of purchases at which Solar will maximize its net benefit. Referring to figure 8.5, Solar's benefit depends on the quantity of its purchases: we suppose that the marginal benefit of a small quantity is very high and that the marginal benefit falls with the scale of purchases.

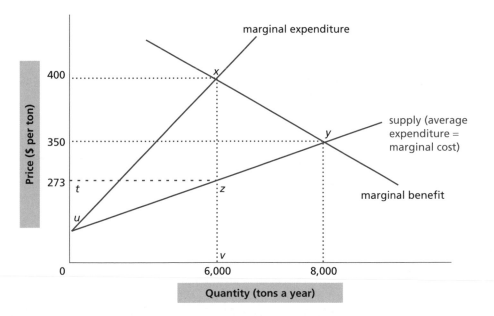

Figure 8.5 Monopsony purchasing
The marginal benefit and marginal expenditure curves cross at a quantity of 6,000 tons. Reading from the supply curve, the price at that quantity is $273. The supply curve also shows the marginal cost. At 6,000 tons, the marginal benefit exceeds the marginal cost.

Also referring to figure 8.5, the supply curve shows, for every quantity, the price at which competitive sellers will provide the leaf. Equivalently, the supply curve represents the monopsony's average expenditure for every possible quantity of purchases. Since the price must be higher to induce a greater quantity of supply, the average expenditure curve slopes upward.

The **marginal expenditure** is the change in expenditure resulting from an increase in purchases by one unit. For the average expenditure curve to slope upward, the marginal expenditure curve must lie above the average expenditure curve and slope upward more steeply.

> The **marginal expenditure** is the change in expenditure resulting from an increase in purchases by one unit.

Maximizing Net Benefit

> The **net benefit maximizing scale** of purchases is where marginal benefit equals marginal expenditure.

We can now state the following rule: a monopsony or any buyer with market power will maximize its **net benefit** by purchasing the quantity at which its marginal benefit equals its marginal expenditure. To explain this rule, consider a scale of purchases where Solar's marginal benefit exceeds marginal expenditure. Then, if Solar steps up purchases, its benefit will increase by more than its expenditure; hence it will obtain a larger net benefit. By contrast, if marginal benefit is less than marginal expenditure, Solar should reduce purchases: its benefit will drop by less than its expenditure. Solar will exactly maximize net benefit when it purchases the quantity where its marginal benefit balances its marginal expenditure.

Referring to figure 8.5, the quantity that maximizes net benefit is 6,000 tons. At that quantity, the price is $273 per ton. Notice that the price of $273 per ton is less than the buyer's marginal benefit. By contrast, if the demand side was competitive and the marginal benefit curve represented the market demand, the equilibrium price would be $350 per ton and the quantity would be 8,000 tons. This illustrates a general point: a monopsony restricts purchases to get a lower price and increase its net benefit above the competitive level.

> **Progress Check 8G** In figure 8.5, shade in an area that represents Solar's total expenditure on the tropical leaf.

⊢ A charitable monopsony ⊣

With an endowment that is worth $28 billion, the Bill and Melinda Gates Foundation is the richest charity in the world. It has several missions, including the improvement of U.S. schools and libraries, benefiting the Pacific Northwest, and, its most ambitious, to eradicate infectious diseases such as malaria, yellow fever, and hepatitis B in the poorest regions of the world.

In January 2005, the Gates Foundation announced that it would donate $750 million to the Global Alliance for Vaccines and Immunizations (GAVI). This donation was the latest of a series of donations intended to combat disease in the tropics. As a result of the foundation's contributions, global spending on research into malaria has almost doubled.

The Gates Foundation received a further boost when Warren Buffet pledged to donate $37 billion of his fortune to the Foundation. According to *The Economist*, Buffet appears to be following the same strategy he used in amassing his fortune – backing good organizations with good management.

The GAVI bundles the infectious diseases requirements of about 70 countries with a GDP per head of less than $1,000. Through bundling these requirements, GAVI "creates a large, reliable demand that stimulates more companies to get involved in manufacturing existing vaccines, provides an incentive to develop new ones, and pushes down unit prices."

A monopsony like GAVI can use its market power to get lower prices than many small competing buyers. In this case, this market power secures two additional benefits – it will encourage the manufacture of existing vaccines and provide an incentive to develop new ones. From a humanitarian perspective, these two results are laudable. With regard to lowering the price per unit, this is a good result for GAVI because more immunizations can be purchased.

Sources: "The World's Richest Charity Confronts the Health of the World's Poorest People," *The Economist*, January 26, 2005; "The New Powers in Giving," *The Economist*, July 1, 2006.

⊣ Videos and Pay-Per-View ⊢

Why do movies come out in video stores before they're available on Pay-Per-View? Answer: Wal-Mart.

The giant retailer, which accounts for over one-third of the studios' video (including DVD) revenues, depends on consumers coming into its stores to rent movies to build traffic for its more profitable merchandise. The studios help maintain this traffic by delaying the release of movies on Pay-Per-View (and other forms of video-on-demand) for 45 days.

If the studios were to change their policy and begin releasing their movies on Pay-Per-View at the same time as they release them on video, a large number of consumers would order them at home at the same price and save themselves a trip to Wal-Mart (and other stores). The big winners from such a change would be the studios. Instead of getting just 40% of the take, as they do from video rentals, they would get 70% of it from Pay-Per-View rentals. The big loser would be Wal-Mart.

Consequently, Wal-Mart has quietly warned studios that if they advance their Pay-Per-View release date, Wal-Mart will retaliate against them. As one top studio executive put it, "They told us, 'Don't bother to call us.'" The message was clear: Wal-Mart might not put a studio's videos and DVDs on their prime shelves if it made Pay-Per-View competitive with video rentals via a simultaneous release.

Not surprisingly, Wal-Mart's monopsony power has caused the studios, so far, to go along with its request, even though it has stifled their more profitable video-on demand option.

There is a corollary question – "Which powerful studio owner will soon be in a position to defy the Wal-Mart monopsony and deliver movies electronically into homes on the same day and date as the store release?" The answer to this is: Rupert Murdoch, who owns both a large studio, Twentieth Century Fox, and the largest satellite TV provider, Direct TV. He has the incentive and the ability to release new films for Pay-Per-View either before, or simultaneous with, video store release.

Sources: www.edwardjayepstein.com/monopsony.htm; www.edwardjayepstein.com/murdoch.htm.

9   Summary

Market power arises from unique resources, intellectual property, scale and scope economies, product differentiation, or regulation.

A seller with market power restrains sales to raise the market price above the competitive level and so, extract higher profits. It maximizes profit by operating at a scale where marginal revenue equals marginal cost. The extent to which a monopoly should adjust the price and scale in response to changes in demand or costs depends on the shapes of both the marginal revenue and the marginal cost curves.

The profit-maximizing advertising–sales ratio is the incremental margin percentage multiplied by the advertising elasticity of demand. The profit-maximizing R&D–sales ratio is the incremental margin percentage multiplied by the R&D elasticity of demand.

A buyer with market power restrains purchases to depress the price below the competitive level and so, raise its net benefit.

Key Concepts

monopoly	promotion	R&D–sales ratio
monopsony	incremental margin	perfectly contestable market
inframarginal units	incremental margin percentage	Lerner Index
contribution margin	advertising–sales ratio	marginal expenditure

Further Reading

References on promotion include the classic by Philip Kotler, *Marketing Management*, 11th ed. (Englewood Cliffs, NJ: Prentice-Hall, 2002), chapter 20, and Paul R. Messinger's *Marketing Paradigm* (Cincinnati: South-Western Publish-ing, 1995), chapter 8. A good discussion of R&D and intellectual property can be found in Hal R. Varian, Joseph Farrell, and Carl Shapiro, *The Economics of Information Technology* (Cambridge, UK: Cambridge University Press, 2004).

Review Questions

1. Give one example of the following sources of market power:
   (a)   a unique human or physical resource;
   (b)   intellectual property.
2. Explain how economies of scale and scope can support market power.
3. Provide an example of market power based on product differentiation.
4. Explain why marginal revenue is less than or equal to price. How does the difference between price and marginal revenue depend on the price elasticity of demand?
5. A software publisher has priced its new spreadsheet program such that its marginal revenue is more than its marginal cost. Advise the company how to raise its profit.
6. A monopoly restrains its sales to maximize its profit. True or false? Explain.
7. Once the patent on a product expires, others can freely manufacture the same product. Suppose that Solar Pharmaceutical's patent on the antiviral drug Beta-4 is about to expire. How will expiration of the patent affect
   (a)   Solar's market power over the drug?
   (b)   Solar's price elasticity of demand?
8. Explain why a seller must take into account both the marginal revenue and the marginal

cost when considering how to adjust price following a change in costs.

9. The profit-maximizing price for a software publisher's spreadsheet program is $100. At that price, the advertising elasticity of the demand is 0.1 and sales are 500,000 units a year. The marginal cost of production is $40 per unit. How much should the publisher spend on advertising?

10. The advertising to sales ratio for some drug exceeds the incremental margin percentage multiplied by the advertising elasticity of demand. How can profit be increased?

11. For which of the following items will the advertising elasticity of demand be relatively higher? (a) item with no substitute; (b) item with several equally popular competitors.

12. Explain the profit-maximizing rule for R&D expenditure relative to sales revenue.

13. How would the Lerner Index for an industry be affected by a reduction in the degree of potential competition?

14. A monopsony restrains its purchases to maximize its net benefit. True or false? Explain.

15. Hospitals are the only large buyer of nursing services in many communities. These hospitals often report "shortages" of nurses – unfilled positions. Reconcile these two facts, using the theory of monopsony.

Discussion Questions

1. Eli Lilly owns the patent to Xigris, which at the time of writing, was the only approved drug for the treatment of sepsis. Bayer manufactures aspirin, which is not covered by patent and is one of several drugs that relieve the symptoms of the common cold.
   (a) Who has relatively more market power: Eli Lilly over Xigris or Bayer over drugs for relieving the common cold?
   (b) How is the difference between price and marginal revenue related to the price elasticity of demand?
   (c) Compare the difference between price and marginal revenue for the two drugs, Xigris and Bayer's aspirin.

2. Table 8.2 describes the demand and costs for Solar Pharmaceutical's Gamma-1 drug. Suppose that the costs have been changed to a fixed cost of $75 million and a constant marginal cost of $50 per unit. The demand remains the same.
   (a) Prepare a new table of revenues and costs according to the new data.
   (b) What is the profit-maximizing price and production scale?
   (c) At that production scale, what are the marginal revenue and the marginal cost?

3. Hong Kong Director-General of Telecommunications Anthony Wong expressed concern about the effect of license auctions on the price of telecommunications: "There's good and bad in auctioning off spectrum . . . it may raise costs for telecoms providers" ("Telecoms Chief Sees Further Fall in Long-Distance Tariffs," *South China Morning Post*, December 31, 1999, Business 1).
   (a) Typically, licenses are transferable, but the one-time license fee, once paid, is not refundable. From an operational standpoint, how does the cost of a license depend on the price, if any, that the owner paid for it?
   (b) How does the one-time license fee affect the marginal cost of providing telecommunications service? How does it affect the profit-maximizing scale of operations?
   (c) Suppose that the one-time license fee is changed to an annual charge based on the telecommunications provider's revenue. How would the new policy affect the service provider's profit-maximizing scale of operations?

4. Eli Lilly holds the patent to the antidepressant Prozac. In 1996, generic drug manufacturer Barr Laboratories challenged Lilly's patent. In January 1999, U.S. District Judge Sarah Barker held in favor of Lilly. That year, Lilly reduced its expenditure on direct-to-consumer advertising

of Prozac from \$37.5 million to just \$151,000, while raising the expenditure on detailing to physicians from \$49.9 to \$60.2 million and advertising in medical journals from \$7.9 to \$8.1 million. Subsequently, the U.S. Court of Appeals overturned the patent, and generic competition was expected to begin in August 2001.

(a) Was Lilly's decision to redirect promotion spending away from consumers to doctors consistent with Judge Barker's decision?

(b) Following the introduction of generic drugs, how should Lilly adjust the price of Prozac?

(c) Following the introduction of generic drugs, how should Lilly adjust the promotion of Prozac?

5. Discount retailer Dollar General targets low and fixed-income families in the midwest and southeast. The majority of the chain's 3,200 items are priced at \$1 or lower. Shoppers spend an average of \$8.06 a trip. The average store size is 6,700 square feet. In 1998, Dollar General discontinued most advertising. While financial analysts worried that sales would drop, the company's profit rose. Chief Executive, Cal Turner, Jr., explained: "Our customer lives within three to five miles of the store, knows we're there, knows who we are and appreciates the everyday low price" ("Dollar General Sticks to Plan for Prosperity," *Wall Street Journal*, August 16, 1999, p. B11E).

(a) How could the cut in advertising raise profit while reducing sales?

(b) Explain Mr Turner's comment in terms of the advertising elasticity of demand.

(c) Relate Dollar General's incremental margin percentage and advertising elasticity of demand to the new advertising policy.

6. Atos Origin, Coca-Cola, Eastman Kodak, General Electric, John Hancock Financial Services, Lenovo Group, McDonalds, Panasonic, Samsung, and Visa are global sponsors of the Olympic Games for the period 2004–08. The eleven companies paid a total of \$866 million to the International Olympic Committee for these rights. The sponsorship period includes the 2006 Winter games in Turin and the 2008 summer games in Beijing. By contrast, total sponsorship for the 2000–04 period, including the winter games in Salt Lake City and the 2004 summer games in Athens, amounted to \$666 million ("For Olympic sponsors, it's on to Beijing," *International Herald Tribune*, August 31, 2004).

(a) Why are global brands such as Kodak and Samsung willing to pay relatively more to sponsor the Olympics than regional or local brands? Explain in terms of the benefit and cost of advertising.

(b) Considering the relative sizes of the Greek and Chinese consumer markets, explain why sponsors paid more for the 2004–08 Olympics than the 2000–04 Olympics.

(c) Atos Origin's customers are primarily other businesses, while Lenovo's market is mainly within China. Compare the benefit from Olympic sponsorship to these two companies with the benefit to other sponsors.

7. In late 2005, software giant Microsoft announced that it would increase R&D spending by \$2.6 billion the following year. Wall Street analysts reacted negatively, worrying that the increased investment would reduce earnings and shareholder return. However, Microsoft CEO Steve Ballmer argued for a long-term view, "We announced [Windows] in 1983 but it didn't make any real money until 1993 and 1994 . . . I don't think any investor should argue about the payback" and further suggested that Microsoft had delayed the update of Windows too long. "Windows is a product that has to be watered periodically . . . We've gone a bigger gap than I'd like to go [this time]." (*Source*: "Ballmer Lobbies for Microsoft's R&D Spending Plan," *Computerworld*, January 6, 2006).

(a) Referring to table 8.6, calculate Microsoft's R&D–sales ratio for 2003–05.

(b) Relate Microsoft's plan to increase R&D expenditure to Mr Ballmer's remark that they had waited too long before updating Windows.

(c) Did Microsoft under- or over-estimate the sensitivity of the demand for Windows to updating?

Table 8.6 Microsoft ($ billion)

Year	Sales (revenue)	R&D expenditure
2005	39,788	6,184
2004	36,835	7,779
2003	32,187	6,595

Source: Microsoft Corporation, Annual Report, 2005.

8. The National Collegiate Athletic Association (NCAA) aims to "govern competition in a fair, safe, equitable and sportsmanlike manner, and to integrate intercollegiate athletics into higher education so that the educational experience of the student-athlete is paramount" (*Source*: NCAA website). The NCAA restricts the amounts that member colleges and universities may pay their student athletes (generally limited to the full cost of their education) and requires student athletes to attend full-time programs of study.
    (a)   What market power does the NCCA have, and what are its source(s)?
    (b)   If the U.S. government were to forbid the NCAA from such restrictive practices, what would happen to: (i) each athlete's earnings, and (ii) the number of athletes?

9. Cricket is India's top spectator sport. Under Indian law, private broadcasters must share any coverage of Indian cricket matches with the national television and radio broadcasters, Doordarshan and All India Radio. However, the law does not require national broadcasters to share their cricket telecasts with private channels (*Source*: "DD May Get a Blank Cheque," *Times of India*, August 13, 2004).
    (a)   How would the Indian law affect the ability of a private television channel to differentiate itself from Doordarshan?
    (b)   How would the law affect the amount that a private television channel would bid for rights to broadcast Indian cricket matches?
    (c)   How would the law affect Doordarshan's degree of market power relative to (i) television viewers, and (ii) the organizers of Indian cricket matches?
    (d)   The *Times of India* predicted that, owing to the law, private broadcasters would not bid for rights to broadcast Indian cricket matches, and so, national broadcasters would be the only bidders. Do you agree?

10. DaimlerChrysler, Ford, and General Motors dominate American automobile production. Some automobile parts, such as batteries and tires, wear out with use and must be replaced at relatively frequent intervals. Accordingly, suppliers of these parts sell their products both as original equipment to auto manufacturers and as replacement parts to car owners. By contrast, air bags and ignition systems wear out relatively slowly. The bulk of such equipment is bought by auto manufacturers.
    (a)   Referring to relevant sources of data, calculate the combined share of DaimlerChrysler, Ford, and General Motors in the American automobile market.
    (b)   Assess the power of automobile manufacturers over sellers of (i) batteries and tires as compared with (ii) air bags and ignition systems.
    (c)   For products like batteries and tires, do you expect prices to be higher in the original equipment market or the replacement market?

11. This question applies the techniques introduced in the math supplement. Suppose that Neptune Music has the copyright to the latest CD of the Heavy Iron band. The market demand curve for the CD is $Q = 800 - 100p$, where Q represents quantity demanded in thousands and p represents

the price in dollars. Production requires a fixed cost of $100,000 and a constant marginal cost of $2 per unit.

(a)   What price will maximize profits?
(b)   At that price, what will be the sales?
(c)   What is the maximum profit?
(d)   Calculate the Lerner Index at the profit-maximizing scale of production.
(e)   Suppose that the fixed cost rises to $200,000. How would this affect the profit-maximizing price?

Chapter 8

Math Supplement

Consider a monopoly that faces the market demand curve represented by the equation

$$Q = 100 - 2p. \tag{8.1}$$

This demand curve is a straight line. Suppose that production requires a fixed cost of 300 and a constant marginal cost of 10 per unit.

Rearranging equation (8.1), the price, expressed as a function of quantity, is

$$p = \frac{100 - Q}{2}. \tag{8.2}$$

Hence, the total revenue

$$R(Q) = pQ = \frac{1}{2}(100Q - Q^2). \tag{8.3}$$

Differentiating, the marginal revenue is,

$$\frac{dR(Q)}{dQ} = \frac{1}{2}(100 - 2Q). \tag{8.4}$$

We can obtain the profit-maximizing production scale by equating the marginal revenue to the marginal cost.

$$\frac{1}{2}(100 - 2Q) = 10. \tag{8.5}$$

Solving, the profit-maximizing production scale is $Q = 40$. By substituting $Q = 40$ into (8.2), we obtain the profit-maximizing price, $p = 30$. Hence, total revenue

$$R(Q) = pQ = 30 \times 40 = 1200. \tag{8.6}$$

It was given that production requires a fixed cost of 300 and a constant marginal cost of 10 per unit. Accordingly, the total cost of producing $Q = 40$ units is

$$C(Q) = 300 + (10 \times 40) = 700. \tag{8.7}$$

Therefore, the monopoly's maximum profit is $1200 - 700 = 500$.

Chapter 9

Pricing

1 Introduction

Established in 1985, Emirates Airline is one of the fastest growing and most financially successful carriers in the world. In 2005, Emirates recorded 24.3 billion United Arab Emirates dirhams ($6.6 billion) in revenue and 2.8 billion dirhams ($762 million) in net profit. Its principal business was the carriage of 14.5 million passengers over an average of 4,295 kilometers each.[1]

Emirates' passenger capacity was 82 billion available seat kilometers. Its fleet comprised 85 Airbus and Boeing aircraft, with an average age of 61 months. Emirates had also placed firm orders for 45 of the jumbo Airbus A380, which will carry over 550 passengers each.

In May 2004, passengers on Emirates flight EK-504 from Dubai to Mumbai who compared tickets might have been surprised at the difference among their fares. The unrestricted economy Dubai–Mumbai round-trip fare was 2,250 dirhams (then equivalent to $613), while the same fare with travel originating in Mumbai was 25,600 Indian rupees (then equivalent to $557).

Even among passengers originating from Dubai, there would have been substantial differences in fares. Emirates offered a Special Excursion fare, requiring a minimum stay of 7 days, with a maximum of 4 months, for 1,900 dirhams ($518), and two Basic Season Special Excursion fares, with the same restrictions but available only in the low season, for 1,550 and 1,200 dirhams ($422 and $327), respectively.

Pricing is crucial for Emirates, as for any airline. Travelers vary widely in the amount that they are willing to pay for the same flight. Moreover, when a plane is about to take off, the marginal cost of filling an empty seat with another passenger is almost zero. Consequently, airlines have invested substantial amounts in reservations and yield management systems to adjust fares and allocate seats. Between 1999 and 2004, Emirate's passenger load factor, which measures capacity utilization, varied between 71.9% and 76.6%.

Besides differences according to origin of travel and restrictions on length of stay, airline fares may also vary on other dimensions, including the passenger's age, requirements for advance purchase, penalties for changes of itinerary, group purchase, and eligibility for frequent flyer miles. The Emirates Group operates its own frequent flyer program, Skywards, for travelers on Emirates Airline and 43.6%-owned Sri Lankan Airlines.

---

[1] This discussion is based, in part, on Emirates Group, *Annual Report*, 2005–06.

Since the marginal cost of filling a seat is almost zero, why doesn't Emirates fill all its seats and earn more profit? Why does it charge different prices for travelers originating in Dubai vis-à-vis Mumbai? What is the purpose of the seven-day minimum stay required for the Special Excursion fare?

In this chapter, we systematically tie threads from previous chapters on demand, elasticity, costs, and monopoly to analyze how a seller with market power should set prices to maximize profit. We first apply the price elasticity of demand and marginal cost. Our rule will explain why Emirates doesn't fill all its seats. Essentially, the reason is that, to fill all the empty seats, it must cut fares to a point that it would reduce overall profit.

Sellers very commonly set the same price for every unit sold. We show how to raise profit by setting different prices that realize different margins from various market segments. This depends on the extent of the seller's information about the individual buyer's demand. We consider situations where the seller has complete information as well as those where the seller has limited information.

Where the seller has sufficient information to directly identify consumer segments, it can apply direct segment discrimination. This explains why Emirates sets different fares for travel originating in Dubai vis-à-vis Mumbai. By doing so, it can earn more profit than if it set the same fare in both cities.

However, even if the seller lacks sufficient information or the ability to discriminate directly, it might have sufficient information to apply indirect segment discrimination. This explains why Emirates requires a seven-day minimum stay for the Special Excursion fare. By doing so, it can earn more profit from travelers who are not willing to stay seven days.

Finally, this chapter presents two specific pricing policies – pricing based on location and bundled pricing, and explains the shortcomings of cost-plus pricing. Any seller with market power can use the methods presented in this chapter to increase profit above the level available from charging the same price for every unit.

2   Uniform Pricing

Whenever managers are asked why do they not set a higher price, the most frequent response is, "Because I would lose sales." This does not, however, answer the question. Unless the demand is completely inelastic, a higher price will always result in lower sales. The real issue is how the increase in price will affect the profit of the business. As we will show, the answer depends on the price elasticity of demand and the marginal cost.

> **Uniform pricing** is a policy where a seller charges the same price for every unit of the product.

In this section, we shall consider only policies where the seller charges the same price for every unit of the product. These are policies of **uniform pricing**. Later in this chapter, we will discuss how a seller can extract higher profit by setting prices so as to realize different margins on various units of the product.

Price Elasticity

Suppose that Mercury Airlines plans to offer air service from Dubai to Mumbai. Assume it incurs no fixed cost in supplying the service. The only cost is a constant marginal cost of 800 dirhams per seat. What price should Mercury set in the Dubai market? One proposal, based on the Dubai price of a fare originating in Mumbai, converted to dirhams, is a price of 1,900 dirhams.

Recall from chapter 3 that the *own-price elasticity of demand* is the percentage by which the quantity demanded will change if the price of the item rises by 1%, other things equal. (For brevity, this chapter refers to the own-price elasticity of demand as simply the *price elasticity*.) When the demand is elastic, a 1% price increase causes the quantity demanded to drop by more than 1%. By contrast, when the demand is inelastic, a 1% price increase causes the quantity demanded to fall by less than 1%.

Suppose that Mercury estimates that, if it were to set the Dubai price 10% higher, at 2,090 dirhams, then sales (which is the quantity demanded) would be 9% lower. This indicates that the demand is inelastic. Since sales fall less than proportionately with the increase in price, Mercury's total revenue will increase, specifically, by 0.1%. Moreover, lower sales mean lower costs. Hence, in this example, a price increase will raise Mercury's profit. Generally, as we showed in chapter 3, if the demand is inelastic, an increase in price will lead to a higher profit. Accordingly, a seller that faces an inelastic demand should raise the price.

Profit-Maximizing Price

We have seen that when the demand is inelastic, a seller should raise the price. But what if the demand is elastic? More generally, what price maximizes the seller's profit? In chapter 8, we showed that, at the profit-maximizing sales, the marginal revenue equals the marginal cost. Figure 9.1 shows the **profit-maximizing price** and sales for Mercury's Dubai business.

> The **profit-maximizing price** is where the incremental margin percentage equals the reciprocal of the absolute value of the price elasticity of demand.

Managers, however, usually do not readily have information about marginal revenue. They usually have better information about the price elasticity of demand. So, it would be more convenient to have a pricing rule based on elasticity.

Fortunately, such a rule is available. This rule applies the concept of the incremental margin percentage. Recall from chapter 8 that the incremental margin percentage is the price less the marginal cost divided by price.

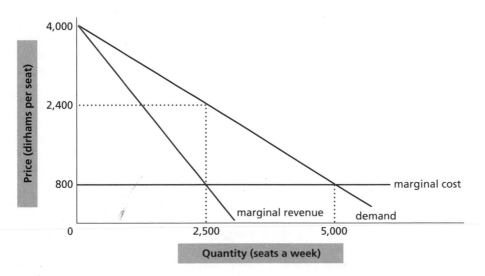

Figure 9.1   Uniform pricing
At the profit-maximizing quantity of sales, the marginal revenue equals the marginal cost. Equivalently, the incremental marginal percentage equals the reciprocal of the absolute value of the price elasticity of demand.

In the math supplement, we show that when the marginal revenue equals the marginal cost, then the incremental margin percentage equals the reciprocal of the absolute value of the price elasticity of demand. Equivalently, a seller maximizes profit by setting a price where

$$\text{incremental margin percentage} = -\frac{1}{\text{price elasticity of demand}} \tag{9.1}$$

The price elasticity of demand is negative; hence, the minus sign on the right-hand side of the pricing rule ensures that the entire right-hand side is positive.

Let us apply the rule to determine Mercury's price for the Dubai market. Suppose that the price elasticity of demand is −1.5. The pricing rule shows that, for Mercury to maximize its profit, the incremental margin percentage must be 1/1.5 = 2/3. Then, representing the price by p, and recalling that the marginal cost is 800 dirhams, the rule implies that

$$\frac{p - 800}{p} = \frac{2}{3} \tag{9.2}$$

By solving this equation, we find that $p = 2,400$. Hence, the price that maximizes Mercury's profit is 2,400 dirhams (as figure 9.1 shows, we get the same price if we look for the quantity where the marginal revenue equals the marginal cost). At the price of 2,400, the quantity demanded is 2,500 seats per week. Hence, Mercury's total revenue is $2,400 \times 2,500 = 6$ million dirhams a week. Mercury's total cost is $800 \times 2,500 = 2$ million; hence, its profit is 6 million − 2 million = 4 million dirhams a week.

The pricing rule highlights the importance of understanding the price elasticity of demand. In chapter 3, we discussed the intuitive factors that underlie the price elasticity. These factors include the availability of direct and indirect substitutes, buyers' prior commitments, and the cost relative to the benefit of searching for more favorable prices.

The price elasticity may vary along a demand curve. Further, the marginal cost may change with the scale of production. Accordingly, determining the profit-maximizing price typically involves a series of trials with different prices until finding a price such that the incremental margin percentage equals the reciprocal of the absolute value of the price elasticity.

Demand and Cost Changes

The pricing rule shows how a seller should adjust its price when there are changes in the price elasticity of demand or marginal cost. Consider changes in the price elasticity. If the demand is more elastic, then the price elasticity will be a larger negative number. So, according to the rule, the seller should aim for a lower incremental margin percentage. For instance, suppose that, in Mercury's case, the price elasticity is −2 rather than −1.5. Then, the profit-maximizing incremental margin percentage will be 1/2 = 50%. Letting the price be p, we have $(p - 800)/p = 0.50$, which implies that the profit-maximizing price is 1,600 dirhams.

By contrast, if the demand were less elastic, say, with an elasticity of −1.33, then the profit-maximizing incremental margin percentage would be 1/1.33 = 75%. Again, representing the price by p, we would then have $(p - 800)/p = 0.75$, which implies that the profit-maximizing price would be 3,200 dirhams.

Next, let us consider changes in the seller's marginal cost. In our original example, the price elasticity was −1.5, while the marginal cost was 800 dirhams. Suppose that the marginal cost is lower at 600 dirhams. How should Mercury adjust its price? Using the pricing rule, the profit-maximizing price must satisfy $(p - 600)/p = 1/1.5$, which implies that $p = 1,800$. Notice that, although the marginal cost is only 200 dirhams lower, the profit-maximizing price is 600 dirhams lower.

Similarly, we can show that, if the marginal cost is higher, Mercury should not raise its price by the same amount. The reason is that Mercury must consider the effect of the price change on the quantity demanded.

These examples demonstrate that the way a seller should adjust its price to changes in either the price elasticity or the marginal cost depends on both the price elasticity and the marginal cost. In particular, this means that a seller should not necessarily adjust the price by the same amount as a change in marginal cost.

Progress Check 9A In the case of Mercury Airlines, suppose that the price elasticity of demand is −2, while the marginal cost is 700 per seat. Calculate the price that maximizes the profit.

Common Misconceptions

The pricing rule applies the concept of incremental margin percentage. In cost accounting, the *contribution margin percentage* is defined as the revenue less variable cost divided by revenue. In the math supplement, we show that the contribution margin percentage equals the price less the average variable cost divided by the price. Accounting systems often assume that costs are proportional; in which case, the marginal cost is the same as the average variable cost. Then, the contribution margin percentage equals what we call the *incremental margin percentage*.

Generally, however, variable costs may increase or decrease with the scale of operations, and so the marginal cost will not be the same as the average variable cost. In this case, it is important to keep a clear distinction between the contribution margin percentage and the incremental margin percentage. Only the latter is relevant for pricing.

A common mistake is the belief that the profit-maximizing price depends only on the elasticity. According to this approach, if the demand is more elastic, the price should be lower, while if the demand is less elastic, the price should be higher. This approach considers only the demand and ignores costs. To maximize profits, however, management should take into account both the demand and costs.

To illustrate the difference between the mistaken thinking and the correct approach, consider the mini-bars provided by many hotels. The mini-bar has considerable market power, especially in the early hours of the morning, when it would be inconvenient if not hazardous to venture out of the hotel for a beverage.

Suppose that the price elasticities of demand of Heineken beer and Coca-Cola in the mini-bar are the same. Should the hotel set the same price for both items? Absolutely not. According to our pricing rule, the hotel should set the same incremental margin percentage on the two items. Since the marginal cost to the hotel of Heineken beer is higher than that of Coca-Cola, the hotel should set a higher price for the Heineken.

⊣ Price elasticity: who is the customer? ⊢

Whenever a damaged car arrives at a repair shop, one of the first questions that the car owner must answer is, "Do you have insurance for the damage?" Why does the repair shop care whether the owner has insurance coverage?

Automobile repair is a case where there are two persons on the demand side: the car owner who makes the buying decision and the insurer who pays the bill. The owner of a damaged car will be relatively less sensitive to the price of repairs. Indeed, the owner may ask the repair shop to fix some other outstanding damage at the insurer's expense. Generally, demand is less sensitive to price whenever there is a split between the party that makes the buying decision and the party that pays the bill. Auto repair shops understand and exploit this split.

Realistically, however, the car owner will be concerned about the price of repairs to the extent that his or her future insurance premium or renewal of the policy depends on past claims.

Another common mistake in pricing is to set the price by marking up average cost. Cost-plus pricing poses several problems. First, in businesses with economies of scale, the average cost depends on the production scale. So, to apply cost-plus pricing, the seller must make an assumption about the scale. But the sales and production scale depend on the price, hence cost-plus pricing leads in a circle.

A further difficulty with cost-plus pricing is that it gives no guidance as to the appropriate mark-up on average cost. Should a seller apply the same or different mark-ups to different products? Suppose that a seller wants to set the mark-up to maximize profits. Then, the seller must go back to considering the price elasticity of demand and the marginal cost. Hence, cost-plus pricing is not so simple after all.

3 Complete Price Discrimination

In the previous section, we introduced a rule for uniform pricing: the seller should set the price so that the incremental margin percentage equals the reciprocal of the absolute value of the price elasticity of demand. In figure 9.2, we illustrate the profit-maximizing uniform price for Mercury Airlines in the Dubai market. On closer examination, however, we can show that uniform pricing does not yield the maximum possible profit. This suggests that we should look for better pricing policies.

Shortcomings of Uniform Pricing

Recall that the demand curve for a product also reflects the marginal benefits of the various buyers. At the price of 2,400 dirhams per seat, the benefit of a flight for the marginal buyer is just equal to the price. For all the other (inframarginal) buyers, who account for 2,499 seats, the benefit exceeds the price. Each of these inframarginal buyers is enjoying some buyer surplus. The market buyer surplus is the shaded area *abd*.

With uniform pricing, the inframarginal buyers do not pay as much as they would be willing to pay. This suggests that, by devising a way of taking some of the buyer surplus, Mercury could increase its profit.

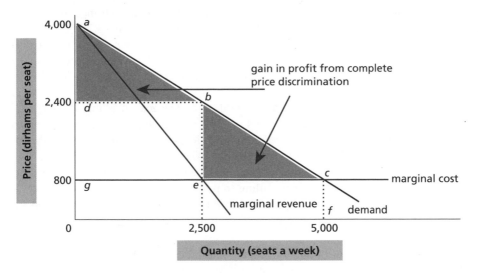

Figure 9.2 Complete price discrimination
With complete price discrimination, the seller prices each unit at the buyer's benefit and sells a quantity such that the marginal benefit equals the marginal cost. The increase in profit over uniform pricing is the shaded area *adb* plus the shaded area *bec*.

Another shortcoming of uniform pricing is that it results in an economically inefficient quantity of sales. (Recall from chapter 6 on economic efficiency that the allocation of an item is economically efficient if the marginal benefit equals the marginal cost.) The marginal buyer derives a benefit of 2,400 dirhams, while the marginal cost is only 800 dirhams. By devising some way to provide the product to everyone whose marginal benefit exceeds the marginal cost, Mercury could also earn more profit.

Progress Check 9B Referring to figure 9.2, shade in the market buyer surplus if Mercury sets a price of 800 dirhams per seat.

Price Discrimination

Ideally, Mercury would like to sell each seat at the respective buyer's benefit. Referring to figure 9.2, this would be like selling down the market demand curve. Then, Mercury would earn a higher incremental margin from buyers with higher benefit and a smaller margin from buyers with lower benefit. Any pricing policy under which a seller sets prices to earn different incremental margins on various units of the same or a similar product is called **price discrimination**.

We give the name **complete price discrimination** to a pricing policy where the seller prices each unit at the buyer's benefit and sells a quantity such that the marginal benefit equals the marginal cost. This policy is called complete price discrimination because it charges every buyer the maximum that he or she is willing to pay for each unit. Hence, the policy leaves each buyer with no surplus.

Price discrimination is a policy where a seller sets different incremental margins on various units of the same or a similar product.

Complete price discrimination is the policy where a seller prices each unit at the buyer's benefit and sells a quantity such that the marginal benefit equals the marginal cost.

To illustrate complete price discrimination, let us consider Mercury Airlines' pricing. Referring to figure 9.2, the demand curve is a straight line with a slope of $-3{,}200/5{,}000 = -0.64$. This means that the first buyer is willing to pay $4{,}000 - 0.64 = 3{,}999.36$ dirhams for a seat; the second buyer, $4{,}000 - 2(0.64) = 3{,}998.72$; and so on. Hence, under complete price discrimination, Mercury should charge 3,998.72 dirhams to the first buyer, 3,998.72 to the second buyer, and so on.

Mercury should *not* stop selling at the 2,500th unit. The reason is that the buyer of the 2,501st seat derives a benefit of $2{,}400 - 0.64 = 2{,}399.36$, which exceeds Mercury's marginal cost of 800. This means that Mercury could increase its profit by selling a seat to that buyer.

Indeed, Mercury should sell up to the quantity where the marginal benefit just equals the marginal cost. Referring to figure 9.2, this balance occurs at a quantity of 5,000 seats a year. The buyer of the 5,000th seat is willing to pay exactly 800 dirhams for a seat, which is Mercury's marginal cost. If Mercury tried to sell beyond 5,000 seats, it would make a loss on additional units. Under complete price discrimination, the buyer of the 5,000th seat is the marginal buyer.

With complete price discrimination, Mercury's total revenue will be the area $0fca$ under the demand curve from the quantity of 0 up to 5,000 seats a year. This area is $(4{,}000 + 800)/2 \times 5{,}000 = 12$ million dirhams a week. As for costs, Mercury's total cost would be area $0fcg$, which is $800 \times 5{,}000 = 4$ million dirhams a week. (Recall that Mercury incurs no fixed cost.) Hence, with complete price discrimination, Mercury's profit would be 12 million − 4 million = 8 million dirhams per week.

By contrast, in the preceding section, we showed that Mercury's maximum profit with uniform pricing is 4 million. So, Mercury's profit with complete price discrimination is higher than the profit with uniform pricing.

Comparison with Uniform Pricing

Under a policy of complete price discrimination, the seller should sell each unit for the benefit that it provides its buyer and sell the quantity where the buyer's marginal benefit just equals the marginal cost. The policy resolves the two shortcomings of uniform pricing. First, by pricing each unit at the buyer's benefit, the policy extracts all of the buyer surplus. Second, the policy provides the economically efficient quantity; hence, it exploits all the opportunity for additional profit through increasing sales.

Specifically, in the case of Mercury Airlines, the policy of complete price discrimination enables Mercury to extract higher prices for the 2,499 seats that would be inframarginal under uniform pricing. This increase in profit is represented by the shaded area *adb* in figure 9.2. Second, with complete price discrimination, Mercury would sell 2,500 more seats than with uniform pricing. These additional seats raise the profit by the shaded area *bec* in figure 9.2. The total increase in profit is the sum of the shaded areas *adb* and *bec*.

Generally, a policy of complete price discrimination yields more profit than uniform pricing. Complete price discrimination extracts a higher price for units that would be sold under uniform pricing, while extending sales by selling additional units that would not be sold with uniform pricing.

Progress Check 9C We can use figure 9.2 to compare the profits from uniform pricing and complete price discrimination. The difference is areas *adb* and *bec*. Calculate the numerical values of these areas.

⊢ Does the doctor really need to know your occupation? ⊢

Price discrimination is common in medical services. Doctors treat patients on an individual basis. A doctor's first step in treatment is always to record the patient's history. This routinely includes questions about the patient's occupation, employer, home address, and scope of insurance coverage. This information is very useful in gauging a patient's ability and willingness to pay as well as the patient's health.

To the extent that a patient is paying her or his own bill, the doctor can easily use this information to charge different prices to various patients for the same treatment. The result is close to complete price discrimination. Indeed, healthcare scholars, Victor Fuchs and Alan M. Garber, have remarked approvingly "Medicine has a long and generally honorable history of price discrimination. Doctors have provided free or heavily discounted care to the needy, and drug companies have charged lower prices to those less able to pay full price."

Source: Victor Fuchs and Alan M. Garber, "Medical Innovation: Promises & Pitfalls," *Brookings Review* 21, no. 1 (Winter, 2003), pp. 44–8.

⊢ Price discrimination, the easy way ⊢

In 1995, British multi-millionaire Stelios Haji-Ioannou founded budget airline, easyJet, in Luton, England. At the end of 2005, easyJet had 109 aircraft and carried almost 30 million passengers on its extensive European network. It earned a profit of £67.9 million on a revenue of £1,341.4 million.

Subsequently, Mr Haji-Ioannou extended the "easy" brand to other industries – car rental, cinemas, and Internet cafes. In all of these businesses, he engages in price discrimination. For example, the first seats sold on easyJet flights are cheap and the last few sold are the most expensive. Similarly, the more individuals rent cars from easyCar, visit the easyInternetcafe, or purchase easyCinema tickets, the higher the price to the remaining customers.

The Economist described Mr Haji-Ioannou's pricing policy as "yield management to the extreme . . . pocket[ing] the extra that the impatient and spendthrift are willing to pay to have just what they want when they want it." The "easy" policy attempts to approximate complete price discrimination, where every buyer is charged the maximum that he or she is willing to pay for each service.

Aside from this pricing policy, costs are ruthlessly contained. Customers get basic service and nothing more, while bookings for all four businesses are online. EasyCinema customers print out a bar-coded entry pass from their own personal computer. EasyCar offers one kind of basic and spartan car at each location. In addition, customers are required to return their rental car within a one hour period, clean and ready for the next user, or pay a penalty. EasyJet only offers short-haul flights from minor airports and provides no food or drink.

While easyJet has been profitable, the other businesses have been less successful. Mr Haji-Ioannou explained that he lost money because he departed from his policy of containing costs. For example, some of the café sites were too expensive. Instead, he has cut costs and branched out to cheaper locations such as Burger King restaurants.

Sources: "Easy Does It," *The Economist*, November 16, 2000; "The Big Easy," *The Economist*, May 29, 2003.

Information

Under complete price discrimination, the seller charges each buyer a different price for each unit of the product. This means that a buyer who is interested in buying more than one unit of the product should be charged a different price for each unit.

Accordingly, to implement complete price discrimination, the seller must know each potential buyer's individual demand curve. It is not enough to know the market demand curve or the price elasticity of the individual demand curves. Rather, the seller must know the entire individual demand curve of each potential buyer. This is a tremendous requirement. In practice, most sellers will not have this amount of information, so, complete price discrimination is usually not feasible.

Selling down the demand curve: Salesforce.com and USi

With Internet service becoming pervasive and more reliable, software producers are mimicking automobile manufacturers and movie studios. Not every potential customer derives enough benefit to justify an outright purchase. Auto manufacturers offer leases to drivers who do not wish to buy. Similarly, movie studios sell videos to rental stores that cater to low-benefit viewers.

The same principle applies to software. Systems for enterprise resource planning (ERP) and customer relationship management (CRM) can be very expensive. Prices are out of reach for many businesses. Yet the marginal cost of software is almost zero. Enter the application service provider (ASP) to offer software "on tap" through the Internet. The ASP charges by usage and so reaches down the demand curve to low-benefit users.

Marc Benioff founded Salesforce.com in 1999 to provide CRM through the Internet to clients of all sizes. By 2004, Salesforce.com served more than 168,000 subscribers at 11,100 companies world wide, earning revenues of $85.8 million and net income of $3.5 million. The company's market value was $1.61 billion.

Founded in 1998, USInternetworking provides ERP by software giants Ariba, Oracle, Peoplesoft, and SAP through the Internet on an ASP basis. Its clients include the Arthritis Foundation, FedEx, Kinko's, and Visa, U.S.A.

It is estimated that ASPs now account for 3–5% of all software sales revenue.

Sources: Lynn Haber, "ASPs Still Alive and Kicking," www.cioupdate.com, January 30, 2004; company websites.

---

4 Direct Segment Discrimination

To implement complete price discrimination, a seller must know the entire individual demand curve of each potential buyer. The seller, however, may not have so much information. Accordingly, we now explore other forms of price discrimination that require less information.

From the viewpoint of the seller's profit, a policy of complete price discrimination is better than uniform pricing, essentially because it sets prices on an individual basis. A seller that lacks sufficient information to price on an individual basis may still be able to discriminate among *segments* of buyers. In the language of marketing, a **segment** is a significant cohesive group of buyers within a larger market.

> A **segment** is a significant cohesive group of buyers within a larger market.

Homogeneous Segments

Suppose that Mercury Airlines transports adults and seniors at the same marginal cost of 800 dirhams. Then, Mercury can divide the market into two segments according to age. We give the name **direct segment discrimination** to the policy of setting different incremental margins to each identifiable segment.

> **Direct segment discrimination** is the policy where a seller charges a different incremental margin to each identifiable segment.

In Mercury's case, there are two identifiable segments: adults and seniors. Suppose that all adults are willing to pay exactly 3,600 dirhams for Dubai–Mumbai round-trip travel, while all seniors are willing to pay just 900 dirhams. Both of these amounts exceed Mercury's marginal cost, which is 800 dirhams.

Accordingly, Mercury Airlines should set the regular adult fare at 3,600 dirhams and the senior fare at 900 dirhams. Mercury would earn incremental margins of 3,600 − 800 = 2,800 dirhams on each adult passenger, and 900 − 800 = 100 dirhams on each senior.

In this simple scenario, Mercury is able to achieve complete price discrimination through direct segment discrimination. However, as discussed next, if the buyers within each segment are heterogeneous and Mercury lacks sufficient information to identify sub-segments, then direct segment discrimination will not achieve complete price discrimination.

Heterogeneous Segments

What if adults differ in their willingness to pay, and seniors also differ in their willingness to pay? Then, the profit-maximizing pricing policy depends on whether Mercury can identify sub-segments within the broader segments of adults and seniors.

If Mercury does not have sufficient information to identify such sub-segments, it has two choices for pricing within the adult and senior segments. One choice is to apply uniform pricing *within* each segment. The other choice is to apply *indirect* segment discrimination within each segment. We will focus on within-segment uniform pricing here and discuss indirect segment discrimination in section 6 below.

As analyzed above, we can determine the profit-maximizing prices for each segment by applying the rule for uniform pricing. The prices are such that the incremental margin percentage for each segment equals the reciprocal of the absolute value of the segment's price elasticity of demand.

Let the adults' and seniors' demands be as shown in figure 9.3. Consider first the demand from adults. Suppose that the profit-maximizing price is a. Through a process of trial and error, we find that, at the price a, the price elasticity of demand is −1.5. Accordingly, Mercury should set the price a so that the incremental margin percentage is $1/1.5 = 67\%$. This means $(a - 800)/a = 0.67$; hence, the price of a an adult fare, $a = 3,200$ dirhams. At this price, the quantity demanded is 2,500 seats.

Next, we consider the demand from seniors. Seniors derive lower marginal benefits; hence, their demand curve is lower than that of adults. Suppose that the profit-maximizing price is s. Through another process of trial and error, we find that, at the price s, the price elasticity of demand is −7/3. Hence, Mercury should set the senior fare so that the incremental margin percentage is 3/7. Then, $(s - 800)/s = 3/7$, which implies that the senior fare, $s = 1,400$ dirhams. At this price, the quantity demanded is 937 seats.

In this example, the adult demand is less elastic. Therefore, Mercury should set a relatively higher incremental margin percentage on regular adult fares. Mercury's profit from the adult segment is $(2,400 - 800) \times 2,500 = 4$ million dirhams. Further, its profit from the

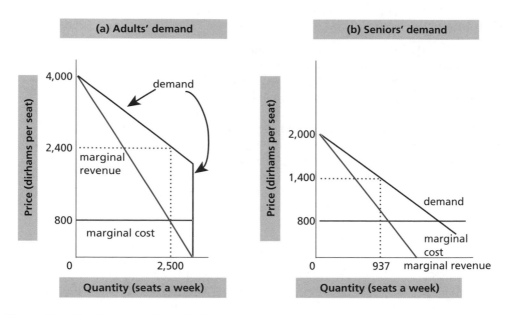

Figure 9.3 Direct segment discrimination
The demand for adult seats is relatively less elastic, so the seller should set a relatively higher incremental margin percentage on adult seats.

senior segment is $(1,400 - 800) \times 937 = 562,000$ dirhams. So, its total profit with direct segment discrimination is 4.56 million dirhams. By contrast, its profit with complete price discrimination is 8 million dirhams, while its profit with uniform pricing is 4 million dirhams.

Implementation

To implement direct segment discrimination, the seller must identify and be able to use some identifiable and fixed buyer characteristic that segments the market. The characteristic must be fixed; otherwise, a buyer might switch segments to take advantage of a lower price.

The second condition necessary for direct segment discrimination is that the seller must be able to prevent buyers from reselling the product among themselves. If the segment to whom the seller sets a relatively low price could resell to other buyers, then the seller will not be able to sell anything at the high price.

Typically, it is more difficult to resell services, especially personal services, than goods. For instance, it is more difficult to resell medical treatment than pharmaceuticals, and it is more difficult to resell tax planning advice than tax preparation software. Accordingly, price discrimination is relatively more widespread in services than goods and is especially common in personal services.

The demand for movies and theme parks varies with such buyer characteristics as income, occupational status, and age. Movie theaters and theme parks cannot observe a customer's income, but they can check a customer's age and whether a customer is a student.

Age is a characteristic that fits the conditions for direct segment discrimination. It is easy to identify and impossible to change. A middle-aged adult cannot buy a senior citizen's ticket.

Accordingly, movie theaters and theme parks set prices so as to extract lower margins from senior citizens and children. Assuming that the marginal cost of serving all patrons is the same, then the result is lower prices for senior citizens and children and higher prices for middle-aged adults.

Resale is the major hurdle to price discrimination between college students and other adults. Service providers recognize this problem. Movie theaters mark their tickets as "Not Transferable." To the extent that theaters can prevent buyers from reselling tickets, they can discriminate between college students and other adults.

Generally, with a policy of direct segment discrimination, prices should be set to derive a relatively lower incremental margin percentage from the segment with the more elastic demand and a relatively higher incremental margin percentage from the segment with the less elastic demand.

⊣ Segment discrimination in e-commerce ⊢

The *New Yorker* famously published a cartoon entitled, "On the Internet, nobody knows you're a dog" (July 5, 1993, p. 61). Clearly, direct segmentation by age, gender, and other personal characteristics is more difficult in business-to-consumer (B2C) e-commerce than conventional retailing.

The degree of difficulty depends on whether the item is delivered through conventional means or the Internet. Many airlines sell tickets through the World Wide Web, either directly through their own websites or indirectly through intermediaries. While passengers may buy tickets over the Internet, they must eventually check in at an airport. Hence, airlines can still set prices to extract different margins from different segments.

Other goods, including newspapers, books, and music, are now delivered through the Internet. Every device connected to the Internet must have an identity so that other devices can communicate with it. For instance, suppose that Max logs on to the Internet and clicks on Amazon.com. Then, Amazon's computers must know where to send its webpage. The Internet standard for identification is the "IP address," a set of numbers that uniquely identifies a device connected to the Internet. For instance, the IP address of one Pacific Internet server is 192.169.41.36.

IP addresses are scarce, and so, Internet access providers typically do not assign users a fixed IP address, but rather assign addresses to users dynamically from a pool, as and when they log on. Users accessing the Internet through organizational networks are identified by the IP address of the organization's computer.

Under these circumstances, segment discrimination is relatively difficult. A middle-aged adult could pose as a child or senior citizen, and someone in Los Angeles could pose as living in New York. To this extent, sellers of goods delivered through the Internet are more likely to fall back upon uniform pricing.

Progress Check 9D Referring to figure 9.3, suppose that the marginal cost is 1,000 dirhams. Use the figure to illustrate the new prices for adult and senior fares.

Heinz ketchup: "not for retail sale"

The market for ketchup consists of a retail consumer segment and an institutional segment. Institutional customers include restaurants, catering services, airlines, schools, and even prisons. The demand curves of retail and institutional customers are quite different. Institutions order larger quantities and often employ professional purchasing staff who aim to secure better deals. Typically, the institutional demand is more price elastic than the retail demand.

Ketchup manufacturers supply retail consumers through distribution channels such as supermarkets and grocery stores. To the extent that manufacturers can prevent institutional customers from reselling ketchup to retail stores, they can implement direct segment discrimination. This means setting prices for a lower incremental margin from institutional customers. It is no coincidence that bottles of Heinz ketchup served in restaurants are marked "Not for Retail Sale."

Residential broadband for home workers

Telecommuting has become common in today's work environment. As cable modems and DSL lines become more prevalent, the opportunity to avoid the commute to the office has greatly increased the number of workers working from home.

Historically, telephone companies charged business subscribers far more than residential subscribers. In the United States, on average, monthly subscription fees for business lines are double those for residential lines. This price discrimination has generally been enforced due to the desire for most businesses to have appropriate directory listings. A business that poses as a residential subscriber will not be listed in the business directory. It will lose potential customers searching in the telephone directory or yellow pages. So, can such price discrimination be sustained in a broadband environment?

Most service providers distinguish between residential and business use of internet services, and use this difference to price discriminate. For example, a typical residential subscriber may pay $30–50 a month compared to over $100 for business use of the same service. This opened the door for businesses to sign up for residential service while using the service for business purposes. Service providers quickly recognized this and started monitoring and managing the traffic on the network.

One example is encrypted tunnel IPSec service, commonly used by enterprises for remote access VPNs (virtual private networks). Because IPSec is used mostly for business applications, service providers shut down the service for those using residential accounts.

In a continuing cat-and-mouse game, businesses have switched their VPNs to SSL (secure socket layer), a service for secure transactions used by both individuals and businesses. Hence, service providers cannot distinguish business users from residential users of SSL. By switching to SSL, business users can pay residential rates.

Source: David Passmore, *Business Communications Review* (November, 2003), pp. 14–15.

⊢ **Microsoft Office** ⊢

Microsoft sells various versions of its hugely popular Office suite of business software. The Standard edition includes Excel, PowerPoint, Outlook, and Word, while the Professional edition includes the three basic programs plus Access, Outlook, and Publisher.

Microsoft's pricing of Office varies internationally. Direct segmentation by country is feasible to the extent that Microsoft can prevent resale across national borders. Table 9.1 reports the regular prices of Office Professional in three countries. Supposing that there are no differences in marginal cost, Microsoft's incremental margin is highest in the U.K. and lowest in Singapore.

Microsoft also segments between students and others through academic discounts. Relative to users in general, students are more sensitive to price. They have low incomes, and possibly, more opportunities to share and copy software. Microsoft has another motivation to provide academic discounts – to lock in users for future purchases at full price. Table 9.1 shows that academic prices for Office Professional 2003 are 64–70% lower than the corresponding regular prices.

Table 9.1 Microsoft Office Professional Edition 2003

	Singapore	United Kingdom	U.S.A.
Regular price	S$859 = $539.23	£484.09 = $884.48	$469
Academic price	S$288 = $180.79	£143.34 = $261.90	$164.99

Singapore and U.K. prices include sales tax; U.S. prices do not.
Sources: Challenger Superstore, Singapore; Insight UK, http://www.insight.com/; author's calculations.

5   Location

To the extent that a product is costly to transport and the seller can identify a buyer's location, the seller can discriminate on the basis of the buyer's location. Generally, there are two ways of pricing to buyers in different locations. One way is to set a common price to all buyers that does not include delivery. Such a price is called ex-works or **free on board (FOB)**. In this case, each buyer pays the FOB price plus the cost of delivery to its respective location. With FOB pricing, the differences among the prices at various locations are exactly the differences in the costs of delivery to those locations.

> A **free on board (FOB)** price does not include delivery.

The alternative way of pricing to different locations is to set prices that include delivery. This practice is called **delivered pricing**, and the price is called **cost including freight** (CF). With delivered (CF) pricing, the differences among the prices at various locations need not correspond to the differences in the cost of delivery to the respective locations.

> **Delivered pricing** is the policy where a seller's price includes delivery.

> A **cost including freight** (CF) price includes delivery.

FOB or CF

Let us compare FOB and CF pricing in the context of pricing to an export market. First, we illustrate FOB pricing. Suppose that Jupiter Bikes sets a price of $350 for an entry level racing bike in its domestic U.S. market. For its price in Japan, it plans to add the freight of $30 and convert the total to yen. Hence, with an exchange rate of ¥100 to the dollar, Jupiter's Japanese price is $380 \times 100 = $ ¥38,000.

FOB pricing, however, ignores the differences between the price elasticities of demand in the various markets. The alternative is CF pricing, which can yield higher profit. In Jupiter's case, assuming that it can prevent buyers in one country from reselling bicycles to the other country, it can implement direct segment discrimination across the two countries. This means setting prices so that its incremental margin percentage in each country balances the reciprocal of the absolute value of the price elasticity of demand.

If the Japanese demand is more elastic than American demand, then Jupiter should set prices so that its incremental margin percentage is lower in Japan than the United States. A lower margin, however, does not necessarily mean a lower price, because Jupiter's marginal cost of supplying the Japanese market includes transportation. Hence, the marginal cost in Japan will be higher than the marginal cost in the United States.

By contrast, if the Japanese demand is less elastic than American demand, then Jupiter should set prices so that its incremental margin percentage is higher in Japan than the United States. Taking into account the higher marginal cost of supplying the Japanese market, this definitely means that Jupiter's price in Japan should exceed that in the United States.

Thus, to the extent that Jupiter can prevent buyers in one country from reselling bicycles to the other country, it can aim for different incremental margin percentages in each market. Then, it will be setting CF prices in the two markets; that is, prices including delivery, rather than FOB prices.

With CF pricing, the difference in the prices between the two markets will simply be the result of the different incremental margin percentages and the different marginal costs of supplying the two markets. In particular, the price difference need not necessarily be the cost of shipping the product from the domestic to the foreign market. Depending on the price elasticities and the marginal costs, the difference may be larger or smaller than the freight cost.

Progress Check 9E Suppose that, for the Japanese market, the price elasticity of demand is −2.5 and the marginal cost including freight is ¥30,000. Calculate Jupiter's CF Japanese price. If Jupiter's U.S. price is $350, and the exchange rate is ¥100 to $1, what is the difference between the Japanese and American prices?

Restricting Resale

If a seller is to succeed in discriminating on the basis of a buyer's location, the various buyers must not be able to adjust location to take advantage of price differences. For most goods, the seller can control only the location at which it sells the product and cannot directly monitor the buyer's location.

If the difference between the prices of a product between two markets exceeds the transportation cost, consumers, and even retailers, might buy the item in one market and ship it to the other. Such parallel importing on an organized basis creates a "gray market." The gray market is a particular problem for lightweight high-price items such as pharmaceuticals and cosmetics.

Manufacturers counteract gray markets in several ways. One is by customizing the product. Products customized for one market will be a poorer substitute for another market. For example, drugs labelled in Greek may not be suitable for the German market. Movie publishers have persuaded manufacturers of DVD players to design their machines so that they will only play movies encoded for the particular region.

Another way to counteract the gray market is to limit sales to the sources of gray-market shipments. Specifically, manufacturers estimate the potential demand in low-price markets and limit sales to such markets accordingly.

In the case of durable goods, manufacturers have another tactic – to restrict warranty service to the country of purchase. This would discourage consumers from buying the good away from home.

Asian Wall Street Journal: print and Internet editions

The *Asian Wall Street Journal* is printed daily in Hong Kong, Singapore, and Tokyo for same-morning delivery. The newspaper charges widely varying prices in the three cities. In May 2006, the prices for a 12-month subscription were HK$2,700 ($348) in Hong Kong, S$525 ($331) in Singapore, and ¥94,500 ($845) in Tokyo.

A business newspaper is particularly suited to discrimination by location. Few business people are interested in trading off a lower price for old news. Hence, the *Asian Wall Street Journal* can maintain a price in Tokyo that is more than double than that in Singapore.

By contrast, it is relatively difficult to pinpoint the location of an Internet subscriber. Accordingly, the *Wall Street Journal Interactive Edition* charges the same price of $99 for a 12-month subscription to every subscriber. Generally, retailers of items that are both sold *and* delivered over the Internet have not been able to discriminate by location.

Sources: Asian Wall Street Journal, www.wsj.com, accessed July 11, 2006.

Emirates Airline's Dubai–Mumbai route: what's your origin?

Price discrimination is especially common in personal services such as airline travel. Airlines are careful to match passengers to tickets, especiallly on international flights. Hence, resale of airline services among travelers is not possible.

By setting different prices for travel originating in Dubai vis-à-vis Mumbai, Emirates Airline is applying direct segment discrimination, with the segments defined by location. The only travelers who might possibly circumvent the discrimination are Dubai residents who travel regularly to Mumbai. They could buy an unrestricted fare to Mumbai, and thereafter, buy all tickets from Mumbai (where the price is lower).

On average, incomes are higher in the United Arab Emirates than India. To the extent that incomes affect the price elasticity of demand, it makes sense for Emirates Airline to set higher prices for travel originating in Dubai as compared with Mumbai.

Table 9.2 Benefits from air travel

Traveler	Segment	Benefit	
		Unrestricted travel ($)	Restricted travel ($)
Maria	Business	1,000	200
Tom	Business	900	180
Robin	Vacation	500	400
Leslie	Vacation	280	224

6 Indirect Segment Discrimination

For a policy of direct segment discrimination, the seller must be able to identify some fixed buyer characteristic that divides the market into segments with different demand curves. A seller may know that specific segments have different demand curves but cannot find a fixed characteristic with which to discriminate directly. Under these circumstances, the seller may be able to apply another policy, which uses an indirect means to discriminate on price.

Suppose that Pluto Airways operates a passenger service between Toronto and Miami. Pluto has four potential customers. Maria and Tom are private bankers based in Toronto who are visiting wealthy clients in Miami. Robin and Leslie are traveling on vacation. Table 9.2 shows the benefit that each of these travelers will derive from (unrestricted) air travel. Clearly, there are two segments, business persons and vacationers, with the business travelers willing to pay more. If traveling to Miami is too expensive, Robin and Leslie could take their vacation elsewhere, so, they are not willing to pay as much.

We use the information from table 9.2 to construct the market demand curve for air travel in figure 9.4. Figure 9.4 shows the market demand curve. (Whether a demand curve is a series of steps or smooth depends on how detailed is the available information about buyers.)

Suppose that Pluto's marginal cost is constant at $200 per seat and the airline has no other costs. Then, each potential traveler gets a benefit that exceeds the airline's marginal cost. If

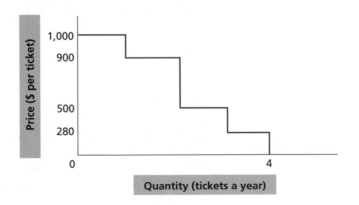

Figure 9.4 Discrete demand
A discrete demand curve consists of a series of steps.

Table 9.3   Air travel, direct segment discrimination

Fare ($)	Sales	Total revenue ($)	Marginal revenue ($)	Marginal cost ($)	Total cost ($)	Profit ($)
Business segment						
1,000	1	1,000	1,000	200	200	800
900	2	1,800	800	200	400	**1,400**
				Maximum segment profit		
Vacation segment						
500	1	500	500	200	200	**300**
280	2	560	60	200	400	160
				Maximum segment profit		

Pluto could implement complete price discrimination, it would set four different fares and sell tickets to each of the four travelers.

It is not likely, however, that Pluto will be able to charge a different price to each traveler. Assuming that Pluto can directly identify business and vacation travelers, the next best alternative is direct segment discrimination. When the segment demands are discrete, the procedure for determining the prices with direct segment discrimination is to calculate the profits from each of the possible prices as in table 9.3. The profit-maximizing prices are a business fare of $900 and a vacation fare of $500. The airline's profit would be $1,700.

We should, however, consider whether Pluto can distinguish business from vacation travelers. The airline's check-in staff might ask every traveler to declare what he or she is planning to do in Miami. Then, every passenger would claim to be going on vacation. Alternatively, Pluto's staff might check whether passengers are wearing casual clothes or business attire. Then, even business travelers would dress casually to check in. Pluto might have to x-ray passengers' luggage to check for business suits and documents.

Clearly, it is very difficult to discriminate directly between business and vacation travelers.

Structured Choice

Let us now consider another form of price discrimination, which uses an *indirect* means to discriminate between business and vacation travelers. Consider the travelers' plans in more detail. Vacationers such as Robin and Leslie can book well in advance and usually want to stay through the weekend. By contrast, business travelers are less able to book early and often prefer to return home for the weekend. So, business travelers and vacationers are differentially sensitive to these features.

Pluto could offer two fares: an unrestricted fare and a fare subject to the restrictions of advance booking and weekend stay. To evaluate this policy, we must know the benefits that the various travelers get from restricted travel. Table 9.2 provides this information. All four get more benefit from unrestricted than restricted travel. The bankers, Maria and Tom, however, get relatively more benefit from unrestricted travel and relatively less benefit from restricted travel.

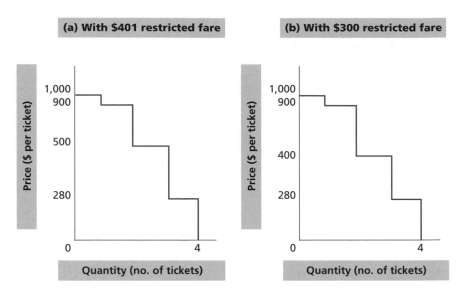

Figure 9.5 Demand for unrestricted travel
If the price of restricted travel is lower, then the demand curve for unrestricted travel will be lower.

Note that unrestricted and restricted fares are substitutes offered by the same seller. Since Pluto cannot directly identify business and vacation travelers, each customer can choose between the two fares. This means that the demand for unrestricted travel depends on the price that Pluto sets for restricted travel. Likewise, the demand for restricted travel depends on the price of unrestricted travel.

Suppose, for instance, that Pluto sets a restricted-travel fare of $401. Table 9.2 shows that this price exceeds the benefit of every traveler from restricted travel. This means that no one will buy the restricted fare. Hence, the demand for unrestricted travel will be the same as if no restricted fare were available. Using the data from table 9.2, we can construct the demand for unrestricted travel when the restricted fare is $401. Figure 9.5(a) illustrates the demand curve.

Next, suppose that Pluto sets a restricted fare of $300. If Robin buys restricted travel, she will get a buyer surplus of $400 − $300 = $100. So, Robin will buy unrestricted travel only if it provides her at least $100 of buyer surplus. By table 9.2, Robin would get a benefit of $500 from unrestricted travel; hence, she will buy unrestricted travel only if the price, u, is sufficiently low that $500 − u \geq 100$, or $u \leq \$400$. Since the restricted fare of $300 exceeds the benefit of each of the other three travelers, they definitely will not buy restricted travel.

Using this information about Robin and the data from table 9.2, we now can construct the demand for unrestricted travel when the restricted fare is $300. If the price of unrestricted travel is between $901 and $1,000, only Maria will buy. If the price is between $401 and $900, both Maria and Tom will buy. If the price is between $281 and $400, then Maria, Tom, and Robin will buy. Finally, if the price is less than or equal to $280, all four travelers will buy. Figure 9.5(b) illustrates the demand curve.

Comparing figures 9.5(a) and (b), we see that the demand for unrestricted travel depends on the price of restricted travel. Generally, if the price of restricted travel is lower, then the demand curve for unrestricted travel will be lower. Accordingly, to calculate the profits from the alternative prices for restricted and unrestricted travel, we must take account of the

Table 9.4 Air travel, indirect segment discrimination

Product	Fare ($)	Sales	Total revenue ($)	Total cost ($)	Profit ($)
Unrestricted	900	2	1,800	400	1,400
Restricted	399	1	399	200	199

substitution between the two products. To find the profit-maximizing prices, we must calculate the profits from every combination of unrestricted and restricted fares.

In table 9.4, we calculate the profit from an unrestricted fare of $900 and a restricted fare of $399. With these fares, Maria would get some buyer surplus from unrestricted travel, while the restricted fare is more than her benefit. Accordingly, Maria would buy an unrestricted fare. Similarly, Tom would buy an unrestricted fare. By contrast, Robin would get some buyer surplus from restricted travel, while the unrestricted fare is more than her benefit. So, Robin would buy a restricted fare. For Leslie, both of the fares are more than the respective benefits, so she will not buy either fare. Thus, Pluto sells two unrestricted fares and one restricted fare.

With the $900 unrestricted fare and $399 restricted fare, Pluto's total revenue would be $900 × 2 + $399 = $2,199. The total cost would be $200 × 3 = $600; hence its profit would be $2,199 − $600 = $1,599. By checking all the other combinations of unrestricted and restricted fares, we can show that this is the maximum profit.

Pluto Airways faces two segments, business travelers and vacation travelers, with different demand curves. The airline, however, has no way to directly identify the segments. Instead, it structures a choice between unrestricted and restricted travel to exploit the differential sensitivity of business and vacation travelers to restrictions on travel. We give the name **indirect segment discrimination** to the policy of structuring a choice for buyers so as to earn different incremental margins from each segment.

> **Indirect segment discrimination** is the policy where a seller structures a choice for buyers so as to earn different incremental margins from each segment.

Implementation

Two conditions are necessary for indirect segment discrimination. First, the seller must have control over some variable to which buyers in the various segments are differentially sensitive. The seller then can use this variable to structure a set of choices that will discriminate among the segments. In Pluto's case, the discriminating variable is the restriction on travel.

The other condition necessary for indirect segment discrimination is that buyers must not be able to circumvent the discriminating variable. Suppose, for instance, that Pluto allowed travelers holding restricted tickets to return without staying over the weekend. Then some business travelers might switch from unrestricted to restricted fares. Such switching will undermine the segment discrimination. Accordingly, Pluto must strictly enforce the conditions of restricted fares.

As we explain later, sellers discriminate indirectly because they cannot directly identify the customer segments. Since indirect segment discrimination means giving every buyer a choice of products, the seller obviously cannot prevent buyers from reselling the product. What is necessary for indirect segment discrimination is that buyers must not be able to circumvent the discriminating variable.

The policy of indirect segment discrimination uses product attributes to discriminate indirectly among the various buyer segments. Essentially, the product attributes are a proxy for the buyer attributes. To determine the profit-maximizing prices, the seller must consider that buyers might substitute among the various choices. Hence, the seller must analyze how changes in the price of one product affect the demand for other choices. Accordingly, the seller must not price any product in isolation. Rather, it must set the prices of all products at the same time.

Ideally, the seller should design each of the alternative product choices to maximize the difference between the buyer's benefit and the seller's cost. The difference between the benefit and the cost is the maximum available profit. It will not always be possible to attain this ideal, however. For instance, in Pluto's case, vacationer Robin chooses restricted travel. The restricted fare gives Robin less benefit than unrestricted travel, but the marginal cost of both fares is the same. If Pluto could implement complete price discrimination, it would make more profit by selling unrestricted travel to Robin. However, with indirect segment discrimination, Pluto must sell Robin a restricted ticket.

Progress Check 9F Referring to table 9.2, suppose that the value of Maria and Tom's benefits from restricted travel change to $600 and $500, respectively. With these changes, can Pluto implement indirect segment discrimination?

Cents-off coupons: consumer time and price elasticity of demand

In 2004, U.S. manufacturers distributed 275 billion coupons, with a face value of over $280 billion. Of these, 190.6 billion and 84.4 billion were distributed by grocery and health and beauty care manufacturers respectively.

However, the number of coupons redeemed was a mere 3.3 billion, yielding a redemption rate of just 1.2%. An intriguing marketing issue is why sellers do not directly cut product prices. Considering the low redemption rate of coupons, direct price cuts would seem to be a more cost-effective way of promoting product sales. From the consumer's viewpoint, a major difference between direct price cuts and coupons is the time and effort needed to redeem a coupon. The more valuable a consumer's time, the higher the cost of redeeming a coupon will be.

Consumers differ in their price elasticity of demand. Ideally, a seller would like to set prices so as to achieve lower margins from consumers whose demand is more elastic and higher margins from those with less elastic demand. To the extent that consumers whose time is more valuable are also those whose demand is less elastic, sellers can use coupons to implement indirect segment discrimination. Buyers whose time is more valuable will tend not to redeem coupons. Only those whose time is relatively cheap will use coupons.

By issuing coupons, a seller can target a discount at the consumer segment that is relatively more price elastic. In contrast, a direct price cut will benefit all buyers, regardless of their price elasticity. Hence, a direct price cut will be less profitable than the policy of issuing coupons.

Source: NCH, *2005 Trend Report*, www.nchmarketing.com/NCHTrendsSample/index.asp, accessed July 11, 2006.

⊣ Delta airlines: unraveling airfare discrimination ⊢

In the U.S. airline industry as a whole, business travel accounts for 40% of passengers but over 50% of revenue. Many business travelers fly at the expense of others. For this and other reasons, they are willing to pay more than leisure travelers. Airlines use reservations and yield management systems to target higher unrestricted fares at business travelers and lower restricted fares at leisure travelers.

Despite the airline's sophisticated systems, many business travelers buy restricted fares. On January 5, 2005, Delta airlines announced "Simplifares," aimed at stemming losses of passengers to low-fare airlines. For travel within the continental United States, Simplifares cut first class airfares by up to 50%, capping unrestricted one-way first class fares at $599 and capped one-way last minute economy fares at $499. Other features were the reduction in change fees from $100 to $50, and the elimination of Saturday night stay requirements.

It was expected that Delta's short-term revenues would decline. Longer-term prospects would depend on how Delta's competitors reacted. The move was aimed at preventing the continued loss of passengers to low-cost rivals. At the time of the change, it was noted that "most of Delta's passengers already fly on fares aimed at the leisure market or low fares offered in response to those of competitors."

Sources: "Delta's Simplifares: Not Simple, But Better," *USA Today*, January 10, 2005; "Inside Delta's Low-Fare Strategy," *BusinessWeek Online*, January 6, 2005.

⊣ Price discrimination and drug patents ⊢

The expiry of the patent for a drug substantially reduces the barriers to entry by competitors. In the United States, 1984 legislation permitted certification of generic drugs as "therapeutically equivalent" to the branded version without expensive and lengthy testing. Since production costs are generally low (compared to R&D costs), generic drugs present competition for the former patent-protected brand name drugs.

What happens to prices and market shares after entry of generic drugs? A study by Grabowski and Vernon of 18 drugs subject to generic competition after the 1984 act documented the rapid market share erosion caused by generic entry. Generics generally captured 50% of the market within two years of entry. However, even while generic prices were falling, brand name prices actually rose. This puzzling phenomenon can be attributed to the fact that generics are not viewed as close substitutes by a particularly price insensitive segment of the market.

As a result, generic entry siphons off the more price sensitive customers, leaving only the inelastic segment of the market. This permits branded drugs to be priced more highly after generic entry, even as they lose significant market share to the generics.

Sources: Henry G. Grabowski and John M. Vernon, "Brand Loyalty, Entry, and Price Competition in Pharmaceuticals after the 1984 Drug Act," *Journal of Law and Economics* 35 (1992), pp. 331–50; Richard G. Frank and David S. Salkever, "Generic Entry and the Pricing of Pharmaceuticals," *Journal of Economics and Management Strategy* 6 (1997), pp. 75–90.

Table 9.5   Benefits from cable television

Segment	Population	Educational channel ($)	Music channel ($)	Bundle ($)
Conservatives	4,000	20	2	22
Middle-of-the-road segment	6,000	11	11	22

7   Bundling

> **Bundling** is the combination of two or more products into one package with a single price.

Indirect segment discrimination usually involves a structured choice that persuades the various buyer segments to identify themselves through their choices. One method of indirect segment discrimination, however, deliberately restricts buyer choices. This is **bundling**, which is the combination of two or more products into one package with a single price.

Pure Bundling

Cable television providers make extensive use of bundling in their pricing. To illustrate this pricing policy, suppose that Venus Cable has an educational channel and a music video channel. There are two segments among the viewer population: conservatives and a middle-of-the-road segment. Table 9.5 shows the segment sizes and their monthly benefits from the two channels. Venus Cable incurs a fixed cost of $100,000 a month, while the marginal cost of providing each channel is nothing.

Suppose that Venus Cable can implement direct segment discrimination. This means setting prices so as to obtain a different margin for each channel from each segment. Since the marginal cost is nothing, Venus should provide both channels to both segments. It should set the prices equal to the segment's benefits. For instance, the prices of the educational and music channels to the conservative segment should be $20 and $2 per month, respectively. The contribution margin will be ($20 × 4,000) + ($2 × 4,000) = $88,000. For the middle-of-the-road segment, both channels should be priced at $11, yielding a contribution margin of ($11 × 6,000) + ($11 × 6,000) = $132,000. Venus's profit would be $88,000 + $132,000 − $100,000 = $120,000.

What if Venus lacks sufficient information to implement direct segment discrimination? Another way to set prices yields an equally large profit. Let Venus offer the two channels as a bundle. Table 9.5 also shows the benefits provided by the bundle. Both segments value the bundle at the same amount of $22 a month. If Venus offers the bundle at a uniform price of $22, then everyone will buy the bundle. The profit will be $22 × (4,000 + 6,000) − $100,000 = $120,000.

In this example, the seller offered only a bundle of the two channels. A pricing policy that offers only a bundle and does not allow the alternative of buying the individual products is called *pure bundling*. Below, we will consider policies that do offer the alternative of the individual products.

With bundled pricing, Venus earns the same profits as from direct segment discrimination. Generally, the bundling strategy will be more profitable than uniform pricing, but less profitable than direct segment discrimination.

Mixed Bundling

In the preceding example, the seller offered only a bundle. Typically, however, the seller can make more profit by allowing buyers a choice between the bundle and the individual products. To illustrate, suppose that Venus incurs a marginal cost of $5 per channel for each customer. The fixed cost remains $100,000 and table 9.5 still represents the buyers' benefits.

Suppose that Venus Cable can implement direct segment discrimination. Consider the prices Venus should set to the conservative segment. Venus should not provide these viewers with the music channel as their benefit of $2 is less than the $5 marginal cost. They should be sold only the educational channel at a price of $20. Venus will earn a contribution margin of $(20 − 5) × 4,000 = $60,000. As for the middle-of-the-road segment, the benefit to these viewers for each channel exceeds the marginal cost. Hence, they should be provided both channels at a price of $11 each, yielding a contribution margin of $(11 − 5) × 6,000 + $(11 − 5) × 6,000 = $72,000. Venus's profit would be $60,000 + $72,000 − $100,000 = $32,000.

Now suppose that Venus Cable lacks sufficient information to implement direct segment discrimination. Pure bundling at a $22 price would be economically inefficient because it would provide both channels to the conservatives. This means that the conservatives would get the music channel, for which their benefit is less than the marginal cost. If it could avoid this inefficiency, Venus could earn a higher profit.

The economic inefficiency can be resolved through *mixed bundling*, which offers buyers a structured choice between the bundle and the individual products. Let Venus offer the bundle at a price of $22, and the educational channel separately at just under $20. What will the conservatives buy? If they buy the bundle, they will get no buyer surplus. If, however, they buy only the educational channel, they will get a little buyer surplus. Hence, they will choose the educational channel, and Venus will earn a contribution margin of just under $(20 − 5) × 4,000 = $60,000.

As for the middle-of-the-road viewers, they will get no buyer surplus from the bundle. Since the price of the educational channel exceeds the benefit, they will not buy the educational channel. Hence, they will choose the bundle, and Venus will earn a contribution margin of $(22 − 5 − 5) × 6,000 = $72,000. Venus's total profit would be just under $60,000 + $72,000 − $100,000 = $32,000. This is only a little less than the profit with direct segment discrimination.

Mixed bundling is a form of indirect segment discrimination. In this example, the conservatives and the middle-of-the-road segments are differentially sensitive to the product structure. The conservatives benefit relatively more from the educational channel, while the middle-of-the-road segment benefits relatively more from the music channel. Through mixed bundling, Venus attracts only the middle-of-the-road segment to choose the bundle, and persuades the conservatives to choose the educational channel.

Implementation

Bundling is relatively more useful under three conditions: where there is substantial disparity among the segments in their benefits from the separate products, where the benefits of the segments are negatively correlated in the sense that a product that is more beneficial to one segment provides relatively little benefit to another, and where the marginal cost of providing the product is low.

With the first and second conditions, the benefit from the bundle will be relatively less disparate across the segments than the benefits from the separate products. The third condition means that relatively little economic inefficiency will accrue from providing the bundle to all buyers.

In the Venus Cable example, each channel provides widely disparate benefits to each of the two segments. The bundle, however, provides exactly the same benefit of $22 to both segments. Accordingly, it is easy to set a price for the bundle.

When provision of the product involves a substantial marginal cost, a seller should consider mixed bundling. This is essentially a form of indirect segment discrimination. By structuring a choice among the bundle and the separate products, the seller can persuade the various segments to identify themselves through their product choice. In this way, the seller can avoid the economic inefficiency of providing a product for which the marginal cost is less than the buyer's benefit.

Ace Rent-a-Car: bundling unlimited mileage

The market for car rentals, like that for airline services, consists of business and vacation segments. To the extent that employers or clients pay for business rentals, the demand of business drivers is relatively less elastic. A challenge for car rental agencies is how to discriminate between business and vacation drivers. Since rental agencies cannot discriminate directly, they need some variable with which to discriminate indirectly.

Suppose that vacationers tend to drive long distances, while business renters drive relatively shorter distances. Accordingly, these segments are differentially sensitive to mileage charges. Then, a rental agency can use mileage charges to discriminate between business and vacation drivers. Specifically, it should structure two choices. One choice combines a relatively high daily charge with a low mileage charge to draw vacationers. In the extreme, this could offer unlimited mileage. The other choice should have a lower daily charge with a higher mileage charge to attract business drivers.

Essentially, the unlimited mileage rate is a bundle of two products: the car and unlimited usage. The time and mileage rate sets separate prices for the two products.

In 2004, Ace Rent-a-Car of Perth, Western Australia offered a Toyota Camry at an unlimited mileage rate of A$288 for four days, or a time and mileage rate of A$216 for four days including 400 free kilometers with additional mileage charged at 25 cents per kilometer. The break-even mileage between the two rates was 688 kilometers. Provided that most business renters drove less than 688 kilometers a day, the Ace pricing policy would succeed in indirect segment discrimination.

Progress Check 9G Referring to table 9.5, suppose that the conservatives derive a benefit of $19 from the educational channel, and $1 from the music channel. The marginal cost of providing each channel is $5. What prices should Venus set with mixed bundling?

---

8   Selecting the Pricing Policy

Generally, the pricing policy that yields the most profit is complete price discrimination. This, however, also requires the most information. The next most profitable pricing policy is direct market segmentation. With direct segment discrimination, the seller discriminates directly

Table 9.6 Ranking of pricing policies

Profitability	Policy	Information requirement
Highest	Complete price discrimination	Highest
	Direct segment discrimination	
	Indirect segment discrimination	
Lowest	Uniform pricing	Lowest

on some fixed attributes of the buyer. The seller can identify each buyer segment and prevent one segment from buying the product targeted at another segment. Hence, the seller can set prices without worrying about buyers switching among the products.

By contrast with direct discrimination, which works through buyer attributes, indirect segment discrimination works through product attributes, and is less profitable. One reason is that the products under indirect discrimination may provide less benefit than those with direct segmentation. For instance, with indirect discrimination, airlines must sell restricted travel to the vacationers, which provides less benefit than unrestricted travel. By contrast, if direct discrimination were possible, airlines would sell unrestricted travel to all passengers, and so earn a higher profit.

Another reason why indirect discrimination is less profitable is that it may involve relatively higher costs. For instance, consumer products manufacturers use cents-off coupons to indirectly discriminate among consumers with different price elasticity. Coupons impose costs on both the issuers and users.

Finally, indirect discrimination relies on the various segments voluntarily identifying themselves through the structured choice. This may not always work perfectly: consumers in one segment may buy the item aimed at the other segments. Such *cannibalization* would reduce the profitability of indirect discrimination.

The least profitable pricing policy is uniform pricing. This involves no discrimination at all. It also requires the least information.

Table 9.6 ranks the various pricing policies in decreasing order of profitability.

Cannibalization

Cannibalization occurs when the sales of one product reduce the demand for another product with a higher incremental margin. Some examples of cannibalization are business travelers flying on restricted economy class fares, high-income consumers redeeming coupons, and wealthy families buying basic sedan cars rather than high-end luxury cars.

> **Cannibalization** occurs when the sales of one product reduce the demand for another product with a higher incremental margin.

The fundamental reason for cannibalization is that the seller cannot discriminate directly, and hence must rely on a structured choice of products to discriminate indirectly. To the extent that the discriminating variable does not perfectly separate the buyer segments, cannibalization will occur.

There are several ways to mitigate cannibalization. One way uses product design. Upgrading the high-margin item would make it relatively more attractive, and hence, less likely to be cannibalized. Degrading the low-margin item would make it less attractive, and so, less likely to cannibalize the demand for the high-margin item.

Another way to mitigate cannibalization also uses product design. The products can be designed with multiple discriminating variables. For instance, airlines specify multiple conditions for restricted airfares, including minimum and maximum stay, limits on stop-overs at intermediate places, and penalties for cancellation or changes in itinerary. Each of these conditions helps to reduce the degree to which the restricted airfare would cannibalize the demand for the unrestricted airfare.

Finally, cannibalization can be mitigated by controlling availability. Limiting the availability of the low-margin item would make it less attractive. Airlines, for instance, limit the number of seats allocated to lower fares.

Discount fares: are seats available?

One way by which airlines manage cannibalization is by controlling the number of seats available at discount fares. Figure 9.6 shows fares available on May 3, 2006 for travel on Southwest Airlines from Los Angeles to San Jose on May 14, 2006.

Clearly, Southwest allocates seats in a way such that the lower the fare, the less likely it will be available.

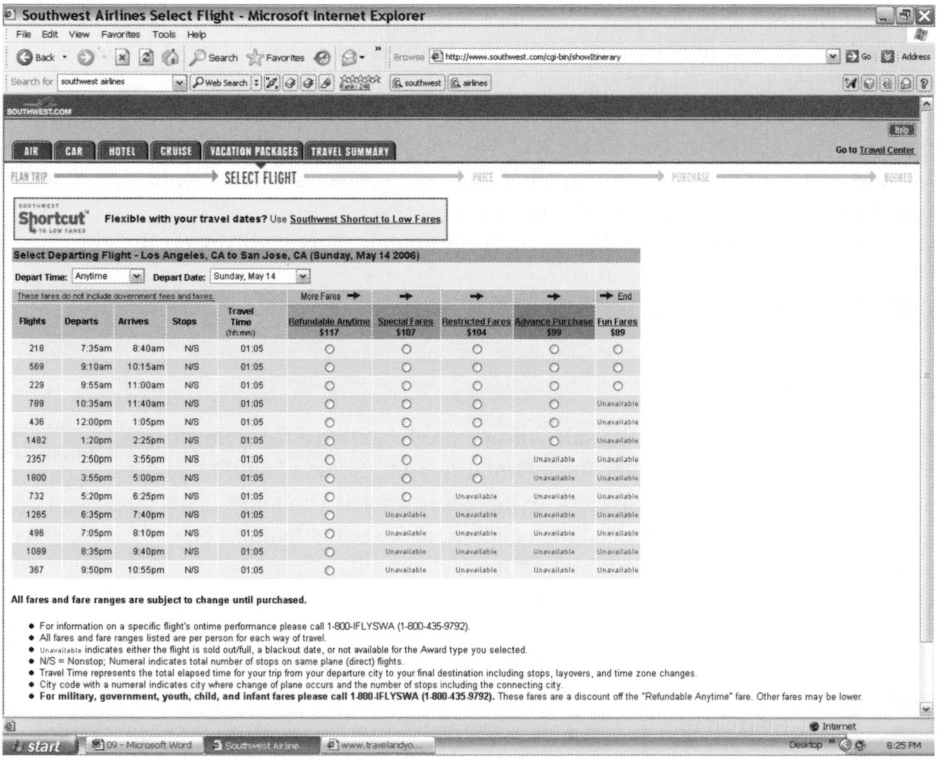

Southwest Airlines Select Flight - Microsoft Internet Explorer

Select Departing Flight - Los Angeles, CA to San Jose, CA (Sunday, May 14 2006)

Depart Time: Anytime   Depart Date: Sunday, May 14

These fares do not include government fees and taxes.

Flights	Departs	Arrives	Stops	Travel Time (hh:mm)	Refundable Anytime $117	Special Fares $107	Restricted Fares $104	Advance Purchase $99	Fun Fares $89
218	7:35am	8:40am	N/S	01:05	O	O	O	O	O
569	9:10am	10:15am	N/S	01:05	O	O	O	O	O
229	9:55am	11:00am	N/S	01:05	O	O	O	O	O
789	10:35am	11:40am	N/S	01:05	O	O	O	O	Unavailable
436	12:00pm	1:05pm	N/S	01:05	O	O	O	O	Unavailable
1482	1:20pm	2:25pm	N/S	01:05	O	O	O	O	Unavailable
2357	2:50pm	3:55pm	N/S	01:05	O	O	O	Unavailable	Unavailable
1800	3:55pm	5:00pm	N/S	01:05	O	O	O	Unavailable	Unavailable
732	5:20pm	6:25pm	N/S	01:05	O	O	Unavailable	Unavailable	Unavailable
1265	6:35pm	7:40pm	N/S	01:05	O	Unavailable	Unavailable	Unavailable	Unavailable
496	7:05pm	8:10pm	N/S	01:05	O	Unavailable	Unavailable	Unavailable	Unavailable
1089	8:35pm	9:40pm	N/S	01:05	O	Unavailable	Unavailable	Unavailable	Unavailable
367	9:50pm	10:55pm	N/S	01:05	O	Unavailable	Unavailable	Unavailable	Unavailable

All fares and fare ranges are subject to change until purchased.

- For information on a specific flight's ontime performance please call 1-800-IFLYSWA (1-800-435-9792).
- All fares and fare ranges listed are per person for each way of travel.
- Unavailable indicates either the flight is sold out/full, a blackout date, or not available for the Award type you selected.
- N/S = Nonstop; Numeral indicates total number of stops on same plane (direct) flights.
- Travel Time represents the total elapsed time for your trip from your departure city to your final destination including stops, layovers, and time zone changes.
- City code with a numeral indicates city where change of plane occurs and the number of stops including the connecting city.
- For military, government, youth, child, and infant fares please call 1-800-IFLYSWA (1-800-435-9792). These fares are a discount off the "Refundable Anytime" fare. Other fares may be lower.

Figure 9.6   Southwest Airlines: Los Angeles–San Jose fares

⊢ Is an Audi worth 40% more than a Passat? ⊢

The Volkswagen Group (including Audi, Skoda, SEAT, and VW) accounts for over 12% of world automobile sales. Like other major car manufacturers, Volkswagen economizes on development and manufacturing costs by using common chassis and engines across its various brands. For instance, the high-end Audi A6 and the lower-end VW Passat share the same 1.8 and 2.8-liter engine and body. The Audi is differentiated through superior paneling, instrumentation, and other electronic equipment.

The Audi is priced at a 40% premium to the VW. Owing to their basic similarities, however, the VW has cannibalized the demand for the Audi. Some German buyers of fleets of cars reportedly switched their purchases to the VW. Having compared the Passat with the Audi A6, automobile reviewer Denis Droppa advised, "In a nutshell, you're getting a car that pampers in a way similar to an Audi A6 . . . but for less money."

Sources: "Let's Make a Deal," *Time*, January 25, 1999, pp. 35–6; "Pssst! Try a Passat for Some Budget Luxury," www.motoring.co.za, April 4, 2002.

9   Summary

The simplest way to set price is through uniform pricing. At the profit-maximizing uniform price, the incremental margin percentage equals the reciprocal of the absolute value of the price elasticity of demand. The most profitable pricing policy is complete price discrimination, where each unit is priced at the benefit that the unit provides to its buyer. To implement this policy, however, the seller must know each potential buyer's individual demand curve and be able to set different prices for every unit of the product.

The next most profitable pricing policy is direct segment discrimination. For this policy, the seller must be able to directly identify the various segments. The third most profitable policy is indirect segment discrimination. This involves structuring a set of choices around some variable to which the various segments are differentially sensitive. Uniform pricing is the least profitable way to set a price.

A commonly used basis for direct segment discrimination is location. This exploits a difference between free on board and cost including freight prices. A commonly used method of indirect segment discrimination is bundling. Sellers may apply either pure or mixed bundling.

Key Concepts

uniform pricing
price discrimination
complete price discrimination
segment
direct segment discrimination
free on board (FOB)

delivered pricing
cost including freight (CF)
indirect segment discrimination
bundling
cannibalization

Further Reading

Thomas T. Nagle and Reed K. Holden provide a comprehensive economic analysis of pricing in *The Strategy and Tactics of Pricing*, 3rd ed. (Englewood Cliffs, NJ: Prentice-Hall, 2002).

Review Questions

1. Many supermarkets sell both branded and private-label merchandise. Suppose that some supermarket estimates that the demand for its private-label cola is less elastic than the demand for Coca-Cola. Does this mean that it should set a higher price for private-label cola?

2. Sol Electric manufactures long-life light bulbs. The marginal production cost is 50 cents per unit. Sol estimates that the price elasticity of demand is −1.25. Assuming that Sol will set a uniform price, what is the profit-maximizing price?

3. Saturn Tire has found a way to reduce the marginal cost of a tire from $50 to $40. Should Sol reduce the selling price of a tire by $10?

4. Book publishers typically set prices by the number of pages multiplied by a standard price per page. Comment on this pricing policy.

5. Give an example of direct segment discrimination. Discuss whether the product meets the conditions for such discrimination.

6. Some department stores offer a free delivery service. For stores that do, is the FOB price of goods less than, equal to, or greater than the CF price?

7. On which of the following products would it be easier to discriminate by the buyer's location? Newspapers or scientific journals? Explain your answer.

8. Microsoft prices Office XP Pro with a higher incremental margin in the United States than in Singapore. Relate this difference to the greater availability of pirated software and opportunities for copying in Singapore.

9. Give an example of indirect segment discrimination. Discuss whether the example meets the conditions for such discrimination.

10. The *Wall Street Journal Interactive Edition* charges a lower subscription fee to those who already subscribe to the print edition. Explain this practice.

11. A wireless carrier offers a menu of pricing plans, such that plans with higher monthly charges include a larger number of "free minutes." Explain this choice in terms of indirect segment discrimination.

12. Typically, car rental agencies charge much higher prices for gasoline than that at nearby gas stations. Explain how this indirectly segments between drivers who are paying for a rental themselves and those who are renting at the expense of others.

13. Use pure bundling to explain the following comment on cable television business strategy: "[I]f every segment . . . was wild about one thing and hated the rest, they have done their job. If all their programmes are mildly, but not very interesting to everybody, they haven't" ("Getting better all the time," *The Economist*, November 21, 1998).

14. Explain the difference between pure bundling and mixed bundling, and the conditions under which each of them should be used.

15. What is cannibalization and how can it be managed?

Discussion Questions

1. In September 2004, HSBC Holdings and Malayan Banking Berhad led a consortium of 13 banks to provide a five-year $200 million load to Optimal Olefins. Optimal Olefins is owned by Petroliam Nasional Berhad, Dow Chemicals Company, and Sasol Limited of South Africa. The interest rate on the loan was set at the London Interbank Offer Rate (LIBOR) plus a spread of 44.5 basis points (0.445%). Banks source funds from demand, savings, and time deposits, as well

as the interbank market. However, interest rates in the interbank market are usually higher than those on demand, savings, and time deposits. (*Source*: "HSBC, Maybank Get 11 Others to Give Optimal $466m Loan," *The Star Online*, September 3, 2004.)

(a)   Does LIBOR reflect a typical bank's average or marginal cost of funds?

(b)   For purposes of pricing, which is relevant – average or marginal cost?

(c)   What factors should banks take into account when setting the spread over LIBOR?

(d)   Explain the banks' pricing policy in terms of the incremental margin percentage and the price elasticity of demand.

2.   Founded in 1995, eBay describes itself as "The World's Online Marketplace." By 2004, with annual revenue of $2.7 billion and net income of $642 million, the company's value exceeded $60 billion. On eBay, items are sold online through an auction-like format. Buyers also have the option of buying at a fixed price before an auction begins. Consider a person who is selling multiple units of some item. Each unit may be listed separately on eBay.

(a)   Compare a seller's revenue from uniform pricing with an eBay auction.

(b)   Should the seller list all items at the same time, or list them one at a time?

(c)   The seller may receive different prices for each unit. Is this a case of complete price discrimination? Why or why not?

3.   Doctors routinely ask patients about their occupation, employer, home address, and scope of insurance coverage. How do the following factors affect the scope for price discrimination in medical services?

(a)   Characteristics such as occupation and home address are quite fixed.

(b)   It is physically impossible to transfer medical treatment from one person to another.

(c)   Doctors treat patients on an individual basis.

4.   Referring to figure 9.1, suppose that Mercury Airlines' marginal revenue and demand curves cross the marginal cost curve at quantities of 3,000 and 6,000 seats a week, respectively. All other data remain the same.

(a)   Calculate the profit under policies of (i) uniform pricing, and (ii) complete price discrimination.

(b)   Suppose that Mercury implements complete price discrimination. Explain why it should sell up to the quantity where the buyer's marginal benefit equals Mercury's marginal cost.

(c)   Explain why Mercury's profit is higher with complete price discrimination than with uniform pricing.

5.   Microsoft offers special discounts to students. Other publishers have developed special "student" editions of their software with fewer features than the regular packages.

(a)   Why do publishers offer discounts to students?

(b)   What is the purpose of developing less powerful "student" editions?

(c)   Should software publishers also offer discounts to senior citizens or develop "senior citizen" editions?

6.   Up to two million U.S. consumers buy pharmaceuticals from online Canadian pharmacies, where prices of are substantially lower than in the United States. Monthly sales reached a peak of $43.5 million in early 2004. Then, U.S. pharmaceutical manufacturers limited supplies to Canadian wholesalers that sold to online pharmacies. In response, like many others, Universal Drugstore of Winnipeg, Manitoba, began to source drugs from wholesalers in Australia, New Zealand and Britain. (*Source*: "Kinks in Canada Drug Pipeline," *New York Times*, April 7, 2006.)

(a)   By considering price elasticities of demand, and production and shipping costs, explain why U.S. pharmaceutical manufacturers set higher prices in the United States than Australia and New Zealand.

(b)   Why does the gray market present a problem for U.S. pharmaceutical manufacturers?

(c)   Compare the gray market problem for drugs administered by medical professionals relative to other drugs.

7. Heinz sells 650 million bottles of ketchup and 11 billion packets of ketchup and dressings annually world wide. (*Source*: "About Heinz," www.heinz.com/About.aspx, accessed, July 11, 2006.) The demand side of the ketchup market comprises a retail segment and an institutional segment. Institutional customers include restaurants, catering services, airlines, schools, and even prisons. Institutions order larger quantities and may employ professional purchasing staff. Ketchup manufacturers supply retail consumers indirectly through distribution channels such as supermarkets and grocery stores.

   (a) Explain why institutional demand for ketchup is likely to be more price elastic than retail demand.

   (b) How would ketchup manufacturers like to apply direct segment discrimination?

   (c) If ketchup manufacturers supply both institutional customers and retail distribution channels through wholesalers, explain how the wholesalers might undermine direct segment discrimination.

   (d) Compare the problem in (c) for ketchup in bottles as compared with packets.

   (e) Why does Heinz mark ketchup sold to restaurants with "Not for Retail Sale"?

8. In 2004, U.S. consumer products manufacturers distributed 27.548 billion coupons, with a face value of over $280 billion, of which a mere 1.2% were redeemed by consumers. Why do manufacturers spend millions of dollars to distribute coupons when the redemption rate is so low? Why don't the manufacturers cut the wholesale prices of the products directly, which would be much cheaper to administer?

   (a) Some say that retailers would absorb a direct wholesale price cut instead of passing it on to consumers. They argue that, by contrast, retailers cannot absorb the value of coupons. Suppose that the retail sector is perfectly competitive. Compare the demand–supply equilibrium in the retail market with (i) a wholesale price cut of 50 cents and (ii) widespread distribution of 50-cent coupons. For this part, you should apply the analysis of tax incidence from chapter 6, treating a price cut or coupon like a negative tax, and may assume that all consumers use coupons.

   (b) Would there be any difference between the wholesale price cut and using coupons if the retailer were a monopoly? (Continue to treat a price cut or coupon like a negative tax, and assume that all consumers use coupons.)

   (c) Explain how coupons may be used to discriminate among consumers on price. Compare this explanation to the argument that retailers would absorb a wholesale price cut.

9. In 2000, the Chinese Embassy in Singapore charged different fees for visas according to the number of times that the visitor wished to enter China and the requested processing time (see table 9.7). Assume that the costs of preparing single and double entry visas are the same, and that the costs of processing over 1, 3, and 5 days are the same.

   (a) Explain the Embassy's pricing policies in terms of indirect segment discrimination between tourists and business travelers.

Table 9.7   Visa fees, Chinese Embassy, Singapore

	Processing time		
	1 day	3 days	5 days
Single entry	75	60	25
Double entry	85	70	35

Source: Chinese Embassy, Singapore, July 2000.

(b)   The Embassy charges a premium of $10 for double entry visas relative to single entry visas. Consider intuitively what premium it should charge for double entry visas.

(c)   Should the Chinese Government set the same schedule of visa fees at all of its overseas embassies?

10.   Singapore holders of the Citibank Cathay Pacific Visa card received a special "Your companion flies for free" promotion in early 2004. Round-trip fares for two persons traveling together ranged between S$500 to Bangkok, S$1,200 to Tokyo, and S$2,900 to Toronto (all amounts in Singapore dollars). These special fares were up to 55% less than regular fares. However, they were subject to a number of restrictions, including tickets being issued by June 15, travel before June 30, "blackout" periods (dates on which travel would not be permitted), and only one stopover allowed, in Hong Kong, and only on the return portion of travel.

(a)   Explain the choice between the special two-person fare and a regular one-person fare in terms of mixed bundling.

(b)   How does the choice between the special two-person fare and a regular one-person fare implement indirect segment discrimination between business and vacation travelers?

(c)   Since travel on Cathay Pacific Airways from Singapore to Tokyo and Toronto required a change of planes in Hong Kong, why did Cathay Pacific limit stop-overs in Hong Kong for the special companion offer?

(d)   The special companion offer did not allow travel to and from Japan between April 9–12 and April 28–May 5, which were peak holiday seasons. Explain this restriction in terms of limiting cannibalization of regular fares.

Chapter 9

Math Supplement

Uniform Pricing

Let us prove the rule for a profit-maximizing price in terms of the price elasticity of demand: the incremental margin percentage equals the reciprocal of the absolute value of the price elasticity. Let Q represent sales, P represent price, MR represents marginal revenue, and MC represents marginal cost.

From chapter 9, we know that, at the profit-maximizing amount of sales, the marginal revenue equals the marginal cost:

$$MR = MC. \tag{9.3}$$

Now the marginal revenue is the additional revenue from selling an additional unit. This is the price that unit is sold at minus the change in price required to sell one more unit multiplied by the previous quantity of sales, or

$$MR = p + \Delta p Q = p + \frac{\Delta p}{\Delta Q} Q = p \left[1 + \frac{\Delta p}{\Delta Q} \frac{Q}{p} \right] = p(1 + 1/e_p) \tag{9.4}$$

where Δ represents "the change in" (note that $\Delta Q = 1$). The definition of the incremental margin %, $IM\%$, is

$$IM\% = \frac{p - MC}{p}. \tag{9.5}$$

Substituting (9.3) and (9.4) in (9.5), we have

$$IM\% = \frac{p - p(1 + 1/e_p)}{p} = 1/e_p. \tag{9.6}$$

This states that, at the profit-maximizing price, the incremental margin percentage equals the reciprocal of the absolute value of the price elasticity.

Contribution Margin Percentage

Using algebra, we can prove that the contribution margin percentage is equal to the price less the average variable cost divided by the price. In cost accounting, the contribution margin percentage is defined as total revenue less variable cost divided by total revenue, or

$$CM\% = \frac{R(Q) - V(Q)}{R(Q)}. \tag{9.7}$$

Dividing both the numerator and the denominator by sales (or the quantity demanded), we have

$$CM\% = \frac{R(Q)/Q - V(Q)/Q}{R(Q)/Q}. \tag{9.8}$$

Consider the first term in the numerator and the same term in the denominator:

$$\frac{R(Q)}{Q} = \frac{p \times Q}{Q} = p. \tag{9.9}$$

Hence, the contribution margin percentage simplifies to

$$CM\% = \frac{p - V(Q)/Q}{p}, \tag{9.10}$$

which is the price less the average variable cost divided by the price.

Chapter 10

Strategic Thinking

1 Introduction

Soft drinks are America's single most popular beverage, accounting for one in four beverages consumed, up from one in five over a decade ago. In 2004, the average American consumed almost 52.2 gallons a year (down from a maximum of 56.1 gallons in 1998), equivalent to 2.3 eight-ounce servings a day. Market shares in the U.S. soft drinks industry have been quite stable, with 2004 shares of 43% for Coca-Cola, followed by Pepsi with 32%, and Cadbury Schweppes with 14.5%. With the top three manufacturers accounting for almost 90% of the market, the industry is highly concentrated.[1]

Despite the high industry concentration, Coke and Pepsi competed intensely on price, and their profits slipped. Then, in November 1999, Coke made a fundamental change in strategy, announcing a 7% increase in the price of concentrate to bottlers, which translated into a 5% retail price increase. Within a week, Pepsi followed suit, raising the price of concentrate by 6.9%, which led to a 5% retail price increase.

Why did the two arch-rivals succeed in raising prices after the long, sustained price war? Standard and Poor's analyst Richard Joy pointed to a significant change in Pepsi's organizational architecture: "The creation of the Pepsi Bottling Group . . . had the effect of reducing price competition at the retail level. . . . Now that it is no longer shielded by the corporate umbrella of PepsiCo, Pepsi Bottling Group needs to produce profits, and thus appears unlikely to discount its brands."

Historically, Coke was vertically separated: the Coca-Cola Company, headquartered in Atlanta, owned the brand and sold concentrate to Coca-Cola Enterprises and other franchised bottlers. By contrast, PepsiCo had been vertically integrated. Then, in March 1999, PepsiCo spun off the Pepsi Bottling Group (PBG). Following the spin-off, PepsiCo managed the brand and sold concentrate. PBG and other franchised bottlers used the concentrate to manufacture soft drinks for sale in supermarkets and other distribution channels.

A *strategy* is a plan for action in a situation where the parties actively consider the interactions with one another in making decisions.

---

[1] This discussion is based, in part, on *Standard & Poor's Industry Surveys: Foods & Nonalcoholic Beverages*, 166, no. 22, section 1 (June 3, 1999), p. 3; "Coca-Cola Shifts Strategy In Effort to Boost Profit," *Wall Street Journal Interactive Edition*, November 16, 1999.

A **strategy** is a plan for action in a situation where the parties actively consider the interactions with one another in making decisions. Consider Coke's decision whether to raise its price. The soft drinks industry is so concentrated that it surely must consider the reactions of Pepsi and Cadbury Schweppes. Coke was making a *strategic* decision.

Sugar is a major input into soft drink concentrate. So, consider a typical sugar beet farmer's choice of how much to plant for the next season. The farmer is too small to affect the price of sugar, hence need not consider her impact on other farms. The farmer's decision is not **strategic**.

In this chapter, we consider how to organize thinking about strategic decisions, choose among alternative strategies, and make better strategic decisions. This chapter is based on a set of ideas and principles to guide strategic thinking called *game theory*.

Game theory explains why competing sellers tend to cut price. Specifically, we develop the model of games in strategic form and apply this to analyze competition in markets with few sellers. We show that sellers tend to compete on price, although collectively, they could raise profit by avoiding price competition.

We then consider games in extensive form, where the focus is on the strategic outcome when parties act in sequence. The analysis explains why Coke and Pepsi were able to raise their prices only after Pepsi vertically separated into independent brand and bottling businesses. Pepsi's vertical separation mitigated the intensity of price competition, and paved the way for the two arch-rivals to raise prices.

Game theory is a set of ideas and principles that guides strategic thinking.

The ideas and principles of **game theory** provide an effective guide to strategic decision-making in many businesses. Corporate financiers apply game theory in takeover contests. Telecommunications and media providers apply it in bidding for licenses. And, of course, game theory is useful to any business with market power in analyzing competitive strategy.

Progress Check 10A Explain why the decisions of a presidential election candidate are strategic.

---

2 Nash Equilibrium

We introduce a framework for strategic decisions that must be taken simultaneously in the context of the following example. Jupiter Transport and Saturn Trailways dominate the market for truck rentals. To restrain competition, the managements of the two companies agreed to limit each company to a specific quota of truck rentals a year. The quotas were set to maintain the market price at the monopoly level.

However, each company makes an independent decision on its sales. Accordingly, it is important to ask: Will the individual companies comply with their quotas?

The situation of the two truck rental businesses is clearly strategic. Jupiter's profit depends on Saturn's action, and likewise, Saturn's profit depends on Jupiter. How should Jupiter act?

Let us try to clarify Jupiter's position in the following way. Recall that a strategy is a plan for action in a situation where the parties actively consider interactions with one another in making decisions. Jupiter must decide on a strategy. Jupiter has a choice of two strategies, follow the quota or exceed the quota, and likewise, Saturn has a choice of two strategies, follow the quota or exceed the quota.

Accordingly, there are four possible outcomes: Jupiter and Saturn both follow the quota; Jupiter follows the quota while Saturn exceeds the quota, Jupiter exceeds the quota while

Table 10.1 Cartel's dilemma

		Saturn	
		Follow quota	Exceed quota
Jupiter	Follow quota	J: 15 S: 10	J: 10 S: 13
	Exceed quota	J: 19 S: 5	J: 12 S: 8

Saturn follows the quota; and both companies exceed the quota. For each of these outcomes, we should calculate the profits of the two companies.

Next, we gather this information in table 10.1 as follows. We mark Jupiter's alternative strategies along the rows, and Saturn's strategies along the columns. The columns and rows delineate four cells, each representing one of the four possible outcomes. In each cell, the first entry is Jupiter's annual profit in millions of dollars and the second entry is Saturn's profit. For instance, in the cell where both Jupiter and Saturn follow the quota, we mark "J: 15" to represent that Jupiter's profit would be $15 million, and then "S: 10" to represent that Saturn's profit would be $10 million.

Table 10.1 is called a **game in strategic form**. It is a very useful way to organize thinking about strategic decisions that parties must take simultaneously. Let us use the game in strategic form to consider how Jupiter should act. First, look at the situation from Saturn's position. If Jupiter follows the quota, then Saturn will earn $10 million if it follows the quota or $13 million if it exceeds the quota, so Saturn prefers to exceed the quota. Now, if Jupiter exceeds the quota, then Saturn will earn $5 million if it follows the quota or $8 million if it exceeds the quota, so, Saturn prefers to exceed the quota.

> A **game in strategic form** is a tabular representation of a strategic situation, showing one party's strategies along the rows, the other party's strategies along the columns, and the consequences for the parties in the corresponding cells.

Hence, regardless of Jupiter's move, Saturn should exceed the quota. For Saturn, the strategy of follow the quota is *dominated* by the strategy of exceed the quota. A strategy is **dominated** if it generates worse consequences than some other strategy, regardless of the other parties' choices. It makes no sense to adopt a dominated strategy.

For Saturn, follow the quota is a dominated strategy. Accordingly, Jupiter can figure out that Saturn will exceed the quota. Similarly, by studying the situation from Jupiter's position, it is easy to see that, for Jupiter also, follow the quota is a dominated strategy. Hence, Jupiter also should exceed the quota.

> A **dominated strategy** is a strategy that generates worse consequences than some other strategy, regardless of the choices of the other parties.

We call the preceding situation the *cartel's dilemma*. As explained in chapter 11, a cartel is an agreement to restrain competition. Both companies know that, if they abide by their quotas, then they can increase their profit. The snag, however, is that when each individual company acts independently, it will decide to exceed its quota. The final outcome is that both companies exceed their quotas and erode the market price below the monopoly level.

⊢ **OPEC: dilemma of an oil cartel?** ⊢

The Organization of Petroleum Exporting Countries (OPEC) includes major oil producers Saudi Arabia, Iran, Kuwait, and Venezuela. Like any other cartel, OPEC suffers from the problem that individual members prefer to exceed their quotas. From a short-term perspective, no matter what others do, each member's best strategy is to cheat.

Predictions of the impending demise of the OPEC cartel or its continued importance abound. As late as 2001, journalist Matt Taibbi described OPEC as a "historically doomed organization." However, the subsequent rise in oil prices to record levels has led many to question this prediction. In April 2006, OPEC members produced at the rate of 27.94 million barrels per day (mbd), almost equal to the total OPEC quota target of 28 mbd, although 6 of the 10 OPEC members (excluding Iraq) were exceeding their individual quotas.

In a recent assessment of the future of OPEC, the Joint Economic Committee of the U.S. Congress concluded that, "Large price swings reveal errors in forecasting and execution, not a lack of power to move the price."

Sources: Matt Taibbi, "The Motherland Arises," *The Exile* 130 (November 29, 2001); Platts OPEC Guide, April 2006, www.platts.com; Theodore W. Boll, "OPEC and the High Price of Oil," A Joint Economic Committee Study, U.S. Congress, November 2005.

Definition

The pair of strategies – for Jupiter, exceed the quota, and for Saturn, exceed the quota – is the obvious way for the two companies to act. Moreover, this pair of strategies is a stable situation in the following sense. Even if Saturn knows that Jupiter will exceed the quota, Saturn's best action is to exceed the quota, so it will not change its strategy. Likewise, even if Jupiter knew that Saturn would exceed the quota, Jupiter would still exceed the quota.

> A **Nash equilibrium** is a set of strategies such that, given that the other players choose their Nash equilibrium strategies, each party prefers its own Nash equilibrium strategy.

In a strategic situation, a **Nash equilibrium** is a set of strategies such that, given that the other parties choose their Nash equilibrium strategies, each party prefers its own Nash equilibrium strategy. In the cartel's dilemma, the pair of strategies in which both Jupiter and Saturn exceed the quota is a Nash equilibrium.

What justifies a Nash equilibrium as a reasonable way for the relevant parties to act? In many typical strategic situations such as the cartel's dilemma, the Nash equilibrium strategies seem like the most reasonable and obvious way to behave. In others, such as the Battle of the Bismarck Sea which we describe below, it is how the parties actually behaved. By extension, this provides ground for believing that, in other, less intuitive settings, the relevant parties should also act according to Nash equilibrium strategies.

Solving the Equilibrium

> **To solve for Nash equilibrium:** first, rule out dominated strategies and, next, check all the remaining strategies, one at a time.

How should parties solve a game in strategic form for the Nash equilibrium? The formal **solution for a Nash equilibrium** is to, first, rule out dominated strategies and, next, check all the remaining strategies, one at a time.

The cartel's dilemma is easy to solve. We first rule out the dominated strategies – for Jupiter, follow the quota is dominated, and for Saturn,

⊣ Prisoners' dilemma ⊢

The cartel's dilemma is just one concrete application of a general strategic situation called the *prisoners' dilemma*. Greg and Susan stole a handbag and have been apprehended by the police. The police do not have sufficient evidence to convict them of theft. The only witnesses to the theft are the two suspects.

The police chief has put Greg and Susan into separate interview rooms. In each room, the police interrogator is offering a deal: "If the other suspect doesn't confess, but you do, we'll give you a reward of $1,000." Each suspect knows that if neither confesses, they will be let off. If one confesses while the other does not, then the confessing suspect will receive the $1,000 reward, while the other will be fined $2,000. If both confess, each will be fined $1,000.

Each suspect must choose between confessing and not confessing. Table 10.2 represents the game in strategic form. For Greg, the strategy of not confessing is dominated by the strategy of confessing. The same is true for Susan. The Nash equilibrium is for both suspects to confess – even though both would be better off if they did not confess.

Source: A. W. Tucker, "A Two-Person Dilemma," mimeo, Stanford University, May, 1950.

Table 10.2 Prisoners' dilemma

		Susan	
		Confess	Do not confess
Greg	Confess	G: −$1,000 S: −$1,000	G: $1,000 S: −$2,000
	Do not confess	G: −$2,000 S: $1,000	G: 0 S: 0

follow the quota is dominated. Then, each company has only one strategy left – exceed the quota – so that must be the equilibrium.

Let us illustrate the solution for Nash equilibrium with a more sophisticated example, which is based on the Battle of the Bismarck Sea in World War II.[2] In late February 1943, Japanese commander Rear-Admiral Kimura had assembled a convoy of 16 transport ships and destroyers at the port of Rabaul. Admiral Kimura's mission was to bring the convoy to Lae, on the mainland of New Guinea. American Lieutenant-General Kenney, commander of Allied Air Forces in the area, was ordered to intercept and destroy the Japanese convoy.

Admiral Kimura had to choose between sailing along a northern route through the Bismarck Sea and a southern route. Meteorologists forecast that there would be rain on the

[2] This example is based on O. G. Haywood, "Military Decision and Game Theory," *Journal of the Operations Research Society of America* 2, no. 4 (November 1954): pp. 365–85; and J. Rohwer and G. Hummelchen, *Chronology of the War at Sea, 1939–45*, vol. 2, trans. Derek Masters (London: Ian Allan, 1974), p. 306.

Table 10.3   Battle of the Bismarck Sea

			Kimura	
			North	South
Kenney	North		Kenney: 2 / Kimura: −2	Kenney: 2 / Kimura: −2
	South		Kenney: 1 / Kimura: −1	Kenney: 3 / Kimura: −3

northern route, which would reduce visibility. Weather on the southern route, however, would be fine.

General Kenney had to decide the direction in which to concentrate his reconnaissance aircraft. Once his aircraft spotted the Japanese convoy, Kenney would dispatch his bombers. The dilemma for Kenney was that his best decision depended on what he believed Kimura would do.

Table 10.3 represents the Battle of the Bismarck Sea in strategic form. In each cell, the first entry represents the number of days of bombing that Kenney could inflict on the Japanese, while the second entry represents the number of days of bombing that Kimura would suffer (as a negative number).

Recall that the solution for a Nash equilibrium is to, first, rule out dominated strategies and, next, check all the remaining strategies, one at a time. First, look at the situation from Kimura's position. If Kenney goes North, then Kimura will suffer 2 days of bombing whether he goes North or South, so Kimura is indifferent between the strategies. If Kenney goes South, then Kimura will suffer 1 day of bombing if he goes North or 3 days of bombing if he goes South, so Kimura prefers to go North. Hence, regardless of Kenney's strategy, Kimura should go North; the South strategy is dominated by the North strategy.

Next, look at the situation from Kenney's position. Knowing that Kimura would go North, his choice is between North, which yields 2 days of bombing, or South, which yields only 1 day of bombing, so Kenney should go North.

Indeed, on February 28, Admiral Kimura set sail on the northern route. General Kenney's reconnaissance planes discovered the Japanese convoy on March 2. In two days of massive aerial raids, Kenney's bombers destroyed the Japanese convoy.

A simple, informal method of finding a Nash equilibrium is to draw arrows between the cells as follows. Supposing that Kenney chooses North, then for Kimura, draw a double-headed arrow between −2 in the top left-hand cell and −2 in the top right-hand cell (this double-headed arrow represents that Kimura is indifferent). Next, supposing that Kenny chooses South, then for Kimura, draw an arrow from −3 in the bottom right-hand cell pointing toward −1 in the bottom left-hand cell (this arrow represents that Kimura prefers North).

Now, supposing that Kimura chooses North, then for Kenney, draw an arrow from 1 in the bottom left-hand cell to 2 in the top left-hand cell (this arrow represents that Kenney prefers North). Finally, supposing that Kimura chooses South, then for Kenney, draw an arrow from 2 in the top right-hand cell pointing toward 3 in the bottom right-hand cell (this arrow represents that Kenny prefers South).

Using this "arrow" technique, we can easily see if a strategy is dominated. A strategy is dominated if the row or column corresponding to the strategy has all the arrows pointing out. From table 10.3, for Kimura, South is dominated. The arrow technique also easily identifies an equilibrium. If there is a cell with all arrows leading in, then the strategies marking that cell are a Nash equilibrium.

By the arrow technique, the Nash equilibrium is for Kenney to fly North and Kimura to sail North.

Progress Check 10B Referring to tables 10.1 and 10.2, use the arrow technique to identify the Nash equilibrium strategies.

Nonequilibrium Strategies

We have explained how to analyze a strategic situation using the concept of a Nash equilibrium. Given that the other players choose their Nash equilibrium strategies, each party's best choice is its own Nash equilibrium strategy. But, what if some party does not follow its Nash equilibrium strategy? Then the other parties may find it better to deviate from their respective Nash equilibrium strategies.

For example, refer to table 10.3, which describes the Battle of the Bismarck Sea. Kenney's Nash equilibrium strategy is North, while Kimura's Nash equilibrium strategy is North. Suppose, however, that Kimura decides, for some reason, to go South and that Kenney has this information. Then, Kenney can score three days of bombing and win a bigger victory by flying *South*.

Accordingly, in the Battle of the Bismarck Sea, if Kimura does not follow his Nash equilibrium strategy, then it is better for Kenney to choose a strategy that is not a Nash equilibrium strategy.

Depending on the circumstances, however, it may be better for a party to stick to its Nash equilibrium strategy even if the other does not follow its Nash equilibrium strategy. These are cases where the other strategies are dominated. For instance, consider Kimura's situation. Suppose that Kenney decides to fly South. Then, Kimura should still go North. The alternative strategy – South – is dominated.

3   Randomized Strategies[3]

When the various parties act strategically, it seems reasonable for them to choose Nash equilibrium strategies. In some situations, however, there is no Nash equilibrium of the type that we have been considering. To illustrate, consider two competing electronics stores, Jaya and Ming. Every week, each store must choose between setting a high price or low price for a flat-screen TV. Suppose that table 10.4 represents the game in strategic form.

By applying the arrow technique to table 10.4, we can see that there is no Nash equilibrium in *pure strategies*: no cell has all the arrows leading inward. A **pure strategy** is one that does not involve randomization. In table 10.4, Jaya has two pure strategies, price high or low, and Ming also has two pure strategies, price high or low.

> A **pure strategy** is one that does not involve randomization.

---

[3]   This section is more advanced. It may be omitted without loss of continuity.

Table 10.4   Retail pricing

			Ming	
			High price	Low price
Jaya	High price		J: $60,000 M: $40,000	J: $40,000 M: $50,000
	Low price		J: $50,000 M: $40,000	J: $50,000 M: $30,000

Although there is no Nash equilibrium in pure strategies, there is another way for Jaya and Ming to act. Essentially, Jaya does not want Ming to know or predict its price. One way by which Jaya can keep Ming in the dark is to randomize the choice between pricing high and low. If Jaya randomizes its choice, the store itself will not know its price. Then, of course, Ming will not know either. Similarly, Ming does not want Jaya to know or predict its price. If Ming randomizes its decision, Jaya cannot guess or learn Ming's price.

> A **randomized strategy** is a strategy for choosing among the alternative pure strategies in accordance with specified probabilities.

Under a **randomized strategy**, the party specifies a probability for each of the alternative pure strategies and chooses a pure strategy randomly according to the probabilities. The various probabilities must add up to 1.

Nash Equilibrium in Randomized Strategies

Suppose that Jaya adopts the following randomized strategy: price high with probability 1/2 and price low with probability 1/2. To implement this strategy, Jaya's president marks a coin with "High price" on one side and "Low price" on the other side, then gives the coin to the store manager. Jaya then orders the store manager to toss the coin and fix the price according to which side of the coin faces up.

Given that Jaya has chosen this randomized strategy, how should Ming act? Referring to table 10.4, let us calculate the expected consequence for Ming from pricing high. Ming's profit would be $40,000 if Jaya prices high, and $40,000 if Jaya prices low. Hence, Ming's expected profit from pricing high is ($40,000 × $\frac{1}{2}$) + ($40,000 × $\frac{1}{2}$) = $40,000. Similarly, we can calculate that, if Ming prices low, its expected profit would be ($50,000 × $\frac{1}{2}$) + ($30,000 × $\frac{1}{2}$) = $40,000.

What should Ming do? Since it gets the same expected profit from its two pure strategies, it is indifferent between the two. Accordingly, it would be willing to randomize between them. Specifically, suppose that Ming prices high with probability 1/2.

Then, we must consider how Jaya will act. If Jaya prices high, its expected profit would be ($60,000 × $\frac{1}{2}$) + ($40,000 × $\frac{1}{2}$) = $50,000. Similarly, if Jaya prices low, its expected profit would be ($50,000 × $\frac{1}{2}$) + ($50,000 × $\frac{1}{2}$) = $50,000. Therefore, given Ming's strategy, Jaya is indifferent between pricing high and pricing low.

A Nash equilibrium in randomized strategies is like a Nash equilibrium in pure strategies: given that the other players choose their Nash equilibrium strategies, each party's best choice is its own Nash equilibrium strategy. The following randomized strategies constitute a Nash equilibrium in the battle of the retail electronics stores: Jaya prices high with probability 1/2 and Ming prices high with probability 1/2.

Suppose that Jaya has adopted the Nash equilibrium strategy of pricing high with probability 1/2. Suppose further that Ming has learned of Jaya's strategy through a spy. How can Ming exploit this information? The answer is that it cannot – as we have calculated earlier, whether Ming prices high or low, its expected profit will be $40,000. Generally, whenever a party adopts a Nash equilibrium strategy, the other parties cannot benefit from learning the strategy.

By contrast, suppose that Jaya decides to price high with certainty, which is not a Nash equilibrium strategy. Then, if Ming learns this strategy, Ming will price low with certainty, thus reducing Jaya's profit to $40,000. For Jaya, this is worse than its profit of $50,000 from the Nash equilibrium with randomized strategies. We should emphasize that the advantage of randomization comes from being *unpredictable*. To implement the randomized strategy, Jaya must leave the direction of its pricing to the coin toss. Jaya must not make any conscious decision on pricing. If it chooses its price in a conscious way, Ming may be able to guess or learn Jaya's decision and act accordingly.

Progress Check 10C Referring to table 10.4, suppose that Jaya prices high with probability 2/5. Calculate the expected consequences for Ming if it (i) prices high, and (ii) prices low.

Solving the Equilibrium

Having understood the usefulness of randomization, we must learn how to determine the Nash equilibrium probabilities. We can do so by using figure 10.1, where the horizontal axis shows the probability with which Jaya prices high, and the vertical axis shows Ming's expected profit.

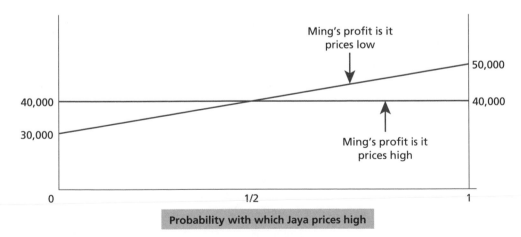

Figure 10.1 Solving randomized strategy equilibrium
If Jaya prices high with probability $1/2$, then Ming will receive the same consequences whether it prices high or low.

We draw two lines in figure 10.1. The sloping line shows Ming's profit if it prices low, as a function of the probability that Jaya prices high. For instance, by table 10.4, if Jaya prices low with certainty (prices high with zero probability), Ming's profit from pricing low would be $30,000. However, by table 10.4, if Jaya prices high with certainty, Ming's profit from pricing low would be $50,000.

Similarly, the horizontal line shows Ming's profit if it prices high, as a function of the probability that Jaya prices high. The two lines cross at one point. At that point, Ming's profit is the same whether it prices high or low. That point marks Jaya's Nash equilibrium probability of 1/2. We can draw a similar diagram for Ming to find its equilibrium probability, which is also $1/2$.[4]

Another way to find the Nash equilibrium probabilities is to use algebra. In equilibrium, both Ming and Jaya must randomize. Suppose that Jaya prices high with probability q. For Ming to be willing to randomize, it must be indifferent between its alternative pure strategies: pricing high and low. This means that Ming must receive the same expected profit from the two pure strategies.

To calculate Ming's expected profit from pricing low, we refer to table 10.4. Ming's profit would be $50,000 if Jaya prices high, which occurs with probability q, while Ming's profit would be $30,000 if Jaya prices low, which occurs with probability $1 - q$. Hence, Ming's expected profit from pricing low would be $50,000 \times q + 30,000 \times (1 - q) = 30,000 + 20,000\,q$.

Similarly, we can calculate Ming's profit from pricing high, which would be $40,000 \times q + 40,000 \times (1 - q) = \$40,000$. In randomized strategy equilibrium, Ming must receive the same expected profit from pricing low and high. This means that $30,000 + 20,000q = 40,000$, which implies that $q = {}^1/_2$.

Likewise, we can determine Ming's Nash equilibrium strategy. Suppose that Ming prices high with probability p. For Jaya to be indifferent between its alternative pure strategies, it must receive the same expected profit from pricing high and low. This means $60,000p + \$40,000(1 - p) = \$50,000$ or $p = {}^1/_2$.

Choosing an auctioneer: a forced randomized strategy equilibrium

Takashi Hashiyama, president of Maspro Denkoh Corporation, a Japanese electronics company, used an unusual method to decide whether Christie's or Sotheby's should sell the company's art collection, valued at more than $20 million. Rather than splitting the collection or using a private dealer, as is usually done, he resorted to a game of chance: rock breaks scissors, scissors cut paper, paper smothers rock.

The two auction houses were informed and asked to choose a weapon (winning could be worth several million dollars, as the fee is usually 20% for the first $200,000 of sales proceeds and 12% above that). Christie's strategy was developed by the 11-year-old twin daughters of the international director of their Impressionist and modern art department. Sotheby's on the other hand, realizing it was a game of chance, "had no strategy in mind."

---

[4]   This technique is based on Avinash Dixit and Barry Nalebuff, *Thinking Strategically: The Competitive Edge in Business, Politics, and Everyday Life* (New York: Norton, 1991), ch. 7.

Christie's chose scissors and Sotheby's chose paper, thereby delivering the auction to Christie's. Mr. Hashiyama said "As both companies were equally good and I just could not choose one, I asked them to please decide between themselves and suggested to use such methods as rock, paper, scissors." In effect, he forced the two auction houses to adopt randomized strategies, although one of the twins claimed the choice of "scissors was definitely the safest . . . adding that if the other side were also to choose scissors and another round was required, the correct play would be to stick to scissors because . . . everybody expects you to choose rock."

Sources: Carol Vogel, "Rock, Paper, Payoff: Child's Play Wins Auction House an Art Sale," April 29, 2005, www.math.toronto.edu/mpugh/Teaching/Sci199_03/RPS_Christies.htm; Listen to the Children, CBS News, May 18, 2005, http://www.cbsnews.com/stories/2005/05/18/opinion/garver/main696175.shtml.

4   Competition or Coordination

In the Battle of the Bismarck Sea (table 10.3), if we add the consequences for General Kenney and Admiral Kimura in each cell, we get a sum of zero in every cell. The situation is a *zero-sum game*. A **zero-sum game** is a strategic situation where one party can become better off only if another is made worse off. A zero-sum game is the extreme of competition: there is no way for all parties to become better off.

> A **zero-sum game** is a strategic situation where one party can become better off only if another is made worse off.

Note that a strategic situation can be a zero-sum game even if the consequences for the various parties do not add up to zero in every cell of the game in strategic form. If the consequences for the various parties add up to the same number (whether negative, zero, or positive) in every cell of the game in strategic form, then one party can become better off only if another is made worse off. Accordingly, such a strategic situation is also a zero-sum game.

Many strategic situations are not zero-sum games. Recall the cartel's dilemma, described in table 10.1. When both companies follow the quotas, their combined profits are $15 + $10 = $25 million; when Jupiter follows the quota, and Saturn exceeds the quota, their combined profits are $10 + $13 = $23 million; when Jupiter exceeds the quota, and Saturn follows the quota, their combined profits are $15 + $5 = $20 million; and when both companies exceed the quotas, their combined profits are $12 + $8 = $20 million. Hence, the cartel's dilemma is not a zero-sum game. Rather, it is a *positive-sum game*. In a **positive-sum game**, one party can become better off without another being made worse off.

> A **positive-sum game** is a strategic situation where one party can become better off without another being made worse off.

Coordination

The following example illustrates a particular type of positive-sum game. Suppose that there are two different instant messaging technologies – Orange and Green – and that they do not interoperate. From the user's viewpoint, the two technologies are equally effective. However, it would be beneficial if all users adopt the same technology, as this would facilitate communication.

Table 10.5 presents a game in strategic form that describes the situation facing two potential users, Venus, Inc., and Sol Corporation. Each must choose between the Orange and Green technologies. The benefit to Venus and Sol is $1.5 million each when they both choose the same technology (whether Orange or Green) which would enable communication between the companies. However, if they choose different technologies, then each will get a benefit

Table 10.5   Positive-sum game

		Venus Inc.	
		Orange	Green
Sol Corporation	Orange	S: 1.5 V: 1.5	S: 1 V: 1
	Green	S: 1 V: 1	S: 1.5 V: 1.5

of $1 million, which is the value of internal communications. Clearly, from adding the benefits in each of the cells in table 10.5, the situation between Venus and Sol is a positive-sum game.

The situation of Venus and Sol is essentially one of coordination rather than competition. If the two users can coordinate on the same technology, both will benefit more. If, however, they fail to coordinate, both will benefit less. Strategic situations involving coordination are positive-sum games.

By applying the arrow technique to table 10.5, we can see that there are two Nash equilibria in pure strategies: in one, both users choose Orange; in the other equilibrium, both users choose Green.[5]

Focal Point

Previously, we discussed why it is reasonable to adopt a Nash equilibrium strategy. In situations of coordination, there is an additional reason to adopt a Nash equilibrium strategy. Suppose that the various parties are able to talk to one another before making their choices and they agree on how to act. Then, a Nash equilibrium is a good basis for discussion because, by definition, Nash equilibrium strategies are self-enforcing in the sense that, if one party expects the others to follow their Nash equilibrium strategies, then its best choice is its own Nash equilibrium strategy.

For instance, in the choice of messaging technologies, there are two Nash equilibria in pure strategies. This presents the companies with the question of which strategy to adopt. Since the essential issue is coordination between the two companies, it is reasonable that they meet to agree on one choice.

If Venus and Sol discuss their choices, they might easily agree on one technology, say, Orange. Then, when they make their purchases, if each expects the other to buy Orange, its own best choice is also Orange. In this way, a Nash equilibrium provides a focal point for discussion and action by the two parties.

---

[5]   In addition to the two Nash equilibria in pure strategies, there is also a Nash equilibrium where both parties randomize with probability 1/2.

⊣ Instant messaging: not ready for prime time? ⊢

Instant messaging (IM) has been used by 42% of Internet users and is used by 12% of Internet users on a typical day. In 2006, the market was dominated by AOL (56% of U.S. users), MSN (25%), and Yahoo (19%). Of the world wide market, 37% is in the United States and 49% is in Europe. Despite rapid growth and rosy forecasts, the market is held back by the lack of interoperability among the different IM systems.

"The most popular IM software programs . . . are mutually exclusive, meaning that users subscribing to a particular IM program can communicate only with instant messengers who use the same software." According to Robert Balgley, CEO of Jabber, "Right now there is a reluctance on the part of a lot of people, both consumers and in business, to use instant messaging because they don't want to get caught in this closed-community conundrum."

Jabber is one of a handful of software developers that have created programs that facilitate open IM. These programs are "gateway technologies," a term coined by Paul David to represent technologies that bridge between two or more incompatible technological standards.

The other development that offers to break the logjam posed by non-interoperable IM systems is agreements between IM providers to link their systems. Microsoft and Yahoo recently agreed to do so, in an effort to overcome AOL's lead in the IM market.

Sources: Evlynn Shiu and Amanda Lenhart, "How Americans Use Instant Messaging," PEW Internet and American Life Projects, 2004; ComScore Media Metrix, "Microsoft, Yahoo Ink Instant-Message Pact," *Wall Street Journal*, October 12, 2005; Paul A. David and J. Bunn, "Gateway Technologies and the Evolutionary Dynamics of Gateway Industries: Lessons from Electricity Supply History," in Mark Perlman and A. Heertje (eds), *Evolving Technology and Market Structure* (Chicago: University of Chicago Press, 1987), pp. 121–56.

Co-opetition

Some situations involve elements of both competition and coordination. Consider a city with two TV stations, Channel Zeta and TV Delta. There are two possible time slots for the evening news – 7:30 p.m. and 8:00 p.m. Market research shows that the demand for news peaks at 8:00 p.m. and is lower at 7:30 p.m.

We construct the strategic form of this situation in table 10.6. Each station has two pure strategies: broadcast at 7:30 p.m. or at 8:00 p.m. In each cell, we present the annual profits to Channel Zeta and TV Delta, in million dollars respectively. By adding the profits of the two TV stations in each cell of table 10.6, we see that the situation is a positive-sum game. The total profit of the two TV stations is not a constant. It is largest when they take different time slots. The next highest total profit arises when both stations broadcast at 8:00 p.m. The total profit is lowest when both stations broadcast at 7:30 p.m. The two TV stations need to coordinate and avoid scheduling their evening news at the same time.

While the battle for the evening news involves coordination, it also has an element of competition. Both stations will be better off if they schedule their news at different times. But one station will benefit relatively more – the station that gets the 8:00 p.m. slot. Accordingly, there are elements of competition as well as coordination.

Applying the arrows technique, we can find the Nash equilibria. As in the situation of choosing the database technology, there are two Nash equilibria in pure strategies: Channel

Table 10.6   Battle for evening news

			TV Delta	
			7:30 p.m.	8:00 p.m.
Channel Zeta	7:30 p.m.		Z: 1 D: 1	Z: 3 D: 4
	8:00 p.m.		Z: 4 D: 3	Z: 2.5 D: 2.5

Zeta gets the 8:00 p.m. slot and TV Delta takes 7:30 p.m., or Delta gets the 8:00 p.m. slot and Zeta takes 7:30 p.m.[6]

> **Co-opetition** is a strategic situation that involves elements of both competition and coordination.

Strategic situations that involve elements of both competition and coordination have been described as **co-opetition**.[7] The battle for the evening news illustrates co-opetition: the two TV stations would certainly cooperate to avoid the outcome where both schedule their news at the same time. They would, however, compete for the 8:00 p.m. slot.

Even the cartel's dilemma (table 10.1) is a situation of co-opetition. Both sellers would like to cooperate and avoid production at the competitive level. The problem, however, is that following the quotas is a dominated strategy, and the result is that both exceed the quotas.

In a later section, we show that cooperation may arise when the strategic situation of co-opetition is repeated. By conditioning their actions on either external events or the previous actions of the other party, the parties involved may be able to avoid the undesirable outcomes of one-shot situations.

> **Progress Check 10D** Check whether the retail pricing scenario (table 10.4) is a zero-sum game.

5   Sequencing

> A **game in extensive form** is a graphical representation of a strategic situation, showing the sequence of moves and the corresponding outcomes.

So far, we have focused on situations where the various parties move simultaneously. However, in many business situations, the parties move one at a time. We shall see that the best strategy may be quite different if the parties move in sequence. To organize thinking about a strategic situation in which the various parties act in sequence, we use the *game in extensive form*. A **game in extensive form** explicitly shows the sequence of moves and the corresponding outcomes. It consists of nodes and branches: a node

[6] There is also an equilibrium in randomized strategies, where each station chooses 7:30 p.m. with probability 1/7 and 8:00 p.m. with probability 6/7.

[7] Adam M. Brandenburger and Barry J. Nalebuff, *Co-opetition* (New York: Doubleday, 1996).

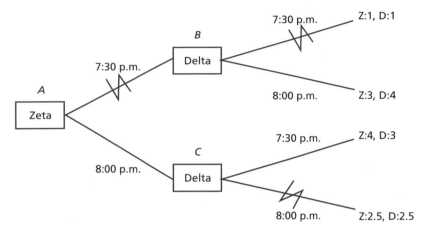

Figure 10.2 Battle for the evening news: extensive form
At node *B*, Delta will choose 8:00 p.m. At node *C*, Delta will choose 7:30 p.m. By backward induction, at node *A*, Zeta will choose 8:00 p.m.

represents a point at which a party must choose a move, while the branches leading from a node represent the possible choices at the node.

Let us apply this concept to the battle for the evening news where Channel Zeta can schedule its news before Delta. Figure 10.2 is a game in extensive form that represents the situation of the two TV stations. The first node, *A*, is on the extreme left. At that node, Channel Zeta must choose between 7:30 p.m. (the upper branch) and 8:00 p.m. (the lower branch). TV Delta has the next move. Delta's node depends on Zeta's choice. If Zeta has chosen 7:30 p.m., then Delta will be at node *B* and must decide between the two branches of 7:30 p.m. and 8:00 p.m. If Zeta has chosen 8:00 p.m., then Delta will be at node *C* and must decide between the two branches of 7:30 p.m. and 8:00 p.m.

The consequences for TV Delta of 7:30 p.m. or 8:00 p.m. depend on Zeta's choice. At the end of each branch, we mark the profits to Zeta and Delta, respectively. If Zeta chooses 7:30 p.m. and Delta also chooses 7:30 p.m., they both earn $1 million. If Zeta chooses 7:30 p.m. while Delta chooses 8:00 p.m., then Zeta makes $3 million and Delta earns $4 million. If Zeta chooses 8:00 p.m. while Delta chooses 7:30 p.m., then Zeta makes $4 million and Delta earns $3 million. Finally, if both stations choose the peak time of 8:00 p.m., they both earn $2.5 million.

Backward Induction

How should the two stations act? We solve the extensive form by **backward induction**, which means looking forward to the final nodes and reasoning backward toward the initial node. We can use this procedure to identify the best strategies for the two stations. There are two final nodes: *B* and *C*. At node *B*, TV Delta can choose 7:30 p.m., which yields $1 million, or it could choose 8:00 p.m., which yields $4 million. Clearly, at node *B*, Delta would choose 8:00 p.m. Accordingly, we cancel the 7:30 p.m. branch. Now, consider node *C*. Here, Delta must choose between 7:30 p.m.,

> **Backward induction** is a procedure for solving games in extensive form, looking forward to the final nodes and reasoning backward toward the initial node.

which yields $3 million, or 8:00 p.m., which yields $2.5 million. It will choose 7:30 p.m., so we cancel the 8:00 p.m. branch.

Having determined how TV Delta will act at each of its two possible nodes, *B* and *C*, we work back to consider the initial node, *A*. At node *A*, if Zeta chooses 7:30 p.m., it can foresee that Delta will choose 8:00 p.m., so Zeta will earn $3 million. On the other hand, if Zeta chooses 8:00 p.m., it can foresee that Delta will choose 7:30 p.m., so Zeta will earn $4 million. Therefore, Zeta should choose 8:00 p.m. Accordingly, in the battle for the evening news, when Zeta can move first, it will choose the 8:00 p.m. slot, while Delta will take the 7:30 p.m. time.

Equilibrium Strategy

An **equilibrium strategy** in a game in extensive form is a sequence of the best actions, where each action is decided at the corresponding node.

In a game in extensive form, a party's **equilibrium strategy** consists of a sequence of its best actions, where each action is decided at the corresponding node. In the battle for the evening news, when Channel Zeta can move first, Zeta's equilibrium strategy is to choose the 8:00 p.m. slot, while TV Delta's equilibrium strategy is take the 7:30 p.m. time.

We have assumed that Channel Zeta could move before TV Delta. If Delta can move first, then the game in extensive form will be like figure 10.2, except that Delta would schedule its broadcast time at node *A*, and Zeta would schedule its broadcast time at node *B* or *C*. Then, Delta's equilibrium strategy would be to take the 8:00 p.m. slot, and Zeta's equilibrium strategy would be to settle for 7:30 p.m.

To decide on a strategy in a situation where the parties move in sequence, the basic principle is to look forward and anticipate the other parties' responses. So, when TV Delta can set its schedule before its competitor, Delta must look forward and anticipate how Zeta will respond to each of Delta's choices. In this way, Delta anticipates that, if it chooses 7:30 p.m., then Zeta would choose 8:00 p.m., while if it chooses 8:00 p.m., then Zeta would choose 7:30 p.m. By this procedure of backward induction, Delta and Zeta can determine their equilibrium strategies.

The concept of equilibrium strategy in a game in extensive form is different from that of the Nash equilibrium strategy in a game in strategic form. In a strategic form, the parties act simultaneously, and a party's Nash equilibrium strategy is the best strategy given that the other parties adopt their respective Nash equilibrium strategies. By contrast, in an extensive form, the parties move in sequence, and a party's equilibrium strategy is the sequence of the best actions for that party, where each action is decided at the corresponding node.

In the battle for the evening news, we have shown that, when the two stations move simultaneously, there are two Nash equilibria in pure strategies. But when the stations move in sequence, there is only one equilibrium. In the battle for the evening news, the equilibrium in the extensive form is also a Nash equilibrium in the corresponding strategic form. In other cases, however, the equilibrium in the extensive form may not be a Nash equilibrium in the corresponding strategic form. Accordingly, when analyzing a strategic situation, it is important to consider carefully the structure of the moves: do the parties move simultaneously or sequentially?

Uncertain Consequences

In some situations, one party may not be certain about the consequences of the various actions of the other party. The situation should still be analyzed by backward induction, using all

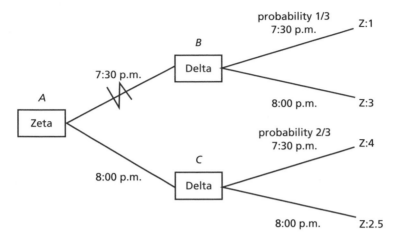

Figure 10.3 Battle for the evening news: uncertain consequences
At node B, Delta will choose 7:30 p.m. with probability 1/3 and 8:00 p.m. with probability 2/3. At node C, Delta will choose 7:30 p.m. with probability 2/3 and 8:00 p.m. with probability 1/3. By backward induction at node A, Zeta will choose 8:00 p.m.

available information. Even if one party does not know the consequences of the various actions for the other party, it may know or be able to assess the probabilities with which the other party will choose between the alternative actions. It can apply backwards induction using these probabilities.

For example, suppose that, in the battle for the evening news, Channel Zeta does not know TV Delta's profits, but Zeta can assess the probabilities of Delta's actions at each node. Figure 10.3 shows the specific probabilities.

Zeta can calculate as follows. At node B, Delta will choose 7:30 p.m. with probability 1/3 and 8:00 p.m. with probability 2/3, hence Zeta's expected profit would be $1/3 \times 1 + 2/3 \times 3 = \$2.33$ million. At node C, Delta will choose 7:30 p.m. with probability 2/3 and 8:00 p.m. with probability 1/3, hence Zeta's expected profit would be $2/3 \times 4 + 1/3 \times 2.5 = \$3.5$ million.

Thus, at node A, looking forward, Zeta should choose 8:00 p.m.

> **Progress Check 10E** Suppose that TV Delta can set its schedule before Channel Zeta. Using a suitable game in extensive form, illustrate this sequence of moves and analyze the two stations' equilibrium strategies.

6   Strategic Moves

Lithography is a process by which an artist creates a stone or metal plate, then treats the plate with ink, and prints pictures. Most lithographers specify the number of copies that they will print from each plate and mark each print with a serial number. For instance, the mark "5/30" means the 5th of 30 copies. Some lithographers destroy their plates after printing the specified number of copies. Why do lithographers engage in such practices?

To address these questions, we consider lithography from the customer's standpoint. The value of a lithograph, like any other work of art or indeed any product in general, depends

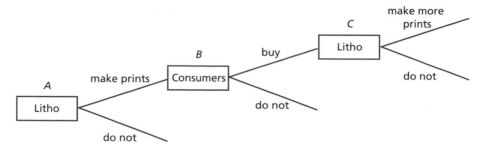

Figure 10.4 Lithographer's incentive
At node *C*, the lithographer will generate more prints. By backward induction at node *B*, consumers will choose not to buy.

on the supply. In the case of a lithograph, the supply is the number of copies that the artist has printed or will print.

Lithography is a business with a substantial fixed cost and low marginal cost. Once the the plate has been made, the lithographer can generate more prints for the minor cost of ink and paper. So, after producing an initial 10 prints, the lithographer may consider selling another 10 at a lower price. Provided that the marginal revenue covers the marginal cost, the lithographer will earn additional profits. Indeed, having sold the second batch of 10, the lithographer may produce a third batch. Generally, the lithographer always has an incentive to continue producing more prints so long as the marginal revenue covers the marginal cost.

We can represent the lithographer's actions by a game in extensive form, figure 10.4. To analyze the situation, we must look forward to the final nodes and reason backward toward the initial node. At node *C*, the lithographer considers whether the marginal revenue of additional sales will cover the marginal cost. If so, she will then generate more prints. Working back to node *B*, consumers will decide not to buy: they would rather wait for the lithographer to cut the price at node *C*.

The lithographer needs some way to convince potential buyers that she will not keep producing more prints. One way is to specify the total number of prints and number each copy; for instance, "5/30" means the 5th of 30 copies. However, potential buyers might still be wary.

A definitive way to resolve this problem is for the lithographer to destroy the plates after printing the initial set of copies. Then, buyers can be confident that there will be no further prints, and they will be more willing to purchase.

> A **strategic move** is an action to influence the beliefs or actions of other parties in a favorable way.

The lithographer's destruction of her plates is an example of a *strategic move*. A **strategic move** is an action to influence the beliefs or actions of other parties in a favorable way. The party making the strategic move may deliberately restrict its own freedom of action. For instance, by destroying her plates, the lithographer prevents herself from producing more prints in the future. This self-imposed restriction is a way to assure collectors that the supply will be limited.

Notice that the lithographer's strategic move involves a real cost. Once the plates have been destroyed, it will not be possible to produce more prints even if all the initial buyers want to have more.

┌─┤ **Pepsi's strategic move: spinning off the bottling group** ├─────┐

Until 1999, Coca-Cola's organizational architecture differed sharply from that of Pepsi. Coke was vertically separated: the Coca-Cola Company, headquartered in Atlanta, owned the brand and sold concentrate to about 100 franchised bottlers, the largest of which was Coca-Cola Enterprises. By contrast, PepsiCo was vertically integrated from brand marketing through production of concentrate to bottling.

Then, in March 1999, PepsiCo spun off the Pepsi Bottling Group (PBG) in one of the largest initial public offerings on the New York Stock Exchange. Following the spin-off, PBG became an independent profit-driven business and responsible to its own shareholders. PepsiCo managed the brand and sold concentrate to PBG and other franchised bottlers. The bottlers used the concentrate to manufacture soft drink for sale in supermarkets and other distribution channels.

PBG accounted for 55% of Pepsi's sales in Canada and the United States and had considerable market power in its territories. Chapter 8 on market power showed that, if a seller with market power experiences a reduction in marginal cost, it would reduce its price by an amount proportionately less than the marginal cost reduction.[8] Accordingly, if PepsiCo reduced the price of concentrate, PBG would reduce its retail price, but by a proportionately smaller amount.

In this light, Pepsi's vertical separation was a critical strategic move to mitigate the intensity of retail price competition. After the spin-off, Pepsi could not directly control retail prices. Further, PBG had an incentive to dampen price cuts. Indeed, Standard & Poor's analyst, Richard Joy, remarked: "Now that it is no longer shielded by the corporate umbrella of PepsiCo, Pepsi Bottling Group needs to produce profits, and thus appears unlikely to discount its brands."

Mr Joy's prediction was soon borne out. In November 1999, Coke announced a 7% increase in the price of concentrate, which translated into a 5% retail price increase. Within a week, Pepsi followed suit, raising the price of concentrate by 6.9%, which led to a 5% rise in retail prices.

Sources: *Standard & Poor's Industry Surveys: Foods & Nonalcoholic Beverages* 166, no. 22, section 1 (June 3, 1999), p. 3; "Coca-Cola Shifts Strategy in Effort to Boost Profit," *Wall Street Journal Interactive Edition*, November 16, 1999.

└──┘

Credibility

The battle for the evening news is another setting where strategic moves are possible. By table 10.6, if both stations move simultaneously, then there are two possible Nash equilibria in pure strategies: one station (either TV Delta or Channel Zeta) gets the 8:00 p.m. slot and the competitor settles for 7:30 p.m. By contrast, if one station can set its schedule before the other, then it can secure the lucrative 8:00 p.m. slot.

Suppose that Delta announces that it wants the 8:00 p.m. slot. Is this sufficient to persuade Zeta to settle for 7:30 p.m.? Probably not. Delta's announcement may prompt Zeta to make its own announcement that it is scheduling its news at 8:00 p.m. A strategic move must be credible to influence the beliefs or actions of other parties. A mere announcement is not very credible.

---

[8]   Strictly, this is true for straight-line market demand curves.

Table 10.7   Competing on production capacity

		Moonlight Water	
		Produce 1 million bottles	Produce 2 million bottles
Agua Luna	Produce 1 million bottles	AL: $750,000 MW: $750,000	AL: $700,000 MW: $1,100,000
	Produce 2 million bottles	AL: $1,100,000 MW: $700,000	AL: $600,000 MW: $600,000

For a strategic move to be credible, it must involve sufficient commitment to persuade other parties to change their beliefs or actions. Suppose that Delta contracts with several major advertisers to broadcast their advertisements during the 8:00 p.m. news. Further, the contracts provide that Delta must pay several million dollars in compensation if the station changes the time of the evening news. Then, these advertising contracts are a commitment and may be enough to persuade Channel Zeta to take the 7:30 p.m. slot.

Let us consider another possible setting for strategic moves. Suppose that Agua Luna and Moonlight Water dominate the market for bottled water. Their products are differentiated: Agua Luna is natural spring water, while Moonlight produces distilled water. Each manufacturer must decide whether to produce 1 or 2 million bottles a year. Table 10.7 presents the game in strategic form.

Assuming that the two manufacturers decide on production simultaneously, there are two Nash equilibria in pure strategies: Agua Luna produces 2 million bottles a year while Moonlight Water produces 1 million, and Moonlight produces 2 million while Luna produces 1 million.

Now suppose that Agua Luna can set its production before Moonlight Water. By analyzing the game in extensive form, we can show that, in equilibrium, Agua Luna will produce 2 million bottles a year, while Moonlight Water will produce 1 million. By contrast, if Moonlight can move first, it will produce 2 million bottles a year, while Agua Luna will produce 1 million.

Moonlight would like to produce 2 million bottles a year and persuade Agua Luna to produce only 1 million. As in the battle for the evening news, a mere announcement would not be credible. A credible commitment would be for Moonlight to sign contracts with major buyers, such as catering services and supermarkets, committing it to supply 2 million bottles a year.

Sunk investments are another strategic move that might persuade Agua Luna to produce 1 million bottles a year. Manufacturing bottled water requires the construction of a production facility and acquiring materials, labor, and utilities. Suppose that the production facility is a large proportion of the total cost and that Moonlight builds a 2-million bottle a year facility. Will this convince the competing manufacturer, Agua Luna, to produce 1 million bottles a year?

The answer depends on the extent to which Moonlight's facility is a *sunk* cost of the bottled water business. Recall from chapter 7 that *sunk* costs are costs that have been committed and cannot be avoided. If the entire facility cost is sunk, Agua Luna will understand that Moonlight is committed to producing 2 million bottles a year. Then, Agua Luna is likely to acquiesce.

By contrast, if Moonlight also intends to expand its beer business and could easily convert the facility from water to beer, then the facility cost will not be so much sunk to the bottled water business. In this case, construction of the facility is not such a strong commitment to producing 2 million bottles of water a year.

Progress Check 10F Suppose that Agua Luna can set its production before Moonlight Water. By analyzing the game in extensive form, identify the equilibrium strategies.

First Mover Advantage

In the battle for the evening news, the station that is first to commit its schedule will make the larger profit. Similarly, in the bottled water example, the manufacturer that is first to commit its production will make the larger profit. In these settings, the first mover has the advantage. There is **first mover advantage** in any strategic situation where a party gains advantage by moving before others. To identify whether a strategic situation involves first mover advantage, it is necessary to analyze the game in extensive form.

> A **first mover advantage** gives a party an advantage if it moves before others.

The first mover advantage is a concept that corporate strategists emphasize a great deal. However, first mover advantage is not a universal rule in business or other strategic situations. In some circumstances, the follower has an advantage. For instance, in retail pricing, if one store sets its price first, then its competitors will have the opportunity to undercut it with lower prices. Similarly, in military confrontations, the party that moves first may reveal its strategy and the other side can take advantage of that information.

In the introduction of a new product category, later movers have some advantage over earlier movers. A business introducing a new product category must make considerable investments in advertising and promoting the entire new category. These expenditures on advertising and promotion of the new category will benefit all businesses introducing new products in the same category. Hence, later movers can piggyback on the advertising and promotion expenditures of the pioneer.

Nokia: first mover advantages and disadvantages

Nokia of Finland is the world's leading maker of mobile telephones. Total industry sales in 2004 were approximately 650 million mobile telephones. Because of the complexity of mobile telephones, it can be argued that Nokia is the leading computer maker in the world. In addition, because half of the mobile telephones sold by Nokia are camera-phones, it can also be argued that Nokia is the leading camera-maker in the world.

In the 1990s Nokia was the first handset-maker to realize that mobile telephones were becoming fashion items and placed a heavy emphasis on design. This helped Nokia become the first in the industry. In addition, the rise of GSM (Groupe Spécial Mobile) mobile phone technology also contributed to this lead. GSM was adopted as a European standard to ensure smooth roaming between countries.

In 2004, Nokia's sales decreased, its market share dropped from 35% to 28.9%. Its stock dropped by over 50% in several months, from March to August, 2004. Nokia

failed to anticipate the popularity of flip-phone or clamshell phones which are especially popular in Asia and North America. In particular, it is argued that Nokia lost its
edge in design when Motorola introduced the sleek and stylish silver "clamshell" phone,
the RAZR V3. In contrast, Nokia has favored the "monobloc" or "candy bar" phones
that do not fold and look staid.

In addition, critics note that Nokia is not leading the switch to third-generation (3G)
networks, which demand more complex handsets. The key feature of 3G is video telephony. Jorma Ollila, the chief executive and chairman of Nokia contended that it is
better to get things right than be the first to market, "Being first is not necessarily a
gateway to heaven." Another commenter remarked, "Being first is very painful" and
"you go through a lot of ugly ducklings." Thus, Nokia is being cautious and taking
more time to develop and offer more 3G handset phones.

Source: "The Giant in the Palm of Your Hand," *The Economist*, February 10, 2005.

⊣ Free "mobile to mobile" calls ⊢

With 44 million subscribers (end of year 2004), Verizon wireless is one of the
leading U.S. mobile telephone carriers. It skillfully uses discriminatory pricing to
consolidate its market share and lock out competitors.

For a monthly fee of $39.99, Verizon's "America's Choice" plan includes 450
minutes of calls at any time, unlimited calls at night and on weekends, and unlimited
"mobile to mobile" ("on-net") calls to any other Verizon Wireless number at any time,
without roaming charges.

The attractiveness of free mobile to mobile calls depends on the carrier's customer
base. With 44 million subscribers, Verizon's offer of free mobile to mobile calls is
very attractive to new customers. This offer can draw customers away from smaller
competitors, and help to entrench Verizon's market position.

On the cost side, a carrier incurs lower costs for calls that terminate on its own
network, as compared with calls that terminate on networks of other carriers.

A study of subscriber behavior in Germany, however, casts doubt on how effective
this strategy is. German mobile operators typically offer lower prices for "on-net" calls
than "off-net" calls. Since the carriers differ in terms of market share, the effective
price they charge will depend on the prices of on-net and off-net calls, as well as the
proportion of calls that will be on-net and off-net. Consumers appear to respond to the
advertised off-net price and not to the effective weighted average price. Carriers
appear to offer comparable off-net prices, even with disparate market shares (and, hence,
disparate effective prices).

Sources: www.verizonwireless.com, accessed on May 6, 2006; Friedel Bolle and Jana Heimel, "A Fallacy
of Dominant Price Vectors in Network Industries," *Review of Network Economics* 4, no. 3 (2005), pp. 197–204.

---

7   Conditional Strategic Moves

Destroying plates is a costly way for a lithographer to convince art collectors that she will
not make more prints in the future. In some situations, it is possible to influence the actions
or beliefs of others at lower cost through *conditional strategic moves*. There are two types

of **conditional strategic moves**: threats and promises. A **threat** is a strategic move that imposes costs under specified conditions to change the beliefs or actions of other parties. By contrast, a **promise** is a strategic move that conveys benefits under specified conditions to change the beliefs or actions of other parties.

> A **conditional strategic move** is an action under specified conditions to influence the beliefs or actions of other parties in a favorable way.

To the extent that a threatened or promised action need not actually be carried out, the conditional strategic move has no cost. A more accurate name for an action like destroying the plates is an *unconditional strategic move* because the party taking the action does not condition it on any eventuality. An unconditional strategic move usually involves a cost under all circumstances.

> A **threat** imposes costs under specified conditions to change the beliefs or actions of other parties.

Threats

To understand threats, let us consider how companies can fend off hostile takeovers. An effective way of deterring a hostile takeover is the so-called scorched earth defense, which means destroying the company. The

> A **promise** conveys benefits under specified conditions to change the beliefs or actions of other parties.

scorched earth defense is a very costly strategic move. Clever bankers and lawyers have devised more sophisticated defenses that are much less costly. One example is the shareholder rights plan, which has also been called the *poison pill*. As we will explain, this plan is a conditional strategic move: it comes into action only in the event of a hostile takeover.

Suppose that Mars Corporation has 1 million shares, with a value of $2 each, hence, a total value of $2 million. The company has adopted a shareholder rights plan that created one right for every share of the company. Under the plan, if any party acquires 100,000 or more of Mars' shares, then Mars' management can activate the rights. Each right could be exercised to buy additional shares in the company at half their value. Any rights owned by the party whose acquisition activated the rights, however, would be canceled.

Pluto, Inc., is potentially interested in taking over Mars Corporation. Let us construct a game in extensive form to analyze the strategic interaction between Pluto and Mars. Referring to figure 10.5, at node A, Pluto must decide whether to acquire 100,000 Mars shares with the attached rights. At node B, Mars' management must choose whether to activate the rights.

Suppose that, at node B, Mars' management activates the rights. This cancels Pluto's 100,000 rights. The holders of the remaining 900,000 rights will now buy an additional 900,000 shares at half their value. The activation increases the number of shares by 900,000 to 1.9 million and also draws more money into Mars as the holders of the 900,000 rights pay for their

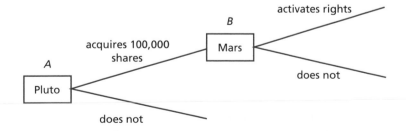

Figure 10.5 Poison pill
At node B, Mars will activate the rights. By backward induction at node A, Pluto will choose not to acquire the 100,000 shares.

additional shares. The number of shares, however, increases proportionately more than the value of the company; hence, the value of each share will fall. Specifically, it may be shown that the activation reduces the value of each share to $1.38.[9]

The activation has two implications for Pluto. First, it raises the cost to Pluto of acquiring 100% of Mars. If Mars' management does not activate the rights, there are 900,000 remaining shares and Pluto must pay $2 × 900,000 = $1.8 million to buy them. By contrast, if Mars' management does activate the rights, there will be 1,800,000 remaining shares, and Pluto must pay $1.38 × 1,800,000 = $2.484 million for them.

Second, the activation of the rights causes a reduction in the value of Pluto's 100,000 shares from $2 × 100,000 = $200,000 to $1.38 × 100,000 = $138,000. So, Pluto will suffer a 31% loss on its investment. It is no wonder that such shareholder rights plans have been given the nickname of a *poison pill*.

In the case of Mars Corporation, a potential bidder will look ahead from node *A* and see how Mars' management could raise the costs of a takeover bid. Accordingly, the establishment of a shareholder rights plan significantly reduces the likelihood of a hostile takeover. If the plan succeeds in discouraging hostile takeovers, the rights need never be activated.

⊣ Threats in corporate finance: two-tier takeover ⊢

In December 1994, Williams Companies, a natural gas producer and pipeline operator, announced a two-tier bid for Transco Energy Co. Williams' first tier offered to buy up to 60% of Transco's common shares for $17.50 in cash. The first-tier cash offer expired within one month and was conditional on Williams securing at least 51% of Transco's shares.

The second tier of the takeover bid would come into effect if Williams received 51% or more of Transco's shares through the cash offer. In the second tier, Williams would exercise its majority control to convert all remaining Transco shares into 5/8ths of a Williams common share. After Williams announced its takeover bid, the price of its shares dropped to $24 on the New York Stock Exchange. At this price, the value of the second tier was 5/8 × 24 × $15 for each Transco share.

The two-tier structure implies a threat: any Transco shareholder who does not sell his or her shares in the first tier would be squeezed out for a lower price in the second tier.

Suppose that Sally owns one share of Transco. How should she respond to Williams's first-tier offer? Figure 10.6 presents the game in extensive form between Williams and Sally. For brevity, the figure shows only the outcomes for Sally at the ends of the final branches.

Suppose that, at node *B*, Sally accepts the $17.50 first-tier offer. At node *C*, we draw a circle to indicate that the ensuing consequences depend on the decisions of the other shareholders. (Neither Williams nor Sally makes a move at node *C*.) If Williams gets

---

[9]   Suppose that Mars' management activates the rights and cancels Pluto's 100,000 rights. Let the value of each share become v. The holders of the remaining 900,000 rights will now buy an additional 900,000 shares at $0.5v$ each. Their payments for these shares will increase the value of the company by $0.5v × 900,000 = $450,000v$ to $2 million + $450,000v$.

Since the activation increases the number of shares by 900,000 to 1.9 million, the value of each share is now $v = \$(2,000,000 + 450,000v)/1,900,000$. Solving, we have $2,000,000 = 1,450,000v$, which implies that $v = 1.38$.

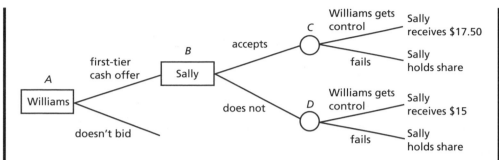

Figure 10.6   Two-tier takeover bid
The outcomes at nodes C and D are uncertain, depending on the decisions of the various shareholders. By backward induction at node B, for Sally, the outcomes if she does not accept are dominated by the outcomes if she accepts, so she will accept. At node A, Williams will make the first-tier cash offer.

51% or more of the shares and gains control over Transco, then it would proceed to the second-tier squeeze out. Since Sally accepted the first-tier offer, she would have $17.50. If, however, Williams fails to secure 51% of the shares in the first tier, it would return all the shares and Sally would be back to holding one share of Transco.

Suppose, instead, that, at node B, Sally rejects the $17.50 first-tier offer. At node D, we again draw a circle to indicate that the ensuing consequences depend on the decisions of the other shareholders. If Williams wins control over Transco, then it would proceed to the second-tier squeeze out. Since Sally rejected the first-tier offer, she would be squeezed out in the second tier and end up with $15. If, however, Williams fails to win control in the first tier, it would return all the shares and Sally would continue to hold one share of Transco.

Looking forward from node B, not to accept the first-tier offer is a dominated strategy for Sally. However the other shareholders act, Sally will be no worse off by accepting the first-tier offer. Accordingly, Sally should accept the first-tier offer. Indeed, all the shareholders of Transco should accept the first-tier offer. Through a two-tier offer, Williams can be assured of winning control of Transco.

Source: "Williams to Buy Transco Energy for $3 Billion," *Asian Wall Street Journal*, December 13, 1994, p. 2.

Strikes

Threats are frequently used in negotiations. In negotiations with employers, unions may threaten a strike: "If you don't agree to raise wages by at least 7%, we will strike." Employers fear the disruption to operations resulting from a strike. The threat of a strike may persuade an employer to concede on wages. The occurrence of strikes, however, varies with the industry.

In professional American football, for instance, strikes are rare. To understand why, we analyze whether a union's threat of a strike is credible. Credibility is an issue because a strike also imposes costs on the workers themselves. During a strike, the workers must forgo part or all of their wages. In figure 10.7, at the node A, where the union decides whether to proceed with a strike, the union must compare the consequences of a strike with those from no strike.

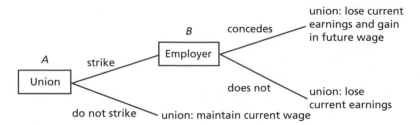

Figure 10.7   Strike

If the workers' union strikes, it will lose current wages and possibly gain higher wages in the future. If it does not strike, then it will maintain the current wage.

If the union proceeds with the strike, the workers will lose some current wages, and they may be able to convince their employer to increase their future wages. If the union decides to cancel the strike, then the workers will continue to receive their current wage. For the threat of a strike to be credible, the workers must expect to gain more from a strike than by continuing to work normally.

In figure 10.7, suppose that, if the union strikes, the workers would lose current earnings of $4 million and the possible gain in future wages is $12 million. Suppose further than the probability that the employer will concede is 0.2, and so the probability that the employer will not concede is 0.8.

Then, at node B, the expected consequences for the union are $(-4 + 12) \times 0.2 + (-4) \times 0.8 = -1.6$, which is a loss of $1.6 million. Hence, the union should not strike.

Compared with many other workers, the career of a professional American football player is relatively short (only four years). Like other workers, if football players strike, they are trading off current loss of income against higher wages in the future. As football players have short careers, they are not so attracted by higher wages in the future. Accordingly, football players are relatively less likely to strike than those in other sports.

Progress Check 10G Referring to figure 10.7, suppose that the loss of current earnings is $2 million, and the possible gain in future wages is $10 million. What is the minimum probability that the employer will concede for the union to strike?

Promises

Besides a threat, the other type of conditional strategic move is a promise. For an outstanding example of a promise, we turn to banking. Most governments are concerned about the stability of their banking systems. Banks take deposits in checking and savings accounts and lend the funds to short- and long-term borrowers. This means that, generally, banks do not have enough cash at hand to repay all their depositors on short notice.

Consider a typical depositor. Every day, she must choose between maintaining her savings account with a bank and withdrawing the deposit to get cash. Cash, of course, is the safest possible investment. It, however, yields no interest. Other things equal, the depositor would rather keep the money in the savings account. If, however, she hears a rumor that the bank is in trouble, she will rush to withdraw her deposit. As all depositors rush to withdraw, the bank may run short of funds. So, rumors can bring down even financially sound banks.

To ensure the stability of the banking system, many governments provide deposit insurance. This means that, if a participating bank cannot repay the money deposited, then the government will pay all its depositors. Deposit insurance is a conditional strategic move: the government pays only in the event that the bank cannot repay.

Official promise: the Federal Deposit Insurance Corporation

In the United States, the Federal Deposit Insurance Corporation (FDIC) guarantees deposits of up to $100,000 at participating banks. The FDIC aim is to forestall bank runs on the scale that exacerbated the Great Depression in the early 1930s. As result of FDIC insurance, holders of insured bank deposits need not worry about the financial condition of the bank. FDIC insurance can effectively prevent bank runs. If the FDIC covers only sound banks, then the banks that it insures will not fail and the FDIC need never pay out any money.

Consider the effect of deposit insurance. The depositor need not worry about rumors. Even if the rumors are true, she will still get her money back, in this case, from the government. Accordingly, depositors will not withdraw their deposits when they hear rumors that their banks are in difficulties. Thus, deposit insurance can effectively prevent bank runs. If the government insures only sound banks, then government need never pay out any compensation. That is the beauty of a conditional strategic move.

---

8 Repetition

So far, we have considered strategic interactions that take place only once. Many strategic interactions, however, are repeated. Generally, the range of possible strategies is much wider in repeated interactions than in one-shot scenarios. In situations that involve coordination, the wider range of strategies may enable the various parties to achieve better outcomes than in interactions that occur only once.

With repeated interaction, a party may condition its action on either external events or the previous actions of the other party. Such conditional strategies may yield a better outcome than the equilibrium of the one-shot scenario.

Conditioning on External Events

Let us consider strategies that condition actions on external events in the context of the battle for the evening news. With simultaneous moves on a one-shot basis, each station will jockey and maneuver for the first-mover advantage. Suppose, however, that the stations look at their situation as a repeated interaction. Then other strategies become possible. In particular, a station could adopt a strategy under which its schedule is conditioned on some independent variable.

For instance, TV Delta could condition its news schedule on the year, as follows: broadcast at 8:00 p.m. in odd years and at 7:30 p.m. in even years. Likewise, one of Channel Zeta's strategies is to broadcast at 7:30 p.m. in odd years and at 8:00 p.m. in even years. These two strategies are an equilibrium in the repeated battle for the evening news.

Essentially, the stations alternate between the two time slots. By alternating, the stations can ensure that they achieve the efficient outcome where one station broadcasts at 8:00 p.m.

and the other broadcasts at 7:30 p.m. Each will have an equal share of the premium 8:00 p.m. slot. The alternating strategy will be better than fighting over the 8:00 p.m. slot on a once-only basis, which might result in both stations broadcasting their news at the same time.

Conditioning on Other Parties' Actions

Strategies in repeated strategic situations can also be conditioned on the previous actions of the other party. Let us see how such strategies can improve the outcome in the context of the cartel's dilemma.

Every member of a cartel knows that, if all sellers cooperate in restricting production, they will collectively be able to increase their profits. In a once-only cartel, however, individual members have an overwhelming incentive to exceed their quotas. Table 10.1 shows the game in strategic form: following the quota is a dominated strategy.

Let us now consider a repeated cartel, that is, a cartel that continues over an extended period of time. In a repeated cartel, a seller can adopt a strategy under which it conditions its production on the actions of another party at a earlier time. One such strategy is "tit for tat": I will begin with following my quota and will continue until you exceed your quota, in which case, I shall produce more than my quota in the following month, and thereafter, I will follow your move.

A tit-for-tat strategy combines a promise with a threat. The promise is to follow the quota if the other seller follows its quota. When all sellers follow their quotas, they can achieve profits above the competitive level. The threat is to produce more than one's quota if the other seller exceeds its quota. Whenever a seller exceeds its quota, it will depress the market price and, hence, reduce the profits of other sellers.

Is tit-for-tat an equilibrium strategy for all parties in the repeated cartel? Referring to table 10.1, suppose that both Jupiter and Saturn adopt a tit-for-tat strategy. Each begins by following its quota, with Jupiter earning $15 million and Saturn earning $10 million. Suppose, however, that in some month, Saturn cheats and exceeds the quota, while Jupiter follows the quota. Then, Saturn will earn $13 million instead of $10 million, gaining $3 million.

In the following month, Jupiter would retaliate and exceed the quota. What should Saturn do? It could continue cheating, and then Jupiter would continue to retaliate. In this case, Saturn would earn $8 million indefinitely. Alternatively, Saturn could go back to following the quota, and so restore cooperation thereafter. In this case, Saturn would earn $5 million for one month and $10 million every month afterward.

Tit-for-tat is an equilibrium strategy for Saturn if the one-time $3 million gain is outweighed by the future losses due to Jupiter's retaliation. This depends on two factors. One is how Saturn values $1 in a future month relative to $1 in the present, which is the concept of discounting introduced in chapter 1. The less that Saturn values money in the future, the more likely it is that Saturn will cheat.

The other factor affecting whether tit-for-tat is an equilibrium strategy is the likelihood that the cartel will be terminated in the future due to the obsolescence of the product or entry of new competitors. The shorter the expected life of the cartel, the more likely it is that Saturn will cheat.

Accordingly, under certain conditions, tit-for-tat is an equilibrium strategy in a repeated cartel. In the tit-for-tat equilibrium, every individual seller will restrict production. Thus, when competing sellers interact over an extended period of time, it is possible to maintain a cartel and achieve profit above the competitive level. A cartel can further improve the likelihood that individual sellers will restrict production if it extends agreement to several different markets. In a cartel that covers several markets, a seller can condition its production on the preceding actions of another party in all the markets.

For instance, in a cartel that encompasses the markets for equipment leasing and truck rentals, a seller could adopt the following tit-for-tat strategy: I will begin with abiding by my quota and will continue until you exceed your quota in any market, in which case, I shall produce more than my quota in both markets; and thereafter, I will follow your move in both markets.

In a cartel that extends to several markets, the tit-for-tat strategy promises a greater benefit: increased profit in all the markets if sellers restrict production. Moreover, the tit-for-tat strategy threatens a greater punishment: reduced profit in all the markets if sellers exceed their quotas.

⊣ Tit-for-tat wins again ⊢

Political scientist Robert Axelrod invited a number of scholars to submit computer programs specifying strategies for a prisoners' dilemma repeated 200 times. Dr. Axelrod pitted each program against the others in a round-robin tournament, and recorded its total score over 200 repetitions against all the other programs.

Programs that were "nice" in the sense of not being first to cheat performed better than those that were not nice. The winning strategy was tit-for-tat. Dr. Axelrod announced these results and held a second tournament. Despite the opportunity to devise better strategies, no scholar could beat tit-for-tat, and the simple strategy also won the second tournament.

Based on the results of his tournaments, Dr. Axelrod put forward four simple rules for success in repeated strategic interactions:

* do not strike first;
* reciprocate both good and bad;
* act simply and clearly;
* do not be envious.

Source: Robert Axelrod, *Evolution of Cooperation* (New York: Basic Books, 1984).

---

9   Summary

In strategic situations, when the parties move simultaneously, there are several useful principles to follow: avoid using dominated strategies, focus on Nash equilibrium strategies, and consider randomizing. When the parties move sequentially, a strategy should be worked out by looking forward to the final nodes and reasoning back to the initial node.

Through conditional or unconditional strategic moves, it may be possible to influence the beliefs or actions of other parties. In some settings, the first mover has the advantage; in others, the first mover is at a disadvantage. Finally, it is important to consider whether the situation will be played just once or repeated. The range of possible strategies is wider in a repeated situation.

In a zero-sum game, one party can become better off only if another is made worse off. In a positive-sum game, one party can become better off without another being made worse off.

Key Concepts

strategy
game theory
game in strategic form
dominated strategy
Nash equilibrium
randomized strategy
zero-sum game
positive-sum game
co-opetition

game in extensive form
backward induction
equilibrium strategy in a game in extensive form
strategic move
first mover advantage
conditional strategic move
threat
promise

Further Reading

Two entertaining and very readable books on strategic thinking are Avinash Dixit and Barry Nalebuff's best seller, *Thinking Strategically: The Competitive Edge in Business, Politics, and Everyday Life* (New York: W. W. Norton, 1991), and Thomas C. Schelling's classic, *The Strategy of Conflict* (Cambridge, MA: Harvard University Press, 1980). Avinash Dixit and Susan Skeath's *Games of Strategy* (New York: Norton, 1999), provides a more formal yet approachable review of game theory.

Review Questions

1. Speedy Snaps is a small public company in the perfectly competitive fastener industry. Which of the following choices by Speedy are strategic?
   (a) Switching deposits from Citibank to J. P. Morgan.
   (b) Hiring another worker for the night shift.
   (c) Adopting a poison pill.
2. Explain the following concepts:
   (a) Dominated strategy.
   (b) Nash equilibrium.
3. Which of the following are reasons to adopt a Nash equilibrium strategy?
   (a) I can minimize my expected loss.
   (b) I can guarantee a minimum outcome.
   (c) Even if the other party knows my strategy, it cannot take advantage of that information.
4. This question relies on the randomized strategies section. Referring to table 10.5, calculate the Nash equilibrium in randomized strategies.
5. This question relies on the randomized strategies section. Some right-handed boxers also train themselves to box with their left hands. Which of the following strategies will be more effective?
   (a) Throw a left-hand punch after every three right-handers.
   (b) Box mainly with the right hand and throw a left-hand punch at random.
6. While shopping at Bloomingdale's in Manhattan, you suddenly realize that you have been separated from your boyfriend. Both your boyfriend and you must simultaneously decide where to look for the other person. Explain why there are many possible Nash equilibria: one corresponding to every place in the store. Explain why the customer service counter is a focal point.
7. Suppose that, in some game in strategic form, the consequences to the two players in every cell add up to -10. Is this a zero-sum game?
8. Recall the choices of Venus and Sol between the Orange and Green instant messaging technologies (please refer to table 10.5). Suppose that Venus can move first. Using an extensive form, analyze the equilibrium.

9. Explain the strategic use of a threat with an example.

10. Compare the following actions by a lithographer. Which is more credible to buyers?
   (a) She announces that she will print only 30 copies.
   (b) She destroys the plates after printing 30 copies.

11. What's wrong with analyzing a game in extensive form by reasoning forward from the initial node?

12. Generally, why are conditional strategic moves better than unconditional strategic moves?

13. Explain the strategic use of a promise with an example.

14. Loan sharks are not allowed to use the legal system to collect debts. Does this explain why they employ violence?

15. How do strategies in repeated strategic situations differ from those that occur only once?

Discussion Questions

1. The National Collegiate Athletic Association (NCAA) restricts the amount that colleges and universities may pay their student athletes. Suppose that there are just two colleges in the NCAA: Ivy and State. Each must choose between paying athletes according to NCAA rules or paying more.
   (a) Construct a game in strategic form to analyze the choices of Ivy and State.
   (b) Identify the equilibrium or equilibria.
   (c) The NCAA rules have government backing. How will this affect the equilibrium or equilibria?

2. Some 85% of online book sales are made by either Amazon or Barnes and Noble. In 2003, Amazon's total online sales were $1.8 billion while Barnes and Noble (.com) had $300 million of sales. It is estimated that the own price elasticity for Amazon is −0.45 and for Barnes and Noble is −3.5. The cross price elasticity for Amazon with respect to the Barnes and Noble price is 0.2, while for Barnes and Noble it is 3.5 with respect to the Amazon price. (*Source*: Judith Chevalier and Austan Goolsbee, 2003, "Measuring Prices and Price Competition Online: Amazon vs. Barnes and Noble," *Quantitative Marketing and Economics* 2.)
   (a) Construct the following game in strategic form. Each online retailer is considering a 1% increase in price. Estimate the revenue impacts for each retailer and speculate on the profit impacts.
   (b) Are there any Nash equilibria in this game?
   (c) Are there any reasons why Amazon would not raise prices, although its demand is estimated to be inelastic? Would you say that Amazon is the dominant firm in online book sales?

3. Since 1982, Malaysia Airlines and Singapore Airlines have operated a revenue pool on the busy air route between Malaysia's capital, Kuala Lumpur, and Singapore. By this arrangement, each airline must pass 50% of its revenue (net of commissions) to the other airline, but bear all of its operating costs. Each year, Singapore Airlines remits millions of dollars to Malaysian Airlines. The two carriers account for 182 of 213 weekly flights, or a staggering 85% market share on the route. Suppose that both airlines charge $400 for a round-trip economy class fare and that each airline sells 500,000 tickets. Each airline believes that, if it cuts its price by 10% while the other airline maintains its price, its sales would increase by 100,000 tickets, half of which would be new flyers, while the other half will switch from the higher-priced airline. If both airlines cut their prices by 10%, then each would increase sales by 50,000 tickets, all of which would be new flyers. Let the unit cost of each seat be constant at $200 for both airlines.
   (a) Suppose that there is no revenue pool and each airline acts independently. For each airline, the possible strategies are to maintain price or to cut price by 10%. Use a game in strategic form to analyze the situation. What will be the equilibrium?
   (b) Use a game in strategic form to analyze the revenue pool. For each airline, the possible strategies are the same as in (a). What will be the equilibrium?

4. The 2004 U.S. Presidential campaign was quite close as election day neared. Florida, Ohio, and Pennsylvania were considered key states, and not surprisingly, both candidates visited those states most frequently. Supposing that George W. Bush has conceded Pennsylvania to John Kerry; then for Bush to win the election, he must win both Florida and Ohio. Suppose that Bush has a 30% chance of winning Ohio and a 70% chance in Florida. Further, assume that Bush can increase his chances by 10% in either state by making a last minute visit there, and that Kerry can do the same. Assume each candidate can only make one more visit before the election. (*Source*: Jordan Ellenberg, "Game Theory for Swingers," October 24, 2004, www.slate.com/id/21086410.)
   (a) Display this game in strategic form.
   (b) Find the Nash equilibrium, if one exists.
   (c) Suppose Bush starts out with a 50-50 chance in each state. Find the Nash equilibrium, if one exists.
   (d) Is there a Nash equilibrium in randomized strategies under the circumstances in (c)?

5. The Organisation of Petroleum Exporting Countries (OPEC) includes Saudi Arabia, Iran, Kuwait, and Venezuela, but not Mexico, Russia, and several major oil exporters. Throughout the 1990s, OPEC sought to raise the price of oil by limiting production without much success. Finally, in 1999, after years of steady decline, the price of oil turned upward to the levels of a decade before.
   (a) Referring to the cartel's dilemma, explain OPEC's difficulty in raising price.
   (b) Compare the incentive of an OPEC member such as Venezuela to cut price with that of a non-member such as Mexico.
   (c) Saudi Arabia's marginal cost of oil production is among the lowest in the world. Traditionally, it played the role of "OPEC policeman," increasing output whenever it detected others cheating on the cartel. Explain why the Saudis were well placed to discipline the cartel.
   (d) During 1998, as the price of oil hit new lows, oil companies throughout the world reduced exploration and production expenditure by $25 billion. How did this cut back affect the effectiveness of OPEC?

6. The demand for most new films peaks in the first few days after opening, then tapers off. Two key factors that affect potential demand are the season (Summer and Christmas are the best times) and the timing of other releases. Suppose that both Studio Luna and Moonlight Movies are producing major action movies. The two studios must choose between release on December 11 or 18. If both films open on December 11, each will sell 200,000 tickets. If one opens on December 11 and the other on December 18, then the early release will sell 350,000 tickets, while the later release will sell 150,000. If both open on December 18, each will sell 100,000 tickets.
   (a) Suppose that the studios choose their launch dates simultaneously. Construct a game in strategic form to illustrate the situation and identify the equilibrium or equilibria.
   (b) Is this a zero-sum game?
   (c) Is this a situation of first-mover advantage? Explain your answer with a suitable game in extensive form.

7. The Estonian government has pegged its currency, the kroon, at a rate of 15.6466 kroons to one euro. The central bank, Eesti Pank, is committed to exchange euros for kroons at this rate. In December 2005, the Esti Pank had issued currency in circulation with face value of 10.1 billion kroons, and Estonia's foreign exchange reserves totalled 25.7 billion kroons. Other things equal, Estonian residents prefer to hold kroons as they are more convenient for daily use than euros.
   (a) Construct a game in extensive form with the following nodes: at the first node, the typical individual chooses between redeeming kroons for euros or not redeeming; at the following nodes, the Eesti Pank either has sufficient assets to meet the redemptions and remains solvent, or has insufficient assets and becomes insolvent.
   (b) As of December 2005, would the typical individual redeem her kroons?

(c)   Suppose, however, that the Eesti Pank increases the currency in circulation to 30 billion kroons. Explain how the typical individual's decision whether to redeem depends on her beliefs about the decisions of other persons whether to redeem.

8.   German telecommunications provider Deutsche Telekom is rated Aa2 by Moody's on a scale ranging from the highest grade of Aaa through Aa, A, Baa, Ba, B, to the lowest grade of Caa. In its June 2000 bond issue worth $14.5 billion, Deutsche Telekom promised to increase the interest payment by 0.5% if its credit rating should fall below A.

(a)   For simplicity, assume that the normal interest on the bonds is $870 million a year. Suppose that, some years later, Telekom will choose between two investments. For the risky investment, it must issue new bonds with annual interest of $130 million. The risky investment will generate a cash flow of $1.5 billion with 50% probability, and $1 billion otherwise. The safe investment will not require additional borrowing and will yield $1.07 billion for sure. Using a game in extensive form, illustrate this choice, while ignoring the promise. At each final node, show the net cash flow (net of interest on all loans).

(b)   Now suppose that the additional borrowings for the risky investment would reduce Telekom's credit rating below A and trigger its promise to raise the interest payment by 0.5% × $14.5 billion = $72.5 million. Suppose that banks will not lend if there is any possibility of negative net cash flow. How does Telekom's promise affect the game in extensive form?

9.   In December 1994, the Williams Companies made a two-tier bid for the common shares of Transco Energy. In the first tier, Williams offered $17.50 per share in cash; in the second tier, Williams offered stock worth $15. Before the bid was announced, Transco shares were trading at $12.625. Williams conditioned its first-tier cash offer on receiving 51% or more of Transco's shares. Only if Williams gained control through the first-tier cash offer would it be able to effect the second-tier squeeze-out.

(a)   Using a suitable extensive form, analyze how a Transco shareholder should respond to the cash offer.

(b)   Suppose, instead, that Williams' first-tier cash offer had been unconditional. How should a Transco shareholder respond under the following conditions:

(i)   She believes that Williams will get control through the first-tier cash offer.

(ii)   She believes that Williams will not get control through the first-tier cash offer.

10.   A major problem for China's large state-controlled commercial banks is loans to state-owned enterprises. Historically, many state-owned enterprises were financed with very high debt and relatively little equity. Most of their loans were from state-owned banks. On a strictly commercial basis, these loans would be classified as "non-performing." Banks should make provision for non-performing loans and, accordingly, reduce their profit and the book value of their assets.

(a)   Use a suitable game in extensive form to describe the following scenario. When a loan is about to mature, the bank must choose between rolling over the loan and demanding repayment. (i) If the bank rolls over the loan, the enterprise continues in business and the bank receives interest and classifies the loan as performing. Then the bank management and staff continue to be employed. (ii) If the bank demands repayment, the enterprise defaults and the bank must write off the value of the loan. The bank might fail to meet capital requirements, and must cut back its other lending and lay off staff.

(b)   What is the equilibrium of the game in (a)?

(c)   In a normal banking market, if a bank demands repayment, the borrower would repay rather than default. How would this change the equilibrium of the game?

Chapter 11

Oligopoly[1]

1 Introduction

On December 10, 2004, Sprint and Nextel, the third and fifth largest wireless telecommunications carriers in the United States announced a merger agreement. The agreement provided that each Nextel common share would be converted into new shares of Spring Nextel and cash. At the close of the merger in August 2005, the conversion ratio was fixed at 1.2675 shares of Sprint Nextel common stock and $0.8463 in cash.

The Sprint/Nextel merger came shortly after the merger of Cingular (itself a joint venture of SBC Communications and BellSouth) with AT&T Wireless, and was followed by a merger of ALLTEL Corp. with Western Wireless Corp. (two of the larger regional wireless providers) less than a month later. Thus began the long-awaited consolidation of the U.S. wireless telecommunications industry.[2]

At the end of 2003, the top five wireless providers in the U.S. accounted for 70% of subscribers. This compared with far greater concentration elsewhere in the world. For example, the top three providers in Italy and Poland had virtually 100% of their respective markets, while the top three providers in Japan and Australia had over 95% of their markets. By contrast, in the U.S., the top three accounted for just over half of the market. In the UK, Germany, Korea, and most other OECD nations, the top four providers accounted for the entire market.

Following the Sprint/Nextel merger, the leading U.S. providers were Cingular/AT&T with 47 million subscribers, Verizon with 42 million subscribers, and Sprint/Nextel with 35.6 million subscribers. T-Mobile was a distant fourth, with 16.3 million.

It was estimated that the merger would reduce operating and capital investment costs by present value of $12 billion, due to increased economies of scale and scope. Also, consolidation offered the potential for three roughly equal-sized competitors to dominate a market

---

[1] This chapter is more advanced. All but sections 5 and 6 may be omitted without loss of continuity. Sections 5 and 6 are relevant background to chapter 15 on regulation.

[2] This discussion is based, in part, on "Sprint And Nextel to Combine in Merger of Equals," Sprint and Nextel, Press Release, December 15, 2004, and "Sprint Nextel Announces Preliminary Stock and Cash Consideration for Nextel Common Stock," Sprint and Nextel, Press Release, August 15, 2005; the *2005 OECD Communications Outlook* and *Telecommunications Reports*, January 1 and 15, 2005.

that was formerly split among two large providers and a number of somewhat smaller ones (including Sprint and Nextel).

A significant question for the merging firms, for investors in the industry, as well as for regulators, was whether the merger would increase or decrease competition within the industry. Opinions varied: "This merger is a positive move for both companies and should create a potent new force in the market," according to Jan Dawson, an analyst at industry consultants, Ovum. By contrast, Gene Kimmelman, Director of Consumers Union's Washington DC office, remarked, "This merger will do little for consumers, but most importantly, it signals the likely end to the possibility of building vibrant wireless competition to the dominant, local Bell telephone companies."

On the day that the merger was announced, Sprint's share price rose by 8% and Nextel's rose by 6.6%, but the share prices of other wireless carriers changed very little.

Would the Sprint/Nextel merger create a third giant to increase competition within the industry, or would the reduction in the number of large competitors from five to four presage less competition and higher prices? How should competing carriers respond to the merger? What would be the impact on consumers?

> A market is an **oligopoly** if it comprises a small number of sellers, whose actions are interdependent.

The U.S. wireless telecommunications industry is an **oligopoly**, which is a situation where a market comprises a small number of sellers with interdependent strategies. Oligopoly is a market structure that lies between the two extremes of perfect competition and monopoly. Recall that, under perfect competition, no seller has market power, while in a monopoly, there is only one seller.

To address the impact of the Sprint/Nextel merger, we must understand competition – how sellers decide capacity, production, and pricing – under conditions of oligopoly. Since there are few sellers, it is important to consider how each seller takes account of the potential reactions of competing sellers. Accordingly, we will apply upon the techniques of game theory, specifically, the concepts of Nash equilibrium and equilibrium in games in extensive form developed in chapter 10.

As in our earlier analyses of perfect competition and monopoly, we distinguish between two time horizons – short and long run. Generally, production capacity is less flexible than pricing, and hence, businesses must decide on capacity (long run) before pricing (short run).

We first study oligopoly in the short run – how competing sellers set price and how their pricing depends on whether the product is homogeneous or differentiated, and how each seller should adjust price in response to competitors' price changes.

We then study oligopoly in the long run – how competing sellers decide on production capacity and how each seller should adjust capacity and production in response to competitors' changes in capacity and production. With these analyses, we can explain the impact of the Sprint/Nextel merger on wireless telecommunications service and prices, and how competing carriers should react to the merger.

Further, we apply the analyses of oligopoly to antitrust law and policy, the aim of which is to regulate competition. We can then explain the impact of the Sprint/Nextel merger on U.S. consumers.

2   Pricing

Typically, in the short run, the strategic variable for oligopolistic sellers is price. The outcome from oligopolistic competition on price depends on whether the product is homogeneous or differentiated. Let us analyze the outcome in each of these two cases.

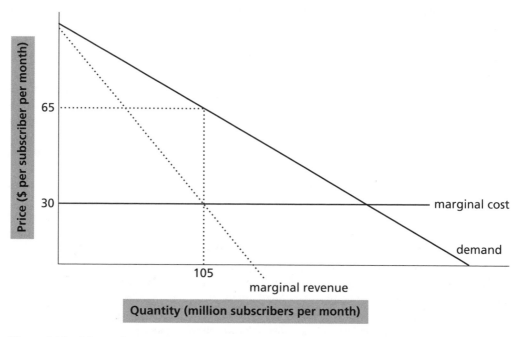

Figure 11.1   Monopoly

Homogeneous Product

Suppose that, in the market for wireless telecommunications, the market demand is represented as in figure 11.1, or mathematically by the equation, $Q = 300 - 3p$, where Q is the number of subscribers in millions, and p is the price or ARPU (average revenue per user) in dollars per month. The marginal cost of service (representing marketing, billing, operations, and usage-based facility investments) is a constant $30 per month per subscriber.

It will be useful to compare the market outcome under conditions of oligopoly with a monopoly scenario. As figure 11.1 shows, the monopoly maximizes profit at the scale of operations where the marginal revenue equals marginal cost. That scale is 105 million subscribers and the corresponding price is $65 per subscriber. The monopoly profit is $65 × 105 million − $30 × 105 million = $3.675 billion per month. In this chapter, all outcomes are solved in the math supplement.

A market is a **duopoly** if it comprises two sellers

For simplicity, we first consider a situation of **duopoly**, which is where there are just two sellers, say, Mars Cellular and Pluto Wireless. Each seller produces under conditions of constant marginal cost of $30 per month per subscriber with no capacity constraint. Consumers consider the services of Mars and Pluto to be identical, i.e., the product is homogeneous. This is the **Bertrand** model of oligopoly, named for the French mathematical economist who published it in 1883.

In the **Bertrand** model of oligopoly, sellers which produce at constant marginal cost with unlimited capacity compete on price to market a homogeneous product.

Under these conditions, the market equilibrium is perfectly competitive pricing. To see this, imagine that Mars Cellular charges some price, p, above marginal cost. Pluto then has three choices: it can price above, equal to, or less than Mars' price p. If Pluto charges above Mars' price, all consumers will subscribe with Mars, and so, Pluto will get no business, hence its profit would be zero. If it matches Mars' price, Pluto would get half of the market demand, which would yield profit equal to the product of the incremental margin, $p - 30$, and sales.

Now, if Pluto charges any price below Mars' price, even slightly lower, then it would get the whole market demand. By marginally undercutting Mars' price, Pluto can almost double its profit. The reason is that its incremental margin is only slightly less than $p - 30$, but its sales would double. Indeed, Pluto faces a demand curve that it is infinitely elastic with respect to a price cut below Mars' price.

The same logic applies to Mars Cellular. Accordingly, the Nash equilibrium in this duopoly is for both competitors to charge a price just equal to the marginal cost of $30, since any higher price would induce the other seller to alter its strategy. (Please refer to chapter 10 for the concept of Nash equilibrium.)

Thus, competition on price in a duopoly with identical products and where sellers have unlimited capacity will result in pricing at marginal cost. This ruinous competitive outcome is essentially the Prisoners' dilemma of chapter 10.

This result is quite dramatic. Even when there are only two competing sellers, each faces a demand curve that is so elastic that the market outcome is identical to that with perfect competition! Moreover, the same analysis applies even if there are more than two competing sellers. Every seller will have a massive incentive to undercut the others – its incremental margin would be only slightly lower, but its sales would double or increase by even more (depending on how many competitors it undercuts).

One way by which oligopolistic competitors can avoid this ruinous outcome is through repeated competition. Then, sellers may adopt "tit-for-tat" strategies – price high, observe competitors' pricing, and cut price only if the competitor cuts price. As shown in chapter 10, in a scenario of repeated competition, "tit-for-tat" may be a Nash equilibrium. Then, the oligopolists would succeed in avoiding price wars and achieve tacit (not explicit) cooperation.

Differentiated Products

What if the competing oligopolists have unlimited capacity but offer differentiated products? With differentiation, if one seller cuts its price below the competitor's price, it would take away only part of the competitor's entire demand. Hence, the price-cutter's demand is not infinitely elastic. We show next that competition on prices need not reduce price to marginal cost, even if the sellers do not face capacity constraints.

Consider the following retail situation. Suppose that consumers are uniformly distributed along "Main Street," and that the linear market is served by two competing stores, Ajax and Bacchus – each located at an endpoint of the street. Consumers must incur travel costs to reach either store, and the travel costs are proportional to the distance to the store. More generally, the line can be thought of as an attribute on which consumers might have different tastes and such that consumers incur disutility from any product whose attribute that differs from the consumer's ideal or most preferred attribute.

The market setting for our two sellers, Ajax and Bacchus, is shown in figure 11.2. Each seller incurs a constant marginal cost of $2 to provide the item.

Figure 11.2 shows Ajax being "located" at point 0 and Bacchus being located at point 1. The consumer shown at location x is some distance from each of the two sellers. The sellers set prices, p_A and p_B, respectively.

Assume that every consumer is willing to pay $10 for her ideal product. However, she incurs a constant marginal cost of travel of $3 per unit of distance to purchase a less than ideal product. (Alternatively, this marginal cost of "travel" may be interpreted as the

Figure 11.2 Product differentiation

In the **Hotelling** model of duopoly, sellers which produce at constant marginal cost with unlimited capacity compete on price to market products differentiated by their distance from the consumer.

marginal disutility associated with the "distance" of the product from the consumer's ideal level of the attribute.) Thus, the consumer located at point x incurs cost $3x to purchase Ajax's product and $3(1 − x)$ to purchase Bacchus' product. This is the **Hotelling** model of duopoly.

What is the Nash equilibrium of this competitive situation? Assume that, in equilibrium, every consumer will be served and each seller will have a positive market share (otherwise, it would be better off cutting price to sell something).[3]

Then, there will be one consumer – the marginal consumer – located at some point, x^*, who would be just indifferent between buying from Ajax and buying from Bacchus. For this marginal consumer, her expected utility from Ajax's product would be $10 − p_A − \$3x^*$, while her expected utility from Bacchus' product would be $10 − p_B − \$3(1 − x^*)$. Since she is just indifferent, the two expected utilities must be equal, which means that

$$10 − p_A − 3x^* = 10 − p_B − 3(1 − x^*) \tag{11.1}$$

The "location" of the marginal consumer is then

$$x^*(p_A,p_B) = \frac{(p_B − p_A + 3)}{2 \times 3}. \tag{11.2}$$

Consumers located to the left of x^* will purchase from Ajax, while those to the right will purchase from Bacchus. So, x^* is the market share of Ajax and $(1 − x^*)$ is the market share of Bacchus.

Referring to equation (11.2), notice that, if the two sellers set the same price, $p_A = p_B$, then $x^* = 1/2$; that is, if the two sellers set equal prices, then each would get half the market demand. Also, referring to equation (11.2), if Ajax reduces its price slightly, say by $0.10, then its market share x^* would change by $−(−0.1)/6 = +0.0167$, that is, its market share would increase by 3.34% from its original level of 0.5%. Accordingly, Ajax faces a demand that is not infinitely elastic with respect to price, and similarly, for Bacchus.

Using equation (11.2), we can calculate Ajax's profit as a function of its own price and marginal cost, Bacchus' price, and the consumers' transport cost (disutility). Ajax should set its price to maximize profit. This profit-maximizing price would be a function of Ajax's own marginal cost, Bacchus' price, and the consumers' transport cost; and we can do similarly for Bacchus. The math supplement shows that the profit-maximizing prices are

$$p_A^* = \frac{p_B + 2 + 3}{2} = \frac{p_B + 5}{2} \quad \text{and} \quad p_B^* = \frac{p_A + 2 + 3}{2} = \frac{p_B + 5}{2}. \tag{11.3}$$

[3]   This also requires that the value of the product to each buyer be sufficient to support a price above marginal cost.

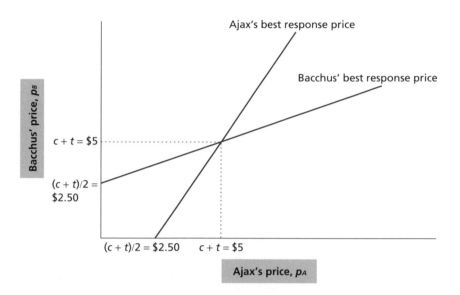

Figure 11.3 Differentiated sellers: best response price functions

Notice that these prices are not absolute numbers, but rather are functions. Each seller's price is a function of the other seller's price. In this context of price competition between oligopolists with unlimited capacity and that offer differentiated products, these functions are called *best response functions*. A seller's **best response function** shows its best action as a function of competing sellers' actions. Figure 11.3 depicts the best response functions.

> A seller's **best response function** shows its best action as a function of competing sellers' actions.

The Nash equilibrium is at the intersection of the two sellers' best response functions. Each seller sets a price equal to $2 + $3 = $5, and they share the market equally. Each seller earns a profit of $2.50 (which is the price, $5, multiplied by the market share of $1/2$) multiplied by market size. As a result of transport costs (disutility), the equilibrium price exceeds marginal cost, and hence sellers earn positive profit. Through product differentiation, sellers can avoid ruinous price competition.

What if the products are relatively more differentiated? Specifically, what if the transport cost (disutility of consuming a less than ideal product) were $4 rather than $3? In general, if the transport cost is t per unit of distance, and the marginal cost of the item is c per unit, then, we can re-calculate equations (11.1) to (11.3) and show that the Nash equilibrium prices would be

$$p_A^* = \frac{p_B + c + t}{2} \quad \text{and} \quad p_B^* = \frac{p_A + c + t}{2}. \tag{11.4}$$

Accordingly, if the transport cost were higher by $1, the equilibrium prices would be higher by $0.50. The incidence of the increase in transport cost is shared between the sellers and the consumers (recall our analysis of incidence in chapter 6). Although the prices are higher, each seller still gets half the market, so serves the same number of consumers.

Generally, the greater are the transport costs, the less price elastic would be the demand that each seller faces. Essentially, greater transport costs cause the products to be more differentiated and hence the demand to be less price elastic. Accordingly, the equilibrium prices would be higher.

Thus, transport costs (disutility of consuming a less than ideal product) serve to dampen the competitive pressure between sellers. Sellers prefer more differentiation since it increases the distance between their products, and hence, would raise the equilibrium prices. But, differentiation can be too much of a good thing, when it moves sellers too far away from the buyers in the market. Differentiation is good for prices, but not necessarily for sales.

At the other extreme as transport costs approach zero, the Nash equilibrium price would approach the marginal cost of the item. This is the outcome with homogeneous products and also the outcome with perfect competition. With zero transport costs, product differentiation no longer pays.

Product Design

If competing sellers in an oligopoly could design their products, how should they do so? In the context of the Main Street setting, the issue is how the sellers should choose their locations (above, these were arbitrarily assumed to be at 0 and 1).

Note that these attributes of "location" are such that some consumers prefer one position while other consumers prefer the other position. There is no position that all consumers prefer. For instance, among competing radio stations, political slant is one such attribute. Some people are conservative while others are liberal. There is no political slant that all people prefer. Similarly among competing furniture manufacturers, design might be an attribute, like location. Some consumers like contemporary design, others prefer traditional. By contrast, with attributes of "quality," all consumers would prefer higher to lower quality.

The simultaneous strategic choice of locations and prices is a complex modeling exercise. Sellers will try to choose different locations in order benefit from differentiation. However, this risks losing too much of the market to competitors. Managers must balance their desire for market share (locating close to their customers) with their wish to avoid head-to-head price competition. The less differentiated are their products, the more direct is price competition, and the lower would be incremental margins.

Progress Check 11A In figure 11.3, draw the best response functions if the transport cost is $1 lower.

Online shopping: lower search costs can lead to higher prices

The introduction of the euro provided a natural experiment to see how lowering search costs might impact pricing. Adoption of the euro facilitated online price comparisons within the euro zone.[4] One study examined price levels in the period leading up to, and following, the adoption of the euro. Surprisingly, it found that prices increased.

In particular, the average price listed (for a variety of products) increased by 3%, while the minimum listed online price increased by 7%. This phenomenon was

---

[4] The euro zone is a subset of the European Union (EU); e.g., Britain is in the EU but not in the euro zone.

explained by there being two market segments. One segment – "shoppers" – will search for the best price they can find. The other segment – "loyal customers" – are loyal to a particular retailer, and will purchase without searching as long as the retailer's price is less than their reservation price. The behavior of loyal customers is unaffected by the adoption of a unified currency.

The introduction of the euro decreased the shopping costs for shoppers, intensifying price competition for this segment. On the other hand, the euro also reduced the probability of any particular retailer making a sale to this segment. Since loyal customers are unaffected by the euro, each retailer's sales would become increasingly concentrated within the loyal segment.

The overall effect of the euro depends on the changes in the number of shoppers and the number of competing retailers. It is the strategic response of retailers that can account for the paradoxical result that a decrease in shopping costs can increase industry prices.

Source: M. R. Baye, J. Rupert, J. Gotti, P. Kattuman, and J. Morgan, "Did the Euro Foster Online Price Competition? Evidence from an International Price Comparison Site," *Economic Inquiry* 44, no. 2 (2006), pp. 265–79.

Strategic Complements[5]

Referring to Ajax's best response function in figure 11.3, if Bacchus were to raise its price, then Ajax should raise its price as well, while if Bacchus were to cut its price, then Ajax should also cut its price. Intuitively, if Bacchus raises its price, the marginal consumer would become one whose ideal product is relatively closer to Bacchus' product and relatively further from Ajax's product. Hence, Ajax's demand would become relatively inelastic, and so, Ajax would raise price.

Likewise, if Bacchus were to cut its price, the marginal consumer would become one whose ideal product is relatively further from Bacchus' product and relatively closer to Ajax's product. Hence, Ajax's demand would become relatively elastic, and so, Ajax would cut price.

Similarly, referring to Bacchus' best response function, Bacchus should always adjust its price in the same direction as Ajax.

Accordingly, in competition between oligopolists with unlimited capacity that offer differentiated products, prices are *strategic complements*. Actions by various parties are **strategic complements** if an adjustment by one party leads other parties to adjust in the same direction.

> Actions by various parties are **strategic complements** if an adjustment by one party leads other parties to adjust in the same direction.

Moreover, we saw above that, in competition between oligopolists with unlimited capacity that offer homogeneous products, if one raises or cuts price, the others should follow suit. Hence, in that setting also, prices are strategic complements. So, generally, in the Bertrand and Hotelling models of price competition between oligopolists, prices are strategic complements.

[5]   This section is based on Bulow, Jeremy, John Geanakoplos, and Paul Klemperer "Multimarket Oligopoly: Strategic Substitutes and Complements," *Journal of Political Economy* 93, no. 3 (June 1985), 488–511.

3 Capacity

Typically, in the long run, the strategic variable for oligopolistic sellers is production capacity. To analyze the outcome of competition on capacity, we return to the setting of wireless telecommunications. We assume that, under all market structures, sellers plan capacity exactly equal to the expected scale of production, hence we treat "capacity," "scale," and "production" as synonymous.

Suppose that Mars Cellular is a monopoly in the market. Then, figure 11.1 describes the monopoly outcome.

> In the **Cournot** model of oligopoly, sellers which produce at constant marginal cost compete on production capacity to market a homogeneous product.

We next consider the outcome under a duopoly: Pluto Wireless enters the market to offer the same homogeneous product at the same constant marginal cost of $30 per month per subscriber. But, now, instead of choosing prices, the two carriers choose service capacities. Assume that the market price is established at a level that equates the market demand with the total service capacity offered by the two carriers. This is the **Cournot** model of oligopoly, named for the French mathematical economist who published it in 1838.

> A seller's **residual demand curve** is the market demand curve less the quantities supplied by other sellers.

In order for Pluto Wireless to choose its capacity, it must make some assumption about Mars Cellular's capacity. The most naïve assumption would be that Mars Cellular will keep providing service to 105 million subscribers. Then, the demand curve facing Pluto Wireless will mirror the market demand curve, but with 105 million customers removed. This *residual demand curve* is described by the equation, $Q_B = 300 - 3p - 105 = 195 - 3p$, drawn in figure 11.4.

A seller's **residual demand curve** is the market demand curve less the quantities supplied by other sellers. Referring to figure 11.4, using its residual demand curve, Pluto can cal-

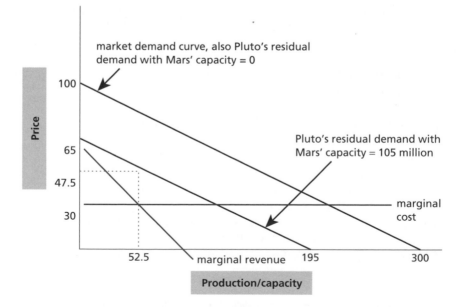

Figure 11.4   Residual demand curves

culate its profit-maximizing capacity by equating its residual marginal revenue with the marginal cost of $30. The profit-maximizing capacity is Q_P = 52.5 million. Then, the total capacity provided by the two carriers would be 105 + 52.5 = 157.5 million. Substituting in the market demand curve, $300 - 3p = 157.5$, the market price would be $47.50 per month.

The problem with this solution is that it does not represent the best decision for Mars Cellular to make. If Mars Cellular knew that Pluto Wireless would choose capacity of 52.5 million, then Mars would not maximize profit with a capacity of 105 million. Rather, Mars should choose its capacity to maximize its profit, given the residual demand curve, $Q_M = 300 - 3p - 52.5 = 247.5 - 3p$. In a similar way as calculated for Pluto, we can show that Mars' profit-maximizing capacity would be Q_M = 78.75 million. This differs from Pluto's belief about Mars' capacity, hence capacities of 105 million for Mars and 52.5 million for Pluto are not a Nash equilibrium.

To find the Nash equilibrium in capacities between Mars Cellular and Pluto Wireless, we must calculate the two carriers' respective best response functions. Pluto's best response function shows its profit-maximizing capacity as a function of Mars' capacity.

We can intuitively derive two extreme points on Pluto's best response function. Suppose that Pluto believes that Mars will choose capacity of 210 million, then Pluto's residual demand curve would be $Q_P = 300 - 3p - 210 = 90 - 3p$, hence the market price would be $30. This price equals the marginal cost of service, $30, hence Pluto would not enter the market. Similarly, if Pluto believes that Mars would choose zero capacity, then Pluto would effectively become a monopoly and should choose the profit-maximizing capacity of 105 million.

Given that the market demand is a straight line and that the marginal cost is constant, Pluto's best response function must be the straight line joining the two extreme points just identified. Mathematically, the equation of Pluto's best response function is $Q_P = 105 - \frac{1}{2}Q_M$. (Please refer to the math supplement for the detailed derivation.) Similarly, we can derive Mars' best response function as $Q_M = 105 - \frac{1}{2}Q_P$. Figure 11.5 illustrates the two best response functions.

The Nash equilibrium of the oligopolistic situation is at the intersection of the two best response functions. Mathematically, the equilibrium is at capacities, $Q_M = Q_P = 70$ million.

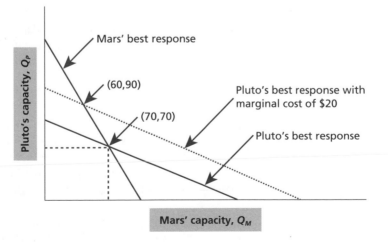

Figure 11.5   Best response capacity functions

If Pluto assumes that Mars will choose capacity of 70 million, then it is best for Pluto to choose capacity of 70 million, and vice versa. Any other combination of capacities will require either Mars or Pluto or both to choose a capacity that is not its best response to their competitor's choice.

In the Nash equilibrium, the total capacity with duopoly is $70 + 70 = 140$ million, which exceeds the monopoly profit-maximizing capacity of 105 million. Further, referring to the market demand, the equilibrium price with duopoly is $^1/_3 \times (300 - 140) = \$53.33$ per subscriber, which is less than the monopoly price of \$65 per subscriber.

Following the analysis of chapter 8, we can calculate that, if the wireless telecommunications market were subject to perfect competition, quantity demanded would equal quantity supplied at a price of \$30 (the marginal cost), and the market equilibrium capacity would be $300 - (3 \times 30) = 210$ million. Hence, the total capacity with duopoly is less than that under perfect competition, while the market price under duopoly is higher than that under perfect competition.

Cost Differences

Over time, sellers may reduce their costs through research and development, outsourcing, and other ways. How should changes in costs affect the sellers' choices of capacity and the market equilibrium? The answer depends on how the changes affect fixed as compared with variable costs.

Generally, suppose that Mars and Pluto have different marginal costs, c_M and c_P. Then, the best response functions will be for Mars, $Q_M = 150 - ^3/_2c_M - ^1/_2Q_P$ and, for Pluto, $Q_P = 150 - ^3/_2c_P - ^1/_2Q_M$.

These are as shown in figure 11.5, except that the lines representing the best response functions will be shifted (parallel) according to the relative marginal costs. For example, suppose that Mars' marginal cost is $c_M = 30$ as before, but that Pluto reduces its marginal cost to $c_P = 20$. Then, Mars' best response curve does not shift, but Pluto's shifts outward, as shown by the dotted line in figure 11.5.

In the new Nash equilibrium, Mars' capacity is 60 million, while Pluto's is 90 million. So, Pluto's marginal cost advantage translates into a significant market share increase. Further, the market price is \$50. Hence, Pluto's cost reduction of \$10 per subscriber results in the market price being lower by \$3.33.

Notice that the best-response functions do not depend on the seller's fixed costs. Accordingly, any change in fixed costs will not affect the sellers' choices of capacity and the market equilibrium.

Multiple Sellers

How does the Cournot model generalize to situations of more than two competitors? Suppose that there are N identical sellers in the market. As shown in the math supplement, the market equilibrium price is given by $100 - 70(N/(N + 1))$ and the total capacity is $(N/(N + 1))(210)$. When $N = 1$ (which is the case of monopoly), price would be 65, and as N becomes very large, the price approaches $\$100 - \$70 = \$30$, which is the price if the industry is perfectly competitive.

Thus, in a market that can be accurately characterized with a Cournot model, the market price decreases and the total capacity increases as the number of sellers in the market increases.

When there are multiple sellers with differing marginal costs, the Nash equilibrium of the best response functions can be written in a way that relates the incremental margin percentage to market demand elasticity and a measure of industry concentration. Intuitively, the more concentrated the industry and the more inelastic the market demand, the higher the incremental margin would be, which is the price relative to marginal cost.

The exact relationship is given by

$$\frac{(p - \bar{c})}{p} = \frac{HHI}{\eta} \tag{11.5}$$

where p is the Nash equilibrium price, $\bar{c}$ is the weighted average marginal cost (weighted by each seller's market share), η is the elasticity of demand, and HHI is the *Herfindahl–Hirschman Index*.

The **Herfindahl–Hirschman Index**, usually represented as HHI, is a measure of industry concentration, specifically, the sum of the squares of the various sellers' market shares. For example, a monopoly would have a market share of 100%, and hence the HHI would be $(100)^2$ or 10,000. In a perfectly competitive industry, each of the many sellers would have almost zero market share, hence the HHI would be close to zero. HHIs exceeding 1,800 are generally viewed as representing significant market concentration. The HHI is usually reported in terms of percentage points (i.e., the maximum value is 100% squared = 10,000), but in equation (11.5) its value is measured in fractions (i.e., the maximum value is 1: $1.0^2 = 1$).

> The **Herfindahl–Hirschman Index** (*HHI*) measures industry concentration as the sum of the squares of the various sellers' market shares.

Progress Check 11B In figure 11.5, draw Pluto's best response capacity function if its marginal cost increases to $c_p = 40$.

⊣ Congested roads: Cournot competition ⊢

Roads are increasingly provided by private, for-profit companies. They are permitted to charge tolls from which to recover their investment and maintenance costs. Critics have claimed that there is a potential for privately provided roads to result in excessive highway congestion, through intense price competition.

Research by Engel et al. suggests a different problem – the result of private road competition is too little congestion, not too much. Essentially, congestion results in Cournot capacity competition. Road providers internalize some of the congestion costs, since they can charge higher prices if their roads are less congested. This softens price competition and results in Cournot outcomes. This entails higher prices and less congestion than would be desirable.

The excessive prices should be reduced in larger markets and with a larger number of private roads (a standard Cournot result). Consequently, the authors suggest that competition will work better in large road networks. They also point out that a toll road competing with a publicly provided (free) and congested roadway, will permit the private road to increase profit by reducing congestion and internalizing the increased willingness of drivers to pay. Again, the congestion would be less than is socially optimal. The private road provider would also intensely oppose any efforts to decrease congestion on the public roadway.

Source: E. M. Engel, R. Fischer, and A. Galetovic, "Toll Competition Among Congested Roads," *Topics in Economic Analysis and Policy* 4, no. 1 (2004), article 4.

⊣ The Las Vegas Strip: evolution of oligopoly ⊢

The Las Vegas Strip is one of the world's major tourist and convention destinations. There are 59,874 hotel rooms in the giant high-quality hotels on the Strip. These comprise about half of the total hotel rooms in the Las Vegas area. The history of the two major hotel groups reveals a pattern of competition on capacity, as shown in table 11.1.

With MGM's purchase of Mirage resorts in 2000, the two major groups had 17,647 rooms (MGM Mirage) and 19,533 rooms (Mandalay Resort Group), respectively, and each had five major properties on the Strip. They attempt to differentiate themselves by identifying each hotel with a theme, although the hotels all have similar amenities and are of similar size.

There was strong competitive pressure for both major hotel groups to mimic each other – in terms of physical location on the Strip, and design concept – both built large-scale luxury hotels combined with casinos. Nevertheless, they did seek to differentiate by applying different "themes" at their respective hotels.

Occupancy rates indicate that capacity was a constraining factor and there was upward pressure on prices. In 2005, two major changes occurred in the Las Vegas Strip. Steve Wynn, developer of many of Las Vegas hotels, opened another megaresort, the Wynn Las Vegas. Entry of new hotels is clearly still feasible on the Strip.

Further, MGM Mirage acquired the Mandalay Resort Group. The merged group (MGM Mirage) now owns 37,180 of the 58,874 large hotel rooms on the Strip, half of the top Strip properties, 44% of the game tables, and 40% of the slot machines. On news of the merger, Mandalay's share price rose by 10.3% and MGM Mirage's rose by 3.4%.

The Federal Trade Commission investigated the merger but permitted it. Apparently, the combined group's dominance on the Strip was mitigated by competitive pressure from other gambling/convention sites and the ease of entry for new hotels.

Sources: Las Vegas Convention and Visitor Authority, http://www.visitlasvegas.com/vegas/Index.asp, hotel and company web sites; "FTC Clears MGM Mirage Buyout of Mandalay Resort Group," *Las Vegas Sun*, February 16, 2005.

Table 11.1 Las Vegas Strip hotels

Group	No. of hotels (1995)	Hotels added (1996–7)	Hotels added (1999–2000)	Average occupancy Jan. 1–June 30, 2004	Average occupancy Jan. 1–June 30, 2005	Average daily room rate Jan. 1–June 30, 2004	Average daily room rate Jan. 1–June 30, 2005
MGM Mirage	1 (MGM Grand)	1 (New York, New York)	3 (Mirage, TI, Bellagio)	96.3%	97.6%	$159	$173
Mandalay Resort Group	3 (Luxor, Circus-Circus, Excalibur)	1 (Monte Carlo)	1 (Mandalay Bay)	92%	93%	$121	$131
Other notables	Caesar's Palace, Aladdin	Stratosphere	Venetian, Paris				

Strategic Substitutes

Referring to Mars' best response function in figure 11.5, if Pluto raises its production capacity, then Mars would reduce its capacity, while if Pluto were to cut its capacity, then Mars would increase its capacity. Intuitively, if Pluto increases capacity, Mars' residual demand curve would shift to the left by the amount of Pluto's increase in capacity. This leftward shift would reduce Pluto's profit-maximizing capacity (at which its residual marginal revenue equals marginal cost). Likewise, if Pluto reduces capacity, Mars' residual demand curve would shift to the right by the amount of Pluto's reduction in capacity. This rightward shift would increase Pluto's profit-maximizing capacity.

Similarly, referring to Pluto's best response function, Pluto would always adjust its capacity in the opposite direction to Mars.

Accordingly, in the Cournot model of competition between oligopolists on production capacity, capacities are *strategic substitutes*. Actions by various parties are **strategic substitutes** if an adjustment by one party leads other parties to adjust in the opposite direction.

> Actions by various parties are **strategic substitutes** if an adjustment by one party leads other parties to adjust in the opposite direction.

A clear understanding of whether particular variables are strategic complements or strategic substitutes is very useful in business strategy. With this understanding, managers can respond to competitor's actions even without knowing the detailed best response functions or even the equilibrium.

Generally, whether strategic variables are strategic complements or strategic substitutes depends on the relevant demand and cost conditions. We have shown that, in the Bertrand and Hotelling models, prices are strategic complements, while, in the Cournot model, capacities are strategic substitutes.

What about other strategic variables – advertising and R&D expenditure? Generally, these may be either strategic complements or strategic substitutes depending on the relevant demand and cost conditions. In the case of R&D expenditure, increased R&D spending can have a similar effect to increasing capacity. On the other hand, an increase in one producer's R&D expenditure may drive competitors to increase R&D as well, particularly when they compete for patents. Similar observations hold for advertising expenditure.

Progress Check 11C Explain how you would determine whether Airbus' and Boeing's investments in the development of new commercial airliners are strategic substitutes or strategic complements.

---

4 Price/Capacity Leadership

So far, we have analyzed oligopolistic strategy assuming that the various sellers move simultaneously. Accordingly, we applied the concept of Nash equilibrium. However, there may be circumstances under which one seller may move ahead of others. In this case, we must consider the actions and consequences in sequence, and apply the concept of equilibrium in a game in extensive form. Referring to chapter 10, sequential actions present the possibilities of first mover advantage and strategic moves.

Price

In an industry where production involves a fixed cost, the leader could use a first mover advantage to deter entry by potential competitors. Suppose that one seller – the "leader" – makes its production decision first, and that any potential entrant assumes that the leader's production will not change regardless of the entrant's actions. We assume that the market price is established at the level that equates the market demand with the total industry (leader plus follower) production. In this case, the leader can control the residual demand curve facing the entrant.

> **Limit pricing** is a strategic move by which an industry leader commits to a level of production so high that any entrant cannot make a profit, and so, will not enter the industry.

If the leader knows the entrant's average cost curve, then the leader can use this information and its first mover advantage to forestall entry. The leader need only produce a quantity sufficient to position the entrant's residual demand curve so that it lies below (to the left of) the entrant's average cost. Then, if the entrant should enter the industry and even if it maximizes its profits, it still cannot cover its costs. Hence, looking forward to this situation, the entrant would not enter. This is known as **limit pricing**.

This situation is illustrated in figure 11.6. The leader chooses its production Q^* large enough to reduce the entrant's residual demand so much that the entrant will not make a profit.

This first-mover advantage – being able to forestall entry – depends on two factors. One is that the leader's first move is viewed as a commitment that will not be reversed regardless of the entrant's actions. The other is that production involves a fixed cost. If there were no fixed cost, then the entrant's average cost curve would slope upward throughout. Then, however large is the leader's production, the entrant would profit from entry to produce at some scale of production, albeit very low.

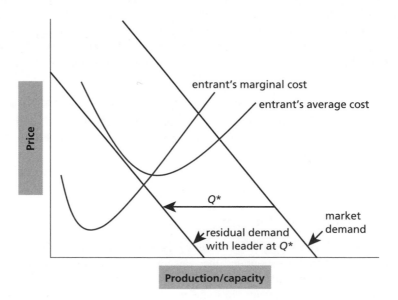

Figure 11.6 Limit pricing

Capacity

What if the industry leader does not completely forestall a potential entrant? It must then take account of the entrant's action. In particular, in a long-run horizon, the leader must take account of the entrant's production capacity.

Consider the following setting. The industry leader and follower produce a homogeneous product under conditions of constant marginal cost. As in the Cournot model, sellers plan capacity exactly equal to the expected scale of production, hence "capacity," "scale," and "production" are synonymous. The industry leader chooses its production capacity before the follower. Note that, when deciding its production capacity, the leader takes account of the entrant's subsequent choice of production capacity. The market price is established at the level that equates the market demand with the total industry (leader plus follower) production capacity. This is the **Stackelberg model**, which is the sequential version of the Cournot model.

> In the **Stackelberg model** of oligopoly, the leader commits to capacity before the follower, and both sellers produce at constant marginal cost and market a homogeneous product.

To apply the Stackelberg model, we return to the example of Mars Cellular and Pluto Wireless, which together face the market demand $Q = 300 - 3p$, as shown in figure 11.1. Both sellers have the same constant marginal cost of \$30 per subscriber. Suppose that Mars is the leader. Then, as the follower, Pluto's best response function is the same as in the Cournot model above. However, Mars' best response function is more complicated: since Mars moves first, it must take account of how its capacity will influence Pluto's choice of capacity.

As shown in the math supplement, in the equilibrium, Mars chooses capacity $Q_M^* = 105$ million, while Pluto chooses capacity $Q_P^* = 52.5$ million. The market price is $= \frac{1}{3} \times (300 - 105 - 52.5) = \$47.50$ per subscriber.

In the Stackelberg model, the total industry production capacity is $105 + 52.5 = 157.5$ million, which exceeds that in the Cournot model (140 million), while the price \$47.50 is lower than that in Cournot (\$53.33).

The major difference is in the relative position of the two sellers. Mars, the industry leader, has twice the market share and twice the profit of Pluto, the industry follower. This is ironic since the follower moves second, and can observe the leader's choice of capacity. The follower fares worse despite its better information because the leader is committed to its production capacity. By contrast, if Mars and Pluto had to choose capacity simultaneously, which is the Cournot setting, a capacity of 105 million for Mars would not be credible. Such is the value of pre-commitment.

The Stackelberg model above assumes a homogeneous product and sellers with identical marginal costs. Oligopoly markets where sellers are differentiated, have different cost structures, and dynamically adjusting their strategies can be complicated to model. They will usually build upon one or more of the models outlined in this chapter.

Progress Check 11D If one seller in an oligopoly is much larger than the other sellers, does this automatically mean that the large seller must behave like an industry leader?

Deregulation changes market structure: insurance in Taiwan

The insurance market in Taiwan was deregulated in 1988. Prior to that time, one insurer, Cathay Insurance, had over 50% of the market, while its closest competitor had 27%. Cathay Insurance was clearly the dominant insurer in that market. Then, in 1988, the Taiwan insurance market was opened to entry of foreign insurers.

After 10 years, Cathay's market share had dropped to 29%, and the second and third largest insurers each had 16% of the market. New entrants had collectively gained 22% of the market.

Wang et al. found that deregulation hurt Cathay Insurance, but helped some of the other incumbent providers in the industry. The outputs of other insurers increased by more than Cathay's output decreased. Prices actually rose in the industry. This was in line with the predictions of a Cournot oligopoly replacing a Stackelberg type market structure.

Source: J. L. Wang, L. Y. Tzeng, and E. Wang, "The Nightmare of the Leader: The Impact of Deregulation on an Oligopoly Insurance Market," *Journal of Insurance Issues* 26, no. 1 (2003), pp. 15–48.

5 Restraining Competition

We have just seen that a monopoly is more profitable than an oligopoly – whether the businesses compete on price or capacity. Further, it can be shown that an oligopoly is at least as profitable as a perfectly competitive industry. Hence, a monopoly is the most profitable of all possible market structures.

Accordingly, rather than compete, sellers can increase profits by restraining competition among themselves. If sellers restrain competition to a sufficient degree, they can achieve the profit of a monopoly. Competing sellers can restrain competition in two ways: through agreement or by integration. We now discuss these ways of restraining competition.

Cartels

A **cartel** is an agreement to restrain competition.

A **cartel** is an agreement to restrain competition. A seller cartel is an agreement among sellers to restrain competition in supply, while a buyer cartel is an agreement among buyers to restrain competition in demand. Typically, a seller cartel sets a maximum sales quota for each participant. By limiting each participant's sales, the cartel restricts the quantity supplied and raises sellers' profit above the competitive level. The more effectively the cartel suppresses competition, the closer the cartel's profit will be to the monopoly level.

A seller cartel restrains sales to raise the market price above the competitive level. The higher the price, however, the more attractive it will be for an individual seller to sell more than its quota. To the extent that any one seller exceeds its quota, the quantity supplied will increase and the market price will fall. So, to be effective, a cartel must have some way to compel each participant to abide by its quota.

Further, if a cartel succeeds in raising the price above the competitive level, it will attract new sellers to enter the market. Hence, another issue for a cartel is how to keep out new entrants. Therefore, the key to an effective cartel, or more generally, effective restriction of competition, is enforcement against existing sellers exceeding their quotas and against the entry of new competitors.

Enforcement

The laws of most developed countries seek to encourage competition and typically do not allow cartels except for specific exemptions. Cartels that are not legal must rely on private enforcement. Generally, the effectiveness of private enforcement depends on several factors. One factor is the *number of sellers* in the market. Enforcement is easier when there are fewer sellers to be monitored. So, a cartel will be more effective in an industry with relatively few sellers than in a fragmented industry.

Another factor in the effectiveness of a cartel is the relation of *industry capacity* to market demand. If all sellers are operating near capacity, then it will be difficult for them to expand; hence, there will be little incentive to exceed the specified quotas. By contrast, a seller with substantial excess capacity will have more incentive to exceed its quota.

A third factor is the extent of *sunk costs*. In the short run, competitive sellers are willing to operate so long as the price covers avoidable cost. Sellers with significant sunk costs will be relatively more willing to cut price and exceed their quotas.

A fourth factor that influences the effectiveness of a cartel is the extent of *barriers to entry and exit*. Recall from chapter 8 that, in a perfectly contestable market, sellers can enter and exit at no cost. Suppose that all the sellers in a perfectly contestable market form a cartel. Despite their monopoly, they cannot raise the price above the long-run average cost, because that would draw new suppliers into the market, which would drive the market price back down.

Finally, the *nature of the product* also influences the effectiveness of a cartel. If the product is homogeneous, then each individual seller faces a relatively elastic demand, so it can easily sell more than its quota. On the other hand, if the product is homogeneous, it is also easier for the cartel to monitor the various sellers. Frequently, sellers circumvent cartels by attributing increases in sales to items not covered by the cartel agreement. If the product is homogeneous, such subterfuge is no longer possible; hence, it will be easier to enforce the cartel. Accordingly, the nature of the product – homogeneous or heterogeneous – has an ambiguous influence on the effectiveness of a cartel.

Labor Unions

Labor unions are probably the most widespread cartels. Unions organize workers to negotiate with employers over wages and conditions of work. Negotiations in which workers are represented by a union are called *collective bargaining*. Unions are explicit seller cartels: their primary purpose is to gain higher wages and better conditions than workers could obtain through individual negotiation. Developed countries have encouraged workers to form unions, and most have laws that specifically allow workers the right to unionize.

Recall from our earlier analysis that a monopoly restrains production to raise the price and gain larger profit. In the case of a labor union, it must restrain the amount of employment so as to raise wages above the competitive level. Accordingly, to the extent that a union succeeds in raising wages, it must restrict employment. This means that it must exclude some workers from work.

Nonunion workers present a major threat to labor unions. To prevent such competition, a union would ideally like to establish a "closed shop." A factory or other place of employment is a closed shop if the employer commits not to hire nonunion workers. A union with a closed shop has a monopoly over the labor supply. At its most extreme, a closed shop means that the employer must dismiss all nonunion workers and cannot hire nonunion workers in the future.

Another challenge to a labor union is the extent to which the employer can automate the production process or shift production overseas. Automation is the substitution of equipment for labor; moving to an overseas location is the substitution of foreign labor for domestic labor.

Progress Check 11E Recall the five factors that determine the effectiveness of a cartel. How do these apply to a labor union?

⊣ American football: how a cartel controls cheating ⊢

The National Football League (NFL) is the most successful sports league in the United States, with revenues of about $6 billion per year and labor costs which have only grown by 9% a year since 1990 (compared with 12–16% annual growth in the other major sports leagues: baseball, basketball, and hockey). This, "one of the world's most effective cartels," can be attributed to a number of structural factors, as well as good management and good luck. Team owners share roughly 70% of their revenues, negotiate television contracts as a single entity, and maintain an effective salary cap, all of which transform the incentives from individual profits to maximizing cartel profits.

The challenge for any cartel is that individual members have incentive to cheat on the cartel. An example is the Cincinnati franchise which was the NFL's fifth most profitable during the 1990s, but which won the fewest number of games. In the NFL's version of cartel cheating, Cincinnati was reported to have skimped on talent scouts and other avoidable costs, and relied on other members of the league to produce revenue.

The NFL limits this problem by allowing individual teams to keep all revenue from a few high-growth segments, such as luxury boxes. Owners have incentives to build new stadiums – 17 of which have been newly constructed or overhauled since 1989. These incentives have also been bolstered by the league leaving at least one major city without a franchise. The threat of teams moving to such cities has been effective in getting cities to provide money and tax breaks for construction of new stadiums. Such incentives provide a counterbalance to incentives by individual teams to free ride on the investments made by other teams.

Source: "In a League of Its Own," *The Economist*, April 29, 2006, pp. 63–4.

Horizontal Integration

Cartels that are illegal must rely on private enforcement to prevent sellers from exceeding their quotas. However, competing sellers can restrain competition in a way that does not raise the difficulties of enforcement. The alternative is for the competing sellers to integrate.

Consider, for instance, a combination of two sellers, each of which has 50% of a market. The combined business will have a monopoly. While it may be illegal for two independent competitors to fix prices between themselves, it is certainly legal for the two parts of the same company to agree on prices. Hence, a combination that creates a monopoly will certainly be able to set price and sales at monopoly levels, subject, of course, to the entry of potential competitors.

Table 11.2 Horizontal integration

Acquirer	Target	Market	Source
AXA	Winterthur	European insurance	a
AT&T	BellSouth	U.S. telecommunications	b
Anheuser-Busch	Harbin Brewery	China beer	c
Bank of America Corporation	FleetBoston Financial	U.S. banking	d
Granada	Carlton	U.K. television broadcasting	e

Sources
a. "Credit Suisse Group sells Winterthur to AXA", Press Release, Winterthur Group, June 14, 2006.
b. "AT&T, BellSouth to Merge," Press Release, AT&T, March 5, 2006.
c. "Anheuser to Bid $720 million for Harbin," *Reuters*, June 1, 2004.
d. "Shareholders approve Fleet, Bank of America merger," *The Business Review* (Albany), March 17, 2004.
e. "Carlton and Granada plan to merge," Press Release ITV, October 11, 2003.

The combination of two entities, in the same or similar businesses, under a common ownership is called **horizontal integration**. This should be distinguished from **vertical integration**, which describes the combination of the assets for two successive stages of production under a common ownership. Chapter 13 analyzes vertical integration.

The horizontal integration of any two businesses with market power will lead to a reduction in the quantity supplied, and hence raise the market price and increase profits. The increase in the market price will benefit competing sellers as they will enjoy higher profits.

Table 11.2 lists recent examples of horizontal integration in various countries.

> **Horizontal integration** is the combination of two entities, in the same or similar businesses, under a common ownership.

> **Vertical integration** is the combination of the assets for two successive stages of production, under a common ownership.

> **Progress Check 11F** Explain the difference between horizontal and vertical integration.

U.S. cellular industry mergers: what can consumers expect?

The Cingular–AT&T Wireless, and Sprint–Nextel mergers have increased concentration within the U.S. cellular industry. Prior to the mergers, the market shares of the top five firms in the industry were 23.6%, 13.9%, 13.8%, 10%, and 8.1%. Using end of year 2003 data, the mergers would cause the top four firms' market shares to become 29.4%, 26.3%, 22.3%, and 10.2% respectively.

If we assume that the remaining market shares are all 5% or less, then the pre-mergers HHI was 1,206, while the post-mergers HHI was 2,207. Assuming the market can be characterized by Cournot capacity competition, and an estimated elasticity of demand for cellular service of -1.2, equation (11.5) implies that the pre-merger mark-up of price over marginal cost was 10.05% while the post-merger markup would be 18.39%.

Does this mean that consumers will see higher prices as a result of the merger? Not necessarily. The mergers were touted to lead to significant operating and investment efficiencies. Thus, the industry average cost should be lower as a result of the mergers. So, consumers should expect a higher markup over cost, but potentially lower prices if costs are reduced sufficiently.

Other cellular providers must view the prospect of lower prices with some concern. If the merged companies have sufficiently lower costs so that market prices decrease, then the smaller firms in the market may be squeezed out. If market prices actually rise due to the mergers, then the profits of all firms in the market (large and small alike) may be expected to rise.

Sources: *OECD Communications Outlook 2005*; A. T. Ingraham and J. G. Sidak, "Do States Tax Wireless Services Inefficiently? Evidence on the Price Elasticity of Demand," *Virginia Tax Review* 24, no. 2 (2004), pp. 249–61.

6 Antitrust (Competition) Policy

Antitrust (competition) policy aims to ensure a degree of competition that maximizes social welfare.

Just as managers and investors need to know how a merger would affect industry profits and market prices, government regulators need to evaluate the same effects. In the United States, the Department of Justice and Federal Trade Commission are responsible for *antitrust policy* and enforcement. The purpose of **antitrust policy** (also called **competition policy**) is to ensure a degree of competition that maximizes social welfare.

Competition Laws

Table 11.3 lists the key laws regarding competition in several jurisdictions. In addition to these laws, individual countries within the European Union and individual U.S. states may have their own competition laws. Table 11.3 also lists the agencies responsible for enforcing competition laws in the various jurisdictions.

Generally, the competition laws prohibit the following: (1) competitors from colluding on price and other means; (2) monopolies and monopsonies from abusing market power; and (3) mergers or acquisitions that would create monopolies or monopsonies. In addition, the laws may prohibit or restrict specific anticompetitive business practices such as control over resale prices and exclusive agreements. What exactly is prohibited varies from one jurisdiction to another.

The role of the competition agency is to enforce the competition laws. Enforcement involves two dimensions. One is prosecution against those who violate the laws. The competition agency will prosecute competing sellers or competing buyers that engage in price collusion. The agency is also responsible for prosecuting anyone involved in anticompetitive practices.

The other major dimension of enforcement is to review proposals for mergers and acquisitions. Each jurisdiction has its own set of criteria regarding mergers and acquisitions. The competition agency must ensure that all proposals meet the criteria. The agency may approve a merger or acquisition subject to specific conditions. For instance, the agency may

Table 11.3 Competition laws

Jurisdiction	Law	Enforcement agency
Australia	Trade Practices Act, 1974 Competition Law Reform Act, 1995	Australian Competition and Consumer Commission
Canada	Competition Act, 1976	Bureau of Competition Policy
European Union	Treaty of Rome, 1957, Article 87	European Commission
Japan	Anti-monopoly Act, 1947	Fair Trade Commission
Korea	Monopoly Regulation and Fair Trade Act, 1980	Fair Trade Commission
New Zealand	Commerce Act, 1986	Commerce Commission
Taiwan	Fair Trade Law, 1992	Fair Trade Commission
United Kingdom	Fair Trading Act, 1973 Competition Act, 1998 Enterprise Act, 2002	Office of Fair Trading Competition Commission
United States of America	Sherman Act, 1890 Clayton Act, 1914 Robinson–Patman Act, 1938 Federal Trade Commission Act, 1915 Cellar–Kefauver Amendment, 1950 Hart–Scott Rodino Antitrust Improvement Act, 1976	U.S. Department of Justice Federal Trade Commission

require divestment of particular businesses to mitigate the anticompetitive impact of a merger or acquisition.

In addition to government enforcement, the competition laws may provide for persons affected by anticompetitive behavior to sue in civil court. Under U.S. laws, for instance, plaintiffs in civil actions can recover three times the damages they suffered. Further, civil plaintiffs can petition the courts for an order to stop anticompetitive conduct.

Merger Guidelines

As we have already observed, competing sellers can increase their profits by restraining competition through horizontal integration, also called horizontal merger. Accordingly, antitrust (competition) authorities are concerned about horizontal mergers.

The U.S. Department of Justice has published Guidelines on horizontal mergers. Under the "Merger Guidelines," the Justice Department would not challenge any horizontal merger in an industry whose Herfindahl-Hirschman Index is less than 1,000, or if the industry HHI is between 1,000 and 1,800 and the merger does not raise the HHI by more than 100 points. However, the Department would investigate any merger in an industry whose HHI exceeds 1,800 and that raises the HHI by 50 points or more. Table 11.4 summarizes these merger guidelines.

A crucial step in determining the competitive impacts of a merger is the definition of the market. This is defined as a product or group of products and a geographic area in which a hypothetical profit-maximizing firm could impose a "small but significant and non-transitory"

Table 11.4   Merger Guidelines and the HHI

Post-merger HHI	Increase in HHI		
	0–50	50–100	>100
>1,800	Safe	Suspect	Suspect
1,000–1,800	Safe	Safe	Suspect
0–1,000	Safe	Safe	Safe

increase in price. The relevant market is no bigger than what is necessary to satisfy this test. Thus, in the Las Vegas Strip case above, the relevant market was found to be larger than the Strip itself, and to include other gambling sites like Indian Reservations. The merger of MGM and Mandalay was found to not impede competition within that larger relevant market, although it probably would have been found to be anticompetitive if the market had been defined to be the Strip itself.

Similarly, in the European Union, the European Commission has responsibility for antitrust policy and enforcement. The Commission typically does not investigate mergers in industries whose HHI is less than 1,000.

The value of the HHI is not determinative in merger policy. Antitrust authorities consider the HHI, along with information about cost efficiencies, innovative effects, and other strategic and dynamic factors. The HHI is an explicit factor used to gauge the extent of potential market power associated with a merger. In that, it is firmly rooted in the Cournot model of oligopoly.

According to equation (11.5), increases in industry concentration (as measured by the HHI) are directly related to the extent to which price exceeds marginal cost. The Cournot model, with a number of sellers and differing costs, also predicts that a seller's market share will be inversely related to its marginal cost. A seller with lower marginal cost will have a larger market share.

So, a merger that increases the HHI and potentially decreases the merged firm's costs, has two of the major ingredients relevant to an antitrust investigation. Regulators must trade off the potential for increased efficiencies against the increased market concentration that would result from the merger.

A multinational marriage: Bertelsmann Music Group and Sony Corporation of America

A merger that creates substantial market power within a jurisdiction may require government approval. A merger that spans several jurisdictions may require the approval of all the relevant competition agencies. Each agency will apply its own criteria and specify its own set of conditions for approval.

In December 2003, Bertelsmann Music Group (BMG) and Sony Corporation of America agreed to combine their recorded music businesses in a 50%–50% joint venture, Sony BMG. The venture excluded the two companies' music publishing, physical distribution, and manufacturing operations, and also excluded Sony's Japanese recorded music business.

The formation of the joint venture reduced the number of major recorded music businesses world wide from five to four. With annual sales of $5 billion, Sony BMG would command 30% of the international market, overtaking the previous market share leader, Universal Music, with 26%.

BMG and Sony sought approval from competition authorities in Australia, the European Union, and the United States. The merger was opposed as being anti-competitive by Apple Incorporated's ITunes online music store, Britain's EMI Group, a group of independent European recording studios, and others.

Despite the objections, the various authorities approved the merger without conditions – the European Commission on July 21, 2004, the U.S. Federal Trade Commission on July 28, and the Australian Competition and Consumer Commission on August 5. The European Court of First Instance recently reversed the European decision and it is now pending appeal.

Sources: "CG Wins EU Antitrust Approval from Sony BMG Merger," Cleary, Gottlieb, Steen & Hamilton, Press Release, July 21, 2004; "FTC Approves Sony–BMG," *Washington Post*, July 29, 2004; "ACCC to Not Intervene in Proposed Merger of BMG and Sony Music," Australian Competition and Consumer Commission, Press Release, August 5, 2004.

Progress Check 11G List some reasons why mergers in highly concentrated industries may not necessarily harm consumers.

Future U.S. air travel: fewer major airlines *and* lower prices?

The air travel industry in the U.S. has witnessed tremendous upheaval. Terrorism, SARS, rising fuel prices, low-cost competition, and bankruptcies have all contributed to uncertainty about its future. The industry is not as concentrated as many others: the HHI in 2001 was 1,180 based on the top 20 airlines. The top 6 airlines alone, however, accounted for an HHI of 1,130. Further consolidation among the major carriers is widely anticipated.

One recent study examined several potential evolutions for the industry structure. They posit that the 6 major airlines will consolidate into 3 or 4. Two scenarios they investigate are one with significant competition coming from low-cost entrants, and one without such competitive entry. They point out that 75% of the current low-fare passengers travel on a single airline, Southwest Airlines. Other low-fare carriers have been far less successful, often exiting the market due to intense price competition from dominant major airlines.

They also point out that 85% of tickets are for leisure travel, and cite an elasticity estimate of −2.4 for such travel. The 15% that is business travel, have an estimated elasticity of −0.1, but has become more elastic over time (due, among other things, to substitution towards videoconferencing and leisure fares).

Future fare levels, in their view, will depend largely on the viability of new low-fare entrants into a consolidating oligopoly. Low fare carriers are particularly important since they can break even when carrying a 60% load, while the larger carriers require load factors of 90% in order to break even. Antitrust protection of new entrants is potentially needed, according to the authors, against selective price pressure from incumbents – selective since new entrants are likely to enter a relatively small number of air markets at one time.

Source: R. M. Rubin and J. N. Joy, "Where are the Airlines Headed? Implications of Airline Industry Structure and Change for Consumers," *Journal of Consumer Affairs* 39, no. 1 (2005), pp. 215–28.

7 Summary

Prices are strategic complements. In an oligopoly, where sellers compete on price, if one seller raises or lowers its price, then others will adjust prices in the same direction. Sellers can dampen price competition by differentiating their products.

Production capacities are strategic substitutes. In an oligopoly, where sellers compete on production capacity, if one seller raises or lowers capacity, then, others will adjust capacities in the opposite direction.

If a seller can commit to its production capacity before others, then it will gain a first-mover advantage. If the leader commits to sufficient production capacity, it can even exclude all potential entrants.

Competing sellers can increase profit by restraining competition – either through agreement or horizontal integration. Antitrust (competition) authorities consider the industry Herfindahl–Hirschman Index in deciding whether to investigate mergers.

Key Concepts

Bertrand model
Hotelling model
best response function
strategic complements
Cournot model
residual demand curve
strategic substitutes

Herfindahl–Hirschman Index (HHI)
limit pricing
Stackelberg model
cartel
horizontal integration
vertical integration
antitrust (competition) policy

Further Reading

R. Preston McAfee, *Competitive Solutions* (Princeton, NJ: Princeton University Press, 2002), provides an intuitive approach to competitive strategy. Massimo Motta, *Competition* *Policy* (Cambridge, UK: Cambridge University Press, 2004), presents the economics of competition policy intuitively and using the relevant mathematical models.

Review Questions

1. True or false? Price will equal marginal cost only in a perfectly competitive industry.

2. Consider two markets, each of which is a duopoly where sellers compete on price. In one market, products are more differentiated. In that market, will prices be higher or lower?

3. Consider the Hotelling product differentiation model where the two sellers are located at points 0 and 1. Explain how the equilibrium would change if the second firm was located at $^2/_3$ instead of point 1.

4. If actions are strategic complements, and your competitor raises its level of that action, how should you respond?

5. Explain the meaning of strategic substitutes.

6. Suppose that, in a particular city, a cable television provider merges with the local telephone company. How would this affect the degree of potential competition in the markets for cable television and local telephone service in that city?

7. Explain why limit pricing is not possible in an industry where production involves no fixed cost.

8. Suppose that you can commit to production capacity before other sellers set their capacity. Should you set a relatively larger or smaller capacity as compared to the situation where you commit to capacity simultaneously with other sellers?

9. What are the five factors that influence the effectiveness of a cartel?

10. Is a cartel easier or more difficult to enforce in a market with less heterogeneous products as compared with a market with more heterogeneous products?

11. Calculate the HHI in an industry with just two sellers: (a) Where each has a market share of 50%; and (b) Where one seller has a market share of 75%.

12. In an industry with a HHI of 1,000, what is the market share of the largest possible seller?

13. Suppose an industry is comprised of three equal-sized competitors and a market demand elasticity of −2. Calculate the HHI and the Cournot equilibrium markup of price over marginal cost.

14. Who is responsible for antitrust policy and enforcement in the United States?

15. What are the "Merger Guidelines"?

Discussion Questions

1. As an analyst of the media industry, consider the extent to which you would apply the Hotelling model of oligopoly to competition between newspapers in any city that are differentiated by:
   (a) the degree of local, national, and international news coverage;
   (b) political positioning – liberal vis-à-vis conservative;
   (c) timeliness of sports news;
   (d) layout – color vis-à-vis black-and-white.

2. Major U.S. carriers including American and United Airlines operate on a hub-and-spoke system, offering many frequent connections through their respective hubs. Travelers may prefer one airline to another depending on which hub is more convenient.
   (a) Suppose that American Airlines were to cut fares on flights to and from its hub at Dallas–Fort Worth Airport. Should United raise or reduce fares at that airport?
   (b) Compare competition between American and United Airlines at Chicago's O'Hare International Airport, which is a hub for both airlines, and at Dallas–Fort Worth Airport, which is a hub only for American Airlines. At which hub would price competition be more intense?

(c)   Suppose that the strength of traveler preferences over alternative hubs were to diminish. How should airlines adjust their prices?

3.   In the wake of expanding demand for their cars, Japanese manufacturers Toyota and Honda have expanded production at existing factories and established new plants in North America. In June 2006, Honda announced that it would build a new $550 million factory, creating 2,000 jobs, at Greensburg, Indiana. Meanwhile, U.S. manufacturers General Motors and Ford have faced falling demand and offered incentives for workers to quit, so that they could reduce production capacity.

(a)   If General Motors increases incentives (price discounts), how should Ford adjust prices in the short run?

(b)   Use the Cournot model to relate the expansion of capacity by Toyota and Honda to the contraction in capacity by Ford and General Motors.

(c)   Suppose that Toyota exercises capacity leadership. How would that affect your explanation in (b)?

4.   The Delhi Noida Direct Flyway is a commercial business that competes with two public bridges that do not charge any toll. All three service traffic across the Yamuna river to India's capital, New Delhi. The public bridges are subject to considerable congestion.

(a)   Consider the likely extent of congestion on the Flyway. Is it likely that congestion is as high as on the public bridge? If you were operating the Flyway, how would you select your capacity in terms of the resulting congestion in comparison with the public bridges?

(b)   Consider two strategies facing the competing links: either keep the current capacity, or increase capacity. Describe the equilibrium (if any) in this capacity game. Why would the Flyway operator attempt to influence the government not to reduce congestion on the public bridges?

5.   The hospitality industry on the Las Vegas Strip has undergone systematic consolidation. In 2005, MGM Mirage acquired the Mandalay Resort Group. The enlarged MGM Mirage has 37,180 of the 58,874 large hotel rooms on the Strip, half of the top Strip properties, 44% of the game tables, and 40% of the slot machines.

(a)   Suppose that the enlarged MGM Mirage will reduce fixed costs. Using the Cournot model, how should other hotels adjust their capacity?

(b)   Suppose that the enlarged MGM Mirage will reduce marginal costs of service. Using the Cournot model, how should other hotels adjust their capacity?

(c)   If the enlarged MGM Mirage exercises capacity leadership, how should other hotels adjust their capacity?

6.   Until 2004, there were no direct flights between Australia and India. In the previous year, passenger traffic, totaling 231,000, passed through Bangkok, Singapore, and other intermediate points. Then, Qantas applied to Australia's International Air Services Commission to provide 2,100 seats per week, the maximum number permitted by Australia's air services agreement with India. Low-cost carrier, Backpackers Xpress, also applied to provide the service, contending that it would "promote fairer pricing, better services and overall efficiency." (*Source*: International Air Services Commission, Determination, 2004, IASC, 104.)

(a)   Typically, bilateral air services agreements allow each of the two countries to designate airlines to provide specified service capacity. How do such agreements affect competition between airlines on price and capacity?

(b)   Compare the incentives of Backpackers Xpress vis-à-vis Qantas to set low fares on routes between Australia and India.

(c)   Should the Australian Government have split the rights to the Indian routes between Qantas and Backpackers Xpress?

7. OPEC has 75% of the world's proven reserves of oil and produces 42% of total production. Fifty-seven % of the world's reserves and 32% of the world's production capacity are within the Persian Gulf region. OPEC operates as a cartel, with mutually agreed production quotas. As of May 2006, total OPEC production stood at 33.33 million barrels per day (mbd), with an excess capacity of between 1.3 and 1.8 mbd. Virtually all of the excess capacity was in Saudi Arabia and several OPEC members were exceeding their production quotas. (*Sources*: U.S. Energy Information Administration, *Short Term Energy Outlook*, June 6, 2006; *Energy Economist*, May 12, 2004; *BP Statistical Review of World Energy*, June 2006.)

   (a) Explain why most, if not all, OPEC members would produce more than their production quota.

   (b) In terms of cartel stability, why is it important that all of the short-run excess production capacity is in Saudi Arabia? Examine the equilibrium strategies within OPEC, using game theory.

   (c) Discuss the importance of non-OPEC production to the effectiveness of the cartel. What is the importance of there being no short-run excess capacity outside OPEC? Why might the long-run outlook differ from the short-run outlook? (Official sources define short-run production capacity as capacity that can be brought on line within 30 days.)

8. DRAMs (dynamic random access memories) are used for storage in a wide range of consumer and industrial electronics, including PCs and mobile phones. DRAM manufacturing is a capital-intensive industry. In 2004, five producers – Elpida, Hynix, Infineon, Micron, and Samsung – controlled 80% of the world wide DRAM market, while the next five accounted for about 17%. In the early 2000s, executives of the five companies agreed to fix prices of DRAMs for sale to computer manufacturers. They held meetings to discuss prices, and exchanged information on sales to particular customers.

   (a) Assess the viability of the DRAM cartel in terms of the five factors.

   (b) Why was it important for the five companies to provide sales information to each other?

   (c) Supposing that the conspirators wished to limit the exchange of information, which customers should they select to monitor?

9. Gesamtmetall is the federation of employers and IG Metall is the labor union in Germany's engineering industry. Under the German system of national collective bargaining, Gesamtmetall and IG Metall negotiate pay and working conditions for the entire industry.

   (a) With respect to labor, does Gesamtmetall serve as a buyer cartel or seller cartel? What about IG Metall?

   (b) Consider large employers such as DaimlerChrysler and Robert Bosch. Why might they prefer to negotiate separate deals with their own workers rather than comply with the national collective agreement?

   (c) If all large employers negotiate separate deals, how will this affect the wages and conditions that small companies must offer?

10. In the U.S. cellular industry, the market shares of the various carriers were 23.6%, 13.9%, 13.8%, 10%, 8.1%, 5%, 5%, 5%, 5% before several important industry mergers, and 29.4%, 26.3%, 22.3%, 10.2%, 5%, 5% after the mergers. (There are over 150 cellular providers in the United States, but most have very small shares and can be ignored.) Assume that the market can be characterized by Cournot capacity competition.

   (a) Estimate the pre-merger markup of price over marginal cost.

   (b) Estimate the post-merger markup of price over marginal cost.

   (c) Estimate the percent decrease in industry marginal cost (this would be the average of each firm's marginal cost, weighted by its market share, as used in equation (11.5)) necessary for market prices to be lower after the mergers than before.

Chapter 11
Math Supplement

We will derive the major results of this chapter for the general case of a linear demand curve $Q = a - bp$, and a constant marginal cost, c. To get the numerical results given in the chapter, substitute $a = 300$, $b = 3$, and $c = 30$.

Monopoly

A monopolist facing the linear demand curve will produce a quantity where marginal revenue equals marginal cost. First, rewrite the demand curve for price as a function of quantity (this is called the *inverse demand function*, which permits us to focus on quantity as the decision variable): $p = a/b - 1/bQ$. Then profit is total revenue minus total cost, or

$$P(Q) = (a/b - 1/bQ)Q - cQ = (a/b)Q - (1/b)Q^2 - cQ \tag{11.6}$$

Taking the derivative with respect to Q and setting it equal to zero gives $Q^* = (a - bc)/2$ as the profit maximizing solution.

Capacity Competition with Homogeneous Products: Cournot Model

With two sellers, M and P, the market demand is given by $p = a/b - 1/b(Q_M + Q_P)$. The market price will be the same for the two sellers, and it will be the price at which the quantity demanded equals the total supplied by the two sellers. Each seller has a profit function that depends on the quantity chosen by the other seller. For example,

$$P_M = [a/b - 1/b(Q_M + Q_P)]Q_M - cQ_M. \tag{11.7}$$

Pluto has an analogous profit function, depending on Q_M. Taking the derivative of each profit function with respect to each seller's quantity choice, and setting these equal to zero for a profit maximum, gives the best response functions:

$$Q_M = \frac{(a - bc - Q_P)}{2} \quad \text{and} \quad Q_P = \frac{(a - bc - Q_M)}{2}. \tag{11.8}$$

The Nash equilibrium is solved by simultaneously solving these best response functions (graphed in figure 11.5):

$$Q_M^* = Q_P^* = \frac{a - bc}{3} \tag{11.9}$$

Differing Costs

If the sellers have different marginal costs, c_M and c_P, then the Nash equilibrium is given (following the same procedure as above) by

$$Q_M^* = \frac{[a - b(2c_M - c_P)]}{3} \quad \text{and} \quad Q_P^* = \frac{[a - b(2c_P - c_M)]}{3}. \tag{11.10}$$

Multiple Sellers

Market demand is given by $p = a/b - 1/b\ (\Sigma Q_i)$ where Σ indicates the sum of the quantities produced by all sellers in the market. Each seller has a profit function which depends on the quantities produced by all other sellers. We show the profit function for a typical seller, seller M:

$$\pi_M = \left(\frac{a}{b} - \frac{1}{b}\Sigma Q_i\right)Q_M - c_M Q_M = \frac{a}{b}Q_M - \frac{1}{b}Q_M^2 - \left(\frac{1}{b}\sum_{i \neq M} Q_i\right)Q_M - c_M Q_M. \tag{11.11}$$

To find maximum profit as a function of the other sellers' production levels, we take the derivative with respect to Q_M and set it equal to zero, or

$$\frac{a}{b} - \frac{2}{b}Q_M - \frac{1}{b}\sum_{i \neq M} Q_i - c_M = 0. \tag{11.12}$$

Each seller has an equilibrium output level determined by a condition such as (11.12) with its own marginal cost and based on all other sellers' output levels. Total industry output, Q_T, is the sum of Q_M^* and ΣQ_i (for the other sellers), so (11.12) can be rewritten as

$$\frac{a}{b} - \frac{1}{b}\sum_{i \neq M} Q_i - \frac{1}{b}Q_M - \frac{1}{b}Q_M - c_M = 0 \quad \text{or} \quad \frac{a}{b} - \frac{1}{b}Q_T - c_M = \frac{1}{b}Q_M$$

or $\quad a - Q_T - bc_M = Q_M \tag{11.13}$

In equilibrium, total output must equal industry demand, given by $a - bp^*$. Substituting this into (11.13)

$$a - (a - bp^*) - bc_M = Q_M \quad \text{or} \quad b(p^* - c_M) = Q_M \tag{11.14}$$

We rearrange (11.14) as follows: divide both sides by b, divide both sides by p^*, and multiply the right-hand side of the equation by Q_T/Q_T to give:

$$\frac{p^* - c_M}{p^*} = \frac{Q_T}{bp^*}\frac{Q_M}{Q_T} = -\frac{s_M}{\eta} \tag{11.15}$$

by noticing that $Q_M/Q_T = s_M$, the market share of seller M, and that the elasticity of demand for a linear demand curve is given by $-b(P/Q)$.

To derive equation (11.5) in this chapter, multiply (11.15) by s_M, do this for each seller in the market, and then add all N sellers' equations together. Noting that HHI is the sum of the squared market shares of the sellers in the market, this gives (11.5).

Price Competition with Differentiated Products: Hotelling Model

With duopolists competing in price, but with differentiated products, the two sellers' profit functions are given by

$$P_A = (p_A - c)\frac{p_B - p_A + t}{2t} \quad \text{and} \quad P_B = (p_B - c)\left[1 - \frac{p_B - p_A + t}{2t}\right] \tag{11.16}$$

using (11.2) to define the marginal buyer. To find the best response functions, we take the derivative of these profit functions with respect to each seller's price variable and set these equal to zero. After some rearranging, this gives (11.3).

To find the Nash equilibrium, we solve the two best response functions, (11.3), simultaneously:

$$p_A = \frac{p_B + c + t}{2} = \frac{\dfrac{p_A + c + t}{2} + c + t}{2} = \frac{p_A + c + t + 2c + 2t}{4}.$$

Hence,

$$\frac{3}{4}p_A = \frac{3c + 3t}{4},$$

and, accordingly, $p_A = c + t = p_B$.

Part III

Imperfect Markets

Chapter 12

Externalities

1 Introduction

General Growth is a real estate investment trust listed on the New York Stock Exchange. With consolidated gross leaseable area (GLA) of 115.2 million square feet, it is one of the largest owners of U.S. shopping malls. General Growth manages over 200 regional shopping centers in 44 states. Among the shopping malls that it owns are the Ala Moana Center in Honolulu, the Fashion Show in Las Vegas, the Northridge Fashion Center in Los Angeles, and the Woodbridge Center in Woodbridge, New Jersey.

As of December 2004, General Growth's three largest tenants in terms of consolidated rental income were The Gap, Victoria's Secret, and Express, which contributed 2.79%, 1.47%, and 1.35% respectively. The Gap, Victoria's Secret, and Express are specialty or mall stores. A typical regional shopping center will include a mix of "anchor" and "mall" stores. An anchor is a department store or other large retail store with GLA of at least 30,000 square feet. Anchors account for 59% of General Growth's consolidated GLA. They include 103 stores belonging to Federated and May, 95 belonging to Sears, and 56 belonging to J. C. Penney.

General Growth acknowledges that anchors pay relatively lower rent as compared with mall stores. However, "Anchors have traditionally been a major component of a regional shopping center ... While the market share of traditional department store anchors has been declining, strong anchors continue to play an important role in maintaining customer traffic and making the centers in the Retail Portfolio desirable locations for Mall Store tenants."[1]

In addition to providing store space, General Growth offers an array of services designed to add value to shopping, including comfortable, controlled environments, entertainment, marketing campaigns, test marketing, and market analysis. General claims to "engage all of the consumer's senses" aimed at a variety of demographic segments (including teens, families, and the mature market). One example is General Growth's sponsorship of the Children's Miracle Network, aimed at partnering with local hospitals and other organizations to raise funds and provide health services for needy children.

---

[1] This analysis is based on General Growth Properties, Inc. SEC Form 10-K, year 2004, page 21; www.general-growth.com; and www.cmn.org.

Why do anchor tenants pay lower rent than specialty retailers? Why does General Growth invest in community-based partnerships, and how do entertainment and event promotion contribute to General Growth's bottom line?

These questions may be answered through the concepts of externality and public good.

> An **externality** arises when one party directly conveys a benefit or cost to others.

An **externality** arises when one party directly conveys a benefit or cost to others (not through a market). Subscribing to an instant messaging service provides benefits to other people that subscribe to that service. The benefit to shoppers depends, in part, on the number of stores in the mall. When an anchor store joins a mall, it generates an externality to all other stores by drawing additional shoppers to the mall. Similarly, investments in the aesthetics of the mall enhance the shopping experience and thereby attract more shoppers to spend more time, hence benefiting all stores in that mall.

The externalities among the stores in General Growth malls tie them strongly to General Growth. General Growth's hold on its lessee stores is further strengthened by externalities among participants in the events that it sponsors, as well as partnerships such as the Children's Miracle Network.

> An item is a **public good** if one person's increase in consumption does not reduce the quantity available to others.

An item is a **public good** if one person's increase in consumption does not reduce the quantity available to others. Fireworks are a public good because provision to one individual does not conflict with provision to another within sight – in fact, once fireworks are provided to one individual, they are provided to everyone in the neighborhood.

Public goods can be privately provided, so the term "public" does not signify who must provide such goods. Many public goods are publicly provided because of problems inherent in supplying them profitably. However, as with General Growth, it is feasible for a private seller to provide public goods and capture enough of the benefits to make a profit.

For instance, in a shopping mall, provision of pleasant aesthetics, entertainment, and security for one shopper does not reduce the quantity of these services for other shoppers (provided that the mall is not congested). By providing such services within its malls, General Growth is able to capture their value through the leasing of retail shopping space, which is not a public good (since provision of space to one store *does* reduce the quantity available to others).

This chapter introduces the concept of an externality, characterizes its economically efficient degree, and discusses how that might be achieved through either merger or joint action by the entities involved. We then discuss the particular concepts of network externalities and network effects, which underlie the rapid growth of the Internet. Finally, we introduce the concept of a public good and discuss how it can be efficiently provided.

2   Benchmark

To introduce the concept of an externality, we consider the following example. Luna, a major department store, is opening a 50,000-square-foot store on Main Street. To obtain the site, Luna outbid several other major chains and raised the general level of rents along Main Street. The increase in rents affects other stores in the area, but this increase is not an externality because it passes through the real estate market.

Luna's new store affects other retailers in another way. Specialty retailers sell smaller ranges of products, for instance, casual wear, flowers, or shoes. Luna's new store will draw more shoppers to Main Street and, hence, generate more business for nearby specialty retailers. There is no market through which specialty retailers pay Luna for the additional business, however. Accordingly, the additional business is an externality from Luna to the specialty retailers.

Alternatively, Luna's new store may take customers away from other department stores on Main Street. The cut in business does not pass through any market; hence, it is an externality from Luna to other department stores.

Externalities can be positive or negative. A **positive externality** arises when one party directly conveys a benefit to others. The additional business that Luna generates for specialty retailers is a positive externality. By contrast, a **negative externality** arises when one party directly imposes a cost on others. The business that Luna's new store takes away from other department stores along Main Street is a negative externality.

> A **positive externality** arises when one party directly conveys a benefit to others.

As the Luna example suggests, there are significant positive externalities in real estate. In Britain, leading banks, insurers, and other financial institutions congregate in the one square mile City of London to benefit from positive externalities among themselves. The same is true in many other countries: financial institutions and associated professionals such as lawyers and accountants tend to cluster in the same area.

> A **negative externality** arises when one party directly imposes a cost on others.

Construction of transportation facilities provides another example of externalities in real estate. Whenever the government builds a mass transportation system, it generates externalities for the owners of nearby property. By improving access, a subway will raise the value of commercial and residential property along the line.

Positive Externalities

By definition, an externality conveys a benefit or cost directly rather than through a market. So, in deciding on the levels of externalities, the source considers only the benefits and costs to itself, while ignoring the benefits and costs to others.

In the case of Luna's investment in its new Main Street store, Luna will consider its own benefit and cost and ignore the benefits and costs to other stores. Let us assume that Luna aims to maximize the profit from its investment. Our analysis will be easier if we segregate the cost of sales from the cost of the investment in the following way. Luna's profit is the difference between its benefit (revenues less the cost of sales) and the cost of the investment. To maximize profit, Luna should invest up to the point that the marginal benefit from an additional dollar in investment equals the marginal cost.

At this level of investment, however, Luna may be ignoring opportunities for additional profit from positive externalities. To understand this point, let us change our earlier setting. Suppose now that the Luna department store belongs to Group Luna and the group also owns a florist shop and a shoe store already on Main Street. Then, when deciding on the level of its investment, the group will consider the benefits and the costs to all of its stores.

The total benefit from Luna's investment is the sum of the benefits to every store in the group, including the new store. The group's marginal benefit from investment in the new store is the increase in benefit to the group resulting from an additional dollar of investment in the new store. The additional dollar of investment will generate benefits for all the stores. Accordingly, the group's marginal benefit is the sum of the individual marginal benefits to each of the stores.

In figure 12.1, we illustrate the marginal benefits from investment in the new store for the new store and the two other stores. Note that each store may receive a different marginal

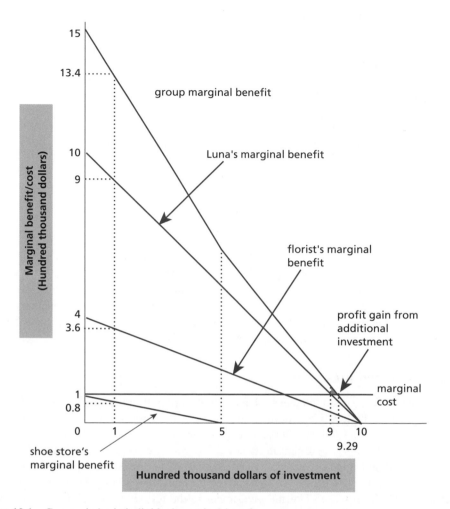

Figure 12.1 Group vis-à-vis individual marginal benefit
The group's marginal benefit is the vertical sum of the individual marginal benefits. At every quantity of
investment, we add the corresponding heights on each of the individual marginal benefit curves. The group
maximizes profit at an investment of $929,000, where the group marginal benefit equals the marginal cost.
If Luna considers only the benefit and the cost for itself, it would invest only $900,000. By increasing its
investment to $929,000, the group could gain the shaded area in additional profit.

benefit. The stronger the positive externality, the higher the recipient's marginal benefit curve
will be.

Graphically, the group's marginal benefit is the *vertical sum* of the individual marginal
benefits. A vertical sum means that, at every quantity of investment, we add the corresponding
heights on each of the individual marginal benefit curves. For instance, referring to figure
12.1, if Luna invests $100,000, the florist's marginal benefit is $360,000, the shoe store's
marginal benefit is $80,000, and Luna's own marginal benefit is $900,000. Hence, the sum
of the marginal benefits is $1,340,000, which marks the corresponding point on the group
marginal benefit curve.

In figure 12.1, we also draw the marginal cost of investment in the new store. If Luna
considers only the benefit and the cost for the new store, it would maximize profit where

the store's marginal benefit equals the marginal cost, which is at an investment of $900,000. This, however, ignores the positive externalities. If Luna considers the benefits and the costs for the entire group, then it would maximize profit at the level of investment where the group marginal benefit equals the marginal cost. Referring to figure 12.1, the profit-maximizing investment would be $929,000.

As this example shows, when the source of a positive externality considers only the benefit and the cost for itself, it overlooks an opportunity for additional profit. Referring to figure 12.1, by increasing its investment from $900,000 to $929,000, the group can gain the shaded area in additional profit.

***

Progress Check 12A Suppose that Luna's investment benefits only the shoe store and does not benefit the florist. Revise figure 12.1 to show the investment that would maximize group profit.

***

⊣ Externalities in talent: Silicon Valley ⊢

There is an exceptional concentration of computer, electronics, and related businesses in the peninsula between the San Francisco Bay and the Pacific Ocean. The area, aptly nicknamed *Silicon Valley*, is home to high-technology leaders such as Apple Computer, Hewlett-Packard, Intel, and Sun Microsystems.

Two institutions, Stanford University and the Xerox Palo Alto Research Center (PARC), played key roles in fostering the development of Silicon Valley. Basic and applied research at the two institutions has provided the foundation for many successful high-tech products.

A local area network links separate personal computers over short distances. Robert Metcalfe and David Boggs invented the Ethernet local area network at the Xerox PARC. In 1979, Metcalfe left the Xerox PARC to found 3Com (the three "coms" being computer, communication, and compatibility), which commercialized the Ethernet technology. 3Com has since grown to become the a leading manufacturer of data networking systems.

Stanford University staff and students personally established several of the most successful Silicon Valley businesses. Routers are devices that link computer networks that use different protocols. Sandy Lerner and Len Bosack started Cisco Systems while working at Stanford University. In 1986, they left the university to run Cisco full time. The company has grown to become the world's largest manufacturer of routers and other data-networking systems.

In April 1994, two graduate students in Stanford's electrical engineering department, David Filo and Jerry Yang, started an index to the Internet. Their hobby quickly grew into Yahoo!, one of the most popular guides to the Internet's multimedia World Wide Web.

More recently, two Stanford computer science graduate students, Sergey Brin and Lawrence Page, launched Google, which is fast becoming the premier search engine for the Web.

Sources: Douglas K. Smith and Robert C. Alexander, *Fumbling the Future* (New York: William Morrow, 1988), pp. 95–103; letter from Robert Metcalfe (July 16, 1996); letter from Cisco Systems (May 23, 1996); world wide web pages www.cisco.com and www.3com.com (May 22, 1996), www.yahoo.com (June 25, 1996).

Negative Externalities

Having considered positive externalities, we next consider how to take account of negative externalities. Recall that Luna's new store will take away business from other Main Street department stores. Changing our earlier setting, let us now suppose that the Group Luna owns two department stores, the Luna as well as the existing Sol store on Main Street, but does not own any specialty retailers. When deciding on its investment in the new Luna store, the group should consider the benefits and the costs to both department stores.

The total cost of investment in the new Luna store is the sum of the costs to both stores in the group. Accordingly, the group's marginal cost of investment in the new store is the increase in cost to the group resulting from an additional dollar of investment in the new store. This group marginal cost is the sum of the individual marginal costs for each store. For the new store, the marginal cost of an additional dollar of investment is just $1. For the existing store, the marginal cost is the reduction in profit arising from an additional dollar of investment in the new store.

In figure 12.2, we illustrate the marginal costs from investment in the new store for the new store itself and the existing store. Graphically, the group's marginal cost is the vertical sum of the individual marginal costs. A vertical sum means that, at every quantity

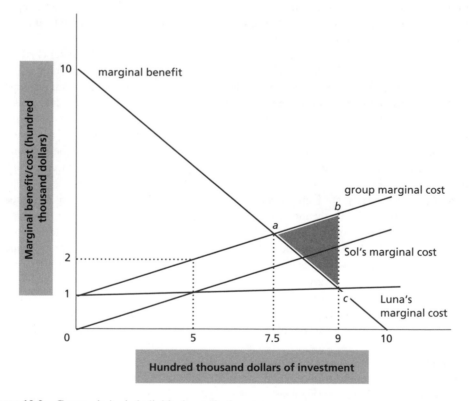

Figure 12.2   Group vis-à-vis individual marginal cost
The group's marginal cost is the vertical sum of the individual marginal costs. The group maximizes profit at an investment of $750,000, where the group marginal benefit equals the marginal cost. If Luna considers only the benefit and the cost for itself, it would invest $900,000. By reducing its investment to $750,000, the group could gain the shaded area *abc* in additional profit.

of investment, we add the corresponding heights on each of the individual marginal cost curves. For instance, at an investment of $500,000, the marginal cost for the Luna store is $100,000, while the marginal cost for the Sol store is $100,000; hence, the group marginal cost is $200,000.

In figure 12.2, we also draw the marginal benefit from investment in the new store. If Luna considers only the benefit and the cost for the new store, it would maximize profit where the marginal benefit equals Luna's marginal cost, which is at an investment of $900,000. If, however, Luna considers the benefits and the costs for the entire group, then it would maximize profit at the level of investment where the group marginal benefit equals the group marginal cost. Referring to figure 12.2, the profit-maximizing investment is $750,000.

As this example shows, when the source of a negative externality considers only the benefit and the cost for itself, its profit will be less than the maximum possible. By figure 12.2, if the group reduced its investment from $900,000 to $750,000, it could increase its profit by the shaded area *abc*.

Progress Check 12B Referring to figure 12.2, suppose that the negative externality to the Sol store is stronger. How will this affect (i) Sol's marginal cost curve and (ii) the level of investment that maximizes the group profit?

Externalities in General

We have separately discussed positive and negative externalities. Generally, if a group has a member that generates positive as well as negative externalities, then the group maximizes profit at the following benchmark: where the sum of the marginal benefits equals the sum of the marginal costs.

We say that an **externality is resolved** when the sum of the marginal benefits equals the sum of the marginal costs. Recall from chapter 6 that this benchmark also defines the economically efficient level of the activity generating the externalities. Hence, we can also say that the externality is resolved at the economically efficient level.

> An **externality is resolved** when the sum of the marginal benefits equals the sum of the marginal costs.

In developing the benchmark, we took the viewpoint of a group that included the source as well as recipients of the externalities. We next show that the same benchmark applies when the source is separate from the recipients.

Consider a positive externality and suppose that the sum of its marginal benefits exceeds the marginal cost. Then, if the source increases the externality, the marginal benefits will be greater than the marginal cost; hence, there will be a net benefit. This is a profit opportunity for an intermediary, which could collect fees from the recipients to pay the source to increase the externality. The set of transactions is feasible since the intermediary could set the fee to each recipient at less than its marginal benefit and the payment to the source to cover its marginal cost.

There will be an opportunity for such a profit whenever the sum of marginal benefits exceeds the marginal cost. The intermediary should pay the source to increase the externality up to the point where the sum of the marginal benefits equals the marginal cost, which defines the economically efficient level of the activity generating the positive externality. At that point, the externality is resolved.

A similar argument applies to negative externalities: an intermediary should pay the source to reduce the activity generating the externality to the economically efficient level. At that point, the intermediary maximizes profit.

Accordingly, the benchmark of economic efficiency applies whether the source of the externality is separate or integrated with the recipients. This benchmark applies whether the externalities can be directly measured in monetary terms or not. To take account of non-monetary externalities, we require only that the recipients be able to measure the benefits and costs in terms of money. We suppose that, rather than maximizing profit, these recipients aim to maximize their net benefit, which is the benefit less the cost. Where all externalities are in monetary form, the net benefit simplifies to the profit.

Academic externalities: a free campus

In May 1995, the regents of the University of California met to choose the location for its proposed San Joaquin campus, to be the tenth branch of the university. The regents considered two alternatives: a 2,000-acre site at Lake Yosemite offered free of charge by the Virginia Smith Trust and another site near the city of Fresno that would be purchased. Swayed in part by the free land, the regents voted for Lake Yosemite.

The Virginia Smith Trust owned 7,000 acres of land by Lake Yosemite. When the trust made the offer to the university, its land was used to graze cattle. The trust projected that, with establishment of the new campus, it could earn $350 million from development of the remaining 5,000 acres of real estate.

The positive externalities generated by the new campus were sufficient to justify the "gift" of 2,000 acres to the University of California. UC Merced opened on September 5, 2005 and is expected to eventually grow to 25,000 students.

Source: "Lake Yosemite Selected for Proposed Campus," *UC Focus* (Office of the President, University of California), 9, no. 5 (June–July 1995), pp. 1 and 7.

---

3   Resolving Externalities

We have identified the benchmark for an externality as the economically efficient level. In chapter 6, we showed that, in a perfectly competitive market, the invisible hand ensures economic efficiency. By definition, however, externalities do not pass through markets. Hence, externalities will be resolved only through deliberate action. We now turn to consider practical ways to resolve externalities.

Merger

In the case of Luna's new store, we saw that, when a single entity owns all the stores along Main Street, it considers all the benefits and costs of its investments; hence, it will invest up to the economically efficient level. This suggests how to resolve an externality: the source and the recipient of the externality could merge into a single entity.

A merger can be effected in one of three ways. Either the recipient of the externality acquires the source, the source of the externality acquires the recipient, or a third party acquires both the source and the recipient. In the case of Luna's new store, either the existing Main Street retailers should acquire Luna, Luna should buy all the retailers presently on Main Street, or Luna and the existing retailers should all sell out to a third party.

From the viewpoint of resolving externalities, it does not matter who buys whom. Once the source and the recipient of the externality are combined, the single entity will take account of all the benefits and the costs of its investments and will invest at the economically efficient level.

Joint Action

We have seen how the affected parties can resolve externalities through merger. Merger, however, is not always feasible. For instance, suppose that Luna's new department store were to impose a negative externality on a nearby church. A merger would mean combining the church and the Luna store under a common ownership. Such a combination may not be feasible.

An alternative approach to resolving an externality is joint action. To resolve an externality through joint action, the source and the recipient of the externality must negotiate and agree on how to resolve the externality. Joint action is a feasible way to resolve the negative externality from Luna's new store to the church. For instance, the church may offer Luna the use of its parking area if Luna agrees not to open on Sunday mornings. Such a deal is a way of jointly resolving the negative externality.

Joint action is also a way by which the positive externalities from Luna to the specialty retailers can be resolved. Since Luna's investment increases the revenues of the florist and the shoe store, the two specialty retailers would like Luna to increase its investment.

Suppose that the florist pays Luna a contribution equal to its marginal benefit from Luna's investment and that the shoe store does likewise. Then Luna's total benefit will be the benefit from its own store plus the contributions from the two specialty retailers. Luna's profit will be its total benefit less the cost of the investment. Therefore, it will maximize profit by choosing the level of investment where the sum of the marginal benefits equals the marginal cost. Referring to figure 12.1, that level of investment is $929,000. Accordingly, joint action can give Luna sufficient incentive to look beyond its own benefits and costs and resolve its positive externalities.

With joint action, the source and the recipient of the externality remain separate entities. Joint action to resolve an externality requires two steps. First, the affected parties must agree on how to resolve the externality. This step involves collecting information about the benefits and costs to the various parties, and then planning the level of the activity that generates the externality. The second step is to enforce compliance with the agreed plan. Enforcement includes monitoring the source of the externality and applying incentives to ensure that the source complies with the planned level of the externality-generating activity.

Cooperative advertising: resolving "Intel Inside"

Hewlett Packard (HP) is one of the world's leading manufacturers of IBM-compatible personal computers. Intel is the dominant manufacturer of IBM-compatible microprocessors. HP spends millions of dollars each year on advertising. Many of these advertisements feature "Intel Inside," the mark that a computer is powered by an Intel microprocessor. By publicizing Intel, these advertisements boost the demand for the products of other manufacturers using Intel microprocessors.

From Intel's standpoint, the economically efficient amount of "Intel Inside" advertising by HP balances the marginal benefit to all manufacturers with the marginal cost to HP. In planning its advertising, however, HP might ignore the positive externalities to other manufacturers.

Intel resolves these externalities through cooperative advertising: it shares the cost of advertising by personal computer makers that features "Intel Inside." This subsidy encourages manufacturers of personal computers to invest the appropriate amount of resources in advertising Intel microprocessors.

Source: "Intel Inside®: Anatomy of a Brand Campaign," www.intel.com/pressroom/intel_inside.htm.

Free Rider Problem

Externalities can be resolved through merger or joint action. There are, however, some hurdles in the way. To illustrate, suppose that Luna and the two specialty retailers aim to resolve the externalities through joint action. Then the three parties must agree on the marginal benefit that Luna's investment will generate for the florist. This will determine the florist's contribution to Luna's investment.

To reduce its contribution, the florist may claim that its marginal benefit from Luna's investment is low. Since the florist will probably have better information than the other two parties about its own marginal benefit, it may be difficult for the other two parties to know whether the florist is bluffing. The result may be that the parties cannot agree and the positive externality would not be resolved.

Further, it is difficult for Luna to exclude the florist from receiving the positive externality. Hence, the florist can still benefit from Luna's investments even if it contributes less than its marginal benefit. When the florist considers its contribution from a purely selfish viewpoint, it will maximize its own profit by underreporting its marginal benefit.

> A **free rider** contributes less than its marginal benefit to the resolution of an externality.

In this example, the florist is taking a free ride on Luna's investment. Generally, a **free rider** contributes less than its marginal benefit to resolution of the externality. In the extreme, the free rider avoids all contribution. The incentive to take a free ride arises whenever it is costly to exclude particular individuals from receiving an externality.

The incentive to take a free ride is stronger when the externality affects many recipients and these recipients differ widely in their marginal benefits. When an externality affects many recipients, the contribution of any particular recipient is relatively small. Hence, the other recipients may resolve the externality even if some recipients take a free ride. When the recipients of the externality differ widely in their marginal benefits, there is relatively more scope for an individual recipient to claim a low marginal benefit.

> **Progress Check 12C** What are the hurdles to resolving an externality by joint action?

⊣ Mickey Mouse externalities ⊢

The Walt Disney Company owns and manages Disneyland in Anaheim, California. This theme park is surrounded by hundreds of businesses, including motels, restaurants, souvenir stores, and transportation services. Disneyland visitors are the major source of income for these neighboring businesses.

In the late 1980s, Disney decided to embark on a large program of investments to upgrade Disneyland. Before commencing construction, the company secretly bought much of the property around the theme park, including the Disneyland Hotel for $200 million. By purchasing the surrounding property, Disney Company ensured that it would capture relatively more of the benefits from new attractions. Consequently, the company had a greater incentive to make the economically efficient level of investment in new attractions at the theme park.

Disney applied the same principle when developing its theme park on Lantau Island, Hong Kong. As a condition of the investment, the Hong Kong government awarded Disney a 20-year option to purchase an adjoining site. The government further agreed to restrict the use of the land, air, and sea in the vicinity. Nearby buildings would be limited in height, aircraft would be banned from flying over the park, and ships would be excluded from the seafront.

Hong Kong Tourism Commissioner Mike Rowse explained, "It is an essential element of a Disney theme park that people outside the park not be able to see in, and those inside not be able to see the 'real world' outside."

Sources: Gary Wilson, Chief Financial Officer, Disney Company, speech at the Anderson School, UCLA, March 15, 1989; "Disney Given Controls over Area around Park," *South China Morning Post*, November 20, 1999.

4 Network Effects and Externalities

As we explained in chapter 1, a **network effect** arises when a benefit or cost depends on the total number of other users. The adjective *network* emphasizes that the benefit or cost is generated by the entire network of users. To illustrate a network effect, consider telephone service. The benefit that one subscriber derives from telephone service definitely depends on the total number of other subscribers. Hence, connections to telephone service generate network effects.

> A **network effect** arises when a benefit or cost depends on the total number of other users.

In chapter 2, we discussed the factors – including price, buyer income, and prices of related products – that affect the marginal benefit and demand for an item. The marginal benefit and demand for an item that exhibits network effects depends on one additional factor, which is the total number of other users. For instance, when another person subscribes to a telephone service, the marginal benefit and demand curves for all other users will shift up.

Related to the concept of a network effect is the concept of *network externality*. To understand the meaning of a network externality, suppose that Joy is the only user connected to the Internet. To whom could she send electronic mail? When Joy is the only subscriber, Internet electronic mail service is worthless.

Suppose, by contrast, that there are 500 million other users on the Internet. Then, Joy could use electronic mail to communicate with 500 million other persons. The benefit of Internet electronic mail to Joy depends on the total number of other users, regardless of how close or distant they may be.

A **network externality** arises when a benefit or cost directly conveyed to others depends on the total number of other users. Accordingly, a network externality is a network effect that is conveyed *directly*, and not through a market. As with externalities in general, the benchmark for an activity that exhibits network externalities is economic efficiency: the sum of marginal benefits equals the sum of marginal costs.

> A **network externality** arises when a benefit or cost directly conveyed to others depends on the total number of other users.

The presence of network effects or network externalities implies that the character of demand and competition will differ from that in conventional supply–demand markets in several important ways.

Progress Check 12D Which of the following are network externalities?

(a) an increase in the number of people speaking French benefits existing French speakers;

(b) one restaurant's advertising attracts more customers to neighboring restaurants.

Critical Mass

> The **critical mass** is the number of users at which the quantity demanded becomes positive.

The first important way in which markets with network effects differ from conventional markets is that the demand is zero unless the number of users exceeds critical mass. The **critical mass** is the number of users at which the quantity demanded becomes positive. For instance, in the case of the Internet, there is some number of users below which the quantity demanded will be zero. Supposing that the number is 10,000, then the critical mass for the Internet is 10,000 users. This means that there will be a positive demand for the Internet only when the price or other factors are sufficient to attract 10,000 users.

> The **installed base** is the quantity of the complementary hardware in service.

The demand for some items depends on the presence of complementary hardware. For instance, the demand for Internet access depends on the number of personal computers, personal digital assistants, and other devices that provide Internet access. Similarly, the demand for telephone service depends on the number of telephones. In these cases, the **installed base** is the quantity of the complementary hardware in service.

Suppose that each user needs one separate unit of the complementary hardware. Then an alternative way to measure the number of users is the size of the installed base. Further, an alternative specification of the critical mass is in terms of the installed base of the complementary hardware. In our earlier hypothetical example of Internet access, the critical mass was 10,000 users. Then, equivalently, the critical mass is an installed base of 10,000 units of personal computers, personal digital assistants, and other access devices.

Expectations

The second important feature of markets with network effects is the role of user expectations. Chapter 10 introduced the concept of Nash equilibrium for games in strategic form. We showed that, in games of coordination, there might be more than one equilibrium.

In the example of the adoption of Internet access, there are two possible equilibria. In the good equilibrium, every potential Internet user expects the others to subscribe to Internet access, and accordingly subscribes. Then demand exceeds critical mass and the service succeeds as expected. By contrast, in the bad equilibrium, potential users are pessimistic. Each person expects fewer than 10,000 others to subscribe, and so, does not subscribe. Then, indeed, demand fails to reach critical mass and the service flops as expected.

The role of expectations is a major difference between markets with network effects and conventional markets. How can the expectations of potential users be influenced? One way is through commitments that effectively guarantee or provide a strong assurance of critical mass. This explains why sellers of items generating network effects often give away large quantities in order to establish a sufficient installed base.

Another way of influencing expectations is hype. For instance, a grand launch attended by dignitaries and movie stars may generate the self-fulfilling prophecy that demand for the item will attain critical mass.

Tipping

The third important feature of markets with network effects concerns the character of competition. The demand in markets with network effects is extremely sensitive to small differences among competitors. Suppose there are several competing products, all of whose demand is close to critical mass. Then, a small increase in the user base of one product can *tip* the market demand toward that product. **Tipping** is the tendency for the market demand to shift toward a product that has gained a small initial lead.

> **Tipping** is the tendency for the market demand to shift toward a product that has gained a small initial lead.

To illustrate the phenomenon of tipping, suppose that there are two global computer networks, the Internet and the Total-Net, each with just 10,000 users. The two networks are incompatible; hence, Internet subscribers cannot communicate with Total-Net subscribers and vice versa.

Now, suppose that 10 users decide to switch from the Internet to the Total-Net. Then, the Internet will have 9,990 subscribers, while the Total-Net will have 10,010 subscribers. Consider Max, a typical Internet subscriber: with 10 users switching, he can now communicate with only 9,989 other people. Hence, the number of Internet users has dropped below the critical mass. So, Max switches from the Internet to the Total-Net. Every other Internet user also switches. Ultimately, the initial switch by 10 users tips everyone toward the Total-Net.

In a market for competing products that generate network effects, the likelihood of tipping means that one product may dominate the market. If demand for some product just exceeds critical mass, any slight movement in demand away from that product will tip all the users away. By contrast, in a conventional market, several competitors of similar size may continue profitably for a long time. Even if one seller gains an advantage in pricing or product quality, the entire market demand will not tip in its favor.

Price Elasticity

Chapter 3 introduced the concept of (own) price elasticity of demand, which is the percentage by which the quantity demanded changes if the price of the item rises by 1%, holding all other factors unchanged. The presence of network effects affects the price elasticity in different ways depending on whether the market demand has reached critical mass and the relation among competing sellers.

When the market demand is below critical mass, the demand will be zero, and hence extremely price inelastic. Neither price increases nor reductions will affect the demand at all.

The demand will be sensitive to price only when it exceeds critical mass. In this case, if the price rises by 1%, the number of users and quantity demanded will be lower. These reductions will feed back through the network effect to reduce the quantity demanded still further. The network effect tends to amplify the effect of a price increase on the quantity demanded. Similarly, the network effect would amplify the effect of a price reduction. Accordingly, the network effect causes the market demand to be relatively more elastic.

If there are several competing products, all of which have just attained a critical mass of demand, then the market demand could tip in favor of one that gains a small advantage. This means that the individual demand for each product will be extremely price elastic.

Microsoft: got Netscape but not AOL

Personal computer software giant Microsoft was relatively late to appreciate the business potential of the Internet. During this window of opportunity, Netscape unseated Mosaic as the dominant web browser and Sun positioned Java as the programming language of choice for the web.

Importantly, the Netscape browser and Java applications were designed to operate on any computer, regardless of the underlying operating system. With the Netscape–Java combination, key software could be moved away from the desktop to powerful machines called servers providing software through the Internet.

Bill Gates recognized the threat to Microsoft's market power over personal computer software: "A new competitor 'born' on the Internet is Netscape. Their browser is dominant, with 70% usage share, allowing them . . . to commoditize the underlying operating system." Microsoft quickly bundled version 2.0 of its Internet Explorer browser free with the Windows 95 operating system.

Microsoft easily defeated Netscape. The reason is that most World Wide Web content was written in simple hypertext markup language (HTML) that could be read equally well with many browsers including Netscape Navigator and Internet Explorer. As such, there was no strong network effect binding users to a choice of web browser. Netscape users could easily switch to Internet Explorer. By the end of 1997, Netscape's market share of usage had fallen below 40%. By June 2002, Internet Explorer had 95.7% of the browser market.

History may be repeating itself. Internet Explorer's market share has now dropped to 85% and the Mozilla Foundation's Firefox has reached over 10%. Other estimates put IE's share down to 58% of the market, with Gecko-based browsers (including Mozilla Firefox and Netscape) at 37%.

By contrast, the battles over instant messaging (IM) and search engines are more long-term. The network effect among IM subscribers is stronger. AOL's lead can be self-enforcing, since the benefits to potential subscribers may be higher than with competitive IM providers, due to the larger installed base of AOL. Microsoft and Yahoo are attempting to make their IM services interoperable in order to challenge AOL's lead in that market.

The search market is more uncertain. Consumers can easily switch search engines, but enhancements have made this more difficult since users invest in their know-how to conduct more advanced searches and use of ancillary features. Microsoft attempted to buy part of AOL, and offered hundreds of millions of dollars if AOL would dump Google in favor of MSN Search. As a defensive measure, Google recently purchased a 5% stake in AOL.

Sources: "America Online: Pricks and Kicks," *The Economist*, August 14, 1999, pp. 52–3; Positive Support Review, Inc., Press Release, January 8, 1998; *U.S. v. Microsoft: Proposed Findings of Fact*, section VII; "Mozilla Gains on IE," *PC World*, July 9, 2004; "Firefox Passes 10 Percent Market Share," www.arstechnica.com; www.safalra.com; "Google to Buy 5% of AOL for $1 Billion," *Washington Post*, December 17, 2005.

5   Public Goods

Every New Year, millions of people gather to watch fireworks. These displays attract more people than football and baseball games and top bands. Clearly, there is a huge pent-up demand for fireworks. Why don't some entrepreneurs provide this form of entertainment on a commercial basis?

To address this question, we apply the concept of a public good. As explained in the Introduction, an item is a public good if one person's increase in consumption does not reduce the quantity available to others. Equivalently, a public good provides *nonrival* consumption. Consumption is **nonrival** if one person's increase in consumption does not reduce the quantity available to others.

> Consumption is **nonrival** if one person's increase in consumption does not reduce the quantity available to others.

Open-air fireworks are an example of a public good. For instance, if Joy comes to watch a show of open-air fireworks, she does not reduce the quantity available for other people. Hence, open-air fireworks provide nonrival consumption and are a public good.

Another way of understanding nonrival consumption is through the concept of scale economies. Given that open-air fireworks are being provided to one viewer, the marginal cost of providing the same display to additional viewers is nothing. There is an extreme economy of scale in providing a public good: provision involves only a fixed cost and the marginal cost of serving additional consumers or users is zero.

As suggested by the question of why there is little or no commercial provision of open-air fireworks, the provision of public goods is a complicated issue. To lay the foundation for an answer, we first discuss the differences between public and private goods, and then consider the economically efficient provision of a public good.

Rivalness

Public goods lie at one end of a spectrum of rivalness, with *private goods* at the other extreme (figure 12.3). An item is a private good if one person's increase in consumption by some quantity reduces the total available to others by the same quantity. Equivalently, a private good provides **rival** consumption, which means that one person's increase in consumption by some quantity reduces the total available to others by the same quantity.

> Consumption is **rival** if one person's increase in consumption by some quantity reduces the total available to others by the same quantity.

Food and clothing, for instance, are private goods. If Lucas eats a four-ounce frozen yogurt, then there will be four ounces less for other consumers. If Max is wearing a new polo shirt, no one else can wear it at the same time. The professional services of accountants and lawyers are also private goods: if an accountant is attending to one client, then there will be less of her time available for other clients.

Figure 12.3   Rivalness
A private good provides rival consumption. At the other extreme, a public good provides nonrival consumption.

> Consumption is **congestible** if one person's increase in consumption by some quantity reduces the total available to others but by less than that quantity.

Some items are neither public nor private. An example is items that provide **congestible** consumption. This means that one person's increase in consumption by some quantity reduces the total available to others but by less than that quantity. Congestible items are public goods when consumption is low but are private goods when consumption is high.

For instance, entertainment by a juggler is congestible: several people can comfortably watch a juggler, but after some number, additional viewers will get in the way and reduce the quantity of entertainment available to other viewers. The Internet is also congestible. At off-peak times, an increase in usage by one person will not reduce the service to others. At peak times, however, the more users connect to the Internet, the slower will be the service for others.

Space in General Growth's malls is rival – consumption by one store precludes using that space by another store. On the other hand, many of the amenities provided by General Growth (e.g., fountains, entertainers, community sponsorship, etc.) are nonrival among the stores located within the mall. It is the private good of mall space that permits General Growth to capture the benefits of the public goods it provides within its malls.

Progress Check 12E On the spectrum of figure 12.3, mark the following items: (1) Internet access, (2) computer monitor, (3) technique for coronary bypass operation, (4) cardiac (heart) surgeon's services, and (5) bottled oxygen.

Content vis-à-vis Delivery

To understand the degree of rivalness, it is important to distinguish between content and delivery. For instance, television programming can be broadcast in a number of ways: over the air from land-based transmission towers, directly to receivers from orbiting satellites, or by cable.

Regardless of the method of delivery, the content of broadcast television is nonrival. If Nancy switches on her television to watch the evening news, she does not affect the quantity of the evening news available to other people. This is true whether the signal comes over the air or by cable.

The method of delivery, however, may be a public or private good. Delivery by over-the-air transmission is a public good. The same signal can serve any number of television sets within the transmission range. Delivery by cable, however, is a private good. One cable serves only one television set.

Scientific knowledge provides another illustration of the distinction between content and delivery. Consider, for instance, this textbook on managerial economics. The intellectual content of this book is a public good. If one more person understands the principles of managerial economics, she or he does not reduce the quantity available to other people.

On the other hand, the principles of managerial economics are delivered through the medium of a textbook. The textbook is a private good: if one person is using a copy of this book, that copy is unavailable to others, at the same time.

As we shall discuss later in this chapter, the distinction between content and delivery is important for commercial provision of public goods. The basis of commercial provision of many public goods is to deliver them in the format of private goods.

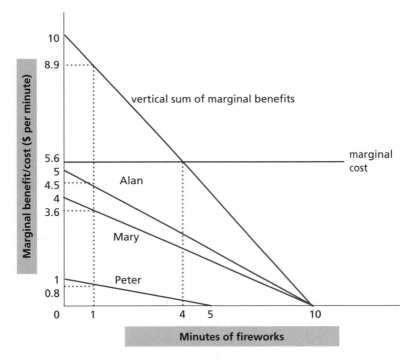

Figure 12.4 Economically efficient provision of public good
At the economically efficient quantity of a public good, the sum of the individual marginal benefits equals the marginal cost. Every individual marginal benefit curve lies below the marginal cost of $5.60; hence, no individual person would be willing to buy even one minute of fireworks. If each individual tries to get a free ride, it might not be possible to provide even one minute of fireworks on a commercial basis.

Economic Efficiency

Previously, we showed that, when an externality is at an economically efficient level, there are no further opportunities to profit from adjusting the activity generating the externality. Let us now show the same for a public good. Suppose that there are three viewers of open-air fireworks – Alan, Mary, and Peter – with marginal benefits as shown in figure 12.4. The figure also shows the marginal cost of open-air fireworks, which we suppose to be a constant $5.60 per minute.

Consider the provision of one minute of fireworks. Since fireworks are a public good, there will be one minute for each of the three viewers. Accordingly, each would be willing to pay her or his marginal benefit for that minute. By figure 12.4, the sum of the marginal benefits to the three viewers is $0.80 + $3.60 + $4.50 = $8.90. The cost of one minute is $5.60, hence there is an opportunity to make a profit by providing one minute of fireworks. This same argument applies for additional quantities up to four minutes.

At four minutes of fireworks, the sum of the individual marginal benefits equals the marginal cost. Can someone make money by increasing provision to five minutes? By figure 12.4, the fifth minute provides an additional benefit to Alan and Mary only. The sum of their marginal benefits is $2.00 + $2.50 = $4.50. Since the cost of each minute is $5.60, providing the fifth minute would result in a loss.

We have shown that opportunities for profit are exhausted at the point where the vertical sum of the individual marginal benefits equals the marginal cost. By the definition in chapter 6, this is the economically efficient quantity of the public good. Accordingly, at the economically efficient quantity, there are no further opportunities to profit from adjusting the provision of the public good.

In figure 12.4, notice that each of the individual marginal benefit curves lies below the marginal cost of $5.60. Hence, no individual person would be willing to buy even one minute of fireworks. The sum of the individual marginal benefit curves, however, lies above the marginal cost curve at quantities of between zero and four minutes. Since a public good provides nonrival consumption, the three persons' willingness to pay is given by the vertical sum of the individual marginal benefit curves. While no single person would buy even one minute of fireworks, they collectively would be willing to pay for four minutes.

Managing congestion: waiting times and the price of gasoline

The pumps at a gasoline station are a congestible facility. At off-peak times, an increase in usage by one driver will not reduce the service to others. At peak times, however, the more drivers are filling up, the slower will be the service for others.

Gasoline stations resolve the congestion through pricing. For many years, at the corner of Le Conte and Gayley Avenues in Westwood, Los Angeles, a Chevron station charged lower prices than the Shell station across the street. A station that sets higher prices will draw fewer customers; hence, it implicitly offers faster service. One estimate shows that, on average, drivers are willing to pay a 1% higher price for a 6% reduction in congestion.

Source: I. P. L. Png and David Reitman, "Service Time Competition," *RAND Journal of Economics* 25, no. 4 (Winter, 1994), pp. 619–34.

---

6   Excludability

Having discussed the nature of public goods and their economically efficient quantity, we are now ready to address the issue of how public goods can actually be provided. Many private goods are provided on a commercial basis. There is a fundamental condition for commercial provision of any product that is easy to overlook. That condition is that, to sell a product, the seller must be able to exclude those who do not pay. The condition is crucial in the commercial provision of public goods.

> Consumption is **excludable** if the provider can exclude particular consumers.

Consumption is **excludable** if the provider can exclude particular consumers. Excludability is a fundamental requirement for commercial provision of any item.

When consumption of an item is not excludable, commercial provision will be difficult. To illustrate the problem, let us suppose that Neptune Entertainment wants to provide one minute of open-air fireworks to Alan, Mary, and Peter. Referring to figure 12.4, Neptune knows that, at that quantity, the individual marginal benefits of Alan, Mary, and Peter are $4.50, $3.60, and $0.80 respectively. If Neptune charges each person a price equal to her or his marginal benefit, then Neptune will collect $8.90 from these three people. Neptune's cost of providing one minute of fireworks is $5.60; hence, it will realize a profit of $3.30.

Peter, however, might reason that if he refuses to pay, while Alan and Mary do pay, then Neptune would collect $4.50 + $3.60 = $8.10, which would be enough to cover the cost of $5.60. Then, Neptune would provide the one minute of fireworks and, since viewing open-air fireworks is not excludable, Peter would enjoy a free show. Alan and Mary, however, might also think in similar ways. If everyone tries to get a free show, Neptune will incur a loss from the fireworks. Hence, in the extreme, the incentive to get a free show prevents the provision of even one minute of fireworks on a commercial basis.

The basic problem is that, whenever consumption of some item is nonexcludable, individual consumers will have an incentive to take a free ride. Free riding will cut into the seller's revenues and, so, reduce the seller's profit and hamper commercial provision of the item.

Many public goods provide consumption that is not excludable. Accordingly, to understand the scope for commercial provision of public goods, we must consider the degree of excludability. This depends on two factors: law and technology.

Law

In the previous section, we explained that scientific knowledge is a public good. An example of scientific knowledge is the formula for an antiviral drug. If a pharmaceutical manufacturer uses the formula to produce the drug, it will not affect the availability of the formula for other users. Hence, the formula is a public good. Similarly, the formulas for other drugs and chemical processes are public goods.

Through the concept of a *patent*, however, the law has made the use of many scientific formulas excludable. A **patent** is a legal, exclusive right to a product or process. It is illegal to manufacture a product or use a process covered by a patent without the permission of the patent owner. Such illegal activity is called *infringement*. The owner of a patent can sue infringers for a court order to stop the infringement as well as an award of damages.

> A **patent** is a legal, exclusive right to a product or process.

With legal authority, the owner of a patented antiviral drug can exclude those who do not pay from getting the drug. Accordingly, commercial production is feasible.

Patents provide the basis for the commercial provision of scientific knowledge in the electrical and electronics, chemicals, and pharmaceutical industries. The development of a new pharmaceutical, for instance, can take a decade and cost several hundred million dollars. Private enterprises are willing to invest large amounts in research and development only because of the profits that are possible with patent protection. Past scientific discoveries that have been covered by patents include aspirin, the light bulb, and the transistor. More recently, patented products include AZT and the Pentium microprocessor.

Like scientific knowledge, artistic, literary, and musical compositions are also public goods. The content of the *Oxford English Dictionary* may be used any number of times without affecting its availability to other users. Similarly, the content of Mozart's piano concertos, Madonna's songs, the movie *Blade Runner*, and computer software is also nonrival.

The law, however, has made the use of artistic, literary, and musical expression excludable through the concept of *copyright*. A **copyright** is a legal, exclusive right to an artistic, literary, or musical expression. It is illegal to reproduce a copyrighted expression without the permission of the copyright owner. The owner of a copyright can sue infringers for a court order to stop the infringement as well as an award of damages.

> A **copyright** is a legal, exclusive right to an artistic, literary, or musical expression.

Copyright gives the owner the authority to exclude those who do not pay from using the material. Commercial provision of literary and musical compositions and computer software is possible only with copyright law. For instance, if there were no copyright protection for personal computer software, all users could freely copy the products and the business of software development would not be commercially viable.

Patent and copyright are two forms of rights over intellectual property, which is the legal concept for ownership of ideas. The law deliberately creates these exclusive rights to encourage investment in creating new scientific knowledge, literary and musical compositions, and computer software.

Patents and copyrights are limited to specific periods of time. Once the patent on a product or process has expired, the owner loses the exclusive right and anyone can freely imitate the item. Similarly, after the expiration of the copyright on a literary or musical work, anyone is free to copy or use the work. For instance, the copyright on Mozart's piano concertos expired long ago, hence advertising agencies and movie studios can freely use Mozart's works. The law can establish excludability through intellectual property. The effectiveness of exclusion, however, depends on enforcement. Consider, for instance, the process for distilling water: heat the water to its boiling point, recover the steam, and then cool the steam and collect the condensate. Even if the law allowed a patent on this process, the right would be nearly impossible to enforce. Imagine trying to exclude particular high-school students, engineers, or household cooks from using the process to distill water.

By contrast, a patent on the formula for an antiviral drug is quite enforceable. The only potential commercial users of the formula are pharmaceutical manufacturers. To make money from the drug, a manufacturer must produce it on a large scale and sell it on the open market. This means that use of the formula will be relatively easy to detect. Accordingly, the owner of the patent can effectively exclude particular persons from usage.

Computer software provides another example of the distinction between establishing and enforcing intellectual property. Millions of people have personal computers and use spreadsheet and word-processing programs. Any one can quite easily copy personal computer software. By contrast, the number of supercomputers is relatively small, which in turn limits the demand for supercomputer software. Accordingly, it is much easier to enforce intellectual property over software for supercomputers than personal computers.

⊢ Uncle Sam – patent infringer? ⊢

"Cheap imitations are killing our business, and destroying thousands of good jobs." Who's complaining? Microsoft? Universal Studios? Bertelsmann? None of the above. It is Rosoboronexport, the company in charge of Russian arms exports.

In 1938, Mickhail Timofeevich Kalashnikov was called up for military service in the Soviet Army. He served as a tank commander and was seriously wounded in October 1941. From his hospital bed, he conceived of a new assault rifle. Upon discharge in 1942, he was posted to a unit responsible for developing small arms and devoted attention to his new idea.assault rifle In 1949, following rigorous competitive trials, the Soviet Army adopted the new assault rifle as the AK-47. Kalashnikov was awarded the Stalin Prize First Class. The AK-47 was then produced by Izhmash, the Russian company which describes itself as "Arms Center of the Russian Federation" as well as East European allies of the Soviet Union.

Fast forward 50 years. Having intervened in Afghanistan and Iraq, the U.S. government has become one of the leading customers of the AK-47. But not the legitimate item produced by Izhmash, which owns the patent for the AK-47.

Rather, the U.S. government buys AK-47s from unlicensed manufacturers in Bulgaria, Hungary, and Romania for supply to its allies in Afghanistan and Iraq. Somewhat helplessly, Rosoboronexport official Igor Sevastyanov declared "We would like to inform everybody in the world that many countries, including the United States, have unfortunately violated recognized norms."

Jordanian-made AK-47s sell for less than one-quarter of the Russian price. Izhmash officials blame such cheap imitations for the decline in employment on arms manufacturing from 12,000 in 1991 to 7,000 in 2004.

Source: "Russians Take Aim at AK-47 Imitators," *International Herald Tribune*, July 26, 2004.

⊣ Patents: 17 years was not long enough for the real thing ⊢

Coca-Cola, one of the world's most famous products, has not been patented, and deliberately so. The reason is that the applicant for a patent must submit a detailed description of the product or process for which it seeks protection. This information becomes part of the public record, so that others can avoid infringing the patent. Potential competitors, however, can refer to the public records for details of the product or process. Once the patent expires, they are free to imitate the product or process.

If Coca-Cola had filed for a patent, it would have enjoyed only 17 years of protection. (Beginning in 1995, U.S. patents were extended to 20 years.) Then, on the expiration of the patent, anyone – even Coca-Cola's arch-rival, Pepsi – could manufacture the "real thing." The Coca-Cola Company decided not to obtain a patent and chose instead to keep its formula a trade secret. Over 100 years later, the company continues to have a monopoly over the real thing.

Technology

In addition to the law, the other factor affecting excludability is technology. Recall Neptune Entertainment's difficulty in marketing an open-air fireworks show: it could not exclude particular persons, so some if not all of the viewers might refuse to pay. Suppose, however, that Neptune could produce fireworks that could be seen only through a special set of viewing glasses. Then, it could charge a price for the special glasses. In this example, a change of technology transforms the consumption of the product from being nonexcludable to excludable.

We have mentioned that the content of television programming is a public good. Whether, however, consumption of broadcast television is excludable depends on the technology of delivery. Consumption of free-to-the-air television is not excludable. The station cannot prevent particular individuals from watching a broadcast.

With scrambling technology, however, the consumption of over-the-air television can be made excludable. If a station scrambles its signal, only viewers who pay for decoding equipment can watch the programs. In this case, scrambling technology has transformed the medium of delivery from being nonexcludable to excludable.

Figure 12.5   Excludability
Consumption ranges from being excludable at one extreme to being nonexcludable at the other extreme.

Consumption of television programming that is broadcast by cable is very easily excludable. A cable television station simply disconnects viewers who do not pay.

Software provides another example. The intellectual content of a new computer program is a public good. Suppose that the publisher distributes the program through the Internet. Whether the delivery is excludable depends on the technology implemented by the publisher. If access is open, then anyone can go to the publisher's site and download the program. On the other hand, the publisher could restrict access to users with an authorized password. Then the delivery would be excludable.

Commercial Provision

Generally, the commercial provision of a public good depends on the extent to which the seller can exclude those who do not pay from consumption. In figure 12.5, we present a spectrum of excludability, with items whose consumption is excludable at one extreme and those whose consumption is nonexcludable at the other extreme.

Considering scientific knowledge, the formula for an antiviral drug is at the excludable end, while the process for distilling water is at the nonexcludable end. With regard to broadcast television, cable television is excludable, while free-to-the-air television is nonexcludable.

We have discussed how excludability depends on law and technology. Neither of these factors, however, is fixed. Like technology, the law can change with time, and so a public good may change from being excludable to nonexcludable or vice versa. Moreover, the scope of intellectual property differs among legal jurisdictions. For instance, discoveries that can be patented in one country may not get protection elsewhere. Accordingly, it is important to pay attention to differences in law and technology over time and place.

Progress Check 12F Using the spectrum of figure 12.5, mark the following items: (1) Internet access; (2) Ohm's Law, which relates electric voltage, current, and resistance; (3) a template contract for sale of real property; and (4) a lawyer's services.

Commercial provision without exclusion? free-to-the-air TV

We have claimed that commercial provision of a public good is difficult when consumption is nonexcludable. Consumption of free-to-the-air television is nonexcludable. In America, however, four major networks provide free-to-the-air television on a commercial basis. Far from limping along, the business has flourished. What is the television networks' secret?

Commercial television networks such as Fox and NBC get no revenues directly from their viewers. Their primary source of revenues is advertising. In 2004, NBC sold 30-second spots during the prime-time Summer Olympics for up to $700,000. While viewers of Fox and NBC do not directly pay for television, they do pay indirectly. They pay by increasing their purchases of the products advertised on television. If television advertising had no effect on consumer demand, would Anheuser-Busch, General Motors, and Visa spend millions of dollars each year on advertising? Obviously not.

Commercial "free" provision when exclusion is possible: Adobe Reader

The Internet provided a medium for provision of public information goods. While exclusion is technically possible, consumption of much software/services have the characteristics of public goods: provision to one person does not reduce the quantity available to others. One example of this is Adobe Reader software.

Adobe has been a leading developer of digital imaging, design and document technologies. The most widely known Adobe product is the Adobe Reader, which is widely advertised and Adobe makes available on the Internet for free download. Adobe Reader is a software for viewing documents in pdf (portable document format).

By providing the Adobe Reader freely, Adobe indirectly promotes the sale of Adobe products to write documents in pdf format. Adobe's marketing strategy has achieved great success: over 500 million copies of Adobe Reader have been distributed world wide and it is estimated that nearly 10% of Internet content is in pdf.

While Adobe provides the Reader free of charge, Adobe earns substantial revenue from other products. With 2004 sales of $1.996 billion and net income of $603 million, Adobe posted annual sales growth of 38.6% and a return on equity of 38.9%. It is the network effects created by the free provision of Adobe Reader which have stimulated the demand for Adobe's other (far from free) products.

Source: www.adobe.com/aboutadobe/pressroom/pdfs/corpbkgdr_June_2005.pdf.

7   Summary

An externality arises when one party directly conveys a benefit or cost to others. A network effect arises when a benefit or cost depends on the total number of other users. A network externality is a network effect that is directly conveyed and not through a market. An item is a public good if one person's increase in consumption does not reduce the quantity available to others. Equivalently, a public good provides nonrival consumption.

The benchmark for externalities and public goods is economic efficiency. At that point, all parties maximize their net benefits. Externalities can be resolved through merger or joint action, but resolution may be hampered by differences in information and free riding. Similarly, the commercial provision of a public good depends on being able to exclude free riders. Excludability depends on law and technology.

Markets with network effects differ from conventional markets in several ways. Demand is insignificant until a critical mass of users is established. Expectations of potential users help to determine the attainment of critical mass. When the demand for competing services are close to critical mass, a small shift in demand towards one service can tip all other users toward that service.

Key Concepts

externality
public good
positive externality
negative externality
externality is resolved
free rider

network effect
network externality
critical mass
installed base
tipping
nonrival

rival
congestible
excludable
patent
copyright

Further Reading

A symposium in the *Journal of Economic Perspectives*, 8, no. 2 (Spring, 1994): pp. 93–150, reviews network effects and externalities. Carl Shapiro and Hal R. Varian analyze business strategy in the new economy more generally in *Information Rules: A Strategic Guide to the Network Economy* (Boston, MA: Harvard Business School Press, 1999).

Review Questions

1. Give one example each of
    (a) negative externality;
    (b) positive externality.
2. What is the condition for the economically efficient level of a positive externality?
3. When the sum of the marginal costs from a negative externality is greater than the marginal benefit to the source, an intermediary could collect fees from the recipients to pay the source to cut back on the externality. Please explain.
4. Explain how the following actions will help to resolve the externalities generated by a new subway line:
    (a) The subway system buys the property around the new stations.
    (b) The owners of property near the new stations buy shares in the subway system.
5. Explain the "free rider problem" in the following context: Luna City lies two miles off Interstate Highway 105. Several of the city's leading property owners have proposed to build an exit from the interstate to attract traffic into the city. One motel refused to contribute any money for the new exit.
6. Give an example of a network externality.

Explain the concepts of a critical mass and tipping.
7. Explain why there are few, if any, network effects in consumers' choice of Web browsers.
8. Does the presence of network effects cause demand to be more or less price elastic?
9. Where are technical standards relatively more important? In markets with network effects or those without? Explain your answer.
10. Give an example of a public good. Explain how the use of the good is nonrival.
11. Which of the following are public goods? (a) CBS, a free-to-the-air network TV channel, and (b) video-on-demand from a broadband service provider.
12. For a public good, why is the group marginal benefit equal to the sum of the individual marginal benefits?
13. In what way does excludability depend on law and technology?
14. Explain the differences between patent and copyright.
15. Give examples of public goods that have been made excludable through
    (a) copyright law;
    (b) patent law.

Discussion Questions

1. A study of leasing practices among U.S. shopping malls reported that, on average, department stores paid rent of $2.24 per square foot. After controlling for differences in sales per square foot among stores of different types, the study calculated that the average rent for a specialty store was $11.88 per square foot. (*Source*: B. Peter Pashigian and Eric D. Gould, "Internalizing Externalities: The Pricing of Space in Shopping Malls," *Journal of Law and Economics* 41, no. 1 (April 1998), pp. 115–42.)
    (a) Compare the development of a new department store along an open street with one in a shopping mall. In which case are the externalities more likely to be resolved?
    (b) Explain why shopping malls charge department stores much lower rent than specialty retailers.
    (c) Explain why shopping malls might charge specialty stores a variable rent that depends on sales revenue.

2. From an economic and technical standpoint, there is an optimal rate at which to extract oil from an oil field. In the mid-1990s, Mobil was producing 60,000 barrels of oil per day (bpd), and Shell was producing 75,000 bpd from adjacent fields in California.
    (a) What are the externalities between the production of the two oil companies?
    (b) If the two companies negotiate an agreement, should they aim to increase or reduce production?
    (c) Assess the likelihood that the externality would be resolved.

3. With populations growing, an increasing number of people are choosing to live in multifamily dwellings including apartments and condominiums. According to the U.S. Census Bureau's *2003 American Housing Survey*, of 105.842 million occupied housing units, 64% were single-family detached homes, and 5% were in condominiums and cooperatives. Condominiums and cooperatives have rules that specify the rights and the obligations of the owners and residents.
    (a) By considering the demand and supply of land, explain why condominiums are becoming relatively more popular.
    (b) Give examples of negative externalities that condominium residents can generate for one another.
    (c) Should the law require the residents of a condominium to comply with the condominium rules?
    (d) Some residents in a condominium are annoyed by the barking of other residents' dogs. How could they jointly resolve this externality?

4. Radisson is an international chain of more than 400 hotels in over 50 countries. Many of the hotels are owned and operated by franchisees with contracts to use the Radisson business format. A franchisee might free ride by compromising on its own service, while depending on the overall Radisson brand to attract customers. To ensure a consistent standard throughout the chain, each Radisson District Director inspects at least one hotel a week.
    (a) Explain the negative externality among franchisees.
    (b) Why would a franchisee want Radisson to inspect other franchisees?
    (c) Will the free rider problem be more or less severe in a chain of hotels that are all in a single city as compared with an international chain?

5. With the growth of international trade and travel, more and more people are learning English. Major European companies have adopted English as a common language. English is also the standard language for communication among aircraft pilots and air-traffic controllers. France, however, has passed a law to restrict the use of English.
    (a) Compare the benefit of speaking a common language among (i) truckers, and (ii) pilots.
    (b) Does the growth of English generate a positive or negative externality for (i) people who are already fluent in English and (ii) people who do not speak English?
    (c) What are the prospects for French as an international language?

6. In 2006, the U.S. market for instant messaging (IM) was dominated by AOL (with 56% of users), followed by Microsoft's MSN (25%), and Yahoo (19%). Despite rapid growth and rosy fore-casts, the market is held back by the lack of interoperability among the different IM systems. In August 2005, Google launched Google Talk, an IM and voice communications service. Two months later, in a radical change of strategy, MSN and Yahoo arranged to make their IM systems interoper-ate by mid-2006. (*Source*: "Microsoft, Yahoo to Link IM Networks," *BetaNews*, October 12, 2005.)
    (a) Use IM to explain the concept of network effects.
    (b) Explain the critical mass problem that Google Talk must overcome.
    (c) Suppose that AOL's users are older and less technically savvy than users of MSN, Yahoo, and Google. Was the decision by MSN and Yahoo more likely directed at Google or AOL?

7. Kevin Kelly, Executive Editor of *Wired* magazine, has written that network effects are per-vasive: "the more plentiful things become, the more valuable they become . . . cotton shirts, bottles of vitamins, chain saws . . . will also obey the laws of plentitude" ("New rules for the new economy," *Wired*, September 1997).
    (a) If more people were to consume some brand of vitamins, how would your marginal benefit from that brand be affected?
    (b) Must the number of chain saw users exceed a critical mass before the demand becomes positive?
    (c) Are there network effects in the demand for vitamins, cotton shirts, and chain saws?

8. Plain text email can be sent and received from a multiplicity of email systems, including those based on the PC like Microsoft Outlook and others provided through the World Wide Web like Hotmail and Yahoo mail. By contrast, email attachments such as Microsoft Word and Lotus Notes files can only be read with the corresponding applications software. This difficulty can be resolved by converting attachments into Adobe Acrobat's pdf (portable document format). Pdf files can be read with the Adobe Reader, which Adobe distributes free through the Web.
    (a) Which demand exhibits stronger network effects? That for text email or that for Microsoft Word and Lotus Notes email attachments?
    (b) How does Adobe Acrobat's pdf affect the network effects in the demand for Microsoft Word and Lotus Notes software?
    (c) Adobe sells the Acrobat program to create pdf files while distributing the Adobe Reader free through the Web. How does the installed base of Readers affect the demand for the Acrobat document creation program?

9. Mikhail Kalashnikov conceived of the AK-47 assault rifle while recuperating from wounds during World War II. Within 50 years, over a 100 million AK-47s had been produced. Izhmash, the Russian company, which describes itself as "Arms Center of the Russian Federation," owns the patent to the AK-47. However, the U.S. government buys AK-47s from unlicensed manu-facturers in Bulgaria, Hungary, and Romania for supply to its allies in Afghanistan and Iraq. Jordanian-made AK-47s sell for a quarter of the Izhmash price. (*Sources*: "Russians Take Aim at AK-47 Imitators," *International Herald Tribune*, July 26, 2004; "AK-47's Inventor Peacefully Retired," *Guardian*, October 26, 2003.)
    (a) Use the AK-47 to explain how engineering design is a public good.
    (b) Patents are only effective within the country in which they are granted. Explain how manufacturers in Bulgaria, Hungary, Romania, and Jordan can free ride on Kalashnikov's design of the AK-47.
    (c) Maxime Piadiyshev, editor of *Arms Export Review* explained the success of the rifle: "Compared to other automatic rifles at the time . . . it was very simple in production, use and main-tenance, with eight moving parts." From Izhmash's viewpoint, does it help or hurt that the AK-47's design is simple yet effective?

10. As of October 2004, Beijing tourists were served by 77 hotels graded one-star and higher. Five-star hotels included international brands like the Grand Hyatt (582 rooms), regional brands like the

ShangriLa (528 rooms), and domestic institutions like the Beijing Hotel (1,000 rooms). Until 2001, Beijing hotels freely broadcast background music without paying any royalties. Then, the hotel sub-association of the Beijing travel industry association signed a three-year agreement with the China music composers' rights association. Under the contract, 63 hotels agreed to pay a lump-sum annual fee ranging from 5,000 yuan for a five-star hotel to 1,000 yuan for a one-star hotel. In 2004, the composers' association insisted on revising the royalty to a monthly fee of 1.75 yuan per bed, regardless of the hotel grade. (*Source*: "Hotel Music Fee to Increase, *Beijing Youth Daily*, June 16, 2004.)

(a) Explain how the royalty depends on the composers' association's ability to enforce the composers' copyright.

(b) Why is it less costly for composers to enforce their copyrights through an association rather than individually?

(c) Compare the 2001 and 2004 pricing schemes in terms of their effect on Beijing hotels' use of background music.

(d) In this context, explain the free rider problem and its consequences.

(e) Is the investment in creating new music likely to be at the economically efficient level?

11. This question applies the techniques presented in the math supplement. Let b represent marginal benefit and q the amount of Luna's investment in the new Main Street store. Suppose that the investment generates marginal benefits, $b = 15 - q$ for Luna, $b = 4 - 0.4q$ for the florist, and $b = 5 - 0.5q$ for the shoe store. Luna's marginal cost is 1.

(a) Calculate the group marginal benefit from Luna's investment.

(b) On a suitable diagram, draw the group marginal benefit and Luna's marginal cost.

(c) Calculate the economically efficient quantity of investment.

Chapter 12

Math Supplement

Let us first show how to obtain the group marginal benefit curve from individual marginal benefit curves. Let b represent marginal benefit and q the amount of Luna's investment in the new Main Street store. Suppose that the investment generates marginal benefits, $b = 10 - q$ for Luna, $b = 4 - 0.4q$ for the florist, and $b = 1 - 0.2q$ for the shoe store.

We draw these marginal benefit curves in figure 12.1. Notice that Luna's marginal benefit is positive for q in the interval [0, 10], the florist's marginal benefit is positive for q in the interval [0, 10], while the shoe store's marginal benefit is positive for q in the interval [0, 5].

Over the interval [0, 5], the vertical sum of the individual marginal benefits is

$$b = (10 - q) + (4 - 0.4q) + (1 - 0.2q)$$
$$= 15 - 1.6q. \tag{12.1}$$

Over the interval [5, 10], the vertical sum of the individual marginal benefits is

$$b = (10 - q) + (4 - 0.4q)$$
$$= 14 - 1.4q. \tag{12.2}$$

Accordingly, the group marginal benefit is

$$b = 15 - 1.6q \tag{12.3}$$

for q in the interval [0, 5], and

$$b = 14 - 1.4q \qquad (12.4)$$

for q in the interval [5, 10]. We draw this in figure 12.1.

Next, given the marginal cost of 1, let us calculate the economically efficient quantity. By figure 12.1, the group marginal benefit will cross the marginal cost with investment in the interval [5, 10]. In that interval, the group marginal benefit is

$$b = 14 - 1.4q. \qquad (12.5)$$

Equating this to the marginal cost of 1, we have

$$q = 13/1.4 = 9.29. \qquad (12.6)$$

Accordingly, the efficient amount of investment is $929,000.

Similarly, we can derive the group marginal cost as the vertical sum of the individual marginal cost curves and calculate the economically efficient investment. We do not elaborate, as the procedure is similar to that for marginal benefits.

Chapter 13

Asymmetric Information

1 Introduction

The state of Massachusetts offers $5,000 worth of basic life insurance to all full-time employees at low cost, as well as optional life insurance.[1] The State has contracted with The Hartford, a financial services group that was founded in 1810 and is listed on the New York Stock Exchange, to provide the insurance.

Effective July 2006, the monthly premium for basic insurance was $1.37 and did not vary by age, gender, or smoking status. The Hartford would only provide optional insurance to a state employee with basic insurance coverage. Any state employee may secure optional insurance coverage of up to eight times her salary without medical review. Table 13.1 reports

Table 13.1   The Hartford: term life insurance premiums (monthly, per $1,000 of coverage)

Age	Massachusetts Group Insurance Commission plan		General public (for coverage of less than $500,000)	
	Smoker	Non-smoker	Smoker	Non-smoker
Under 35	$0.09	$0.05	$0.10	$0.06
35–44	$0.13	$0.06	$0.15	$0.08
45–49	$0.24	$0.09	$0.26	$0.13
50–54	$0.38	$0.15	$0.35	$0.18
55–59	$0.58	$0.23	$0.43	$0.25
60–64	$0.88	$0.34	$0.58	$0.36
65–69	$1.57	$0.83	$0.89	$0.57
70 and over	$2.81	$1.30	$1.16	$0.75
			(age 70 only)	(age 70 only)

Sources: State of Massachusetts, Group Insurance Commission, www.mass.gov/gic/bdg/bdgrates.htm, accessed, July 15, 2006; "Annual Renewable Term Life Insurance Rates", *The Hartford*, June 30, 2006.

---

[1]   The following discussion is based, in part, on information from the State of Massachusetts, Group Insurance Commission, www.mass.gov/gic.

The Hartford's premiums for the optional life insurance. Monthly premiums varied with the applicant's age and smoking status, and ranged from $0.05 and $0.09 per $1,000 of coverage for non-smokers and smokers respectively aged less than 35 to $1.30 and $2.81 per $1,000 of coverage for non-smokers and smokers respectively aged 70 and above.

The Hartford also offers term life insurance to the general public. All applications are subject to completing a medical questionnaire and possibly a physical examination. The premiums for term life insurance to the general public vary with each year of the insured person's age. Table 13.1 reports the average premiums for the general public within each of the age brackets set for the Massachusetts Group Insurance Commission plan. Clearly, the group insurance plan is much cheaper than policies offered to the general public.

Why does Hartford limit Massachusetts state employees seeking optional insurance to coverage of up to eight times salary without medical review? Why are Hartford's premiums with the group insurance plan lower than on individual policies offered to the general public for persons aged below 60, but higher for persons aged 60 and above? Why doesn't Hartford publish rates for term life insurance to the general public aged above 70? Why does Hartford subject all applications from the general public to a medical review and possibly a physical examination?

Sellers of most goods and services do not limit the quantity that a customer may buy. Rather, they tend to offer quantity discounts – the more that a customer buys, the lower is the unit price. Business practices in life insurance are quite different: group insurance schemes limit the amount of insurance cover, but do not generally require medical examinations. Employees who seek higher coverage must buy an individual policy, which is generally more expensive than the group scheme, and which recognizes any number of risk factors.

> In a situation of **asymmetric information**, one party has better information than another.

The basic reason for the puzzling discrepancies between group and individual insurance is **asymmetric information** between the insurer and the party seeking life insurance. In a situation of asymmetric information, one party has better information than another. A person's likelihood of death depends on his or her health. She or he has better information about her own health than The Hartford. Accordingly, there is asymmetric information between the insurer and the applicant for life insurance.

Many other markets are characterized by asymmetric information. In credit markets, borrowers have better information about their ability to repay than lenders. In labor markets, workers have better information about their productivity than potential employers. In retail markets, buyers have better information about their preferences than retailers.

Recall from chapter 5 that a condition for perfect competition is that buyers and sellers have symmetric information. Hence, a market where information is asymmetric cannot be perfectly competitive. The better-informed party will take advantage of its superior information, and the allocation of resources will not be economically efficient.

This chapter focuses on business practices that resolve asymmetric information. We use asymmetric information to explain the systematic difference in premium between group and individual insurance policies. Essentially, individual insurance policies tend to attract applicants with relatively worse health or who are relatively more pessimistic about their life expectancy. One reason is that insurers provide larger coverage through individual than group policies.

Insurers like The Hartford require applicants for individual policies to undergo a medical review and possibly a physical examination. This is one way to resolve the asymmetric information between the insurer and applicant for insurance. The medical review illustrates the use of appraisal to resolve asymmetric information.

Appraisal does not always resolve asymmetric information completely. Accordingly, we also discuss three alternative methods of resolving asymmetric information – screening, signaling, and contingent contracts. These are indirect ways to resolve asymmetric information. They play a major role in credit, labor, insurance, and other markets characterized by asymmetric information.

2   Imperfect Information[2]

Before analyzing situations of asymmetric information, we should understand the concept of *imperfect information*. To have **imperfect information** about something means not having certain knowledge about that thing. Most people have imperfect information about future events such as

| Imperfect information is the absence of certain knowledge. |

next Monday's Standard & Poor's 500 Index, the severity of the coming winter, and the next year's growth in employment. It is also possible to have imperfect information about things in the present or past. For instance, do you know precisely the height above sea level of Mount Kilimanjaro or the distance between Berlin and Kansas City?

Imperfect vis-à-vis Asymmetric Information

A single person can have imperfect information. By contrast, asymmetric information involves two or more parties, one of whom has better information than the other or others. Asymmetric information will always be associated with imperfect information, because the party with poorer information definitely will have imperfect information. For instance, if the seller of an antique knows whether the item is genuine or fake but a potential buyer does not, then the buyer has imperfect information. The item could be a genuine antique or a fake, but the buyer does not know which for sure.

Although the concepts of asymmetric and imperfect information are related, it is important to remember the difference between the two. The reason is that a market can be perfectly competitive even when buyers and sellers have imperfect information, so long as they all have symmetric but imperfect information. In a perfectly competitive market, the forces of demand and supply will channel resources into economically efficient uses; hence, no further profitable transactions are possible.

For instance, the current demand for heating oil depends on expectations about temperatures in the coming winter. Buyers and sellers have equal access to meteorological forecasts. Based on these forecasts, each buyer determines its demand for heating oil. In a market equilibrium, the quantity demanded equals the quantity supplied and the marginal benefit equals the marginal cost. Hence, any further sales would be unprofitable.

By contrast, a market where information is asymmetric cannot be perfectly competitive. This means that, if buyers and sellers can resolve the information asymmetries, they can increase their benefits by more than their costs.

Risk Defined

When information is imperfect, there is risk. To understand the meaning of *risk*, let us consider the following example. Nancy knows, with probability 1.5%, that someone will steal

---

[2]   Please refer to the chapter 1 subsection on bounded rationality.

her $20,000 car within the next 12 months. If that were to happen, Nancy would lose $20,000. If Nancy's car is not stolen, however, Nancy would lose nothing. The probability that her car will not be stolen is $100 - 1.5 = 98.5\%$.

Nancy has imperfect information about her future losses, because she does not know for sure whether her car will be stolen. Nancy bears a risk: either she will lose $20,000 with probability of 1.5% or she will lose nothing with probability of 98.5%. **Risk** is uncertainty about benefits or costs and arises whenever there is imperfect information about something that affects benefits or costs.

> **Risk** is uncertainty about benefits or costs.

If Nancy knew for sure that her car would not be stolen within the next 12 months, then she would not bear any risk. Similarly, if she knew for sure that her car would be stolen, she would also not bear any risk. It is because her information is imperfect that she faces risk.

To explain the distinction between risk and imperfect information, consider Max, who is unrelated to Nancy. Max also has imperfect information about whether Nancy's car will be stolen. But the fate of Nancy's car does not affect Max's benefits or costs. Hence, Max does not bear any risk with regard to Nancy's car.

Risk Aversion

A risk neutral person is indifferent between a certain amount and risky amounts with the same expected value.

Insurance is the business of taking certain payments in exchange for eliminating risk.

> A **risk averse** person prefers a certain amount to risky amounts with the same expected value.

How a person responds to situations involving risk depends on the extent to which he or she is *risk averse*. A person is **risk averse** if she or he prefers a certain amount to risky amounts with the same expected value. A person is *risk neutral* if she or he is indifferent between a certain amount and risky amounts with the same expected value.

Given Nancy's possible losses and the probabilities, her expected loss is ($20,000 \times 0.015$) + (0×0.985) = $300. If Nancy is risk averse, she will prefer to lose $300 for certain than to lose $20,000 with probability of 1.5%, or lose nothing with probability of 98.5%. If Nancy is risk neutral, she will be indifferent between losing $300 for certain and the risk of losing $20,000 with probability of 1.5%, or losing nothing with probability of 98.5%.

Risk-averse persons will pay to avoid risk. *Insurance* is the business of taking certain payments in exchange for eliminating risk. Suppose that an insurer offers Nancy an insurance policy that pays her $20,000 if her car is stolen but pays nothing if her car is not stolen. If Nancy has the policy and her car is stolen, she loses the car but receives $20,000, so on balance, she gains and loses nothing. If her car is not stolen, the insurer will not pay her anything, so she gains and loses nothing. Thus, the insurance policy eliminates the risk that Nancy must otherwise bear. Recall that, without insurance, Nancy's expected loss is $300. Hence, if she is risk averse, she would pay at least $300 for the insurance policy.

How much risk-averse persons are willing to pay for insurance depends on their degree of risk aversion in that situation. A more risk-averse person will be willing to pay a larger amount to avoid risk. By contrast, a risk-neutral person will not pay anything to avoid risk. For instance, suppose that Lucas faces the same situation as Nancy. If Lucas is risk neutral, he would pay no more than $300 for the insurance policy.

It is important to understand the meaning of risk and risk aversion because, whenever information is asymmetric, the less-informed party has imperfect information. To the extent that this means uncertainty about benefits or costs, the less-informed party faces risk.

3 Adverse Selection

The cost of producing a fake antique can often be very low compared to the value of the genuine article. If fakes are sufficiently convincing, they present a serious problem for the legitimate market. Under such circumstances, potential buyers will be concerned whether they are getting a fake or the genuine article. By contrast, sellers will be much better informed about the true provenance of what they are selling. In these circumstances, information is asymmetric.

Let us use the antiques example to understand the implications of asymmetric information. Specifically, we will consider the nature of market equilibrium and the effect of price changes on the quantity demanded and supplied.

Demand and Supply

Initially, suppose that sellers offer only genuine antiques. The stock of antiques is fixed (or almost fixed, since a small number are always being discovered). The supply for sale at any one time, however, is more elastic: it depends on existing owners' willingness to sell. In figure 13.1, we show the supply and the demand for genuine antiques. In equilibrium at point *b*, the price would be $500 per unit and 3,000 units of antiques would be sold each month.

Now suppose that forgers produce a quantity of 1,000 fakes at no marginal cost. In principle, there could be two markets: one for fakes and another for genuine antiques. Suppose, however, that potential buyers cannot distinguish genuine antiques from fakes. Then, there will be only one market. In that single market, fakes trade alongside genuine antiques, so the supply of genuine antiques and fakes is combined.

Figure 13.2 illustrates the market with both fakes and genuine antiques. Since forgers produce 1,000 fakes at no marginal cost, the combined supply of genuine antiques and fakes begins with 1,000 fakes at no cost, and then, at that quantity, the supply curve jumps up and runs parallel to the supply of genuine antiques.[3]

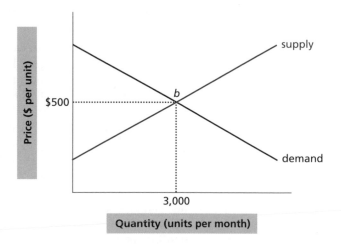

Figure 13.1 Market with symmetric information

---

[3] This model is adapted from B. Peter Pashigan, *Price Theory and Applications* (New York: McGraw-Hill, 1995), pp. 520–6.

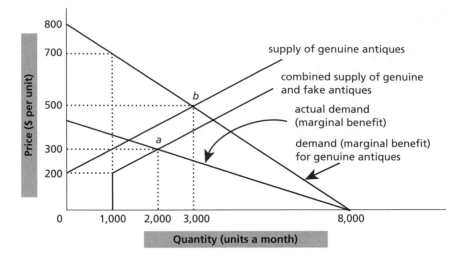

Figure 13.2   Market with adverse selection
The supply and demand for genuine antiques is in equilibrium at point *b*, with a price of $500 per unit and a quantity of 3,000 units. The combined supply of genuine antiques and fakes begins with 1,000 fakes at no cost, then jumps up and runs parallel to the supply of genuine antiques. The actual demand, which reflects the probability of getting a fake, is the demand curve for genuine antiques shifted down by the proportion $1/Q$. The actual demand and the combined supply cross at point *a*, where the price is $300 per unit, and the quantity is 2,000 units a month.

Progress Check 13A Suppose that Nancy buys the insurance policy that pays her $20,000 if her car is stolen but pays nothing if her car is not stolen. Who of the following has imperfect information and who faces risk: (i) Nancy; (ii) the insurer?

What about the demand side of the market? Each individual buyer has a marginal benefit curve for genuine antiques. Buyers, however, know that they might get fakes. Suppose that all buyers derive no marginal benefit from a fake. So, taking into account the probability of getting a fake, the actual marginal benefit is lower than the marginal benefit from a genuine antique.

Suppose that all buyers are risk neutral and that they purchase a total of Q thousand pieces, of which 1,000 are fake. Then each buyer has a probability $1/Q$ of getting a fake and a probability $(Q - 1)/Q$ of getting a genuine antique. Since all buyers are risk neutral, each buyer's actual marginal benefit is only $(Q - 1)/Q$ of the marginal benefit for genuine antiques. So, a buyer's actual marginal benefit curve, which reflects the probability of getting a fake, is his or her marginal benefit curve for genuine antiques, shifted down by the proportion $1/Q$ at every quantity.

Accordingly, the actual demand for antiques, which reflects the probability of getting a fake, is the demand curve for genuine antiques shifted down by the proportion $1/Q$. Equivalently, at every possible quantity, the buyers' actual willingness to pay is only a fraction $(Q - 1)/Q$ of their willingness to pay for the same of quantity of antiques that are definitely genuine.

Market Equilibrium

Having laid out the demand and the supply, we can study the equilibrium. The actual demand and the combined supply cross at point *a*, where the price is $300 per unit and the quantity is $Q = 2,000$ units a month. Hence, the probability that a buyer gets a fake is $1,000/2,000 = 50\%$ and the probability of getting a genuine antique is 50%.

What if the quantity of fakes were different? If, for instance, there are 500 fakes, then the actual demand will be higher and the combined supply of genuine antiques and fakes will be further to the left. Then, the equilibrium will have a higher price. The equilibrium quantity, however, may be higher or lower: the demand is higher, but supply is further to the left.

By contrast, if the quantity of fakes is larger, then the actual demand will be lower and the combined supply will be further to the right. Hence, the market price will be lower. Again, sales may be higher or lower, depending on the balance between demand and supply.

Let us consider the effect of a price reduction on the antiques market. The marginal cost curves of legitimate sellers slope upward. So, when the market price is lower, each of them supplies a smaller quantity. By contrast, a drop in the market price does not affect the quantity of fakes supplied. Hence, the drop in the market price increases the proportion of fakes, leaving buyers with a more serious case of *adverse selection*.

The problem of an **adverse selection** arises in situations of asymmetric information: the party with relatively poor information will draw a selection with relatively less attractive characteristics. In the antiques case, the buyers have less information and draw a mixture of fakes and genuine antiques, which is an adverse selection of items.

> In an **adverse selection**, the party with relatively poor information draws a selection with relatively less attractive characteristics.

Progress Check 13B Using figure 13.2, illustrate the market equilibrium with 500 fakes. Will the market price be higher or lower than when there are 1,000 fakes?

Economic Inefficiency

How does the introduction of fakes affect buyer and seller surplus? Buyer surplus falls as some buyers receive fakes. On the other hand, buyer surplus rises to the extent that the market price falls. Buyer surplus may also increase if sales are higher. Accordingly, the effect on buyers is ambiguous. As for sellers, we must distinguish those who sell fakes from those who sell genuine antiques. Legitimate sellers are definitely worse off: they get a lower price and they sell fewer units (as genuine antiques get crowded out by lower-cost fakes). Sellers of fakes are the only group that are definitely better off from the entry of fakes into the antiques market.

Is the market equilibrium with fakes economically efficient? Each buyer purchases up to the point that its actual marginal benefit (adjusted for the probability of getting a fake) balances the market price. Similarly, each legitimate seller supplies up to the point that its marginal cost balances the market price. Since fakes provide no marginal benefit, in equilibrium, buyers who get fakes will have a marginal benefit less than the legitimate sellers' marginal cost. On the other hand, buyers who get genuine antiques will have a marginal benefit higher than the legitimate sellers' marginal cost. Accordingly, the equilibrium is not economically efficient.

Specifically, referring to figure 13.2, if sellers offered only genuine antiques, then in equilibrium, the price would be $500 per unit and 3,000 units would be sold. At this quantity, the marginal benefit and the marginal cost are both $500.

When the supply includes 1,000 fakes, however, the price falls to $300 per unit and the equilibrium quantity drops to 2,000 units. The equilibrium quantity of genuine antiques is 2,000 − 1,000 = 1,000 units. The supply curve for genuine antiques shows that the marginal cost of the 1,000th unit is $300. The demand curve for genuine antiques shows that the marginal benefit of the 1,000th unit is $700. Hence, in equilibrium, the marginal benefit exceeds the marginal cost, so the quantity traded is not economically efficient.

If, somehow, another genuine antique could be sold, then there would be a buyer willing to pay almost $700 for that item and there would be a seller willing to provide it for a little above $300. Accordingly, there is potential gain of just under $400.

We can relate this analysis to chapter 12 on externalities. Sellers of fakes impose a negative externality on sellers of genuine antiques and buyers. From our study of externalities, we know that, unless it is resolved, there will be too much of a negative externality relative to the economically efficient level. This means that a profit can be made by resolving the externality, which in this case, means resolving the information asymmetry.

Market Failure

Before considering how to resolve an asymmetry of information, let us look at an extreme possibility in the antiques example. Suppose that there are F fakes. Referring to figure 13.3, the combined supply of genuine antiques and fakes has a kink at point c. Now suppose that the number of fakes is so large that the actual demand crosses the combined supply at some

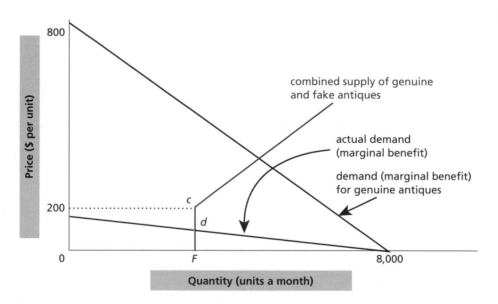

Figure 13.3 Market failure
Supposing that the actual demand crosses the combined supply at point d, then the entire supply will be fakes. The actual demand curve must coincide with the horizontal axis, so the actual demand cannot cross the combined supply at point d. Generally, there cannot be an equilibrium with the actual demand curve crossing the combined supply above but close to the kink.

point d below the kink. In this case, there will be no supply of genuine antiques and the entire supply will be fakes. Then, a buyer's probability of getting a genuine antique is 0. This means that the actual marginal benefit and the actual demand curve must coincide with the horizontal axis. Thus, the initial supposition that the actual demand crosses the combined supply at some point d is not valid.

This discussion shows that there cannot be an equilibrium with the actual demand curve crossing the combined supply below the kink. Indeed, the same logic also shows that there cannot be an equilibrium with the actual demand curve crossing the combined supply above but close to the kink. If there cannot be an equilibrium, then buyers and sellers cannot trade. This means that the intrusion of fakes has caused the entire market to fail!

Let us view the market failure from another perspective. We will show that a change in price has very different effects in a perfectly competitive market as compared with a market subject to adverse selection. Suppose that, in a perfectly competitive market, the quantity supplied exceeds the quantity demanded. Then, a price reduction will reduce the quantity supplied and raise the quantity demanded. A sufficient reduction of the market price will restore equilibrium.

By contrast, suppose that the antiques and fakes market is out of equilibrium, with the quantity supplied greater than the quantity demanded. Consider a reduction in the price. This will cause some genuine sellers to withdraw, hence increasing the proportion of fakes. Thus, buyers will face a worse adverse selection, and hence, their willingness to pay and the demand curve will drop. Reducing the price cuts the demand as well as the quantity of supply, so it will not necessarily restore the equilibrium. In the extreme, if the price is sufficiently low, the actual demand curve will drop down to zero and there will be no sales at all. In this case, the fakes have destroyed the market completely.

Generally, the market equilibrium will belong to one of two classes. In one class, the number of fakes is sufficiently small that the actual demand will balance the upward sloping portion of the combined supply well above the kink at point c. Then, in an equilibrium, the supply consists of both fakes and genuine antiques. In the other class, so many fakes have flooded the market that the actual demand curve will drop down to zero and the market will fail.

Lending and Insurance

In the antiques market, sellers have better information about their own characteristics than buyers. In other markets, it is the buyers who have better information than sellers. Consider the market for residential mortgages. One question is at the forefront of any lender's mind: if the value of the property falls below the amount of the outstanding principal, will the borrower default? To *default* means to stop paying the interest and principal.

When the property value is less than the outstanding principal, the borrower's equity in the property is negative. If he or she then defaults on the loan, the borrower is effectively selling the property to the lender for the outstanding principal. Some borrowers will not hesitate to default, while others will continue to make payments, even when they have negative equity.

To the extent that borrowers have better information about their personal willingness to default, there is asymmetric information between borrowers and lenders. Generally, a lender will have some chance of lending to a (bad) borrower who would readily default and some chance of lending to a (good) borrower who would be reluctant to default. If the lender raises the interest rate, it will draw an adverse selection of borrowers: the higher the interest rate, the fewer good borrowers will want loans and the higher will be the proportion of bad borrowers. This explains why a bank will not necessarily agree to lend more if a borrower offers a higher interest rate.

Insurance is another market where buyers have better information about their own characteristics than do sellers. Life insurance is insurance against the possibility of death. (It would be more accurate, but much less appealing, to call it *death insurance*.) The likelihood that a person will die within the next 12 months depends on her or his state of health and style of life.

The price that an insurer charges for an insurance policy is called a premium. Life insurers face an adverse selection problem: if an insurer charges a high premium, it is likely to draw applicants who know that they are in relatively poor health or who maintain risky lifestyles.

Insurers collect information about applicants for life insurance – whether they smoke, their age and their medical history, and their employment, sports, and other activities. However, it is difficult for an insurer to obtain all the relevant information about an applicant's state of health and style of life. Hence, there remains asymmetric information between insurers and applicants for insurance.

Progress Check 13C Suppose that a life insurer presently has a high percentage of high-risk policyholders. If the insurer reduces its premiums, what will be the effect on the percentage of high-risk policyholders?

Resolving adverse selection in insurance: State of Massachusetts, Group Insurance Commission

A person's likelihood of death depends on health and lifestyle. People differ in health and lifestyle. The Hartford, like other life insurers, fears that its policies will attract an adverse selection of applicants. Accordingly, it subjects individual applicants for the term life insurance to a questionnaire on their health, employment, and activities, and possibly a physical examination. Further, Hartford controls risk by limiting individual insurance policies to persons aged 70 and below. Otherwise, Hartford sets no limit to the insurance coverage available to individual applicants.

By contrast, the group insurance plan offered to Massachusetts state employees does not require any medical review and covers employees of any age. By covering a large number of persons, a group plan may avoid the adverse selection arising from individual applications. For persons aged below 60, Hartford charges a lower premium with the group insurance plan than with individual policies. However, for persons aged 60 and above, Hartford charges a higher premium with the group insurance plan. Apparently, Hartford believes that, among state employees, the possible adverse selection from no medical review and no age limit is relatively serious from age 60 onward.

In addition, Hartford limits its risk from the group plan through a ceiling of eight times annual salary for coverage without medical review.

Sources: State of Massachusetts, Group Insurance Commission, www.mass.gov/gic/bdg/bdgrates.htm, accessed July 15, 2006; "Annual Renewable Term Life Insurance Rates," *The Hartford*, June 30, 2006.

⊢ China's quiet export: baby girls ⊢

In just ten years, the number of Chinese children adopted by U.S. parents grew from under 1,000 in 1994 to almost 8,000 in 2005. The explanation for this export boom is minimal adverse selection.

An adoption service, Great Wall China Adoption, states: "Chinese children have been well cared for and are generally healthy." In a web posting, Fred and Margaret Bazzoli who adopted Ellen from Nanching, Jiangxi province, in November 1995, added: "compared to domestic adoptions, the process is . . . unlikely to result in a birthparent returning to claim the child."

The more fundamental explanation is China's one-child policy, implemented in 1979. Many Chinese parents still favor sons, and would rather abandon their only child if it turns out to be female. These girls are sent to orphanages and then made available for adoption.

By contrast, in other countries, relatively more children are given up for adoption because they are unwell, or they are born to a parent who is unable to care for them. Accordingly, adverse selection is relatively more serious among adoptive children from sources other than China.

Sources: *Great Wall China Adoption*, http://www.gwcadopt.org; "International Chinese Adoption," *Shared Blessings*, Winter, 1998, http://www.night.net/rosie/9802-acs-article1.html; U.S. Dept. of State, http://travel.state.gov/family/adoption/stats/stats_451.html.

⊢ Hurricane Katrina exposes adverse selection problems ⊢

In 1968, the U.S. government established the National Flood Insurance Program (NFIP), due to the relative absence of privately provided flood insurance. Adverse selection was immediately apparent, as few people signed up for the insurance. Legislative changes made flood insurance mandatory for mortgages on homes within Special Flood Hazard Areas (SFHAs). It is estimated that compliance is around 75%–80% within SFHAs. Outside flood zones, however, voluntary purchase of flood insurance is around 1%. The NFIP is not permitted to use past claims history in setting flood insurance rates or deciding what properties to cover.

The NFIP encounters a double asymmetric information problem. Flood hazard maps are often inaccurate, so that homeowners often have superior knowledge of actual flood hazards compared with government officials. On the other hand, some homeowner behavior exhibits cognitive limitations of the type studied by behavioral economists.

A recent study reveals that the penetration rate of flood insurance is 70% in communities with flood events within the past 5 years, but only 15% in those that have no recorded flood event. Similarly, 37% of homes have flood insurance in communities where less than 10% of homes are in a SFHA, but 78% are insured in communities where over half of the homes are in a SFHA. Communities subject to coastal flooding have 69% penetration rates for flood insurance, while communities subject to river flooding have only 42% penetration rates.

Hurricane Katrina has brought these issues to a head. Nearly half of the flood victims were not insured, and of those insured, the $25 billion of claims bankrupted the system.

A number of attempts to restructure the system by expanding mandatory flood insurance have been blocked by real estate interests that are concerned about the extra costs of flood insurance stifling development. Mandatory insurance is often a useful remedy for an adverse selection market failure. Consumers often resist mandatory insurance, however: "You've got people living in dry areas paying for people who want to keep living in wet ones."

Sources: "Fix Doubtful for Insuring Flood Areas," *New York Times*, May 15, 2006; L. Dixon, N. Clancy, S. A. Seabury, and A. Overton, *The National Flood Insurance Program Market Penetration Rate* (Santa Monica, CA: Rand Corporation, 2006).

4 Appraisal

Our discussion of fakes in the antiques market illustrates that, when information is asymmetric, the market outcome will not be economically efficient. Generally, if the information asymmetry can be resolved, then benefits will increase by more than costs and, hence, there is room to make a profit.

The most obvious way to overcome asymmetric information is to obtain the information directly. In the antiques market, a collector could engage an expert to appraise a potential purchase. Referring to figure 13.2, in the equilibrium at point *a*, the marginal benefit of a genuine antique is $700, while the market price is $300. For that marginal buyer, there is a potential gain of almost $400 by identifying a genuine antique. Provided that an appraisal costs less than the potential gain, then the buyer will purchase the appraisal.

To the extent that buyers obtain appraisals, there will be a separate market for genuine antiques. In that market, buyers and sellers will have equal information and, so, perfect competition will lead to economic efficiency. The buyers, however, must pay the cost of appraisals. (Recall from chapter 6 the distinction between paying and incidence. Who bears the cost of appraisals depends on the elasticities of demand and supply.)

There are some buyers whose marginal benefit from a genuine antique is relatively low, however, so that the difference between their marginal benefit and the market price does not cover the cost of appraisal. These buyers will choose not to get appraisals; hence, they cannot distinguish genuine antiques from fakes. The information asymmetry means that they will suffer from an adverse selection.

For an information asymmetry to be resolved directly, the asymmetry must satisfy two conditions. First, the characteristic about which information is asymmetric must be objectively verifiable. If an expert cannot objectively distinguish genuine antiques from fakes, then appraisals will not resolve the information asymmetry between buyers and sellers. The verification must be objective: if different appraisers give different opinions, then buyers' and sellers' information will still be asymmetric.

The second condition is that the potential gain from resolving the asymmetric information must cover the cost of appraisal. This, in turn, depends on two factors. One is the proportion of fakes. The other is the difference between the marginal benefit and the marginal cost. Buyers, however, focus on the difference between the marginal benefit and the market price, which is a smaller difference. Sellers focus on the difference between the market price and their marginal cost. Generally, if the potential gain is too small, then the information asymmetry will not be resolved.

┌───┐

⊣ Making a business out of appraisal: Verisign secure site ⊢

Despite its rapid growth, e-commerce still holds out significant risk in the security of information provided during a transaction. As may as 64% of online shoppers decided not to complete a purchase online because of a lack of security of the purchase transaction.

Items of concern include personal information; address, phone number and credit card number. Although companies have many tools available to provide secure transactions, there is more trust in a third party specialist to provide the required security. Verisign has a strong reputation in security and provides secure transaction solutions to businesses. The Verisign brand helps to assure customers of the safety of their private information and provides third party authentication of the seller.

In 2005, Verisign reported revenues of $1.66 billion (42% growth over 2004) and net income of $406 million.

Source: www.verisign.com/products-services/security-services/ssl/ssl-information-center/ecommerce-trust-ssl/index.html.

└───┘

Procuring the Appraisal

In the antiques example, we supposed that the buyers procured expert appraisals to resolve the information asymmetry. Recall that the intrusion of fakes hurts sellers of genuine antiques. Hence, sellers of genuine antiques may pay for expert appraisals to distinguish themselves from sellers of fakes.

Indeed, it is more economical for sellers to procure the appraisals. The seller of an item can obtain one appraisal and present the results to many potential buyers. The appraisal is a public good: any number of potential buyers can use the same information. Hence, it is less costly for the seller to get an appraisal than for every potential buyer to procure an appraisal of the same item.

Under what circumstances should a seller rather than potential buyers obtain the appraisal? One factor is the number of potential buyers. If there is only one potential buyer, then the expenditure will be the same whether the seller or the buyer procures the appraisal. By contrast, if there are many potential buyers, then there will be a relatively greater saving if the seller procures the appraisal.

Another factor is the extent to which the various potential buyers seek the same information about the item. If different potential buyers have different considerations, then it may be difficult for the seller's appraisal to provide all the required information. In this case, each potential buyer might prefer to obtain an individual appraisal.

Appraising Borrowers

In the market for loans, borrowers have better information about their ability and willingness to repay than potential lenders. To guard against adverse selection, lenders can also appraise applicants for loans. One input into the appraisal is a credit evaluation. This shows the applicant's outstanding debts and record in repaying loans and other forms of credit. A credit evaluation provides information about a borrower's ability and willingness to repay. Many lenders will also check a loan applicant's employment record, which is another indicator of ability to repay.

Credit evaluations and employment reports can help borrowers with some history to resolve their asymmetry of information with lenders. What about borrowers such as new immigrants and graduating students who have little prior credit history or employment record? They may have no way to directly resolve the information asymmetry.

> **Progress Check 13D** Will appraisals be more common in the market for cheap or more expensive antiques?

Moody's: appraising debt

Private and public corporations, municipalities, sovereign governments, and international organizations raise funds through issuance of debt obligations such as commercial paper and bonds. These securities may be sold to numerous investors, dispersed all over the world. A major concern for investors is the possibility that the issuer will default. Issuers, however, have better information about their own financial condition and likelihood of default.

Issuers can address this asymmetry by obtaining an independent rating of their debt. Moody's Investors Service was founded in 1909 to rate railway bonds. At the request of an issuer, Moody's will rate a debt obligation on a scale ranging from the highest grade of Aaa through Aa, A, Baa, Ba, B, to the lowest grade of Caa. The issuer can then provide the rating to potential investors.

Empirical studies show that issuers with lower Moody's ratings have been systematically more likely to default. Over the period 1920–99, the average 10-year default rate was 4.85% among investment-grade (Baa and higher) issuers, and 25.31% among speculative-grade (Ba and lower) issuers.

Sources: "Rating the Rating Agencies," *The Economist*, July 15, 1995, pp. 61–2; Moody's, www.moodys.com, accessed, March 10, 1999.

5 Screening

We have discussed how asymmetric information can be directly resolved through appraisal. Since appraisal is costly and not always feasible, however, it is important to consider indirect alternatives. Generally, asymmetric information can be resolved in three indirect ways. We discuss one in this section, and the others in later sections.

Screening is an initiative of a less-informed party to indirectly elicit the other party's characteristics.

In a situation where one party has better information about its own characteristics, the less-informed party may be able to elicit another party's characteristics indirectly through *screening*. **Screening** is an initiative of a less-informed party to indirectly elicit the other party's characteristics. It exploits the sensitivity of the better-informed party to some variable that the less-informed can control. The less-informed party must design choices around that variable to induce **self-selection**, meaning that parties with different characteristics choose different alternatives.

In **self-selection**, parties with different characteristics choose different alternatives.

To explain the concept of screening, let us consider again the market where buyers cannot distinguish fakes from genuine antiques. The unknown characteristic is the true nature of the item. With the intrusion of fakes, the market outcome is not economically efficient. Since buyers suffer from the fakes, they may take the initiative to resolve the asymmetry of information. Suppose that all buyers insist that they pay the purchase price into escrow, which will be released to sellers only after a period of five years. Can this escrow arrangement effectively screen fakes from genuine antiques?

The answer depends on whether sellers of fakes will agree to the escrow arrangement. Assume that buyers of fakes discover the truth within five years. Then, a dealer who sells fakes would not get any money. Accordingly, sellers of fakes would not agree. Agreeing to the escrow arrangement makes sense only for sellers of genuine antiques. Thus, it credibly screens sellers of genuine antiques from sellers of fakes.

Then, the escrow arrangement would separate the market for genuine antiques from the market for fakes. With the two markets separated, the genuine market is described by figure 13.1. Screening is possible only if the less-informed party can control some variable to which the better-informed parties are *differentially* sensitive. In the antiques example, sellers of fakes were more sensitive to the escrow arrangement than sellers of genuine antiques.

By contrast with direct appraisal, screening elicits the characteristics of the better-informed party indirectly. Screening is an indirect way of resolving an information asymmetry. Buyers do not directly ask sellers whether their items are genuine. Rather, buyers force sellers to make a choice that indirectly yet credibly communicates their information.

A key business application of screening is to pricing. In chapter 9, "Pricing," we discussed policies of *indirect segment discrimination*. These are pricing policies that apply screening to induce self-selection among buyers with different price elasticities of demand.

⊣ Solomon: who's the real mother? ⊢

The ancient Jewish king Solomon provided the classic example of screening. Two women came before him, one holding a dead boy and the other a living boy. Each woman claimed the living boy to be her son. Solomon had to decide:

> [T]he king said, "Bring me a sword . . . Divide the living child in two, and give half to the one, and half to the other." Then the woman whose son was alive said to the king, because her heart yearned for her son, "Oh, my lord, give her the living child, and by no means slay it." But the other said, "It shall be neither mine nor yours; divide it." Then the king answered and said, "Give the living child to the first woman, and by no means slay it; she is the mother."
>
> (1 Kings 3.16–27, RSV)

In this famous case, Solomon was the less-informed party: he did not know which woman was truly the mother of the living boy. He did know, however, that the true mother would not allow her son to be killed, while the false mother might be indifferent. The two women were differentially sensitive to Solomon's proposal to divide the boy. The king exploited this differential to good effect. The true mother and the false mother quickly identified themselves.

⊢ "Points": screening home mortgage borrowers ⊢

In the United States, financial institutions making residential mortgage loans face borrowers with different horizons. Some borrowers plan to repay within a short time, while others intend to keep their loans for a longer period. The longer the period, the more profit the lender will earn from the loan.

Lenders, however, cannot directly distinguish borrowers with different horizons. They do so indirectly through an up-front charge called "*points*." The charge is set as a percentage of the principal. So, for instance, the charge on a $100,000 loan that bears 1.5 points is $1,500.

Lenders typically offer borrowers a choice among loans with different interest rates and points. Loans with lower interest rates bear higher points. For instance, in May 2006, Digital Federal Credit Union (DFCU) of Marlborough, Massachusetts, advertised 30-year fixed interest loans as follows: a rate of 6.25% with 2 points, a rate of 6.5% with 1 point, and a rate of 6.75% with 0 points.

By offering these alternatives, DFCU can screen among borrowers according to how long they plan to hold their loans. A borrower who plans to repay his or her loan within a short time horizon will prefer a loan with low points. Such a borrower would rather pay a higher interest rate for a relatively short period of time. By contrast, a borrower who plans to hold the loan for a long time will prefer a loan with a lower interest rate and higher points. The savings on interest will make up for the higher up-front charge in points.

The choice between high points or a high interest rate effects self-selection among the borrowers. Loans with high points and low interest rates draw longer-term borrowers, while those with lower points and higher interest rates attract borrowers with shorter horizons.

Differentiating Variable

In some instances, the less-informed party may have the choice of several differentiating variables. Ideally, the less-informed party should structure the choice that drives the biggest possible wedge between the better-informed parties with the different characteristics.

The less-informed party must consider the effectiveness of each differentiating variable in driving a wedge between the various segments. This means comparing the differential sensitivity of the segments to each variable. The less-informed party should place relatively more emphasis on the more effective variable.

For instance, airlines could use clothing as a differentiating variable, offering a lower fare to travelers wearing casual clothing and a higher fare to travelers in business attire. Business travelers could easily circumvent this differentiating variable; hence, it is not effective. By contrast, airlines have found advance booking and weekend stayover to be effective differentiating variables.

The most effective screening may involve a combination of the differentiating variables. For instance, airlines use a combination of restrictions, advance booking and weekend stayover, and frequent flyer benefits to screen leisure from business travelers.

Multiple Unobservable Characteristics

In some cases, the information asymmetry between two parties concerns not just one but several characteristics. Then, if the less-informed party screens on a single differentiating variable, the resulting choices may not resolve the asymmetry.

Consider the following example. Comprehensive automobile insurance covers loss or damage to a car arising from all causes, including fire and theft. The likelihood of loss or damage depends on the driver's behavior. It is lower for a careful driver who parks in secure, well-lighted places and uses a steering lock and car alarm. By contrast, the likelihood of loss or damage is higher for less careful drivers.

The demand for comprehensive insurance arises from risk-averse drivers: they would rather pay a fixed premium than face the risk of loss or damage. The insurer, however, cannot directly observe either the driver's carefulness or degree of risk aversion.

Many automobile insurers offer comprehensive insurance with a choice of several deductibles, where the insurer compensates loss or damage only in excess of the specified deductible. Insurers charge relatively higher premiums for policies with lower deductibles.

The choice of deductible can screen drivers by their carefulness. Careful drivers will select cheaper policies that carry higher deductibles. Less careful drivers will prefer expensive policies with low deductibles. The choice of deductibles, however, also screens drivers by their degree of risk aversion. Less risk-averse drivers will prefer cheaper policies with high deductibles, while more risk-averse drivers will prefer policies with lower deductibles.

The choice of deductibles screens two characteristics: carefulness and risk aversion. A single variable, the deductible, cannot resolve the asymmetry of information over two characteristics. For instance, the insurer will not know whether those choosing the high-deductible policies are more careful drivers or less risk averse.

Generally, to resolve information asymmetries through screening, the less-informed party needs as many differentiating variables as there are characteristics that it cannot observe.

> **Progress Check 13E** Collateral is property that a borrower provides to a lender as a security for a loan. If the borrower defaults on the loan, the lender can seize the collateral. Explain how a lender can use requirements for collateral to screen among borrowers with different willingness to repay.

6 Auctions[4]

We have understood how businesses can apply screening to discriminate among buyers who are willing to pay different prices. Let us now discuss auctions, a pricing technique that screens by exploiting strategic interaction among potential buyers.

Consider the following example. Venus Paper wants to sell a tract of forest. There are many potential buyers and Venus wants to get the highest possible price. In this case, it does not seem feasible to apply indirect segment discrimination: what set of choices would induce self-selection? One feasible approach is to negotiate with all the possible buyers on an

---

[4] This section is more advanced. It may be omitted without loss of continuity.

individual basis. Individual negotiation, however, would take a lot of time. An alternative is for Venus to conduct an auction.

An auction applies competitive pressure to the participating bidders. Each bidder must act strategically since its best bid depends on the competing bids: if the other bids are low, then a bidder can win with a relatively low bid, while, if the other bids are high, then a bidder must bid relatively high to win. Each bidder faces a fundamental trade-off. By bidding more aggressively, it will improve its chances of winning the auction. On the other hand, if it bids more aggressively, it will get a smaller profit from winning the auction.

The differentiating variable in an auction is the probability of winning. A bidder with a higher value for the item will gain relatively more from winning the auction, and hence will pay relatively more for a higher probability of winning. Thus, the auction induces self-selection among the participants according to their respective values for the item.

Auction Methods

The **reserve price** is the price below which the seller will not sell the item.

There are various methods of conducting an auction. The bidding could be open or sealed. The seller may or may not specify a **reserve price**, below which it refuses to sell the item. In an auction for multiple items, each winning bidder could be required to pay the price that she or he bid, or the price bid by the marginal winning bidder.

How the method of auction affects bidding depends on various factors, including the extent to which bidders share the same value for the item on sale, the bidders' uncertainty about the true value, and bidders' risk aversion. Rather than investigate all of these factors in detail, we discuss some implications that apply generally.

Auction houses such as Christie's and Sotheby's use open auctions to sell jewelry, real estate, and works of art. The auctioneer calls out prices in an ascending sequence, and the bidders indicate whether or not they wish to continue participating. By contrast, other auctions allow only sealed bids. One factor in the choice between open and sealed-bid auctions is the potential for collusion among the bidders. Competing buyers can increase their net benefit by colluding to depress the price. This principle applies to auctions as well: competing bidders can benefit by agreeing on a low price.

The bidders in an open auction can see each other's behavior. This means that colluding bidders can observe whether they are each abiding by their collusive agreement. If one bidder cheats by bidding above the agreed price, another bidder can raise the price and prevent the cheater from winning the auction. By contrast, in a sealed-bid auction, a bidder can easily cheat on the collusive agreement with a bid exceeding the agreed price. The other bidders will learn about the cheating only when the seller announces the result of the auction. At that time, it would be too late to rein in the cheater.

Another difference between open and sealed-bid auctions concerns the character of information revealed during bidding in an open auction. We consider this difference later in this section.

We have discussed how open auctions are more vulnerable to collusion among bidders than sealed-bid auctions. The seller in open auction, however, can counteract collusion by applying a reserve price. A bidder must exceed the reserve price to get the item. The major reason for a seller to set a reserve price is to defeat collusion among the bidders. A reserve price forces bidders to bid higher or face the prospect of not getting the item.

The downside of a reserve price is that all the bids may fall below the reserve price. In this case, the sale will fail and the seller gets no revenue. Accordingly, in setting a reserve price, the seller must balance the increased revenue from a sale against the probability of no sale. A factor in this trade-off is the number of bidders: when there are many bidders, it is more likely that at least one bidder will exceed the reserve price.

In a nondiscriminatory auction, each winning bidder pays the price bid by the marginal winning bidder.

In a *discriminatory auction*, each winning bidder pays the price that she or he bid. By contrast, in a **nondiscriminatory auction**, each winning bidder pays the price bid by the marginal winning bidder. Since a winning bidder at a nondiscriminatory auction pays the price of the marginal winning bidder, a bidder at a nondiscriminatory auction should bid relatively higher than at a discriminatory auction.

> In a **discriminatory auction**, each winning bidder pays the price that she or he bid.

This, however, does not necessarily imply that the seller will get higher revenue from a nondiscriminatory auction. Although bidders make relatively higher bids, the seller collects only the price bid by the marginal bidder for each item sold. Whether a seller gets a higher revenue from a discriminatory or nondiscriminatory auction depends on the balance between the two factors.

Winner's Curse

In addition to not knowing their competitors' strategies, the bidders participating in an auction may also be uncertain about the value of the item for sale. For instance, in the example of Venus Paper, the various bidders may be unsure about the quantity of wood pulp that the trees will yield. Let us see how this uncertainty can affect the outcome of bidding.

Suppose that Joy is one of four bidders at the auction and that her estimate of the yield is 400,000 tons of pulp a year, while the other bidders have lower estimates. Then, Joy will probably make the highest bid and win the auction. On the basis of the information of all four bidders, however, Joy probably has overestimated the true yield. It is even possible that Joy's estimate is so high that her bid exceeds the true yield, so that she will incur a loss on the deal.

Joy's example illustrates the *winner's curse*. The **winner's curse** arises in an auction where the various bidders are uncertain about some common element in the value of the item for sale. A bidder whose estimate of that common element is high has a higher probability of winning. Hence, on average, the winning bidder is one who has overestimated the true value of the item.

> The **winner's curse** is that the winning bidder overestimates the true value of the item for sale.

A bidder should take account of the possibility of the winner's curse by bidding more conservatively, that is, aiming for a larger margin between her estimate of the value of the item and her bid. By bidding conservatively, she can reduce the likelihood of overbidding for the item.

The winner's curse is more severe when the number of bidders is larger, when the true value of the item is more uncertain, and in a sealed-bid compared with an open auction. If there are 20 bidders, then the winner will probably be one whose estimate is higher than 19 other estimates. By contrast, if there are four bidders, then the winner's estimate is probably higher than three other estimates. An estimate that is higher than 19 others is more likely to exceed the true value than an estimate that is higher than three others.

If the true value of the item is more uncertain, then the probability that the highest estimate exceeds the true value will be higher. Consider, for instance, an ounce of gold. There is no uncertainty about the true value of an ounce of gold. Every bidder would know the value to be the prevailing market price, and hence all their estimates and bids would be the same. The winner's curse arises only when there is uncertainty about the true value of the item for sale. The greater the uncertainty about the true value, then the greater will be the extent of the winner's curse.

In an open auction, bidders with relatively low values for the item will drop out progressively as the price ascends. Since the record of bidding is open, the remaining bidders can see the prices at which the various bidders drop out. The price at which a bidder drops out reveals information about her estimate of the true value of the item. The remaining bidders can use this additional information to refine their estimate of the true value. Hence, open bidding mitigates the winner's curse.

We have discussed three factors that affect the extent of the winner's curse. Whenever the winner's curse is relatively more severe, a bidder should adjust by bidding more conservatively.

Winner's curse: the Marina Line

Governments frequently use auctions to procure goods and services. The principles of an auction to buy are exactly the same as for an auction to sell. In an auction where the bidders are competing to supply an item and they are uncertain about some common cost element, the winner's curse is the prospect of bidding *less* than the true cost. The following example illustrates the winner's curse in a procurement auction.

Singapore's Land Transport Authority received six bids to build the 5.4 kilometer Marina Line subway. This included the construction of the Nicoll Highway and Boulevard stations and tunnels from downtown Marina to Stadium Boulevard.

Following a technical evaluation, the Authority eliminated three bidders. The remaining contractors and their bids were: Nishimatsu-Lum Chang Joint Venture (NLC), S\$275 million (Singapore dollars); Impregilo SPA-Hua Kok Realty Joint Venture, S\$343 million; and Samsung Corporation Engineering and Construction, S\$345 million.

The Authority awarded the contract to NLC in May 2001. However, NLC engineers under-estimated the difficulty of the project. By January 2004, the project was 12 weeks behind schedule, and the contractor faced the threat of paying \$46,000 per day in liquidated damages. Further, NLC engineers over-estimated the strength of the soil and provided inadequate temporary structures. On April 20, 2004, the structures collapsed at a critical point, causing the deaths of four workers.

Sources: "LTA's Choice of Lowest Bid Queried – Selection Panel Not Influenced by Costs: Official," *Today Online*, August 24, 2004; "24-hour Work Order: Nishimatsu Exec Denies Ignoring Danger Signs to Meet Deadline," *Straits Times*, October 9, 2004; "LTA Man Denies Delay Fears Led to Inaction: Contractor Told of Design Flaws 17 Months Later," *Today Online*, August 25, 2004.

Progress Check 13F Venus Paper has procured an independent appraisal of the tract that it is selling by auction.

(a)   Should it provide this information to the bidders?

(b)   How will this affect the extent of the winner's curse?

7   Signaling

In a situation where information is asymmetric, the marginal benefit does not equal the marginal cost; hence, a profit can be made by resolving the asymmetry. We have considered an indirect solution – screening, an initiative of the less-informed party to elicit the characteristics of the better-informed party.

Another indirect way of resolving an information asymmetry is through the initiative of the better-informed party. **Signaling** is an action by the better-informed party to communicate its characteristics in a credible way to the less-informed party.

> **Signaling** is an action by the better-informed party to communicate its characteristics in a credible way to the less-informed party.

To explain the concept of signaling, let us consider again the antiques market where buyers cannot distinguish between genuine items and fakes. In this market, the unknown characteristic is the true nature of an item. With the intrusion of fakes, the market outcome is not economically efficient. Since sellers of genuine antiques clearly suffer from the fakes, they may take the initiative to resolve the asymmetry of information.

Suppose that an antiques dealer guarantees to buy back anything that it sells at the original sale price at any time. To assure potential customers that the offer is legitimate, the dealer posts a sufficiently large bond with a reputable bank. Can this buyback offer effectively signal that the dealer is indeed selling a genuine antique? Equivalently, is the buyback offer a credible signal?

The answer depends on whether the seller of a fake will also make such a buyback offer. Assuming that buyers of fakes eventually discover the truth, a dealer who sells fakes and makes the buyback offer would eventually have to buy back all the fakes that it has sold. Accordingly, sellers of fakes would prefer not to make buyback offers. The buyback offer makes sense only for sellers of genuine antiques. Thus, it credibly distinguishes sellers of genuine antiques from sellers of fakes.

By contrast with appraisal which is direct, signaling indirectly communicates the characteristics of the better-informed party and thereby resolves the information asymmetry. The antiques dealer does not directly declare its item to be genuine. Rather, the dealer makes a commitment that indirectly and credibly communicates that it is selling a genuine item. Because sellers of fakes would not make the same commitment, the buyback offer is a credible signal. Thus, the buyback offer separates the market for genuine antiques from the market for fakes. With the two markets separated, the genuine market is described by figure 13.1.

Credibility

To be credible, a signal must induce self-selection among the better-informed parties. Specifically, the cost of the signal must be sufficiently lower for parties with superior characteristics than for parties with inferior characteristics. Then, only those with superior characteristics will offer the signal. For instance, in the case of the antique dealers, if buyers of fakes eventually discover the truth, then the cost of the buyback offer is lower for sellers of genuine antiques than for sellers of fakes. This cost difference drives the self-selection among the various sellers.

Suppose that an antiques dealer posts a sign "All genuine" outside its store. Will this be a credible signal? The answer depends on whether it is relatively more costly for the seller of a fake to post the sign. The cost of posting an "All genuine" sign is the same for sellers of genuine antiques and fakes. Hence, such a sign alone will not induce self-selection among sellers and cannot be a credible signal.

Advertising and Reputation

We have just claimed that an "All genuine" sign cannot be a credible signal that a seller is offering genuine antiques. Let us next consider a somewhat different proposal. Suppose that Mercury Antiques spends several thousand dollars to advertise that it deals only in genuine articles, and that the advertising expenditure is a sunk cost. Suppose that if Mercury pushes out fakes, then buyers will discover the subterfuge and the word will spread. If the word spreads quickly enough, Mercury will not recover the investment in its advertising. In this case, the advertising expenditure is an investment that pays off only if Mercury does indeed deliver genuine antiques.

A sunk investment that pays off only if the seller does indeed deliver good quality can be a credible signal. This signaling depends on three conditions. First, the investment must be sunk. If the advertising expenditure is reversible, then a seller of low quality can also make the same investment, pass out inferior products, and get its money back. A reversible investment would not be a credible signal.

Second, buyers must be able to detect poor quality fairly quickly. If a seller can fool buyers for a long time, then even one offering poor quality can afford the sunk investment. Many car owners purchase rust treatment: It is almost impossible for any individual driver to tell whether the treatment is effective. Automobile rust treatment is a product for which a sunk investment may not be a credible signal.

The third condition is that word of poor quality must spread and cut into the seller's future business. A one-time seller can afford to pass off poor quality because it will never face the punishment of losing repeat business. Fast-food restaurants along highways serve many customers on a one-time basis. If a restaurant provides poor quality, its customers may notice but they might never pass the same way again, so the restaurant does not lose.

⊢ Branding: signaling service station quality ⊢

Service stations market a variety of products ranging from hot dogs to gasoline and repair service. The seller's reputation is a potentially credible signal of good product quality. But, it would be credible only to customers who are likely to come back. What about one-time customers?

The asymmetry of information can be resolved through branding. A brand attaches its reputation to many service stations, all over the country. Hence, if one station provides poor service, it affects the reputation of the entire brand, and customers will cut back their patronage of all the stations with the same brand. The owner of the brand will invest effort in monitoring the various stations to maintain quality, and so avert a brand-wide drop in business.

Service stations along highways have a higher proportion of one-time relative to repeat customers. Hence, they have greater need for branding as a way to assure customers of product quality. An empirical study of service stations in eastern Massachusetts showed that stations along highways were 19% more likely to be affiliated with a major brand than stations off highways.

Source: I. P. L. Png and David Reitman, "Why Are Some Products Branded and Others Not?", *Journal of Law and Economics* 38, no. 1 (April, 1995), pp. 207–24.

Any investment that meets these three conditions can be a credible signal of good product quality. An "All genuine" sign may not be meaningful for a seller with a short time horizon. By contrast, a seller who has been in business for many years can build up a reputation. This is a sunk investment that would not make sense for a seller offering inferior quality.

> **Progress Check 13G** Explain the difference between screening and signaling.

8 Contingent Payments

We have discussed two indirect ways to resolve an information asymmetry: screening and signaling. Let us now consider a third indirect approach, which is to use a *contingent payment*. A **contingent payment** is a payment made if a specific event occurs. Bets are contingent payments: you get a dollar from me if the coin turns up heads, while I will get a dollar from you if it turns up tails. In this bet, the specific event is the side of the coin that faces up after the toss.

> A **contingent payment** is a payment made if a specific event occurs.

All insurance policies make use of contingent payments. A life insurance policy makes a payment in the contingency of death, a health insurance policy makes payments in the contingency of illness, and a driver's liability policy makes a payment in the contingency of an automobile accident.

Let us consider how contingent payments can be used to signal information. Recall Venus Paper's auction of a tract of forest. Suppose that Venus knows that these trees will yield an exceptional quantity of wood pulp, say, 600,000 tons a year. It, however, has no independent appraisal or other information that would directly convince potential buyers.

What if Venus were to specify that it would sell the tract for a share of the pulp production rather than a straight cash payment? By asking for a share, Venus is taking a payment that is contingent on the yield from the tract. If the tract produces a high yield, then Venus will get a higher payment, while if it produces a low yield, then Venus's payment will be low.

Selling the tract for a share of the production is a way by which Venus can signal its information to potential buyers. Other things equal, sellers of average or relatively low-yielding trees would prefer to sell for straight cash. Hence, those selling relatively better trees can distinguish themselves by selling for a share of the production. Accordingly, the share induces self-selection among sellers offering products of different quality.

Contingent payments can be used to screen as well as signal. In the example of Venus's trees, the seller can retain a share of the production as a way of signaling its information. On the other hand, a potential buyer could take the initiative of offering the seller a choice between payment in a share of the production or straight cash. A seller who chooses straight cash is implicitly admitting that the production will be relatively low. A seller of relatively high-yielding trees is more likely to choose the payment with a share of production.

The market for legal services provides another example of how contingent payments can resolve asymmetries of information. Suppose that Heather was hurt in an automobile accident. She has consulted a lawyer about suing the other driver. The lawyer has advised Heather that she can get at least $100,000 in damages.

Realistically, an experienced lawyer will be better informed than Heather about the amount that she can expect to recover in a law suit. In the United States, lawyers may be paid a contingency fee, under which the lawyer receives a percentage of the amount recovered from the other side. A lawyer on a contingency fee who loses the case will receive nothing.

The contingency fee can help to resolve the asymmetry of information between client and lawyer about the expected recovery from a law suit. A lawyer on a contingency fee will not have an incentive to exaggerate the expected recovery.

⊣ Buyback in international investment ⊢

Many developing countries want to boost their exports of manufactured products. With this aim, they actively promote the acquisition of production technology and equipment from foreign suppliers. The developing countries use these to produce manufactured items for export to the world market.

Compared with large multinational companies, however, developing countries suffer from an information asymmetry. They have relatively poor information about current technology and world market conditions. They worry that foreign suppliers are palming off old write-offs rather than providing the most cost-effective technology and equipment. They also worry that the foreign suppliers may exaggerate the market potential for the manufactured product.

One way to resolve the information asymmetry is to require the foreign supplier of production technology and equipment to buy back a specified quantity of future production of the manufactured item. The foreign suppliers' sales will depend on the quality of production technology and facilities that it had supplied to the developing country. The sales will also depend on the world market conditions.

Through the arrangement, the payment to the foreign supplier becomes contingent on the quality of production technology and equipment supplied and the supplier's estimate of world market conditions. The foreign supplier will then have a strong incentive to supply the most cost-effective technology and equipment and provide a realistic projection of the market potential for the manufactured product.

Source: Jean Francois Hennart, "The Transaction-Cost Rationale for Countertrade," *Journal of Law, Economics, and Organization* 5, no. 1 (Spring, 1989), pp. 127–53.

---

9   Summary

In situations of asymmetric information, the allocation of resources will not be economically efficient. The asymmetry can be resolved directly through appraisal or indirectly through screening, signaling, or contingent payments. The indirect methods depend on inducing self-selection among parties with different characteristics. Screening is an initiative of the party with less information, while signaling is an initiative of the party with better information.

A key business application of screening is indirect segment discrimination in pricing. A related application is auctions, which exploit strategic interaction among competing bidders to force bidders with higher values to pay higher prices.

When the distribution of information is asymmetric, one or more parties will have imperfect information and hence bear risk. The distribution of risk may conflict with the self-selection needed to resolve the asymmetric information.

Key Concepts

asymmetric information	insurance	discriminatory auction
imperfect information	adverse selection	nondiscriminatory auction
risk	screening	winner's curse
risk averse	self-selection	signaling
risk neutral	reserve price	contingent payment

Further Reading

For more on the economics of asymmetric information generally, see Eric Rasmusen, *Games and Information: An Introduction to Game Theory* (Cambridge, MA: Basil Blackwell, 2001) chapters 7–9 and 11. Paul Milgrom and John Roberts apply the economics of asymmetric information to corporate finance in chapter 15 of *Economics, Organization, and Management* (Englewood Cliffs, NJ: Prentice-Hall, 1992). Paul Klemperer applies the economics of asymmetric information to auctions in *Auctions: Theory and Practice* (Princeton, NJ: Princeton University Press, 2003).

Review Questions

1. Explain the difference between imperfect information and risk.
2. In the following situations, explain the asymmetry of information, if any.
   (a) Investors cannot perfectly predict the next day's Standard & Poor's 500 Index.
   (b) Acquirer is planning a takeover bid for Target at $50 a share, which is 25% above the current market price of $40. Directors of Acquirer are secretly buying shares of Target for their personal accounts.
3. True or false?
   (a) Where there is asymmetric information, there will be imperfect information.
   (b) Whenever people face risk, they will seek insurance.
4. Bohemian Clothing, a manufacturer of women's fashions, pays its production workers through a piece rate. The human resources manager has proposed to offer workers the alternative of a fixed salary. Will this alternative draw an adverse selection of workers?
5. Jill is about to buy a secondhand car. The seller is offering a below-market price. The seller has assured Jill that the car is in perfect mechanical condition. Explain why Jill should get an expert to evaluate the car.
6. Give an example of screening. Explain
   (a) the asymmetry of information;
   (b) how screening works through self-selection.
7. An automobile insurance policy with a $2,000 deductible only covers loss in excess of $2,000. Typically, automobile insurers offer policies with a choice between higher deductibles and higher premiums. Explain how this choice can screen among drivers with different probability of accident.
8. During peak hours, the demand for road space exceeds the available capacity. Drivers differ in their value of time. From the standpoint of economic efficiency, the road space should be allocated to the drivers who value time most highly. Explain how a toll on road usage can screen among drivers with different value of time.
9. This question relies on the auctions section. Explain the impact of the following on collusion among bidders at an auction:
   (a) using open bidding vis-à-vis sealed bids;
   (b) setting a reserve price.
10. This question relies on the auctions section. In which of the following auctions for the

rights to extract oil will the winner's curse be more serious?
- (a) The seller provides all available geological information to the bidders.
- (b) The seller has made a geological study but is keeping it secret.

11. Give an example of signaling. Explain
- (a) the asymmetry of information;
- (b) how signaling works.

12. A publisher of PC-based financial management software offers full refunds to any dissatisfied purchaser. Is the refund policy a credible signal of product quality?

13. If a borrower defaults on a secured loan, the creditor can seize and sell the item against which the loan is secured. Explain why the interest rate on secured loans is lower than that on unsecured loans.

14. Explain the meaning of a contingent payment.

15. Acquirer is interested in making a takeover bid for Target. Acquirer, being unsure about Target's true value, decides to offer an exchange of shares rather pay cash for Target. Explain how the exchange of shares resolves asymmetric information between Acquirer and Target.

Discussion Questions

1. Southwest Airlines pioneered the concept of a low-cost airline, operating from secondary airports with short hops and quick turn-arounds. Unlike the major U.S. network carriers, Southwest has succeeded in being consistently profitable for three decades. In 2005, Southwest increased net income by 75.1% to $548 million, or by 76.3% to $0.67 per share. One reason for Southwest's financial performance despite the sharp spike in the price of oil is that in 2005, the airline had hedged 85% of its fuel requirements at $26 per barrel of crude oil. Hedging saved the airline almost $900 million. Table 13.2 reports selected financial and operating information.
- (a) Referring to Southwest's fuel consumption in 2005. Explain how a 10-cent increase in the price of jet fuel would affect Southwest's costs and income.
- (b) Southwest is averse to risk. Explain why it has purchased crude oil derivatives to hedge the price of jet fuel.
- (c) Suppose that the actual price of crude oil turns out to be *lower* than the price at which Southwest hedged. Was Southwest wrong to have hedged?

Table 13.2 Southwest Airlines

	2005	2004
Total operating revenues ($ million)	7,584	6,530
Operating income ($ million)	820	554
Net income ($ million)	548	313
Available seat miles (billions)	85.2	76.9
Average fuel cost (cents per gallon)	103.3	82.8
Fuel consumed (million gallons)	1,287	1,201

2. Under California law, the owner of car must show proof of valid insurance to renew automobile registration. Drivers with poor records have difficulty securing insurance. Fortunately for them, Save-On Insurance Services of Los Angeles advertises "Lowest Rates, Low Monthly Payments, No One Refused."
- (a) What type of drivers will Save-On attract?
- (b) Consider the premiums for automobile insurance provided to all applicants ("No One Refused") with that for a select group such as government employees. Which would be higher? Explain why.
- (c) Is Save-On offering a good or bad deal?

3. Hong Kong University of Science and Technology has contracted with HSBC Insurance to provide medical insurance to university staff. Medical insurance covers the cost of the treatment and prescriptions necessary for the insured party to recover from an illness or accident.

    (a) Explain the asymmetry of information between the insurer and insured party.

    (b) Why do some insurers require a minimum co-payment for each treatment, even on the most expensive policies?

    (c) Unlike falling sick or meeting with accidents, in many cases, women voluntarily enter into pregnancy. Explain why HSBC covers pregnancy as part of the basic coverage, rather than as an option.

4. Many countries have a consumers' association that evaluates the quality and prices of consumer goods and services. Consumers pay for most of these assessments. Such associations include Which? (previously called the Consumers' Association) in the U.K. and the Consumers Union in the United States. Some countries also have institutions that test products according to specified standards. Testing institutions include the British Standards Institute, the TUV in Germany, and the Underwriters' Laboratory in the United States. Typically, manufacturers pay for their products to be tested.

    (a) Which are relatively more subjective: (i) product assessments by a consumer association or (ii) standards tests by a testing institution?

    (b) Based on your answer to (a), can you explain why consumers pay for most product assessments by consumer associations, while manufacturers pay for most tests by testing institutions?

5. At the request of an issuer, Moody's Investors Service will rate a debt obligation on a scale ranging from the highest grade of Aaa through Aa, A, Baa, Ba, B, to the lowest grade of Caa. Moody's studies show that issuers with lower ratings have been systematically more likely to default. Over the period 1920–99, the average 10-year default rate was 4.85% among investment-grade (Baa and higher) issuers, and 25.31% among speculative-grade (Ba and lower) issuers.

    (a) Explain the asymmetry of information between issuers of securities (borrowers) and their potential investors.

    (b) Explain why it is issuers of securities rather than potential investors who commission Moody's for ratings.

    (c) Why is it important that, historically, issuers with lower ratings have been systematically more likely to default?

6. Some mortgage borrowers plan to repay within a short time, while others intend to keep their loans for a longer period. The longer the period, the more profit the lender will earn from the loan. In May 2006, Digital Federal Credit Union of Marlborough, Massachusetts, advertised 30-year fixed interest loans as follows: a rate of 6.25% with 2 points, a rate of 6.5% with 1 point, and a rate of 6.75% with 0 points. The "points" are an up-front charge which is set as a percentage of the principal.

    (a) Mortgage lenders generally check borrowers through one of the three major consumer credit bureaus – Equifax, Trans Union, and Experian (formerly TRW). Will such credit reports help to resolve the lender's uncertainty about the borrower's repayment horizon? Considering only the interest and points paid on the basis of simple interest paid monthly, and assuming no repayment of principal, what is the break even time horizon between a loan at 6.25% with 2 points and a loan at 6.5% with 1 point? (Use the following formula: the interest and points paid on a $100,000 loan at 6.25% with 2 points over 24 months would be $(0.0625 \times 24/12 + 0.02) \times \$100,000 = \$14,500$.)

    (b) Explain how the choice of loans with different combinations of interest rates and points serves to screen among borrowers with different repayment horizons.

7. This question relies on the auctions section. In 2001, Singapore's Land Transport Authority shortlisted three contractors to build the Marina Line subway, which included two stations and

5.4 kilometers of tunnels. NLC bid S$275 million (Singapore dollars), Impregilo SPA-Hua Kok Realty Joint Venture bid S$343 million, and Samsung Corporation Engineering and Construction bid S$345 million. Three years later, in May 2004, the bids for contract 855 of the Circle Line were much closer. The contract included the construction of three stations and 4.35 kilometers of tunnels. In ascending order, the bidders were NLC (S$376–389 million), Woh Hup-Shanghai Tunnel Engineering Co. – Alpine Mayreder consortium (S$390–398 million), Obayashi (S$400.3 million), SembCorp Engineers (S$399–404 million), and Shimizu with United Engineers (S$449–453 million).

(a) Explain the winner's curse in the context of the bidding for the Marina Line.
(b) Explain how a contractor's degree of risk aversion would affect the amount that it bids.
(c) What experience from the Marina Line bidding did NLC apply in bidding for contract 855?
(d) Explain why the Authority should provide all available information about the soil conditions to the bidders.
(e) In projects subject to substantial uncertainty, such as tunneling, should the Authority agree to share part of the contractor's cost over-run? How would such sharing affect the contractor's bids?

8. In the late 1990s, Korean auto manufacturer, Hyundai Motor, was vilified by U.S. talk shows for producing tinny, unreliable cars. Chairman Chung Mong Koo decided to raise quality to "Toyota levels." Chairman Chung initiated twice-monthly meetings to review quality, and expanded the staff from 100 to 865 persons. In a shock to the U.S. auto industry, Hyundai extended its warranty to 10 years or 100,000 miles for the power train and 5 years or 60,000 miles for all other parts. By April 2004, J.D. Powers reported that Hyundai's initial quality – the number of complaints in the first 90 days of ownership – had climbed to rank with Honda at 102 per 100 cars, which was second only to Toyota. (*Source*: "Hyundai: Kissing Clunkers Goodbye," *BusinessWeek Online*, May 17, 2004.)

(a) Explain the asymmetry of information between Hyundai and its potential customers.
(b) Under what conditions would an extended product warranty be a credible signal of superior quality? In Hyundai's case, did the extended product warranty meet these conditions?
(c) How would the publication of the J.D. Powers report in 2004 have affected the asymmetry of information between Hyundai and its potential customers?

9. A major obstacle to business-to-consumer (B2C) e-commerce is Internet consumers' concern about privacy. BBBOnline's Privacy Seal, TRUSTe, and other services have arisen to certify Web-based vendors' compliance with privacy guidelines. BBBOnline was established by the Council of Better Business Bureaus, while TRUSTe was founded by CommerceNet, the Electronic Frontier Foundation, and the Boston Consulting Group.

(a) Would a certification service started by some college students be as effective as BBBOnline's Privacy Seal and TRUSTe?
(b) TRUSTe systematically "seeds" participating Web sites with user information to monitor whether the data are collected and used in conformance with stated privacy policies. Why does TRUSTe do this?
(c) Some major e-commerce vendors, including Amazon and Yahoo!, do not carry any third-party privacy seal. Explain why they have less need for external certification than less well-known vendors.

10. Established after World War II, the Long-Term Credit Bank of Japan (LTCB) helped to finance Japan's industrial miracle. LTCB, however, strayed from its original mission into real estate lending. When the Japanese real estate market collapsed, many of LTCB's loans turned sour. In June 1998, with its share price at ¥50, down more than 90% in nine months, LTCB tried but failed to merge with Sumitomo Trust and Banking, The Japanese government had to take over LTCB. In late 1999, American investor group Ripplewood Holdings bought LTCB with the government's promise to buy back LTCB's outstanding loans at book value if their value fell by more than 20%.

(a) Explain the asymmetry of information between the managements of LTCB and Ripplewood.

(b) Explain how the government's buyback guarantee could resolve the asymmetry of information.

(c) Compare the government's buy-back promise with an alternative scheme under which Ripplewood paid for LTCB in shares rather than cash.

11. This question applies the technique for deriving a market equilibrium with adverse selection presented in the math supplement. Suppose that the demand for genuine antiques is $D = 4 - p$ and the supply is $S = p - 2$, where D and S are in thousands of units a month and p represents price in hundreds of dollars. In addition, some sellers produce 500 fakes at no marginal cost.

(a) In a market of purely genuine antiques, what will be (i) the buyers' marginal benefit from a quantity Q, (ii) the sellers' marginal cost of providing a quantity Q, and (iii) the market equilibrium price and quantity.

(b) In a market including both genuine antiques and fakes, what will be (i) the buyers' marginal benefit from a quantity Q, (ii) the sellers' marginal cost of providing a quantity Q, and (iii) the market equilibrium price and quantity.

Chapter 13

Math Supplement

In an early section of the chapter, we presented a market equilibrium with adverse selection. Let us now derive the equilibrium precisely using algebra. Suppose that the demand for genuine antiques is

$$D = 8 - p \tag{13.1}$$

and the supply is

$$S = p - 2, \tag{13.2}$$

where D and S are in thousands of units a month and p represents price in hundreds of dollars.

Since the demand for genuine antiques is $D = 8 - p$, the buyers' marginal benefit from a quantity Q of genuine antiques is $(8 - Q)$. Since the supply of genuine antiques is $S = p - 2$, the sellers' marginal cost of providing a quantity Q of genuine antiques is $(2 + Q)$.

In a market of purely genuine antiques, the market equilibrium will be at the price where $D = S$; that is,

$$8 - p = p - 2, \tag{13.3}$$

or $p = 5$. At this price, $D = S = 3$.

Now, suppose that some sellers produce 1,000 fakes at no marginal cost. The market equilibrium includes both genuine antiques and fakes. Suppose that the equilibrium quantity is Q (in thousands of units a month). Then, a buyer's probability of getting a genuine antique is

$$(Q - 1)/Q. \tag{13.4}$$

We have shown the buyers' marginal benefit from a quantity Q of genuine antiques is $(8 - Q)$. Hence, with the fakes, the buyers' actual marginal benefit is

$$(Q - 1)/Q \times (8 - Q). \tag{13.5}$$

On the other side, the market supply consists of 1,000 fakes plus the genuine supply. Referring to figure 13.2, for any quantity Q, the marginal cost of the genuine and fake antiques is $2 + (Q - 1)$.

At the market equilibrium, the buyers' actual marginal benefit equals the sellers' marginal cost, which in turn is the market price:

$$(Q - 1)/Q \times (8 - Q) = 2 + (Q - 1), \tag{13.6}$$

or

$$2Q^2 - 8Q + 8 = 0, \tag{13.7}$$

which implies that $Q = 2$. By (13.5), the buyers' actual marginal benefit, and the market price, is $1/2 \times 6 = 3$.

Thus, the market equilibrium with both genuine antiques and fakes is at a price of $300 per unit and quantity of 2,000 units a month.

Previously, we also showed that the antiques market will fail if the quantity of fakes is too large. We can illustrate this with the mathematical model. Suppose that, in the preceding scenario, there are 2,000 rather than 1,000 fakes. Then, the buyers' actual marginal benefit will be

$$(Q - 2)/Q \times (8 - Q). \tag{13.8}$$

The sellers' marginal cost will become $2 + (Q - 2) = Q$.

In equilibrium, the buyers' actual marginal benefit equals the sellers' marginal cost:

$$(Q - 2)/Q \times (8 - Q) = Q, \tag{13.9}$$

or

$$2Q^2 - 10Q + 16 = 0. \tag{13.10}$$

This equation has no real roots, which implies that there is no equilibrium. In intuitive terms, the market has failed.

Chapter 14

Incentives and Organization

1 Introduction

Until 1970, Boeing, McDonnell Douglas, and Lockheed dominated the world market for large commercial aircraft.[1] Then, the governments of France and Germany established Airbus, Lockheed exited the industry, and Boeing acquired McDonnell Douglas. Today, Airbus and Boeing are the world's two leading commercial aircraft manufacturers. Until 2001, however, they had very different organizational architectures. Boeing was an integrated manufacturing company that is publicly traded on the New York Stock Exchange.

By contrast, Airbus was a sales, marketing, and customer-support organization, established under French law as a tax-free "groupement d'interêt economique." Airbus was owned by Aerospatiale-Matra (37.9%), British Aerospace (20%), Construcciones Aeronauticas (4.2%) and Daimler Aerospace (DASA) (37.9%). The four partners performed dual roles as shareholders of Airbus and industrial contractors, carrying out most of the design and all aircraft manufacturing.

Most major decisions required unanimous approval of the shareholders. Owing to its shareholders' dual role, Airbus was obliged to distribute production work among the partners according to political as well as economic considerations. For instance, when final assembly of the new A-318 was assigned to DASA's Hamburg plant, Aerospatiale demanded a share of DASA's work on the older A-319 model. Consequently, A-319 production was split between DASA in Hamburg and Aerospatiale in Toulouse. Another symptom of Airbus's peculiar organization was that it operated a dedicated fleet of huge transport aircraft to shuttle aircraft fuselage sections among the various production facilities.

The governments of Britain, France, Germany, and Spain recognized the difficulties with Airbus's organizational structure. They pressed for Airbus to be converted into a limited company that integrated design and production with sales, marketing, and customer support. Airbus' Chief Executive at the time, Noel Forgeard, was hopeful about the benefits of injecting a private-sector culture. They included estimated annual savings of 350 million euros through

---

[1] This discussion is based on "European Aerospace: Airbusiness as Usual," *The Economist*, June 19, 1999, p. 73; "BAe Expects Value of its 20% Holding in Airbus to Double," *Asian Wall Street Journal*, October 27, 1999, p. 23; "Airbus Rolls the Dice, Prepares to Make Bold Moves," *Seattle Times*, August 8, 1999; "Survey: Partners in Wealth," *The Economist*, January 21, 2006; Airbus web pages, www.airbus.com; and "Airbus' Crisis Looks Like Boeing's in 1997," Society of British Aerospace Companies, September 10, 2006.

elimination of duplicative management, streamlining of production, and reduction of inventories. For instance, the various Airbus partners could save a substantial sum by consolidating their purchases of aluminum alloy.

Some, however, resisted the organizational change. Former Aerospatiale Chairman, Yves Michot, dismissed corporatization as merely a "legal" issue and preferred Airbus to continue as an "industrial project." The corporatization of Airbus was also hampered by disagreement among the partners on the values of their respective assets that would be pooled into the new company.

> **Organizational architecture** comprises the distribution of ownership, incentive schemes, and monitoring systems.

Organizational architecture comprises the distribution of ownership, incentive schemes, and monitoring systems.[2] The Airbus example demonstrates the importance of organizational architecture: management estimated that corporatization could reduce costs by 350 million euros, which was significant for an entity with 17.8 billion euros annual revenues.

In 2001, Airbus became a fully integrated company, with the European Aeronautic Defence and Space Company (EADS) owning 80% and BAE Systems owning 20%. Nevertheless, Airbus continues to face organizational problems. Owing to a split in production of the jumbo A-380 between Hamburg and Toulouse, deliveries have been delayed by over two years, costing the company $6 billion in penalties and lost revenue. Tom Enders, co-CEO of the parent company, EADS, remarked that further restructuring, including overhaul of the entire supply chain would be required: "Airbus must change and change quite radically."

This chapter presents a framework for analyzing organizational architecture. An efficient organizational architecture resolves four internal issues – holdup, moral hazard, monopoly power, and economies of scale. A holdup is an action to exploit the dependence of another party. For instance, when Aerospatiale demanded a share of A-318 production, it exploited Airbus's dependence on it for supply of cockpits and forward fuselage sections.

Moral hazard arises when one party's actions affect but are not observed by another party, and the two parties have different interests. Airbus's production partners sold their services at fixed transfer prices. Each production partner had more incentive to economize on its own work, where it would enjoy the whole gain, than on the product of Airbus as a whole, from which it derived only a part of the gain.

As the management of Airbus well knows, changes in organizational architecture can help to resolve moral hazard and the potential for holdup. These changes can also influence costs through their impact on internal monopoly power and the extent of economies of scale and scope. The framework of analysis presented in this chapter can also be applied to address the important managerial issue of vertical integration and how to manage the related question of whether to "make or buy."

2   Moral Hazard

Suppose that Marie is a sales representative with Neptune Financial Advisors. By the very nature of her job, a salesperson operates independently. Hence, it is difficult for Neptune to monitor Marie's work.

---

[2] Brickley, Smith, and Zimmerman, *Managerial Economics and Organizational Architecture* (Maidenhead, UK: McGraw-Hill, 1997) coined the term "organizational architecture." This chapter draws heavily from chapters 9 and 10 of their book, and chapters 5–7, 9, and 16 of Paul Milgrom and John Roberts, *Economics, Organization, and Management* (Englewood Cliffs, NJ: Prentice-Hall, 1992).

Marie alone decides how many customers to visit, what routes to take, and how many breaks to take. Another feature of Marie's job is that she and her employer may disagree over how hard she should work. Neptune wants her to exert the maximum effort – to be patient and persuasive, yet persistent.

In this example, Marie is subject to *moral hazard*. A party is subject to **moral hazard** if its actions affect but are not observed by another party with whom it has a conflict of interest. There is a conflict of interest between Marie and her employer over her level of effort since she prefers less effort while her employer prefers her to exert more.

> **Moral hazard** exists when one party's actions affect but are not observed by another party with whom it has a conflict of interest.

Senior management in large publicly listed corporations are also subject to moral hazard. A large publicly-listed company may have many diverse shareholders ranging from pension funds with million-dollar holdings to individuals with several hundred shares. Few shareholders consider it worthwhile to monitor the managers of the company. Further, there may also be a conflict of interest between shareholders and management. While shareholders are primarily concerned about the value of their shares, senior managers may have other objectives such as building a large corporate empire or hobnobbing with fashionable artists.

Asymmetric Information about Actions

If Marie's employer could freely monitor her at all times, then it could direct her on how many customers to visit, what routes to take, how many breaks to take, etc. Then Marie would not be subject to moral hazard. As this discussion shows, moral hazard arises because information is asymmetric. The employer depends on the worker's effort but cannot observe it.

In chapter 13, we discussed asymmetric information in situations such as buying and selling antiques, an application for life insurance where the applicant has better information about his or her health, and an application for a loan where the borrower has better information about prospective repayment. In these cases, the asymmetry of information concerned some individual characteristic of the better-informed party.

By contrast, in the example of Neptune Financial Advisors, the salesperson has better information about her future actions. In this case, the asymmetry of information concerns some future action of the better-informed party. This information asymmetry is a necessary condition for there to be moral hazard.

Economic Inefficiency

In the case of Neptune Financial Advisors the degree of effort that a salesperson exerts at work affects the employer's revenues and costs and, hence, profit. Let us separate the wages and other incentives that the employer pays to the worker from the employer's other costs. We call the employer's revenue less the other costs, the employer's benefit. Then the employer's profit is its benefit less the wages and other incentives paid to the worker.

For the worker, her net benefit is these wages and incentives less the cost of her effort. Considering the worker and the employer as a group, the group's net benefit from the worker's effort is the employer's benefit less the worker's cost of effort.

If a salesperson increases her effort, the resulting change in the employer's profit is its marginal benefit from the worker's effort. The additional cost required to increase effort is the worker's marginal cost of effort. In figure 14.1, we draw the employer's marginal benefit from the salesperson's effort and the worker's marginal cost of effort.

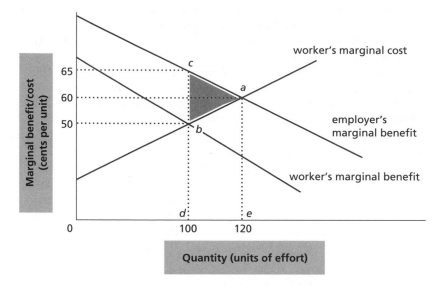

Figure 14.1 Economically efficient effort
The economically efficient level of effort, 120 units, balances the employer's marginal benefit with the worker's marginal cost. The worker chooses 100 units of effort, which balances her personal marginal benefit with her marginal cost. The lower the worker's marginal benefit is relative to the employer's marginal benefit, the lower will be the effort that the worker chooses relative to the economically efficient level.

From the perspective of maximizing the group's net benefit, the worker should put in the amount of effort that balances the employer's marginal benefit with the worker's marginal cost. By the definition in chapter 6, this also characterizes the economically efficient level of effort. Referring to figure 14.1, the employer's marginal benefit equals the worker's marginal cost at an effort of 120 units. There, the employer's marginal benefit is 60 cents per unit of effort, which equals the worker's marginal cost of 60 cents per unit of effort.

Recall, however, that the worker acts independently. Hence, the worker does not consider the employer's marginal benefit but rather her personal marginal benefit from effort. Her personal marginal benefit depends on the structure of her wages and other incentives. In figure 14.1, we also draw the worker's personal marginal benefit from effort. The worker chooses the level of effort that balances her personal marginal benefit with her marginal cost. This is the level of effort that will actually be realized.

Referring to figure 14.1, the worker's marginal benefit equals her marginal cost at an effort of 100 units. At that level, the worker's marginal benefit and marginal cost are both equal to 50 cents. At 100 units of effort by the worker, however, the employer's marginal benefit is 65 cents. This exceeds the worker's marginal cost of 50 cents.

Generally, a party that is subject to moral hazard will choose to act according to its own marginal benefit and marginal cost. As a result, its behavior will diverge from the economically efficient choice.

Suppose that the worker could be induced to increase her effort to 120 units. Then the additional benefit to the employer would be the area *cdea* under the employer's marginal benefit curve, between 100 and 120 units of effort. The additional cost to the worker would be the area *bdea* under the worker's marginal cost curve, between 100 and 120 units of effort. Hence, the additional benefit to the employer would exceed the additional cost to the worker by the shaded area *acb*. This represents the amount of profit that can be earned by resolving the worker's moral hazard. The challenge then is how to resolve the moral hazard.

Degree of Moral Hazard

Suppose that there was no conflict of interest between Marie and Neptune Financial Advisors. This means that the worker's marginal benefit from effort would coincide exactly with the employer's marginal benefit from effort. Then, the worker would choose the economically efficient level of effort. Under these conditions, there will be no moral hazard.

Referring to figure 14.1, the lower the worker's marginal benefit is relative to the employer's marginal benefit, the lower will be the effort that the worker chooses relative to the economically efficient level.

This example suggests that we can measure the degree of moral hazard by the difference between the economically efficient action and the action chosen by the party subject to moral hazard. The larger this difference is, the greater will be the degree of moral hazard and the gain in net benefit that can be realized by resolving the moral hazard.

Progress Check 14A Suppose that the worker's marginal cost of effort in figure 14.1 were higher. Draw the new marginal cost curve. How does this affect (a) the economically efficient level of effort and (b) the effort that the worker actually chooses?

⊣ Moral hazard can be costly: alternative fuels ⊢

In 2000, the state of Arizona initiated an alternative fuels tax credit program aimed at increasing purchases of hybrid vehicles that run on alternative fuels, as well as on gasoline. The cost of the program was orginally estimated to be $3–$10 million. In its first year, the cost ballooned to an estimated $600 million – more than 20,000 people signed up. The tax credit applied to retrofits of old vehicles and purchases of new vehicles than could use alternative fuels, such as propane, hydrogen, or compressed natural gas.

An earlier state tax credit had already shown signs of moral hazard problems. A tax credit for electric plug-in vehicles prompted people to buy the electric vehicles for $6,000–$12,000, apply for a $10,000 tax refund, and then donate the vehicles to charity in exchange for tax deductions. The new program expanded the range for moral hazard.

Small car conversion companies proliferated. A state official claimed "It's amazing how many people get concerned about air quality when they get a vehicle for 45 cents on the dollar." People purchased gas guzzling SUVs, retrofitted them for alternative fuels (that they did not actually have to use), and received tens of thousands of dollars of tax credits. The most extreme case may have been the credits for vehicles to run on compressed natural gas, for which the entire state had only one filling station at the time.

Facing a budget nightmare, the state finally scaled back the program to reduce the estimated cost to $200 million. Many consumers, having arranged to buy vehicles eligible for the rebate, were left unhappy.

Sources: "The Making of a Quagmire: Alt-Fuel Flap a Tale of Legal Drama, Fiscal Tragedy," *The Arizona Republic*, November 3, 2000; "Hull Signs Alt-Fuels Remedy Says She Expects Some Lawsuits Over Change," *The Arizona Republic*, December 15, 2000.

⊣ **Moral hazard in medicine: what did the doctor order?** ⊢

Patients rely on doctors for advice and, often, get treatment from the doctor providing the advice. Consequently, the doctor is subject to moral hazard. The more treatment a doctor recommends, the more he or she will earn.

Obstetricians are doctors who specialize in treating pregnant women and delivering babies. Babies can be delivered either naturally through the vagina or by cesarean section. A study of pregnant Brazilian women focused on those who preferred vaginal delivery. Of those who delivered in public hospitals, 30% (81 of 269) received cesarean sections. Of those who delivered in private hospitals, 66% (117 of 177) received cesarean sections.

The researchers offered three possible interpretations of the large discrepancy between public and private hospitals. One was that Brazilian obstetricians might believe that a cesarean section is safer for the baby and more comfortable for the mother. Another was that the obstetricians did not know the patients preference for vaginal delivery. The final reason was that cesarean deliveries were faster and more convenient for the obstetrician.

Very politely, the researchers did not mention that obstetricians also earn more from cesarean sections than vaginal delivery.

Source: Joseph E. Potter et al., "Unwanted Caesarean Sections among Public and Private Patients in Brazil: Prospective Study," *British Medical Journal* 232 (November, 2001), pp. 1155–8.

⊣ **Flood insurance: natural hazard or moral hazard?** ⊢

Hurricane Katrina focused attention on the problems with Federal Flood Insurance. Not only does the NFIP suffer from adverse selection, but has moral hazard problems as well. Two types of moral hazard are apparent.

Just 1% of the NFIP policies have generated 30% of the total claim amounts, mostly through repetitive losses. Often these are older structures that do not meet current flood mitigation standards. NFIP rules require that mitigation measures be taken if structure damage exceeds 50%. This is difficult to enforce, and irrelevant to many of these properties. Often the damage is less than 50%, but the property suffers repeated damage from flood events. There is no requirement to take preventative action, and little incentive to do so with subsidized flood insurance.

The second type of moral hazard does not result from the behavior of people with insurance. It provides an additional reason why people might opt not to purchase insurance. Past efforts to expand the pool of insured households have required flood insurance in SFHAs (as described in chapter 13). Households may come to believe that the government will require flood insurance if it is really necessary.

This may partially explain why voluntary purchase of flood insurance is so rare. It is estimated that there is a 25% chance of a home being flooded by a 1% chance flood at some time during the term of a 30-year mortgage, while there is only a 1% chance of a fire within that same time frame. Yet most homeowners purchase fire insurance and few purchase flood insurance (voluntarily). It is estimated that only 25% of structures in flood hazard areas are covered.

Source: Rawle O. King, Congressional Research Service, Library of Congress, *Federal Flood Insurance: The Repetitive Loss Problem*, June 30, 2005.

3 Incentives

We have identified the potential gains from resolving moral hazard. Generally, there are two complementary approaches to resolve moral hazard. One is to invest in monitoring, surveillance, and other methods of collecting information about the behavior of the party subject to moral hazard. The other approach is to align the incentives of the party subject to moral hazard with those of the less-informed party.

Monitoring systems and incentive schemes are two elements of organizational architecture. They are complementary because all incentives must be based on behavior that can be observed, so the better the available information is, the wider the choice of incentive schemes will be. Ideally, the relevant parties would like to completely resolve the moral hazard, so that the better-informed party will make the economically efficient choice. Let us now discuss how to resolve the moral hazard of a worker relative to her employer.

Monitoring

The simplest monitoring system focuses on objective measures of performance. Most employers require workers to punch a card to record the time at which they arrive and depart work. The time clock is a basic and almost universal monitoring system.

Hours on the job, however, is distinct from effort. A worker can arrive at 8:00 a.m. and leave at 5:00 p.m., but do nothing during that time. Accordingly, employers need monitoring systems that provide more than basic objective information.

One method that employers frequently use to collect information is supervision. It is not cost effective for supervisors to monitor workers all the time, however. Hence, supervisors should make only random checks. In chapter 10, we discussed the advantages of randomization. The same principle applies to supervision: the supervisor should check workers at random, rather than according to some regular pattern.

Employers can also enlist customers to monitor worker performance. Customers have a natural advantage in monitoring workers, such as sales representatives, who spend more time with customers rather than at the employer's location. Employers can encourage customers to report worker performance and then follow up by investigating reports of especially poor or good performance.

Monitoring truck drivers: onboard computers

Truck drivers must operate independently and may travel far from base. Some trucks are equipped with onboard computers. There are two types of onboard computers – trip recorders and electronic vehicle-management systems (EVMSs). A trip recorder provides an electronic record of speed, idle time, and other data. An EVMS includes the functions of a trip recorder and, in addition, provides real-time information about the vehicle location and a communications system to allow the dispatcher to direct the driver.

The management of a trucking business can use trip recorders and EVMSs to monitor its drivers. A study of the U.S. trucking industry found significant differences in the adoption of onboard computers between owner- and employee-operated trucks, and between trucks driven over short as compared with long distances.

Only 7% of owner-operated trucks were equipped with onboard computers, as compared with 19% of employee-operated trucks. An owner-operator would not need to monitor himself, hence derives less benefit from an onboard computer.

Only 6% of trucks that operated at fewer than 50 miles from base were equipped with an onboard computer. By contrast, 19% of trucks that operated at distances of 100–200 miles had onboard computers. Truckers who operate at greater distance will be more difficult to monitor through personal supervision. Hence, management derives a greater benefit from installing an onboard computer to monitor such drivers.

Source: Thomas N. Hubbard, "The Demand for Monitoring Technologies: The Case of Trucking," *Quarterly Journal of Economics* 115, no. 2 (May 2000), pp. 533–60.

Performance Pay

The counterpart to monitoring systems is incentive schemes. Incentive schemes resolve the moral hazard by tying payments to some measure of performance. The schemes depend on a link between the unobservable action and some observable measure of performance. Generally, the scope of incentive schemes depends on what indicators of the unobservable action are available.

An employer can use the information provided by monitoring systems to structure incentives for its workers. For instance, in the case of Neptune Financial Advisors, the employer cannot observe Marie's effort. But it can monitor the value of financial products sold. Then it could base incentives on Marie's sales revenue.

Performance pay is an incentive scheme that bases pay on some measure of performance.

One common incentive scheme is **performance pay**, which bases a worker's pay on some measure of performance. Let us consider performance pay in the Neptune example. Suppose first that Neptune pays Marie a fixed monthly wage of $3,000 and that Neptune does not monitor Marie at all, not even using a diary of sales calls.

Then, Marie cannot affect her earnings in any way, whether she starts early or late and whether she persists or not. Her personal marginal benefit from effort will be zero. In figure 14.2, the worker's personal marginal benefit with a fixed wage is the horizontal axis. This is lower than the worker's marginal cost at all levels of effort. Hence, with a fixed wage, the worker chooses no effort. (Realistically, she chooses the level just exceeding the level that the employer can freely observe.)

Now, suppose that Neptune pays Marie a 10% commission on each financial product sold. This is an example of payment based on performance. The more products that Marie sells, the more she will earn. With this incentive scheme, her personal marginal benefit from effort will be positive. The height and slope of the personal marginal benefit curve depend on how the worker's effort affects the number of deliveries.

In figure 14.2, we also show the worker's personal marginal benefit with a 10% commission. This crosses her marginal cost at an effort of 80 units. With a 10% commission, the worker chooses effort of 80 units. Accordingly, the commission helps to resolve the worker's moral hazard.

An incentive scheme is relatively "stronger" if it provides a higher personal marginal benefit for effort. Suppose that the employer strengthens the incentive scheme by raising the commission to 15%. Then the worker's personal marginal benefit curve would be higher, and it would cross the marginal cost curve at a higher level of effort, say, at 100 units of

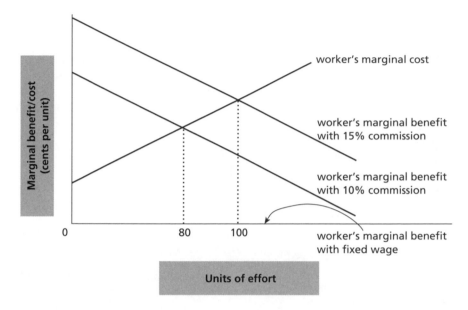

Figure 14.2 Performance pay
With a fixed daily wage, the worker's personal marginal benefit is the horizontal axis. A commission of 15%
leads the worker to choose more effort than a 10% commission.

effort. This shows that the stronger the incentive scheme is, the higher the worker's effort
will be.

> **Progress Check 14B** Using figure 14.2, draw a personal marginal benefit curve such
> that the worker would choose the economically efficient level of effort.

Performance Quota

If Neptune paid a large enough commission, Marie's personal marginal benefit would be
sufficiently high that she would choose the economically efficient 120 units of effort. This,
however, may mean paying a large sum of money in commissions.

Let us explore another way to induce a worker to choose the economically efficient level
of effort. Suppose that Neptune establishes the following incentive scheme: Neptune will
pay a fixed monthly wage provided that the salesperson sells a specified
quota of sales revenue; otherwise, she will be dismissed.

The incentive scheme just described is a *performance quota*. A **performance quota** is a minimum standard of performance, below which a
worker is subject to penalties. The penalties could include deferral of
promotion, reduction in pay, or even dismissal.

> A **performance quota** is
> a minimum standard of
> performance, below
> which penalties apply.

To apply a performance quota, Neptune Financial Advisors must identify the sales revenue
that would result if Marie chose the economically efficient 120 units of effort. Suppose that
120 units of effort would generate sales revenue of $300,000. Then the employer should

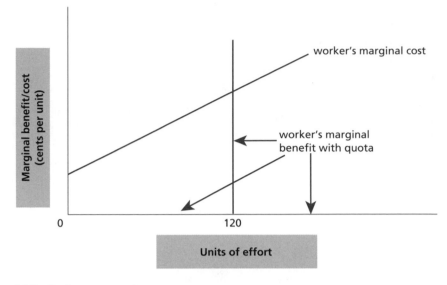

Figure 14.3 Performance quota
With a quota of $300,000 per month, the worker's personal marginal benefit curve has three parts, and the worker chooses 120 units of effort.

set the performance quota at $300,000 per month. In figure 14.3, we show the worker's personal marginal benefit curve with such a quota.

The worker's personal marginal benefit curve has three parts. Recall that the employer pays the worker a fixed monthly wage provided that he or she meets the quota; otherwise that worker will be dismissed. At 119 units of effort and below, the worker will be dismissed. Additional effort does not affect her earnings; hence, her personal marginal benefit is zero.

The incentive scheme pays the worker no extra for additional effort above 120 units. Accordingly, at 121 units of effort and above, the worker's personal marginal benefit also is zero. The personal marginal benefit, however, is very high at exactly 120 units of effort. An increase in effort from 119 to 120 units is just enough to satisfy the quota and hence allows worker to retain her job.

Thus, the worker's personal marginal benefit curve follows the horizontal axis from 0 to 119 units of effort, spikes up at 120 units, and then follows the horizontal axis again at 121 units of effort and above. Therefore, the personal marginal benefit curve crosses the marginal cost at 120 units of effort. Accordingly, the worker chooses 120 units of effort.

A performance quota is a cost-effective way of inducing the worker to choose the economically efficient level of effort. It is cost-effective because it does not reward effort below or above the economically efficient level. It focuses the incentive at the economically efficient level of effort.

Progress Check 14C Suppose that 100 units of effort would generate $250,000 worth of sales. Using figure 14.3, illustrate the worker's marginal benefit if the employer specifies a sales quota of $250,000 per month.

⊢ Performance incentives ⊢

Harold D. Stolovitch, Richard E. Clark, and Steven J. Condly undertook a comprehensive study of the impact of performance incentives. They conducted a meta-analysis of 45 published studies on incentives, which were identified as being adequately designed and reported from a pool of over 600 studies.

Further, they surveyed U.S. organizations that had used incentive schemes. Of these, 145 of 400 (37%) responded to a full-length survey. The research team also conducted 90 structured interviews with designers and selectors of incentive schemes, and persons subject to incentives and their supervisors.

They found that, on average, tangible incentives (money, gifts, travel) to individuals increase performance by 27%. In decreasing order, the most to least effective incentive schemes were: performance quotas, performance pay, relative performance pay, and fixed wages.

The research team also found long-term incentives to be more effective than shorter-term incentives.

Source: "Incentives, Motivation and Workplace Performance," Harold D. Stolovitch and Associates, Performance Newsletter, Winter/Spring, 2002, www.hsa-lps.com/Performance_WS_2002.htm.

⊢ When incentives are too weak – real estate agents ⊢

Superficially, it would seem that real estate agents and home sellers would have their interests aligned – the agent typically gets a fee of 6% of the sales price of the house. Thus, the seller would like to get as high a price as possible, and the agent would as well.

However, home sales are also a situation of asymmetric information. The real estate agent typically has better information about the actual market value of a home than does the home seller.

A closer look at the agent's incentives casts doubt on the alignment of incentives. For example, consider the sale of your $300,000 house. The agent would receive a fee of $18,000 (6%), usually split equally between the seller's and buyer's agents. Then, each agent gives half of their fee to their respective agency. The agent is still left with $4,500 – though this is only 1.5% of the sales price.

If the agent could sell the house for $310,000 with more effort, you would receive an additional $9,400 while the agent would get 1.5% of the extra $10,000, or $150. For this additional payment, the agent would need to spend additional time, money, and energy.

This hypothetical example was presented by Steven Levitt, who then proceeded to examine data on 100,000 Chicago homes, some of which were sold on behalf of clients and some which were owned by the agents themselves. On average, the agent-owned homes stayed on the market an average of 10 days longer and sold for an extra 3%. On her own house, an agent would earn all of the additional benefit from the 10 extra days of marketing.

Source: Steven D. Levitt and Stephen J. Dubner, *Freakonomics* (London: HarperCollins, 2005), pp. 8–9.

Multiple Responsibilities

Until this point, we have focused on situations where the moral hazard concerns a single action or responsibility. In many cases, however, the party subject to the moral hazard has multiple responsibilities. For instance, a sales representative may be responsible for selling as well as providing post-sales service to the customer. In a factory, production supervisors may be responsible for meeting output targets as well as maintaining quality.

Consider situations where the moral hazard concerns multiple responsibilities. This means that the party subject to moral hazard takes multiple actions that affect but are not observed by another party with whom it has a conflict of interest.

Ideally, an incentive scheme should aim to balance the multiple responsibilities. This means that there should be some investment in monitoring each of the unobservable actions and incentives based on the corresponding indicators.

Balancing multiple responsibilities becomes harder when it is more difficult to measure performance for some responsibilities than others. An incentive scheme may focus on a particular responsibility because that dimension is relatively easier to monitor. As we emphasized previously, the scope of an incentive scheme depends on the available indicators of the unobservable action.

Suppose that the incentive scheme focuses on just one responsibility. Then, it will induce better performance on that dimension but have the side effect of aggravating the moral hazard with regard to the other responsibilities.

For instance, a factory wants its production supervisors to meet output targets as well as maintain product quality. Output is easy to measure. However, product quality may be difficult to measure. If the factory adopts a strong incentive scheme for output, the supervisors would tend to focus on output, and quality would fall.

⊣ Balancing multiple responsibilities: teaching to the test ⊢

Teachers are expected to pursue multiple objectives: helping students learn basics, helping students achieve their potential, and addressing student moral development are among the most important. Efforts to improve school performance frequently involve standardized testing and rewarding teachers and schools on the basis of (improvement in) test scores. The "No Child Left Behind" legislation in the U.S. is a notable example.

Critics of these developments often point to the potential substitution of the more easily measured test performance for more difficult-to-measure goals, such as moral development. These concerns are compounded by the troubling evidence that the easily measured test performance is itself inaccurate, due to cheating. In fact, one study reports that cheating may have occurred in 3.4%–5.6% of all classrooms where "high stakes" testing was being used.

The study points out that this cheating by teachers, test administrators, or principals can be easily prevented through better testing procedures. However, "the challenge for educators and policymakers will be to develop a system that captures the obvious benefits of high-stakes testing as a means of providing incentives while minimizing the possible distortions that these measures induce."

Source: A. Jacob and Steven D. Levitt, 2004, "Rotten Apples: An Investigation of the Prevalence and Predictors of Teacher Cheating," www.educationnext.org/unabridged/20041/68.html.

Incentive schemes focus on actions for which there are reliable measures of performance. If, however, there are important responsibilities for which it is difficult to measure performance, then it will be better to adopt relatively weak performance incentives in general. A deliberate use of *weak incentives* is a way to achieve a balance among multiple responsibilities.

Progress Check 14D Suppose that a department store has switched its sales clerks from a fixed salary to a salary plus a commission on sales. How will this affect the sales clerks' incentive to process returns?

---

4 Risk

Incentive schemes resolve moral hazard by tying payments to some observable indicator of the unobservable action. But, what if the indicator is affected by factors other than the unobservable action? Then, the payments will depend on these other factors. A party who is subject to moral hazard and has imperfect information about these factors will face risk.[3]

For instance, in the example of Neptune Financial Advisors, Marie's incentives may be based on her monthly sales revenue. But her monthly sales revenue may also depend on other factors such as the general state of the economy, traffic congestion, and the weather. An incentive scheme based on monthly sales revenue will impose a risk on Marie. Specifically, it is possible that, even when she puts in a great deal of effort, her sales will be hindered by factors outside her control.

Risk arises whenever incentives are based on an indicator that depends on extraneous factors and the party subject to the moral hazard has imperfect information about those factors. The incentive scheme that maximizes net benefit, that is, the economically efficient scheme, must balance the incentive for effort with the cost of risk.

Costs of Risk

The cost imposed by risk depends on three factors. The first is the structure of the incentive scheme. Generally, as we showed in the preceding section, a stronger incentive scheme would induce the worker to increase her effort. A stronger incentive scheme, however, would impose a heavier burden of risk on the party subject to moral hazard.

For example, in figure 14.2, if the commission per sale were raised from 10% to 15%, the worker would increase the effort from 80 to 100 units. With the larger commission, however, a bigger part of worker's income will depend on sales revenue. This means that the worker will bear more risk.

The second factor that affects the risk-bearing cost is the degree of risk aversion in the party subject to moral hazard. If the party is risk neutral, then the risk imposes no cost. Risk imposes a cost only if the party is risk averse. The more risk averse that the party is, then the larger will be the cost imposed by risk.

The third factor is the effect of the uncertain, extraneous factors on the indicator that forms the basis for the incentive scheme. If the indicator is sensitive to these extraneous factors and the factors are subject to wide swings, then the risk would be relatively large. By

---

[3] The reader may wish to refer to the section on imperfect information in chapter 13.

contrast, if the indicator is not sensitive to these factors or the factors do not vary much, then the risk would be relatively smaller.

Generally, the incentive scheme should be stronger if the party subject to moral hazard is relatively less risk averse and the extraneous factors are weaker. Conversely, the incentives should be weaker if the risk aversion is higher and extraneous factors have a stronger influence.

Progress Check 14E Alan and Marie are sales persons for Neptune Financial Advisors. Alan is more risk averse than Marie. Whose incentive scheme should be stronger?

Relative Performance Incentives

In some situations, the moral hazard can be resolved in a very natural way without imposing risk. Suppose that Marie is just one of many salespersons working for Neptune Financial Advisors. Then Neptune could adopt the following incentive scheme, which is based on *relative* performance. Using sales records of the various salespersons, Neptune can calculate the average sales revenue. It can then pay each salesperson a fixed monthly wage plus a 10% commission for all sales revenue in excess of the average for all salespersons.

Neptune's incentive scheme will not penalize Marie for an extraneous factor like a bad economy. If the economy weakens, this would affect all salespersons. If Marie exerts relatively more effort, she will still achieve higher sales than the average and hence will earn the commission.

By gauging performance on a relative basis, the incentive scheme cancels out the effect of extraneous factors to the extent that they affect all workers equally. This reduces the risk due to extraneous factors.

Even with a relative incentive scheme, however, a worker must continue to bear the risk due to idiosyncratic factors that do not affect all workers to the same extent. For instance, if Marie's territory is relatively more prone to traffic congestion, she will suffer relatively more risk from this factor.

Generally, an incentive scheme based on relative performance will eliminate the risk due to extraneous factors that affect all parties equally. Relative incentive schemes are most useful where common extraneous factors are important.

⊢ Evaluating managerial performance: Medtronic ⊢

Headquartered in Minneapolis, Medtronic manufactures medical devices for a wide range of conditions, including cardiac rhythm disease, coronary artery and peripheral vascular disease, diabetes, and neurological illnesses. In 2005–6, Medtronic earned net income of $2.55 billion (or $2.09 per share) on revenue of $11.29 billion.

A common way of evaluating the performance of company management is through total shareholder return, which includes dividends and appreciation in the stock price. Between 2001–5, Medtronic yielded total shareholder return of 20%. Should investors have cheered?

Not if they considered their alternatives. Figure 14.4 shows the cumulative total shareholder return from a $100 investment in Medtronic shares as compared with the Standard & Poor's Healthcare Equipment Index, which is an index of shares of manufacturers

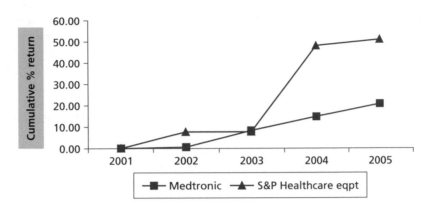

Figure 14.4   Medtronic: relative performance

of healthcare equipment. An investment in the Index would have been much more profitable.

This example suggests that a more reasonable way of evaluating managers is to measure their performance against that of other companies in the same industry. Relative performance evaluation cancels out background factors over which managers have no control. This yields a more accurate measure of management's performance.

Yet, in 2005, Medtronic paid Chairman and CEO Arthur D. Collins, Jr, over $1.27 million in long-term incentive awards. These awards are based on "performance goals of diluted earnings per share, revenue growth and after-tax return on net assets." For the period 2003–5, the Compensation Committee of Medtronic's Board of Directors awarded 110% of the target award to all executive officers including CEO Collins.

Source: Medtronic, Inc., "Proxy Statement," July 21, 2005.

5   Holdup

The architecture of an organization includes incentive schemes and monitoring systems. It can help to resolve holdup as well as moral hazard.

To understand the meaning of a *holdup*, suppose that Luna Supermarket engages Speedy Deliveries to deliver grocery orders. According to their contract, Speedy makes two rounds of deliveries a day, one beginning at 12:00 noon and another at 4:00 p.m. One day, however, Luna received so many delivery orders that it asked Speedy to make a third round. Sensing that Luna was in a desperate situation, Speedy refused to make the additional delivery unless Luna paid twice the usual price.

In this example, Speedy took advantage of Luna's special need to *holdup* the supermarket. A **holdup** is an action to exploit another party's dependence. A holdup is distinct from moral hazard in that it does not require asymmetric information. For example, when Luna requested the extra delivery, Speedy openly refused. Luna could clearly observe Speedy's action: hence, there was no asymmetry of information. A holdup is similar to moral hazard in that it arises only when there is a conflict of interest between the parties.

> A **holdup** is an action to exploit another party's dependence.

Speedy's holdup has implications beyond the exceptional price that Luna paid on that one occasion. The prospect of a holdup in the future will lead Luna to take precautions and avoid depending too much on Speedy. For instance, Luna might warn customers that delivery cannot be assured on the same day, it might limit the number of orders for delivery each day, or it might establish its own delivery service.

Limiting the number of orders for delivery each day will reduce Luna's benefit from Speedy's service. Establishing its own delivery service will add to Luna's costs. Luna's precautions either reduce its benefit from Speedy's service or increase its own costs.

Generally, whenever there is the potential for holdup, other parties will take precautions to avoid dependence. These precautions either reduce the benefit from the relationship or increase costs. Thus, the potential for a holdup reduces the group's net benefit.

Specific Investments

One particular type of precaution against a holdup is not so obvious and, hence, should be highlighted. Suppose that, to optimize delivery time and fuel, Speedy has installed a computerized route planning system on every truck. To use this system, every package must be marked with a suitable barcode strip. Then, the driver scans the packages so that the onboard computer can prepare the optimal delivery route.

Luna must prepare a delivery order for each package. The easiest way of preparing the route planning barcodes is to generate them with the delivery orders. This, however, requires Luna to integrate Speedy's bar codes with its delivery system. Integration will make Luna relatively more dependent on Speedy and, hence, more vulnerable to a holdup. Accordingly, Luna will be reluctant to invest in such integration.

> **Specificity** is the percentage of the investment that will be lost if the asset is switched to another use.

In this example, integrating the barcodes is an investment by Luna that is specific to its relationship with Speedy. The **specificity** of an investment in an asset is the percentage that will be lost if the asset is switched to another use.

For instance, suppose that Luna must spend $5,000 to integrate Speedy's barcodes with its delivery system. Of the $5,000 investment, $2,000 is for a barcode printer, while the remaining $3,000 pays for tailor-made software specified by Speedy. If Luna switches to another delivery contractor, it will lose the $3,000 specialized investment. Hence, the integrated barcode system is 3,000/5,000 = 60% specific to the relationship with Speedy.

By contrast, suppose that Luna buys several mobile phones to contact delivery persons when they are on the road. The same phones, however, can be used by any delivery contractor. Hence, these are nonspecific assets. The prospect that Speedy might act opportunistically will have relatively little impact on Luna's investments in such nonspecific assets.

Specific assets can be physical; for instance, plant and equipment. Specific assets also encompass human capital. Many businesses provide new recruits with introductory training. Through on-the-job training programs, employees are making investments in specific human capital. The prospect of a holdup will deter investments in all forms of specific assets.

Progress Check 14F Which of the following requires you to invest relatively more in specific human capital: a university degree program or on-the-job training?

Avoiding specificity in electric power investments: floating power plants

Smith Cogeneration International of Oklahoma City manufactures electric power plants. In 1993, the company was invited to supply a power plant in the Dominican Republic. However, it learned that over 20 other potential suppliers had refused to bid. Owing to the political and economic risks of investment, the other suppliers could not secure the several hundred million dollars of financing necessary for construction.

Taking inspiration from sailboat racing, company president Donald Smith contracted to supply a *floating* plant. The company built a gas turbine plant on a barge at a Beaumont, Texas, yard and then towed it across the Caribbean Sea to the Dominican Republic.

The barge had two advantages over a conventional land-based plant. First, in the event of default by the host government, Smith could actually float the plant away. The extent of its specific investment was much lower than with a land-based plant. The second advantage was faster delivery. Smith did not have to send personnel to the Dominican Republic and thus saved six months in construction time.

Source: "Power Plants atop Barges Will Make Waves in Asia," *Asian Wall Street Journal*, May 23, 1996, pp. 1 and 6.

Incomplete Contracts

Suppose that the contract between Luna and Speedy had specified conditions under which Luna could request an additional delivery and the corresponding price. Then, Speedy would not have been able to holdup Luna. Generally, the scope for a holdup depends on the extent to which a contract is incomplete. A **complete contract** specifies what each party must do and the corresponding payments under every possible contingency. By contrast, a contract is incomplete if it does not specify duties or payment in some contingency.

> A **complete contract** specifies what each party must do and the corresponding payments under every possible contingency.

It would be extremely costly for Luna and Speedy to prepare and agree on a complete contract. A huge number of contingencies would have to be covered: the need for a fourth delivery, the possibility that Speedy's truck may break down, and the possibility of an earthquake are just a few. Rather than consider every such detail, the two parties will probably agree on an incomplete contract.

As this example suggests, in practice, all contracts are incomplete, and deliberately so. The issue then is how incomplete the contract should be. Generally, the answer depends on two factors: the potential benefits and costs at stake and the extent of the possible contingencies.

Let us consider the first factor: the potential benefits and costs at stake. The larger the stakes, the more the parties should invest in preparing the contract. Compare, for instance, Luna's purchases of sundry hardware and dairy products. Sundry hardware such as nails and screws is a minor item in Luna's sales. By contrast, dairy products account for a large part of Luna's sales and are much more important. Accordingly, Luna might not need a contract with its supplier of sundry hardware, but it will need a detailed contract with its supplier of dairy products.

The second factor in the incompleteness of the contract is the extent of the possible contingencies. Consider again Luna's purchases of sundry hardware and dairy products.

Hardware is a durable item with relatively slow sales. By contrast, dairy products are perishable and sold in high volume, hence Luna needs frequent supply. Moreover, the supply of dairy products is relatively more vulnerable to disruptions by bad weather, transportation problems, and labor disputes. Accordingly, Luna will seek relatively more assurance about the supply of dairy products. This means a relatively more detailed contract.

Gains from Resolution

In general, contracts are deliberately incomplete. This incompleteness gives rise to the possibility of a holdup. In turn, this leads the affected parties to take precautions such as avoiding investments in specific assets. These precautions reduce the net benefit of the various parties from the relationship. If, however, the potential for holdup can be resolved, then the additional benefit will exceed the additional cost. Accordingly, a profit can be made by resolving the potential for holdup.

An obvious way to resolve the potential for holdup is for the relevant parties to specify contracts in greater detail. We have already discussed the factors to consider when deciding on the degree of contractual incompleteness.

Another way to resolve holdup is through changing the ownership of the relevant assets. In the next section, we discuss the meaning of ownership.

How detailed the contract? watch the movies

A common dispute between movie producers and actresses and even actors concerns how much flesh to show. Actress Kirsten Dunst played the leading role of Nicole Oakley in the teen movie, *Crazy/Beautiful*. Cranky Critic interviewed Ms Dunst about the movie and asked whether her contract included a "no nudity" clause. Ms Dunst was emphatic, "Yeah, I'm always very careful about that, definitely . . . [a nude scene] was in the script, but I would never do that and they knew that."

Rick Schroder, previously the child star of the 1980s television sitcom, *Silver Spoons*, played Detective Danny Sorenson in the hit TV series, *NYPD Blue*, from 1998–2001. The producers of *NYPD Blue* made sure to specify the degree of exposure required in Mr Schroder's contract: "You may be required from time to time to show the buttocks. No genitalia will be shown."

Sources: "Rick's Secret Weapon," *Cosmopolitan*, January 1999, p. 154; "Kirsten Dunst – Cranky Critic StarTalk: Movie Star Interviews," www.crankycritic.com/qa/pf_articles/kirstendunst.html, accessed, July 18, 2006.

Contracting before sinking costs: PNG–Queensland gas pipeline

The Highlands are the most densely populated area in Papua New Guinea (PNG). The area is rich in mineral resources, including oil, gas, and gold. The Highlands Gas Project includes conversion of the Kutubu oil fields to gas production, and development of the Hides, Juha, and Angores gas fields.

The Project was first mooted in 1996 and estimated to cost A$6–7 billion (Australian dollars). The Project is owned by a consortium led by ExxonMobil. The main shareholder is Oil Search, which owns 70% of PNG's oil reserves and over 50% of Highlands Gas Project. Other shareholders are MRDC and Nippon Oil Exploration.

To bring the gas to market, the consortium proposed 3,000 kilometers of pipeline from the Highlands and under the Coral Sea to Queensland, Australia. The construction cost is estimated to be A$1.8 billion for the PNG section and A$1.38 billion for the Australian section. In 1997, the consortium awarded an international tender to build and operate the pipeline, if approved, to the Australian Gas Light Company and Malaysia's national oil company, Petronas.

In October 2004, the consortium signed two conditional 20-year sales agreements, one with Queensland Alumina Limited for 12–20 petajoules of gas per year, and the other with CS Energy for 10 petajoules per year. The consortium had earlier secured agreements with Energex (Comalco and others) and Western Mining Company to sell 36–80 petajoules per year.

The consortium then engaged the Australian Gas Light Company and Petronas for front-end engineering and design (FEED) work on the pipeline. The FEED work in PNG would cost A$34.5 million.

However, the contracts secured were not sufficient to justify approval of the Project. Chairman of the Highlands Gas Project Owners Group, Rob Franklin, cautioned "While entry into FEED is an important milestone, securing additional customers remains the focus for the Highlands Gas Project."

Sources: "PNG Gas Pipeline Enters New Phase," *Courier-Mail* (Brisbane, Queensland), October 7, 2004; "PNG–Australia Gas Pipeline Gets Major Boost," *ABC Online*, October 7, 2004; Oil Search Ltd, www.oilsearch.com/html/, downloaded October 18, 2004.

6 Ownership

Ownership means the rights to **residual control**, which are those rights that have not been contracted away. To explain the meaning of **residual control**, suppose that Saturn Properties borrowed $5 million from a bank to develop a supermarket, which it has rented to Luna on a five-year lease.

> **Ownership** means the rights to residual control.

The bank has a mortgage against the building. This means that, if Saturn fails to make the loan payments on time, the bank will have the legal right to take possession of the building. This is a right that Saturn contracted away to get the loan.

> The rights to **residual control** are those rights that have not been contracted away.

Saturn has also entered into a five-year lease with Luna Supermarket. Through the lease, Luna has the right to use the property for five years. This is another right that Saturn has contracted away.

As owner, Saturn has residual control. This means that it has all rights except those contracted away. For instance, it may have the right to enter into a second mortgage on the building, and it has the right to use the building after the expiration of Luna's lease.

A transfer of ownership means shifting the rights of residual control to another party. Suppose that Luna buys ownership of the supermarket building from Saturn. Then Saturn will no longer have the right to enter into a mortgage on the building. Such rights now belong to the new owner, Luna.

Residual Income

| **Residual income** is the income remaining after payment of all other claims. |

One dimension of residual control is particularly worth emphasizing. The owner of an asset also has the right to receive the **residual income** from the asset, which is the income remaining after payment of all other claims.

To illustrate, suppose that Saturn collects $100,000 a month in rent from Luna. Saturn's expenses include $50,000 in interest and principal to the bank as well as $20,000 in taxes and other expenses. As owner of the building, Saturn receives the residual income of $100,000 − $50,000 − $20,000 = $30,000.

As the recipient of the residual income, the owner gets the full benefit of changes in income and costs. For instance, if Saturn can raise the rent by $5,000 to $105,000, then its profit will increase by $5,000 to $35,000. Similarly, if Saturn can reduce expenses by $2,000, then its profit will increase by $2,000 to $32,000. On the other hand, if Saturn's expenses increase by $5,000, then its profit would fall by $5,000 to $25,000.

Vertical Integration

| **Vertical integration** is the combination of the assets for two successive stages of production under a common ownership. |

Chapter 8 introduced the concept of vertical integration. To recall, **vertical integration** is the combination of the assets for two successive stages of production under a common ownership. Table 14.1 lists some recent examples of vertical integration, while table 14.2 lists recent examples of vertical disintegration.

Vertical integration is downstream or upstream, depending on whether it involves the acquisition of assets for a stage of production nearer to or further from the final consumer. Suppose, for instance, that a food manufacturer acquires a supermarket. Since the supermarket operates a stage of production nearer to the final consumer, this is an example of downstream vertical integration. By contrast, if the food

Table 14.1 Vertical integration

Acquirer		Target		
Company	Business	Company	Business	Source
SBC	Local telephone service	AT&T	Long-distance telephone service	a
Amgen	Biotechnology	Abgenix	Human therapeutic antibodies	b
China National Petroleum Company	Integrated oil (production, refining, and marketing)	Petro Kazakhstan	Oil exploration and production	c

Sources
a. "SBC to Acquire AT&T," Press release, SBC, January 31, 2005.
b. "Amgen to Acquire Abgenix for $22.50 Per Share; Provides Amgen With Full Ownership of Panitumumab and Eliminates a Denosumab Royalty", Amgen, Press Release, December 14, 2005.
c. "Petro Kazakhstan Inc. shareholders approve CNPC offer", Xinhua, October 19, 2005.

Table 14.2 Vertical disintegration

Owner		Divested entity		
Company	Business	Company/asset	Business	Source
International Paper	Paper manufacturing	6.8 million acres of forests	Timber	a.
Alltel Corp.	Wireline and wireless telecommunications	Alltel – Valor Communications	Wireline communications	b.
Air India	Airline and related services	Air-India Engineering Services	Aircraft maintenance and repair	c.
Seiko Epson (Japan) and Sanyo Electronic (Japan)	Diversified electronics manufacturing	Sanyo Epson Imaging Devices	LCD manufacturing	d.

Sources
a. "A Promising Paper Route", *Business Week*, November 21, 2005, p. 14.
b. "Alltel to spin off wireline holdings, merge busines with Valor in $4.9 billion deal," *The Detroit News*, December 10, 2005.
c. "Air-India to engineer a spin-off," *Rediff.com*, June 21, 2004.
d. "Epson, Sanyo Join Forces," *Electronic News*, March 30, 2004.

manufacturer were to acquire a grower of fresh fruit, it would be vertically integrating upstream.

The decision to vertically integrate upstream is often characterized as the choice of whether to "make or buy." The food manufacturer can either *buy* fruit from growers or establish its own fruit-growing operation to *make* the input for its production.

Vertical integration or disintegration changes the ownership of assets, and hence alters the distribution of the rights to residual control and residual income. As we explain in the next section, these in turn affect the degree of moral hazard and the potential for holdup.

> **Progress Check 14G** Referring to table 14.1, identify the examples as upstream or downstream vertical integration.

7 Organizational Architecture

In chapter 1, we discussed the vertical and horizontal boundaries of an organization. An oil company that produces crude, refines it, and markets gasoline is more vertically integrated than one that only produces crude. A media organization that publishes newspapers and provides cable television and Internet service has wider horizontal boundaries than one that specializes in cable television service.

Vertical and horizontal boundaries are just two implications of the architecture of the organization, which comprises the distribution of ownership, incentive schemes, and monitoring systems. From the viewpoint of managerial economics, the design of organizational architecture depends on a balance among four issues – holdup, moral hazard, internal monopoly, and scale and scope economies – and the mechanisms by which these issues may be resolved.

Holdup

First, let us consider how the potential for holdup can be resolved by changing the ownership of the relevant assets. Recall that, when Luna requested an additional delivery on short notice, Speedy extracted double the usual price for the service. What if Luna had an in-house delivery service? To make the additional delivery, it might have to order a driver to work overtime. The driver could respond by striking to demand a special overtime payment. By doing so, however, the driver runs the risk that Luna may replace her with another worker.

If the driver strikes, the cost imposed on Luna is the cost of hiring a replacement driver on short notice. This will be lower than the cost of hiring a replacement truck and driver which would be necessary if Speedy should withhold its services.

As this example suggests, even an employee can engage in holdup. However, an employee is less likely than an external contractor to engage in holdup and would impose lower costs if it did so. The reason is that the external contractor owns the assets necessary to provide the service. Residual control of an asset includes the right to withhold its services. Hence, an external contractor has the power to withhold the services of its assets.

By contrast, an employee has no such power since the assets on which she works belong to the employer. With less power, the employee is less likely to behave opportunistically and engage in a holdup and would impose lower cost if it did so. Accordingly, the potential for holdup can be mitigated through vertical integration into the relevant stage of production.

Moral Hazard

We have discussed how a change in the ownership of an asset can affect the likelihood and cost of a holdup. A change in ownership will also affect the degree of moral hazard.

If Luna Supermarket vertically integrates into the delivery business, it must engage people as delivery persons. It would change from dealing with an owner who supplies a service to dealing with an employee. As we showed above, employees are subject to moral hazard. Generally, the employer's marginal benefit diverges from the worker's personal marginal benefit. Since the worker chooses effort according to her personal marginal benefit, she chooses less than the economically efficient level of effort.

By contrast, suppose that the employee owns the business. In this case, the worker receives the residual income of the business. Hence, if the worker exerts an additional unit of effort, she will receive the entire marginal benefit. If she reduces effort by one unit, she will suffer the entire reduction in the marginal benefit. Thus, when balancing her marginal benefit with the marginal cost, the worker will choose the economically efficient level of effort. Giving ownership to the worker will resolve the moral hazard.

This explains why many businesses pay senior managers through shares and stock options. To the extent that these managers have a share of ownership, their interests will be more closely aligned with those of the business, which reduces the degree of the moral hazard.

Vertical integration changes ownership. Since an employee is subject to relatively greater moral hazard than an owner, vertical integration increases the degree of moral hazard.

⊣ Corporatizing Airbus ⊢

Airbus's organizational architecture required it to divide manufacturing work among its shareholders. For instance, Aerospatiale manufactured cockpits and forward fuselage sections, DASA was responsible for major fuselage sections and the tail, while British Aerospace manufactured the wings. These sections were then transported to either Hamburg (DASA) or Toulouse (Aerospatiale) for final assembly. To support this division of work, Airbus operated a dedicated fleet of huge transport aircraft.

Airbus purchased sections and services from its production partners at fixed transfer prices. Each production partner had more incentive to economize on its own work, where it would enjoy the whole gain, than on the product of Airbus as a whole, from which it derived only a part of the gain.

In 1999, Airbus decided that the newest A-318 model would be assembled in DASA's Hamburg plant. Aerospatiale threatened to withdraw from the program unless it received an equal share of work. Airbus management succumbed and agreed to re-assign a share of A-319 final assembly from DASA to Aerospatiale. The result of the holdup was that Airbus split assembly of the A-319 between two locations, and hence diluted economies of scale in manufacturing.

Despite all these anomalies, Airbus claimed to have one of the most efficient production systems in the world, with about 95% of its manufacturing work performed by its shareholders.

Source: "Airbus Rolls the Dice, Prepares to Make Bold Moves," *Seattletimes.com, Business*, August 8, 1999.

Internal Monopoly

Another consideration in organizational architecture is the extent to which an internal provider exploits monopoly power. If Luna establishes its own delivery service, it will prefer using its own delivery service to engaging an external contractor. This is a reasonable policy to the extent that some of the costs of the in-house delivery service are sunk.

The preference in favor of an internal provider, however, means creating an internal monopoly. In chapter 8, we showed that a seller with market power will restrict production and raise price. An internal provider may also use its market power to raise its price. Then, the organization as a whole will find that the cost of internal provision may rise above the price charged by external contractors. This higher cost must be borne by the organization.

One way of resolving the problem of an internal monopoly is to outsource whenever the internal provider's cost exceeds that of external sources. *Outsourcing* is the purchase of services or supplies from external sources. It subjects internal providers to the discipline of market competition and, so, limits the extent to which the cost of internal provision diverges from the competitive level.

Economies of Scale and Scope

Finally, a decision on organizational architecture should also take account of scale and scope economies. Recall from chapter 7 that, if there are economies of scale, then the average cost of provision will be lower with a larger scale. Typically, an internal provider will operate at a smaller scale than an external contractor. It then is necessary to consider how the average cost varies with the operating scale.

For instance, in Luna's case, the supermarket's deliveries may occupy a truck and driver for only four hours a day. If Luna were to set up its own delivery service, its utilization of the assets and human resources would be relatively low. By contrast, an external delivery contractor may get 10 or 12 hours a day of work from its equipment and personnel. The external contractor would have better capacity utilization and hence a lower average cost. To this extent, it would be less costly to purchase the service from the external contractor.

We can also illustrate the significance of scale economies by comparing a supermarket's need for delivery service with that for armored truck service to convey cash and checks. While some supermarkets have their own delivery service, almost none have their own armored trucks. A major reason for this difference is economies of scale. It hardly would be efficient for a supermarket to buy an armored truck that makes one daily trip to the bank.

From chapter 7, if there are economies of scope across two products, then the total cost of production will be lower when the two products are produced together than when they are produced separately. Economies of scope are a key reason for the growth of super-markets at the expense of traditional stores. A supermarket can supply items at a relatively lower cost than more specialized stores such as bakeries, groceries, and newsstands.

Economies of scope are the major factor in favor of wide horizontal organizational bound-aries. However, for an individual company, scope economies have countervailing effects. If the company already produces one item, then it can reduce total cost by producing the other one as well. However, if the company does not already produce either item, then economies of scope imply that it should outsource both.

Balance

The decision on organizational architecture depends on a balance among all the factors that we have discussed: the scope for holdup, the degree of moral hazard, internal monopoly power, and the extent of economies of scale and scope. Further, it also depends on other ways to resolve these issues. Specifically, holdup can be resolved through investment in more detailed contracts, moral hazard can be resolved through incentives and monitoring, and inter-nal monopoly power can be resolved through outsourcing. Generally, the economically efficient solution will involve a mix of all policies.

Let us illustrate the application of this framework with two examples. One concerns the vertical boundaries of the organization, while the other concerns its horizontal boundaries. The two examples show that the same framework can be applied to address both vertical and horizontal dimensions of organizational architecture.

A function that many organizations consider whether to "make or buy" is information technology services. As figure 14.5 shows, this decision resolves to a balance among four factors. The factor in favor of "make" is the extent to which the potential for holdup can-not be cost-effectively reduced through more detailed contracts. There are three factors in favor of "buy." The first is the extent to which moral hazard among the internal informa-tion technology group cannot be cost-effectively resolved through incentive schemes and monitoring systems. The second is the extent to which the internal group's monopoly power cannot be cost-effectively redressed through outsourcing. The third is the extent to which the internal group will lack economies of scale.

Decisions whether to "make or buy" concern the vertical boundaries of the organization. An organization must also consider its horizontal boundaries. For instance, should a bus oper-ator also be in the trucking business? As the businesses are not vertically related, holdup and internal monopoly power are not major issues. The key factor in favor of owning both

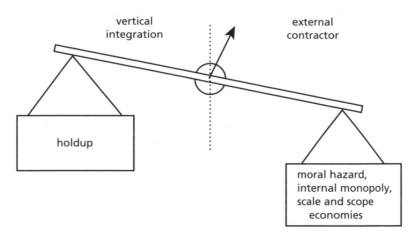

Figure 14.5   Vertical integration
The scope for a holdup weighs in favour of vertical integration, while the degree of moral hazard, internal monopoly power, and the extent of economies of scale and scope, weigh against it.

businesses is economies of scope, while the factor against is the extent to which moral hazard in the trucking group cannot be cost-effectively resolved through incentive schemes and monitoring systems.

Progress Check 14H What are the four factors that should be considered in the decision whether to "make or buy"?

⊢ B2C e-commerce: to build warehouses or not to build ⊢

Established in 1995, Amazon.com quickly became the world's leading online retailer of books, music CDs, and videos, and one of the preeminent B2C (business-to-consumer) portals. Founder Jeff Bezos began with the sale of books and located his new business in Seattle, close to a major wholesaler of books. In this way, Amazon could economize on inventory.

By late 1998, with annual sales exceeding $600 million and a product line extending into toys, electronics, and tools, Amazon changed its strategy to embrace bricks and mortar. Amazon already had two relatively old warehouses, in Seattle and Delaware. It then decided to invest $300 million to build five state-of-the-art warehouses across the country – in Georgia, Kansas, Kentucky, and Nevada.

Amazon justified the vertical integration into distribution in terms of control over holdup. Vice President Andrew N. Westlund feared that independent distributors would pass on Amazon's innovations in customer service to competing retailers: "We would be the teacher and then they would offer those services to our competitors." By 2006, Amazon had seven fulfillment centers in the United States and five in other countries.

By comparison with Amazon, online video retailer BigStar Entertainment is a minnow. Commenting on Amazon's integration into distribution, BigStar Chief Executive, David Friedensohn, remarked, "I don't want 1,000 hourly workers sitting in a warehouse wrapping presents. There are plenty of people bidding for that business." One factor in the difference in the degree of vertical integration between Amazon and BigStar is the difference in their scale and scope.

The online video rental business places a higher premium on time-to-delivery. As a result, Netflix maintains a nationwide system of distribution centers serving all major metropolitan areas. This is necessary in order to rapidly process exchanges of rentals. Netflix offers unlimited rentals, but with a maximum number at any time (up to 3 at a time for $17.99 per month; 2 at a time for $14.99 per month; or 1 at a time for $9.99 per month). This means that Netflix must be able to receive old videos and exchange them for new ones fairly rapidly. Since customer satisfaction is so tied to timeliness, it would be dangerous to outsource fulfillment in this business.

Sources: "Amazon's Risky Christmas," *New York Times*, November 28, 1999, Money and Business, p. 1; "Amazon.com to Open Two Kentucky Distribution Centers to Meet Rapid Growth," *PRNewswire*, May 25, 1999; Amazon and Netflix 2005 annual reports.

Samsung Electronics: second-sourcing color filters

Samsung Electronics is one of the world's leading manufacturers of LCD panels. By 2004, Samsung was fabricating LCDs at three lines at Chonan in Chungchong South Province, South Korea, and was building another fabrication facility in nearby Asan, also in Chungchong South Province.

A key component in LCD manufacturing is the color filter. Samsung is vertically integrated and manufactures color filters internally. However, Samsung has also committed to a policy of buying half of its filter needs from Sumitomo Chemical Company. Sumitomo Chemical President Hiromasa Yonekura remarked, "They really press these departments to compete." Samsung's commitment to Sumitomo helps to limit the monopoly power of its internal color filter factories.

In May 2003, Sumitomo Chemical announced a 28 billion Yen investment in its color filter plant at Pyungtaek in the southern part of Kyonggi Province. With the investment, Sumitomo would double production to 1.44 million filters per year, in line with Samsung's expansion plans.

Sources: "The Samsung Way," *Business Week*, June 16, 2003; "Samsung Electronics Announces 7th-Generation TFT LCD Glass Substrate," Samsung Electronics, Press Release, May 27, 2003.

8 Summary

The architecture of an organization comprises the distribution of ownership, incentive schemes, and monitoring systems. Ownership means the rights to residual control. Incentive schemes and monitoring systems are related as incentives must be based on behavior that can be observed. An efficient incentive scheme balances the incentive for effort with the cost of risk.

An efficient organizational architecture resolves four internal issues – holdup, moral hazard, monopoly power, and economies of scale and scope, and how these can be resolved. Holdup and moral hazard arise between parties with a conflict of interest. Additionally, moral hazard depends on one party not being able to observe the actions of the other. Holdup can also be resolved through more detailed contracts, moral hazard through incentive schemes and monitoring systems, and internal monopoly power through outsourcing.

Key Concepts

organizational architecture	relative performance	ownership
moral hazard	holdup	residual control
performance pay	specificity	residual income
performance quota	complete contract	vertical integration

Further Reading

The key reference is Paul Milgrom and John Roberts's *Economics, Organization, and Management* (Englewood Cliffs, NJ: Prentice-Hall, 1992). They apply state-of-the-art scholarship to the issues of incentives and organization. See especially their chapters 5–7, 9, and 16.

James A. Brickley, Clifford W. Smith, Jr., and Jerold L. Zimmerman, *Managerial Economics and Organizational Architecture*, 3d ed. (Boston, MA: Irwin McGraw Hill, 2004), chapter 11, provides a complementary perspective.

Review Questions

1. In the context of your business or organization, explain the meaning of organizational architecture.

2. Explain the moral hazard in the following situation. Leah has just bought comprehensive insurance on her car. This covers loss and damage for any reason including theft. Her insurer is concerned that she may take fewer precautions against theft.

3. By considering benefits and costs to the various parties, explain why a profit can be made by resolving moral hazard.

4. Compare the following ways of paying a lawyer in terms of the incentive for effort.
   (a) Hourly rate, in which the lawyer receives a fixed dollar amount for each hour of work on the case.
   (b) Contingency fee, in which the lawyer receives a portion of the amount that the client recovers. If the client loses the legal action, the lawyer gets nothing.

5. Explain how a taxi company can structure incentives based on relative performance to motivate its drivers to maintain their cars carefully and avoid breakdowns.

6. A secretary's job includes typing letters, answering telephone calls, and handling visitors as well as other responsibilities. Comment on a proposal to pay a secretary according to the number of letters that he types.

7. For each of the following investment funds, suggest an appropriate benchmark against which the fund performance might be measured:
   (a) a fund specializing in small stocks;
   (b) a U.S. Government bond fund;
   (c) a Japanese stock fund.

8. Maria is a pilot. Which of the following investments is the relatively more specific?
   (a) An executive MBA program for middle managers.
   (b) Training on an Airbus A-340 simulator.

9. Why do businesses enter into contracts that are deliberately incomplete?

10. In the context of an incorporated business, explain the meaning of (a) residual control, and (b) residual income.

11. Give an example of a holdup. Explain how this will induce the affected parties to avoid specific investments.

12. True or false? An aircraft manufacturer has experienced holdup by its supplier of avionics. The aircraft manufacturer could resolve all incentive problems by producing the avionics internally.

13. How can outsourcing resolve the monopoly power of an internal supplier?

14. A property management business is considering whether to set up its own cleaning service to replace an outside contractor. What are the arguments for and against this proposal?

15. Explain the roles of economies of scale and scope in decisions about horizontal integration.

Discussion Questions

1. CapitalMall Trust is a real estate investment trust that owns and manages the IMM Building, a Singapore shopping mall. Until 2004, tenants of the IMM Building paid a fixed monthly rental. Then, for new tenancies and renewals, CapitalMall set a two-part rental, comprising a fixed monthly payment of S$35–38 (Singapore dollars) per square foot, and a variable payment of up to 1% of the tenant's gross revenue. Tenants complained about the variable payment, but CapitalMall asserted that it was a common practice and aligned the interests of landlord and tenant. ("Seeing RED over RENT," *Straits Times*, October 20, 2004, H24.)
   (a)   As manager of the IMM Building, how is CapitalMall subject to moral hazard with respect to its tenants?
   (b)   How would the variable payment align the interests of landlord and tenant?
   (c)   How should the variable payment depend on the landlord's attitude towards risk?
   (d)   Should the variable payment be based on the tenant's gross revenue or net revenue (gross revenue less cost of goods sold)?

2. In 1996, the Aetna Life and Casualty Company acquired U.S. Healthcare for $8.8 billion. At the time, Aetna was a leading provider of medical insurance. Medical insurance allows the insured party a relatively free choice of doctors and treatment centers. By contrast, U.S. Healthcare specialized in managed healthcare, under which covered patients could get treatment only from specific doctors and at specified facilities ("Aetna to Buy U.S. Healthcare in Big Move to Managed Care," *New York Times*, April 2, 1996, p. A1).
   (a)   A medical insurer pays the bills, while a doctor decides on tests, treatment, and prescriptions. Explain the moral hazard between doctors and medical insurers.
   (b)   A managed healthcare plan may restrict coverage to treatment by the plan's own employees and facilities. Compare the extent of a doctor's moral hazard under managed healthcare relative to medical insurance.
   (c)   Using your answer to (b), explain why managed healthcare is less costly than medical insurance.

3. Bristol–Myers Squibb is a global manufacturer of pharmaceutical and related healthcare products. Its top-selling drugs are Plavix (clopidogrel bisulfate) and Pravachol (pravastatin sodium) tablets. In March 2005, the company awarded Chief Executive Officer Peter R. Dolan 125,000 options to buy Bristol–Myers Squibb common shares at an exercise price of $25.29. (*Source*: Bristol–Myers Squibb Company, Proxy Statement, March 22, 2006.)
   (a)   Explain how the stock options were intended to motivate Mr Dolan.
   (b)   Suggest an incentive scheme based on relative performance and compare it with Bristol–Myers Squibb's stock option scheme.
   (c)   Mr Dolan also received a salary and bonus from Bristol–Myers Squibb. How would the stock options affect the risk that he bore?

4. SGS, an international leader in inspection, verification, testing, and certification, sends inspection reports from all of its world wide operations to two facilities for processing. It requires the processing offices to meet targets for on-time completion, productivity (number of reports per employee), and accuracy. In 2002, it implemented an incentive scheme with increasing levels of monetary reward: lowest level to any team achieving any target; higher levels to any team achieving multiple targets or to multiple teams achieving the same target; highest level to all teams achieving all three targets. Although the scheme implicitly weighted each target equally, the targets differed in their difficulty and also their importance to the company.
   (a)   How would employees allocate their effort with respect to the various targets?
   (b)   Did the incentive scheme align the company's interests with those of the employees?
   (c)   How would you revise the incentive scheme?

5. Exxon Mobil leads an energy consortium that is developing the Highlands Gas Project in Papua New Guinea. The consortium has proposed to build 3,000 kilometers of pipeline to transport gas from the Highlands fields to Queensland, Australia. Australian Gas Light and Petronas lead an engineering consortium to build and operate the pipeline. By October 2004, four Australian companies had signed 20-year conditional sales agreements to buy gas from the Highlands Project.
    (a) In the context of the new Project, explain the meaning of "sunk costs."
    (b) In the consortium's sales agreements with gas customers, how important is it that gas prices are fixed in advance?
    (c) What are the potential holdup problems among the three parties – gas producer, pipeline, and gas customers?
    (d) If Exxon Mobil decided to build and operate the pipeline itself, what problems would be resolved, and what new problems would arise?

6. Rick Schroder, previously the child star of the 1980s television sitcom, *Silver Spoons*, played Detective Danny Sorenson in the hit TV series, *NYPD Blue*, from 1998–2001. The producers of *NYPD Blue* made sure that Mr Schroder's contract specified the degree of exposure required: "You may be required from time to time to show the buttocks. No genitalia will be shown." (*Source*: "Rick's Secret Weapon," *Cosmopolitan*, January 1999, p. 154.)
    (a) Explain the potential holdup that the *NYPD Blue* producers might be concerned about.
    (b) What specific investments do the producers make in Mr Schroder?
    (c) Compare the need for such a specific clause in Mr Schroder's contract to act in *NYPD Blue* with any contract between a club featuring male strippers and the strippers.

7. Wärtsilä, with headquarters in Helsinki, Finland, builds electric power plants and also dual-fuel diesel-electric engines and machinery for ships. The company's brochure, "Power for a changing world," advertises that its power plants offer maximum operating flexibility: "The design of the plants enables you to incrementally change the plant size as your needs change. If you need to relocate, modular construction will make the move easier. Or you can choose a Wärtsilä floating power plant or a Wärtsilä Power Module and become truly mobile." The brochure features a 114 Megawatt plant floating off Puerto Quetzal, Guatemala.
    (a) How is the specificity of an investment related to sunk costs?
    (b) Explain the concept of specific investments in relation to building an electric power generation facility.
    (c) Do you expect the demand among investors for floating power plants to be greater or less in countries with high political risk? Explain why.

8. Until 2001, Airbus was owned by Aerospatiale-Matra (37.9%), British Aerospace (20%), Construcciones Aeronauticas (4.2%) and DaimlerChrysler Aerospace (DASA) (37.9%). Most major decisions by Airbus required unanimous shareholder approval. In 1999, Airbus decided to assemble the newest A-318 model in DASA's Hamburg plant. Aerospatiale threatened to withdraw from the program unless it received an equal share of work. The organization succumbed and agreed to re-assign a share of A-319 final assembly from DASA to Aerospatiale.
    (a) The potential for holdup by a supplier may lead a customer to contract with a back-up supplier, a practice called "second-sourcing." Explain why second-sourcing may be inefficient in terms of scale economies.
    (b) Explain how the potential for holdup by a customer may lead a supplier to avoid specific investments.
    (c) Upon corporatization, the management of Airbus would need unanimous shareholder approval only for three-year business plans, corporate changes exceeding $500 million, and a few other major business decisions. Referring to the episode with Aerospatiale over the A-318 and A-319, explain how corporatization might increase Airbus's earnings.

9. In 1995, the Walt Disney Company acquired Capital Cities/ABC Inc. for $19 billion. Through the acquisition, the Disney Company, which produces films and television shows, gained ownership

of a major customer, the ABC television network. *Business Week* remarked that the deal would give Disney "a guaranteed platform for its first-run syndication programs – shows that might otherwise die on the vine" ("Disney's Kingdom," *Business Week*, August 15, 1995, p. 33).

(a) Use this example to explain the meaning of downstream vis-à-vis upstream vertical integration.

(b) Considering the ABC television network as a division of the Walt Disney Company, explain the meaning of outsourcing.

(c) From the perspective of maximizing the company's overall profit, does it make sense for Disney to force ABC to broadcast programs that "might otherwise die on the vine"?

10. In 2000, BP began outsourcing all of its human resources (HR) services to Exult, Inc. At the time, it was the biggest HR outsourcing contract on record – BP agreed to pay Exult $600 million for a seven-year contract. A primary justification for the outsourcing was that a series of mergers in the late 1990s left BP with 100,000 new employees and a number of incompatible systems. Exult was to handle all administrative elements of compensation, benefits, payroll, performance management, organizational and employee development, and labor relations while BP would retain things that require judgment and policy. (*Source*: Paul S. Adler, "Making the HR Outsourcing Decision, *MITSloan Management Review* 45, no. 1, 2003.)

(a) Compare the outsourcing of services with outsourcing production activities. How do they compare in terms of the opportunities for greater scale economies to be achieved through outsourcing? How do the risks of holdup compare?

(b) BP took an 8% stake in the startup, Exult. Evaluate the specificity of this investment. Why might BP have made this investment?

(c) How important was the fact that BP had undergone significant expansion through a series of mergers? Does this make it more or less likely that BP would outsource its HR function compared with more stable (in terms of size) firms?

(d) Why are activities such as payroll processing frequently outsourced while others, such as HR planning rarely are?

Chapter 15

Regulation

1 Introduction

Until the late 1990s, the Consolidated Edison Company of New York had a legal monopoly over the market for electricity in New York City and Westchester County. Like many other U.S. electric power utilities, Con Edison was vertically integrated from generation of electric power through transmission and distribution to retail sale.[1]

Under the terms of its franchise, Con Edison was subject to regulation by the New York State Public Service Commission. The Commission restrained Con Edison's exercise of monopoly power by limiting the company to a maximum rate of return on its investments.

Despite regulation, the price of electricity in New York State rose steadily through the 1980s and into the early 1990s. By 1995, the average price reached 12 cents a kilowatt, which exceeded the national average by over 50%. Moreover, the disparity between New York State and the national average was on an increasing trend.

The State then decided on two changes. First, it re-directed the focus of regulation from an allowed rate of return to a price cap. The State linked Con Edison's prices to those of a peer group of other Northeast electric utilities.

Second, and more fundamentally, the State decided to re-structure the entire electric power industry. Con Edison and other electric power utilities were required to divest their power generation businesses, and to focus on transmission and distribution. The State encouraged the entry of new Energy Service Companies and required Con Edison and other utilities to transport their electric power supply.

Between 1996 and 2004, New York State energy prices declined by 14% in real terms, compared with an 8% average decline in states that did not introduce any competition. As of January 1, 2006, New York State's average residential electricity rate was 14.54 cents per kwh (kilowatt hour), while the average U.S. rate was 9 cents per kwh.

Under Con Ed's price cap plan, the company is permitted a rate of return of at least 11.4%; earnings between 11.4% and 13% are to be shared 50/50 with consumers; while earnings above 13% are to be shared 75/25 with consumers. According to company reports, "The

---

[1] Data comes from *Con Edison 2005 Annual Report*; *Staff Report on the State of Competitive Energy Markets*, New York State Public Service Commission, March 2, 2006; other data from New York State Public Service Commission and U.S. Energy Information Administration documents.

company does not consider it reasonably likely that another company would be authorized to provide utility delivery service where the company already provides service."

Why did New York State award Con Edison a monopoly over electricity in New York City and Westchester County? Why did the State shift from rate of return regulation to a price cap? Why did the State re-structure the entire industry, forcing Con Edison to sell all of its electric power plants? Why did the State permit competition in generation of electricity, but not its delivery?

This chapter addresses these and other issues that arise where the invisible hand fails. Buyers and sellers, acting independently and selfishly, do not equalize marginal benefit and marginal cost; hence, the allocation of resources is not economically efficient.

If the resource allocation is economically inefficient and private action fails to resolve the inefficiency, then there may be a role for government action. The government can act through regulation. If government regulation can resolve the divergence between the marginal benefit and the marginal cost, then it will increase net benefit for society.

To understand the role of government regulation, we consider the various sources of economic inefficiency: market power, asymmetric information, externalities, and public goods. In each case, we then analyze the conditions under which the government should intervene and the appropriate form of regulation.

In our analysis of economic inefficiency due to market power, we explain why a government may award legal monopolies for businesses with significant economies of scale or scope relative to demand. One example is electricity distribution. This explains Con Edison's monopoly over electricity in New York City and Westchester County, and the monopoly structure of the U.S. electricity industry until the late 1990s, as well as Con Edison's continued monopoly in the delivery of (but not the generation of) electricity.

We compare regulation by rate of return with direct regulation of price. The difference explains why New York State shifted from rate of return regulation to a price cap. We also discuss how to regulate an industry in which some parts have strong economies of scale or scope, while other parts do not. This explains why New York and many states and countries have re-structured electricity industries to separate power generation from transmission and distribution.

The invisible hand may also fail because of information asymmetries. We consider how these may be resolved through regulation of disclosure, conduct, and business structure. The third group of reasons for failure of the invisible hand is externalities and public goods. We consider how the government can resolve externalities through standards and user fees, and resolve the provision of public goods through an appropriate legal framework.

2   Natural Monopoly

Recall from chapter 8 that a monopoly will restrict sales to a quantity where the price exceeds the marginal cost. If buyers have no market power, they each purchase a quantity where the price equals the marginal benefit. Hence, at the monopoly price, some buyers will be willing to pay more than the seller's marginal cost but cannot get the product. This outcome is not economically efficient.

If monopolies cause economic inefficiency, why have governments all over the world awarded exclusive franchises to electricity distributors? To address this question, we must consider the technology of the business and, specifically, the presence of substantial economies of scale or scope.

Electricity is distributed through a network of cables running from a central source to every user. Consider a town in which there are two separate electricity distributors. Then, two sets of cables would run into every home, office, and factory. In the electricity distribution business, having more than one provider could mean wasteful duplication.

A market is a **natural monopoly** if the average cost of production is minimized with a single supplier. Examples of natural monopolies include distribution and transmission of electricity, gas, and water, and collection of sewage. In all of these markets, the economies of scale may be large relative to the market demand. Consequently, the average cost of production is lowest when there is only one supplier. Similarly, in a market with economies of scope that are large relative to the market demand, the average cost of production will be minimized with a single supplier.

> A **natural monopoly** is a market where the average cost of production is minimized with a single supplier.

If a market is a natural monopoly, the government should prohibit competition and award an exclusive franchise to a single supplier. This will establish the conditions for production at the lowest average cost.

The monopoly, however, might exploit its exclusive right to raise its price at the expense of its customers. The increase in the price will force the marginal benefit above the marginal cost. Accordingly, to ensure economic efficiency, the government must establish controls on the monopoly.

A monopoly can be controlled in two ways: the government itself can own and operate the business, or a monopoly franchise could be awarded to a commercial enterprise that would be subjected to government regulation. Historically, government ownership of natural monopolies was relatively more common in Europe and developing countries, while private ownership subject to government regulation was more common in the United States. Since the 1980s, however, there has been a world wide trend to adopt the U.S. model and privatize government enterprises.

Government Ownership

The major reason for privatization is that government-owned enterprises tend to be relatively inefficient. One problem is that they are more prone to be coopted by employees, so that the enterprise serves its employees rather than its customers. Some symptoms of employee control are high wages and over-staffing, both of which inflate the cost of production.

Another problem for government-owned enterprises is their dependence on the government for investment funds. The national government budget must finance everything from social welfare to military equipment. A government-owned enterprise must compete with other priorities for an allocation from the budget.

Unlike a commercial enterprise, a government-owned enterprise cannot borrow or raise capital independently. The reason is that lenders cannot prevent the government from spending the funds on social welfare, military equipment or other purposes. By contrast, a privately owned enterprise can commit to invest borrowed funds or capital in its own business.

Owing to these problems, government-owned natural monopolies may fall far short of resolving economic inefficiency in their respective markets. We have mentioned that there has been a world wide trend toward *privatization*. **Privatization** means transferring ownership from the government to the private sector. It does not necessarily mean allowing competition. Indeed, many privatized enterprises continue to have exclusive franchises in their respective businesses.

> **Privatization** is the transfer of ownership from the government to the private sector.

⊣ Privatization without liberalization: Gazprom ⊢

In 2005, with production of 547.9 billion cubic meters (bcm) and reserves of 28,900 bcm, Gazprom is the largest producer of natural gas and has the largest reserves in the world. Gazprom earned 203 billion rubles (or 8.58 per share) on sales of 1.231 trillion rubles. Gazprom's 463,400 kilometer network of gas pipelines is the world's largest. Gazprom exported 156.1 bcm of gas to Europe and 76.6 bcm to the former Soviet Union countries.

Gazprom was established from the Ministry of Gas Industry in 1989, privatized as a Russian joint-stock company (RAO "Gazprom") in 1993, and then as an Open joint-stock company (OAO "Gazprom") in 1998. In 1996, it was listed on the London Stock Exchange with an offering of 1% of its equity in the form of London Depository Receipts. After privatization, Gazprom continued to be majority-owned by the Russian government.

As the successor to the government ministry, Gazprom held an effective monopoly of Russia's exports of natural gas. In July 2006, Russia's parliament, the State Duma, enacted a bill to award Gazprom a legal monopoly over all exports of gas, including natural gas, liquefied natural gas, and liquefied petroleum gas. The bill cited "the necessity of defending Russia's economic interests, fulfilling international gas export obligations, securing federal budget revenues and supporting Russia's energy balance." Within days, President Vladimir Putin signed the bill into law.

The new law allows exceptions only for companies in production sharing agreements with the Russian government. In the 1990s, consortia led by ExxonMobil and Royal Dutch Shell entered into such agreements for the development of the Sakhalin-1 and Sakhalin-2 fields respectively in the Russian far east.

Sources: Wikipedia, accessed July 19, 2006; "Energy of the State," *Financial Times*, March 14, 2006; "Gazprom's Export Monopoly Cemented," *Moscow Times*, July 6, 2006.

Price Regulation

If the government awards an exclusive franchise for a natural monopoly to a commercial enterprise, then the government must regulate the monopoly. How should the government carry out the regulation?

Recall from chapter 6 that the provision of any good or service will be economically efficient at the level where the marginal benefit equals the marginal cost. Suppose that the government awards an exclusive franchise for gas distribution to Pluto Gas. Pluto's costs include a fixed cost and a constant marginal cost of 15 cents per cubic foot. Figure 15.1 shows the distribution cost and the demand for gas.

Suppose that the government requires the franchise holder to set its price equal to its marginal cost and to meet the quantity demanded. Then, referring to figure 15.1, at every possible quantity, the price will be the marginal cost. In effect, the government's policy forces the franchise holder to behave like a perfectly competitive supplier. This policy is called **marginal cost pricing**.

Marginal cost pricing is the policy in which the price is set equal to the marginal cost and the provider must supply the quantity demanded.

The demand curve crosses the marginal cost curve at point *a*. If Pluto sets a price of 15 cents a cubic foot, the market quantity demanded will be 9 million cubic feet. Under the regulation, Pluto must meet the quantity demanded; hence, it must produce 9 million cubic feet. Recall that each

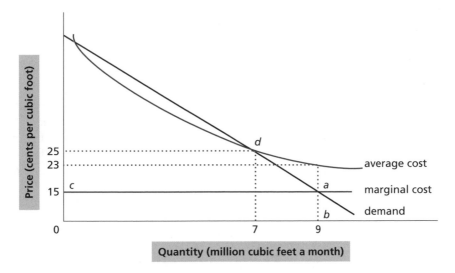

Figure 15.1 Marginal cost pricing
The demand curve crosses the marginal cost curve at point *a*. Under marginal pricing, the provider sets a price of 15 cents per cubic foot and the market quantity demanded is 9 million cubic feet a month. The demand curve crosses the average cost curve at point *d*. Under average cost pricing, the provider sets a price of 25 cents and the market quantity demanded is 7 million.

customer buys the quantity that balances the marginal benefit with the price. Thus, the marginal benefit equals the marginal cost, which is the condition for economic efficiency.

Pluto's revenue is represented by area 0*bac*, which is $0.15 × 9 million = $1.35 million a month. The average cost at the 9 million production rate is 23 cents per cubic foot, which means that the total cost of production is $0.23 × 9 million = $2.07 million. Accordingly, the government must provide a subsidy of $2.07 − $1.35 million = $720,000 a month to ensure that the franchise is financially viable. In this case, the subsidy is necessary to achieve economic efficiency.

How should the government regulate Pluto if it does not wish to provide a subsidy? In this case, the regulation must allow the franchise holder to break even. This can be achieved by requiring the franchise holder to implement **average cost pricing**, which means setting the price equal to average cost and meeting the quantity demanded. With average cost pricing, the franchise holder will exactly cover its costs.

> **Average cost pricing** is the policy in which the price is set equal to the average cost and the provider must supply the quantity demanded.

Let us illustrate average cost pricing in the case of Pluto Gas. In figure 15.1, the demand curve crosses the average cost curve at point *d*. If Pluto sets a price of 25 cents a cubic foot, the market quantity demanded would be 7 million cubic feet. Under the regulation, Pluto must meet the quantity demanded: it must produce 7 million cubic feet. Its total revenue would exactly balance its total cost; hence, it would break even.

Where there are economies of scale in production, the average cost curve will be higher than the marginal cost curve. Then, average cost pricing leads to a lower level of provision than marginal cost pricing. Pluto Gas illustrates such a situation. With average cost pricing, it would produce 7 million cubic feet, while it would produce 9 million with marginal cost pricing.

Generally, the provision under average cost pricing is not economically efficient. The reason is that, with this regulation, buyers purchase up to the quantity where their marginal benefit equals the price. The franchise holder's price is set so that the price equals the average cost. Hence, the quantity of provision is such that the marginal benefit equals the average cost and not the marginal cost.

In Pluto's case, with average cost pricing, the franchise holder produces a quantity of 7 million cubic feet. At this quantity, the marginal benefit is 25 cents per cubic foot, while the marginal cost is 15 cents. Hence, the provision is not economically efficient.

A major difficulty arises in the implementation of price regulation based on the franchise holder's costs: the franchise holder has a strong incentive to persuade the regulator that its costs are higher than they actually are. Then the regulator will allow the franchise holder to set a higher price, closer to the monopoly level, which means a higher profit.

Note that the incentive is for the franchise holder to exaggerate its *reported* costs. Since the regulated price is fixed, the franchise holder will not try to inflate its actual costs. An increase in the franchise holder's actual costs would cut into its own profit.

Progress Check 15A Referring to figure 15.1, suppose that the franchise holder is subject to average cost pricing. It reports to the regulator that its average cost curve is 10% higher than the true curve. Draw the new regulated price and show the franchise holder's profit.

⊣ Australia: price regulation of trunk telecommunications ⊢

In April 2004, the Australian Competition and Consumer Commission (ACCC) declared transmission capacity services with 2 Megabits per second or greater bandwidth subject to regulation. The ACCC exempted a number of markets, including those between Adelaide, Brisbane, Canberra, Melbourne, Perth, and Sydney from regulation.

Under regulation, providers of transmission capacity services must provide service to carriers or carriage service providers in accordance with standard access obligations under the Trade Practices Act of 1974.

The ACCC decided to regulate the price of transmission capacity according to Total Service Long-Run Incremental Cost (TSLRIC). The TSLRIC is essentially the marginal cost of service based on commercially available efficient technology, and taking account of scale and scope economies.

The ACCC gave four justifications for regulating according to TSLRIC:

- If the service provider faced effective competition, its prices would approximate TSLRIC;
- TSLRIC provides a risk-adjusted return on investment, and so, it provides incentives for efficient investment in infrastructure;
- TSLRIC encourages the efficient use of existing infrastructure; and
- TSLRIC allows the service provider to fully recover its efficient costs of providing service.

Source: Pricing Principles for Declared Transmission Capacity Services – Final Report, Australian Competition and Consumer Commission, September 2004.

Rate of Return Regulation

To implement price regulation, the regulator needs information about the franchise holder's costs. However, this gives the franchise holder an incentive to exaggerate its reported costs. The alternative to price regulation is rate of return regulation. This avoids the issue of costs by focusing on the franchise holder's profit. The regulator allows the franchise holder to set prices freely, provided that it does not exceed the maximum allowed profit.

Under rate of return regulation, the regulator specifies the franchise holder's maximum allowed profit in terms of a maximum rate of return on the value of the **rate base**, which is the assets to which the regulation applies. Whenever the franchise holder's rate of return exceeds the specified maximum, it will be required to reduce its prices.

> The **rate base** is the assets to which the rate of return regulation applies.

Suppose, for instance, that Pluto Gas is subject to rate of return regulation with a maximum 12% rate of return, and the rate base consists of all plant and equipment used for producing and distributing gas. The value of this plant and equipment is $100 million. Then, Pluto's maximum allowed profit will be $0.12 \times \$100$ million = $12 million a year.

Rate of return regulation presents three major difficulties for the regulator. The first is determining the maximum permissible rate of return. Since the rate base is typically a very large number, a small difference in the allowed rate of return will translate into a large sum of money. There is considerable room for dispute over the appropriate rate of return because the franchise holder is a monopoly, which means that there will be few comparable investments.

The second problem is that there will be disputes over what assets are needed to provide the regulated service and, hence, should be counted in the rate base. The franchise holder will seek the widest possible definition to increase its profit.

The third problem with rate of return regulation is that it creates an incentive for the franchise holder to invest beyond the economically efficient level. Specifically, if the franchise holder enlarges its rate base, the allowed rate of return will be applied to a larger base; hence, the franchise holder can earn a larger profit.

For example, the demand for electric power varies over time: the peak demand from commercial and industrial customers occurs during working hours, while the peak demand from residential customers occurs in the early morning and late evening. Suppose that there are two neighboring electric power utilities, one catering to mainly commercial and industrial demand and the other serving mainly residential users. It would be efficient for the two utilities to share generating capacity to meet differences in their peak demands. However, if they are subject to rate of return regulation, each may prefer to build more generating plants to increase its rate base.

⊣ Hong Kong's power failure ⊢

In Hong Kong, the supply of electric power is monopolized by two vertically integrated companies. Hong Kong Electric supplies Hong Kong Island, while China Light and Power supplies Kowloon and the New Territories. The Hong Kong Government subjects each company to a "Scheme of Control" that limits its profit to a maximum rate of return on its rate base. The maximum is generally 13.5%, except for investments funded by shareholder equity, in which case it is 15%.

Since the adoption of the Scheme of Control, the Hong Kong economy has been transformed. Many manufacturers shifted their factories to mainland China, to benefit from lower costs of labor, real estate, and other resources. Consequently, the industrial demand for electricity steadily declined. This decline had a relatively larger impact on China Light as most factories were located in Kowloon and the New Territories.

Meanwhile, Hong Kong's population and household incomes continued to grow. This increased the residential demand for electricity and benefited both China Light and Hong Kong Electric.

For China Light, the fall in industrial demand outweighed the growth of residential demand, and by 2000, it had over 50% excess generating capacity. Yet, the company sought government approval to invest HK$30 billion to upgrade its Castle Peak power plant and network. Its motivation was clear – to increase its rate base and hence its allowed profit. Rapid demand growth has continued, with 15% growth in electricity consumption in 2004.

Another symptom of the Scheme of Control is that the networks of China Light and Hong Kong Electric are not interconnected. Although their networks are less than a mile apart, the two companies have not arranged to transmit electric power to each other. Interconnection would have increased economic efficiency but reduced both companies' rate bases.

Testifying on the electric power industry before Hong Kong's Legislative Council, senior regulator, Maria Kwan, remarked, "I feel like I am a little bit of a failure."

Sources: "The SAR's Greatest Power Failure," *South China Morning Post*, June 10, 2000, p. 16; "China's Power Sector: Can Supply Meet Demand?", *China Business*, October 7, 2005.

3   Potentially Competitive Market

By contrast with a natural monopoly, a potentially competitive market is one where economies of scale or scope are small relative to market demand. A market can switch from a natural monopoly to potentially competitive or vice versa with changes in demand or technology. The math supplement provides a formal analysis of such a change.

If perfect competition prevails over a potentially competitive market, the invisible hand will ensure economic efficiency. Some potentially competitive markets, however, have government protection through exclusive franchises or restrictions against foreign imports. From the standpoint of economic efficiency, these markets should be opened to competition.

In most jurisdictions, the policy regarding competition depends on whether the industry is subject to government regulation. (A jurisdiction could be a state, country, or group of countries such as the European Union.) Unregulated industries are subject to general competition law, while regulated industries may be subject to laws specific to the industry. Please refer to chapter 11 for a discussion of competition law.

⊢ Cable television: still a natural monopoly? ⊢

For over three decades, AT&T Cable Services and its predecessors held San Francisco's only franchise for cable television services. In mid-2000, AT&T Cable, whose franchise was valid until 2005, had over 190,000 subscribers. Then, the city of San Francisco licensed a competitor. It granted RCN Telecom Services a 15-year franchise to provide cable television, broadband Internet, and telephone service.

In many cities across the United States, competition in cable television was permitted. For years, however, the cost of laying new cables deterred the entry of new providers. In effect, the cable television market was a natural monopoly.

After passage of the Telecommunications Act of 1996, the Federal Communications Commission deregulated the local telephone service industry to allow competition, and consumer demand for high-speed Internet service took off. With these two developments, cable providers could expect revenues from two additional sources – telephone and Internet service. Existing cable companies like AT&T had to re-build their legacy networks to provide telephone and Internet service.

At the same time, satellite television was granted access to local television stations and it captured 15% of the cable television market. More recently, traditional telephone service providers, like SBC (now AT&T after a merger of the two companies), are upgrading their legacy networks to provide video service as well as telephone and internet services.

Sources: "First for S.F. – Cable TV, Phone, Internet Rivalry," *San Francisco Chronicle*, July 21, 2000; numerous submissions in FCC *Notice of Proposed Rulemaking 05-189*, MB Docket no. 05-311, 2005–6.

Structural Regulation

The fact that one market is a natural monopoly does not necessarily mean that related upstream or downstream markets are also natural monopolies. In natural gas, for instance, production may be potentially competitive even while distribution is a natural monopoly. Likewise, distribution of water may be a natural monopoly, while production is potentially competitive.

Under such circumstances, the government must consider how to preserve the benefits of monopoly in one market while fostering competition in the other. A special challenge to the regulator arises when the monopoly franchise holder also participates in the potentially competitive market.

To illustrate the issues, suppose that the government awarded a monopoly franchise for water distribution to Saturn Water, while allowing competition in production of water. Since Saturn has a monopoly over distribution, it has a monopsony over the purchase of water. Hence, the government must regulate Saturn's monopoly over water distribution as well as its monopsony over water purchases.

Now, suppose that Saturn has vertically integrated upstream into the production of water. Then, Saturn may have an incentive to extend its monopoly upstream by discriminating against external water producers. An external source of water might offer a lower price with slightly different technical specifications. It may not be easy for the regulator to distinguish legitimate engineering reasons against the outside source of water from spurious arguments. Hence, external sources may be at a disadvantage.

This particular problem arises when the monopoly and the potentially competitive market occupy successive stages of production. One solution is structural regulation to separate the natural monopoly from the potentially competitive market. Applied to the example of Saturn Water, the regulator may require Saturn to separate its water distribution and production businesses. An extreme form of structural regulation would be to require that Saturn divest itself of the production business.

⊢ Re-structuring the electric power industry ⊢

Table 15.1 reports the world wide pattern of electricity deregulation. The common thread has been the vertical separation of power generation from transmission and distribution. A major reason for re-structuring has been a change in power generation technology. Traditionally, utilities had generated electricity in large-scale fossil fuel (coal, fuel oil, natural gas, or nuclear) or hydro-electric plants.

New generation technology based on natural gas, however, allowed cost-efficient generation on a much smaller scale. It allowed industrial users to generate their own power at a lower cost than the prices charged by the electric power utility. Consequently, power generation ceased to be a natural monopoly.

While power generation is deemed to be potentially competitive, many regulators continue to view transmission and distribution as being natural monopolies. Accordingly, New York State government and others have required electric power utilities to be vertically disintegrated, and opened power generation to competition.

Similar deregulation in the State of California attracted much attention, as it was associated with blackouts and huge price increases. California appears to be unique in its debacle, as at least 25 U.S. states and numerous countries have successfully re-structured their electricity industries.

Source: Robert Thomas Crow, "What Works and What Does Not in Restructuring Electricity Markets," *Business Economics* 37, no. 3 (2002).

Table 15.1   Electric power: world wide deregulation examples

Year	Jurisdiction	Actions
1990	England	Central Electricity Generating Board divided into two generating companies (National Power and PowerGen), a transmission company, and 12 regional electricity distributors. Competition allowed in power generation. Each regional distributor granted exclusive franchise for its territory.
1993–4	Victoria, Australia	State Electricity Commission of Victoria divided into five generating companies, two transmission companies (PowerNet Victoria and Victorian Power Exchange), and five distribution companies. Each regional distributor granted exclusive franchise for its territory.
1996	California, United States	Deregulation of wholesale electricity markets; required investor-owned utilities to separate generation from their transmission and distribution businesses, and to divest their thermal generation assets. Wholesale prices were deregulated, retail prices were not, and limits were placed on risk mitigation measures by utilities, such as use of futures contracts.
1998	Ontario, Canada	Ontario Hydro divided into three parts: nonprofit Independent Electricity Market Operator, and two commercial organizations, Ontario Power Generation and Ontario Hydro Services Company. Competition allowed in power generation, while Ontario Hydro granted monopoly in transmission and distribution.
2002	Delhi, India	Delhi Vidyut Board divided into a generation company, a transmission company, and three regional distribution companies.

Progress Check 15B Suppose that the production of natural gas is potentially competitive and its distribution is a natural monopoly. Explain how structural regulation can ensure economic efficiency in the two markets.

4 Asymmetric Information

The second situation in which the invisible hand may fail is where there is asymmetric information about some characteristic or future action. Then, from chapters 12 and 13, we know that, if the information asymmetry is not resolved, the marginal benefit will diverge from the marginal cost, and the allocation of resources will not be economically efficient.

Consider, for instance, the market for medical services. Patients rely on doctors for advice as well as treatment. Owing to the asymmetry of information between doctor and patient, the doctors are subject to moral hazard. Specifically, doctors can over-prescribe treatment and so increase their incomes.

Figure 15.2 illustrates the market equilibrium. The true demand reflects the patients' marginal benefit if they and their doctors had equal information. The inflated demand is the demand that is actually realized and reflects the asymmetry of information. The inflated demand is higher than the true demand to the extent that doctors induce patients to get excessive treatment.

The inflated demand crosses the supply of medical services at point *a*. In the market equilibrium, the price is $140 per hour and the quantity of treatment is 210 million hours a month. At that quantity, the true marginal benefit of medical services is $50, which is the height of the true demand curve. The marginal cost of medical services is $140, the height of the supply curve at the equilibrium quantity. In equilibrium, the marginal cost exceeds the true marginal benefit by $90. This economic inefficiency is the result of the asymmetry of information between doctors and patients.

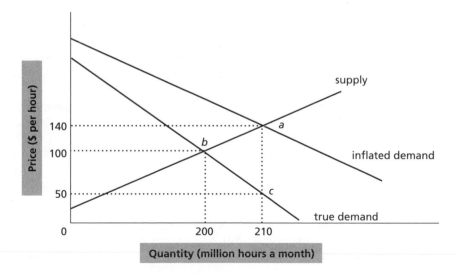

Figure 15.2 Moral hazard in medical services
The inflated demand is higher than the true demand. The market equilibrium lies at point *a*, where the inflated demand crosses the supply. The price is $140 per hour and the quantity is 210 million hours a month. If the moral hazard can be resolved, the inflated demand will shift down to the true demand and the equilibrium will be at point *b*, where the true marginal benefit equals the marginal cost.

Supposing that doctors and patients could not privately resolve the information asymmetry, how can regulation help? In markets with asymmetric information, the regulator can resolve the asymmetry in three ways. First, the regulator can require the better-informed party to disclose its information. Second, it can regulate the conduct of the party with better information. Third, it can impose regulations on the business structure of the better-informed party.

Disclosure

The most obvious way to resolve asymmetric information is to require the better-informed party to disclose its information truthfully. In an unregulated market, parties may supply false information. For instance, service stations may pass off regular low-octane gasoline as high-octane premium, financial advisors may hard-sell risky investments to widows and orphans, and an obstetrician may exaggerate a pregnant patient's need for a cesarean section.

A regulatory requirement for disclosure will be meaningful only if the information can be objectively verified. Of the three examples mentioned – substituted gasoline, unnecessary cesarean section, unsuitably risky investment – disclosure works best for the substituted gasoline. The regulator can require service stations to mark each pump with the octane content of the gasoline and randomly inspect the pumps to ensure that the gasoline matches the specified octane level.

Whether disclosure can resolve the asymmetry of information between financial advisors and their clients depends on whether the clients' preferences between risk and return can be objectively measured. As for the cesarean section, the patient's need is a matter of professional judgment, hence, disclosure may not resolve the information asymmetry.

⊢ Avoiding SIN: New Zealand's used-car dealers ⊢

In December 2003, new regulations on the sale of used motor vehicles came into effect in New Zealand. The new regulations required that the seller display a Supplier Information Notice (SIN) prominently on the vehicle.

Six months later, however, the Fair Trading Branch of the Commerce Commission found that 64% of used vehicle dealers in the Auckland, Wellington, and Christchurch areas did not comply with the new regulations.

Many dealers did not complete the SIN or provided inaccurate information. The information that was missing or inaccurate included current price, expiry date of warranty, chassis number, odometer reading, and seller registration.

Director of the Fair Trading Branch, Ms. Deborah Battell, emphasized: "SIN cards were designed to provide a standard set of information to consumers. It is important their format is consistent and that all information is filled out so that consumers can easily make comparisons and therefore make better informed purchasing decisions."

Source: "It's a SIN – 64% of Vehicle Dealers Inspected Not Complying with New Regulations," New Zealand Commerce Commission, Media Release, July 29, 2004.

Regulation of Conduct

Instead of directly resolving an information asymmetry, an alternative is to regulate the conduct of the better-informed party and limit the extent to which it can exploit the informational advantage. If parties with better information cannot exploit their advantage, then they are more likely to assist in resolving the asymmetry.

For example, in the market for medical services, a regulation may prohibit doctors from advertising. This may help to prevent further inflation of demand. Another possible regulation is a requirement that doctors recommending major procedures must advise their patients to get a second opinion. The second opinion provides a check against excessive treatment. To the extent that these checks are effective, the inflated demand in figure 15.2 will shift down toward the true demand and the equilibrium will be closer to point b, where the true marginal benefit equals the marginal cost.

Another example of asymmetric information arises in the market for real estate. Typically, a seller will have better information about her or his property than potential buyers. A seller may use this advantage to pressure a potential buyer. For instance, the seller may say, "Ten other people came this morning, and three of them are making offers. You'd better move fast or you'll lose this house." A regulator can restrict such high-pressure sales tactics by stipulating a minimum "cooling period" during which a buyer can cancel a purchase at no cost. Further, the law might require that real-estate agreements be in writing and witnessed. This would restrict the scope for a seller to provide misleading information and rush potential buyers into a purchase.

Structural Regulation

In addition to regulating conduct, a way to limit the extent to which a better-informed party can exploit an informational advantage is structural regulation. By enforcing separation of different businesses, a regulator may reduce the opportunities for exploiting superior information.

The market for medical services provides one example of structural regulation. Doctors providing medical advice will have much less incentive to over-prescribe if the treatment is provided by others. Hence, a structural regulation requiring doctors to specialize in either providing advice or providing treatment would mitigate the moral hazard problem. While reducing the demand for medical services, this mandatory specialization would increase the cost of the services actually provided. Accordingly, the benefit of the specialization would have to be weighed against the cost.

Mandatory specialization is not as outlandish as might be thought. In some jurisdictions, doctors are allowed to sell medicines and medical supplies in their clinics. Under these circumstances, the doctors will have an incentive to over-prescribe these items. In other jurisdictions, doctors are prohibited from selling medicines and medical supplies. This regulation effectively separates medical services from retailing of medicines and medical supplies and dissuades doctors from excessive prescriptions.

Another example of structural regulation arises in the market for real estate transactions. Suppose that one agent represents both the seller and the buyer of some real estate. Then, the agent will suffer a conflict of interest between the seller and the buyer. The agent, for instance, may learn how much the buyer is willing to pay and convey that information to the seller. Such conflicts of interest can be prevented by a regulation requiring that the seller and the buyer must have separate representation.

Self-Regulation

To forestall direct government regulation, some industries subject themselves to *self-regulation*. **Self-regulation** is the regulation of industry members

> **Self-regulation** is the regulation of industry members by an industry organization.

by an industry organization. The organization may regulate various aspects of commercial activity, including entry and exit, business structure, investment, production, products, pricing, and advertising. The self-regulatory organization may or may not have legal powers.

Self-regulation is particularly widespread among professions such as accountants, lawyers, financial advisors, doctors, architects, and engineers. Typically, as a quid pro quo for self-regulation, the government gives the professional organization an exclusive right to license practitioners. This means that any unlicensed practitioner would be violating the law and liable to be prosecuted.

The professional organization may set conditions for licensing and rules of conduct. The licensing conditions may include specific preparatory education and training, and examinations. The professional organization may also regulate conduct such as advertising, pricing, and business structure. For instance, some professional organizations prohibit their members from incorporating with limited liability. Other organizations publish set prices and restrict advertising.

One important issue is whether industries and professions use self-regulation as a cover to limit competition. Some rules may have anticompetitive effects. For instance, restrictive standards may pose a barrier to new entry, and guidelines on pricing and limits on advertising may restrict competition.

Self-regulation of lawyers: the State Bar of California

The State Bar Association of California is the self-regulatory authority for lawyers in California. The Bar's admission requirements include a specified number of years of law school and a membership examination. The Bar regulates advertising by lawyers. This may be a way to prevent lawyers from inflating the demand for their services. However, it has not prevented ambulance chasers from promoting their services on late-night television.

The Bar also prohibits lawyers from sharing fees and forming partnerships with people who are not licensed lawyers, such as accountants. This restriction is a structural regulation to ensure that clients receive independent opinions on legal issues.

The Bar Association will not automatically grant admission to lawyers from other states. Each state bar sets its own standards of admission. The differences in these standards hinder lawyers from crossing between states, hence, constitute a barrier to competition.

National Advertising Review Council

The National Advertising Review Council (NARC) was established in 1971 by the Association of National Advertisers, the American Association of Advertising Agencies, and the American Advertising Federation, together with the Council of Better Business Bureaus.

The NARC is an independent self-regulatory body administered by the Council of Better Business Bureaus (CBBB). It provides guidance and sets standards for national advertisers and advertisements.

The Children's Advertising Review Unit oversees advertising and promotion directed at children to ensure compliance with the Self-Regulatory Guidelines for Children's Advertising. The Electronic Retailing Self-Regulatory Program oversees direct response advertising. The National Advertising Division oversees all other nationwide advertising. The National Advertising Review Board hears appeals from decisions by the National Advertising Division and Childrens' Advertising Review Unit.

While the NARC has no legal power, it may refer advertisers who fail to comply with NARC decisions to the relevant federal authorities.

Source: National Advertising Review Council, www.narc.org, accessed, July 19, 2006.

5   Externalities

Externalities arise when the markets for some costs or benefits fail to exist. Absent a market, the invisible hand cannot work. Chapter 12 discussed how externalities can be resolved through private action. Some externalities, for instance, aircraft noise and automobile emissions, involve hundreds if not thousands of parties. In these cases, the difficulty of organizing all the sources and the affected parties means that private action will probably fail to resolve the externality. Government regulation may be the only solution.

To analyze how to regulate such widespread externalities, consider the emissions that create smog. Chapter 6 showed that, for an economically efficient allocation of resources, every good or service must be provided up to the level that the marginal benefit balances the marginal cost. Although emissions are bad, the same principle applies: the economically efficient quantity of emissions balances the marginal benefit of emissions with the marginal cost, taking into account both private benefits and costs and external benefits and costs.

The major benefit of emissions is that the sources can avoid the cost of technologies that generate fewer emissions. Smog causes harm to people and damage to crops. Smog is ambient: it affects victims over a wide area and each victim is equally exposed. If one victim increases her exposure to the emissions, this does not reduce the exposure to others. Accordingly, the marginal cost to society is the *sum* of the marginal costs to the various victims.

As depicted in figure 15.3, the economically efficient rate of emissions is 800,000 tons a year, where the marginal benefit equals the marginal cost to society. How can this be achieved?

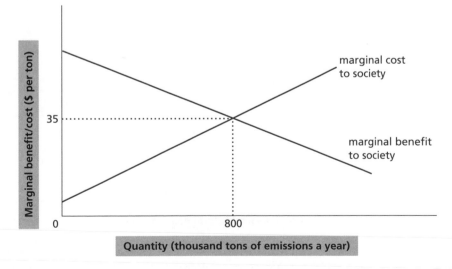

Figure 15.3   Economic efficiency in emissions
The economically efficient rate of emissions is 800,000 tons a year, where the marginal benefit and the marginal cost to society are both equal to $35 per ton.

Generally, there are two approaches. One aims to mimic Adam Smith's invisible hand: allow all sources to emit as much as they like provided that they pay a user fee. The other approach is to control emissions directly through standards.

User Fees

Referring to figure 15.3, at the economically efficient rate of emissions, the marginal cost to society is $35 per ton. Suppose that the regulator sets a user fee for emissions of $35 per ton and allows every source (user) to buy as much emissions as it would like at that price.

Consider an oil refinery that emits pollutants. To maximize profits, the refinery should buy emissions up to the rate where the marginal benefit of emissions balances the $35 fee. Suppose that, as shown in figure 15.4, the refinery's marginal benefit balances the $35 fee at an emissions rate of 50,000 tons a year.

To see why 50,000 tons maximizes profit, consider emissions of less than 50,000 tons a year, say, 40,000 tons. Then, as figure 15.4 shows, the marginal benefit will be $45, which exceeds the $35 fee; so, by increasing emissions, the refinery can increase profits. Consider, instead, emissions of more than 50,000 tons a year, say, 60,000 tons. Then, the marginal benefit will be $25, which is less than the $35 fee; so the refinery should cut back on emissions. Accordingly, the refinery maximizes profit at the emissions rate where its marginal benefit equals the fee.

Other sources of emissions such as furniture manufacturers will make the same calculation: each will emit up to the point that its marginal benefit equals $35. Since the regulator charges the same $35 fee to all sources, the marginal benefits of all sources will be equal.

Since the regulator set the fee at the social marginal cost of emissions, it balances the marginal benefit with the marginal cost of emissions to society. Accordingly, the user fee achieves the economically efficient rate of emissions.

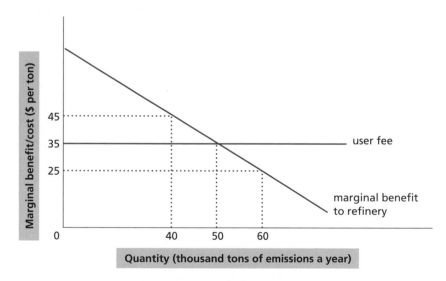

Figure 15.4 User fee
The refinery's marginal benefit equals the $35 fee, at an emissions rate of 50,000 tons a year. If the refinery emitted 40,000 tons, the marginal benefit would be $45, which exceeds the $35 fee, so by increasing emissions, the refinery could increase profits. If the refinery emitted 60,000 tons, then the marginal benefit would be $25, which is less than the $35 fee, so the refinery should cut back on emissions.

Standards

The alternative to charging a fee for emissions is to regulate directly through standards. From figure 15.3, the economically efficient emissions rate is 800,000 tons a year, which is the appropriate standard. There are many sources of emissions, however. How should the regulator allocate the 800,000 tons a year among the various sources?

The answer depends on the cost of monitoring. Suppose that the emissions of all sources can be monitored at relatively low cost. The regulator could issue licenses for 800,000 tons of emissions a year and sell them through public auction. Potential sources of emissions will provide the demand for the licenses. The demand of each source for licenses will be the same as its marginal benefit from emissions. The market demand will be the horizontal sum of the individual demand curves. So, the market demand curve will be identical to the social marginal benefit curve in figure 15.3.

The supply of licenses would be perfectly inelastic at 800,000. In equilibrium, the market demand will balance the supply at a quantity of 800,000 licenses a year. Now, by figure 15.3, the marginal benefit of the 800,000th ton of emissions is $35. Thus, the equilibrium price of a license will be $35. Each source will buy licenses up to the point that its marginal benefit balances the price of $35. As a result, each source's emissions will be economically efficient and the total emissions will be at the economically efficient rate of 800,000 tons a year.

By selling emissions licenses, the regulator is effectively charging a user fee that is determined by a competitive market. The license scheme, however, may be difficult to implement for small mobile sources such as power-boats and lawn mowers. It will be relatively expensive to monitor emissions from these sources. In such cases, it may be better for the regulator to specify directly the type and size of engine and fuel.

Progress Check 15C Referring to figure 15.3, compare the social welfare with user fees of $25 per ton and $45 per ton.

⊢ Japan and the Kyoto Protocol ⊢

In December 1997, representatives of more than 160 countries met in Kyoto, Japan, to negotiate binding limits on greenhouse gas emissions. This meeting followed the United Nations Framework Convention on Climate Change of 1992.

The meeting agreed on the Kyoto Protocol, in which the developed countries committed to reduce their greenhouse gas emissions relative to 1990 levels. Japan committed to a 6% reduction in emissions by 2012.

The Kyoto Protocol encouraged the reduction of greenhouse gas emissions in various innovative ways. For instance, sources of emissions could achieve their targets by reducing emissions elsewhere in the world.

In 2002, Tohoku Electric Power of Japan signed a long-term contract to buy coal from Powercoal of Australia. Methane is a by-product of coal mining. Under the contract, Powercoal agreed to reduce the release of methane into the atmosphere, and so, cut annual carbon dioxide emissions by 1.6 million tons. The methane would be used to generate electricity. Powercoal would then transfer the emissions credits to Tohoku.

Despite voluntary action by industry, Japanese emissions continued to rise. By 2000, emissions already exceeded the 1990 levels by 8%. Consequently, the Environment Ministry came to the view that a carbon tax was necessary for Japan to meet its Kyoto Protocol commitment. Finland, Germany, the Netherlands, and Britain had already imposed carbon taxes.

The Ministry advocated a tax of 3,400 yen per ton of carbon. If all the revenues were used to finance measures to counter climate change, the Ministry estimated that the tax would reduce carbon dioxide emissions to 97% of 1990 levels. The tax would translate to 2 yen per liter of gasoline.

Sources: "A Primer on the Kyoto Protocol: The Climate's Changing, Now What?", http://about.com/ downloaded October 14, 2004; "Environment Panel Calls for Carbon Tax in 2005," *Japan Times*, August 28, 2003.

Regional and Temporal Differences

The efficient degree of an externality balances the marginal benefit with the marginal cost. Many externalities that need regulatory action are regional problems. For instance, smog above Los Angeles does not affect Chicago. Further, the marginal benefit and the marginal cost of an externality may vary from one place to another.

If the benefits and costs of an externality are confined to a region, then it is economically efficient to allow each region to determine its own degree of the externality. Uniform national standards may result in economic inefficiency.

National or international standards, however, are necessary for externalities that cross boundaries. For instance, sulfur dioxide emitted by coal-fired electric power plants in the American Midwest causes acid rain in the Northeast and Canada. Chlorofluorocarbons from all over the world damage the ozone layer in the atmosphere. Federal regulation is necessary to resolve externalities among states, and international regulation for externalities among countries.

If the marginal benefit and the marginal cost of an externality vary over time, then the efficient degree of the externality will also vary with time. This is most obvious with noise. Society may be relatively more willing to tolerate noise during working hours than at night or on weekends. The same principle also applies over longer periods of time. As victims become more sensitive to air pollution or new technologies to reduce emissions become available, the economically efficient rate of emissions will fall.

Accidents

As discussed earlier, private action may fail to resolve externalities that involve large numbers of parties. A specific class of such externalities is accidents. When Joy drives out of her house onto the main road, she joins an anonymous stream of other cars, buses, and trucks. She has no way of knowing the other drivers, let alone negotiating and agreeing with them on how to deal with an accident.

Yet each driver influences the likelihood and severity of accident by the care that she takes in driving. The economically efficient degree of care balances the marginal benefit to society (in terms of the reduced expected damage from accidents) with the marginal cost of care to the driver. We illustrate this balance in figure 15.5.

Private action, however, may fail to resolve the externality imposed by one driver on another. It is difficult for every driver to negotiate with every other driver about their respective degrees

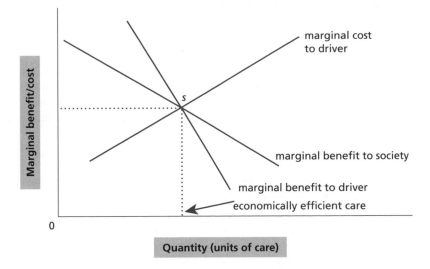

Figure 15.5   Care
At the economically efficient degree of care, the marginal benefit to society equals the marginal cost of care to the driver. If the marginal benefit of care to the driver balanced the marginal cost at the economically efficient level, then the driver would choose the economically efficient degree of care.

of care in driving and even more difficult to enforce compliance. Accordingly, government intervention is necessary to balance the marginal benefit and the marginal cost.

Typically, the government does not intervene directly. Rather, the government establishes a legal framework to deal with accidents. The legal framework consists of laws and the court system. The **law of torts** governs interactions between parties that have no contractual relationship. The court system provides the mechanism by which the victim of an accident can enforce her or his legal rights.

> The **law of torts** is the law governing interactions between parties that have no contractual relationship.

The law of torts specifies the *liability* of the parties to an accident. **Liability** is the set of conditions under which one party must pay damages to another party. The law regarding liability varies from one jurisdiction to another. For instance, in some jurisdictions, the injurer is liable only if she was negligent, and in other jurisdictions, the injurer is not liable if the victim contributed to the occurrence of the accident.

> **Liability** is the set of conditions under which one party must pay damages to another party.

The law of torts also specifies the amount that the injurer must pay in damages to the victim. Generally, the damages include compensation for the victim's loss, including medical expenses and lost earnings. Again, the precise rules on damages vary among jurisdictions.

In effect, by specifying liability and damages, the law of torts establishes a price for causing an accident or, equivalently, a price for failing to take care. Unlike prices in competitive markets, the price for an accident is paid only after the event. This legal framework is less costly than requiring every potential injurer to negotiate and agree with every potential victim in advance.

Within this framework, each potential injurer will balance the private marginal benefit of care (in terms of the reduced expected liability for damages) against the marginal cost. If the law specifies liability and damages appropriately, then the potential injurer will choose the economically efficient level of care. Referring to figure 15.5, this will happen if the marginal benefit of care to the driver balances the marginal cost at the economically efficient level.

Progress Check 15D Suppose that, relative to the situation in figure 15.5; the courts double the damages that injurers must pay accident victims. How will this affect a driver's choice of care?

---

6   Public Goods

A public good provides nonrival consumption or use. Private enterprises provide many public goods, including free-to-the-air television, literary and musical works, and software on a commercial basis. Usually, a public good can be provided commercially only if the consumption or use of the item is excludable. If a provider could not exclude free riders, then it would be very difficult to sell the item. As we discussed in chapter 12, excludability depends on law and technology.

Here, we discuss the legal framework for excludability and show that regulators must balance two factors: that excludability is necessary for private provision and that private provision may result in less than the economically efficient level of provision. We then discuss the alternative to private provision, which is provision by charity or the government.

Legal Framework

Chapter 12 presented two forms of intellectual property – copyright and patent – that make the use of knowledge excludable. A copyright is a legal, exclusive right to an artistic, literary, or musical creation. The concept extends protection to software. Similarly, a patent is a legal, exclusive right to a product or process invention.

Suppose that the owner of a copyright or patent aims to maximize profit and applies uniform pricing. Each individual user will purchase the quantity of the copyrighted or patented item where the marginal benefit equals the price. Hence, the marginal benefit equals the price. But the profit maximizing uniform price exceeds the marginal cost. This means that each user's marginal benefit will exceed the marginal cost and the use will be less than economically efficient.

For economic efficiency, a public good should be provided up to the quantity that the marginal benefit equals the marginal cost. A public good provides nonrival use; hence, the marginal cost of additional provision is zero. Thus, the public good should be provided up to the quantity that the marginal benefit is zero for each user. A profit-maximizing owner applying uniform pricing will not achieve this level of provision.

We have just shown that copyright and patent protection may result in use at less than the economically efficient level. On the other hand, without such protection, there would be little incentive for commercial creation or invention. Accordingly, society faces a trade-off between the incentive to create and invent and inefficient use.

This trade-off explains why copyrights and patents have limited lives. Under U.S. law, copyrights last for the life of the creator plus 70 years, while patents are valid for 20 years. On the expiration of a copyright, anyone can freely copy or use the material. Similarly, once a patent has expired, anyone can freely imitate or use the product or process.

The expiration of a copyright or patent allows free use of the formerly protected creation or invention. Usage will extend to the point where the marginal benefit equals zero, which is the economically efficient level. During the life of a copyright or patent, however, the owner has an exclusive right and society bears the cost of less than efficient usage.

Progress Check 15E If society wants to increase the usage of existing scientific knowledge, should it reduce or extend the validity of copyrights and patents?

Public Provision

For some public goods, it would be difficult or impossible to exclude people who do not pay. For instance, if the air circulating above London becomes cleaner, it would be difficult to exclude specific persons from enjoying the cleaner air. The same is true of national defense: during an enemy bomb raid, anti-aircraft batteries cannot protect some people without protecting everyone else in the neighborhood.

For other public goods, exclusion may be possible but only against some users. Consider the process for distilling water. Suppose that the law allowed a patent on this process. The owner of the patent could probably enforce it on large-scale users such as commercial suppliers of distilled water. It would be nearly impossible to exclude high-school students or household cooks from using the process, however.

Typically, if use of a public good is nonexcludable or difficult to exclude, it can be provided only by charities or the government. Some of the public goods provided by charities are medical and scientific research, public health, and free-to-the-air radio and television.

⊢ Global Alliance for Vaccines and Immunizations (GAVI) ⊢

The scientific formulas for vaccines are public goods. GAVI was launched in 2000 to enhance the distribution of existing vaccines and to accelerate the development of new vaccines for 75 low-income countries with a gross domestic product per head of less than $1,000. Through bundling the requirements of these countries, GAVI "creates a large, reliable demand that stimulates more companies to get involved in manufacturing existing vaccines, provides an incentive to develop new ones, and pushes down unit prices."

GAVI supports existing vaccines which target diphtheria, tetanus, pertussis, tuberculosis, measles and polio, and also supports underused vaccines where needed (hepatitis B, Hib and yellow fever). GAVI supports the development of vaccines against rotavirus, pneumococcal disease and meningitis (types A and C).

As of September 2005, GAVI had disbursed a total of $672 million, including $419 million to purchase vaccines and supplies, $203 million for immunization services and safety, and $39 million on the development and introduction of new vaccines. GAVI estimated that, by the end of 2005, its programs would have averted almost 1.7 million deaths from Hib disease, pertussis, and hepatitis B.

Sources: "The World's Richest Charity Confronts the Health of the World's Poorest People," *The Economist*, January 26, 2005; GAVI, "GAVI Alliance: Progress and Achievements," accessed, July 21, 2006.

The public goods that are provided by government include civil laws, environmental protection, and national defense.

In addition to the issue of excludability, there is another reason for charitable or government provision of a public good. To the extent that these providers do not charge a price for the use of the good, it will be used up to the quantity where the marginal benefit equals zero. Hence, the use will be economically efficient.

It is important to distinguish public goods from goods provided by the government, however. Not all items provided by the government sector are public goods. Compare, for instance, public health programs such as the eradication of communicable diseases with medical treatment. The eradication of communicable diseases such as tuberculosis is a public good. Once tuberculosis is wiped out, everyone benefits to an equal degree. By contrast, medical treatment is a private good: a doctor who spends more time treating one patient will have less time for other patients.

Governments provide many private goods such as food, education, housing, and medical services. By providing these private goods, the government may be aiming to equalize the distribution of wealth and provide equal opportunity for future generations.

Congestible Facilities

The use of facilities such as bridges and tunnels is excludable. Such facilities often have a capacity that is relatively large compared with demand, causing them to be natural monopolies. Hence, for economically efficient usage, they must be prevented from exercising monopoly power. In principle, these facilities could be provided by a commercial operator subject to regulation. Some, however, are provided by the government.

The demand for such facilities usually varies with time. Outside of peak hours, the facility provides nonrival use. By contrast, during peak hours, each additional user adds to congestion, the costs of which include delays, additional fuel, and an increase in accidents; hence, usage is a private good.

Consider a tunnel that can smoothly convey up to 30 vehicles a minute. When, however, 30 vehicles a minute are already entering the tunnel, additional drivers will cause congestion. From the standpoint of economic efficiency, traffic through the tunnel should be managed so that the marginal benefit of each user balances the marginal cost. When there are fewer than 30 vehicles a minute, the marginal cost of a crossing is nothing. So, the tunnel should not exclude any driver.

When, however, 30 vehicles per minute are in the tunnel, the marginal cost becomes positive. For economic efficiency, the tunnel should set a toll equal to the marginal cost. This will ensure that the only drivers who enter the tunnel are those whose benefit exceeds the marginal cost.

What if the tunnel does not charge a toll? Consider the decision of a marginal driver (the 31st) whether to enter the tunnel or wait until there is less traffic. If the driver enters immediately, she will save some time. In making the decision, that driver compares her private benefit from crossing at that time with her private cost and ignores the additional costs on other drivers. Owing to this negative externality, the number of drivers entering the tunnel tends to exceed the economically efficient number. The solution is for the tunnel to charge a toll equal to the marginal cost of a crossing.

Generally, for economic efficiency, congestible facilities should levy a price, set equal to the marginal cost of use, where the cost includes the externalities imposed on other users. As the marginal cost varies with the time of day, so should the price. This pricing would ensure economically efficient usage of facilities such as bridges, tunnels, roads, and subways.

Progress Check 15F Suppose that a local telephone service provider sets the same price for local calls at all times of the day. Would this lead to economically efficient usage?

⊣ Congestion of the airwaves? ⊢

Historically, governments have regulated radio spectrum as a scarce resource. They awarded exclusive use of particular frequencies to particular users. More recently, they have used auctions (see chapter 13 for the discussion of auctions) to determine the value and users of different frequencies. The analogy often used is that of land: private property rights in land are needed to prevent the overuse that occurs with common property resources.

Other experts believe that new technology has made spectrum resources almost unlimited. Their analogy is shipping lanes on the open sea: no exclusive property rights are needed, only rules that prevent interference among ships. Numerous electronic devices can use the same spectrum if they use technology to prevent interference.

Thomas Hazlett observes that the successful use of unlicensed spectrum often results from complementary exclusive *real property* rights. For example, ownership of houses limits the potential interference from low-power devices, such as garage openers, cordless phones, and home WiFi networks. However, unlicensed spectrum continues to lead to inefficiencies, in the form of increased investment costs for uses which require higher-powered devices (such as wireless networks). He maintains that more flexible, but exclusive, specturm rights would permit technological advance as well as preventing inefficiencies that can accompany common property.

The FCC appears to be hedging its bets: it is advocating more spectrum auctions for exclusive uses, as well as increasing the availability of unlicensed spectrum.

Sources: Eli Noam, 1998, "Beyond Auctions: Open Spectrum Access," CATO Institute; Thomas Hazlett, 2005, "Spectrum Tragedies," *Yale Journal on Regulation*, 22, no. 2, pp. 242–75.

Social versus Private Benefits

Intellectual property strategy, and patents in particular, play a strong role in R&D decisions. In the example of Neptune Tech from chapter 8, assume that Neptune will procure a patent from its R&D activity. Neptune will invest less in R&D than is socially efficient. In the multi-stage decision problem, where Neptune makes an initial investment and has the option for subsequent development, Neptune would invest whenever the probability of the favorable market condition is at least 67%. In this calculation, however, Neptune is only accounting for its profits ($3 million), and not the value of the innovation to buyers.

Society would value the profits to Neptune as well as the buyer surplus it would generate. The total buyer and seller surplus will be larger than the profits to be earned by Neptune. Suppose that the buyer surplus is an additional $2 million. Then, society would like to see Neptune undertake the R&D project if its NPV $= -1 + p(3 + 2 - 1.5) + (1 - p)0 = 3.5p - 1 > 0$. This occurs for any value of $p > 28.6\%$.[2] The situation may be worse, given that patents are usually limited to 20 years, while the social benefits of invention may continue

---

[2] Neptune's solution is found using the same calculation, with the $2 million of buyer surplus omitted.

indefinitely. Much of the rationale for patents hinges on the tradeoff between the inefficiency of granting monopoly power to the inventor and providing adequate incentives for invention.

There are two important countervailing factors to the finding that investment in R&D will be less than socially optimal. First, the above example assumes that the invention will not take place unless Neptune engages in the R&D. In fact, most invention and innovation is simultaneously pursued by a number of organizations. Thus, the effect of much R&D is to accelerate invention and innovation, but not to determine whether or not it occurs. In this case, the actual social benefit generated by Neptune's R&D may be smaller than the private benefit that would be realized by Neptune, if it is successful.

Second, many patented products are substitutes for products that are currently provided at a price that exceeds marginal cost (due to patents on the currently available substitute products). This enhances the private benefits available to Neptune from invention, without a commensurate increase in the social benefits of the invention.

Hence, patents are a rich area for analysis, strategy, and public policy.

7   Summary

The marginal benefit of an item may diverge from the marginal cost for three basic reasons: market power, asymmetric information, and externalities and public goods. This divergence results in economic inefficiency. Government regulation may help where private action fails to resolve the economic inefficiency.

Generally, the government can regulate conduct, information, and structure. Specifically, the conduct of a franchised monopoly may be regulated directly through price or indirectly through the rate of return. Competition law regulates the conduct and structure of businesses in general. In situations of asymmetric information, mandatory disclosure is one form of regulation.

Externalities may be regulated through fees or standards. The efficient degree of an externality depends on location and time. The government can help to resolve inefficiency in accidents and public goods by providing an appropriate legal framework. The laws regarding copyrights and patents must balance the incentive for new research against inefficient use of existing knowledge.

Key Concepts

natural monopoly
privatization
marginal cost pricing
average cost pricing

rate base
self-regulation
law of torts
liability

Review Questions

1. Using relevant examples, explain the concept of a natural monopoly.
2. Define price and rate of return regulation.
3. What are the problems with price regulation?
4. What are the problems with rate of return regulation?

5. Explain the differences between
   (a) privatization;
   (b) allowing competition.

6. Name one self-regulated profession. Does it regulate disclosure, conduct, or structure?

7. At one time, U.S. law prohibited movie producers from owning theaters. Use this example to explain structural regulation.

8. True or false? Mandatory disclosure is always the best way to resolve asymmetric information.

9. Explain how regulation of conduct and business structure can resolve asymmetric information.

10. Explain how the following policies can be used to control noise pollution from a construction site:
    (a) user fee;
    (b) standard.

11. True or false? The economically efficient degree of an externality can only be achieved through a standard.

12. How do copyrights and patents contribute to excludability of usage of a public good?

13. Which of the following situations involves externalities?
    (a) The workers in a factory may injure themselves on the production equipment.
    (b) Two ships may collide while passing through a narrow channel at night.

14. A charitable foundation sponsored the development of a drug that cures bone-marrow cancer. The foundation has patented the drug and is selling it on a commercial basis. Will the use of the drug be economically efficient?

15. Explain the differences among a private good, congestible facility, and a public good.

Discussion Questions

1. In July 2000, the San Diego Water Authority charged its 23 member agencies a uniform price of $439 per acre-foot of water. (An acre-foot is the volume of water that would cover one acre to a depth of one foot, or about 326,000 gallons.) Suppose that the Water Authority practices marginal cost pricing and its marginal cost of water is increasing and begins at $0.
   (a) Illustrate the current price and quantity on an appropriate diagram.
   (b) The Water Authority negotiated with the Imperial Irrigation District to buy 200,000 acre-feet of Colorado River water at $245 per acre-foot. Show how this purchase would affect the Authority's marginal cost of water.
   (c) Assume that the Water Authority continues to practice marginal cost pricing. On your diagram, show the increase in buyer and seller surplus that San Diego as a whole will achieve from the acquisition of the water rights to 200,000 acre-feet.

2. With over 21 million subscribers, Comcast is the nation's largest cable television provider. The cable industry also includes many small operators that serve a few thousand subscribers each.
   (a) For over 20 years, there was only one cable television provider in Louisville, Kentucky. Explain how the cost of laying a network causes cable television to tend towards a natural monopoly.
   (b) Considering an area with a single cable service provider, discuss whether the provider would have greater market power over its consumers if it were Comcast or a small independent operator.
   (c) With deregulation of the local telephone industry and growing demand for the Internet, cable companies found new opportunities in providing local telephone and Internet access services. Existing cable providers, however, had to re-build their legacy networks to provide the new services. Has the cable business ceased to be a natural monopoly?

3. In 2002, the Delhi Vidyut Board was divided into separate generation, transmission, and distribution companies. The distribution companies were partly privatized. North Delhi Power Limited, a 51%–49% joint venture of Tata Power and the Delhi Government, secured the franchise to distribute electricity in the north and northwest areas. The franchise contract fixed retail prices for five years until 2006–7. However, the Delhi Government agreed to subsidize

North Delhi Power's purchases of electric power, so that the company would earn at least 16% return on net worth.

   (a)   Why did the Delhi Government break up the Delhi Vidyut Board into separate generation, transmission, and distribution companies?

   (b)   Referring to North Delhi Power's costs, explain conditions under which the Delhi Government could reasonably fix retail prices below average cost.

   (c)   Did North Delhi Power's franchise contract apply price regulation or rate-of-return regulation?

   (d)   Suppose that Tata Power was concerned about holdup by the Delhi Government. Explain how the 51%–49% shareholding structure could resolve the potential for holdup.

4.   In the United States, all stockbrokers must insure customer accounts up to a minimum level with the Securities Investor Protection Corporation (SIPC). This insurance covers customers against default by the broker.

   (a)   What is the minimum required level of SIPC insurance?

   (b)   Can you explain this requirement in terms of asymmetric information between brokers and investors?

   (c)   Many brokers purchase private insurance to cover losses that exceed the minimum SIPC cover. Please explain this practice as a way by which brokers can signal their financial reliability.

5.   Consider the following practices of the Hong Kong medical profession. Do they serve to resolve economic inefficiency or limit competition?

   (a)   Doctors are not allowed to advertise.

   (b)   Doctors can sell medicines from their clinics. At one time, they could dispense drugs in unmarked containers, and were not required to mark the expiration date of the medicine.

   (c)   Doctors admitted in Ireland can practice freely in Hong Kong, but doctors who are qualified in California must undergo special training and a rigorous examination.

6.   On January 29, 1999, the tank vessel *Chelsea* collided with the container ship, *Manzanillo* in the vicinity of Miami Harbor Sea Buoy. In any harbor with significant marine traffic there may be a significant risk of collision between passing vessels.

   (a)   Using a suitable diagram, analyze the marginal benefit and marginal cost of care to society in navigation through the harbor.

   (b)   Suppose that the law of torts provides that any ship that fails to take due care must bear liability for accidents. Using the diagram in (a), explain how a typical ship's master will choose care.

   (c)   Suppose that the courts reduce the damages that ships must pay to victims of accidents. How will this change affect masters in their degree of care in the harbor?

7.   The U.S. Federal Aviation Administration (FAA) classifies all civil transport aircraft according to noise. The categories range from stage 1, which is the noisiest, to stage 3, which is the quietest category.

   (a)   If one airport prohibits landings by stage 1 and 2 aircraft, will it impose externalities on other airports?

   (b)   Who should regulate aircraft noise: the federal government or local airport authorities?

   (c)   Suppose that an airport has specified standards for aircraft noise. Some airlines operate older, noisier aircraft than others. Should the airport create permits for aircraft noise and allow airlines to trade these permits?

8.   Dan Brown owns the copyright to his best-seller *Da Vinci Code* (2003). He earns revenues from sales to individuals and libraries world wide.

   (a)   Explain the sense in which the content of *Da Vinci Code* is a public good.

   (b)   Students who photocopy a library copy of the book are breaching Mr Brown's copyright. Compare the following proposals in terms of rewarding authors and administrative cost:

(i) The government imposes a levy on all copies made on library photcopying machines. It distributes the revenues from the levy to authors. (ii) The government bans photocopying machines from libraries.

9. GAVI was launched in 2000 to enhance the distribution of existing vaccines and to accelerate the development of new vaccines for 75 low-income countries with a gross domestic product of less than $1,000 per head. GAVI subsidizes the distribution of existing vaccines and underused vaccines, and the development of new vaccines. By bundling purchases of vaccines and supplies, GAVI "creates a large, reliable demand that stimulates more companies to get involved in manufacturing existing vaccines, provides an incentive to develop new ones, and pushes down unit prices." (*Source*: "The World's Richest Charity Confronts the Health of the World's Poorest People," *The Economist*, January 26, 2005.)
    (a)   How would GAVI affect the economically efficient use of vaccines?
    (b)   How would GAVI affect investments in the development of new vaccines?

10. Internet users connect either by dial-up service, or continuously through digital subscriber line, cable modem, or corporate network. Among those who dial up, some pay a usage charge for each minute, while others subscribe to unmetered service for a flat monthly fee. Usage of the Internet varies with the time of day.
    (a)   Explain why unmetered service results in economically inefficient usage of the Internet.
    (b)   Some Internet access providers charge per minute usage fees that are fixed throughout the day. Should they charge fees that vary with the time of the day?
    (c)   While users do not mind if email is delayed, they do care about the speed of Web pages. Do the existing pricing mechanisms cater for this difference?

11. This question applies the mathematical technique for analyzing a natural monopoly presented in the math supplement. The demand for electric power in Sol Province is $p = 20 - 20q$, where p and q represent the price in thousands of dollars and the quantity in megawatt-hours, respectively. Suppose that an electricity plant generates power at a constant marginal cost of $1,000 per megawatt-hour up to a capacity of 10 megawatt-hours. The government requires the plant to implement marginal cost pricing.
    (a)   Illustrate the price and quantity with marginal cost pricing.
    (b)   Suppose that demand grows to $p = 20 - 0.1q$. At a price of $1,000 per megawatt-hour, what is the minimum number of plants needed to produce the quantity demanded?

Chapter 15

Math Supplement

Let us apply a numerical example to see how a natural monopoly can evolve into a potentially competitive market. Suppose that the demand for electric power is

$$p = 10 - q, \tag{15.1}$$

where p and q represent price in thousand dollars and quantity in megawatt-hours, respectively. All generating plants have a capacity of 10 megawatt-hours. Generation involves a fixed cost of $50,000 and a constant marginal cost of $1,000 per megawatt-hour.

Figure 15.6 depicts the demand and costs. The demand curve intersects the marginal cost at the quantity where

$$1 = 10 - q \tag{15.2}$$

or $q = 9$.

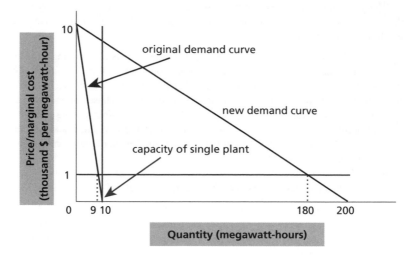

Figure 15.6 Demand and market structure
With the original demand curve, generation is a natural monopoly. With the new demand curve, the economies of scale are now small relative to the market demand; hence the market is close to being potentially competitive.

Hence, at the intersection, the quantity demanded is 9 megawatt-hours. A single plant can produce this quantity at a total cost of $50,000 + $1,000 \times 9 = $59,000, or an average cost of $59,000/9 = $6,556 per megawatt-hour. If, however, two plants were generating, then each would incur the fixed cost of $50,000, hence the total cost would be $109,000, implying an average cost of $109,000/9 = $12,111 per megawatt-hour. In this case, generation is a natural monopoly.

Now, suppose that the demand grows to $p = 10 - 0.05q$. This new demand curve will cross the marginal cost at a quantity of $1 = 10 - 0.05q$, or $q = 9/0.05 = 180$. If every plant operates at full capacity, 18 plants would be needed to meet this quantity demanded. The economies of scale are now small relative to the market demand. The market is no longer a natural monopoly but is close to being potentially competitive.

Answers to Progress Checks and Selected Review Questions

Chapter 1 Introduction to Managerial Economics

1A. The managerial economics of the "new economy" emphasizes network effects in demand and scalability.

1B. NPV = $3 - 2/(1.02) = 2/(1.02)^2 = -0.880$, or $-\$880,000$.

1C. Vertical boundaries delineate activities closer to or further from the end user. Horizontal boundaries are defined by the scale and scope of operations.

2. No, models must be less than completely realistic to be useful.

3. (a) Average price per minute = $(20 + 14.70 \times 4)/5$ = HK\$15.76 per minute.
    (b) Price of marginal minute = HK\$14.70.

5. False, in general. For a project where the costs come first and the benefits later, the statement is true.

8. With strong economies of scale, the business should produce on a large scale, and hence its horizontal boundaries would be broader.

10. (a) The electricity market includes buyers and sellers.
    (b) The electricity industry consists of sellers only.

12. (a) Intel.

13. (b).

14. (a) and (b).

Chapter 2 Demand

2A. The theater must cut its price by $3 from $11 to $8.

2B. (1) It slopes downward because of diminishing marginal benefit.
    (2) Assuming that all-in-one stereos are an inferior product, the drop in the consumer's income will cause the demand curve to shift to the right.

2C. Video rentals are a substitute for movies. A fall in the price of video rentals will cause the demand curve for movies to shift to the left.

2D. An increase in the price of a complement would cause the market demand to shift to the left.

2E. If the price of movies is $8, Joy's buyer surplus would be the area under her demand curve above the horizontal line at the price of $8.

3.   Introduction of the new product will
     (a)   reduce the demand for male condoms;
     (b)   reduce the demand for birth control pills.

7.   (a)   The demand for Marriott rooms will increase.
     (b)   Assuming that Motel 6 rooms are an inferior product, the demand for Motel 6 rooms will decrease.

9.   (a), (b), and (c).

10. The carrier should set the price so that the consumer has no buyer surplus.

Chapter 3 Elasticity

3A. The residential demand for water is relatively less elastic than the industrial demand.

3B. The demand curve is a straight line. At a price of $110,000, the quantity demanded would be 14,000 while at a price of $120,000, the quantity demanded would be 12,000. Accordingly, the proportionate change in the quantity demanded is −2/13 and the proportionate change in the price is 10,000/115,000 = 10/115. Hence, by the arc approach, the own-price elasticity of demand is (−2/13)/(10/115) = −1.77.

3C. The demand for liquor is relatively more income elastic than the demand for cigarettes.

3D. For a durable, the short-run demand could be more or less elastic than the long-run demand.

3E. The advertising elasticity of demand is $0.03 \times 446.67/88.93 = 0.15$.

5.   Rise.

7.   (a)   True.
     (b)   True.

8.   (b)   Complements.

10. The increase in quantity demanded would be $1.3 \times 5 = 6.5\%$.

11. Advertising by one particular brand will draw customers of other brands as well as increase the demand for beer in general. Advertising of beer in general can only increase the market demand.

12. More elastic in the long run.

15. A cross section records all the data at one time, while a time series records changes over time.

Chapter 4 Supply

4A. The total cost curve would be higher but the variable cost curve would not change.

4B. The marginal and average variable cost curves would not change, but the average cost curve would be lower.

4C. To maximize profit, Luna must produce at the rate where marginal cost equals 75 cents. Please refer to figure 4C.

4D. If the market price of eggs is $1.31, Luna should produce 8,000 dozen eggs a week and its revenue would be $1.31 \times 8,000 = \$10,840$, hence its profit would be $\$10,480 - \$7,232 = \$3,248$.

4E. See figure 4E.

4F. Proportionate change in quantity $= (6,500 - 5,800)/6,150 = 11\%$. Proportionate change in price $= (90 - 80)/85 = 12\%$. Hence, the price elasticity $= 11/12 = 0.9$.

1.   The short run is a time horizon within which a seller cannot adjust at least one input. By contrast, the long run is a time horizon long enough that the seller can adjust all inputs. Assuming that all fixed costs are also sunk, while all variable costs are not sunk, then there are fixed costs only in the short run, while all costs are variable in the long run.

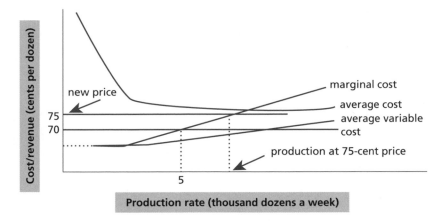

Figure 4C   Answer to progress check 4C

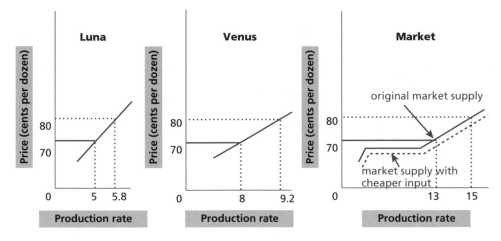

Figure 4E   Answer to progress check 4E

2. This statement confuses average with marginal cost. The average cost is $2. The marginal cost may be greater than, equal to, or less than $2, depending on the production technology.

5. Since the price is less than the marginal cost, the producer can raise profit by reducing production.

6. The analysis underestimates the increase in profit: it considers only the increase in profit on the existing production, and ignores the increase in profit resulting from an increase in production.

7. (a) Increases both average and marginal cost curves.
    (b) No effect.
    (c) Reduces both average and marginal cost curves.

11. (a) Movement along the market supply curve.
     (b) Shift of the entire market supply curve.
     (c) Shift of the entire market supply curve.

12. The buyer should design its order to leave the seller with zero seller surplus.

13. (a) False.
     (b) True.

15. The supply will be relatively more elastic in the long run.

Chapter 5 Competitive Markets

5A. A seller with market power could affect the selling price; hence, it could not answer the question, "How much would you sell, assuming that you could sell as much as you would like at the going price?" Thus, it is not possible to construct a market supply curve.

5B. See figure 5B.

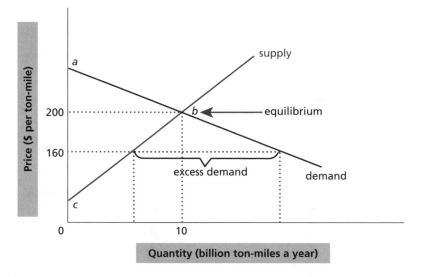

Figure 5B   Answer to progress check 5B

5C. (1) False.
    (2) True.

5D. See figure 5D.

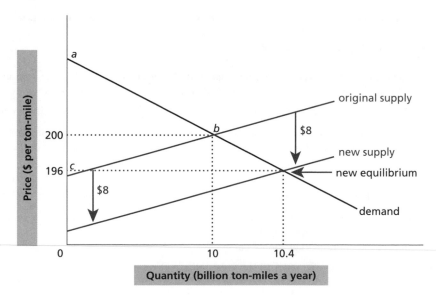

Figure 5D   Answer to progress check 5D

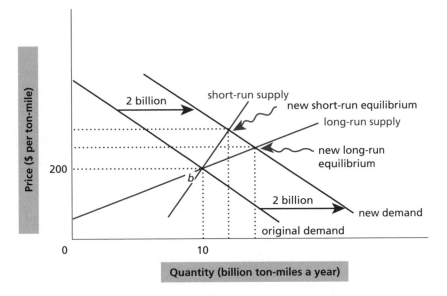

Figure 5E   Answer to progress check 5E

5E. See figure 5E.

1. (b)

3. True, because a seller with market power cannot sell as much as it would like at any particular price.

5. False.

7. The quantity supplied will exceed the quantity demanded.

9. (a) Reduce the supply.
    (b) Increase the demand (unless it causes a shift from apartment rentals to home ownership, in which case demand could decrease).

10. If the demand is extremely elastic or the supply is extremely elastic.

13. The supply of new housing is more elastic in the long run than the short run. Hence, the price will rise further in the short run than the long run, while the quantity will increase more in the long run than the short run.

14. False. If sunk costs are substantial, sellers will quit production only if the price drops by a large amount. Hence, prices will be more volatile.

Chapter 6 Economic Efficiency

6A. Technical efficiency means producing wheat at the minimum possible cost, while economic efficiency requires providing the quantities such that all users have the same marginal benefit, all producers operate at the same marginal cost, and the marginal benefit equals the marginal cost.

6B. The invisible hand increased the price of grain, which encouraged consumers to conserve and producers to grow more.

6C. With decentralization, Jupiter should set the transfer price equal to the market price of semi-conductors. Then, both divisions will use semiconductors up to the point where marginal benefit equals the transfer price. This will ensure economic efficiency.

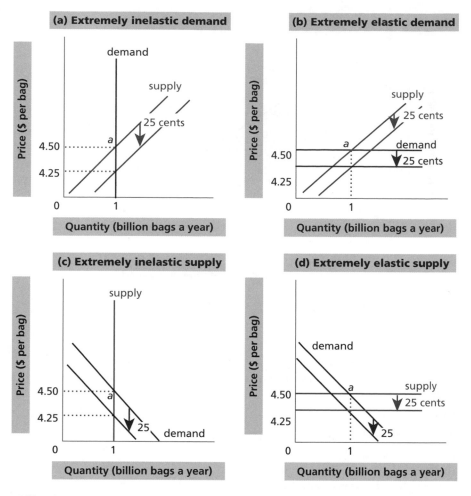

Figure 6D   Answer to progress check 6D

6D. See figure 6D.

6E. See figure 6E. The buyer's price increases relatively more. Hence, the incidence of the tax on travelers will be relatively higher.

1. Children were using bread (in sport) up to the point that the marginal benefit equaled the very low price. This price was less than the marginal cost. Hence, the marginal benefit of use was less than the marginal cost and not economically efficient.

2. The condition that all users receive the same marginal benefit.

3. In a competitive labor market, all buyers (employers) purchase up to the quantity where the marginal benefit equals the wage, and all sellers (workers) supply up to the quantity where the marginal cost equals the wage. Buyers and sellers face the same wage; hence, the allocation of labor is economically efficient.

6. The juice division should be charged the market price of apples.

8. The retailers receive the wholesale price cut. In a competitive retail market, however, the wholesale price cut will increase the supply. The new equilibrium will have a lower retail price. Consumers benefit from a lower retail price, so part of the wholesale price cut will be incident on consumers.

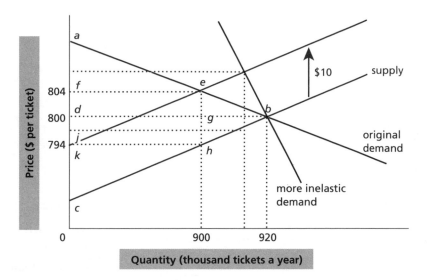

Figure 6E   Answer to progress check 6E

10. Retail supply will decrease and demand will increase. The new equilibrium price (with free shipping) should be higher than without free shipping.

12. Since demand is inelastic and supply is very elastic, the tax will be incident mostly on the demand side. Manufacturers would not be much affected.

13. Demand is elastic relative to supply, so most of the sales tax in Philadelphia will be paid by the electronics store.

Chapter 7 Costs

7A. See figure 7A.

7B. Neither economies nor diseconomies of scope.

7C. See figure 7C.

7D. The revenue from a shutdown in table 7.5 would become $460,000 and the opportunity cost in table 7.6 would become $680,000. Eleanor should continue in the warehouse business.

7E. In table 7.7, the columns for "Cancel Launch" would have zero in every cell. In table 7.8, the advertising agency cost would be $50,000, and the Road Runner would charge $250,000. Sol should cancel the launch.

7F. The cost would be $-5.51 + (21.20 \times 0.75) + (19.63 \times 1.5) + (0.04 \times 40) + (2.19 \times 10) = 63.335$ thousand dollars, or $63,335.

2. Southern Power's average fixed cost will rise.

3. Economies of scale are more significant in (a).

4. No.

6. Diseconomies of scope.

8. Two reasons: first, the client's time must be spent getting a sales pitch, and second, the cost to the salesman will be reflected in the final price paid by the client.

10. The "profit" should be reduced by the opportunity cost of the facilities.

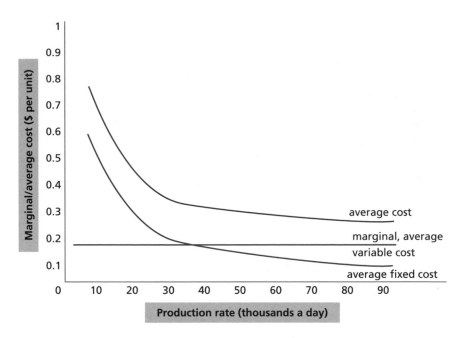

Figure 7A   Answer to progress check 7A

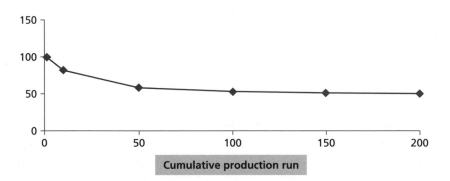

Figure 7C   Answer to progress check 7C

12. No. They are sunk costs.

13. (a).

15. Capacity, speed, and landings – the statistically significant variables.

Chapter 8 Monopoly

8A. No difference: the price would be identical to the marginal revenue.

8B. It should raise price, so reducing sales up to the quantity where its marginal cost equals its marginal revenue.

8C. See figure 8C.

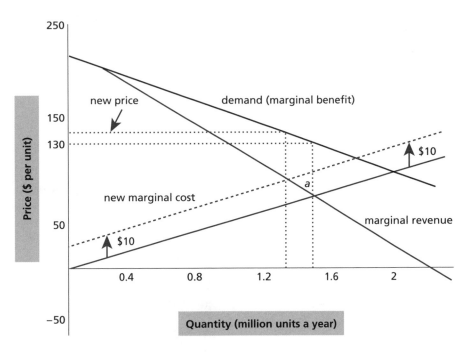

Figure 8C   Answer to progress check 8C

8D.   The advertising expenditure should be $(140 − 70) × 0.01 × 1.4 = $0.98 million.

8E.   If price and marginal cost increase by an equal *percentage*, then R&D expenditure should not change. If price and marginal cost increase by an equal *dollar amount*, then R&D expenditure should be reduced (the incremental margin will be lower).

8F.   Lerner Index = (130 − 70)/130 = 0.46.

8G.   Solar's total expenditure is represented by either the area *u0vx* under the marginal expenditure curve from a quantity of 0 to 6,000 tons or the rectangle *t0vz*.

2.   Economies of scale or scope give a firm a cost advantage over other sellers in the market. As the firm expands its production, its marginal costs will be lower than its competitors, enhancing its ability to price lower and gain even more sales, lowering cost further. Large economies of scale or scope will tend to cause the firm to dominate its market.

4.   To sell additional units, a seller must reduce its price. So, when increasing sales by one unit, the seller will gain the price of the marginal unit but lose revenue on the inframarginal units. Hence, the marginal revenue is less than or equal to the price. If the demand is very elastic, then the marginal revenue will be close to the price. If, however, the demand is very inelastic, then the marginal revenue will be much lower than the price.

7.   Expiration of the patent will
    (a)   reduce Solar's market power;
    (b)   raise the price elasticity of demand.

9.   Advertising expenditure = (100 − 40) × 0.01 × 500,000 = $0.3 million.

11.   Advertising elasticity would be higher for item (b).

13.   A reduction in the degree of potential competition would lead to higher prices, thereby raising the Lerner Index for the industry.

15.   Hospitals with monopsony power will hire a quantity of nurses for which their marginal benefit exceeds the marginal supply price of the labor. This permits the hospital to offer lower wages. Therefore, there will be an excess demand at the wage rate that the hospital is willing to pay.

Chapter 9 Pricing

9A.   The profit-maximizing price is 1,400 dirhams.

9B.   The market buyer surplus is the area *agc*.

9C.   Area *adb* = 2 million dirhams. Area *bec* = 2 million dirhams.

9D.   See figure 9D.

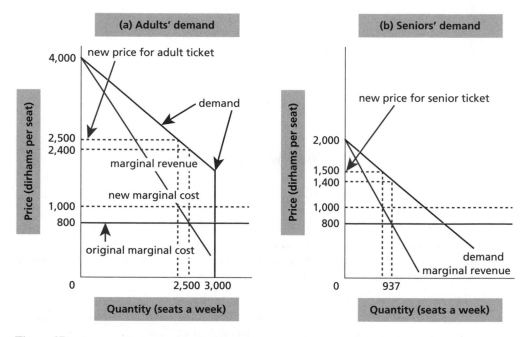

Figure 9D   Answer to progress check 9D

9E.   Japanese CF price = ¥50,000 = $500. The difference from the American price = $150.

9F.   No, the two segments will not be differentially sensitive.

9G.   Price the bundle at $22 and the educational channel at $19.

1.   Not necessarily. The price also depends on the marginal cost.

2.   The profit-maximizing price = $2.50.

3.   No.

6.   Equal.

7.   It would be easier to discriminate against newspapers because they have time value and are priced low relative to transportation cost.

10.   Current print subscribers will have a lower willingness to pay, since they already have access to the content of the publication.

12.   Drivers who are on an expense account are not likely to care enough (i.e., they have a more inelastic demand) to spend the time to get gas at a nearby station, where it is cheaper. Thus, the higher price for gas from Hertz indirectly segments the market between those that are paying for themselves and those that are not.

14. Pure bundling requires a buyer to purchase the bundle or not purchase any of its components; mixed bundling permits an option for consumers to purchase components of the bundle separately or together. In general, bundling is profitable when buyer tastes are negatively correlated across the components. Mixed bundling should be used when production is costly (so that it is not profitable to force buyers to purchase low-valued components) or when some buyers have extreme tastes (where some buyers have such a low value on one component of the bundle that the bundle price would need to be decreased too much in order to induce a sale to such buyers).

Chapter 10 Strategic Thinking

10A. A presidential election candidate must consider how other candidates will react to her or his decisions. Accordingly, these decisions are strategic.

10B. See figure 10B.

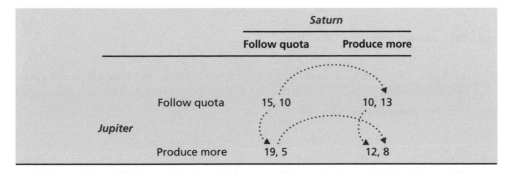

Figure 10B   Answer to progress check 10B

10C. (1) If Ming prices high, its expected profit would be $(40{,}000 \times 2/5) + (40{,}000 \times 3/5) = 40{,}000$.
    (2) If Ming prices low, its expected profit would be $(50{,}000 \times 2/5) + (30{,}000 \times 3/5) = 38{,}000$.

10D. It is not a zero-sum game.

10E. See figure 10E. Delta would choose 7:30 p.m.

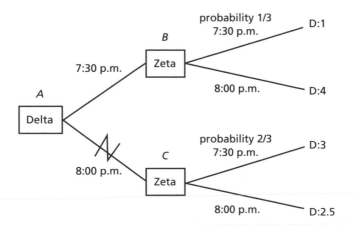

Figure 10E   Answer to progress check 10E
At node B, Zeta will chose 7:30 p.m. with probability 1/3 and 8:00 p.m. with probability 2/3. At node C, Delta will choose 7:30 p.m. with probability 2/3 and 8:00 p.m. with probability 1/3. By backward induction at node A, Delta will choose 7:30 p.m.

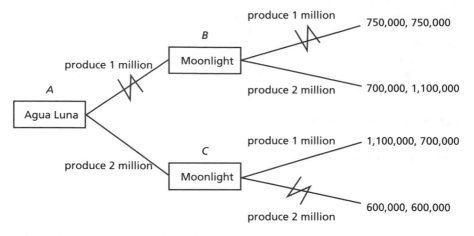

Figure 10F   Answer to progress check 10F

10F.   See figure 10F. Agua Luna would produce 2 million bottles, and Moonlight would produce 1 million bottles.

10G.   Minimum probability is 2/10 = 1/5.

   1.   (c).

   3.   (c).

   4.   Venus chooses Orange with probability 0.5 and chooses Green with probability 0.5; and Sol does the same.

   8.   Venus will choose either Orange or Green – either way, it will receive 1.5. Please refer to figure 10R Q8.

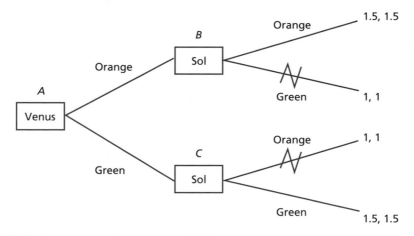

Figure 10RQ8   Answer to review question 10R Q8

   10.   Strategy (b) is more credible.

   12.   Conditional strategic moves may be less costly.

   15.   In repeated situations, strategies may be conditioned on external events or the actions of other parties.

Chapter 11 Oligopoly

11A.   See figure 11A.

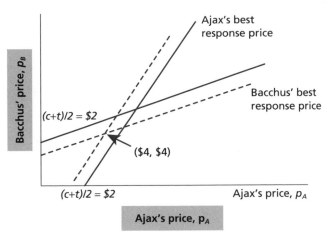

Figure 11A   Answer to progress check 11A

11B.   See figure 11B.

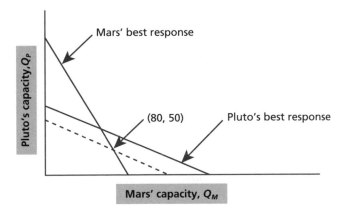

Figure 11B   Answer to progress check 11B

11C.   When one of the firms increases R&D, does the other firm respond by increasing its R&D (strategic complements) or decreasing it (strategic substitutes)?

11D.   No, it also depends on their relative costs and whether or not their product is differentiated from that of other sellers. It also depends on the potential competition available from sellers not currently in the market – if they can enter easily, then the seller may not be dominant, regardless of its size relative to the other sellers presently in the market.

11E.   The union will be more effective the less available is nonunionized labor in the industry. It will be more effective the less available additional workers are, and the less feasible it is for current workers to expand their hours (i.e., their capacity). Sunk costs, in the form of specialized training, will make unions less successful (other things being equal). On the other hand, any barriers to entry or exit (such as specialized training) will tend to make unions more effective. Finally, the more homogeneous the labor (repetitive easily monitored tasks), the more effective the union.

11F. Horizontal integration combines two entities that were selling similar products while vertical integration combines two entities that sell different stages in the production of a single product.

11G. If the merger were to reduce costs significantly, consumers may benefit from a merger that substantially increases concentration. Also, if a merger creates a more viable competitor for other significantly larger sellers in the market, it may become more competitive even while the measure of market concentration increases.

1. False. For example, price should equal marginal cost under Bertrand competition even in a duopoly.

3. Shortening the distance between the sellers is the same thing as decreasing product differentiation in the market. The result should be lower prices, and possibly lower consumer benefits (if the differentiation was valuable to consumers).

7. If there are no fixed cost, then it is not possible for the dominant firm to choose a price below the minimum average cost point of a potential competitor. That is, there is no price that will preclude entry, since entry will not involve any fixed cost.

10. A cartel is easier to enforce with less heterogeneity since it is easier to monitor the sales of the sellers.

11. 5,000. 6,250.

13. HHI = 3,333. Markup is 16.67%.

Chapter 12 Externalities

12A. Same as figure 12.1, except that the group marginal benefit is the same as Luna's marginal benefit. The profit-maximizing investment is now $900,000.

12B. (1) Sol's marginal cost curve will be higher, and (2) the level of investment that maximizes the group profit will be lower. Please refer to figure 12B.

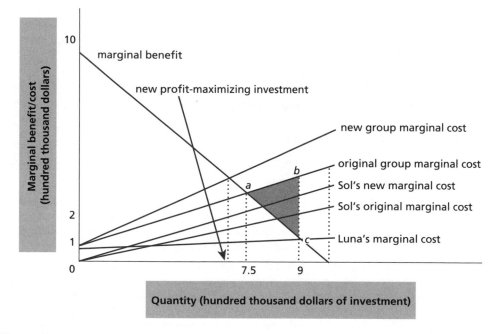

Figure 12B Answer to progress check 12B

12C. Transactions costs (information, monitoring, and enforcement). Also, the parties must be convinced that the potential benefits of joint action exceed the private benefits available through free-riding.

12D. (a) is a network externality;

(b) is not a network externality, as the benefit is limited to the neighborhood.

12E. See figure 12E.

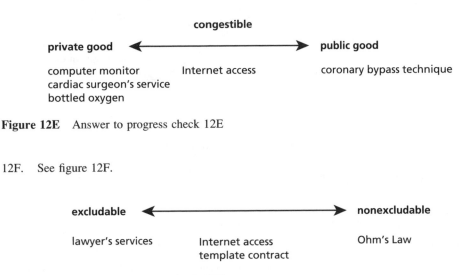

Figure 12E Answer to progress check 12E

12F. See figure 12F.

excludable ←————————————————→ nonexcludable

lawyer's services   Internet access   Ohm's Law
                       template contract

Figure 12F Answer to progress check 12F

3. The amount that the recipients of the negative externality are willing to pay for a marginal reduction is less than or equal to the marginal cost. The amount that the source is willing to accept for a marginal reduction is greater than or equal to the marginal benefit. Since the sum of the marginal costs exceeds the marginal benefits, the intermediary could make money.

5. The motel understands that if the exit gets built, it will reap the benefits whether it has contributed to the cost or not. It cannot be excluded from benefiting, as long as the exit is built.

7. A user interacts directly with their network browser and uses it to access web pages – any browser is capable of reaching the same web pages. Hence, there is little value to be gained by using the same browser as others. Indeed, on the Internet, nobody knows what browser you are using.

11. (a) but not (b).

12. Since public good consumption is nonrival, whatever quantity is provided to one consumer is provided to all consumers (at least, those that cannot be excluded). Since they are all consuming the same quantity of the public good, the marginal benefit to the group is the sum of the marginal benefits to the individuals.

Chapter 13 Asymmetric Information

13A. Nancy has imperfect information but does not face risk. The insurer has imperfect information and faces risk.

13B. The market price will be higher, as shown in figure 13B.

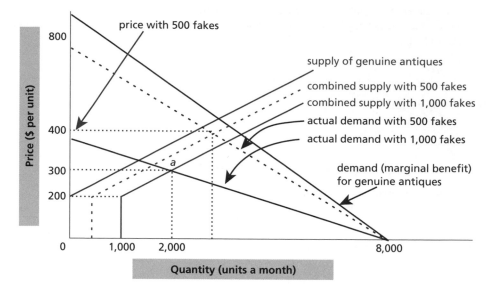

Figure 13B   Answer to progress check 13B

13C.   The percentage of high-risk policyholders will fall.

13D.   Appraisals will be more common in the market for more expensive antiques.

13E.   Borrowers who are more willing to repay will be relatively more likely to post collateral.

13F.   (a)   It should provide the information to the bidders.
       (b)   This information will reduce the extent of the winner's curse.

13G.   Screening is an initiative of the less-informed party, while signaling is an initiative of the better-informed party.

   2.   (a)   No asymmetry.
        (b)   The directors of Acquirer have better information than the general investor.

   4.   Yes, this will draw relatively less hardworking persons.

   5.   The seller has an interest not to reveal negative information about the car.

   7.   Drivers with a higher probability of accident will prefer a lower deductible as they are more likely to make a claim.

   9.   (a)   Open bidding allows the participants to observe the bids of others. This supports collusion.
        (b)   Setting a reserve price will put a limit to collusion.

  12.   Yes.

  15.   By accepting payment in Acquirer's shares, the amount that Target receives will depend on Target's true value.

Chapter 14   Incentives and Organization

14A.   The new marginal cost curve lies above the original. Please refer to figure 14A.
       (a)   The economically efficient effort will be lower.
       (b)   The effort that the worker actually chooses will be lower.

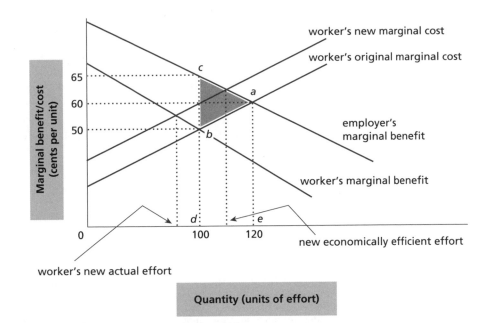

Figure 14A   Answer to progress check 14A

14B.   Draw any personal marginal benefit curve that crosses the marginal cost curve at 120 units of effort.

14C.   See figure 14C.

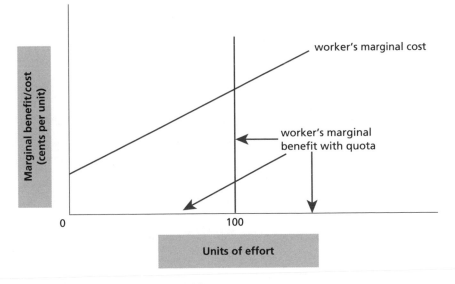

Figure 14C   Answer to progress check 14C

14D.   The sales clerk's incentive to process returns will be reduced.

14E.   Marie's.

14F.   On-the-job training.

14G.   SBC and Amgen integrated downstream. China National Petroleum Company integrated upstream.

14H.   The potential to reduce holdup through detailed contracting; the potential to resolve moral hazard through incentives and monitoring; the potential for outsourcing to reduce internal monopoly power; and the extent of economies of scale for the internal group.

  2.   Regarding asymmetry, it is costly for the insurer to monitor Leah's precautions. There is a conflict of interest because, with insurance, Leah bears the cost of precautions but receives only part of the benefit.

  4.   Method (b) provides more incentive to the lawyer.

  6.   The scheme will reduce the secretary's incentive for effort in the other tasks.

  7.   (a)   Index of small stocks.
       (b)   Index of U.S. government bonds.
       (c)   Index of Japanese stocks.

  8.   (b).

 12.   False. It would resolve the potential for holdup, but increase moral hazard by the internal producer of avionics.

 14.   For: reduces potential for holdup. Against: increases moral hazard, creates internal monopoly, does not benefit from scale economies.

Chapter 15 Regulation

15A.   See figure 15A.

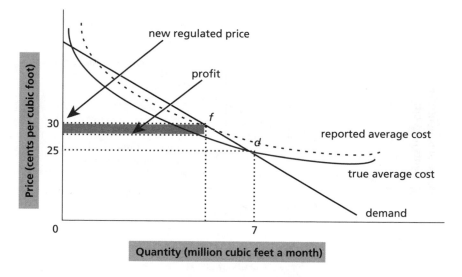

Figure 15A   Answer to progress check 15A

15B.   One operator should be given a monopoly franchise for distribution of gas. It should be either not allowed to produce natural gas or required to separate its distribution and production businesses.

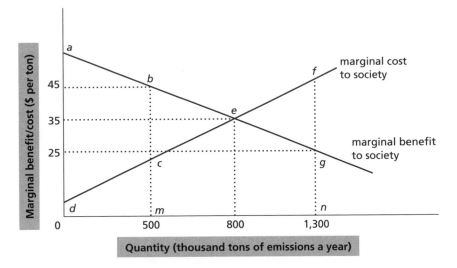

Figure 15C   Answer to progress check 15C

15C.   See figure 15C. With a $25 per ton user fee, sources of emissions will emit 1.3 million tons a year. Social benefit would be area 0*agn*, under the marginal benefit curve up to 1.3 million tons a year. Social cost would be area 0*dfn*, under the marginal cost curve up to 1.3 million tons a year. There would be a net social gain of area *aed* less area *efg*.

With a $45 per ton user fee, there would be a net social gain of area *abcd*. Neither the $25 nor the $45 fee is optimal. Which is preferable depends on the balance between area *bec* and area *efg*.

15D.   The new level of care would exceed the economically efficient level.

15E.   Reduce.

15F.   Assuming that demand varies over the day, the marginal cost of usage will also vary. Economically efficient usage requires the price to vary with the marginal cost.

4.   Rate of return regulated companies have little incentive to minimize costs and have exaggerated incentives to increase their rate base. There are also significant administrative costs with implementing such regulation (determining the rate base, the rate of return, and monitoring costs).

5.   Privatization means transferring ownership from the public to the private sector. Allowing competition means removing an exclusive right.

7.   (a)   A movie producer that owns a theater is vertically integrated into the exhibition business.
      (b)   The law that prohibited movie producers from owning theaters is a structural regulation to separate the movie production and exhibition businesses.

8.   False.

10.   (a)   The regulator could charge a fee for noise generated by the construction equipment.
       (b)   The regulator could set a standard and make it illegal for construction equipment to generate noise exceeding the standard.

13.   (a)   Not an externality because all the parties belong to the market for production workers.
       (b)   This is an externality.

14.   No.

Index of Companies and Organizations

Subject Index